THE WRITER'S HANDBOOK

The *Writer's* Handbook

Edited by
SYLVIA K. BURACK
Editor, The Writer

Publishers   THE WRITER, INC.   Boston

"Plot and Character in Suspense Fiction," by Joan Aiken. Copyright © 1988, by Joan Aiken Enterprises, Ltd.

"What Works for Me in Writing Science Fiction" by Poul Anderson is reprinted by permission from the *Bulletin* of the Science Fiction Writers of America. Copyright © 1989 by Poul Anderson.

"Always a Storyteller," by Mary Higgins Clark, Copyright © 1987, by Mares Enterprises, Inc.

"Dick Francis: In Interview" is reprinted by permission of the author from Writers' Monthly (England)

"Grilling Ed McBain," by Evan Hunter, Copyright © 1989, by Hui Corp., published by permission of the author, c/o John Farquharson, Ltd.

"To Be a Writer: What Does It Take?" Copyright © 1986, by John Jakes

"No Gore, Please—They're British," by P. D. James, is reprinted by permission. Copyright © 1988, by The New York Times Company.

"Inside a Poem," Copyright © 1989 by Eve Merriam.

"Ballad of the Boneless Chicken" and "Euphonica Jarre" from *The New Kid on the Block* by Jack Prelutsky. Copyright © 1984 by Jack Prelutsky. Reprinted by permission of Greenwillow Books, a division of William Morrow & Co.

"I Wave Good-bye When Butter Flies" from *Something Big Has Been Here* by Jack Prelutsky. Copyright © 1990 by Jack Prelutsky. Reprinted by permission of Greenwillow Books, a division of William Morrow & Co.

Library of Congress Catalog Card Number: 36-28596
ISBN: 0-87116-163-X

Printed in The United States of America

CONTENTS

BACKGROUND FOR WRITERS

WHAT EVERY WRITER SHOULD KNOW

HOW TO WRITE—TECHNIQUES

GENERAL FICTION

SPECIALIZED FICTION

NONFICTION: ARTICLES AND BOOKS

THE WRITER'S HANDBOOK

1

WHAT WRITING HAS
TAUGHT ME—THREE LESSONS

BY KATHERINE PATERSON

SOMEWHERE IN THE MIDDLE OF WRITING my tenth novel, it occurred to me that I had been at this business for twenty-five years. Since the book was moving along about as rapidly as a centipede with corns, I was not in the mood to celebrate the silver anniversary of my life as writer—not published writer, mind you, just writer. The silver anniversary of publication will be a few more years coming. But now the book is in the mail at last, and I am wracking my brain for lessons gleaned along the quarter-century journey. They seem pitifully few, but here they are:

1. *One idea doth not a novel make.* In answer to the often-asked question, Where did you get the idea for this book? I have at long last come to realize that a novel is not born of a single idea. The stories I've tried to write from one idea, no matter how terrific an idea, have sputtered out and died by chapter three. For me, novels have invariably come from a complex of ideas that in the beginning seemed to bear no relation to each other, but in the unconscious began mysteriously to merge and grow. Ideas for a novel are like the strong guy lines of a spider web. Without them the silken web cannot be spun.

The ideas that came together for *Park's Quest* were a long time in process. I had wanted for years to set a story on the Virginia farm where my father grew up and where I had spent many summers of my childhood. Once I even tried setting a short story there which never quite jelled. In one of those flashes that writers are prone to, I saw a scrawny Oriental-looking girl standing in the dark hall of that farmhouse. It was a child I didn't know, and I had no idea what she was

3

doing there, so I tucked her away until I had the other strands for her story.

The second came when my husband and I happened to visit old friends the day after they returned from the dedication of the Viet Nam memorial. Their eldest son had been killed during the war, and it was evident that the memorial and the services surrounding its dedication had been a time of real healing for their whole family. I went to visit the memorial myself soon afterwards and felt something of that power that all its visitors seem to experience. But still I was not ready to begin a novel.

The final strand began as an almost off-hand remark made by a speaker at the National Women's Conference to prevent Nuclear War in 1984. She warned those of us concerned about the nuclear threat that we could not simply frighten our friends and neighbors into responsibility: People who are frightened tend simply to deny the fact that any danger exists. "I think what we must do," she said, "is to ask the question of Parzival."

A shiver went through my body. I didn't know what the question of Parzival was, but I knew I had to find out. And, of course, when I found Wolfram's Medieval romance, which climaxes in Parzival's powerful question, "Dear Uncle, what aileth thee?" I found why my story would tie together our ancestral farm and the Viet Nam War. For surely for all Americans, not just for those who went to war, that conflict is "the wound that will not heal" and will never heal until we ask ourselves Parzival's question.

2. *My target audience is me.* Since I write primarily for children, people often ask me for what age child a book is intended. I have trouble answering the question, partly because I know very little about developmental psychology, but mostly because I know that people, even people of the same age, vary enormously in their interests and abilities. To try to "target an audience," as we writers for children are urged to do, would be impossible for me. I decided years ago it was not my job to decide who could or would read my books. If the publisher needs to suggest age or grade level designations in the catalogue, fine, but I will simply try to tell a story as well and as truly as I can. It would then be up to each reader to decide if my story was for him or her.

I suppose this truth came home to me after *Bridge to Terabithia* was

4

published. I had written the book after a year during which I had had surgery for cancer and our youngest son's best friend had been killed by lightning. I wrote the book because I could neither bring back the little girl my son had loved nor could I seem to comfort him. In order to keep going, I needed, somehow, to make sense for myself of senseless tragedy. I truly thought that no one whose name was not Paterson would understand the book. I was very much in doubt that my editor would even want to publish it. Over the years the book has not only sold millions of copies and been published in at least seventeen languages, it is the book that prompts readers of all ages to write me and pour out the pain of their own lives. I keep learning that if I am willing to go deep into my own heart, I am able, miraculously, to touch other people at the core.

But that is because I do have a reader I must try to satisfy—that is the reader I am and the reader I was as a child. I know this reader in a way that I can never know a generic target out there somewhere. This reader demands honesty and emotional depth. She yearns for a clear, rhythmically pleasing language. She wants a world she can see, taste, smell, feel, and hear. And above all she wants characters who will make her laugh and cry and bind her to themselves in a fierce friendship, as together they move through a story that pulls her powerfully from the first word to the last.

O.K. So she's a fussy reader. I've never fully satisfied her, but I would love to spend the next twenty-five years trying.

3. *A novel can be finished.* Some years ago I was having lunch in a crowded restaurant with a writer friend who has been at this business a lot longer than I. I was moaning that I was stuck—that this book I had poured two years of my life into was going nowhere. "This is my seventh novel! All these years and I haven't learned anything!" I cried out, eliciting a few stares from the diners at the next table.

"Yes, you have," my friend said. "You've learned one thing. You've learned that a novel *can* be finished." I cling to that knowledge every time I hit the invariable stone wall in the middle of a novel. I have finished nine of them now. I can finish another. And when it is done, given time and several sturdy guy lines, I may even be able to begin weaving yet another. There is always the hope that within the next twenty-five years I will be able to fully please my reader.

2

Cultivating Surprise

By Donald M. Murray

IN RETIREMENT, I HAVE RETURNED TO the reflective life of childhood, spending hours alone, cultivating surprise.

I used to try to mean, then say, but through fifty years of writing I have learned to allow the saying to come first and then to accept, develop, shape, and clarify the unexpected meaning. To encourage such surprise, I *have* to create an environment, internal and external, that is conducive to unexpectedness.

Quiet. Reception of surprise begins with quietness and aloneness. Not loneliness. I am lonely at parties but I have never felt alone when writing. Or perhaps it is that I treasure such aloneness. I have grown a portly body around myself, a public person with a public smile, but I am never as comfortable in that social costume as I am sitting by myself trying to hear a sentence that runs true and clear. To hear that sentence, I must surround myself with quiet, a calculated escape from busyness and a return to the emptiness all people feel when writing. In the cleansing terror of "I have nothing to say" I am freed from what I have said before and can begin to hear fragments of language, words, phrases, lines, not yet sentences and paragraphs, that entice and inspire pursuit.

Awareness. My world is twice, thrice, a dozen times experienced. I have instant replay of all the lives I have lived and imagined I have lived, and this increases my awareness of the world around me. Each day is filled with potential columns, poems, stories, and books that I might begin to discover. I am the watcher who is never bored for I am alwaya armed with the questions, "I wonder who that person is? I wonder what would happen if. . . ?

6

Play. No struggle, not any more. Play. It took me years of working hard to learn to work easy. To live a life of craft, I have had to recover the ability to play, to try to hook things together that may not go together, to try to make the large block balance on the small one—and to laugh when it tumbles down. I play with words and ideas, talking nonsense to myself, making music of words, even creating words that may catch meaning in flight.

Tools. My office is filled with writers' toys. I cannot remember when I was not fascinated with paper, the feel of paper, the smell of paper, the possibility of paper, white or tinted, unlined or lined. My pens are my right hand's sixth finger, a rebellious extension that leads me toward meaning. I am surrounded by notebooks, spiral, bound, looseleaf. In these books and in my hanging files I have captured surprise and the questions that will lead to more surprise.

Craft. In the corporate world of business—or government, science, the university, the church—most of us are denied the delight of making, with our own hands, something that was not there before. The writer feels a text forming in the hand, something that the writer has never heard before. And in making this text, which is more like the skill of the midwife assisting the birth, the writer exercises all the craft of language and form for which the writer has been apprenticed for years. Old in experience, I continue to learn restraint, what not to do, how to give language its head, as I put in, take out, reorder with such a gentle touch the evolving text is never forced to my meaning but teaches me its own surprises as I continue to learn to write.

Concentration. One of the great gifts of art or craft is that the maker becomes lost in the work. I step through my page to the other side and live so intensely that the imagined life is more real, for the moment, than the life of reality. In this way I live many lives and escape the familiar to places where I see what I have not seen before, inhabiting the mind and the skin of strangers who are closer to me than neighbors.

Sharing. I write first for myself, then for my wife and daughters, then a small roomful of friends who live in New Hampshire, Florida, Ohio, Utah, Maine, Idaho, Wyoming, Virginia, Massachusetts. Some of my books, articles, poems, stories reach strangers and they, by what they make of the text, become associates in the making of meaning. None of them hears just what I hear from my page. I try to make myself clear, not to force my reading on them but to stimulate their own thinking. Our texts, once published, are no longer ours any more than we own the children we have led into the world. My readers make what they will of what I have said, as I take the pages of other writers and read them in such a way they become my own.

Each morning I wake wondering what I will write today. And then words appear on the page or the screen. Hesitantly at first, then more surely the words lead to further words, accelerate into sentences and paragraphs as I race to capture surprise.

3

BETWEEN AGENT AND WRITER

By Anita Diamant

THERE NEVER HAS BEEN A TIME when news of the publishing world had more press than the present. *The New York Times, The Wall Street Journal,* and similar papers throughout the country have been devoting space daily to stories about changes in the publishing world, mostly portending news of major setbacks, mergers, firings, reorganizations, buyouts, etc. We see endless essays on the diminishing power of the editor, the increasing power of the agent. New writers reading all of this must be deeply concerned. How will all of this affect them?

From my perspective as an agent, it is interesting to assess the power the agent wields today, probably more than any other period in publishing. Agents have been facing the changes in publishing for some time.

On one hand, we are getting very large advances for some manuscripts, and on the other, fighting for low four-figure advances on books by authors with weaker track records. We are increasingly aware that the publisher paying a six-figure advance might have a particularly difficult time recouping such an investment, but we also realize that when we ask a seven-figure advance for a writer with approximately 50 million books in print, this is no gamble for the publisher. We all agree that there are too many books being published, too many marginal books, the publication of which pleases neither the writer nor the publisher, but not every feasible work can promise to be a best seller. That is where the midlist book comes into play. These books do not normally reach the best-seller lists, but they usually earn out the smaller advances and continue to sell for a reasonable period. Often these books become backlist items that publishers keep in print for many years, selling a small number of copies each year and providing a satisfactory return for the author. Publishers and agents are going to have to consider building more midlist books at midlist advances.

9

Today, publishers rely greatly upon legitimate agents for salable properties. While at one time publishers resented the intrusion of the agent in making a deal, today the agent has assumed a far more powerful and invaluable role. First of all, the agent screens everything that is sent to a publisher. The fact remains that editorial staffs have been cut considerably, leaving fewer first readers and editors who are very much overworked. The complaint—well justified—by writers is that editors take an interminably long time to respond to their manuscript submissions. As agents, we have some of the same problem, although because of our working relationship with publishing houses, we can be more insistent on receiving a speedier decision.

The recent mood of the industry reflects publishers who are concerned that if they do not enter into a bidding situation for any major property, the agent will auction the property off to a higher bidder, in spite of the fact that one publisher may have been bringing out the work of that author for some time. Is there any loyalty left in the field? Very little: Money has become the name of the game. Every now and then a writer of prominence, like Scott Turow, will stay with his publisher and his editor, but even Bill Cosby, whose book *Fatherhood* sold innumerable copies for Doubleday, now has gone to another house. Ironically, the sale of this new book has declined immeasurably!

Many of the problems have stemmed from the large number of takeovers of publishing houses—in many cases by foreign companies. Hardly a week goes by that we do not hear of a change of editor or forthcoming change in ownership. Also, there have been some horror stories in the business, most recently about the closing of the trade department of an old established firm and the firing of much of the staff. This uneasiness on the part of personnel has, of course, affected the business, and a successful writer takes this into consideration in determining which publisher he wants to work with again, keeping his eye on the advance rather than the house or editor.

All these problems have placed greater emphasis on the client-agent relationship. Most writers feel lost without some representation, even in category or genre writing, where the agent can do only so much for a writer. The writer feels more secure with good representation, but must select an agent carefully: There has to be good rapport between the writer and the agent, and a feeling of mutual trust. A great many agents who represent top-selling authors are experts in securing large advances, but they do not actually offer a writer any real editorial services. We like to think that an agent must be able to place himself or herself in the role of an editor and have a strong enough background and experience to do this successfully on behalf of the writers. Personally, I have spent many a weekend working over a manuscript for one of our best-selling writers before even showing it to the editor, who I know has an entire list to deal with. But again, the agent's focus should depend on the need of the writer and what the writer's priorities are.

I do not feel that an agent should be paid a fee from a writer other than the cost of return postage and the commission for selling a manuscript. Any experienced agent can look at a part of a manuscript and determine whether the property is worth handling. A legitimate agent makes a livelihood only from charging a percentage—today usually 15%—for handling a manuscript, and this in itself makes the representation a remunerative one. Many writers today approach several agents at the same time with their manuscript. How do I feel about this? I have no objection to receiving intelligent letters asking us about representation, but all agents resent receiving manuscripts, spending time reading them, only to find out later that the writer has decided to accept representation by another agent. A writer should always make this procedure clear *before* sending material to an agent, and if asked for exclusivity, should set a time limit. This differs from multiple submissions made to publishers, which all agents do today when they are submitting books with wide sales potential, mostly because of the great length of time editors take in reading manuscripts and making decisions. After all, the only thing an agent has to offer, besides good contracts, is his or her time.

At writers conferences, writers usually ask me just how to go about getting an agent and what one should submit to an agent. The good news is that good agents are constantly on the lookout for new talent. While it is comforting to represent name writers, we are all very much aware that *they* had to make a first sale, too. All agents will read query letters sent to them (with an SASE!). An intelligent letter explaining a project and indicating that the writer has the background and authority to write such a book should be sufficiently impressive for the agent to ask to see the manuscript or some part of it. Usually, we ask for an outline and a couple of chapters to determine whether there is sufficient material for a book and whether the writer has the talent to complete it successfully. A writer who cannot write an intelligent letter probably cannot write a salable manuscript!

While I have been talking primarily about books and the way in which agents handle book submissions, it is also true that there are other types of material for which it would be exceedingly difficult to obtain agent representation. This is basically due to the economics of the business, for while agents may enjoy reading fine verse, essays, sketches, etc., they know it is impossible to find a ready market for such writing, and the existing markets pay very small amounts for it. A writer who wishes to place short pieces and poetry will find lists of suitable publications in libraries and in leading writers' magazines.

There are other kinds of books and short pieces that some agents will handle—religious materials, juvenile stories and books—and indeed there are a few agents who specialize solely in books for children. Almost all agents handle young adult books (ages 8–15). This is a very open market today, and there is also the possibility of developing a series. But even though most unpublished writers of stories for young children sell directly to juvenile editors, the young adult novel is a very important field today. Sales reports indicate that juveniles continue to offer very wide potentialities for the writer as well as the publisher. So, once a writer is established in the juvenile field, it would then be possible, even advantageous, to interest an agent in representation.

For the most part, I would advise writers of short pieces slanted for regional or inspirational markets to try to sell these pieces themselves. Very few agents would be interested in selling to small markets, nor do they really have the necessary expertise in any of these fields. Often the writer can do very well in approaching editors directly.

Agents today rarely want to take on a short story writer or a writer who devotes time solely to articles. Since many magazines have either eliminated the publication of short stories or publish only a limited number, this has become a very small market for the short fiction writer. We do handle articles and stories for some of our clients whose main effort is writing books, but again it is possible for a writer to contact magazine editors directly and build up a satisfactory relationship for selling nonfiction.

What, then, is the agent's role in this business? Of course, an agent's main role is selling a manuscript for a writer, but most important of all, an agent must know the market and keep up with all of its changes; must have contacts with the new editors as they come to the various established houses; and have intimate knowledge of publishing contracts, for it is through negotiation that a writer can hope to receive the best possible terms. And many publishers really prefer to work with agents, for there is less difficulty in working with someone who really knows the publishing business.

Many writers wonder whether it is better to use a lawyer than a literary agent. Of course, there are some people who are well versed in both areas, but I feel that it is far better to have a really good agent than an average attorney, who is not experienced in publishing. Agents can not only negotiate contracts, but they also have the facilities to handle all subsidiary rights for the writer. And many times sales of foreign rights, first serial rights and film and TV rights amount to a great deal more than the sale of the initial book publication rights.

In the last months of 1989, there were major changes in the publishing industry—Dutton, a longtime publisher, cut their trade department and fired many people; Contemporary Books closed their New York office, and fired their staff who had been hired to start a fiction list; McGraw-Hill closed their trade department and let go 1,000 employees. The hysteria of publishers bidding enormous advances is obviously over. Writers will have to recognize the fact that this is a profession and the carnival, big-book aspects are fast disappearing. A writer who wants to become successful will have to face the fact that a professional presentation of his work is necessary. And while agents are assuming more and more power, still an agent is only as powerful as the manuscripts he or she represents: An agent cannot sell a bad manuscript, and we will all have to continue to rely on competent writers for our stables.

The writer—the agent—and eventually the editor may find that he or she has to work harder to assure success in this business today. Does this all portend disaster for our profession? I do not think so. Once we acknowledge that books are still selling well in spite of the attention given to TV, video, and films, we'll realize that there is a solid future for writers in every aspect of the media. And real talent will always find recognition and success.

4

To Be A Writer: What Does It Take?

By John Jakes

You can answer the question two ways.

If you're an aspiring fiction writer, you might say something like, "It takes the ability to sense, imagine, and tell a strong story. It also takes talent for writing efficient dialogue that gives the illusion of reality and carries a lot of plot or characterization freight at the same time. Besides that, it takes good powers of description. . . ." You could spin out your answer to cover all the basic tools and techniques of the fiction writer's craft, and you would be right.

If you're an aspiring poet, you might mention meter and form first. A dramatist would think of structure and exposition. Those answers, too, would be right.

There's a second answer, though, equally correct but more fundamental. An answer that actually precedes the learning of technique, no matter what sort of writing you prefer.

By way of illustration, think about golf. I think about it a lot, because I love it, and I play badly. Obviously, good golf calls for certain skills. Strong, straight drives based on a good swing. Dependable putting. A keen eye for reading greens. Expert chipping to rescue your ball from a trap. But you can achieve none of that without certain broader fundamentals. Excellent hand-eye coordination and muscle memory (I don't have either one). Ability to concentrate. A liking for the game itself. All these underlie technique.

So, too, do certain attitudes underlie all the skills a writer must have. I call those attitudes states of being. During a professional career that spans thirty-seven years, I've thought about these states of being a lot. Added some, subtracted others. Finally distilled and described seven. I believe a writer must "be" all seven, even before taking the first steps toward technical mastery. Indeed, so crucial are these seven states of being, I believe that if you lack them, you will never be a professional, only an eternal novice.

Each of the seven is simple to describe, but profound in its impact on your life. Here they are, then . . . the seven "states of being" that support a writing career.

1. BE SURE. Do you really want to pay the price? It isn't small. Are you willing to isolate yourself day after day, session after session, year after year, in order to learn your craft the only way you can—by writing?

There are much easier, more pleasant ways to pass the time, though few so rewarding intellectually and spiritually. But it's no sin to be honest and admit it if you'd rather garden, fish, or socialize with friends than go it alone as a writer, with no guarantee of success. If you aren't sure you're up to all that writing demands of a person, go no further.

2. BE DETERMINED. This is a re-statement of one of my "three P's" of a writing career—practice. You must have guessed by now that I believe many parts of the writing process (though not all) can be learned, just as golf can be learned. It's true. You may never be a Fuzzy Zoeller or a Nancy Lopez—there are few out-and-out champions in any field—but, with determination and practice, you can probably become at least a part-time professional. To do it, however, you must write and keep on writing, trying to improve all the time.

3. BE PATIENT. This equates with the second of my "three P's," persistence. The writing profession is not, thank God, the record business. Idols are neither born nor made on the strength of a single three-minute album cut. A more substantial body of work is required. Nor do many stars emerge in the writing field at eighteen (only to be forgotten six months later). Except for a very few, a solid writing career usually arrives later in life.

Also, you must remember that publishing, like any other art that is part industry, changes constantly. Editorial people change jobs. A house or publication that rejects you this year may, under a new editor, say yes the next. Failure to realize this can increase your impatience to the danger point . . . the point at which you say, "What's the use?"

We live in an age of instant gratification. You won't get it writing . . . except for the joy in the work itself.

15

4. BE OPEN. This is the last of my "three P's"—professionalism. By being open, I mean being willing and eager to have all the flaws in your work exposed, so that you can fix them. I mean being anxious to have a working partnership with an editor who admires your strengths but won't spare you criticism of your weaknesses.

Don't let the editor do all the work, though. You must want to find the weak places for yourself, before the editor sees them. It is this rather cold-blooded attitude that sets most money-earning writers apart from dabblers and those who would rather talk about being a writer than do what it takes to be one. "No pain, no gain," runners say. It's the same with writing. Unless you're open to tough criticism and willing to do something about it, you'll never go the distance.

5. BE CURIOUS. Read everything you can read. Read widely, not merely in your chosen field of writing. Spend as much time as you can with your mouth shut and your eyes and ears open. Don't strive for attention . . . strive to go unseen in a crowd, on the beach, at a party. Watch people. Watch the sky. Watch a baby's repertoire of expressions. Watch the way sun puts shadow on a wrinkled garment. Nothing should escape your notice. Everything eventually contributes to what you write, even though the way it contributes is totally unknown to anyone, including you.

6. BE SERIOUS. Give unstintingly of yourself when you write. The kind of effort NFL players casually refer to as "110 percent." There's something to it.

Once again, if you dabble . . . withhold part of your energy . . . refuse to commit your whole mind and heart to the work . . . that will be reflected in a lackluster creative product. Give your work the best you have to offer at the moment you do it. Give it a clear head, and a body that's fit and rested.

On the other hand, while you're taking the work seriously, don't take yourself seriously. I abhor the kind of writer who can't laugh at himself . . . who can't avoid pretentious pronouncements (probably to cover a raging insecurity) . . . who carries "the gift" like a royal scepter and never stops waving it about for others to see.

Too many writers unwittingly play what I call Immortality Roulette. They get involved in worrying about their own reputations. How will they be remembered in a hundred years? They grow desperate, sometimes almost maniacal about it. They write nasty letters to harsh critics—or at least talk about doing it. They are happy or sad depending on a few words from a total unknown (most reviewers). The result of all this is often compensation in the form of overweening self-importance.

The saddest cases are the most marginal . . . those very competent popular writers who probably will be largely forgotten, except by a few trivia scholars or aficionados, as time goes by. Since most of us can't answer questions about posterity—a Hemingway, acknowledged a genius in his own lifetime, is a rarity—just do the best you can. No one can ask more, and what more can you logically ask of yourself? Posterity will take care of itself, with or without you.

7. BE YOURSELF. Above all, let who you are, what you are, what you believe shine through every sentence you write, every piece you finish. I don't mean preach. Just be natural. The originality and power of Tolstoy's *War and Peace* do not lie in the fact that he was the first to write a mammoth novel about Imperial Russia facing Napoleon. I don't know whether he was first or not. I suspect so; it doesn't matter. What matters is that he was unique, a singular person, and his great novel emerged from what *he* had to say about his homeland and its people in wartime. One of my favorite statements about writing, encountered so long ago I can't even acknowledge the source, is this:

"True originality lies not in saying what has never been said, but in saying what you have to say."

So there you are. Seven "states of being" you must achieve before you start your work in order to master the specific tools of your craft. Again, if you honestly feel these requirements are too tough—simply not for you—no one will blame or criticize you. But if you say, "Yes, I will be a writer because I can be all of those things . . . I am all of those things . . . or I'm willing to try to become them," then I predict eventual success for you.

Not enormous wealth, mind you. Not a best seller every year. Not immortality—just the solid satisfaction of being a *writer*. It's a proud and ancient profession . . . and it's a great feeling to achieve even a little success in the business of entertaining and enlightening millions with your own words. It's a calling very much worth the price.

17

‖ 5

How to Find Time to Write When You Don't Have Time to Write

By Sue Grafton

Early in my writing career, I managed to turn out three novels, one right after another, while I was married, raising two children, keeping house, and working full time as a medical secretary. Those novels were never published and netted me not one red cent, but the work was essential. Writing those three books prepared the way for the fourth book, which *was* published and got me launched as a professional writer. Ironically, now that I'm a "full-time" writer with the entire work day at my disposal, I'm often guilty of getting less work done. Even after twenty-five years at it, there are days when I find myself feeling overwhelmed . . . far less effective and efficient than I know I could be. Lately, I've been scrutinizing my own practices, trying to determine the techniques I use to help me produce more consistently. The underlying challenge, always, is finding the time to write and sticking to it.

Extracting writing time from the fabric of everyday life is a struggle for many of us. Even people who are technically free to write during an eight-hour day often can't "get around" to it. Each day seems to bring some crisis that requires our immediate attention. Always, there's the sense that tomorrow, for sure, we'll get down to work. We're uncomfortably aware that time is passing and the job isn't getting done, but it's hard to know where to start. How can you fit writing into a schedule that already *feels* as if it's filled to capacity? If you find yourself lamenting that you "never have time to write," here are some suggestions about how to view the problem and, better yet, how to go about solving it.

First of all, accept the fact that you may never have the "leisure" (real or imaginary) to sit down and complete your novel without interruption. Chances are you won't be able to quit your job, abandon your family, and retire to a writers' colony for six weeks of uninterrupted writing

18

every year. And even if you could, that six weeks probably wouldn't get the job done. To be productive, we have to make writing part of our daily lives. The problem is that we view writing as a luxury, something special to allow ourselves as soon as we've taken care of the countless nagging duties that seem to come first. Well, I've got news for you. It really works the other way. Once you put writing first, the rest of your life will fall into place.

Successful writers disagree about how much time is needed per stint—ranging anywhere from one to ten hours. I feel that two hours is ideal and not impossible to find in your own busy day. One of the first tricks is to make sure you use precious writing time for *writing* and not for the myriad other chores associated with the work.

"Writing" is made up of a number of sub-categories, each of which needs tending to. A professional doesn't just sit down and magically begin to create prose. The process is more complex than that, and each phase requires our attention. Analyzing the process and breaking it down into its components will help you understand which jobs can be tucked into the corners and crevices of your day. In addition to actual composition, writing encompasses the following:

Planning—initiating projects and setting up a working strategy for each.

Research—which includes clipping and filing.

Outlining—once the material has been gathered.

Marketing—which includes query letters, manuscript typing, Xeroxing, trips to the post office.

And finally, *follow-up* for manuscripts in submission.

All of these things take time, but they won't take *all* of your time, and they shouldn't take your best time. These are clerical details that can be dispatched in odd moments during the day. Delegate as much as possible. Hire someone for these jobs if you can. Have a teen-ager come in one day a week to clip and file. Ask your spouse to drop off a manuscript at the post office on his or her way to work. Check research books out of the library while the kids are at story hour. Use time waiting for a dental appointment or dead time at the laundromat to jot down ideas and get them organized. Take index cards with you every place.

Now take a good look at your day. Feel as if you're already swamped from dawn to dark? Here are some options:

19

1. *Stay up an hour later each night*. At night, the phone doesn't ring and the family is asleep. You'll have fewer distractions and no excuses. You won't drop dead if you cut your sleep by an hour. The time spent creatively on projects important to you will *give* you energy. Eventually, you can think about stretching that one hour to two, but initially, stick to a manageable change and incorporate it thoroughly into your new schedule before tackling more. I used to write from ten at night until midnight or one a.m., and I still find those hours best for certain kinds of work.

2. *Get up an hour earlier,* before the family wakes. Again, shaving an hour from your sleep will do you no harm, and it will give you the necessary time to establish the habit of daily writing. Anthony Trollope, one of my favorite writers, worked for most of his adult life as a postal clerk, on the job from eight until five every day. His solution was to get up at five a.m. and write 250 words every fifteen minutes till eight— three hours. If he finished a book before the time to go to work, he started a new project at once. In his lifetime, he turned out forty-six full-length books, most of them while he earned a living in another capacity.

3. *If you're employed outside your home, try working en route.* British crime writer Michael Gilbert wrote 23 novels . . . all while riding the train to his work as a solicitor. He used the 50-minute transit time to produce 2 to 2½ pages a day, 12 to 15 pages a week. Buses, trains, commuter flights can all represent productive time for you. Use those periods for writing, while you're inaccessible to the rest of the world.

4. *What about your lunch hour?* Do you go out to lunch every day to "escape" the tensions and pressures of the job? Why not stay at your desk, creating a temporary haven in your own head? Pack a brown bag lunch. It's cheaper, among other things, and if you limit yourself to fruit and raw vegetables, you can get thin while you pile up the pages!

5. *Look at your week nights.* See if there's a way to snag one for yourself. You'd make the time if you decided to take an adult education class. Invent a course for yourself, called "Writing My Novel At Long Last" and spend three hours a week in the public library. I heard about a writer who finished a book just this way, working only on Tuesday nights.

6. *Weekends generally have free time tucked into them.* Try Saturday afternoons when the kids are off at the movies, or Sunday mornings when everyone else sleeps late.

7. *Revamp your current leisure time.* Your schedule probably contains hidden hours that you could easily convert to writing time. Television is the biggest time-waster, but I've also realized that reading the daily paper from front to back takes ninety minutes out of my day! For a while, I convinced myself that I needed to be informed on "current events," but the truth is that I was avoiding my desk, squandering an hour and a half that I desperately needed to complete a manuscript. I was feeling pressured, when all the while, the time was sitting right there in front of me . . . literally. Recently, too, I took a good look at my social calendar. I realized that a dinner party for six was requiring, in effect, two full days of activity . . . time I now devote to my work. I still have friends. I just cut my entertainment plans by a third.

Now.

Once you identify and set aside those newly found hours, it's a matter of tailoring the work to suit the time available. This can be done in four simple steps:

1. Make a list of everything you'd like to write . . . a novel, a short story, a film script, a book review for the local paper, that travel article you outlined during your last trip.

2. Choose three. If you only have one item on your agenda, how lucky you are! If you have more than three projects on your list, keep the remaining projects on a subsidiary list to draw on as you complete the items on your primary list and send them out into the marketplace. I generally like to have one book-length project (my long-term goal) and two smaller projects (an article, a short story . . . short-term goals) on my list.

3. Arrange items on the list in the order of their true priority. Be tough about this. For instance, you might have a short story possibility, an idea you've been toying with for years, but when you come right down to it, it might not seem important enough (or fully developed enough) to place among the top three on your list. My first priority is

always the detective novel I'm writing currently. I work on that when I'm at my freshest, saving the smaller projects for the period after my first energy peaks. Having several projects in the works simultaneously is good for you psychologically. If you get stuck on one, you can try the next. As you finish each project, the feeling of accomplishment will spur you to renewed effort on those that remain. In addition, by supplying yourself with a steady stream of new projects, you'll keep your interest level high.

4. Once you select the three projects you want to work on, break the writing down into small, manageable units. A novel isn't completed at one sitting. Mine are written two pages at a time over a period of six to eight months. Assign yourself a set number of pages . . . 1 or 2 . . . and then meet your own quota from day to day. Once you've completed two pages, you can let yourself off the hook, moving on to the next task. By doing a limited amount of work on a number of projects, you're more likely to keep all three moving forward. Don't burden yourself with more than you can really handle. Assigning yourself ten pages a day sounds good on the surface, but you'll soon feel so overwhelmed that you'll start avoiding the work and won't get *anything* done. Remember, it's persistence that counts, the steady hammering away at the writing from day to day, day *after* day, that produces the most consistent work and the greatest quantity of it.

Essentially, then, all you need to do is this:

> Analyze the task.
> Scrutinize your schedule.
> Tailor the work to fit.

I have one final suggestion, a practice that's boosted my productivity by 50%. Start each day with a brief meditation . . . five minutes of mental quiet in which you visualize yourself actually sitting at your desk, accomplishing the writing you've assigned yourself. Affirm to yourself that you'll have a good, productive day, that you'll have high energy, solid concentration, imagination, and enthusiasm for the work coming up. Use these positive messages to block out your anxieties, the self-doubt, the fear of failure that in fact comprise procrastination. Five minutes of quiet will reinforce your new determination and will help you make the dream of writing real.

6

TRUSTING THE READER

BY LOIS LOWRY

I'M SOMETHING OF A SKEPTIC. I'm skeptical about oat bran and I'm skeptical about Tammy Bakker's newest church; I don't believe that Oil of Olay will halt the aging process—it didn't for me—and I don't believe that blondes have more fun—I'm one, and I didn't, and more fun than *what*, anyway?

And I don't believe everything that Henry James is reputed to have said. But Henry James once said (or so I was told in graduate school) that a writer is a person "on whom nothing is lost."

I do believe that.

It means that we writers are noticers. We are perceivers. We don't miss much. We see the details, the nuances, the flyspecks.

Most easy truths have hard corollaries, though. And so does this one.

The truth is that we are, as James said, people on whom nothing is lost.

The hard part, which he neglected to add, is that we, as writers, then face the task of sifting and selecting. What do we point out to the audience? What do we hint at? What do we lie about? What do we shout? What do we hide?

Here, in a book of mine called *Rabble Starkey*, a twelve-year-old girl hears Steinbeck's book *The Red Pony* (one of my own personal favorites) read aloud, for the first time:

I knew that each one of us could see it in our own minds. And probably we each saw different things. A book with no pictures lets you make your own pictures in your mind. A guy who writes a book like that really trusts the people who read it to make the kind of pictures he wants them to. Of course he helps them along, with the words. Like Mr. Steinbeck told us all about that old dog named Smasher having only one ear because the other got bit off by a coyote, and how his one good ear stood up higher than the ear on a regular collie. So we

23

could all picture Smasher in our minds, just the way he was supposed to be, but at the same time each of us had our own private Smasher, built out of all the dogs we had ever known.

We can't ask the late John Steinbeck about the dog he saw in his own mind when he wrote the passage. But we can guess that he had a collie clearly envisioned, and that perhaps the collie he saw had a lame leg, or scruffy fur, or unusually bright and wary eyes.

But if that's what he saw, that's what he chose to hide.

He only mentioned the ears.

So the child, hearing the story, builds upon those two clearly described ears and goes on to create, as she says, her own private Smasher in her mind. And she is grateful for the trust Steinbeck had in her to do that.

(It's difficult, trusting the readers. Who *are* those people, anyway? We've never been properly introduced. Maybe they have bad taste. Maybe they're dumb. Maybe they don't understand, or have the proper sense of values, or appreciation of the visual, or—)

Not so. I said I'm a skeptic, but I am not a skeptic about the capacity of the reader, particularly the young reader. A sense of wonder comes built in with every child. Powers of absorption greater than the most up-to-date Pampers are part of youth's standard equipment. Memory begins at birth, or perhaps even before.

How do you trust those things? Let's say that you, as writer, sit down and begin to present something—maybe a classroom—to your audience. You can, of course, see it in your mind. You are, after all, a person on whom nothing is lost. So you can see an entire classroom: its dimensions, the number and arrangement of its windows and desks, the color of the shavings in the gerbil cage, the fabric of the teacher's dress; the alphabet strip that is mounted above the blackboard; the Christmas (or Spring, or Halloween) decorations; the countless other things which, combined, create the classroom you perceive, a classroom which probably comes from your own memories.

Years ago, writing a book called *Autumn Street,* I called on my own memories of first grade in a small Pennsylvania school. All of those details were there: the stored bits and pieces, maybe thousands, that combined to make my own first grade class.

I chose five:

—Ticonderoga pencils in an orderly yellow row.

—A daub of mint-scented paste on a square of construction paper.

—Miss MacDonald in a flowered dress, bending to whisper.

—Furry erasers thick with chalk dust.

—Dick and Jane and Baby Sally skipping through the pages of a book.

I trusted the reader to add the rest. The classroom each reader made in his own mind was not the classroom I could see in mine.

And why should it be? Television provides that—the exact, specific image—and lets the audience loaf.

In contrast, the printed word asks—and trusts—the reader to contribute from his own memory, imagination, and dreams.

It is very tough to be skeptical about *that*.

7

A Writer's Education

By Rick DeMarinis

I WASN'T RAISED IN A FAMILY of book readers. My mother worked in a fish cannery, and my stepfather drove a bread truck. There were a few books in the house—a library copy of *Forever Amber* no one had bothered to return, some mildewed paperbacks with racy covers, an ancient encyclopedia, and, amazingly, a beautiful, gold-embossed, wonderfully illustrated copy of the Koran! (My mother was Lutheran, my stepfather Baptist, and I, at sixteen, was a fallen-away Catholic.) This small and exotic collection of books didn't make much sense, but it contained an essential message for a young aspiring writer: don't expect things to make sense. Expect surprise.

In high school English class, we were introduced to something called, with unmistakable reverence, Literature. I hated it. I remember having to read novels such as *Silas Marner*. But the nebulous minds of sixteen-year-old California kids were hardly prepared for such fare. We traded copies of Mickey Spillane out in the parking lot, away from the snooping eyes of teachers. A novel about gang warfare called *The Amboy Dukes* was hugely popular with us. We saw reading as an extension of our internal lives, and could not make the great leap to the world of George Eliot.

Something happens to people destined for a life of writing that has nothing to do with Literature. It happens early in life, and is probably the psychological equivalent of scarlet fever. It has to do with pain. In answer to the question, "How does one become a writer?" Ernest Hemingway is said to have replied, "Have a lousy childhood." I believe this, but I also know that people who have had wonderful childhoods— on the surface at least—have become, in spite of this handicap, first-rate writers. Even so, something happened to them. Maybe *birth* happened to them and that was disaster enough. Someone sensitive to his or her surroundings, sensitive in the sense of always being aware, of noticing the details, and of being affected imaginatively by the force of these impressions—i.e., a person destined to be an artist—will find trauma waiting around every corner. A childhood doesn't have to be lousy to be traumatizing. As Flannery O'Connor said, ". . . anybody who has survived his childhood has enough information about life to last him the rest of his days."

Then something else happens. We find that words can be an escape from the pain of social impotence. Words became, for me, a bright mantle of power. I discovered that pressing a #2 pencil into a sheet of clean white paper was a sensual experience. And as that pencil moved, a world was created. What power *that* was! Creating fictional worlds is a natural refuge for the powerless, since it *confers* power. There, on the clean white page, all power is restored. My English teachers (except for that one fine teacher all of us seem to encounter, that mythic "helper" who appears just at the right time with the right kind of encouragement) had no perceivable passion for words. It was as if the Literature we were asked to read were made of rarefied ideas breathed directly onto the page by pure mind from the slopes of Olympus. It was the rock solid clatter and bang of our raucous and flexible language that moved me like small earthquakes. Rarefied ideas were a vapor that would be condensed in college and graduate school much later on. Besides, at sixteen I had no apparatus for absorbing serious ideas, and surely none for expressing them. Writing was a physical exercise, as pleasureful as bench pressing heavy weights, but not as socially acceptable. There was something shameful about a strong, healthy boy spending long hours in his room *writing stories.* And so writing, like all suspect activities, had to be done in secret. But how lovely it was, putting down those blocks of words until I and my perplexing, misperceived world were redefined on *my* terms. I became a middleweight boxer, on his way to the championship, when a beautiful girl (who looked remarkably like Jean Simmons in one of her Christian epics) convinced me that boxing was brutal and inhuman—hours before my title fight! Or I became a jet fighter pilot, touring MIG alley in Korea with a vengeance unknown to modern warfare, or a professional quarterback playing in the NFL title game against a team who had dropped me from their roster.

My English teachers and I regarded each other through the wrong ends of our private telescopes. We shied away from each other, and yet they gave me an occasional B or A for my awkward but imaginatively untethered "essays" that twisted the world out of its expected shapes. This habit of twisting the world persisted. If you twist hard and long, it surrenders its truths. George Eliot knew that. All writers know that. Too often, English teachers, even college English teachers, don't know that or they don't see it as the central mission of fiction writing.

Is the writer therefore anti-intellectual? Not necessarily. The intellect, however, wants to be "right." It wants answers and it wants certainty. A writer operates in a different atmosphere, an atmosphere charged with uncertainty and surprise. I heard E. L. Doctorow say, in a recent speech, that the writer, *as* a writer, is someone who places equal value on the objects of his experience. The latest cosmological theory is of no more intrinsic importance than the way sunlight passes through a Japanese fan. This democracy of the objects of experience is a necessary state of mind for the writer. It opens the gates and lets a whole world in where things won't necessarily make sense. For example, you might find your mother in such a world, just home from the cannery and smelling like fish—your mother who quit school at fourteen—sitting at the kitchen table reading a gold-embossed, illustrated edition of the Koran.

8

EVERYTHING YOU NEED TO KNOW ABOUT WRITING SUCCESSFULLY— IN TEN MINUTES

BY STEPHEN KING

I. *The First Introduction*

THAT'S RIGHT. I know it sounds like an ad for some sleazy writers' school, but I really am going to tell you everything you need to pursue a successful and financially rewarding career writing fiction, and I really am going to do it in ten minutes, which is exactly how long it took me to learn. It will actually take you twenty minutes or so to read this essay, however, because I have to tell you a story, and then I have to write a *second* introduction. But these, I argue, should not count in the ten minutes.

II. *The Story, or, How Stephen King Learned to Write*

When I was a sophomore in high school, I did a sophomoric thing which got me in a pot of fairly hot water, as sophomoric didoes often do. I wrote and published a small satiric newspaper called *The Village Vomit*. In this little paper I lampooned a number of teachers at Lisbon (Maine) High School, where I was under instruction. These were not very gentle lampoons; they ranged from the scatological to the downright cruel.

Eventually, a copy of this little newspaper found its way into the hands of a faculty member, and since I had been unwise enough to put my name on it (a fault, some critics would argue, of which I have still not been entirely cured), I was brought into the office. The sophisticated satirist had by that time reverted to what he really was: a fourteen-year-old kid who was shaking in his boots and wondering if he was going to get a suspension . . . what we called "a three-day vacation" in those dim days of 1964.

I wasn't suspended. I was forced to make a number of apologies— they were warranted, but they still tasted like dog-dirt in my mouth—

and spent a week in detention hall. And the guidance counselor arranged what he no doubt thought of as a more constructive channel for my talents. This was a job—contingent upon the editor's approval—writing sports for the Lisbon *Enterprise,* a twelve-page weekly of the sort with which any small-town resident will be familiar. This editor was the man who taught me everything I know about writing in ten minutes. His name was John Gould—not the famed New England humorist or the novelist who wrote *The Greenleaf Fires,* but a relative of both, I believe.

He told me he needed a sports writer and we could "try each other out," if I wanted.

I told him I knew more about advanced algebra than I did sports.

Gould nodded and said, "You'll learn."

I said I would at least try to learn. Gould gave me a huge roll of yellow paper and promised me a wage of ½¢ per word. The first two pieces I wrote had to do with a high school basketball game in which a member of my school team broke the Lisbon High scoring record. One of these pieces was straight reportage. The second was a feature article.

I brought them to Gould the day after the game, so he'd have them for the paper, which came out Fridays. He read the straight piece, made two minor corrections, and spiked it. Then he started in on the feature piece with a large black pen and taught me all I ever needed to know about my craft. I wish I still had the piece—it deserves to be framed, editorial corrections and all—but I can remember pretty well how it looked when he had finished with it. Here's an example:

Last night, in the ~~well-loved~~
~~gymnasium of~~ Lisbon High School, partisans
and Jay Hills fans alike were stunned by
an athletic performance unequalled in school
history: Bob Ransom, ~~known as "Bullet" Bob~~
~~for both his size and accuracy,~~ scored
thirty-seven points. He did it with grace
and speed...and he did it with an odd courtesy
as well, committing only two personal fouls
in his ~~knight-like~~ quest for a record which
has eluded Lisbon ~~thinclads~~ *is basketball team* since 1953...

When Gould finished marking up my copy in the manner I have indicated above, he looked up and must have seen something on my face. I think *he* must have thought it was horror, but it was not: it was revelation.

"I only took out the bad parts, you know," he said. "Most of it's pretty good."

"I know," I said, meaning both things: yes, most of it was good, and yes, he had only taken out the bad parts. "I won't do it again."

"If that's true," he said, "you'll never have to work again. You can do *this* for a living." Then he threw back his head and laughed.

And he was right: I *am* doing this for a living, and as long as I can keep on, I don't expect ever to have to work again.

III. *The Second Introduction*

All of what follows has been said before. If you are interested enough in writing to be a purchaser of this magazine, you will have either heard or read all (or almost all) of it before. Thousands of writing courses are taught across the United States each year; seminars are convened; guest lecturers talk, then answer questions, then drink as many gin and tonics as their expense-fees will allow, and it all boils down to what follows.

I am going to tell you these things again because often people will only listen—really *listen*—to someone who makes a lot of money doing the thing he's talking about. This is sad but true. And I told you the story above not to make myself sound like a character out of a Horatio Alger novel but to make a point: I saw, I listened, and *I learned*. Until that day in John Gould's little office, I had been writing first drafts of stories which might run 2,500 words. The second drafts were apt to run 3,300 words. Following that day, my 2,500-word first drafts became 2,200-word second drafts. And two years after that, I sold the first one.

So here it is, with all the bark stripped off. It'll take ten minutes to read, and you can apply it right away . . . if you *listen*.

IV. *Everything You Need to Know About Writing Successfully*
1. *Be talented*

This, of course, is the killer. What is talent? I can hear someone shouting, and here we are, ready to get into a discussion right up there

31

with "What is the meaning of life?" for weighty pronouncements and total uselessness. For the purposes of the beginning writer, talent may as well be defined as eventual success—publication and money. If you wrote something for which someone sent you a check, if you cashed the check and it didn't bounce, and if you then paid the light bill with the money, I consider you talented.

Now some of you are really hollering. Some of you are calling me one crass money-fixated creep. And some of you are calling me *bad* names. *Are you calling Harold Robbins talented?* someone in one of the Great English Departments of America is screeching. *V. C. Andrews? Theodore Dreiser? Or what about you, you dyslexic moron?*

Nonsense. Worse than nonsense, off the subject. We're not talking about good or bad here. I'm interested in telling you how to get your stuff published, not in critical judgments of who's good or bad. As a rule the critical judgments come after the check's been spent, anyway. I have my own opinions, but most times I keep them to myself. People who are published steadily and are paid for what they are writing may be either saints or trollops, but they are clearly reaching a great many someones who want what they have. Ergo, they are communicating. Ergo, they are talented. The biggest part of writing successfully is being talented, and in the context of marketing, the only bad writer is one who doesn't get paid. If you're not talented, you won't succeed. And if you're not succeeding, you should know when to quit.

When is that? I don't know. It's different for each writer. Not after six rejection slips, certainly, nor after sixty. But after six hundred? Maybe. After six thousand? My friend, after six thousand pinks, it's time you tried painting or possibly computer programming.

Further, almost every aspiring writer knows when he is getting warmer—you start getting little jotted notes on your rejection slips, or personal letters . . . maybe a commiserating phone call. It's lonely out there in the cold, but there *are* encouraging voices . . . unless there is nothing in your words which warrants encouragement. I think you owe it to yourself to skip as much of the self-illusion as possible. If your eyes are open, you'll know which way to go . . . or when to turn back.

2. *Be neat.*

Type. Double-space. Use a nice heavy white paper, never that erasable onion-skin stuff. If you've marked up your manuscript a lot, do another draft.

32

3. *Be self-critical*

If you *haven't* marked up your manuscript a lot, you did a lazy job. Only God gets things right the first time. Don't be a slob.

4. *Remove every extraneous word*

You want to get up on a soapbox and preach? Fine. Get one and try your local park. You want to write for money? Get to the point. And if you remove all the excess garbage and discover you can't find the point, tear up what you wrote and start all over again . . . or try something new.

5. *Never look at a reference book while doing a first draft*

You want to write a story? Fine. Put away your dictionary, your encyclopedias, your World Almanac, and your thesaurus. Better yet, throw your thesaurus into the wastebasket. The only things creepier than a thesaurus are those little paperbacks college students too lazy to read the assigned novels buy around exam time. Any word you have to hunt for in a thesaurus is the wrong word. There are no exceptions to this rule. You think you might have misspelled a word? O.K., so here is your choice: either look it up in the dictionary, thereby making sure you have it right—and breaking your train of thought and the writer's trance in the bargain—or just spell it phonetically and correct it later. Why not? Did you think it was going to go somewhere? And if you need to know the largest city in Brazil and you find you don't have it in your head, why not write in Miami, or Cleveland? You can check it . . . but *later*. When you sit down to write, *write*. Don't do anything else except go to the bathroom, and only do that if it absolutely cannot be put off.

6. *Know the markets*

Only a dimwit would send a story about giant vampire bats surrounding a high school to *McCall's*. Only a dimwit would send a tender story about a mother and daughter making up their differences on Christmas Eve to *Playboy* . . . but people do it all the time. I'm not exaggerating; I have seen such stories in the slush piles of the actual magazines. If you write a good story, why send it out in an ignorant fashion? Would you send your kid out in a snowstorm dressed in Bermuda shorts and a tank top? If you like science fiction, read the magazines. If you want to write confessions stories, read the magazines. And so on. It isn't just a matter of knowing what's right for the present story; you can begin to catch on, after awhile, to overall rhythms, editorial likes and dislikes, a magazine's entire slant. Sometimes your reading can influence the *next story*, and create a sale.

7. *Write to entertain*

Does this mean you can't write "serious fiction"? It does not. Somewhere along the line pernicious critics have invested the American reading and writing public with the idea that entertaining fiction and serious ideas do not overlap. This would have surprised Charles Dickens, not to mention Jane Austen, John Steinbeck, William Faulkner, Bernard Malamud, and hundreds of others. But your serious ideas must always serve your story, not the other way around. I repeat: if you want to preach, get a soapbox.

8. *Ask yourself frequently, "Am I having fun?"*

The answer needn't always be yes. But if it's always no, it's time for a new project or a new career.

9. *How to evaluate criticism*

Show your piece to a number of people—ten, let us say. Listen carefully to what they tell you. Smile and nod a lot. Then review what was said very carefully. If your critics are all telling you the same thing about some facet of your story—a plot twist that doesn't work, a character who rings false, stilted narrative, or half a dozen other possibles—change that facet. It doesn't matter if you really liked that twist or that character; if a lot of people are telling you something is wrong with your piece, it *is*. If seven or eight of them are hitting on that same thing, I'd still suggest changing it. But if everyone—or even most everyone—is criticizing something different, you can safely disregard what all of them say.

10. *Observe all rules for proper submission*

Return postage, self-addressed envelope, all of that.

11. *An agent? Forget it. For now*

Agents get 10% of monies earned by their clients. 10% of nothing is nothing. Agents also have to pay the rent. Beginning writers do not contribute to that or any other necessity of life. Flog your stories around yourself. If you've done a novel, send around query letters to publishers, one by one, and follow up with sample chapters and/or the manuscript complete. And remember Stephen King's First Rule of Writers and Agents, learned by bitter personal experience: You don't need one until you're making enough for someone to steal . . . and if you're making that much, you'll be able to take your pick of good agents.

12. *If it's bad, kill it*

When it comes to people, mercy killing is against the law. When it comes to fiction, it *is* the law.

That's everything you need to know. And if you listened, you can write everything and anything you want. Now I believe I will wish you a pleasant day and sign off.

My ten minutes are up.

9

THE WRITER'S COMPASS

BY WILLIAM STAFFORD

WE WRITERS try to help each other, sometimes. But there is a catch in this generosity: if you begin to rely only on what others say about your work, you may become like a compass that listens to the hunches of the pilot. You may be good company, but you are useless as a compass.

So, when we meet, say at a conference or workshop, we look each other in the eye with an estimate hovering between us. We know that our kind of activity has some complexities not evident to others, and we wonder if those complexities will be recognized in any interchanges about our craft.

For instance, we know that our work is insufficiently judged if much time is given over to assessing the topics of our work. We know that a critic who discusses whether we talk enough about Nicaragua or not, or human rights or not, or the general topic of enlightenment or not, is missing the mark.

We know that there is something supremely important in the creating of a story or poem that all too often will escape the attention of an outsider trying to assess it. And for those outsiders, general readers, even critics, it may not be devastating if they talk at large: the main point is that such readers be affected, no matter what they ascribe our influence to. But for us writers it would be fatal to be misled by superficial assessments; and in fact one of the main hazards for a "successful" writer may be the insidious intrusion of those outer assessments on the inner process that allows us writers to find our way.

We must have an inner guide that allows us to rove forward through the most immediate impulses that come our way. For us, our whole lives are our research; and caught up by our best subjects we become not just an expert, but the only expert there is. We have to be the sole authority for what comes toward us, where we are, with our unique angle of seeing.

Though this inner guide is difficult to talk about, it is supremely important; and it is different from that urge for money, publication, recognition, that is glibly identified as the bait for a writer. You can get lost, following the whims of the public. And the public can give you recognition, or withhold it; but afterward you must set forth again, alone.

If the most significant writing comes from this inner guidance, who will help you find it? Would it be someone who interposes the considerations of the marketplace while the delicate time of discovery is going on? Would it be the person who puts primary emphasis on your imitation of forms and strategies?

Let me plead, not for ignoring advice from wherever it comes, but for allowing in your own life the freedom to pay attention to your feelings while finding your way through language. Besides that audience out there in the world, there is some kind of ideal audience that you have accumulated within your individual consciousness—within your conscience!; and abiding guidance is your compass, one that constitutes what you have to contribute to discourse with others.

Moving back and forth from the inner to the outer world might be the way to your best writing.

Into the unknown you must plunge, carrying your compass. It points at something more distant than any local guidance. You must make "mistakes"; that is, you must explore what has not been mapped out for you. Those mistakes come from somewhere; they are disguised reports from a country so real that no one has found it. When you study that country, shivers run down your back—what a wilderness out there! What splendid stories flicker among those shadows! You could wander forever.

Odd words keep occurring to you—pauses, side glances—mysterious signals. What hidden prejudice brought that next word into your mind? If you hastily retreat to an expected progression, what shadowy terrain might you be neglecting? What revelations might you miss by any "expert" weaving of another well-crafted poem or story?

Like Don Quixote on his unorthodox steed you must loosen the reins and go blundering into adventures that await any traveler in this multi-level world that we too often make familiar by our careful threading of its marked routes between accustomed places.

And like Don Quixote you must expect some disasters. You must write your bad poems and stories; for to write carefully as you rove forward is to guarantee that you will not find the unknown, the risky, the surprising.

Art is an activity in which the actual feel of doing it must be your guide; hence the need for confidence, courage, independence. And hence the need for guardedness about learning too well the craft of doing it.

By following after money, publication, and recognition, you might risk what happened to the John Cheever character who in like manner "damaged, you might say, the ear's innermost chamber where we hear the heavy noise of the dragon's tail moving over the dead leaves."

10

THE ABC's OF COPYRIGHT

BY ELIZABETH PRESTON

THOUGH THE AREA OF COPYRIGHT PROTECTION and infringement tends to concern and often confuse many writers, the copyright law is actually quite straightforward, easy to comprehend, and generous in terms of copyright protection of literary property. The law was revised in 1978—the first complete revision since 1909—and the changes dramatically increased the rights of creators of copyrightable work. In this chapter we'll discuss some copyright basics, including what may be copyrighted, who may apply for copyright, duration of protection, and the rights of copyright owners. For answers to more complicated copyright questions, writers should get in touch directly with the Copyright Office.

What is copyright? What works can be copyrighted?

The copyright laws of the United States protect "original works of authorship"—both published and unpublished—including literary, dramatic, musical, artistic, and certain other "intellectual" works. Under the law, a work is protected as soon as it is set down on paper, or recorded, for the first time, and it becomes the sole property of the author who created it. What this means to you as the writer or "creator" of a work is that you own and control the rights to its publication and use, whether it's a four-line limerick, a story, an article, a play, or a novel.

There are several categories of material that may not be copyrighted, however: speeches or performances that have not been written or recorded; titles, names, and slogans; ideas, concepts, principles or devices, as distinguished from a description, explanation, or illustration; and works that consist entirely of information that is in the public domain and contains no original authorship, such as standard calendars, material from public documents or other common sources.

What's the procedure for copyright registration?

As noted earlier, your work is automatically protected by copyright from the time that it's put onto paper or in another physical form, and actual registration with the Copyright Office is not a requirement for protection. Nonetheless, there are several advantages to registration, and failure to register your work could be detrimental, particularly if the work becomes commercially valuable and there is increased possibility of infringement (unauthorized reprinting, filming, recording, or other uses). Among these advantages are the following:

• Registration establishes a public record of the copyright claim

• Registration is ordinarily necessary before any infringement suits may be filed in court

• If made before or within five years of publication, registration will establish evidence in court of the validity of the copyright

• If registration is made within three months after publication of the work or prior to an infringement of it, the court may award statutory damages and attorney's fees to the copyright owner. Otherwise, only an award of actual damages and profits is legally available to the copyright owners.

To register a work, send the following (in the same envelope or package) to the U.S. Copyright Office, Register of Copyrights, Library of Congress, Washington, DC 20559:

1. A properly completed application form (supplied free of charge by the Copyright Office)

2 A fee of $20 for each application (recently increased from $10)

3. A deposit (copy) of the work being registered (one if the work is unpublished, two if already published)

Be sure the application form is completed legibly, preferably type-written; since it becomes a part of the official permanent records of the Copyright Office, it must meet archival standards.

In general, you should register book manuscripts, play scripts, and other long works when they're completed. It's well worth the $20 registration fee to make sure that there's a public record of your copyright ownership. It's not necessary to register articles, short stories, poems, or other short work individually; you may use one application—and pay a single fee—to register several individual published works of the same nature. For instance, 20 short stories published in a single year may be registered on one $20 application. Write to the Copyright Office for further details on group registration.

Most writers will use application form TX—for published and unpublished non-dramatic literary works—or PA—for published and unpublished works of the performing arts. Other forms available include RE (for claims to renew copyright in works copyrighted under the old law); CA (for supplementary registration to correct or amplify information given in the Copyright Office record of an earlier registration); and GR/CP (an adjunct application for registration of a group of contributions to periodicals). When requesting forms from the Copyright Office, indicate exactly what type of work you wish to copyright so that you'll receive the proper information. The effective date of copyright registration is the day on which a completed application, deposit, and fee have been *received* in the Copyright Office. Once your application has been processed, you will receive an official certificate of copyright registration.

Who may file an application form?

The following individuals may submit an application form for a particular work:
- The author
- A person or organization that has obtained ownership of all the rights under the copyright initially belonging to the author
- The owner of exclusive right(s). Under the new law, any of the exclusive rights that make up a copyright—and any subdivision of them—can be transferred and owned separately, even though the transfer may be limited in time or place. For example, a magazine or book publisher that has purchased first rights in a work may apply for registration of a claim in the work for this use only.
- The duly authorized agent of an author, other copyright claimant, or the owner of exclusive right(s). For instance, book publishers usually apply for copyrights on behalf of their authors; of course, the author should always be sure that the work is copyrighted in his or her name.

How long does copyright last?

One of the major innovations in the U.S. copyright law is that it adopts the basic "life-plus-fifty" years system already in effect in most countries; that is, *a work created and "fixed in tangible form" after January 1, 1978, is protected for a term of the author's life, plus 50 years after the author's death.* Works created before January 1, 1978, but neither published nor registered for copyright before that date, are also automatically protected by statute for the life of the author plus 50 years.

The protection available for works copyrighted before 1978 depends on whether the copyright had already been renewed and was therefore in its second term when the new law came into effect, or was still in its first term on December 31, 1977. The copyright law before 1978 allowed for a work to be copyrighted for a first term of 28 years from the date it was secured, followed by a renewal for a second term of 28 years. This system of computing the duration of protection for works copyrighted before 1978 has been carried over into the present law, with one major change: the length of the second term is increased to 47 years. Thus, the maximum total term of protection for works already copyrighted (i.e., prior to 1978) is increased from 56 years (28-year first term plus 28-year renewal term) to 75 years (28-year first term plus 47-year renewal term).

Any copyright in its second term as of January 1, 1978 was automatically extended up to a maximum of 75 years from the end of the year in which it was originally secured, without the need for further renewal. Copyrights still in their first term as of January 1, 1978, must be renewed by the end of their 28th calendar year, or else they will expire, and the work will go into public domain. (For instance, the first term of a copyright registered for a work in 1970 will come up for renewal in 1998; if renewal is made by the end of that year, the work will then be protected for an additional 47 years.)

Should you put a copyright notice on your work?

Writers often wonder whether they should affix a copyright notice to unpublished works before submitting them to publishers. Technically, such a notice is not required on unpublished works, but most would agree that it's a good idea to include a copyright notice on the first page of a short manuscript, or the title page of a book manuscript. The notice should include the following three elements:

- The symbol © and/or the word "copyright"
- The year of first publication of the work
- The name of the owner of copyright in the work

Example: © 1990 by John Doe or Copyright © 1990 John Doe

Most magazines are copyrighted, so if your work is published in such a publication, it will automatically be protected. Even so, *you* remain the copyright owner of the work, since in most cases, periodicals buy "first rights" only.

What are the rights of copyright owners?

Copyright owners have the right to reproduce their work; to prepare derivative works based upon their work; to distribute copies of the work to the public by sale, rental, lease or lending; and to perform or display the work publicly, as in the case of literary, musical, and dramatic works and pantomimes, motion pictures, and other audiovisual works.

As the author of a copyrighted work, you may sell or transfer rights to it in any way that you choose. For example, you would usually sell "first rights" only to a magazine in which your poem, story, article, or filler is to be published. Later, you may choose to sell reprint or "second" rights in that work to another publication, or for some other use (movie or TV filming, for instance). The permission of the original publisher is not required, although it may be necessary for certain works copyrighted under the old law. A publisher may not buy "all rights" to your material unless you agree to such a sale and signify it in a signed written statement or "instrument of conveyance." In the absence of this signed statement, the publisher owns only first rights, or one-time use of your work.

A work written or prepared by an employee within the scope of his or her employment—called "work for hire"—is the property of the employer, who may register the work in his name or that of the company. However, as the result of a recent Supreme Court decision, the "work for hire" stipulation applies only to those writers who are actually in an employer-employee relationship with a publisher; it cannot be applied to the work of those who write on a free-lance basis unless they specifically agree to it.

If you're selling a book manuscript, be sure the contract your publisher offers specifically states the terms of the sale and which rights are included. Book contracts are somewhat standardized, though the language and terms will vary. For instance, as author you would declare that your work is original; that you are granting the publisher the right to publish your book; that you will deliver your manuscript in final form on a specified date; that you will be responsible for obtaining permissions if the manuscript includes copyrighted work. The publisher promises to make timely payment of royalties; to give you as author a specified number of free copies of your published book; to share in the proceeds from sales to book clubs, and so forth. It's important to remember that the time to discuss any terms that are not satisfactory to you, or are at all unclear, is *before* the contract is signed. In most cases, the terms of book contracts are somewhat negotiable, and you shouldn't shy away from discussing possible changes with your editor.

A final note: Infringement of copyright is a relatively rare occurrence, and although writers should take precautions to protect their work, they should find reassurance not only in the fact that the revised copyright law represents their best interests, but also that reputable publishers will deal fairly and honestly with authors in all matters relating to the publication of their work.

‖11

JOURNAL KEEPING

BY HEIDI VANDERBILT

LAST AUGUST—WHICH WAS EVEN HOTTER than this August—I was writing a scene in a story in which a woman walks in moonlight across an ice-crusted field. In August it's hard to remember what four feet of snow feels like. I tend not to believe snow exists if I'm not right in it. It was a great help to pull out an old journal and find some weather-appropriate entries:

December 31: Day before yesterday we had a blizzard, 12 inches of light dry snow, followed by a hard freeze. Temperatures around zero . . . I am reminded of the snows in Connecticut winter '78, when the little thaws and hard freezes left the snow crusted and shiny as sunburned skin and I slid down on my boots as if I were skating or skiing. . . . The moon last night near full, the snow lavender-gray, striped with the shadows of branches. . . . In bed I looked through our new glass door, over the indigo snow, across the pond with its slate shadows, up the far wooded hill. At the top of the glass door, one perfect, fat star.

I used this entry as the base for the snowy night I was inventing. Reading what I had written, I was able to recreate the particular moonlit coldness I needed.

This is how it came out in the story:

The moon was nearly full, the snow lavender-gray, striped with the shadows of branches. Marta could see her way perfectly past the pond, over the fences and fields that separated her from the Timms. The boys ran around as if it were daylight. She clutched the warm foil-wrapped cake in her mittens, its scent mingled with the smell of snow.

They crunched over bare sloping fields to the Timms'. The snow's surface had already crusted. With each step Marta's feet hesitated, then broke through. The children pretended to ski on the soles of their boots, leaving silvery trails behind them.

I have kept a journal—written longhand in lined notebooks—since I was fourteen, recording in it the details of my life. Since I began writing and publishing in 1981, I have expanded my use of my journal to help my fiction. I now use it to help me remember, to loosen up, and to deepen and develop character and setting—as well as to keep track of myself. Because journal writing is so personal, my suggestions here will be personal, too. They are what work for me.

Let me start right off with the myth that writers should write every day. Why? Who on earth wants to do anything every day? How much do you enjoy brushing your teeth? O.K., brushing your teeth never was very exciting. How about making love? Every day? Even when you're sick? Of course not. Anything done day after day, week after week grows tiresome. We grow bored and mutinous. We need—and allow ourselves—a break, even from love.

I write most days. It's August as I write this, it's raining, a great day to work. But there are days on this island where I live when the humidity's up, the sun's out, there is a breeze and I don't write a word—I go to the beach or shopping or see friends I won't see again until next summer.

So writing in your journal *most* days is really good enough. In fact, it's perfect. That will allow you to write with interest and energy.

Sometimes you need just to live.

The same goes for this business of writing at the same time every day. What for? Do it when you want. Some people find a schedule reassuring. Others don't. There is no one right way to live—or to write.

The fiction writer creates a universe out of characters, situations, emotions, and problems which, to be effective, must be fundamentally recognizable to readers. This can come only from the writer's personal experience and personal truths: from being personal, it becomes universal.

Where does one find the universal? In the specific. Look at what's around you. Look, especially, at yourself.

I use my journal to record what I see and hear and feel: events, conversations, emotions. I keep a record of surprises and passions, of secrets I allow myself to find out about myself. I use it as a way to record and remember. When I see something marvelous, I write it down. When I hear some special bit of colloquial humor, some odd exchange between children in a bookstore, some fabulous insult screamed from a truck window, I write it down. Otherwise it's hard to recall what happened yesterday, last week, last month.

When my son Jack was little, I marked each of his accomplishments.

"Today he said his first word," I wrote in a tiny spiral notebook. " 'Wire'."

But for all the things I wrote down about him, there were others I didn't. I knew, for absolute certain, that I would never forget what he and his friend Abby said to each other in the park that Monday. Well, I did forget. Not everything, but some—too many—of the specifics.

Good fiction is built on specifics. "Show, don't tell." It's the details that show, the specifics. Grab them while you can. Write them down. I often carry a notebook with me, in case. I'm always glad later.

Of course, there is the problem of time, as in, "I have no time to write." The quotes which follow come from a diary I kept when Jack was three years old. I had no time then to keep a full journal, so that notebook consists of nothing but dialogues with him, written as they happened (I kept a notebook in his stroller).

JACK: Did you know that there is a medium-sized beach in New York City?
ME: What's it called?
JACK: New Hampshire.
ME: New Hampshire is a state.
JACK: No, it's not. It's a beach. And there are *no* crabs and *no* lobsters and *no* sharks and *no* whales and *no* dolphins.
ME: What do you think would be a good present for Jonathan while he's sick? Something for while he's feeling quiet and not all there?
JACK: A ghost. Next year I want a coat with fur on the outside and on the inside. And a fur hat to match. Isn't that disgusting?

Any time I need the flavor of conversation with a child that age, I have only to turn to that book.

What should a fiction writer include in a journal that will be particularly helpful for developing character?

First, secrets. All the things you think you shouldn't or couldn't say.

Listen to what Elia Kazan says about his early work on his first novel, *The Arrangement:*

Since it never occurred to me that anyone would see it, I set down what I thought and felt without self-censoring. A true expression of anger, love, and bewilderment . . . moving closer and closer to the bone. (Elia Kazan, *A Life,* p. 730)

Then, include anything that interests you enough to write about it— what you did, thought, said, felt.

I jot down ideas to be worked up later—interesting names, great title ideas, and quick character sketches. My journal has become a pantry of sorts, where I store supplies for later use.

But I don't always wait to get to the computer before working up an idea. I play right there, in longhand, in my journal.

I say "play" because when I write in a particular way, which I'll describe in a moment, the primary, exciting, enlightening experience I am writing about, the insight on which good fiction depends, can happen right on the page. It's fun. And what comes out of me then is fresh and free. I am in touch with myself.

In *Crossing to Safety,* Wallace Stegner writes, ". . . great writing is just trial and error tested by time, and if it's that, then above all it has to be free, it has to flow from the gift, not from outside pressures."

Let it flow into your journals. That is the one place where we are—or can work to be—free of the constraints of censorship by self and others. Your journal is private, remember?

The trick to this kind of writing is simple: Write fast. Write very fast. Write so fast you don't think about what you're writing, you don't worry if it's good or bad or even sane. Don't worry if it's deep or accurate or useful. Just write very, *very* fast.

If you are thinking about a character—I'm working on one named Tony Moon—whom you want to develop and get to know better, you might decide to write for fifteen or twenty minutes on him. Write his name at the top of the page. Then just scribble, *Go*! Say anything that comes into your head without worrying if it's pertinent. Some of it will be, some of it won't. But when your fifteen or twenty minutes are up, you'll have several pages about your character, with some interesting insights about him you would not get otherwise.

Here's the first thing I ever wrote about Tony Moon, who became the protagonist in the book I'm working on now. When I wrote this I knew only his name and that he worked on the New York City streets with child prostitutes:

Tony is scarred. The word like scared with an extra r, the added growl, the sound of teeth clenching, of endurance. The scar runs the length of his leg, from waist to ankle, stapled, white where it's healed, red where it hasn't, never has, never will. This scar is Tony . . . and the scar runs into his sleep, links his waking hidden movements—the way he keeps his right side to the wall, keeps his pants on at the beach—to his dreams to the taste of pain in his sleep, the cement weight of sheets and blanket. . . .

At the end of that burst of writing, I knew all about how Tony got his scar, about his father and mother, his marriage, his sense of self, his sexuality.

When I write this way about my characters (and about myself) I discover things I didn't know I knew; I slide into their souls (and mine).

I also write a lot, cover many pages, many topics. So here is a final *important* piece of advice:

I number my journals along their spine (a piece of tape across a wire spiral works fine). In the front of each book I write the date I start it and the date I finish it. I number the pages. At the back of each book I write the word Index and after every entry I jot down the topics I wrote about and the page numbers.

This way I can find things again.

On my shelves, I have way over a hundred journals. I can't find a damn thing in the early ones, which I didn't index, unless I reread every word. Two years ago, I began this simple system to help locate things. As I worked on this article I was able to go to the shelf, open a book, know instantly when I'd written in it, flip to the back and see if the material I was looking for was there.

Writing is hard, hard work. We fiction writers struggle to show what is specific and true about ourselves and, through ourselves, the world. Our journals are private places in which we can safely be savage, opinionated, perverse, derivative and brilliant. They are our havens, schoolrooms, rehearsal halls, pantries.

The uses I've suggested are perhaps broader than those generally thought appropriate to a journal. But they are still limited. I use my journals in ways that suit me. You should do the same for yourself. Find ways I haven't suggested, ways that free and support you and what you want to do. A journal is as broad and as deep and as varied as the person who writes it. Stretch yourself until you are loose and free.

Keep a journal.

12

THE WRITER'S EYE

BY RANDALL SILVIS

A PART of every successful writer is, and must be, amoral. Detached. Unfeeling. As nonjudgmental as a tape recorder or camera. It is this capacity to stare at pain or ugliness without flinching, at beauty without swooning, at flattery and truth without succumbing to the lure of either, which provides the mortar, the observable details, to strengthen a story and make it a cohesive unit. This capacity I call the writer's eye.

As a child, I was and still am fascinated by the peaks and valleys of people's lives. I was blessed—or cursed—with what was often referred to as "morbid curiosity." At the scene of a funeral, I would be the one trying to inch a bit closer to the coffin, one ear turned to the dry intonations droning from the minister; the other to the papery rustle of leaves overhead. I would take note of how the mourners were standing, where they held their hands, if there were any clouds in the sky, who wept and who did not even pretend to weep, which shoes were most brilliantly shined, the color of the casket, the scent of smoke from someone's backyard barbecue, a killdeer whistling in the distance.

This is how I would remember and record the day, the event. In the details themselves, unbiased, unvarnished and pure, was every nuance of emotion such a tragedy produced. The same held true for weddings and baptisms, for joyous moments as well as sad. Almost instinctively I seemed to know that every abstraction had an observable form: To remark that my neighbor, a tired and lonely man, was drunk again, said nothing; to say that he was standing by the side of the road, motionless but for his gentle, oblivious swaying even as the cars zipped by and blasted their horns at him, his head down, eyes half-closed, hands shoved deep in his pockets as he sang a mumbled "Meet Me Tonight in Dreamland," said it all.

The writer's eye discriminates. It does not and cannot record every detail in a particular scene, only the most telling ones. It is microscopic in focus, telescopic in intent. If, for example, you wish to depict a woman who is trying to look poised despite her nervousness, does it deepen the depiction to say that she wears a two-carat diamond ring on her left hand? Probably not. But if she is shown sitting very straight, knees and feet together, a pleasant smile on her lips as her right hand unconsciously and repeatedly pulls at and twists the diamond ring on her left? These details are in and of themselves emotionally pallid, but in sum, they add to a colorful, revealing whole. In such a description, the word *nervous* need never be uttered. Yet the conclusion is inescapable, and all the more acute because the reader has not been informed of the woman's uneasiness but has witnessed it for himself.

In my novel *Excelsior* (Henry Holt, October, 1987), one of the most important scenes is a moment of closeness between an inept father and his six-year-old son. The scene takes place in a YMCA locker room minutes after the father accidentally knocked the terrified boy, who cannot swim, into the pool. Bloomhardt, the father, despises himself for his own incompetence, and believes that his son does, too. But during a rare moment of openness, six-year-old Timmy admits *his* feelings of frustration and failure. At this point, it would have been quick and easy to state simply that Bloomhardt was relieved, grateful that his son did not despise him, and was filled with a fervent, though awkward, desire to reassure the boy. Instead, I chose to show his state of mind as evidenced in observable details:

> Bloomhardt blinked, his eyes warm with tears. He leaned sideways and kissed his son's damp head. . . . He faced his open locker again, reached for a sock and pulled it on. He smiled to himself.

Bloomhardt's actions are elemental and, on their own, nearly empty of emotional value. But in the context of this passage and in relation to the man's and boy's characters as defined prior to this scene, these details are all that are needed to show the beginnings of a mutual tenderness, trust, and love.

The writer's eye is not merely one sense, but every power of observation the writer possesses. It not only sees, but also smells, tastes, feels, and hears. It also senses which details will paint the brightest picture, which will hint at an unseen quality, which will allow the reader to see beneath the surface of a character to the ice and fire of emotion within.

51

Think of each phrase of description, each detail, as a dot of color on a Seurat landscape. Individually, each dot is meaningless, it reveals nothing, neither laughter nor sorrow. But if you choose your dots carefully and arrange them on the canvas in their proper places, you might, with luck and practice, compose a scene to take the breath away.

¶ 13

Six Myths That Haunt Writers

By Kenneth T. Henson

AMONG THE MANY THINGS I have learned in conducting writers workshops on campuses across the country is that there are several false ideas, myths, that haunt most writers and often impede and/or block beginners. The following are six of these myths—and some suggestions for dealing with them.

1. *I'm not sure I have what it takes.*

I have found that on each campus, coast to coast, there is a superstar writer who, I am assured, has only to put his fingers to the keyboard or pen to paper and, presto, words, sentences, and paragraphs—publishable ones—flow. And, it is thought, these creations are effortless.

These tales are as ridiculous as ghost stories, but more damaging, since most people *believe* them. And like ghost stories, their purpose is to frighten.

If I were a beginning writer and believed that writing comes so effortlessly to some, I would be totally discouraged.

You admit that you, too, have heard of such a superwriter? You may even know such a person by name. Well, don't believe it. It's probably the creation of a person who doesn't intend to write and therefore would prefer that you don't either. The next time someone mentions this super-person, think of Ernest Hemingway, who wrote the last chapter of *Farewell to Arms* 119 times. Or think of the following definitions of writing: "Writing is 10 per cent inspiration and 90 per cent perspiration" and "Successful writing is the ability to apply the seat of the pants to the seat of the chair." Contrary to the myth, all writers perspire; some even sweat!

2. *I don't have time to write.*

You have heard this many times, and if you're like most of us, you have even said it yourself: "If only I had time to write." Ironically, most would-be writers have more time to write than most successful writers do. Some writers even have 24 hours a day to do as they please. But they represent only a small fraction of all writers. The vast majority of writers are free lancers who have either part-time or full-time jobs and pick up a few extra dollars, a little prestige, and a lot of personal satisfaction through writing articles.

The reason behind the bold statement that you have more time than most successful writers have to write is that, probably like you, most of them must earn a living some other way. Yet, these individuals have allotted themselves some time for writing: they took it away from their other activities. Good writers don't *make* time, and they don't *find* time. Rather, they reassign part of their time to writing. And that part of their lives is usually some of their leisure time.

I don't suggest that you stop golfing or fishing or jogging or watching TV, but if you are to be a successful writer, you must give up part of the time you spend (or waste) in the coffee room or bar and you must also give up the idea that you are too tired to write or that watching a mediocre TV show relaxes you. Writing is far more relaxing to most of us who return from our work emotionally drained; it provides an outlet for frustrations, a far more effective release than our more passive attempts to escape from them.

The next time you hear people say, "I don't have time to write" or "I would write for publication if I had time," observe how those persons are spending their time at that moment. If writing is really important to you, replace the activities that are less important with writing. Let your friends and family know that this is your writing time and that you're not to be disturbed. Then tell yourself the same thing. Disciplined people have much more time than do undisciplined people.

3. *I don't have anything worth writing about.*

We've all heard this for years. A significant percentage of aspiring writers really believe that they don't know anything that is worthy of publication. If you are one of them, you're not learning from your experiences: either you don't make mistakes or you don't adjust your behavior to avoid repeating them.

The truth is that you possess a lot of knowledge that would be valuable to others. And you have the abilities that successful writers have to research the topics you wish to write about. I don't know any successful writers who don't feel that they need to research their topics. Start with the subjects that are most familiar, then enrich your knowledge of these subjects by periodic trips to the library, or by interviewing people, or by conducting surveys on these topics.

4. *The editors will reject my manuscript because my name isn't familiar to them.*

Of all the excuses that would-be writers give for not writing, none is weaker than, "If my name were James Michener or Stephen King, editors would listen to me."

But these people don't consider the fact that the Micheners and Kings didn't always have famous names; they started as unknowns and made their names known through talent and hard work. And they would probably be first to say that they have to keep earning their recognition through hard work. Of course, these writers have unusual talent, but you can be equally sure that they work hard and continue to do so to sharpen their skills, research their topics meticulously, and to create and invent new, fresh ways to express their ideas.

There's no guarantee that any of us can earn similar status and acclaim, but we can improve our expertise in our areas of interest and improve our communication skills.

5. *My vocabulary and writing skills are too limited.*

Many people equate jargon, unfamiliar words, complex sentence structure, and long paragraphs with good writing. Actually, though a good vocabulary is a great asset to writers, so are dictionaries and thesauruses, for those who know how to use them and who are willing to take the time to do so. Jargon and long sentences and unnecessarily complex paragraphs harm writing more than they help it.

The sooner you replace words like *utilize* and *prioritize* with words like *use* and *rank,* the faster your writing will improve. Remember, your job is to communicate. Don't try to impress the editor. Editors know what their readers want, and readers seldom demand jargon and complexity.

6. *In my field there are few opportunities to publish.*

If your area of specialization has few professional journals (actually, some fields have only one or two), you may feel trapped, knowing that this uneven supply/demand ratio drives up the competition for these journals.

You might deal with this by searching for more general journals that cover your field, or journals whose editors often welcome articles written by experts in outside but related fields. For example, a biologist or botanist might turn to wildlife magazines, U.S. or state departments of conservation publications, forestry magazines, hunting and fishing publications, or magazines for campers and hikers.

Again, you could consider writing for other audiences, expanding your areas of expertise by taking courses in other disciplines, reading widely, and doing research in other fields to help you develop a broader range of subjects to write about.

Some fields have more journals than others, and some writers are luckier (and more talented) than others. But for those who are willing to work hard at their craft, writing offers a way to reach many professional and personal goals.

14

A GOOD AGENT IS NOT HARD TO FIND—
If You Know How, When, and Where to Look

BY TIMOTHY SCHAFFNER

THE INCREASED VOLUME OF SUBMISSIONS versus the limited time in which an editor has to consider manuscripts has caused many publishers to close their doors to unagented material. In the eyes of these publishers, the work has passed muster only when submitted by a reputable agent. Therefore, today, more than ever, writers need the services of a good literary agent. So, before even attempting to make a sale, the writer must find a good agent to represent his work.

Finding a good agent can, in many respects, be more difficult than getting the book published. Agents these days are a lot more choosy than they might have been in the past because of stricter publication standards, the narrowing list of viable publishers, and the decrease in the number of books published by each house within a given year. An agent's select list must be honed down to include only those writers of the highest quality in any given area of literature; for not only must the agent be able to place work successfully, he must also maintain a reputation among the publishers with whom he works in order to continue to do business with them in the future.

When submitting a manuscript to an agent, the writer must observe a high level of professionalism. Make sure all spelling, typing, and punctuation are correct; type on one side of each page, leave wide margins (2–2¼"), and be sure to paginate throughout. If using a word processor, use only a letter quality or "near-letter quality" printer—dot matrix is discouraged by most agents as it is extremely hard on the eyes. A full manuscript should be submitted unbound in a sturdy typing paper box; be sure to enclose a self-addressed, stamped envelope with sufficient postage for the manuscript's return.

Always query first. A six-hundred-page manuscript, even if it is the greatest work of literature since *War and Peace,* will not be looked upon favorably if it arrives unbidden at an agent's door; chances are, if it does not have the requisite postage for its return, it may very well end up in the trash. In the query letter, briefly describe the nature of the work in one paragraph, and include a short biography and any information that might be helpful to the agent: previous writing credentials and awards received in the last five years, a brief description of your background not only as a writer, but in general terms as well, i.e., where you live, your age, your profession other than writer, interests, etc.

There are several publications on the market to aid the writer in finding an agent. I suggest the *Literary Market Place* (a guide to publishing brought out annually by R. R. Bowker and available in every library reference department), *The Literary Agents of North America* (published by Author Aid Associates, 340 E. 52nd St., New York, NY 10022, this is especially helpful, as it gives a detailed list of each agent's interest as well as a brief rundown of recent titles sold through that agency), and the various books and pamphlets made available through such sources as the Society of Authors' Representatives (10 Astor Pl., 3rd Fl., New York, NY 10003), The Authors Guild (for members), Poets & Writers (72 Spring St., New York, NY 10012), and others. Some of these will provide a detailed description of a particular agent's field of activity. It will be fairly easy to glean from these which you should or should not try. Many of the bigger agencies will not take on any new clients unless they have been referred by someone they know, or better yet, someone who is already a client at that agency. Some agents will work only in a specific area, while others are more generalized. The guides will also point out who accepts unsolicited material, who charges reading fees, and what commission each agent takes. Though many of the big agencies still charge ten percent, most of the independent agents are now charging fifteen.

Trade magazines—such as *Publishers Weekly,* which often gives brief rundowns on the deals of the week (on the "Rights" page) and the agents involved—are also helpful, and you can always look for mention of an agent's name in the acknowledgments of a book you've recently enjoyed. If working in a particular genre, such as romance, science fiction, or mystery, you'll often find agents who are active in that field mentioned in the pages of the various fanzines. Word of mouth is always helpful if you know an agented author who can recommend some agents. Try not to call the agent to ask what kind of work he handles, as this can be determined easily in your research, and such calls can often interrupt the agent in his day-to-day tasks. An agent might be more receptive to your work if you inform him of the source through which you got his name and if you show that you know a little about his special interests.

Once you've selected a group of agents or a particular agent to query, write to them in the manner previously described. If you enclose a self-addressed stamped envelope, you'll be assured of a quick response. Some writers include a postcard with spaces for the agent to check off whether he or she wants to see the work, and if so, in what form, i.e., partial manuscript or complete manuscript. In the case of fiction, I generally ask to see the full manuscript, as it is essential to read the beginning, middle, and end to judge the work. But many agents ask only for partial manuscripts. With a partial, a full synopsis is required, or if it is a nonfiction work, sample chapters plus an outline and table of contents. When an agent asks to see your work, expect a good amount of time to elapse before you hear from him. I usually take between four to six weeks to respond, sometimes less if the author indicates the work is being submitted to more than one agent. When submitting your work to several agents simultaneously, be sure to inform each agent of this fact, and to keep each abreast of any early interest that may develop. Though simultaneous submission is an increasingly common practice, many agents refuse to consider an author's work unless offered to them exclusively.

Once an agent has offered to represent a writer, it is very important to determine the extent to which such representation is offered and under what terms. Many agents work in conjunction with co-agents in the areas of foreign dramatic rights, so it is a good idea to find out a little about this arrangement. Some agents might insist on handling all the author's work or on having a "first look" option, while others might not wish to peddle the writer's short fiction or articles to those magazines and literary journals that tend to offer little or no money and are slow to respond. Some agents have long binding contracts, while others work purely on the basis of a handshake or verbal agreement.

It is always a good idea to get to know the agent either by phone, correspondence, or ideally, in person. Arrange a brief appointment at the agent's office to judge the size of his operation and the sorts of books he has handled recently. The way the agent conducts business is by far the most important factor in your decision, but it is essential for you and the agent to see eye to eye. Though you may be primarily interested in getting your work-at-hand sold, bear in mind that you'll be working with each other for a long period of time beyond the first book. The agent you select should be interested in working with you as a *writer,* and not just in representing you for this one particular book.

Equally important to knowing *how* to find an agent is knowing *when* to get one. Virtually every writer, with the exception perhaps of beginning free-lance magazine writers, juvenile writers, and poets, needs an agent. Once you've reached the point in your career at which a book is evolving, for instance, you will need someone to protect your rights in negotiations and promote your work to insure its greatest possible success. Many well-known writers prefer to handle their books themselves, and some use the services of a lawyer. But, no matter how skilled you or your lawyer might be, it would be extremely difficult to exploit successfully all the additional rights in your work, and to market your book through all the necessary channels. An agent provides services beyond the preliminary negotiations and sale of a work that are vital to an author's career and success. Much of the agent's activity on your behalf is conducted in the day-to-day course of events and does not require the author's participation. The agent is there to handle all your literary business affairs so you can attend to the business of writing without worries and distractions.

Bringing an author out of obscurity into the literary limelight does not happen overnight, and the agent must therefore be thinking long term, beyond the first book, toward building an author's career. Sometimes that much-anticipated first novel might receive glowing reviews but sell only two thousand copies. It then becomes the agent's job to assure both editor and author that there is more to look forward to after the initial frustration and disappointment inherent in the publication of any first book. Similarly, an agent must be able to determine that point in an author's career at which it is necessary to make the great leap forward, to auction the new "break-out" novel for huge sums, and to take the daring gambles that he or she knows from experience will pay off for the writer. Over time, an author can develop a special relationship with his or her agent, a state of symbiosis based on trust, friendship, and an intuitive understanding by the agent of the writer's potential for the present and the future.

15

WRITER'S GAMBIT

BY SCOTT D. YOST

CHESS OPENINGS AND FICTION HAVE MORE IN COMMON than you might think. In fact, if you learn the rules of good opening play for chess and apply them diligently to your writing, you'll end up with winning stories and novels. Just take a look at these chess maxims and their fiction analogues.

• *Grab the center.* The two most common (and best) first moves in chess involve taking a central pawn and putting it right smack in the middle of the board. You should do this in your writing, too: *Begin your story in the middle.* Get to the heart of the matter. Open with a bang. A good chess player doesn't fool around with side pawns at the beginning—there'll be time for those less important pawns in the middle of the game. And a good writer hooks the reader from the first page. Later, you can use flashbacks or dialogue to fill in background material. Time is precious in both a game of chess and a good story. So don't waste it.

• *Get the pieces out fast.* "Pieces" in chess are anything other than pawns—knights, rooks, bishops, the queen, and the king. They are your army, what you play the game with. As soon as you've moved a few pawns and cleared lanes of passage for the pieces, *get the pieces out.* In fiction, your "pieces" are your main characters—and you should introduce them early and get them out quickly, doing whatever it is they'll be doing.

• *Make moves that threaten something.* When you move a piece, always think: *Attack!* Cause problems for your opponent; make moves that hinder his or her opening. When writing, pretend your protagonists are opponents in a chess game: give them problems. Put obstacles in their way. Make each new event apply additional pressure to your protagonist. In chess and in stories, don't be afraid of conflict. Good stories are tales of struggle.

• *Don't bring the queen out too early.* The queen is the most powerful piece on the board. It should be used when the time is right, not before. Get your opponent on the ropes with deft moves of the minor pieces *and then* bring out the queen. Keep this strategy in mind when you write also. Hinder your protagonist, and make his or her goal difficult to attain. Then, when their situation can't get any worse, make it worse. Knock the characters down and hold them there; *then start kicking them.* That is: Bring out the queen—the Big Problem—to menace them, making a solution appear impossible. Set the stage with other events, but save that knockout punch for the end, when it can be most effective.

• *Make each move accomplish several things.* Each chess move should have more than one purpose: ideally it opens lines of attack, gets a piece out, influences the center, attacks the opponent, and fortifies your defenses. All in one move.

Each passage of writing should also do as much as it can. A description, for instance, should not only describe, but progress the plot and characterize as well. Dialogue can perform several functions—characterize, give exposition (though be careful here), move the story, etc.

• *Castle.* Castling is a special move that allows a player to tuck the king away safely, keeping it free from attack until it's needed at the end of the game. When writing, don't reveal your strategy. The solution to the protagonist's problem should be there, on the board and in plain sight, but safely tucked away. Then, when the time is right, use it to help you win the game.

So next time you sit down to write fiction, remember your chess: grab the center, get the pieces out.

16

Dialogue—The Fizz in Fiction

By Peter Lovesey

DIALOGUE OUGHT TO FIZZ like champagne. It should be the guarantee that our writing doesn't go flat.

As a child deciding what to read, I would flick through books to see how much the characters talked. I wasn't attracted by pages dense with prose. I was impatient to get on with the story. A page of dialogue with its lines of different length was more engaging than solid text. Still is, both to read and write. And dialogue also appealed to me because it gave me a direct link with the characters in a book. I wasn't conscious of the writer at work, as I was in descriptive sections. I heard the words of the characters and they came alive. I would sometimes skip sections of description; dialogue, never.

So let's brighten up this page with the opening lines of Gregory Mcdonald's *Fletch*:

"What's your name?"
"Fletch."
"What's your full name?"
"Fletcher."
"What's your first name?"
"Irwin."
"What?"
"Irwin. Irwin Fletcher. People call me Fletch."
"Irwin Fletcher, I have a proposition to make to you. I will give you a thousand dollars just for listening to it. If you decide to reject the proposition, you take the thousand dollars, go away, and never tell anyone we talked. Fair enough?"
"Is it criminal? I mean, what you want me to do?"
"Of course."
"Fair enough. For a thousand bucks I can listen. What do you want me to do?"
"I want you to murder me."

For me, that opening has the rhythm and power of poetry. It is tense, sonorous writing that conveys vital information and ends with a surprise. The writer gives it conviction with naturalistic touches. It is believable as speech.

I used this example because it is pure dialogue. It could be a film script, or the speech bubbles in a cartoon strip. It dispenses with all of the props conventionally used to support direct speech. The identity of the one character we need to know is contained in the first lines, so the writer doesn't need to have *Fletch said* at the beginning or end of any of the lines.

Of course the to and fro of dialogue isn't usually so clear. We need to identify the speakers at some point; they won't necessarily supply their names in the words they speak. But as soon as we add explanatory words, we are dealing in artifice as much as art. The *he/she said* that we tag on is just a device to help the reader distinguish between the speakers. It should be unobtrusive.

The common variations of *he said* are so familiar that they, too, can do their work almost unnoticed: *he remarked/commented/asked/inquired/answered/responded*. But beware. It's a short step to words that may appear strained when you use them: *he questioned/interposed/interrogated/enunciated/averred*. Such words can distract from the dialogue. So, also, can the group often used to portray speech in animal terms: *he snapped/growled/barked/whimpered/yelped/howled/squawked*.

All of us use such words occasionally for color. The danger is that color can clash. My own preference is to stay with the simple *said* in most cases. If the dialogue is sufficiently interesting, the reader can stand the repetition. Occasionally, variations seem appropriate. Fine—but they shouldn't distract. Brilliant writers from Jane Austen to Raymond Carver have been content for the most part to settle for the stark *he/she said*.

The same principle can be applied to the adverbs writers often tag on to the *he said*. Used with discretion, they are effective. It's easy, however, to overdo it, to emulate the writer of the Tom Swift stories. We have all come across writing in which every *he said* is followed by an adverb—and sometimes a redundant adverb: *"I'm sorry," she said apologetically./ "I wonder," he said thoughtfully*.

It *is* a problem, particularly when you want the reader to be conscious of the characters and their response to the things being said. It can be helpful to study the techniques of writers you admire. Graham Greene, one of my favorites, makes regular use of the construction *he said with* . . . The examples that follow are from *The Human Factor*:

> . . . *he said with his habitual guilty grin.*
> . . . *he said with formal politeness.*
> . . . *he said with a sharp note of accusation.*

Raymond Chandler's solution in *The Big Sleep* is frequently to give a short sentence describing some gesture or facial expression of the speaker:

> *Sudden panic flamed all over her face.*
> *His mouth became a hard white grimace.*

In giving these examples, I have over-simplified. Writers as skillful as Greene and Chandler employ a variety of techniques. My point is that if you analyze successful authors' methods of presenting dialogue, you may well be inspired to try different techniques of your own, for nowhere else in the writing of fiction does it come down so obviously to the nuts and bolts. Make yourself aware of well-tested methods and adapt them to your own creative output.

Let's turn from the externals to the dialogue itself. The English thriller-writer, Len Deighton, once wrote that he didn't want to be so famous that people recognized him. "I like to be able to listen to conversations without people turning around to look at me over their shoulders. I want to be the man behind you in the fish shop." All writers should be eavesdroppers. We dignify it by saying that we have to cultivate an ear for dialogue, but it comes down to listening to other people's conversations. If our characters are to talk like real people, the speech-patterns must be in our heads. When we come to write conversations down, it's sensible to speak them aloud and see how they compare with what we overheard in the fish shop or on the train.

What you end up with is not quite what you heard in the fish shop. Anyone who has tape-recorded and then transcribed a conversation knows how banal most of it appears. You have to delete the ums and ers, the tedious repetitions of "you know" and "as I say." A few may stay in, but many would be tedious unless used for some special purpose. You compress and select. You are in charge—up to a point. Here we enter controversial territory.

Almost all novelists, as they write their books, have experienced the phenomenon of having a character grow and develop in an unplanned way. "The characters have their own lives and their own logic, and you have to act accordingly," is the way Isaac Bashevis Singer expressed it. This mysterious process is often at work when you compose dialogue. A character almost demands to say something. And quite frequently this can reveal new possibilities to the writer. Not all writers are comfortable when it happens. Jorge Luis Borges put it this way: "Many of the characters are fools and they are always playing tricks on me and treating me badly." However, it can be worth submitting to the treatment, if only in a draft, just in case serendipity hands you a pearl.

Time for some more of the real thing, from *The Silent Salesman,* by Michael Z. Lewin:

As I opened the door, I saw a girl sitting behind my desk. Late teens, with slightly reddish-brown hair, dark brown eyes, and freckles. She looked vaguely familiar. I took two steps inside and stumbled over a knapsack that I hadn't left in the middle of the floor.

I hadn't left it anywhere; it wasn't mine.

"This yours, Miss?"

She nodded. Then she opened the middle drawer of my desk. "Hey, there's nothing in here," she said. "Why don't you keep anything in it?"

"Because when I'm out working I leave the office open. To offer a moment's rest for strays and waifs and the occasional client. Which might you be?"

She smiled at me until she saw that I wasn't smiling. "I don't think I'm any of those categories. Do you?"

"Look here, young lady, it's hot. I've had a hard day—"

She stood up with a sense of urgency. "Don't you really recognize me?"

I frowned. She did look . . .

"Daddy!" she said.

"Oh my God," I said. It takes a wise father to know his own child.

"I recognized *you*! And all I've had is a picture from more than twelve years ago."

"My God," I said. "My God."

Leaving aside what I called the nuts and bolts, let's concentrate on the effectiveness of the dialogue. First, the voices sound right: the Private Eye, suave, capable of handling most emergencies, but getting a severe jolt here; and his daughter, casually playful until she senses that this reunion isn't working out exactly as she planned. Dialogue works best when there is disharmony between characters. By disharmony I don't necessarily mean conflict. I mean the friction between two points of view.

In the extract you have just read, the story is written in the first person, from the point of view of the man. Yet Michael Lewin makes us conscious of the girl's unease *(She smiled at me until she saw that I wasn't smiling)* swiftly turning to alarm *(She stood up with a sense of urgency),* and we are engaged by her vulnerability in this situation as much as her father's. They are two people with different expectations.

There ought to be friction of some sort in most dialogue. Even in situations where characters have an identity of interest—say, a love scene—you don't want them echoing each other's words. They are individuals with their own perceptions, and the more conscious we are of their different personalities, the more effective will the scene become. So it is essential to *know* the characters, their hopes and hang-ups, before you attempt to give them speech.

The pace and rhythm of dialogue must be a matter of judgment. We've looked at examples of tense dialogue using short speeches. Difficulties can arise when you need a longer piece of exposition. Crime writers like me usually face this problem in the last chapter of a book, when everything has to be explained. A protracted speech calls for an effort of concentration that the reader isn't always prepared to give at that stage, so we have to devise ways of breaking up those long speeches. Occasionally writers will divide a long speech into paragraphs, but that is the least satisfactory remedy. It is preferable to have another character interrupt the speaker with some question or comment, and to prevent this becoming too obvious a device you might change the pace for a few lines with a staccato exchange:

> ". . . and left the gun in his hand."
> "And a note in his pocket."
> "Yes."
> "Why?"
> "Why the note?"
> "The gun."

Such an exchange may seem artificial as you write it. However, it's worth noting that in real conversations people rarely allow anyone to talk on for very long, and when an interruption comes, the original speaker can be thrown for a moment. The floundering before order is restored provides a convenient pause for the reader.

The need to be realistic, to make people sound believable as they speak, has to be reconciled with your wish as a writer to move the story in a particular direction. As I have said, it can be helpful sometimes to let the characters take over, particularly when their voices demand to be heard. But ultimately dialogue must be controlled by the writer. It is not conversation, but the semblance of conversation. It is a distillation of what might have been said in real life, selected and shaped to a degree that the reader shouldn't begin to suspect.

The quotations from *Fletch*, by Gregory Mcdonald, and from *The Silent Salesman*, by Michael Z. Lewin, are reprinted here by permission of the authors.

17

Emotion in Fiction

By Rosamunde Pilcher

I WAS, AS A CHILD, extremely emotional. Almost anything or anybody could make me cry. I wept copiously as I listened to Paul Robeson singing "Ol' Man River." Soggy with sentiment, I begged my Scottish mother to oblige me with a rendering of "Loch Lomond," swearing that I wouldn't blub. But when she got to the bit, "But me and my true love will never meet again," my good resolutions went with the wind and the tears poured down.

There were books as well. A dreadful Victorian drama for children called *A Peep Behind the Scenes*. I have no recollection of the plot, but I know that almost everybody, in some way or another, died. Mother had tuberculosis, and a saint-like child who crossed the road in order to pick buttercups in a field was squashed flat beneath the wheels of a passing cart. When I found myself with an empty afternoon and no one to play with, I would find myself drawn, with hideous inevitability, to the bookshelf, and the dismal book. Sitting on the floor, I would turn the pages, scarcely able to see the print for weeping.

In other words, I, like an awful lot of other people, enjoyed a good cry.

The poem, "The Raggle, Taggle Gypsies" had the same effect on me, and, oddly enough, so did Beatrix Potter's "Pigling Bland." I say "oddly enough," because Beatrix Potter was always marvelously unsentimental and thoroughly practical about the seamy side of life. Jemima Puddleduck, laying her eggs in the wrong places, was deemed a simpleton. Squirrel Nutkin, teasing the owl, got his deserts and lost his tail. And right and proper, too. But Pigling Bland was different. He and his little girlfriend Pig Wig finally escaped the dreadful fate of being sent to market, and sent off on their own, running as fast as they could.

> They came to the river, they came to the stream,
> They crossed it, hand in hand,

Then over the hills and far away,
She danced with Pigling Bland.

It made me cry, not because it was sad, but because it was beautiful. I still think it is beautiful, and I still get a lump in my throat when I read it aloud to my grandchildren.

The most subtle form of arousing emotion is to slip the reader, with little or no warning, from laughter to tears. James Thurber wrote a piece entitled "The Dog That Bit People." It was about an Airedale called Muggs. He didn't simply bite people, but terrified the life out of deliverymen and was regularly reported to the police. Told in Thurber's laconic style, it was marvelously funny.

But in the last paragraph, Muggs dies, quite suddenly, in the night. He is duly buried, in a grave alongside a lonely road. Mother wants a marble headstone erected, but finally settles for a smooth board, on which Thurber wrote, with an indelible pencil, "Cave Canem," and his mother was pleased with the simple classic dignity of the old Latin epitaph.

All right; so the death of any faithful animal is a sure-fire tear-jerker, but it still gets to me, every time I read it.

Emotion, conveyed by the written word, is a delicate business. Like humor, it cannot be pushed, or it slips into sentimentality. Hemingway, that master of reported speech, could wring the heart by the bare bones of his painful dialogue. He never stressed the fact that he was telling you something that went beyond ordinary feelings, and yet you read the mundane, oft-used words, and hear his voices, and recognize the poignancy of the frailty of man, and there comes the lump in the throat and the sting of incipient tears.

Some years ago, I wrote a three-act play, with a single set; not a very accomplished piece of work, but it was produced by our local repertory theater, and for a few weeks I enjoyed a mild local fame. For the first time in my life, I was invited to open fetes, judge competitions, and hand out prizes for various contests. I found none of this too daunting. But then I was approached by a woman famous for her good works, and asked if I would make an appeal on radio to raise funds for her pet project—a training center for young mothers (scarcely more than schoolgirls) unfit to care for their unwanted babies. Touched by the plight of these little families, I agreed. Only then was I told that not only

71

would I have to deliver the appeal, but would have to write the message myself.

It was the first time that I had been faced with a situation in which I deliberately had to drag emotion out of the bag. For without emotion, I should not touch hearts, and if I didn't touch hearts, I would not touch pockets. I engaged the help of a bright girl who was involved in the project, and for two days we sat at our typewriters, finally bashing out five minutes' worth of heartbreak, sentiment, and crying need. I duly read this out over the radio one Sunday morning, and by the end of the week the center was about a hundred and fifty pounds to the good. It wasn't much, and it wasn't enough. They struggled on for a month or two, and then closed down. We had tried, but it hadn't worked.

Much more recently, the very opposite occurred. In Dundee, Scotland, a small boy was desperately ill. Specialized neurosurgery was required, but the Dundee Royal Infirmary did not have the necessary equipment. In Boston, Massachusetts, however, the equipment was available, and this was flown, in some urgency, to Scotland. The two neurosurgeons had never used the device before, but they operated, with total skill, and the small boy's life was saved.

The story appeared the next day in our local paper, *The Dundee Courier and Advertiser*. A plain, factual account of what had taken place. We learned that the reason the equipment had had to be borrowed was that the Infirmary could not afford the £60,000 necessary to purchase it. With some idea of expressing my gratitude and admiration for the two doctors, I put five pounds in an envelope and posted it to the Infirmary. So did just about everyone else, who, that morning, took the paper. A fund had to be hastily set up, without an appeal ever having been launched, and within the next two weeks, the £60,000 target had been achieved. Which proves that if you've got a good story to tell, you don't need to play your sobbing violin at the same time.

Sadness, bravery, beauty, all touch our heart strings. Great happiness can be deeply touching, else why do we sometimes weep at weddings, or that moment when an old gentleman heaves himself to his feet at his Golden Wedding party and raises his champagne glass to his wife?

My novel *The Shell Seekers* covered a span of fifty years, and because of this, the varying ages of the characters, and the intrusion of two terrible wars, I found myself writing, more than once, about death. The demise of an elderly person I do not, in fact, find particularly sad. A shock and a loss, certainly, to be followed by a period of grieving, but death is part of life, and just about the only thing we can all be certain of.

However, the death of the young officer, Richard Lomax, killed on Omaha Beach, with all his life ahead of him, I found quite agonizing to set down. And worse was endeavoring to describe the reactions of Penelope Keeling, who when told of his tragic end, knew that their brief love was finished, and that the rest of her life would have to be lived without him. Struggling, as she struggled, for words, I gave her only the most banal of sentences to utter. And then cheated, and instead let her recall the final passage of the Louis MacNeice poem which they had both known and loved.

> . . . the die is cast
> There will be time to audit
> The accounts later, there will be sunlight later,
> And the equation will come out at last.

Cheating, perhaps. But it seemed to me to say it all.

To sum up, an analysis of what touches the writer is what will eventually get through to the reader. Understated, underplayed, unexaggerated, and yet totally sincere. There has to be rapport, a chime of instant recognition, clear as a bell. If you don't produce tears, you will at least kindle understanding, identification, and so forge a bond with the reader. And, at the end of the day, perhaps this is what writing is all about.

18

FICTION WRITING: TWENTY QUESTIONS AND ANSWERS

BY SIDNEY SHELDON

Q. *Many stories start out well, but then lose momentum midway through. What are some techniques you use to keep your stories moving along, or as they say, to keep the reader turning the pages?*

A. It's very important to me that my books never lose momentum. I try not to let anything slow the pace of the plot and a trick I use is to end each chapter on a note of suspense so the reader has to keep turning pages.

Q. *Is there such a thing as purely spontaneous or inspired writing? Do you experience it at some point in your work, say, usually in the first draft?*

A. The answer is yes. I feel as though my books are given to me and I know that many other writers feel the same way. In writing a book, the greatest joy is having the characters take over and race away with the story.

Q. *Can you recall a published novel or a screenplay that gave you particular trouble? How was it worked out?*

A. All my novels give me trouble. Usually in the middle of a novel I'm tempted to give it up. Somehow they always seem to work out.

Q. *What, if any, basic changes have taken place in your writing from when you first began? How do you account for those changes—were they the result of a deliberate intent or of a slow evolution?*

A. My first book, *The Naked Face,* was a straightforward, simple story. Since then, my books have become more complex, written on larger canvasses. Like Topsy they just growed.

Q. *At what point does your own, internal critic step into your writing? Do you dictate pages upon pages in a stream of consciousness manner, and then go back, or is this critic always on the lookout?*

A. I think it's very important for a writer not to be critical while he's creating. I do my first drafts without criticizing anything. When I'm finished I become a critic and will write up to a dozen complete drafts.

Q. *How well do you know your characters when you begin writing a novel? Do they develop as you go along?*

A. When I begin a novel I start with one character, usually a woman. I learn about her and about the other characters as I begin writing the novel. I have no plot in mind when I begin, and again I want to warn the young writer that this is a precarious way to write. I would suggest doing a step outline before starting a novel.

Q. *First impressions are widely believed to be of the utmost importance in day-to-day life. Is this true when introducing characters to the reader? What sort of device do you rely on most for first introductions between character and reader?*

A. I don't rely on any devices in introducing a character. My characters are always very clear in my mind and each behaves in his own distinctive way.

Q. *Do you keep a journal, and if so, what sorts of things are recorded in it? If you don't, why not—have you ever tried?*

A. I do not keep a journal but I fervently wish that I had and I would advise all writers to do so.

Q. *As a self-taught writer, how do you feel about the current trend toward enrolling in university writing programs?*

A. I don't think enrolling in a university writing program can harm anyone. You can learn some of the basics. But if you don't have any talent for writing, the program won't help.

Q. *Many writers, beginning writers especially, believe the place where they write (a big city, or a cabin in the woods) must have romantic overtones for them to write well. How elemental is a writer's habitat to maintaining a high level of creativity? If it is a myth, what is it about the writing profession that perpetuates such fantasy?*

A. The only important thing about where a writer works is that it should be comfortable for him or her. If a mountain or a desert gives you inspiration, fine. I learned long ago when I was working in a studio that when you get a paycheck every week, the studio doesn't want to hear that you're waiting to be inspired. They want pages.

Q. *How much of your writing is from memory—whether from overheard conversation, characters drawn from people you know—and how much can you attribute entirely to imagination? Is it possible to separate memory from imagination?*

A. Some wise man once said that all writers paper their walls with themselves. In one way or another, we use everything we see, hear, read, smell. Having said that, all good stories come from the imagination.

Q. *Do you ever knowingly write about people who would be identifiable, say, well-known figures barely disguised, or friends and relatives? Have you ever experienced any backlash from people who've recognized themselves, or thought they had, in your work?*

A. In *The Other Side of Midnight*, I based the character of Constantin Demiris on Aristotle Onassis. Mr. Onassis read the book, recognized that the character was based on himself and objected to some of the characteristics.

Q. *Are there topics that are so close to you that you won't or can't write about them? Family history, for example. Do you wait for certain emotions or emotional situations to settle before writing about them, or is it best for you to commit them to paper immediately?*

A. There are no topics that I will not write about. The most painful scenes I wrote were the death scenes in *Windmills of the Gods*. My wife had died shortly before I wrote the book and writing the scenes was a catharsis for me.

Q. *Do you have any strong feelings about the use of flashbacks, how they should be used, or when? What devices do you use for transitions from past to present?*

A. Flashbacks are very tricky and have to be handled carefully. When you jump backward or forward in time, it is easy to confuse the reader. There are mechanical devices like asterisks and leaving extra space between paragraphs, but it is a mistake to rely solely on those methods. You have to phrase your sentences so that it is clear to the reader that you are now taking him back in time or forward in time, or that you have returned to the present. These are important guideposts, so handle them carefully.

Q. *Should writers at the outset of a novel believe they are going to write "the great American novel," or, as one writer once said to us, "I'm going to write a classic."*

A. If the question is "should one aim high?" the answer is "yes." Not every writer has it in him to write "the great American novel." The trick is to do your best. It is an unfortunate fact of life that too many writers—like too many people in other fields—are satisfied with less than their best.

Q. *How attentively should a beginning writer listen to his critics? How seriously do you take reviews of your works?*

A. I learned long ago never to ignore a specific criticism of my work. I used to say, "but don't you see what I meant was," but I realized that if you have to explain, it's not the reader's problem, it's your problem. As far as how seriously I take reviews of my books, it depends on the reviewer. I look for constructive criticism. I don't hold the general critical community in very high regard.

Q. *What impact do you hope your books will have on your readers?*

A. My books seem to have a great deal of impact on my readers. A woman came up to me in a restaurant and told me that she became a lawyer because she had read *Rage of Angels* about a woman lawyer. Another example of reader impact was also in *Rage of Angels*. I let a little boy die and I received so many letters from distraught readers that, when we made the miniseries, I let the little boy live.

Q. *What do you think about the increasing reliance of publishers on literary agents to "discover" new talent and the growing number of major publishers who refuse to read unsolicited manuscripts?*

A. Many publishers refuse to read unsolicited manuscripts partly because of fear of lawsuits, and partly because so much of the material is a waste of time. I don't think it matters whether literary agents discover new talent or publishers discover new talent. Just keep discovering them!

Q. *Do you think the growing problem of illiteracy in America has or will eventually have an effect on the types of books published here? If so, what will it be?*

A. Illiteracy is a tremendous problem in this country. Twenty-six million adults are unable to read. Libraries and national organizations are trying hard to reverse that trend and I think we are beginning to make progress. I think we will go on publishing the same types of books we publish now.

Q. *Are there limits to what types of books should be kept from children at certain ages, and if so, who should control the restrictions— librarians, teachers, school boards, parents, bookstores? Given what children are exposed to today in the newspapers, movies, and television, is any kind of "censorship" of reading materials ever justified?*

A. I think it is up to the parents to control the reading habits of minors. I do not believe in censorship. A little censorship is like being a little bit pregnant; it's going to grow.

19

THE READER AS PARTNER

BY TONY HILLERMAN

SOMETIME VERY EARLY in my efforts to make a living as a writer, I noticed an odd little fact, trivial but useful: People just back from seeing the Rocky Mountains didn't describe the Front Range. They told me about the clump of mountain iris they'd seen blooming through the edge of a dwindling snowbank. Witnesses of a train wreck I interviewed when I was a reporter would describe the women's clothing scattered along the right-of-way and ignore the big picture. The fellow drinking beer after watching the rodeo would talk about the sounds the bulls made coming out the gate—not the derring-do of the champion rider.

I noticed my own brain worked that way, too: It would store a scattering of details in full color and with every stitch showing, but the general scene would be vague and ill-defined. I presumed that this was the way run-of-the-mill men and women remembered things, and thus, it would be useful for writers in the process of converting a scene that exists in our minds into words that would recreate it in the imagination of those who read what we write.

I doubt if there is anything new or original about this thinking or this tactic. Selecting significant details to cause the reader to focus attention exactly where it's wanted was being done with quill pen on papyrus and probably before. Except for those dilettantes of the "art for art's sake" school, every writer is engaged in a joint venture every time he writes. He looks at what's behind his own forehead and translates it into words. At the other end of the crosscut saw, the reader drinks in those words and tries to transmute them back into images.

It's a partnership. We work at it. So does the reader.

But we're getting paid for it, in money, fame (if we're lucky), and in the fun of controlling the process. The reader expects a different reward for the cash and time he or she invests. Even so, that reader is a working member of the team.

I always write with some clear notions about those for whom I write. They are, for example, a little more intelligent than I am and have a bit better education. They have good imaginations. They enjoy suspense. They are impatient. They are middle-aged. They are busy. They know very little about the specific subject I'm writing about. They are interested in it only if I can provoke that interest.

Given that, how should I go about my business? For example, how should I describe in physical terms this benign character I am about to introduce in chapter three? Not much, probably, if that character is to be important to the plot, and the reader is to come to know him from repeated meetings. But quite a bit if said character takes the stage only briefly.

Why this odd inversion? Because my intelligent, well-educated, middle-aged, imaginative reader knows from personal experience what various sorts of people look like. Therefore, if you use a character a lot, the reader paints his own portrait. For example, as far as I can remember, I have never given more than the vaguest descriptions of either Joe Leaphorn or Jim Chee, the two Navajo tribal policemen who are often the protagonists in my mystery novels. Yet scores of readers have described them to me. Tall and short, big and little, plump and lean, handsome and homely. The reader's imagination creates the character from his or her own experience, making the policeman look exactly the way he should look. Why should the writer argue with that? Why should the person who is investing money and time in reading my story be denied his role in the creative process?

Minor characters, I think, need more description. The reader is likely to see them only briefly through the eyes of the protagonist. He should be as curious about minor characters as is the viewpoint character—looking for the spot of gravy on the necktie, the nervous twitch at the corner of the eye, the dark roots of the bleached blonde hair, the scar tissue on the left cheek. Our reader won't see this minor actor enough to fit him into any personal mold.

Sometimes, of course, the writer must exercise more control over the image the reader would create. The story line may demand that the reader know the character is burly, has an artificial hand, and that his eyes tend to water if he stands too long reading the sympathy cards in the Hallmark shop. Otherwise, I count on the reader to perform his half of the task with no interference from me. I think he enjoys it more.

This notion of the reader as partner in a game of imagination affects how I write in many other ways. For example, there's that hard-to-define something that I think of as "mood." It exists in my mind as I write a scene. Sometimes it is merely the mental state of the viewpoint character through whose eyes whatever is happening is seen. But it can be more than that, or even different from that. For example, I may need to send signals to the reader that it is time for nervous anxiety, while the protagonist is still happily remembering that there's nothing left to worry about.

I tend to take on the mood of the scene—writing with lower lip gripped between my teeth when doom is impending, writing with a grin when all is well in chapter nine. I want the reader to join me in this mood. And here I'm on shaky ground. I simply have no way of knowing if my tactics work.

They involve engaging the reader's senses. I interrupt the dialogue or the action to show the reader through the eyes of the protagonist the dust on the windowsill, the grime on the windowpane, the tumbleweeds blowing across the yard, the broken gate creaking in the wind, the spider scurrying toward the center of its web, the stuffed weasel in its frozen leap toward the cowering quail in the taxidermy display. I have the reader notice the odors of old age, of decay, and of air breathed too often in a closed and claustrophobic room. I have him hear the sort of vague sounds that intrude into tired, tense silences. These are the sorts of signals my senses are open to when I am in this certain mood. If they don't contribute to causing it, at least they reflect it. Perhaps the same will be true for the reader.

Another mood. Another set of sensory signals. Take satisfaction-contentment-happiness (what my Navajo characters might call "hozro"). There's the smell of rain in the air (remember, I write mostly about a landscape where rain is all rare and a joyful blessing), the aroma of brewing coffee, the promising voice of distant thunder, the sound of birds, the long view through slanting sunlight of sage and buffalo grass, and the mountains on the horizon, a sense of beauty with room enough and time enough to enjoy it, and the good feeling of fresh-baked bread under the fingertips.

Unless some psychologist can come up with a universal catalogue of which objects/smells/sounds are connected in the mind of Average

Human with which mood, neither you nor I will ever know how effective this technique is. My conversations with those who have read my work suggest that sometimes I can make it work, and sometimes I fail. But I am working at it, using my only laboratory animal—myself—as guinea pig.

Someone I meet pleases me. I think I would like them. Why? Well, you know . . . there was just something about him. But specifically, exactly what was it? Go back, you sluggard, and remember. What was it, specifically and exactly, that first caused you to start looking at and listening to this stranger? It was the body language, the expression, that told you he was really and intently listening when you talked to him. Interested in you and in what you were saying. So how can that be described most effectively? And what else was there? The way he said things? The turn of phrase. To defer. Not to interrupt. The tendency not to overdescribe, to presume his listener was intelligent and informed. Whatever it was, isolate it. Remember it. Have it handy the next time you want to introduce this sort of person to the reader.

A scene depresses me, leaves me out of sorts and angry. Why? The coldness of the room, the dim, yellow light, the tarnish on the gold tassel on the rope, the arrogant stare of the hostess, the slick, clammy coolness of the surface of this table. . . . What else?

I awake at night from a bad dream, tense and anxious. Quick. Dissect the mood before it evaporates. Nightmares are rare these days for me. For a man who deals in suspense, fear, and tension, they are too valuable to waste. What was in it and in the darkness around the bed that provokes this uneasiness and anxiety? Specifically, what do you hear, or smell, or feel or see that causes this painful tension?

I have been doing this for years: stripping down people and places, dissecting their looks and their mannerisms, filling the storage bins of imagination with useful parts; doing the same with street scenes, with landscapes, with the weather. When I wrote only nonfiction, such stuff was jotted in my notebook—the telltale details I trained my mind to isolate and collect. The anthropologist squatted on a grassy slope beside an anthill, his callused fingers sifting through those tiny grains ants bring to the surface, frowning in his fierce hope of finding a chip from a Stone Age artifact. The same fingers sorting through the residue left on the sifter-frame over his wheelbarrow, eliminating the gravel, roots, and rabbit droppings, saving the tiny chips flaked from a flint lance point; finding a twig to fish out the angry scorpion and return him to the grass. And that final detail, I hope my reader will agree, does more than put him on the scene with me. It gives him insight into the character of the man who owns the callused fingers.

20

SO YOU WANT TO WRITE A BESTSELLER?

BY BARBARA TAYLOR BRADFORD

WHEN I'm on tour to promote a new novel, I meet many people in bookstores, TV audiences, and lecture halls, who tell me they want to be a bestselling novelist. They seek my advice. Generally, I tell them to sit down and do it, because that is the only way a book is ever written. However, I usually make a point of asking each one the same question: Why do you want to be a novelist?

Invariably they tell me that they want to make a lot of money and become a famous celebrity.

These are the wrong reasons.

There is only one reason to write a novel and that is because writing fiction is absolutely essential to one's well-being. It is to mine and it always has been. In other words, it is the work that really counts, the sense of creation that is the important thing to me.

Don't misunderstand me. Of course I want readers, every author does. But I have never sat down at a typewriter and told myself that I'm about to write a great bestseller. I have no idea if a book of mine is going to sell in the millions when I actually start it. How could I know, since I don't have a secret recipe? All I have is a story to tell about a number of characters who are very real people to me. I knew I wanted to be a novelist when I was a child in Yorkshire. I had no brothers or sisters so I invented playmates and told them stories. When I was ten, my father bought me a second-hand typewriter and I typed out these little tales and stitched them in a folder with a hand-painted title.

When I was 12 I submitted one—about a little horse, I think—to something called *The Children's Magazine* and it was actually published. I got ten and six for it. I have never stopped writing since.

The first novel I attempted was about a ballet dancer named Vivienne Ramage who lived in a garret in Paris! By this time I had managed to get

84

a job on the *Yorkshire Evening Post* and had been to the Paris fashion shows with the women's page editor.

Paris totally overwhelmed me. I came back, and began this story. My ballet dancer was desperately poor and it was all terribly dramatic and suspiciously reminiscent of Dumas' *La Dame aux Camélias*! Anyway, I got to about page ten and suddenly thought: I've a feeling I've read this somewhere before.

I kept experimenting like that all though my girlhood. Being on a newspaper, doing the police beat, covering the coroners' courts, exposed me to life in the raw and taught me that you can't just write about the landscape or a room setting—a story is only interesting if it's about people. Their tragedies, their dramas, their joys.

That's what I'm dealing in now, human emotions. The hope is that I can get them down on paper in such a way as to touch a nerve in the reader so that he or she identifies and is moved. At 17 I was very much in love with being a newspaperwoman—a newspaper*man* I should say—even down to wanting a dirty trench coat. My mother accused me of having dragged it round in the street to make it grubby.

But my newspaper career didn't begin as a reporter. The only job I could get at the start was in the typist pool. First day I was still typing away long after everybody had gone home. As I was leaving I saw the wastepaper basket overflowing with the company's crumpled, vellum-like notepaper and I thought, I'm going to get fired for wasting their stationery. So I took a handful into the ladies' room, lit a match to it and threw it down the toilet.

Well, the blaze was so enormous I then thought: this way I'll be fired for being an arsonist! So I collected up the rest, smoothed it out and hid it in the bottom drawer of my desk.

For a week after that I took one of my mother's shopping bags to work with me and brought the telltale paper home in batches. I think I eventually got a job as a cub reporter because I was such an awful typist.

But I worked at getting moved, too—I did little stories and handed them in to my editor, who finally put me in the newsroom.

At 18, I became women's editor. When I was 20 I left Upper Armley, Yorkshire, for London and a job on *Woman's Own* as a fashion editor, followed by a stint as a reporter and feature writer on the *Evening News*.

Naturally, that was a job in which I met actors, film stars, novelists, screenwriters, politicians—people who were "achievers"—but I never expected to find success or be rich and famous myself. However, when I look back, I realize my mother always instilled in me a desire to do my best. I wanted to please her. She loved the theatre, movies, music and art and she got me my first two library tickets when I was still very small. When she died in 1981—only 5 weeks after I lost my father—I found those tickets in her purse.

I continued writing after I moved to the United States, where I have lived since my marriage in 1963 to a Hollywood film producer, Robert Bradford. I wrote non-fiction books between 1963 and 1974, mostly on interior design, and two books for children.

Between 1968 and 1974, when I was writing a syndicated column for American newspapers, I started four novels but discarded them all after a few hundred pages. One was set in Paris and North Africa. It was called *Florabelle*. I liked strong heroines from the start. That one was an actress.

Yet another novel was set in North Africa—I was smitten with Morocco at that time—and that tale was about a woman photo-journalist. My next was sited in the South of France. But the one I was writing when I thought of *A Woman of Substance* was called *The Jasper Cypher*. It was a Helen MacInnes-type suspense novel starting in New York and moving to Spain.

But obviously I was wrong, wasn't I? I should have been writing about Yorkshire, not Morocco. I got to chapter four and I thought, this is boring. I asked myself a lot of questions that day. It was like a dialogue with myself. I said: Well, what *do* you want to write about? What *sort* of book do you want to write? Where do you want to set it? And of course I knew, suddenly, that I really wanted to set it in England, specifically Yorkshire. Then I said: And I want to write about a strong woman.

So, having decided to write about a Yorkshire girl who emancipates herself and creates a big business empire, I could see it would be more effective if she were born poor and in an age when women were not doing these things, and to have her working for a rich family who falls as she rises.

After a couple of hours of thinking along these lines I had the nucleus of my plot and started to jot down a few notes and I thought, yes, she becomes a woman of substance. And I looked at that on my pad and thought, that's a marvelous title.

At a point like this I put paper in typewriter and tap out a few details. I might take two days experimenting with a name for the character. It has to have just the right ring. Then I create the other protagonists, maybe draw a family tree, listing names and ages, their relationships.

All the time I'm asking myself questions and answering them on paper. When is it going to start, how old is she, what is her background, what motivates her, why did this woman do what she did, become what she became? All my characters are totally analyzed, as if I were a psychiatrist.

I then transpose these notes onto index cards, and I maintain these character cards as if I'm dealing with real people—and they become very real to me. As I develop them, somehow the plot falls into place almost automatically.

Once I have title, characters and story line in note form, I divide the book into parts. It's a way to organize the material. In *A Woman of Substance* I got titles for the sections from the land—the valley, the abyss, the plateau, the pinnacle, the slope. It was a method of tracing the rise and fall of a life. In *Voice of the Heart,* I used the stage— overture, wings, Act 1, downstage right and so on. In *Hold the Dream,* the phases are entitled "Matriarch"—that's Emma Harte in old age— and "Heiress and Tycoon," which is the ascent of her granddaughter, Paula.

At this stage I write a piece like the copy on a novel's dust jacket, the bare bones of the story. Then I finish the outline, which is ten to 20 pages. That takes me about a week to ten days.

Once I get going on a novel, a good day is when I've written five finished pages. I usually start in longhand, using a fine nibbed pen (Sanford's Expresso, if you like to know that sort of thing) and then move to the typewriter.

Someone once asked me what a novel is and I said: It's a monumental lie that has to have the absolute ring of truth if it is to succeed.

It's easy to know when something is good and, in a way, it's easy to know when something is bad. But to know *why* it's bad, that's the thing. And how do you change it?

I've gone back and looked at my first attempts at fiction, and there wasn't too much wrong with them, except that I wanted basically to write about Yorkshire and didn't know it. So I wouldn't say to the would-be novelist: press on with *anything* you start. You could be on the wrong subject matter, as I was.

However, I now realize that as I labored, I was in effect honing my craft, teaching myself how to write a novel. I truly believe that learning the craft of fiction writing is vital and that you can't do that at classes. You can perhaps learn techniques—I borrowed library books on journalism when I was trying to become a reporter—but no one can teach you to write a novel. You have to teach yourself.

Basic writing ability is still not enough. A would-be novelist must also observe what I call the five Ds:

D for desire—the desire to want to write that novel more than do anything else.

D for drive—the drive to get started.

D for determination—the will to continue whatever the stumbling blocks and difficulties encountered on the way.

D for discipline—the discipline to write every day, whatever your mood.

D for dedication to the project until the very last page is finished.

Finally, there is a sixth D—to avoid! This is for distractions—perhaps the most important D of all, the enemy of all writers, whether would-be or proven.

Writing novels is the hardest work I've ever done, the salt mines, really. I sit long hours at my desk, starting out at six in the morning and finishing around six or seven in the evening. And I do this six and a half days a week, till my neck and shoulders seize up. I make tremendous social and personal sacrifices for my writing, but after all, I chose to be a novelist. Nobody held a gun to my head.

But in all truth, it's not possible to be a full-time novelist and a social butterfly, living the so-called glamorous existence of the bestselling novelist.

There's nothing which faintly resembles glamour about the work I do. I spend all of my working hours alone, facing a blank sheet of paper, and myself. For I have to dredge through my soul and my memories every day of my life.

When a book is finished I have to go on promotion tours. This may sound exciting. But it isn't. Taking a different plane or train every day and heading for another city is hardly my idea of fun; neither are crowded airports, poor hotels or bad food eaten on the run.

Then there are the fairytales. When reporters come to interview me they sometimes have a preconception. It's nothing to do with what they've learned about me, it's what they've decided without knowing me. They want to make me into Emma Harte. They want a rags-to-riches story. Somebody asked me the other day about my enormous change of lifestyle since I wrote a bestseller. Well, I started off simply enough but, to be truthful, my lifestyle changed when I married 22 years ago and went to live in Manhattan and also had an apartment in Beverly Hills.

But whatever I say, they're determined to write the story they want to tell. So the only thing I can do when I read a misleading story is smile and say, well at least they spelled my name right! But I'm not Cinderella, and never was.

Still, I admit that a bit of fiction about oneself is not much to put up with. I've been accused of dressing my Bichon Frisé puppy, Gemmy, in a diamond-studded collar and of wearing a £25,000 dress. I was due to go and stay with an old friend in Ripon and she roared with laughter when she read that. "Do I have to get a burglar alarm installed?" she kidded me. She knew a Yorkshire girl would never spend £25,000 on a dress, that she'd be doing something extraordinary if she paid £250!

So why do I go on? The answer is easy. I can't *not* do it. Writing is a means of self-expression for me, and it gives me great gratification. Especially when I know that a novel I have striven over truly works, not only for me, but for readers all over the world . . . readers who have derived enjoyment from my work, who have seen life through my angle of vision . . . who have been touched, enlightened and entertained. That is the greatest satisfaction of all.

And if you are a would-be novelist, hellbent on pursuing this career, then what better inspiration is there?

Ten Questions for Would-Be Novelists

Let us assume that the would-be novelist has both ability and a talent for using words. What else is required in the writing of fiction? I think I would have to ask you these questions.

1. Are you imaginative?

If you create characters in your imagination that are interesting and different and yet with whom the reader can identify, then you have a good start. If you can picture scenes between characters you create and can also feel caught up in their emotions, that's what I call imagination.

2. Have you got insight?

A novelist must be able to understand what makes people tick. Insight is being able to weigh someone up, to understand why they do the things they do. You must have compassion, and be willing to understand all points of view.

3. Can you get under the skin of a character, express his or her nature?

You have to be able to put the feeling and thought processes of your characters on paper effectively. I think writing up character studies is helpful. It teaches you how to develop a *whole* person on paper, remembering that nobody is all good, nobody is all bad; we are all made up with many complexities in our nature.

4. Can you make readers care about your characters?

That depends on whether you can flesh them out so that the reader believes they truly exist. I've found reading biographies very useful since they are about real people.

5. Can you really tell a story?

If it's to be compelling, make the reader want to turn the page to find what happens next, a novel has to combine structure, plot and action in a way that produces narrative drive. I have what I call my "loving ears"—two girlfriends I can ring and say: May I read you these few pages? That's what I sometimes do if I'm trying to say something complex, and their reaction helps me know if I've refined it enough. Do they want to "hear on"? Some feedback is helpful if you're feeling unconfident.

Structure is very important. Studying favorite books is good homework here. The structure of *Tai Pan* by James Clavell, who also wrote *Shogun,* is marvelous. And Wilbur Smith did a trilogy, *Flight of the Falcon, Men of Men* and *The Angels Weep,* which are all well-constructed novels. And the classics of course. There's nothing better than studying Dickens. And Colette. Colette, by the way, said: Two things are important in life. Love and work. I like that. Yorkshire people have the work ethic. My mother was always polishing a chair or making a stew and I still feel I must work all day, every day, or God will strike me dead.

6. Have you a talent for plots?

Working out story lines and getting them down in, say, ten pages is the best way of finding out. For myself, an event will trigger a plot. For instance, a former friend who was dying and wanted to make peace with me and other friends she had once hurt led to my plot for *Voice of the Heart.* The story line may "unreel" in the bath or on a bus in anything from ten minutes to an hour.

I never use anything exactly as it has befallen me or my friends, but I've seen so much of what happens to people that I know my plots are not too far-fetched, not larger than life. Nothing is larger than life.

7. Can you create a sense of time and place, mood and atmosphere?

I rely on memory for scenes from nature but I have occasionally taken snapshots for interiors. For *Voice of the Heart,* I photographed a *schloss* in Germany, to help me keep the mood of the place in my mind. Note-taking is another helpful tool, and sensible for people who don't have photographic memories.

I can't explain how you create atmosphere. I mean, Stephen King, the "horror" writer who wrote *Carrie* and *The Shining,* among many others, is brilliant when he creates an atmosphere of horror, and I think he does it with his choice of words. Atmosphere is not something visual, it's a feeling, and it's conveyed by particular words, so I too feel I must find the *exact* word and I'll spend hours sometimes to arrive at it. But, having said that, it's hard for a writer to analyze how he or she writes: I always fear I might analyze it away!

8. Do you have the knack of writing dialogue?

Dialogue has to do several things. It has to move the plot along and provide information of some kind. It has to delineate the character of the person speaking—or somehow reflect his personality. It should add to the flavor of the book, convey emotion or feeling. So it has to be very structured, even though it must sound natural.

Ask yourself if the dialogue you have written does all of these things, and if in all honesty you have to answer "no" you will almost certainly find that you can throw it out without loss—indeed it will be an improvement—to your book.

Written dialogue is totally different from spoken dialogue—write down a taped conversation and you'll see it's unreadable.

9. Are you organized enough?

If you want your novel to have a feeling of authenticity, then you must write from strength, from knowledge—and that means research. But the important thing about research is to be able to throw it away! Put it all in and it slows down the narrative drive. I might do a day's research just for a few lines of dialogue but it has to be integrated so it's not apparent.

An efficient filing system is vital, as are good reference books and address books that record sources—or you will waste precious time and work in a muddle. I have a table next to my desk where I keep handy a large dictionary and the *Columbus Encyclopaedia,* along with a thesaurus, *Bartlett's Familiar Quotations,* a world atlas, and maps of England.

10. Do you have a sense of drama?

There's so much drama every day in the newspapers, surely everyone has. Reading plays, watching movies helps to sharpen a dramatic sense, teach you what makes a "story." A book I go back to time and again is *Wuthering Heights.* Every time I read it I find something I hadn't noticed before. It is extremely emotional to me, a very Yorkshire book—though structurally it's said *not* to be good.

21

"WHERE DO YOU GET YOUR IDEAS?"

BY ELIZABETH PETERS

ONE OF THE QUESTIONS most often asked of writers by readers and interviewers is, "Where do you get your ideas?" I used to sputter and roll my eyes when this query was put to me; there was in it the implication that ideas were physical objects, like avocados, and all one had to do was go to the proper store in order to pick up a supply.

However, my prejudice began to diminish when I started thinking seriously about the question. It is not a silly question. I thought it was silly only because I didn't know the answer. I still don't know the answer, but I have arrived at some answers—the sources from which I derive many of my ideas. I can't answer for other writers, but perhaps some of these will work for you.

First, let's define the term: An idea is not a plot. This distinction may seem so obvious that it isn't worth mentioning, but many of the earnest souls who offer me "plots" or "ideas" ("You write the book, and we'll split the royalties") don't know the difference. What I call an idea is not a plot. An idea is the germ from which a plot may one day develop if it is properly nurtured and tended. For me, the "idea" has two distinct stages.

It begins with a "one-liner"—a single sentence or a visual image, characterized by brevity and vividness. Since an idea is not an avocado, you can't simply go out and get one. In fact, the technique of finding a usable idea is more akin to birdwatching than to chasing butterflies: There are ideas all over the place, the trick is to recognize one of the elusive creatures when it flits past. I'm not being whimsical. It is certainly possible to search actively for an idea, but unless you know one when you see one, there is no point in looking.

The most obvious source of inspiration is your own hobby or profession or job specialty. My training is in archaeology and history, so I derive a good many plot ideas from those fields. The archaeology themes have been particularly prominent in my Elizabeth Peabody novels.

My hobbies—cats, needlework and gardening—have also provided me with ideas. Once when I was absorbed with collecting and embroidering samplers, I thought vaguely, "I wonder if I could use a sampler as a clue in a book?" This idea ended up as *House of Many Shadows*. I usually have an animal, or three or four, in my books, but cats have played seminal roles in the inspiration of ideas. "How about a ghost cat, who shows up in the nick of time to save the heroine?" That one turned out to be *Witch*.

Ideas don't always come from nonfiction reading. Sometimes irritation spawns a plot idea—when I read a book with a smashing twist that doesn't quite come off, prompting me to mutter, "I would have done that differently. . . ." And I do. Sometimes admiration of a particular book prompts not imitation so much as emulation. *Sons of the Wolf,* one of my early Gothics, was inspired by Wilkie Collins's *The Woman in White*. I took his two heroines, one dark and homely and competent, the other beautiful and blond and fragile. . . . Or so she seemed. It surprised me as much as it did some of my readers when the fragile blond came to the rescue in a moment of crisis, but her development was probably the result of my unconscious resentment of Victorian assumptions about women, which affected even so sensitive and gifted a writer as Collins. I turned his stereotype around to produce different characters and a different plot.

When you are looking for a plot idea, it is helpful, therefore, to read as widely as possible. I got one idea from the *Smithsonian Magazine,* not from an article but from a reader's letter that described a black rainbow. I had never heard of such a thing, but the image was so evocative I knew I had to use it.

Since I am by nature and by training a reader, I derive most of my ideas from books. However, visual images can also be useful. The most obvious visual image is physical—a handsome old house, a quaint village, a medieval town. The dark closes of old Edinburgh, the triple-layered church of San Clemente in Rome, a country inn in Western Maryland—these and other locations have inspired books of mine.

Other images from which I have derived ideas are also physical, but

93

they are one step removed from reality. They are, in fact, misinterpretations of what I actually see. (Being absent-minded and/or nearsighted helps here.) The commonest misinterpretation, with which most of us are familiar, occurs when we wake in the night and see some familiar object in the room transformed by shadows and moonlight. A robe hanging on the bedpost becomes a dangling body or a looming spectre. A rocking chair appears to have an occupant, misshapen and frightening. My most recent stimulus of this nature came when I was driving alone a narrow country road and saw a bundle of trash lying in a ditch. (At least I hope it was a bundle of trash.) The shape suggested a human body, and all at once I had a mental image of a skeleton, dressed in a pair of overalls, sprawled by the road. The exigencies of the plot that I developed from this image demanded a female rather than a male skeleton, and the overalls turned into a calico dress.

Once you learn to spot ideas, you see them all over the place—remarks overheard on planes or buses, unusual signs in shop windows, street names, those one- or two-line fillers newspapers sometimes insert to fill out a column. Then there are satires and take-offs. Hundreds of ideas there! Having once attended a Romance Writers Convention, I knew I had to do a book about such a group. Nothing personal—I plan eventually to satirize cat shows, sci-fi conventions, and my own professional society meetings.

One purely mechanical technique you may want to develop is to write down or clip anything that seems to have potential, and file it away. I have a file bulging with cryptic notes. A few examples: a scribbled description of a mourning gown once worn by the Empress of Austria. It is a fantastic outfit, all black without a speck of color, featuring a face mask of black lace. What am I going to do with this? I don't know yet. But I have a hunch that one day a lady dressed in this fashion will make a marvelous ghost. In my file, there is also an eerie story told me by a local antique dealer about one of her customers; a notation on nuncupative wills; notes on an article on early American gravestones; and a list of terms for groups of animals (a kindle of kittens, a shrewdness of apes) from a book published in 1614. (Goodness, what a mess; I must clean this file out!)

Another file, labeled "miscellaneous," contains newspaper clippings. I keep separate files for clippings on archaeology, the supernatural, and crime. In the miscellaneous file I find, among many others, articles with the following headlines: "Twins May Have One Mind in Two Bodies"; "Switzerland's Dying Language (Romansh)"; and my personal favorite, "The Tree That Ate Roger Williams." Sooner or later I'll get a book out of one of these—maybe all of them.

But—I hear you, the reader, complain—it's a long way from your one-liner to a finished book. True, I told you that in the beginning, remember? An idea is not a plot. A "one-liner" may not even turn out to be an idea! For me, the second stage of the process loosely termed "getting an idea" is to encourage the initial image or brief sentence to develop into something a little more substantial. It's a difficult process to describe or define; perhaps an example will demonstrate what I mean.

Legend in Green Velvet started with a visual image—a view of a steep winding street in the Old Town of Edinburgh. The "idea" that popped into my mind was a single sentence: "What a super setting for a heroine to be chased in." (Grammar never concerns me at such moments.) But I was getting tired of reading and writing books about pursued heroines. Mulling this over, I thought, "How about having the heroine do the chasing for a change?"

Then I turned to my most useful source—books. I started reading about Edinburgh and its history. Before long I came across the old story of Mary, Queen of Scots' illegitimate baby, who was carried off and adopted by one of her ladies-in-waiting. If the story were true (I doubted it, but that wasn't important), Mary was not only an ancestress of the present British royal house, she was also an ancestress of a Scottish noble family. How about one of those close physical resemblances, between a young man (hero or villain, I hadn't decided which) and a Prominent Royal Personage?

I needed more. For one thing, if I decided to make my young man the hero, I needed villains. My reading turned up another intriguing story—that of the Scottish students who swiped the Stone of Scone from Westminster Abbey. The memory of a delightful conversation with an Edinburgh taxi driver who treated me to a fiery lecture on Scottish rights reinforced the idea of using a Scottish Nationalist group in my book. But I couldn't bring myself to make the Nationalists real villains. From what I knew of them, they were an amiable lot. They would, however, provide a useful red herring, and my heroine could safely pursue one of them, since he would not be inclined to harm her.

I still needed villians—genuine, wicked, evil villains. Back to the history books and eventually another piece of the plot. The ancient regalia of Scotland—vanished, during one of the periods of warfare.

By this time my original one-line idea of a heroine chasing a villain through the streets of Edinburgh had developed, not into a plot as yet, but into the skeleton of a plot. I had a heroine, a hero who bore an uncanny resemblance to a Royal Personage, and two sets of villains who were interested in the same treasure for different reasons. The Nationalists wanted the lost royal regalia for its symbolic importance; the genuine villains planned to steal it and sell it. I had strengthened and encouraged my original idea to a point where, or from which, it could be developed into a genuine plot.

There is another technique I often employ when engaged in this second stage of idea development. It is almost the exact antithesis of the active, reading-research method; one might call it a variety of free association. First, it is necessary to find an ambiance in which your mind is free to wander as it will. For me, the ideal situation is a form of mild physical activity (I never engage in strenuous physical activity) that requires minimal mental effort. Walking is ideal. Some types of housework, such as ironing, necessitate a blank mind. (If I thought about what I was doing, I wouldn't do it.) Total relaxation, flat on my back, doesn't work, because when I am relaxed I promptly go to sleep. But as I walk or push the iron across the fabric, a goodly portion of my mind takes off on a tack of its own. With a little encouragement I can turn that detached section down the track I want it to follow. "What about that girl chasing a man up a flight of stairs in Edinburgh? Why the dickens would she do that? Why do people chase people? Did she think he was someone she knew? Did she see him drop his wallet or his handkerchief?"

These methods work for me. They may not work for you, but something else will, if you experiment. And the most encouraging thing about writing is that, as with any other talent, your skill will improve with practice.

I still become irritated when people ask me where I get my ideas, not because it is a silly question, but because it is too complex to be answered in a few words. And also, perhaps, because to a writer getting an idea is the easy part. The hard part is turning that ephemeral one-liner into thousands of actual words on hundreds of actual pages in a connected, coherent manner.

22

Let's Do It Over

By Phyllis A. Whitney

Revision has become, for me, the interesting part of writing. Setting a story down the first time around is often hard and discouraging work. Unable to see the woods for the immediate trees, I never have complete confidence in what I'm doing. It's wonderful when it flows, but that can't be counted on, so I plug along doggedly. What keeps me going is the knowledge that what I'm writing doesn't need to be perfect in the first draft. No piece of fiction is. Despite our intentions, we can't always be sure we have succeeded. There are still improvements to make, once we see what we have really done.

However, before you consider letting an "outside eye" look at your manuscript, there are certain elements you can analyze for yourself; private challenges you can make. The process of learning to criticize your own work in a constructive way may take years of practice, and in some aspects should take all your writing life.

Here are a few items you can think about between your first writing and the revision of your manuscript.

Everything depends on the imaginary people who inhabit your novel. Know them well. Not just how they look—that's easy and superficial. What do they think? How do they relate and react to all the other characters? This is important and will help you know each person in your book. I don't care for lists. Lists never represent characters who are alive. Talk to yourself on paper. Where are your people going? What are their goals? This is something you must know, not only about your main character, but about all of the others, minor and major. You never know when a minor character you hadn't thought much about will come to life and make some useful move.

Motivation means *what-do-they-want-and-why?* With strong motivation, you'll have strong conflict. Your main character, first of all, should be wrestling with a life-or-death issue. Perhaps literally; perhaps only because happiness is at stake. In the long run, happiness is always at stake, and that goal may take many forms, depending on the nature of the person and the situation. If there is nothing your main character wants passionately, you can be sure you'll have a weak story, and consequently, low reader interest. At the outset, be sure to check for strong desires and interests in all your characters. These will, of course, clash—no conflict, no story!—and you must let these opposing forces collide. Part of good revision is to avoid some of the pitfalls ahead of time!

Psychological conflict can often be stronger than the physical kind, and much more interesting. An action story can be strengthened by the struggle of characters whom readers come to love or hate because the author has made them "real" people.

If you reach a place in your story where the main character cannot take action—for good reason—introduce a character who has a special drive that will threaten or oppose your protagonist. You will be surprised at how quickly your main character will discover specific action that must be taken to help him achieve what he wants. Sometimes you don't see these effective touches until you reread and revise.

Perhaps every plot, boiled down, is the same: Character wants something desperately; character is strongly opposed by outer or inner forces, or both; character gets what he or she *deserves*.

The first two are obvious. You can check for them in every piece of fiction you read, as well as in what you write. The third is just as important, but a bit more difficult to appraise and follow through with. Stated simply: If your main character's motivation leads her to do dreadful things, then she'd better get her comeuppance at the end of the story. *Frankly, Scarlett, I don't give a damn,* is the strongest punishment the heroine could receive in *Gone With the Wind,* and she has certainly earned it. (Even though we're a smidge sorry for her by that time.)

If your main characters are sympathetically portrayed, and their struggle is justified so readers want them to succeed, then there will be disappointment if you do a flip and let them down at the end.

Sometimes when I view old movies on television, I am struck by the unhappy endings that governed the screen for a long while. Bogie died, Cagney died, Robinson died, and sometimes Barbara Stanwyck died—

and we didn't always cheer. There now seems to be more of an emphasis on reader satisfaction—the upbeat. Perhaps because there is so much downbeat in our lives that we want to be entertained and inspired by our fictional people. Escape into other people's lives can help to heal our own.

The novel that makes us happy usually builds to some satisfying and well-earned triumph in the conclusion—thus bringing readers back for more—something editors like. Nevertheless, we can only write those happy endings we believe in. What we do with our characters must never go against what *we* believe, or we will only turn out pot-boilers.

In my own writing I learned very soon that emotion is the most important ingredient in any piece of fiction. If your characters feel nothing strongly, neither will your reader. The degree of emotion usually depends on the importance of the stake. Make the stakes high. The more your characters stand to lose or gain, and the more they *care,* the more powerful the effect on the reader. This is the great difference between journalism and fiction writing. Journalism reports; it stands back and watches. Fiction writing is subjective and takes sides.

I have found that the best way for me to begin a novel is to make sure my heroine is quickly immersed in an emotional situation that she needs to do something about. Looking over past novels, I find that I usually start out with some critical problem about which my main character feels strongly and which she must confront with action on her part.

In *Snowfire* a brother has been imprisoned for murder, and his sister must prove his innocence. (Remember, happiness is always at stake.) The heroine's father in *Vermilion* has died under mysterious circumstances, and she must find out how and why. In *The Golden Unicorn* the protagonist is driven to learn about her own heritage, and she discovers she was adopted. In *Silversword* my main character, on learning that the mother she believed was dead is still alive, must go to Hawaii, where she confronts a heartbreaking situation. All these complications involve strong emotion—an absolutely essential element. Make sure from the start that a reader's reaction will never be, "Who cares?"

Suspense is another revision check point—to make sure it's present. Any number of devices can help you here. "Secrets" that your characters are hiding are always a good ploy, whether you are writing a mystery or a straight novel. Is everything too out-in-the-open, too obvious or predictable? If your characters conceal secrets that take unexpected turns, and are gradually revealed, you have a good chance to hold your reader. All readers love a surprise.

The revision process—shaping all that clumsy, groping material—can be deeply satisfying for a writer. This is the way to carry your story to the heights you intended in the first place.

In the final aspects of revision, you'll need that outside eye I spoke of earlier. Eventually a critic whom you can trust will come into your life because you'll be seeking and watching for one. In the beginning, when you most need helpful criticism, you probably won't have access to an editor. Before that happy acquisition, however, there are several steps you can take to help you find an objective critic.

In the beginning we all write alone. When someone (usually family or friends) reads our story, we get conflicting advice and have no idea which way to turn. Here are some suggestions.

Join a small writers' group, where manuscripts are read aloud and discussed. Often we learn to criticize our own work by criticizing others. We learn mistakes not to make. Be careful, however, since not all the criticism offered will be of equal value. Perhaps the first advantage of such a group is the stimulation it offers. You are with others who are engaged in the same struggle you are going through, and you help encourage one another. If there is no such group near you, start one. Eager writers will come out of the woodwork when you whistle!

A second type of writing group will be larger and will come together to hear lectures from professional writers or editors. Often selling writers belong to such groups and can be helpful to the beginner.

A writers' conference can provide similar experience, with the added advantage of having your manuscript read by a professional writer or editor. Lectures are apt to be of high caliber and valuable. Sometimes a contact made at such a conference may even lead to publication— providing you are ready.

Another step is to enroll in a writing class, if one is offered in your area. It is a good idea to look into the background of the person who is teaching such a course and make sure that the type of writing you wish to pursue will be covered.

Somewhere there is help if you search for it. There are also many books on writing in your public library, and there are writers' magazines to offer you information, shortcuts, and inspiration.

There is a simple rule to follow in dealing with outside criticism. Whether you agree with it or not, accept it with your mind, not your emotions. I have suffered a few emotional traumas myself, and I have also witnessed them in young writers who blew up in my face because I dared to criticize some darling word-child. *Calm down and think.* See whether the criticism might even help the "child" to be better accepted by some editor.

When it comes to the matter of criticism, another factor enters in. All writers begin with a resistance to those who point out faults in their work. We all have a sense of proprietorship about our writing, and when an "outsider" makes suggestions (as a good critic should) we may fear that what we have created will no longer belong to us. These are other people's ideas and we want nothing to do with them, lest we lose the authorship of our own writing. You needn't worry. There is a certain "magic" that takes place in a writer's imagination—an alchemy that exists for every writer of fiction. As you think about what your critic has said, you will see wonderful new ways to use these suggestions as you incorporate them into your revision. The result will be as much yours as what you wrote originally, and your fiction will profit from this expansion of your early ideas. Often the result will be better than you ever imagined, yet it will still be entirely yours.

When you make "doing it over" a regular part of your writing life, you will find yourself well on the way to becoming a published writer.

23

THE MAJOR ROLE OF MINOR CHARACTERS IN FICTION

BY HANS OSTROM

AFTER READING AN EARLY DRAFT of a novel I had submitted, my editor—as I expected—commented on several areas that needed improvement. One of her responses to the novel surprised me, however. She said that she had had some difficulty with several of the minor characters. In her view, I had not depicted these characters vividly enough, and when a significant amount of time had elapsed between appearances of some secondary characters, she found that her sense of those characters had become cloudy.

To be sure, the remarks about the novel's minor characters came toward the end of the editor's written evaluation, after she had commented on larger elements of the novel. I do not want to imply that a concern for minor characters should outweigh a concern for the plot, primary characters, threads of suspense, setting, and other crucial aspects of a novel.

Ironically, however, because novelists must focus so intently on these obvious concerns, minor characters may not receive the attention they deserve, especially in early drafts. And poorly conceived minor characters can weaken a novel substantially. As a newcomer to writing novels, I realized after reading my editor's letter that concentrating on the major areas of my novels did not mean that I could afford to neglect minor characters. I also realized that, perhaps unconsciously, I had made the mistake of equating "minor" with "incidental."

Revising the manuscript in response to my editor's concerns was not difficult, but my interest in the topic of minor characters did not stop there. I thought further about the essential ways in which minor characters contribute to novels in general, and I offer my observations here in hopes that they might help other new novelists.

Perhaps the most obvious function of minor characters is in advancing the plot. In basic terms, the plot consists of events in which the main character(s) take part. Nonetheless, minor characters can often play major roles in constructing the plot.

In mystery novels, they can provide a crucial bit of information to the sleuth, or they can become unwitting obstacles to the success of either a detective or a criminal, or they can trigger a memory on the part of a detective that will allow him or her to solve a puzzle or to take the right action. In mainstream novels, the contribution of minor characters to the plot can be just as important but in an even greater variety of ways. Virtually any element of crisis or resolution can be enhanced by a minor character.

Charles Dickens's novels remain an excellent example of this potential; even though ideas about "the novel" have evolved since his era, the range of ways in which he used minor characters to contribute to intricate plots still offers a model to novelists for what it is possible to do with minor characters. Compared with many contemporary novels, Dickens's works may sometimes seem crowded or "overpopulated" with minor characters, and yet the portraits and functions of those characters are always painstakingly precise. Dickens is beyond imitation, but he may be the best example of how seriously a novelist must take lesser characters. His works reinforce the platitude about a chain being as strong only as its weakest link: A minor character, even one with a bit part, can be the most important link in a chain of events that constitutes the plot of your novel.

A second major contribution minor characters can make to a novel is to enhance the development of the main character(s). We learn much about main characters *only* from main characters—from seeing them in action or from listening to their interior voices. However, we can learn as much about them from the way they behave in encounters with secondary characters. Even when such brief encounters are not crucial to the plot (and they often are), they show us how the main character functions in "ordinary life." Furthermore, the whole concept of "round" or "three-dimensional" characters depends on the existence of "flat," "two-dimensional" characters who allow primary characters to stand in relief. As in motion pictures, such characters literally "support" the major roles in novels.

Another way of describing this function of minor characters is to say that they add texture to a novel. In fact, one of the discoveries I made in my transition from writing short fiction to writing novels is that novel writing allows me more latitude to work to enrich the texture of my fiction. Generally speaking, one can employ a larger cast of characters in a novel than one can in a short story. This situation makes for more freedom, but it also asks the writer to think more extensively about what to *do* with the freedom and, more specifically, what to do with additional minor characters in the cast.

Minor characters can also contribute to the development of suspense, either in a scene or in a whole novel. Consider one example from a classic of the suspense genre, Dashiell Hammett's *The Maltese Falcon*. In Chapter 16, when "the black bird" suddenly falls into the hands of Sam Spade, it is delivered by a mysterious, dying stranger:

> The corridor door opened. Spade shut his mouth. Effie Perine jumped down from the desk, but a man opened the connecting door before she could reach it. . . . The tall man stood in the doorway and there was nothing to show that he saw Spade. He said, "You know—" and then the liquid bubbling came up in his throat and submerged whatever else he said. He put his other hand over the hand that held the ellipsoid. Holding himself stiffly straight, not putting his hands out to break his fall, he fell forward as a tree falls.

The scene itself is suspenseful, for as readers we sense the mixture of confusion and terror that Spade and his secretary feel when the dying man appears at their door. Moreover, in relation to the entire plot, the appearance of this minor character adds enormously to the suspense. Who is he? How did he get the Maltese Falcon? Who killed him? Will Spade be accused of killing him? What should Spade do now? To a great extent, suspense is uncertainty, and Hammett uses a minor character to dump a truck load of uncertainty on Sam Spade's doorstep.

Minor characters can contribute to suspense not just in mystery and action fiction but in virtually every kind. Rust Hills, in *Writing in General and Short Story in Particular,* applies the idea of suspense to all good fiction, saying that it "can function in literature as subtly and effectively as it does in music." Minor characters are one important source of such subtlety and effectiveness. In James Joyce's classic story "Araby," for example, the minor character of the uncle is an enormous problem for the main character, the boy who wants to go to the bazaar to buy something for the girl he worships. In coming home late and generally being difficult, the uncle delays the boy's departure, adding to the suspense of the story (will the boy make it to the bazaar or not?)

and to the sense of disillusionment and disappointed desire that Joyce creates.

Still another way minor characters can be useful to fiction writers is to help evoke a sense of place and atmosphere. Whether it's Conan Doyle's London, Raymond Chandler's Los Angeles, William Faulkner's Mississippi, or Ann Beattie's New York, our sense of place depends on the people in the place. Authors can use minor characters to help convey the flavor of a region or a city quickly and convincingly. Fog and gaslights add to our sense of Holmes's London, but Mrs. Hudson, cabbies, bobbies, and a legion of other minor characters contribute as much, if not more, to our mental picture of the fictional London Conan Doyle creates.

Finally, minor characters can be interesting in and of themselves. A quick sketch of a minor character can (and should) be vivid and entertaining—should stand on its own in some way. Moreover, like all characters, minor ones grow in surprising ways, demanding more attention from the author during revisions, competing for greater roles as novels or stories take shape. In my own novel, a bartender (of all people) who I thought would be almost incidental became more crucial to the plot and to the sleuth (a sheriff) than I had ever imagined. He became more of a confidante and a representative of sorts of the ordinary people in the rural county. Such "independence" on the part of minor characters may be even more likely to occur in novels than in short stories.

These, then, are several significant roles minor characters can play in fiction. In addition, there are some rules of thumb a writer should keep in mind during the revision process:

1. Beware of stereotyping. Because minor characters *are* minor, and because authors cannot afford to spend more than a few sentences describing them, a stereotype can be tempting. A waiter or a cop or a librarian need not be a stock character. Don't call Central Casting; instead, draw on your own experience and your notebook for a not-so-typical sketch.

2. Beware of the time lapses between appearances that minor characters make. If the interval between appearances is substantial (several chapters, for instance), it is even more necessary for the first appearance to be striking. As mystery novelist Lillian O'Donnell has remarked, "Clue: If I have to go back into the early pages of a first draft

to find out a character's name, that character is not real." O'Donnell's observation applies to mainstream fiction as well, of course, and one might add that if a reader's memory of a minor character's first appearance is fuzzy, how well is that character really functioning in the novel?

3. Give minor characters memorable but not outlandish names, and make sure the names and initials of your minor characters are sufficiently different to avoid confusing the reader. Don't make your reader wonder which character was Ron Ryan and which was Bryan Ray. Most of us are unconsciously attracted to a very narrow range of names, and we need to broaden that range in our fiction.

4. Don't be afraid to eliminate a minor character entirely. The fact that minor characters can themselves be interesting cuts both ways because a minor character can upstage a major one without contributing to plot, character development, suspense, or atmosphere. He or she may be engaging without being genuinely functional.

Ask yourself whether the character ought to appear at all. (If you are moving from short fiction to a novel, you may find that the comparative freedom of the novel creates a greater temptation to clutter the stage with characters; the clutter springs not so much from the number of characters as from the purposelessness of characters.) Such characters need not disappear forever. They may turn out to be useful in other stories and novels, and may even become main characters in other works.

Ultimately, the nature of minor characters in fiction is something of a paradox: although such characters are by definition secondary and often two-dimensional, they add depth to various elements of stories and novels.

24

How Do You Learn to Write?

By Ruth Rendell

POPULAR FICTION no more needs a formula than does the highest art in the mainstream novel. Indeed, I have always maintained that genre fiction, so-called, is better written as if it were mainstream fiction and that fitting it into a category is best forgotten. And one should write to please oneself. When I consider the number of readers who have written to me to ask why I bother about style and characters when all they need is the mystery, others who have written asking for more murders or fewer murders, those who have demanded only detective stories, and those who have asked for anything but detective stories, I wonder where I should be now if I had aimed to please a public rather than suited my own taste.

One myth I used to believe in has been thoroughly debunked. This is the illusion that writing cannot be taught. The truth of it is that the desire to write cannot be taught, and that desire, that longing, must be there. Perhaps it is all that must be there, for with care and awareness, and yes a certain humility, the rest may be learned. Innumerable books exist on the writing of fiction. There are more and more courses available. But I believe that the aspiring writer—come to that, the working writer—cannot do better than learn by reading other works of fiction. I read and read, more now than ever, and if my attitude to what I read has changed over the years, it is in that gradually I have brought to bear on my reading an analytical eye, a developing critical faculty, a hunger to learn more of the craft. Perhaps I have lost something thereby. Escape in fiction is less easy for me; identification with characters comes less readily; I no longer lose myself in the story. But I am first a writer. And I think these things well lost for my gain in knowledge of how to write, though I see how far I still have to go.

So what kind of fiction do I as a writer of crime novels read? Not crime fiction, not mysteries. Not any longer. I used to, and then I became afraid that I would come upon the plot I was currently writing or the twist in the tail I was so proud of. The best crime fiction anyway—always excepting the pure detective story—is simply fiction with crime in it. I read and reread the great Victorian classics that once afforded me sheer pleasure and now teach me how to evolve and develop a story and cliff-hang my protagonist at the end of a chapter. I read the best contemporary British and American masters of fiction, every novel that comes out and gets acclaimed by reviewers or wins a prize or gets itself talked about, everything we see adapted for television. My favorite novel used to be Samuel Butler's *The Way of All Flesh*, and I still love it and reread it, but its place in my top admiration stakes has for two or three years been occupied by *The Good Soldier*, by Ford Madox Ford. It has been called the finest novel in the English language, at least the best constructed. I read it once a year. Its structure, its author's skill in dealing with time, the smooth swift movements of its narrative through and in and out of the years, its curiously intimate, despairing, aghast creating of suspense—these are all marvels.

I recommend *The Good Soldier* to everyone who asks me how to write. I hope it has taught me something. It ought to have imparted some of its own subtlety, its wonderfully understated withholding from the reader—until nearly the end—of a chain of secrets, an interwoven carpet of mysteries. Victorian ghost stories also have a lot to teach us. M. R. James knew all about the power of reticence in building tension that is an essential element in my kind of fiction. And more than any modern master of horror, Perceval Landon teaches the writer all he needs to know about fear and how to create it in "Thurnley Abbey," the most frightening story I have ever read.

I am always a little dismayed by people who ask me where I get my ideas and go on to say that though they want to write, they don't know what to write about. Any aspiring writer of the sort of fiction that aims to entertain and be exciting should begin at any rate with more ideas than he or she knows what to do with. They want to tell a story, don't they? Isn't this what it's all about?

I never base my characters on real people. I mean this; I am being quite sincere. And yet, and yet . . . all we know of people is through the men and women we are close to or have met or those we have read of or seen on film. Heaven forbid that we should base our characters on those printed or celluloid personages others have created. So only reality and living people remain. I suppose that we create amalgams, taking an appearance here, a quality there, and eccentricity from elsewhere. Increasingly, I look through books of pictures, the works of old or modern masters, for my characters' faces: to Rembrandt's "Juno," Greuze's "The Wool Winder," Picasso's "Acrobats," and Titian's dark sorrowful handsome man with the gloves. And for characters' names I go not to the telephone directory but to the street names in the back of a gazetteer.

It is interesting how a character begins to form itself as one gazes at some marvelously executed portrait. Slyness must lurk behind those eyes surely, cruelty in that thin-lipped mouth, subtlety and finesse revealed by those long thin fingers. I wish I had known of this method when I first began and struggled unwisely to make a character fit the plot instead of the plot growing naturally out of the behavior of the characters. I wish I had known then the abiding satisfaction of contemplating, say, Umberto Boccioni's self-portrait and seen there a young man's inner doubts, suspiciousness, intellect, hyper-nervousness, and begun to see my way to putting his counterpart into a book.

From the first, though, I listened to people talking. My friends tell me that my books are full of the things they have said. "We had that conversation in your house with such-and-such and so-and-so." It's true. I don't use my friends for my characters, but I use what they say for my dialogue. I listen in pubs to people talking and in restaurants and at airports, in trains, in shops. And when I write down what they say, I repeat it in my head, listening with that inner ear for the right cadence, the ring of authenticity. Is this how it really sounds? Is this the rhythm? Would my man with the thin body and sad face of Picasso's harlequin, the thin lips and the delicate upturned nose, would he use quite that word in quite that way? And if not, it won't do, must be changed and listened to all over again.

A publisher friend once said to me that the next time he received a manuscript that began with the protagonist waking up, feeling depressed, and going down to make himself a cup of tea, he wouldn't read on. All too many first books do begin like this. My experience of reading the manuscripts of unpublished writers is not that they are badly written or unreal or silly or badly constructed, but they are deadly boring. They are dull. The characters have no life and are undifferentiated; every piece of information is fed to the reader in the first chapter; no care has been taken over accuracy or authenticity. If they are not exactly plagiarisms of other more exciting works, they are deeply derivative. Originality is absent. There is no evidence of the writer's own experience being put to use.

Of course, few of us have first-hand knowledge of violence, even fewer of murder. How many of us have had a child kidnapped or know of anyone to whom this has happened? We should be thankful for our lack of experience. And the writer's imagination will supply what is needed here. We all know what it is like to walk alone along a dark road at night, be alone in a house and suspect the presence of a marauder outside, hear a footfall or a door close where there should be no footfall and no closing door, suffer the suspenseful anxiety of waiting for some loved person who is late home, long for the phone to ring yet dread it, miss a train and a date, fear flying, suffer jealousy, envy, love, and hate.

These are the raw materials the writer must use. Journalists ask me if I have known many murderers, visited courts and prisons. I have known none, and it is twenty-five years since I was in a court. But I can read the great psychiatrists, the newspapers, look at faces in pictures, and I can use my imagination. If a would-be writer doesn't have an imagination, he or she should find it out young and serve the world in perhaps a worthier way by making a career in a government office or a hospital. Newspapers as sources of stories and portraits of psychopathic perpetrators of violence have their value but to my mind have been overrated by teachers of mystery writing. Sociological case histories and transcripts of trials supply better models.

I have never been much interested in writing about heroes and villians, and I think the time for a blackness and whiteness of characters, a Dickensian perfect good and utter evil, has long gone by. We have all read novels in which our attention has flagged halfway through. Sometimes this is because the characters are all so unpleasant that we lost interest in their fate. For even the worst character in a novel should inspire in the reader some fellow-feeling. It is an intriguing fact that in order to make readers care about a character, however bad, however depraved, it is only necessary to make him love someone or even something. A dog will do, even a hamster will do. I once had a character called Finn in a novel, a psychopathic hit man, almost irredeemable, one would have said. My aunt read the book and told me that for all his vices and all his crimes, she couldn't help liking Finn because he loved his mother.

Structure and the movement of my characters I used to find hardest. Moving people about I still find hard. It was Graham Greene, I think, who in giving advice on how to write about violent or dramatic action, recommended the paring down of the prose into brief sentences without adjectives or adverbs. And nothing else must be allowed to intervene, no descriptions of the room or the terrain or the people or the weather. While X is killing Y, let him do it bare, in Anglo-Saxon nouns and verbs, in short brisk sentences. This way the action will come across swift and shocking.

I've never had problems moving my characters in time. The associative process takes care of this beautifully for the writer. We all understand it; it works for us in reality. The stray word, the seldom-heard name of person or place, the sight of something or the scent—all these can evoke the past, and in fiction at any rate carry the protagonist back in time days, months, or years to when that was last heard, smelt, mentioned. There are subtler ways, but these will be learnt along the way.

Writing begets writing. Successful writing—and I mean not only worldly success but that private satisfaction that comes from doing something well—inspires the writer to do better, to attempt the scaling of greater heights, hitherto daunting obstacles. So when a technique has been mastered, instead of sitting back to rest and preen himself or herself, the writer should investigate more subtle methods. Smoother transitions in the matter of flashbacks, for instance, subtler differentiations of character by means of dialogue alone, atmospheres created without violent words or hyperbole but on a lower, more fearful key. And how to make that which is very, very hard look easy.

25

THE MISSING PIECE SYNDROME

BY RICHARD MARTIN STERN

NO PROFESSIONAL WRITER I KNOW will challenge the need for discipline. It is the *sine qua non* of the trade, craft, business, call it what you will, of setting thoughts and ideas down on paper and selling them. A writer's place is at his desk facing his typewriter or word processor, *not* finding reasons why today he cannot write. And yet. . .

I speak here only of and for writers of fiction. Writers who deal with facts have, or should have, the facts in front of them before they sit down to write. The fortunate ones can wrestle with those facts, arrange and rearrange them, in effect play with their material as with the pieces of a jigsaw puzzle until the picture finally becomes whole and clear and ready to be presented as effectively as the writer can manage.

Fiction writers are in a somewhat different situation. We deal not with facts but with dreams and smoke and mirrors, and these *on occasion* refuse to fit together in a way that will make the illusion you are attempting to create, the illusion of reality, even inevitability in your tale, come off.

It is always possible that somewhere along the way your hand has slipped, and the picture you have presented of this character or that has thrown your entire story out of whack. Reading and rereading and frequently rereading again can usually turn up the cause of this aberration. You can then stifle the guilty character's propensity for taking center stage and shove him or her back into his proper niche in the story.

Or you may have made the mistake (all too easy to make) of putting certain scenes in the wrong sequence, thereby destroying the effect of building suspense, and what you intended to be a crashing climax fizzles like a wet match because you have told too much too soon.

It is also possible that in the delicately tangled web of your narrative you have overlooked a complete contradiction and, say, had Character A behaving on the basis of knowledge he could *not yet have had*. It does happen. You might even have already killed off a character you now bring on stage to catch your reader's attention with his brilliant performance.

These, of course, are only a few of the possible flaws in your tale that have brought you to the discouraging but unavoidable conclusion that the story as written will not wash. To return to the jigsaw analogy, what I am talking about is the *missing* piece syndrome, the missing twist of plot, the character emphasis, the single, cohesive fact of feeling or force that can bring the entire story into sharp focus. In short, you do not yet have the handle, and this is when discipline, that *sine qua non* of writing, as I said, simply does no good at all.

This is one of the most discouraging of times for a writer. You *know* something is wrong, badly, basically, damnably wrong, but you don't know what it is. Reading and rereading what you've written turns up nothing but emptiness. You sit and stare at the machine and the blank page or screen. You go over and over the entire story as it first appeared in your mind—that shining, whole, flawless concept—and you realize that it does not even vaguely resemble what you have put down on paper, but you don't know why.

All of the characters are there, and the situations, the conflicts, the interplay of emotions and even the drama, carefully contrived. But the whole picture is askew, out of focus, whopperjawed, simply *not right*.

If you plow on, you tell yourself, it will all come out the way it should. If at first you don't succeed . . . But there also comes to mind the conclusion W. C. Fields put to that dictum: "Give up; stop making a fool of yourself." And sometimes W. C. Fields was right; a small voice tells you so, and *sometimes* you had better listen to that small voice, because if you do not, you are headed for nothing but disaster.

In every successful story there is something—and I will not even try to put a name to it because it is too nebulous, no more than a feeling—that binds the story into a whole, brings it alive, draws the reader into it page after page and in the end lets him put the tale down, satisfied.

Without that feeling, that binder, that whatever it may be called, there is nothing. And until you have found that essential force and have it firmly in mind, you will do well to throw discipline out of the window and wait for something within you, perhaps your unconscious, to come up with what is needed.

Only then, after balancing conscience against reality, is apparent sloth not only justified, it is mandatory.

I have recently begun the third complete revision of a new 135,000-word novel, and it has struck me with stunning force that I do not yet have the handle; in short, I do not know yet what the hell I am doing. I will now do nothing until the answer appears out of nowhere, as it will, bright and clear and good, tying everything together, bringing the story off the paper and into reality, making the entire tale *alive*.

Then, and only then, will I be able to proceed with confidence.

26

MAKING YOUR READER FEEL: YOUR STORY'S HIDDEN POWER

BY MARION DANE BAUER

WHY DO PEOPLE, YOUNG OR OLD, read stories? For entertainment, for escape, to gather information about other people, places, cultures, times, to find meaning that can be applied to our own lives. These are the answers fiction writers give when I ask them why they read stories, why does anyone? But the most important reason for reading stories is seldom mentioned.

People read fiction in order to *feel,* to have strong feelings in a context of safety. The thrill of danger without the threat of harm. Cleansing tears, but without loss. Even laughter, dignity intact.

And you, the fiction writer, must be the one to satisfy this unarticulated but very real need in readers. How can you guarantee that will happen? Through the strong feelings of your central character, one who is individual, fully rounded, and involved in a conflict important to him or her.

Nothing could be more obvious than that the main character of your story must be an individual, not a mob. If you tell me that five hundred people were left homeless by the ravages of a hurricane, I will respond because my attention is caught by struggle, but my response will be abstract and brief. I don't know those people, and thus I don't feel their hurricane.

If you narrow that down to one victim of the storm, with a name and perhaps a face but without any emotional history, and if you tell me how she struggled against the hurricane, you will catch my attention on a deeper level. Human interest newspaper and television stories achieve that all the time. But you won't hold me for very long.

If, however, you go farther and let me know your character, her history and her hidden terrors, the hopes and dreams she brought into the confrontation with the hurricane, you will have not only my attention, but my empathy as well. You will be satisfying my deep need for safe, vicarious feeling.

Your story begins, then, with somebody who has a problem he must struggle to resolve or who wants something he must struggle to get. The somebody (character) and the struggle (plot) are inseparable. The problem doesn't have to be as large as a hurricane; in fact, it probably won't be life threatening in any way. Many of the most interesting story problems occur entirely on an inner, psychological level. But the key is, whatever the problem, it must be important to your main character. In other words, your main character must have strong feelings about the conflict he is involved in.

And in order to have strong feelings (and therefore to elicit strong feelings in the reader), your main character must *be* somebody. Stick figures evoke little emotion, no matter what contortions they go through. To elicit empathy, your character must give the illusion of being like us . . . complex, even contradictory, someone with preferences and prejudices, hopes and fears, someone with a history upon which the story is based.

How do you create such a person and bring your character to life? You begin with the richest and most mysterious source of all . . . yourself.

Your self-knowledge will be your primary source for every character, particularly every central, perceiving character you create. If you are going to write a story from the perspective of a murderer, you must look into yourself and find that place where you, too, given the right personal history or circumstances, could be capable of murder. To write about greed or fear, passion or loss, you must first touch those qualities in yourself.

You may find that the deepest feelings, the ones that set off your strongest stories, are the ones you yourself don't yet understand. That is often the case for me. And in fact, I decide which story I am going to write, which character I am going to explore, far more on the basis of what I *feel* when I am sifting through story ideas than on what I *understand* about my reasons for responding to one idea over another.

The most important question I find I must answer is not, why do I care? Rather it is, do I care passionately enough to continue exploring

117

this character and her problem for the months or even years it will take me to complete the novel? My strong feelings will not only hold me throughout the story, but they will, ultimately, give me an opportunity to draw an emotional response from the reader. Lack of such feelings in me will leave my main character—and consequently my reader—emotionally flat.

However, while your own feelings are the richest resource you have for creating good fiction, your feelings alone will not be enough to guarantee a reader's response. In fact, the strength of your own emotion, if you are too close to it as you write, can keep you from knowing whether you are touching the reader or not. Good fiction, fiction capable of drawing response from the reader, is neither a therapeutic exercise for the writer nor a vehicle for emotional flashing. And it is the hard lessons of craft that can keep it from being either.

The core of your character's struggle will come out of the mysterious jumble of your own psyche, that place where you yourself may still be struggling in your own life. But you will need to assemble the flesh and bones from the most accessible regions of your imagination.

First, begin, very consciously, to distance your main character from yourself. Preserve the core of feeling related to your central story problem, but give your character a history, or pieces of a history, different from your own. Change the gender or create life circumstances for your character that separate her from you. Make him much older or younger than you are or modify the superficial manifestations of the problem he faces. If you are, for instance, drawing energy for a story from a long-standing battle you have had with a childhood friend, alter the conflict so that it is with a sister or change the occasion for it entirely, while retaining the feelings the conflict generates in you.

How much distance you will need will depend upon many factors, one of which is how vulnerable you feel to the story issue you have taken on, how much distance you have already established within yourself. I have found that the more crucial the issues are to me, the more distance I need, and some distancing mechanisms give me more freedom and perspective than others. Sometimes I can give myself the most freedom of all by making my perceiving character male (since I am female); two of my strongest novels are perceived through the eyes of a young boy.

Most writers' first work of fiction is intensely and sometimes even embarrassingly autobiographical, which is natural enough. But few first stories are published, because there is a kind of blindness in most autobiography, a self-indulgence, that fails entirely to evoke reader response. The more I write, the deeper I reach into my own core to locate the energy for my stories, but the smaller are the fragments of my own life or history that make their way onto the page.

The first question I am usually asked by my readers, young or old, is, did that really happen? And the fact is that only one of my books, *On My Honor,* is based on an actual event—and that even occurred to a childhood friend of mine, not to me. *On My Honor* is the story of two boys who go swimming in a forbidden river, and one of them drowns. The boy who is left is so terrified and feels so guilty, knowing he was doing something he wasn't supposed to do, that he goes home after the accident and tells no one of the other boy's death. The last half of the book involves the working out of his guilt as the survivor.

The remembered incident began to work in me as a story for reasons I don't fully understand. I know only that I have a strong emotional response to the issue of survivor guilt that made the story *feel* important to me. I could easily have created the incident itself, because none of it came from my own experience. I had never gone swimming in that river or been involved in a serious accident or witnessed a death. I had to imagine my way into my main character's thoughts and feelings. And in order to do that, I reached deeply into that place in myself where my own unexplained survivor guilt resides, and used it to bring to life a character created from my imagination. (No, I did not try to reproduce the boy actually involved in the original incident, because his reality would have gotten in the way of my attempt to inhabit him with my own feelings.)

But I don't always find that core immediately. Sometimes my early ideas of a character are all surface, and sometimes they remain surface through the first, or even several, drafts. That happened with Steve, the main character in my novel *Rain of Fire.* After about the third draft a friend read the manuscript and told me that by the end of the story she liked Celestino, the story's villain, better than she liked Steve. Naturally, I sat down to figure out where I had gone wrong.

What I discovered was that I had given Steve a lot of my own life's surfaces, more than usual, in fact, because I had put him in my own childhood setting and time. But perhaps because he was the first male I had used as a central character, he shared none of my inner reality. Knowing that I needed to give him some of my own substance, I decided to make him a liar. Not a vicious liar, but the liar every storyteller is, the kind for whom a good story, any good story, can be far more attractive than mere truth. And once I invested that emotional part of myself in my character, Steve sprang to life.

The difference between melodrama, which brings amused tolerance, embarrassment or even disdain, and drama, which the reader feels, is not mysterious at all. If the action of your story is imposed upon flat figures, you will have melodrama. If it rises out of grounded, believable, complex characters, characters whom you both feel and stand apart from, you will have drama. You will have a story that lives, that produces the purging of pity and fear which Aristotle spoke of.

If you want your readers to feel—and if you want them to read, you must want them to feel—start with what you yourself feel most strongly. But don't end there. Shape and control and distance your feelings through craft. Work with them as though they were diamonds to be mined and cut—which is exactly what they are. And if you do this, your readers will give you the greatest compliment of all. They will tell you that your story made them laugh or cry or shiver with terror or sigh with relief.

And you will have readers—first, that most important of readers, an editor—who will be waiting anxiously for your next story.

27

WRITING ABOUT REAL PEOPLE

BY JANET LEMBKE

WRITING ABOUT REAL PEOPLE, using their true names and exact words, seemed at the outset to be a simple undertaking. When I began collecting stories and oral history for *River Time,* I thought that all I'd need do would be to mosey around armed with notebook and tape recorder, chat with friends and neighbors, and later sort our conversations into logical, readable order.

But, why write about them in the first place? Why try to create a verbal portrait of a tiny, nameless community tucked away at the back of beyond? Because the microcosm of the riverworld represents something larger and precious.

Rural isolation fosters a feisty independence in the people, past and present, who have chosen to live with its hardships. My friends and neighbors are survivors, and, from my writer's point of view, the way of life relished by our community differs only in its details from that enjoyed in other remote pockets throughout the country.

Let me put you briefly on the scene. Shacks, cottages, elderly mobile homes, a few substantial houses—the community sprawls for two leisurely miles on a bank of North Carolina's lower Neuse River. Road maps have never bothered to notice us, but the nautical chart for the river identifies the area as Great Neck Point. We have modern conveniences, such as indoor plumbing and air-conditioning, but police, firefighters, and doctors ply their trades in more accessible places. The people at the Point must therefore rely on their own resourcefulness. They can grow anything, repair anything, form ad hoc fire brigades, render emergency medical services, and mete out a rough, frontier-style justice.

Our freedom is hard-earned, but not limitless. Here, as in every isolated enclave, it waxes or wanes according to how scrupulously the community observes two commandments. The first is to be neighborly (even if the neighbor is detestable). The second is to honor the environment. At the Point, the river that gives us fish, blue crabs, and contentment may also be deadly.

Just what kind of people thrive under these conditions? When we moved here, I set forth with my writer's implements and began asking questions of everyone in sight to learn about the people and to preserve the stories that would otherwise be lost as suburban development erodes this wilderness. I chatted with "newcomers" who have lived on the riverbank for thirty years; also with old-timers, including sixth generation members of the large farm family that once grew corn and tobacco.

As a writer must when soliciting personal information from living people, I told friends and neighbors at the outset that I was gathering material for publication. Instead of formal interviews, we sat on porches, leaned on fences, stood in yards, messed around in boats, and simply talked.

And, oh, how people talked! My notebook and busy pen fazed no one. The requisite permission to use the tape recorder was invariably granted. I heard about old-time Christmas celebrations, children's games, and the hot, dirty work of growing and harvesting tobacco. I heard about gill nets, long-haul fishing, and hurricanes. I also heard about the seamier sides of life: who had tumbled whom in the haymow and when, who had "bought a beef"—rustled a cow or two—for the family larder, who had jinxed an enemy and how, and who had served time in jail for making moonshine. Nor did my informants always agree: They would tell the same basic story with distinctly different twists. One tale about a fire, for example, appeared in three wildly conflicting versions. They furnished discordant characterizations of each figure important in the Point's history. Was the grande dame of the farming days a lady or a cheating wife, a tyrant or a saint? Take your pick. There were as many views of her personality as there are people who remembered her. And everyone who talked with me vowed that he or she was telling the truth, the whole truth, and nothing but the truth. It soon became clear that truth comes in as many colors as bantam chickens.

The project no longer seemed simple. What is a writer to do with a muddle of variations on the "truth"? I was lost in a wilderness of opinions and impressions, nor had anyone provided map and compass.

By then, however, the project had found its own momentum, and I received a contract from a publisher. The vital questions I had to answer became clear:

1. Which version of the story could I trust?
2. From lawbreaking to infidelity, crimes and sins kept coming up in conversation. They're part of the life of every community. But, to what extent would I betray the confidences of friends by mentioning these matters? To what extent would I betray my story by leaving them out?
3. Would this person's remarks advance the overall story, or were they nothing more than fascinating but extraneous gossip?
4. Would my perceptions of the truth seem true to anyone else?

There were no tidy answers to any of these questions. I made my decisions about which version of a story to trust on a case-by-case basis. Sometimes they came easily. Objective statements—those dealing with facts on which everyone agreed or with details that I could verify with research—presented no problem whatsoever. The difficulties arose when I had to determine the accuracy of subjective impressions or of memories filmed over by the fine dust of time. A majority vote often came to my rescue: If five people held their noses and stated that the local hermit had been averse to bathing, while only one said he'd been clean as a baby, then I felt it was safe to write that he'd had a powerful aroma. For many tales, however, there was no majority vote. Some I regretfully scrapped because the facts could not be distinguished from fiction. In other instances I chose the version based on firsthand information rather than hearsay. Another solution was to present two or more diverse opinions without comment from me as the writer.

Though the question of possibly betraying confidence may seem to pose a dilemma, I found some ground rules. If a seamy, steamy episode, past or present, was *truly* common knowledge, then the matter of betrayal did not arise, and the story could be transmitted to readers. If certain people were spoken of with the admiration accorded heroes, while others were uniformly cussed out as villains, then I could accept the neighborhood's consensus and record its views. On the other hand, if a secret happened to spill out in the cascade of conversation—whoa! My job was to keep the confidence from seeping into print.

I gave one safeguard to everyone who contributed tales: When I wrote about their lives and quoted their words, I identified them only by their first names. No need to give strong, capable people pseudonyms; they deserved the dignity of being acknowledged directly as who they are. But to protect the privacy they also merit, I omitted surnames.

The third question—substance or gossip?—is the crucial one. It provides a further guideline for answering the second. What information did I really need to portray my wild, freewheeling neighbors and the lives they've led? What tidbits served no purpose? To be kept in the book's final draft, a story needed to convey something about its subject's character, whether shining or grievously flawed. Some tales were cast out at once because they centered not on personality but on sensational or scandalous events. It was more difficult to decide what to do with widely repeated references to the grande dame's "sweetheart" or "lover." I chose to keep them. Not only was that long-ago romance common knowledge, but it added a living, breathing fullness to the account of a pivotal figure in the Point's history. To write only about her marriage at the age of thirteen and her hardscrabble years as a farm wife would be to settle for a cardboard woman. To include the sweetheart of her later years endowed her with humanity—a capacity for friendship, an ability to grasp joy amid general hardship.

Once these three questions were addressed, the stories tumbled to the page like ripe pears falling from a tree. The actual writing took me a short three months. Whether my perception of the truth would seem true to readers had to await the book's publication.

Writing about real people is a scary business. It becomes more so still when the book is published, and the people written about come knocking at the door to read about themselves. Friends and neighbors whose lives I wished to celebrate had poured out their stories, opinions, and secrets because they're sociable people who like to talk. Before sending the manuscript to my editor, I'd offered to let each of them see the pertinent portions to check details, correct errors, or delete material that was upsetting. No one had accepted the invitation: "I trust you." Now they could examine my trustworthiness.

When they'd read the book, however, they gave an almost unanimous Yes to the fourth question. The exception was one of the grande dame's granddaughters, who was appalled that I'd made bold to mention her granny's lover. But another granddaughter said, "Oh, for heaven's sakes, everybody's been talking about that for twenty-five years." It was the living subjects of the stories who made the book a success.

To tell the truth about real people is to avoid distortion, evasion, and guesswork as much as possible. It is to prefer the mundane to the sensational. It is to play fair with prickly feelings and intricate life histories. Most of all, it is to let people have their say without interference from the writer.

What is the truth, anyway? In the end, *River Time* tells the only kind of truth it can—a subjective truth formed of my kaleidoscopic impressions of how the frontier spirit and its concomitant freedom endure and triumph today in a tiny community deep in the boondocks.

28

THE BREATH OF LIFE

BY EDITH KONECKY

WHO ARE THESE PEOPLE?" I asked a new writer-friend who was showing me the workplace in her apartment, an erstwhile dining room, now serving up the kind of commercially successful novels that are gobbled up as fast as she can get them out of the oven. The desk she works at is actually a large glasstopped oak table. Beneath the glass, surrounding her typewriter, were color pictures of a dozen people, apparently culled from the pages of magazines.

"Oh, those," she said, a little embarrassed. "That's Harry Gilbert, and this one is Dolly Davis, isn't she unusual? Those eyes! And this . . . but that's not who they really are. I don't know who they really are in the real world. They're characters in the book I'm doing now. It helps me write about them when I can see them."

I was charmed. Such a simple, useful device. When I thought about it, though, I realized that it was one that wouldn't have occurred to me, since I tend to create my characters from the inside out, and prefer not to see my characters so set in physical line and color before I've really found out who they are. I would worry that, given such definition at the outset, they would dominate me. But my friend's way of giving her people reality was to have them right there before her eyes. If Harry looks like that, then she would have some notion of how his voice would sound, how he would stand or slouch, sit, walk, dress, how others might respond to him, at least initially. It is, after all, the responsibility of the author to make his fictional characters real, no matter how he goes about it.

My own way of going about it—since character has always interested me more than plot—has almost always been to begin with a name: Allegra Maud Goldman, Rachel Levin, Prudence Dewhurst, Ralph,

Magda Wickwire . . . almost all my stories began this way. I couldn't tell you where the names come from, and, at the time, I don't consciously know who these people are, though my unconscious apparently does. Finding out who they are, where they are, what they're in the middle of doing, is what gives me the beginning of my story. Sometimes a name won't stick, or the character refuses to reveal himself and must remain stillborn.

Too often, characters in fiction fail to become distinguishable from others in their fictional world, except perhaps by name, gender, and possibly some physical description quickly forgotten by the reader, and occasionally, by the writer as well. This blurring of characters is an all-too-common problem among neophytes, and often not-so-neophyte writers, usually because they are so intent on moving the plot along. These writers may have given labels and costumes to their people, but they have forgotten to provide them with flesh and voice, blood and breath. They have failed to imagine them properly, to create them fully rounded in all their dimensions. They have given the reader stick figures. This, I would think, must be more boring to the writer than to his putative reader, since the writer must live with these created people over a much longer period of time.

Interchangeable characters don't belong in a novel, any more than interchangeable friends belong in your life. It's their differences that make one's friends interesting and valuable. I love Alpha because, even though she is sharply critical and often judgmental, she is intensely moral and responsible, has read everything, has perfect taste and wit, and can always be counted on to do the correct thing. I value Beta because, while she is sometimes less than honest in her self-evaluation and isn't always a faithful friend, she is great fun to be with, sees things in a fresh, original way, and has a daring and adventurous spirit. Epsilon is a homely man who had a troubled childhood, but he is tender and sympathetic and understanding and insightful. Zed is terse, brusque, with military bearing and an evil smile, but he is not evil; he is powerful and successful and sexy, and he can be counted on to give very good practical advice.

Characters are invented out of the people in our lives—friends, family, acquaintances, people we know only through gossip, people we've read about in the newspapers—and then transformed for the purposes of our story. But, when we as writers create our characters, we have an advantage that we don't have in life; we can know *everything* about them. Unlike even those we are closest to, the people we create can't hold anything back from us; they have absolutely no privacy. It is our business to decide just how much of them we need, how much to reveal, how much to keep hidden, how much to allow the reader to imagine. What power! But, then, writing fiction, indeed all creativity, gives a kind of power, as does any form of play, since we are making something where nothing was. In a novel, even in a story, we make a world, we make the people in that world, we make what happens to them; we dictate, out of the kinds of people we have made them, their actions and reactions, and we go even further—we give, or at least we try to give, some meaning to it all (and this may be why we do it in the first place).

In our fiction as in our dreams, we are in for surprises. Our characters, if we have pumped enough blood into them, develop minds and wills of their own. When this happens, when we surprise ourselves, we experience what I believe is the real joy of writing: "The book, or story, has come alive, and we can be fairly confident that it's going to succeed. Our fictional people sometimes won't go where we send them or say the things we meant them to say. It's important, then, to listen to them carefully, to follow where they lead, to make the compromises they demand of us, to trust them. If we have created a powerful person then we must allow him to exercise his power.

"Go marketing," I once instructed a troubled young married woman named Jane. "You have a family to feed." But she wouldn't go. "The hell with that," she said. "It's too beautiful a day. It's spring. I'm going to the Bronx Zoo with Willie." Willie was her little boy. "What's the point of that?" I asked her, meaning within the context of my story. She wasn't sure herself, but I let her go. When we got to the zoo, she ran into an old lover with his two little girls. All sorts of things I wasn't expecting were raked up at the zoo on that bright day, and there put to rest. Jane was right; she knew what she was doing. She had found the metaphor for me.

Of course, there is always the risk that a character, given her head, may bludgeon the book to death. If this happens, then we must decide which is at fault, our original premise for the book or something in the character that doesn't belong there and may have to be altered.

What a writer does when she puts herself into her characters is what actors do—not merely interpret the characters but become them: the woman, the man, the child, the beggar on the corner, the old woman in the attic, even the cat. While we have only the baggage of ourselves to bring to these roles, that baggage holds much more than we can ever remember packing into it. Writing, letting the mind roam free, is like foraging through an almost bottomless old trunk in the attic; much of what we pull forth may be drab, moth-eaten, discardable, but we never know what bright, lovely unremembered treasure lies hidden, waiting to be found. The great pleasure of writing lies in these discoveries. They can happen only when we imagine and experience our characters deeply and honestly, and give them the kind of integrity that demands that they act and speak and think and feel in ways consonant with their own individuality.

29

MAKING COINCIDENCE BELIEVABLE

BY WILLIAM SCHOELL

IMAGINE YOU'RE READING A NOVEL in which the heroine has been repeatedly terrorized by her psychopathic cousin, who has escaped from a mental hospital. Toward the end of the book, the heroine, alone in her house in the country while her boyfriend has been delayed in town, hears a noise on the second floor and goes upstairs to investigate.

"Now, wait a minute!" you say. This woman knows her cousin is on the loose. She has no weapon, is not physically strong, and has shown no evidence of being especially brave. She's an ordinary person. It's not believable for her to go upstairs alone rather than run out of the house or hide until her boyfriend returns.

Although scenes like this do occur in published books, they irritate the reader. But while readers can't return such novels to a bookstore for a refund, book editors can and will return those manuscripts with too many scenes—or even just one scene—that makes them say, "Now, wait a minute!"

Authors must strip their manuscripts of all coincidences or contrivance, or make such instances work *for* the plot. When we plot a novel, we should think ahead to the scenes that the storyline will engender and that cry out to be written: confrontation between heroine and psychotic; the climactic moment when the disadvantaged hero finally socks it to the wealthy villain who seems to hold all the cards. Too often, however, we make the mistake of twisting events and contriving situations to *force* those scenes to occur instead of letting them flow naturally from the storyline and characters. The novelist must decide when these scenes are totally inappropriate and cut them out, however painful the process, or make them convincing and plausible enough to fit smoothly into the basic framework.

130

In my first published novel, *Spawn of Hell,* the murders of the early victims go unwitnessed. I had in mind a scene in which a small town police chief, who goes alone into an underground cavern to investigate an area where a corpse has been discovered, is himself killed. But on further thought, it didn't seem credible to me that he would do this on his own. So, how could I *logically* get him to go down there alone?

Easy. First, most of his men are on other assignments and cannot be spared. Second, the middle-aged chief is bored and lazy and needs to prove that he can handle any challenge or physically demanding activity. Finally, he has always been embarrassed by his claustrophobia and wants to confront and overcome this weakness. If he should not be able to handle it and loses control, he clearly wants no one around. Although his actions may seem foolish, they are also human and understandable, and the scene is therefore convincing.

In this way, you can realistically explain why people do things that may at first seem unlikely. Sound motivation, clearly delineated, can do much to get a writer out of a jam: It can turn contrived situations into scenes that are inventive and exciting; can make scenes that could have seemed contrived ring true; explain a character's presence in your story; and make a book's whole premise believable.

In my novel *The Dragon,* about an archaeological expedition in New Mexico, I had to ask myself why Ellen Foster, a chic, sophisticated woman who hated dust and dirt, would go to an out-of-the-way site with her husband. It certainly couldn't be just out of love. She was amusing and sharp-tongued, and I wanted to make it logical for her to go on this trip to play a strong, if only a supporting part in the novel. Solution? She goes to New Mexico because she learns her husband is having an affair with one of the young women on his team and wants to make sure both of them are made utterly miserable by her presence. Just the sort of thing Ellen would do, too.

In Peter Straub's *Koko,* several Viet Nam veterans chase across the globe after a former comrade, neglecting lives, lovers, and businesses to do so. Why don't they simply leave things up to the authorities? Straub makes the camaraderie among these men who served on the same battlefield a *palpable* thing. The man they are looking for, who may be a murderer, is one of their own, and they have a duty to find him first. Straub drives home the point that an unbreakable bond exists among these men.

131

Nothing will make a prospective editor toss aside a manuscript faster than a premise that seems ludicrous or contrived . . . unless the writer takes the trouble to make the outré situation convincing. Piling up lots of significant details can bolster a farfetched premise and provide motivation for the actions of the individual characters. Glossy, pampered executives' wives in the jungle, fending for themselves? Absurd. But Shirley Conran makes it perfectly believable in her engrossing book *Savages.* These women flee into the jungle after terrorists attack the hotel to which they have come with their husbands on a company vacation. They don't just decide improbably to trek into the wilds for "kicks"; they're there by accident.

Related to contrivance are *coincidence* and *convenience,* when problems are solved too easily for the protagonist, as if the writer can think of no other way of getting his or her hero out of a predicament. (For instance, the ordinary guy in the spy novel who somehow manages against all odds to outwit trained government agents.) Yet coincidences do happen in real life. The trick in writing fiction is to make them plausible, or to make them the very *basis* of spellbinding sequences or even a book's whole premise.

One might turn coincidence into irony as Kenneth Fearing did in his classic suspense novel, *The Big Clock.* A magazine editor just happens to have spent time with his publisher's mistress earlier on the same night that the publisher kills her. The publisher wants to pin the murder on the "other man" and audaciously gets his editor to organize a manhunt (without knowing that this editor is the very man he's after). The editor, therefore, winds up organizing a manhunt for himself! There are coincidences to spare in the storyline, but they actually propel the novel along, giving it twists and turns and many moments of top-notch suspense. It works in spite of being "farfetched," because the characters and their motivations are real and the details totally convincing. The author makes you believe that, yes, it *could* happen.

Sometimes a coincidence can add just that touch of drama that your story needs. If a detective happens to see the felon he's just been assigned to look for as he crosses the street, it might be pretty boring. But if a weary detective takes the commuter train home because his car broke down (a perfectly believable situation) and at the station sees the fugitive he's been hunting down for months, you have not only another believable situation but an ironic and exciting one. It's coincidental, yes—and yet it's not. The detective saw his man only because his own routine had been altered. It *could* happen.

Because "ordinary" characters in thrillers usually have to overcome the odds and ultimately triumph over their opponents, they often seem to succeed too easily. The solution to this problem is to have the protagonist seem less of a superman by making his antagonist flawed, uncertain, and human. But don't pull these flaws out of nowhere. Let your reader know in advance, for instance, that the guards surrounding the adversary's fortress have been partying all night, so it won't seem farfetched later when the housewife-heroine sneaks by them without being seen. Let your readers know that the evil dictator, vampire, or what-have-you occasionally undergoes seizures, so that it won't seem too convenient for him to have a seizure at the climactic moment and thus allow the hero to escape.

Don't make things seem too easy; often the more hopeless the odds, the more desperate the situation, the harder and more desperately your hero has to fight. He or she may triumph—convincingly—simply because there is more at stake. There is no need for *deus ex machina* or a "convenient" solution. This is not to say that police or agents cannot arrive at some point as they might in real life, but they shouldn't show up—if at all—until the hero has had a pretty hard time of it, has almost used his own ingenuity to survive up until that point, and is close to taking his very last breath.

Having your protagonist face "unimaginable horrors" or a truly overwhelming and petrifying antagonist, means that you must explain how he can carry on to the end, when in real life most people would collapse or go mad. This can be accomplished in several ways. In my novel *Saurian,* I explained the characters' ability to cope and continue their campaign to eradicate the threat (an intelligent saurian-human hybrid of staggering proportions), by showing how they summon up their courage, even as they're quaking with terror. They do what they do because they *have* to. If they give up, who will take their places?

How would *you* solve the problem of the terrified heroine who goes upstairs to investigate a footfall? It is dramatically right for the woman to face this psychotic relative on her own, without the boyfriend's assistance. Yet at the same time it is totally unbelievable that she would do so.

Or is it? Here is how I would handle it, through *motivation.* The

133

young woman has been hounded by her insane cousin for so long that she just can't take it any more. Although she is terrified, her primary emotion as she goes up the stairs is not fear but anger. Why should she cower downstairs waiting for him just because she's a woman? Though she doesn't have a gun, she can always get a knife from the kitchen. Maybe she does wait for the boyfriend to return, but as more and more time goes by, she's afraid something's happened to him, and feels that she has no choice. She has no car, and she is determined not to be driven from her home to tremble in the woods and dark. She decides to face up to her greatest fear.

By using this technique, you can not only make "contrived" scenes believable, but convince the reader that it is the only way the scene could have been written; that what occurs is the only thing that *could* have happened. It is up to the writer to suspend the reader's disbelief, to make sure the story flows smoothly, and that there are few, if any, moments when an editor stops and says, "Now, wait a minute!"

¶ 30

KNOWING YOUR FICTION CHARACTERS

BY SONIA LEVITIN

YOU HAVE PLOTTED YOUR NOVEL effectively. The main scenes are well laid out. The beginning is clear in your mind, and you know pretty much where you're headed. You realize that writing a novel is like embarking on a journey, with departure and destination known to you. What will happen in between is still uncertain. That's what makes the trip worth taking and the novel worth writing.

With plot in hand and characters assigned their various roles, you grant yourself a block of time, provide the essential resources, and enthusiastically launch into Scene One.

But the scene dies on the page as you write it. Words, just words, flow, without the vigor of conflict or the excitement of discovery. What's wrong? You started too soon, that's what. You don't really know your people.

"But I'll get to know them as I write," you may respond. And many writers do it that way. A fine novelist of my acquaintance has confessed to writing her first chapter *seventy* times. "I was getting to know my characters," she explained somewhat sheepishly. If that works for her, fine. I prefer another technique—analysis.

Before you can really launch your characters into that first encounter, you have to know what they're all about. Delve into their backgrounds. Where were they born? To what kind of parents? How do they usually solve their difficulties? Do they fight or do they retreat? Do they mask their true feelings or are they perhaps too open, courting hurt?

That first encounter, while it seems simple, sets the tone of a relationship that must last throughout the novel. The way your characters react is a microcosm of everything to follow, hinting at the broad range of motives and quirks that define their personalities. This is the way they always react to each other: They will harbor the same grudges, tell the same lies, attempt the same manipulations over and over again, each time with a different little twist, but they will behave according to the nature you have shown us at the start—until they have grown sufficiently to break out of their pattern and can take control of their lives.

That is, basically, what every novel is about. Hero and heroine, acting upon inner or external pressures, learn to break out and take control of their lives, thereby finding happiness and often, too, love.

It is an accepted rule of dramatic presentation that for a story to move ahead, the characters must change and grow. Therefore, when the reader first meets your fictional people in Scene One, they must be presented with all their flaws and masks, all their rationalizations and self-delusions. That makes it tricky, for they will not always say what they really mean, nor will they be entirely honest with each other. Like real people in difficult situations, they will get at a problem obliquely. They'll hide their true feelings. They'll rationalize, counterattack, play games. All this maneuvering for position is touched upon in the first scene. All the hidden, underlying motivations are implied by the ways the characters first appear—by their clothes, their mannerisms, their speech patterns, the way each tries to attain his own end.

Remember that in every scene somebody must want something; somebody gets something. And, of course, while the character continues with his quest, the reader is also gaining something—information.

Sometimes when I discuss a character with a writer friend, I realize that many of the things I know about the character will never actually appear in the book. For example, in my young adult novel, *The Return,* the main character, Desta, is raised by her Aunt Kibret and uncle. Aunt Kibret is unwilling to let Desta and her siblings go, even to escape the persecution that they, as Jews in Ethiopia, face daily. Why is the aunt so adamant? To understand the conflict and give dimension to the scenes between aunt and children, I had to give the aunt a specific personality and special motives.

Aunt Kibret is seen from the start as a noncommittal person. She is always uncertain about how to react and nervous about what the neighbors will think. Added to this aspect of her personality are the usual motives about adults and children, but it is not quite enough to say that she loves them and relies on them to assist her in old age. I added a more compelling fact to her background. Her husband, when he was beaten by the Marxist thugs, was made not only lame, but impotent. This fact is never expressly stated in the book. But for me, the writer, it haunts all of Aunt Kibret's actions and her pain comes through whenever she appears. Kibret will never have children of her own, so she has very strong reasons for wanting these children to remain with her. Strong reasons like these make her a character of depth and allow her to express real courage and love when at last she does let the children go.

I am deeply interested in characters who, when the reader first meets them, say one thing but mean another. That is the way readers understand them—by seeing how their actions are opposed to their words. It is also how readers see them change and grow—or fail to grow. In *Incident at Loring Groves,* Ken Farquar is seen as an all American fellow, a school leader, son of a popular candidate for local office. But all is not as it seems. If it were, there wouldn't be a novel. Beneath the hail-fellow-well-met exterior there are terrible tensions. Readers learn that Ken's mother left the family a few years earlier, that Ken's dad is now remarried to a much younger woman. Behind the scenes—in my notebook—I worked out exactly what sort of woman Ken's mother was, even though she never appears in the pages of the book. I created her because I had to visualize how Ken was torn between his mother and father, the one who loved the limelight, and the other who was shy and a little afraid of life but who, to save her sanity, at last had to leave. I know how Ken suffered when his Mom left, how he tried in his way to help patch things up, and how the father nearly abandoned the family before he found a new wife, Nancy.

In the novel, I used very few words to indicate these deep and fundamental feelings. But as the writer, I had to *know* them completely, or else those few words could never be written, and the novel would lose its impact and its depth. But most important, without this background knowledge, the characters could never have really come alive in the fullest possible dimension.

So, before I launch into my story, I write other stories, sometimes dozens of them, in my notebooks. I begin by giving him or her a name. Where did that name come from? Names are important, because everyone is named by the people closest to him. The name expresses the parents' expectations. It also conjures up memories and symbolizes the family's hopes. Ken's brother was named P. J., meaning Peter Junior, which showed immediately that the father tried to replicate himself through his son. Ken is not named for his father—therefore he's at a disadvantage from day one. He always has to struggle to prove himself, to be as good as P. J.—and as good as Dad.

Names can, therefore, become an essential part of the plot, certainly part of the total metaphor. In *Smile Like a Plastic Daisy*, the main character is Claudia. She wages a struggle for independence, expressed in an unexpected protest she launches at school. The protest follows her first awareness of the oppression of women.

Among the feminist books Claudia reads is one about the history of the women's struggle. She learns that in ancient Rome girls were not given names of their own, but were called, for example, "Claudia," meaning, "of Claudius." It is the first time Claudia has ever seen her name in a book. Further, it provides sharp, dramatic verification of her present dilemma: All her life she has known and endured a subtle form of persecution for being female. Now she's ready to rebel. Reading that small fact in the book crystallizes everything for her.

Strangely, I had named her "Claudia" before I came upon that historic item in a book about feminism. Often the things already in the story can be exploited to greater advantage if only we will stop to think about them. It often seems that our unconscious mind has already prepared the material for us, ready to use when we dig a little deeper.

Sometimes, in an effort really to know a character before I let him appear on the "stage," I question him. I ask him his dreams, his memories, his fears. Or I have him write me a letter about what he most desires or most fears in life. How can you really know a person, unless you know his strongest emotions?

In *Incident at Loring Groves*, a minor but important character, Ivan, is the sidekick to a murderer. "What makes you tick?" I asked Ivan. "What do you want out of life?" I had him write me a letter.

"What I really want most," Ivan wrote, "is to go down to the beach at Venice and watch those chicks roller skate in their bikinis." What a sad character! That was all he wanted out of life—and he'd never get even that.

Every good story is really two stories. There is the obvious external quest for a goal—to survive a danger, to succeed in a career, or to find love and self-esteem. Beyond the obvious desire lies something deeper, which we can uncover only if we know our characters well. A good book provides a bonus, not only to the reader, but to the characters as well.

For example, in *A Season for Unicorns*, my main character, Inky, must come to terms with her father's betrayal. Like all of us, Inky has certain fears. She is afraid of heights. And Inky's mother is agoraphobic. Now, the story of the father's infidelity and Inky's disillusionment could certainly have been told without this added dimension. But I think it would not have been as satisfying. Knowing that Inky has this inner problem, I can help her understand herself better. She must learn to equate her mother's problem with her own. She can do this only when she is able to face two truths: that her father is unfaithful, but that she cannot change him or her mother. She can change only herself. By understanding her fears, I, as novelist, can make Inky overcome them; thus both she and the novel will grow beyond rudimentary requirements of the plot. Inky does gain self-esteem. She finds love when she meets a boy with whom she can be honest. And, as a bonus, she overcomes her fear of heights.

Students often ask me what to do about writer's block. I tell them— with a smile—that I don't believe in it. What I do believe in is being prepared. To me that means that if you get stuck, you are lacking something. And usually it is something you don't know about your people. Because if you really know your characters, then when you have them confront each other in a scene, they will work against each other—which is, after all, the essence of drama.

Before you can write a good story, you have really to know your people, not superficially, but well enough to invite them into your home and make them part of your life. Then they'll come across for you and make things happen.

31

WRITE THE STORY <u>YOU</u> WANT TO TELL

BY SUSAN ISAACS

SO THERE I WAS, at a "Meet the Author" luncheon in Detroit, my speech about how I became a writer finished, the question-and-answer segment concluded, when this ferociously determined woman with shoulder pads bulldozed a couple of innocent bystanders, came up beside me and announced: "Susan, you give me *such* confidence!" I smiled and began work on a modest thank you, but she cut me off: "If *you* can do it, anybody can."

Condescending? Sure. But also correct. If I could do it, so could she . . . or, if not, her neighbor . . . or you.

Of course, any literate person can write, but writing that *lives* is a gift; the earth is not teeming with billions of potential novelists, waiting only for time and a typewriter. Writing is a talent you're either born with or have acquired by the time you're eight or nine years old. Where does the gift come from? I don't know. How do you know if you have it? Only one way: you write.

This takes enormous courage. We all have successful writer dreams: exchanging bon mots with Johnny Carson, delivering our Nobel address. You will always be great in these dreams, but let me tell you: The reality of actually writing will wake you up. Nothing I've written is as clever, brilliant (or as well received) as my original conception of it. Deep down I think we all sense this disparity, this abyss between our dreams and our talents, so actually sitting down and writing an entire novel takes guts.

I used to think: Who am *I* to be a writer? Writers don't wear makeup. And they're gaunt, haunted-looking, like Virginia Woolf or Joyce Carol Oates or Joan Didion. Or else, writers are incessantly witty, urbane— even glamorous. Well, all that is nonsense, pure stereotype. A writer can look like Christie Brinkley or a troll. As for sophistication, a writer is not necessarily someone who can get a good table at Elaine's. In fact, life in the fast lane probably does more to destroy talent than nurture it; look at F. Scott Fitzgerald, Truman Capote. Further, a writer is not someone who touts his or her genius or vulnerability. Nor is he or she someone who goes from writer's conference to writer's conference, year after year, working over the same fifteen pages of exquisitely refined prose.

A writer can be *anyone*—pretty or not, a sophisticate or a creep. As for writing, like making chicken soup or making love, it is an idiosyncratic act. There is no one right way to do it. I can only tell you how I do it.

Writing is a job, and I go to work every morning: nine o'clock, five days a week. I quit about noon when I'm working on a novel (creating a universe being somewhat fatiguing), although I might edit the two or three pages I've written the rest of the day, or go to the library: What did most women do about birth control in 1940? How did the OSS screen potential agents?

(Writing a screenplay is less taxing, and by the time production rolls around I am so familiar with my characters that I can, on occasion, write whole scenes on the set while electricians drag cables over my sneakers and the grips look over my shoulder and critique my dialogue.)

But back to the beginning writer. When I decided to start my first novel, which was to be *Compromising Positions,* I thought about taking a fiction workshop. Lucky for me, I couldn't get a baby-sitter at the time the New School's best course was being offered. So instead I bought a copy of John Braine's *Writing A Novel.*

Like the Montessori method of tying a shoelace, the book broke a complicated task into a lot of idiot steps, so that the job didn't seem overwhelming. *Make an outline of no more than four pages:* When I began all I knew was I had a housewife-detective who lived on Long Island. When I finished, I not only knew who'd done it, I knew where, how, and why. In writing those few pages, putting down ideas that had probably been whizzing around my unconscious for months or years, I discovered that my heroine, Judith Singer, and the homicide lieutenant were soulmates, while her husband . . . Well, you get the point. *Draw up a list of characters:* I did, and suddenly Judith's best friend, an ex-Southern belle with an earthy sense of humor, jumped up and winked at me. The victim? I considered who most deserved to die: a periodontist.

141

You know that old platitude: *write about what you know*. Well, it's not a bad idea. You can use what you know—computers, mahjongg, Harlem, or parakeets—either as the core of the novel or as a background. And write about what you care about. I care about people, character. For me, writing a novel is fashioning an intimate biography.

In *Compromising Positions,* I used my home, suburban Long Island, as the setting, and bestowed my then-job, housewife, on my heroine. In *Close Relations,* I drew on Brooklyn and Queens, the world I grew up in, the world of New York City ethnics. I also took my (brief) experience as a political speech-writer, as well as my passion for New York Democratic politics and gave them to Marcia Green. In *Almost Paradise,* I wrote about show business (this was before I became a screenwriter) and celebrity. Wasn't that writing about what I didn't know? Well, in America show business *is* everybody's business. And celebrity? I took my own minor exposure to it, my twelve-city book tour for *Close Relations,* and puffed it up: being on a TV talk show; being recognized by an effusive reader in the ladies' room; having mere acquaintances feel my sex life—to say nothing of my tax return—is their property.

By the time it came to writing *Shining Through,* I was secure enough in my proficiency as a novelist, in my imaginative ability, to write about what I didn't know: speaking German, being a spy in World War II. But what I *did* know was what it's like to look at the rich and powerful through the eyes of someone who was neither. Linda Voss, my heroine, like me, started as an outsider. Like Linda, I worked as a secretary and knew what it was like to be thought of as something more than a typewriter—but less than a human being. (Later when Linda became a spy, her "cover" was a cook. Listen, I was still writing about what I know. I was a housewife. I know from pot roast. I just transferred it to Germany and made it sauerbraten.)

In other words, in *Shining Through,* I was writing about *people.* I was writing about love—real and unrequited—and passion, honor, deceit, friendship, patriotism, courage, terror. In other words, having lived for over forty years, I *was* writing about what I knew.

Another suggestion: *write for yourself.* I was among the blessed. I never went to a writers' conference, never took a fiction workshop. I learned to write for *me,* not for a teacher, a critic, an editor or even that amorphous, intimidating mass, the "audience." I never allowed myself to worry: What will my mother think? The minute you write to please someone, or not to offend someone, or to take big bucks, or to be taken seriously, you're gazing outward, not inward, and you're doomed to lose sight of what is unique and true in you.

So then, what does it take to be a novelist? Well, a gift for writing. A willingness to sit alone in a room for one or three or ten years, telling yourself a story. Then you must be able to *become your toughest critic*. Ask yourself the blunt questions: What is there about this protagonist that would make someone else besides me, the creator, care about his or her fate? What propels the novel, what will drive the reader to turn the page? This may be the most difficult task of all. With all four of my novels, there were days I was embarrassed—no, mortified—at the drivel I was passing off as fiction; and there were days that I was jolted by the force of my own brilliance. You will discover, after many readings, that the truth lies somewhere in that broad range in between.

If you want to write, expect criticism, some of it personal. If you write about sex, someone will inevitably tell you that you have a dirty mind. If you are a woman and you write about something other than glitz or, on the other hand, quiet, domestic lives, you run the risk of being criticized for *chutzpah* or naiveté. ("Serious" American female novelists are almost all experts at literary petit point; the big canvas is left to the men with their broad strokes.) Don't be afraid of what They say. *Write*. Don't write the story you think they want to listen to. Write the story you want to tell.

I know, it seems overwhelming. But then again maybe that nagging thought—if *she* can do it, I can too—is really a good, honest gut feeling about your own talent. Do you think it's worth taking the chance to discover the truth?

32

FROM RAW MATERIAL TO STORY

BY MAYA SONENBERG

IDEAS FOR STORIES STRIKE FROM ANYWHERE, spring from anything—dreams, newspaper articles, paintings, relatives' lives, the words of a song, the encyclopedia—and then we set out to transform them into fiction. "Write what you know," we've all been told. But we know things in so many ways, from so many sources, and any one of these can start a train of thought that ends with a story.

We limit ourselves by thinking that "what we know" means only what we've lived intimately, daily, for it can also mean what we've read, what we've been told, what we've observed in the woods, on Main Street, in museums. We limit ourselves, too, by thinking that these germs of stories must already contain a compelling plot and fully rounded characters; the raw material of fiction can as easily be image, idea, metaphor, language—plot and characters growing only as necessary from these sources. The less we limit ourselves, the more chance we have of finding the trigger for what may be a fantastic story.

How do we transform these scraps of experience—all kinds of experience—into fiction? For the art resides not in the experience itself but in what we do with that raw material. Often personal experience serves as the catalyst for a story. The place you live can spark the imagination. A quirky aunt who forgets to wash behind her ears; lives in an empty apartment because she's given all her furniture to refugees; does cartwheels down Fifth Avenue; and is also an unrivalled success as a trial lawyer can inspire a story about a young nephew who discovers the evils of conformity and the importance of independent thinking.

This material is immediate. Making a story from it seems easy enough, but the first draft may be little more than a journal entry, a memoir, or a character sketch instead of a full-fledged story. We've all faced the criticism—or realized ourselves—that a character, setting, or image is vague, dead, unconvincing. It does no good to tell ourselves, "But it really happened that way. She's really like that." Instead, it may help to think of this as a problem of transformation, or really lack of transformation. Close your eyes and you see Aunt Edith so clearly that the words "crazy, quirky, and successful" seem to describe her perfectly. She's so real to you that you don't need to create her with words; you can't see the fictional character for the actual person, and such lack of vision makes your story murky and keeps you from using language accurately. This, I think, is why writing fiction based on auto-biographical material can be so deceptively easy and so hard to do well.

It takes special care to make the transformation from life to art successfully. The first step may simply be to pretend you've never met Aunt Edith. After you've convinced yourself of this, reread your story. Is she clear to you? Do you feel you've been introduced to a new person? If not, this is the time to cut out the hackneyed words and the too-broad images, the outlines you can fill in as you read because you know Aunt Edith but that fail to create a picture for anyone else. Replace them with specific description and action—old advice, I know, but especially important to remember when writing about things and people we're close to. Don't just say Aunt Edith was a bit strange; describe her doing pirouettes on the escalators in Bloomingdale's.

My story "Quarry Games" grew out of visits to an abandoned quarry near the ocean. In part, I simply wanted to describe a place I loved. I also wanted to write about sensing the past, the way I could imagine so clearly how other people had walked and worked there. In the story, a young girl uses the quarry as a springboard for her imagination and brings to life everything she sees, only to have an older boy disparage these fantasies until she abandons them. But if readers can see neither the actual quarry nor the girl's inventions, they will not find the loss of her imagination compelling. Early versions of this story were bland, threadbare. I was taking for granted that everyone already found old quarries intriguing and knew which games could be invented there. I needed to forget my own reactions to the place and imagine the girl's— from inside.

Personal experience is just one example of raw material that needs to be transformed to become a story. While all fiction writing demands the exactitude I've described, stories that arise from other sources present other opportunities and problems. You may find an idea in a newspaper, a book, or a conversation you overhear on the bus. The problem here is to write something new, to transform something that already exists in language. I once gave students a newspaper article about a Czechoslovak family who escaped to Austria in a hot air balloon and asked them to turn it into fiction. "Don't tell the whole story," I suggested. "First, figure out what intrigues you most about the account." The seven-year-old son's fear as he steps into the balloon? The way the earth looks from above on a moonlit night? The father's sorrow at leaving his own parents behind? The idea of pursuit? The workings of the balloon? The surprise of the Austrian border guards when the balloon lands? This decision made, point of view, voice, tense, time frame, start to fall into place.

With a story you've heard hundreds of times before—a myth, fairy tale, or history book standard—you can start by choosing a different point of view, perhaps that of the character you feel has been slighted in the original, and see where that takes you. Tell "Rapunzel" in the witch's voice. Describe the assassination of Abraham Lincoln through the eyes of John Wilkes Booth. In "Ariadne in Exile" I decided to retell the story of Theseus and the Minotaur through the Minotaur's sister and found I was writing a story about a woman abandoned on an island and haunted by her memories.

Of course, more unusual things can serve as sources and subjects for fiction—a visual image, a painting, for example. In "Nature Morte," I tried to bring a cubist baby to life. As a cubist painting depicts its subject from many points of view at once, I approached my cubist baby through the voices of a number of characters—mother, doctor, school-yard friend, and the baby himself—in order to create a verbal equivalent of a visual experience.

Day-to-day images also trigger stories of all types. You see a bowl sitting on a table with the light from a lamp throwing its interior into shadow, and this image refuses to let you alone. "Who owns that bowl?" you ask yourself. "Is it whole or cracked? New or old? What color is it? Where was it purchased? Who made it? Was it a gift? What does it hold?" In inventing answers to these questions, you're starting a story—perhaps a story about the bowl's owner, the bowl's maker, or the bowl itself, passing from hand to hand, affecting lives.

Sometimes we start making up a story when a phrase buzzes in our

146

ear, the way a mosquito hovers in the dark as we try to sleep. The phrase can be a bit of conversation that leads us to invent the speaker, a sentence whose music makes us think of water kissing the side of a ship, or a metaphor waiting to be given flesh. What if that sound of kissing becomes a real kiss between two passengers on the ship? What if two map-makers carry on a love affair the way they make and read maps, the way the imagination relates to "reality"—recreating, interpreting, inventing, failing to communicate? In "Cartographies," I explored these metaphors in trying to answer that question. What triggered these meditations on maps, map-makers, and imagination that ended in a love story? The title of a poem by Adrienne Rich—"Cartographies of Silence." Just a few words can be raw material if we work out the ramifications: Just what is a map of silence and how can it be expressed as a relationship between people?

Questions often goad us into writing, but they are not always questions about characters, places, or events. They can also question abstract ideas. What is the nature of loneliness? What if immortality were a reality? In the stories we write, characters can ask these questions. Characters' lives can represent possible answers. Or, the form of the story can embody both questions and answers. If you decide there are twelve varieties of loneliness, you might write a work in a dozen sections, exploring in each a different facet of that emotion. I started the story "Dioramas" when I asked myself about the different ways one might relate to nature. In "Cartographies," my mapmakers end by finding a peace and wholeness in nature, but in "Dioramas" I wanted to explore less romantic ways of relating to landscape. What if someone preferred an industrial park to a national park? What would it be like to feel beholden to a place, tied to it against one's will? To fear a place? To be seduced by countryside? To be cursed by a location? To be obsessed with a landscape? To be literally absorbed by land? To simply be bored? Eventually I chose seven settings and peopled each with a different couple whose relationship mirrored the relationship between them and the land. These questions may be only the framework I use to build the piece, no longer visible, but still necessary to the construction. In this way, writing fiction can be a dialogue *with*—though not necessarily *about*—yourself, one story acting as the impetus for the next, a give-and-take on whatever images, characters, metaphors intrigue you.

Writing fiction based on material that at first seems distant does not mean avoiding the things you care about, but expands the range of those materials. Learn to pounce on whatever starts you thinking about a new story, however unlikely (for me it's very often a visual image), and you've found your catalyst.

Still, it's only a catalyst, a moment of inspiration that needs to be shaped by imagination and verbal ingenuity. What prevents writing about personal experience from being a diary? What prevents writing about current events from being an essay? Or an idea from being philosophy? The boundary lines—thank goodness—are rarely clear, but one distinction may be this: With fiction, the experience or idea resides *in* language and form, in image, voice, character, scene, and is inseparable from these things rather than explained by them. Fiction is language the way an ice sculpture is ice; dissolve the ice surface to search for supports, disregard the verbal surface to find another meaning, and the whole thing disappears. With language, we create a fictional equivalent, a parallel or not-so-parallel universe, rather than describing the one that already exists.

Fiction may be far indeed from the event or image that triggered it. In revisiting a setting I've used in a story, I'm always surprised by how different it is from what I've described, how much more space there is, simply how physical it is. By now, I should expect this to happen, but I always sit up with a jolt, gasp at the beauty or ugliness that didn't make it to the page, and realize again that writing fiction is not a process of holding a mirror to the world and transcribing what one sees, but a process of transformation by language and into language, a creation rather than a *re*creation, an experience of great and terrible freedom more than anything else. It matters little that the granite quarry I described doesn't match the one I see; that day exploring ledges by the ocean was only the trigger for a story, not its reason for being.

33

CREATING SHORT FICTION FROM CHARACTER: FIVE RULES

BY LUCIA NEVAI

FEW OF TODAY'S GREAT SHORT STORIES achieve their power from strong plots. If you are at work on a story or want to try your hand at one, keep in mind the importance of fully conceived characters. Vladimir Nabokov in the chapter on Dickens in his *Lectures on Literature* says that every Dickens character has his attribute, *a kind of colored shadow that appears whenever the person appears.* To me, the important phrase is *whenever the person appears.* If you introduce your main character with an adjective-filled paragraph on page one, that may not be enough to bring him to life.

The reader has to smell his hair oil when he sweats on page two, worry about his excess weight when he trudges heavily up the fire escape on page four. A common exercise used to help writers get to know about characters that interest them is to have them write a brief biography of each one. Sounds easy, sounds obvious. Try it once, and you will see how little you know about your character at the outset. Even if you don't use the material discovered in your biography in the actual story, the reader will know how well you know whom you're writing about. It's O.K. to know more than you tell—in fact, it creates a pleasant suspense between you and the reader.

After you've written the biography (or -phies), revise your plot—it will need revision. If you don't have a plot, don't berate yourself for not being a real writer. Some writers do not conceive plots and characters in a single spontaneous stroke of inspiration. List events that might test, reveal, ruin, or redeem the major character. If you discover through writing, write first. Then reread and rethink the structure and purpose of the story. If you prefer to think first, fine. Try to extract the story—a sequence of deeds—from the character's essence. Then write. Your folders will be thinner. Both routes require you to think; both routes require you to rewrite. Short fiction today is extremely accomplished. Editors are used to reading tightly written, professionally edited material.

It goes without saying that you will have numerous drafts of almost any story. In order to keep in focus the purpose and the music of the story, I can recommend these five rules for rewriting and editing your drafts:

• **One.** *Always keep in mind the image that first led you to want to write about this character.* If a character has mystery, power, and subtlety, the reasons for this are in the sensory details of the image that has led you to want to write about him. Return to these details when you feel the story wobble off track. Remind yourself what time, what season, what mood are in the image. Where is the character? What has just happened, what is about to happen? This image probably appears in the story, but it doesn't have to. Whether or not it does, nothing emotional that happens in the story should contradict the gist of this image. This image remains greater than the sum of its parts and may function as an after-image, lingering with the reader when the story is over.

• **Two.** *Isolate one strong central action that symbolizes this character's resolution of a dilemma.* The only difficulty presented by this rule is that first you must know the character's dilemma; you must know how he or she would resolve it emotionally; and you must know the action options afforded by the plot. If you really know all that, it's usually easy to isolate an action that formally depicts or symbolizes the resolution. If isolating this action seems difficult or arbitrary, it's probably because you have either too much action or too little—a common problem among beginning writers. If you have too much, use restraint. Choose one gesture, one reaction, emphasize it and play down the others. If you have little or no action, go back to the biographies to see if there is an act or idea in the minds and histories of your characters. Do not force a deed on a character, or you'll end up with a stereotype or an inconsistency. The deed, remember, can be passive: a thought, a decision, a withholding of help or harm.

• **Three.** *Keep the tone of the story consistent throughout and reflective of the vision you offer.* This is not easy. From draft to draft, you have to become very adept at editing your work for consistency. The reason is that as a story finds its tone, language will have survived from previous drafts (descriptions, dialogue, narration) that detracts from or contradicts the emerging tone. If you love your sad description of a lake in late afternoon, you may have to force yourself to eliminate it or adapt it when the scene turns out to be ironic. Conversely, if you discover your humorous sketch has a poignant underbelly, you may have to relinquish some of your broader jokes. Tone, remember, is tone of voice. Someone can ask you how you are, but the real meaning of the question is in the tone: sarcastic, sympathetic, habitual, romantic, wary, threatening. The second part of the rule, the relation between tone and vision, is also tricky. They don't have to match, but they have to be appropriate and consistent. A sarcastic portrayal of a girl's naïve fling with a self-help group is appropriate, but you would have to be very clever to depict with sarcasm a weighty event like an abortion.

• **Four.** *Is the emotional progress of the story satisfying to the reader?* Now that you've had your fun, said what you had to say, take a look at the progress of emotion in the story to see if it works and makes sense. A short story should begin at one point emotionally and end at another. Your sad story should not read like the Book of Job; your happy story (much harder to write, by the way) should find its happiness. *Show, don't tell* is an important exercise in evoking emotion in a story. If, for example, a woman goes to work at the office even though she's grieving over the death of her mother, the reader should recognize her emotional state in the language you choose—and not by reading the sentence, "She felt sad." Imbue the woman's actions with her feelings, and the reader will come with you. Emotional progress is satisfying and the basis of much entertainment. This rule keeps you from jumping around too much, leaving scenes too quickly, jumbling up your story with episodes that derail the narrative.

• **Five.** *Could anyone but you have written this story in just this way?* Depending on your weaknesses and strengths as a writer, you may have more faith in your ability to sound like other writers you've read than to sound like yourself. In this case, *yourself* is the feeling, observing person who is mystified or curious, impassioned or outraged, fascinated or mortified by life and wants to articulate something of the experience. You can always go back to your imagination, where both your experience and your love of language have their source. Look and listen one last time to make sure the characters and images have the unique stamp of *your* character, and that your colored shadow, to use Nabokov's phrase, appears on every page.

Although it is difficult to separate the elements that contribute to the power of successful short fiction, the element of character is especially strong in the following twelve stories by very different authors, male and female, legendary and emerging. Go to the library and browse through the collections and anthologies that include stories like these. When you find two or three voices that please and excite you, read those authors.

Some questions to ask as you read include: How does the author use description and dialogue to set up contrasting characters? What is the social relationship of the characters—does it differ from the moral relationship? How does the relationship change during the story? What is the progress of emotion? And finally, whose story is this? Although the action may center on one character, the purpose of the story might be to reveal another character, or even the narrator who seems to stand outside the action.

TWELVE GREAT SHORT STORIES

"Alaska," Alice Adams
"The Privy Councilor," by Anton Chekhov
"Mr. Burdoff's Visit to Germany," by Lydia Davis
"Water Liars," by Barry Hannah
"Patriotic," by Janet Kaufman
"Labor Day Dinner," by Alice Munro
"The Artificial Nigger," by Flannery O'Connor
"How Can I Tell You?" by John O'Hara
"The Saint," by V. S. Pritchett
"Bad Characters," by Jean Stafford
"The Gift of the Prodigal," by Peter Taylor
"The Rich Brother," by Tobias Wolff

34

Too Good To Be True: The Flawless Character

By Mary Tannen

My mother once bought a new table that came with a card printed on buff-colored heavy stock explaining that the table had been "distressed" with artful gouges and well-placed worm holes to give it a patina of age. We (her four children) thought this was hilariously funny and said that if we had only known she wanted distressed furniture we would have been happy to oblige and that clearly we had misinterpreted her screams of anguish every time we left a soda bottle on the coffee table or ran a toy car up the leg of the Duncan Phyfe chair.

The very phrase "character flaw" makes me think of that distressed table, as if characters were naturally shiny new and perfect and needed only the addition of a flaw or two, artfully placed, to make them more realistic. To me, a personality, whether actual or fictional, is not solid but liquid, not liquid but airborne, as changeable as light. What looks like a flaw might turn out to be a virtue. Virtue might, under certain circumstances, prove to be a fault.

When my daughter was reading *Billy Budd* and having a hard time with it, she came storming into my room to protest, and seeing the book I was working on in galleys, took it into her room to read. She brought it back the next day and announced that it was "better than *Billy Budd*."

"Better than *Billy Budd*!" I could see it emblazoned across the book jacket. Actually, my novel isn't better than *Billy Budd*, but the style was a lot more congenial to my daughter. She was appalled by Melville's heavy symbolism, by the way Billy Budd was the representation of an idea, not an actual man.

Billy Budd had no flaws, physical or moral (except for his stutter). He was illiterate, of noble but unknown birth, untainted by the corrupting influence of either family or literature. He was a myth, "Apollo with his portmanteau"! Melville never intended to create a realistic character. Billy Budd was Adam before the fall.

Sometimes when reading over a draft of a fiction piece I am working on, I realize that one of my major characters is suspiciously lacking in flaws. She is usually a person like me, but she is lacking in defects as well as in color and definition. When this happens in a piece of fiction I'm writing, it is a sign that I am identifying too closely with her. Just as I try to show my good and hide my bad, I am protecting this fictional person.

Recently I discovered a trick that helped me correct this. I was working with a character, Yolanda, a woman my age who ran a bookstore. Yolanda was nice. She was good. A nice good woman, and very bland. I couldn't get a grip on her or who she was. I went to my local swimming pool to do a few laps and take my mind off my troubles, when I saw a woman I'd seen many times before but don't know very well—a tall skinny woman with short elfin hair and wide-awake eyes. I decided to steal this woman's body and give it to Yolanda.

It worked miracles because now Yolanda was no longer me. She was this woman I didn't know very well. She began to exhibit all kinds of personality traits. She was allergic to almost everything and purchased her meals at the New Age Take-Out Kitchen. This explained why she was so thin. She spent lonely nights watching the families in the apartments across the street. The strange thing was that although Yolanda had many more weaknesses than she did before I discovered she wasn't me, I liked her better.

Another way to break the spell of the flawless character is to elicit the opinion of another character in the novel or story, one who dislikes, resents, or holds a grudge against the paragon of virtue. In *Second Sight,* I had a perfectly lovable older woman, Lavinia, who refused to believe that her philandering husband, Nestor, had left her for good. Instead of selling the house and investing the proceeds in order to live off the income, she managed on very little so that she could keep the house intact for Nestor's return.

Nestor (who had flaws to spare) had another version of the story. Lavinia's loyalty enraged him. He saw it as a ploy to make him feel guilty and remain tied to her. Indeed, at the end when Nestor asked Lavinia to take him back, Lavinia realized she no longer wanted to

154

return to her old life with Nestor. She wondered if perhaps instead of being noble and true all those years, she hadn't actually been taking out a genteel and subtle revenge.

A character without flaws has nowhere to go. He can't change or grow. In Philip Roth's *The Counterlife,* the novelist Zuckerman, who used himself as a character in his books, was writing about his younger brother Henry. Because Zuckerman had given all the faults to himself-as-character, he had doomed his brother-as-character to a life of virtue. Henry had always been the good son, the good husband, father, dentist. Writing about Henry at thirty-nine, Zuckerman imagined him as the suffocating prisoner of his perfect but shallow life. The only way Henry could break the pattern was to escape altogether, leave his family and practice in New Jersey and begin anew in Israel. Zuckerman went to visit Henry in his kibbutz on the West Bank and found that his younger brother had simply exchanged one slavish system for another. He was still the good brother. He could change the scene, but he couldn't change himself because he was a character without flaws.

I realize I have been using the term "flaw" as if it could mean anything from nail-biting to one of the Seven Deadly Sins. I think of a flaw as a personality trait I wouldn't confess to, except on a dark and stormy night to a stranger passing through. And then there are the flaws we hide from ourselves, or lack the insight to see, but which help determine the course of our lives.

When I'm writing, the flaws that interest me are not the ones I assign ("Q kicks small dogs"), but those that emerge in the course of the story. Take Yolanda, who tries to be good, to be virtuous, to do no harm to others: I was amazed to discover, somewhere near the end of the first draft, that she had used someone, a man, a friend, to get over a wound suffered long ago, and in using him had hurt him. Yolanda didn't see how she could hurt this friend whom she considered much more powerful and attractive than she. The more I work on that novel, the more I see that Yolanda's major flaw is her modesty. She lets people down because she cannot conceive that she means as much to them as they do to her.

In *Second Sight,* the opposite was true: a character's flaw proved to be her saving grace. Delia, the widowed mother of a twelve-year-old son, lacked all marketable skills. She lived on welfare and whatever she could make telling fortunes over the phone. Everyone, but especially

155

Delia's career-minded sister Cass, faulted her for not taking her life in hand and finding a way out of the dead-end life of poverty she and her son had fallen into.

But Delia operated on another level from her more rational friends and relatives. She was watching for signs and portents, for signals that the time was right. She refused to force the unfolding of her life.

Delia did manage finally to bring about a change for herself and her son, to the amazement of the others, who began to see a glimmer of wisdom in her otherworldliness. Cass, however, could never accept that Delia's passivity had enabled her to recognize and receive love when it came her way. Cass would continue to take charge of her life, as Delia said, captaining it as if it were a ship, but never allowing for the influence of wind or tide or current.

People, fictional and real, are not perfect, like fresh-from-the-factory tables. They come with their faults built in, mingled and confused with their virtues. Whenever I find I am dealing with a character without flaws, and I am not intending a twentieth-century rewrite of *Billy Budd,* I take it as a sign that I have not done my work. I have not imagined my character fully, have not considered her through the eyes of the other characters. Finally, I have not cut the umbilical cord. I am protecting her, shielding her, and, at the same time, imprisoning her in her own virtue. It is time to let her go so she can fail and change and grow.

35

LET FICTION CHANGE YOUR LIFE

BY LYNNE SHARON SCHWARTZ

THE LURE OF USING our own experiences in fiction is almost irresistible—not only for beginners but for seasoned pros as well. What could be more natural, or more inevitable? To tell what has shaped us, to cast the incidents of our lives in the form of narrative, with ourselves as heroes and heroines, is instinctive: It shows itself as soon as children acquire language. And personal experience is a vital source of fiction, one might even say the only source: what else *can* we write of but what we have seen, felt, thought, done, and as a result, imagined? As readers, we're touched most deeply by stories that possess, in Henry James's phrase, the sense of "felt life," stories the author has cared about and lived with and presented in all their intensity; the others lie stone cold on the page. Indeed, a corollary to the old saw, "write what you know," could be, "write what you care about."

But if all of the above is true, then fiction might be no more than faintly disguised autobiography, an indulgent exercise in self-expression. Fiction would be a sorry, impoverished thing indeed, deprived of the rich and incomparable offerings of the imagination and the unconscious, with their enigmatic leaps and turns. Thankfully this isn't so.

How do we make use of the tremendous stores of material our lives provide, and at the same time avoid boring our readers by being that most tedious of companions—the kind we all know and dread—who talks only of himself, by himself, and for himself?

The lamest excuse beginning fiction writers give in response to criticism is, plaintively, "But that's what really happened." Who cares, I'm tempted to ask. To put it more tactfully: If you want to write fiction that others will love to read, you have to be willing to sacrifice parts of your life. Or if that sounds rather extreme, let's call it giving up "the way it really happened" in favor of a greater truth. For a story, in some

157

unaccountable fashion, makes its own demands, like a child outgrowing the confines of the parental home. When you're willing to let the story's life take precedence over your own and go its way, you've taken the first step to becoming a successful writer.

Once you've embarked on that journey, the urge to tell what happened is slowly transformed into the desire to give events pattern and significance, to construct a *thing*, almost like a free-standing sculpture whose shape and contours are clear to all, with the power to delight, or amuse, or provoke, or disturb. Above all, to draw in an entrance. In its final form, while the construction may have been inspired by happenings in the writer's own life and may still contain their germ, it has taken on its own life. It has, sometimes in most surprising ways, gone beyond the writer's experience.

This doesn't mean you can't allow your deepest concerns into your fiction—quite the contrary. Look at the work of Jane Austen, who has left us the most witty, thorough, and painstaking account of nineteenth-century courtship and marriage rites in the middle classes; no sociological study could be more informative, not to mention enchanting. Little is known of Austen's personal life; we cannot say for certain who were her suitors or why she did not marry; we cannot point to episodes in her novels and trace their origins. What we do know is that she scrutinized the mating game in all its aspects, with a unique blend of irony, skepticism, and mellow acceptance. In other words, Austen managed to put her individual sensibility into her work in a far more profound way than by merely drawing on actual events.

As a humbler example, since it's what I know best, I'll use my own novel, *Rough Strife,* which also happens to be about a marriage. The story follows some twenty years in the life of a couple, Caroline and Ivan, who meet in Rome then return to the United States to live in Boston, Connecticut, and finally New York City—settings I chose because I knew them and felt on "safe" territory. During the time I was writing *Rough Strife,* a spate of novels appeared in which married women, weary and disgusted with the inequities of family life, were cutting loose to find independence and adventure. Something about the ease and abruptness of their flights from home bothered me; much as I sympathized with the problem of constraint, the solution seemed oversimplified. I was determined to write about a heroine who stayed to see it through, to learn where that route could lead. At the same time I, too, was determined not, fashionably, to abandon my marriage, a fact that surely influenced the book.

I suppose I planned, in some imprecise way, to have Caroline and Ivan face many of the issues my husband and I faced. But in the end the couple bypassed me to lead their own lives. Caroline, for example, surprised me by having a difficult time conceiving their first child. A mathematics professor, she has an affair with a graduate student, which leads to an abortion; later on, her second child with Ivan turns out to be hyperactive. Why, I wondered as I wrote, did I invent all that? Why did it invent itself, might be more accurate. Well, I wanted to illustrate the enormous effects that bearing and raising children have on a marriage, and those events heighten the illustration. They apply pressure and create tension. They arose from the imagination, wisely, I think, to serve the story.

At still another point the characters escaped me, quite against my will. I was writing a scene of a marital quarrel, with some rather acidic repartee. No one could have been more alarmed than I when Ivan suddenly turned violent, pushing Caroline to the floor. It was not at all what I had intended—not with these characters, anyway, civilized people, incapable of such behavior. In shock and horror, I watched a rape scene unfold. How much more shocking that it was coming from my own pen! And Caroline's reaction was equally horrifying. Instead of being indignant and repelled, she thinks she invited it in some way. She even feels sorry for Ivan in his guilt and remorse! The whole incident contradicted my beliefs as well as my experience—in real life I would have shaken them both to their senses. But this was not real life. This was the utter mystery and excitement of fiction, where characters rebel and demand their own errors and their own destiny, and we had best not stand in their way.

In the end, I had a novel about a couple whose story barely resembled my own. The only autobiographical elements left were a certain analytical turn of mind and a sense of the complex, ambiguous accommodations involved in living with another person. Whatever my original aims, I had written about the gradual process of accepting the results of one's uneducated choices. With the benefit of several years' hindsight, I can see that this notion of process, not the details of the plot, is what makes the book personal as well as, I hope, universal.

The same shifts occur in writing stories, only on a smaller scale. How well I remember lying awake one entire night with a gray spot jiggling before my eyes—something the doctors call a "floater," I later learned. It didn't let me sleep, and as the hours passed, I slipped into a miserable, unreasonable state of mind, berating myself for all the mistakes of my past, wondering what it all meant, if anything. . . . Anyone who's spent a sleepless night recently will know what I mean. The experience was so powerful and disturbing that naturally I wanted to write about it. The result was a story, "Acquainted With the Night," whose main character turned out to be a male architect ten years older than I. Why, I can't say. He too lies awake, victim of a floater, examining and agonizing over his past, which, needless to say, has nothing in common with my own. (I took the opportunity to give him a life full of moral crisis, without the straints I might have felt about detailing mine.) Again, the common and personal element, as well as the universal one, is simply the insomniac's painful and—in the light of day—distorted trip, a trip almost every reader has taken at one time or another.

The path leading to a newer story was more circuitous. Several years ago, a fire forced my husband and me out of the apartment building where we had lived for twenty years and raised our two daughters. Besides the shock and pain of losing our home, we and our fellow-tenants were outraged at the behavior of the landlord, Columbia University, in the aftermath of the fire. A lengthy court case ensued, with the tenants ranged against the power and willfulness of a large institution. Two years later I completed a book about the fire, the legal proceedings, and the social implications of institutions as landlords. Since I had written mainly fiction till then, I was prepared when friends asked why I hadn't turned my experience into a novel—what an ideal story it seemed, full of drama and conflict. My answer was, first, that the truth was topically urgent and needed to be told precisely as it happened; and second, that the story (plus the research it would entail) really didn't interest me as a novelist. I had been writing long enough to know that real estate practices, demographics, and the nature of bureaucracy were not my subjects.

Some time later, though, probably under the influence of many newspaper and magazine articles about homelessness in New York City, an imaginary family moved into my mind. Little by little their features became clear: they were newcomers from the Virgin Islands, the father was an electrician but temporarily working at a lunch counter, they were black, they were very proper and conventional, there were three young children. . . . They too had been forced out of their apartment by a fire, but unlike my family, they had had to accept the city's offer of a welfare hotel, a dismal and dangerous environment. The father, a proud man, found that intolerable, but with so little money what could he do? I became obsessed with the family until their story virtually wrote itself—"The Last Frontier," in which George and Louise Madison and their children move onto the stage set of a situation comedy, contrasting the whitewashed TV image of family life with their own reality.

None of the details about the Madisons corresponded to my own life—none, that is, except their condition of homelessness, and the resulting anger, frustration, and bewilderment. In those feelings that give the story its life, we were identical. One might say it is auto-biographical in the deepest sense.

The ability I've been discussing—giving up the facts for the broader reaches of the imagination—may sound daunting, but it comes with experience, and with the confidence and willingness to let the story take control. For almost always, at some point in the arduous process, the inner voice will whisper, "What if . . . instead of . . . ?" The secret is to listen, and to yield.

But that's not the only way. Some fiction gets written backwards, so to speak. In the case of *Balancing Acts* (my first novel, though it was published second), I was on the third draft and puzzled over why it wouldn't come right, when I finally grasped what the book was about and what its connection was to me.

I had begun it after a friend told me about her ten-year-old daughter's strong attachment to an elderly man, a volunteer teacher in her school. The man had just died, and the child was suffering the sort of grief—for the loss of a close friend—that most of us don't know till later in life. The story stayed with me—I didn't know why; one often doesn't—and I constructed a novel around it, with background and details far different from those of my own life. I couldn't help but notice, though, that the man in my novel had much in common with my father, and the thirteen-year-old heroine, with me. Not circumstantial matters in common, but affinities of temperament and attitude. Only on that third draft, when I realized that book was a particular emotional struggle on my part, connected with my aging father, could I rewrite it with coherence and conscious design. Plot, setting, and characters all remained the same, but I had found the autobiographical impulse at the core and could work outwards, using its energy.

Giving the imagination free reign, or conversely, locating the fertile source of a story, is exhilarating as well as productive. But it has its negative side (doesn't everything?). The upshot of letting fiction change the events of your life is losing parts of your past. It's not an overstatement to confess that looking over my work, I occasionally note bits that sound familiar, yet I can't quite remember whether they happened or whether I made them up. Did the neighbors down the street when I was nine years old really shout those awful things out the window, or did I imagine it? Or exaggerate it? Did that man in the boat really look at me in that seductive way? Was the path behind the country houses really as dark and lush with greenery as I wrote? And were my grandmother's glasses of tea with lumps of sugar as wonderful as I've made out? The line between memory and invention blurs; I can't say for sure what happened, and I have the sinking feeling that I've erased parts of my life in order to write stories over them. I may have given up more than I expected, becoming a writer. The only relief for such doubts is to go back and write some more. Because in the end, as the Roman poet said, life is short, but art is long.

36

GETTING YOUR NOVEL STARTED IN TEN DAYS

BY GENNI GUNN

YOU'VE always wanted to write a novel but can find neither the time nor the starting point. You have unique experiences to record, hundreds of characters struggling to come out of your pen on to paper. What you need to do is make time to write and, perhaps most important, have a clear idea of *what* you are going to write.

A book is not written in one sitting. Even assuming you have a busy schedule, you need not wait to begin until you can afford to take a year's vacation from work. If your ideas are well organized, you can begin your novel now, by setting aside one hour a day in which to write.

Think of your novel as a jigsaw puzzle. Every day, you will examine one piece and put it in its proper place. The events, characters, and actions that first appear as a jumbled mass too big to tackle can be organized to make sense. You will need discipline and persistence.

Here's how to begin:

1) Set aside one hour a day for writing, if possible, the same time every day, so that eventually writing will become a habit.

2) Set up a place to write (preferably a desk where you can leave notes, typewriter, and necessary files) and return there every day to write.

Now you're ready to explore your novel idea. Where do you start? It is important to set realistic, achievable goals for each day. Here is a sample schedule for the first ten days:

Day 1. DEFINE YOUR IDEA. A novel begins as an idea. This can take the form of a character, an isolated event, or a lifetime struggle worth recording. Begin by asking yourself, "What is my novel about?" Write a one-sentence summary. If you can't do this right away, write down all the things you think your book is about. Read these over and condense them until you have *one sentence only.* Try to be as specific as possible.

At the end of your hour, type your finished sentence and tape it over your desk so it will always be visible as you write.

Day 2: LIST YOUR CHARACTERS under two headings: *Major Characters* and *Minor Characters*. Describe their relationship to one another. New characters may emerge as you write. Add them to your list. Fill in their descriptions later.

Day 3: LIST LOCATIONS AND SETTING in your novel: cities and towns (real or imaginary), houses, fields, roads, schools, etc., in which major events will take place. Fill in the detailed descriptions later.

Day 4: DEFINE YOUR CHARACTERS' GOALS. Your main characters must want something that they are unable to get. In one sentence, define *what* each of your main characters wants—tangible or intangible. As an example, here are three characters from an unwritten novel, and their three goals. At the end of Day 4, you should have a completed page that resembles the following:

GOALS

Paul wants: 1) money to settle pressing debts.
2) a means to live; a job.
3) a way to defend himself against his sister's accusations.
Alice wants: 1) to prove Paul's a swindler. She believes that before their aunt's death, Paul took money from their aunt that rightfully belonged to Alice.
2) her share of the money.
3) to keep Paul away from her adopted daughter, Judy.
Judy wants: 1) Paul.
2) her mother (Alice) to like Paul.
3) Paul to make a new start.

Day 5: LIST OBSTACLES that will prevent the main characters from getting what they want. These should be difficult for your characters to overcome; they can be other characters or physical or emotional impediments. Here, for example, are obstacles the characters described may have to surmount:

OBSTACLES

Paul: 1) Aunt Sophia, who was to leave him an inheritance, died penniless.
2) He has no skills with which to make a living. He is in his late thirties and feels he is too old to begin a trade.
3) His sister Alice.
Alice: 1) Paul won't divulge any information regarding his relationship with their Aunt Sophia prior to her death.

164

2) Paul is secretive about his financial affairs—she can't prove he has the money.

3) Her adopted daughter, Judy, is in love with Paul.

Judy: 1) Paul is not in love with her—he considers her his little niece.

2) Her mother distrusts Paul and won't let Judy see him.

3) Paul doesn't believe in his own ability to make a fresh start.

Day 6: PLAN THE CONCLUSION. Make up an ending for your novel. Write it in paragraph or point form and tape it over your desk. Characters often take on a life of their own and do things that are not what you had originally intended. Don't be afraid to rewrite the ending if your original version doesn't ring true.

Day 7: MAKE AN OUTLINE. The outline will serve as your guide while you're writing. (Update your outline if your story plot changes along the way.) When you are stuck in a chapter, choose something from the outline that interests you and begin writing about that event. It is not necessary to write chronologically. You may prefer to write separate sections of your novel and fill in the transitions later.

List the major events that will occur in your novel, not necessarily in detail.

Day 8: MAKE CHAPTER HEADINGS. Examine the events you listed yesterday. Separate them into chapters—with each chapter covering one major event. Now, write a one- or two-sentence summary description of what happens in each chapter. Tape the revised outline over your desk.

Day 9: SET UP FILES. Today will be an organizational day. Take blank file folders (either letter or legal size) and make a label for each one, using the following headings:

1) Characters
2) Locations
3) Chapters (one for each chapter heading)
4) Mannerisms
5) Speech patterns
6) General observations

These files will give you easy access to your information as well as suggest what to write about on those days when you lack inspiration. When you begin writing your novel, fill these files with the following information:

165

a) *Characters:* Write detailed descriptions—physical characteristics, emotional needs, family background, etc.—*know* your characters.

b) *Locations:* Where do your characters live? Where does the action take place in your novel? Think of writing as a visual art—write pictures for the reader.

c) *Individual chapters:* For your chapters in progress, notes, and ideas.

d) *Mannerisms:* Be observant. Record the way people show their emotions by body movements. To say, "He was angry" is vague and weak, but "He stamped his foot" *shows* the anger.

e) *Speech patterns:* Listen to people speak—the sound of their voices, the way they shape sentences, etc. This will be invaluable when writing dialogue, but remember that conversation is not dialogue. Give each of your characters distinct characteristics, perhaps a favorite phrase to repeat, short clipped sentences—whatever seems appropriate.

f) *General observations:* Keep a record of any thoughts you have about your novel or about human nature. You can always use these, even if not in your current project.

Make up you own file headings for other things that are important to your novel.

Day 10: WRITE YOUR OPENING PARAGRAPH. Begin your novel at that point at which your main character is faced with his or her major problem. Try to make your opening paragraph intriguing. Here is a possible opening for the novel example given earlier:

Paul had waited twenty years for his inheritance. He had squandered his time and what little money he'd earned with odd jobs on gambling and physical pleasures. After Aunt Sophia's funeral—a dull, dreary affair in which he'd been unable to feign sorrow—the will was read. Aunt Sophia died penniless.

This opening includes:
1) The main character
2) His predicament—therefore his problem
3) The necessary background to show the reader the gravity of his problem

If you're dissatisfied with your opening paragraph, put it aside and as you get new ideas, revise it.

166

From now on, each day, when you sit at your desk, you'll have a choice of things to write about. Look through your files for something that interests you. Describe characters, locations, mannerisms, or speech patterns and fit these into your novel later. Don't worry about the order. Get your story down on paper. You can fine-tune when you begin rewriting.

Set yourself realistic goals: One page a day for a year will yield 360 pages—a book-length manuscript. Half a page each day is even more realistic. Some days you'll write several pages; other days you'll struggle just to fill one. Most important, *stick with it*! Do nothing but write in the hour you've set aside, even if you only repeat a word to fill the page.

There are no easy ways to write a novel, no secrets, no shortcuts. It takes hard work, perseverance, and the belief that you have a story to tell.

37

DICK FRANCIS: AN INTERVIEW

Q. *Did your journalistic training provide a good background to novel writing?*

A. Journalism was a wonderful school for book writing. Newspapers will never print an unnecessary word because they're always pushed for space. I used to think I was a pretty good editor and, in the end, it annoyed me intensely if I took my article up to Fleet Street and the sub found an unwanted word.

Q. *Why didn't you write your first thriller until five years after your autobiography?*

A. Writing for the *Sunday Express* was quite hard and I didn't think I had a story to tell. But as we passed the book stands in a railway station once I suddenly said to my wife, "I'm going to write one of those thrillers one day."

Some time later, the carpets were wearing out and we had two sons to educate. Although I had a good job on the newspaper, it wasn't as lucrative as being a successful jockey had been. Mary said, "Well, you always said you were going to write a novel. Now's the time." So I sat down and wrote *Dead Cert,* which took about a year.

Q. *Do you carry a notebook around and jot down ideas?*

A. Before I go to bed, I sometimes put a note down about something. But my wife Mary and I have quite good memories. Mary especially. I'm always asking her to reel off what happened at such and such an event.

Mary also takes photos of things like telephone kiosks and buses. These help to describe the scene when I am writing a story.

Q. *How do you plan your books? Do you know how they will end when you start?*

A. I have a good idea of the main crime upon which I'm basing the story. But I create many sub-plots as I go along. I often describe things I hadn't thought of before or introduce new characters.

I do only one draft. I hear of people doing two or three but I couldn't possibly do that. I write it all in longhand in a notebook and then put it onto a word processor. My procedure hasn't changed in the past 25 years. Even when I wrote the racing articles, I only ever did one draft.

Q. *As you write one chapter, then, you can't know what will happen in the next.*

A. That's right. I can't really be sure. But when I'm halfway through a chapter, I know I've got to start warming it up. I try to finish at an exciting spot, so that the reader can't put the book down and starts the next chapter.

Q. *There's a good balance in the scenes between action pieces—full of shocks and climaxes—and descriptive pieces. How do you create this?*

A. I don't know. I suppose it comes from experience. I like to grab the reader on the first page. It's rather like riding a race. You keep your high moments until the last furlong and then you produce your horse to win. When you're jumping the big fences, you're placing your horse to meet that fence. When you're writing your story, you're placing your words so that the reader will be excited at the right moment and, then, easing off after you've jumped the fence.

Q. *All your novels are written in the first person. Are there any limitations with this?*

A. I write in the first person because that's how I like to describe things. I had great difficulty in writing the Lester Piggott biography because I had to write in the third person.

I think this is one of the reasons no films have been made of the books, although options have been taken on them all. As they're written in the first person, a lot of each book describes what's in the hero's mind. It would be difficult to portray on screen.

Q. *Do you identify with your heroes?*

A. Probably, yes, though I'm not as tough and brave as my main characters are. They usually have some cross to bear but I try to make them compassionate and likeable, with a sense of humor and a lively eye. I wouldn't want to write about a miserable, depressing character. I get on well with people myself and I try to make my hero do the same.

My heroes aren't like James Bond superstars throughout. I try to make them human and make them develop in the book.

Q. *Do you ever get writer's block?*

A. Not really. Nowadays I do most of my writing in Florida, sitting on the balcony looking out to sea. I spend hours looking at the ocean, thinking. Often I've got a character in a certain position and I don't know how I'm going to get him out of it. I think out all the pros and cons of one way and then another and, eventually, find the right one.

38

SETTING IS MORE THAN PLACE

BY WILLIAM G. TAPPLY

AN INTERVIEWER RECENTLY ASKED ME WHY I choose to set my mystery novels in New England instead of, say, Nebraska. I was tempted to answer with the old vaudeville punchline: "Everybody's got to be somewhere." Every story has to have a setting.

Instead I told the interviewer the simple truth: My choice of New England was easy—New England is where I've lived my entire life. It's what I know best. I couldn't write about Nebraska.

I define setting broadly. It's more than place. Setting comprises all the conditions under which things happen—region, geography, neighborhood, buildings, interiors, climate, weather, time of day, season of year.

I feel fortunate. My New England provides me with a rich variety of settings from which to select. I can send my narrator/lawyer/sleuth Brady Coyne from the inner city of Boston to the wilderness of the Maine woods, from the sand dunes of Cape Cod to the farmland of the Connecticut Valley, from exclusive addresses on Beacon Hill to working class neighborhoods in Medford. New England has whatever my stories might call for.

New England also gives me the full cycle of the seasons and all the weather and climate that accompany them. It gives me Locke-Ober and pizza joints, museums and theaters, factories and office buildings, mansions and apartments, skyscrapers and fishing lodges, condominiums and farmhouses.

I don't know about Nebraska. I suspect that if I lived there and knew it as intimately as I know New England I'd find a similar wealth of possibilities. I have, in fact, sent Brady to parts of North Carolina and Montana that I'm familiar with. What's important is knowing my settings well enough to invoke the details that will bring them to life and be useful in my stories.

Settings must strike our readers as realistic. A realistic setting persuades readers to suspend their disbelief and accept the premise that our stories really happened. The easiest and best way to do this is to write knowledgeably about real places, places where our readers live or have visited, or, at least, places they have read about or seen pictures of. Readers, I have learned, love to find in a novel a place they know. They enjoy comparing their impressions of Durgin Park or the New England Aquarium with Brady Coyne's. They like to hear what strikes Brady as noteworthy about Newbury Street, the Combat Zone, the Deerfield River, or the Boston Harbor.

You must get actual places precisely right or you risk losing your readers' trust. No matter how much you might dislike it, you cannot avoid research. You *must* hang out in the places you intend to write about. Observe the people, listen to the sounds, sniff the smells, note the colors and textures of the place. I have spent hours loitering in Boston's Chinatown and prowling the corridors in the East Cambridge courthouse. I've wandered around the Mt. Auburn Hospital and the Peabody Museum, looking for the telling detail that makes the place unique and that will allow me to make it ring true for every reader who has been there.

Research need not be unpleasant, in fact. I make it a point to eat in every restaurant I write about, no matter how familiar it already is to me, at least twice—once just before writing the scene to fix it in my mind, and once again afterward to make sure I've rendered it accurately.

A realistic setting doesn't really have to exist, however, and the fiction writer shouldn't feel limited to using actual places if doing so will alter the story he wants to tell. A fictional setting can still be true. My rule of thumb is this: If the setting you need exists, use it; if it doesn't exist, make it up but make it true. I built Gert's on the North Shore and Marie's in Kenmore Square—where no such restaurants stand—because my stories demand there be restaurants like them there. Readers are continually asking me how to find Gert's and Marie's, which I take to mean that I have rendered them realistically.

I made up a hardscrabble farm in Lanesboro and a horse farm in Harvard—fictitious but realistic places in actual Massachusetts communities. In my first Brady Coyne novel, I moved a rocky hunk of Rhode Island coastline to Massachusetts, committed a murder there, and named it Charity's Point because that storyline required it. I've had readers tell me they believe they have been there. In *The Vulgar Boatman,* I invented the town of Windsor Harbor. Had I tried to set that tale in a real community north of Boston, too many readers would have known that no events such as the ones I invented actually happened there. They would have been unable to suspend their disbelief.

Gert's and Marie's, the farms in Lanesboro and Harvard, Charity's Point, and Windsor Harbor were like the characters that populated the books. Although they were not *real,* they were all *true*—places like them exist, and they *could* be where I put them.

Setting can—and should—serve as more than a backdrop for the action of the story. The conditions under which the action occurs should do double or triple duty for you. Setting can create mood and tone for your fiction. The places where they live and work can reveal the personalities and motivations of your fictional characters. Places, weather, climate, season of year, and time of day can cause things to happen in a story as surely as characters can.

Shakespeare and Conan Doyle understood how setting can establish mood and foreshadow events. The "dark and stormy night" had its purpose, as did the spooky mansion on the remote moor or the thick fog of a London evening. Contemporary writers can use thunderstorms and abandoned warehouses and the barrooms and alleys of city slums in the same way. Robert Louis Stevenson once said, "Some places speak distinctly. Certain dank gardens cry aloud for murder; certain old houses demand to be haunted; certain coasts are set apart for shipwrecks." Find such places. Use them.

But be wary. Such obvious settings can too easily become literary clichés. Misuse them, or overuse them, and they lose their punch. Clever writers understand the power of going against stereotypes. Seek subtlety and irony. Murder can be committed on a sunny May morning in a suburban backyard, too, and when it does, the horror of it is intensified by the contrast.

Carefully selected details of setting can delineate the characters who populate the place. Match the pictures or calendars that hang on every office wall with some trait of the man who works there. Is the policeman's desk littered with half-empty styrofoam coffee cups? What kind of tablecloths does your restaurant use? What music is piped into the elevator of the office building? Does a week's worth of newspapers litter the front porch of that Brookline mansion? Does a specimen jar containing a smoker's lung sit on the desk of the forensic pathologist? Does the lawyer keep a bag of golf clubs in the corner of his office? Does a stack of old *Field & Stream* magazines sit on the table in the dentist's waiting room? Such well-chosen particulars can reveal as much about a character as his dress, manner of speech, or physical appearance.

Think of your settings as characters in your stories. Settings need not be passive. They can act and interact with your characters. Rainstorms cause automobile accidents. Snowstorms cover footprints and stall traffic. Laboratories contain chemicals that spill and release toxic fumes. The bitter cold of a Boston winter kills homeless people. Water released from a dam raises the water level in a river and drowns wading fishermen.

Your choice of setting may, at first, be arbitrary and general—the city where you work, the village where you live. But as you begin writing, you will need to search out particular places where the events of your story will unfold. Visit them often enough to absorb them. If you're lucky, you'll find that your real settings will begin to work for you. You'll see a person whose face you'll want to use. You'll overhear a snatch of conversation that fits a storytelling need. You'll note a detail you didn't expect that suggests a new direction for your plot. On one background-ing mission to a rural farmyard, I came upon a "honey wagon" pumping out a large septic tank. This suggested to me an unusually grisly way for a villain to dispose of a dead body; this murder method found its way into my story.

The secret of a successfully rendered setting lies *not* in piling ex-haustive detail upon repetitive particulars. There's no need to lug your typewriter around a room describing the designs of the furniture, the colors of the rugs and drapes, the brands of the whiskey on the sidebar. Extended descriptive passages, no matter how poetic and clever, only serve to stall the momentum of your story and bore your reader.

Setting is important. It serves many purposes. But don't get carried away. It *is* only a setting, the conditions in which your characters can play out their conflicts. The key to creating effective settings lies in finding the *exactly right* detail that will suggest all of the others. Be spare and suggestive. Look for a water stain on the ceiling or a cigarette burn on the sofa. You may need nothing else to create the picture you want in your reader's imagination. As Elmore Leonard says, "I try to leave out the parts that people skip."

39

ALWAYS A STORYTELLER

BY MARY HIGGINS CLARK

THERE'S A THEORY that our lives are set in seven-year cycles. Vaguely, I remember that the basis for that belief is that in seven years every cell in our bodies has replaced itself. In case that's mountain-folk legend, I hasten to apologize to the more learned in the scientific fields. Recently I reread an article on suspense writing that I wrote just seven years ago to see what I've learned since.

My conclusion is that the more you know, the more you don't know. I've written four books, short stories, a novella, and film treatments since then, and I'm not sure I've gained any greater insight into this wondrous, complex and tantalizing field we call writing.

However, we must start somewhere, so let's go with the basics. How do you know that you are supposed to be a writer? The first necessity is that utter yearning to communicate, that sense that "I have something to say"; reading a book and knowing, *knowing* that you can write one like it; the sense that no matter how well ordered your life is, how thoroughly you delight in your family and friends and home and job, something is missing. Something so absolutely necessary that you are constantly swallowing ashes. You want to write. You must write.

These are the people who just might make it. That yearning is usually accompanied by talent, real talent, often native, undisciplined, unfocused talent, but certainly it's there. The degree of yearning separates the *real* potential writer from the truism that everyone has one story in them. How many times are professional writers approached at seminars or parties with the suggestion, "I've got a great story to tell. You jot it down for me, and we'll split the royalties."

Face the yearning. At some point, you'll have to or else eventually go to that great beyond unfulfilled. My mother always told me that my grandmother, struggling to raise her nine children and an orphaned

176

niece, used to say, "Oh, how I'd love to write a book." On her deathbed, she was still regretting that she'd never tried.

Now you've acknowledged that you've simply got to try. Where do you begin? Most of us have a sense of what we want to write. If you don't, a terrific clue is to analyze what you like to *read*. I hadn't the faintest idea that I could write suspense, but after my first book was published, a biographical novel about George Washington that was read by the favored few, I knew that if I tried again, I'd really want to look forward to that lovely mailing from the publisher known as a royalty statement. I cast about for a story idea and looked at the bookshelf. I was astonished to realize that ninety percent of the books I'd read in the last couple of years had been mysteries. I did further soul-digging and began naming my favorite authors: Mary Roberts Rinehart, Josephine Tey, Agatha Christie, Charlotte Armstrong, and on and on. That was the clue that helped me decide to try a suspense novel. The one I launched was *Where Are the Children?* It's in its forty-second printing right now.

Footnote, just so I don't forget. Judith Guest's first novel was turned down by two publishers. She then looked at her bookshelf and realized that many of the books she read were published by Viking Press. She sent her manuscript to them. Months later she received a telegram. "Viking Press is honored to publish *Ordinary People*." The point is that the books you like to read give you a clue to what you may write best. The publisher of the books you read may turn out to be the best potential publisher for you.

Back to the beginning. Having determined whether you want to begin the writing adventure in the field of suspense or romance or science fiction; mainstream novels or books for children or adolescents; or poetry or articles, the next step is to treat yourself to several subscriptions. *The Writer* is the best at-home companion for the aspiring and/or achieving writer I can suggest.

I sold my first short story on my own. It went to forty magazines over the course of six years before it found a home. Which leads to the next question the new writer invariably asks. "How do I get an agent?" It's the chicken-and-egg query. In my case, in 1956 a young agent read the story and phoned me, saying, "I'd like to represent you." We were together thirty years until she retired two years ago. I'm still with her agency and the terrific people she put in her place. The point is, I think it's a lot easier to get an agent after you've proven yourself, even if your success is a modest one. That story brought me one hundred dollars. But remember. No story or book should ever sit in your drawer. If you get it back from one editor, send it out to the next. And don't sit in never-never land waiting for that one to sell. Start on the next project.

O.K. You have the determination; you know what you want to write; you're gathering the tools. I think it's fundamental to set aside time every day. Even one hour a day creates a habit. When my children were young, I used to get up at five and work from five until seven. I have the whole day to write now and don't get up that early, but I'm tempted to start setting the alarm again. There is something exhilarating about the world being quiet and you're somehow alone in it knowing that the phone won't ring or someone won't stop by. On the other hand, maybe you work best at night. Take that extra hour after everyone else in the family has been tucked in and use it to work on the story or poem or novel. No matter how tired you are when you start, I promise you that the sense of accomplishment of seeing even a page or two completed will make your dreams blissful.

I urge you to join some kind of writing group. Writing is one of the most isolated professions in the world. Your family can be marvelously supportive, but it's not the same. One of two things happen. They see the rejection slips and urge you not to keep banging your head against a wall. "Give it up, dear. It's just too tough to break into that field." Or they think that every word you write is gospel and expect a massive best seller any minute. Your local college or library may have writing courses available. Sign up for one of them. Don't worry about the fact that you'll inevitably miss three or four classes during the semester. You'll make the other ten or twelve. Listening to a professional, getting to know people who are in the field or aspiring to it is balm to the soul. When you begin having contact with others who share your need, you'll experience the feeling Stanley must have had when he said, "Dr. Livingston, I presume."

Be aware that there is probably an organization in your general area you should join: mystery writers, science writers, poets, among others. They're waiting for you. After that first story sold, I joined the Mystery Writers of America. I still remember my first meeting. I didn't know a soul. I was in awe of the name writers around me. Many of my best friends today I met at MWA meetings. And oh the joy of talking shop! Besides that, at these professional organizations you get to meet editors and agents who otherwise would be behind closed doors.

That's how it should be in the beginning. The determination. The quest to know what to write. The studying of the craft. The fellowship of other writers. And then in the quiet of that study or the space you cleared for yourself in the corner of the kitchen or bedroom, begin to write. Always remember that what you are is a storyteller. No matter how elegant your prose, how descriptive your passages, how insightful your eye, unless you tell a story people want to hear, you're not going to make it. A story has a beginning and a middle and an end. It tells about people we all know and identify with. It tells of their hopes and dreams and failures and triumphs. It tells of the twists of fate that bestow fortune on one person and rob another who is equally deserving. It makes us laugh and mourn and hope for the people whose lives we are sharing. It leaves us with a sense of catharsis, of emotion well spent. Isaac Bashevis Singer is a dedicated mystery reader. Several years ago at the Mystery Writers annual banquet, he received the award as Mystery Reader of the Year. This great writer offered simple yet profound advice. It was that the writer must think of himself or herself primarily as a storyteller. Every book or story should figuratively begin with the words "Once upon a time." Because it is as true now as it was in the long ago days of wandering minstrels, that when these words are uttered, the room becomes quiet, everyone draws closer to the fire, and the magic begins.

40

WHAT WORKS FOR ME IN WRITING SCIENCE FICTION

BY POUL ANDERSON

—may be of no use at all to you. Over the decades, I've met a number of fellow writers and made a hobby of collecting their working methods. No two have been alike. Besides, I have no grand scheme or basic system of my own, just a bag of tricks. Some I learned from other professionals, some from study of literature, most the hard way, by making mistakes. Herewith a few. Perhaps one or two will be helpful to somebody.

In early days, I wasted a lot of energy because of inadequate preparation. I'd start a story, realize that I didn't know what would happen next or how to solve a problem that had arisen, put it aside, and never get back to it. Often this was due to a loss of interest. It would have been smarter to go fishing; that might have put food on the table.

Now I usually spend considerably more time thinking about a piece beforehand than in the actual writing. After all, this is supposed to cast the illusion of a complete reality. Science fiction has its special problems, countless details that should be known to the author; frequently a little mathematics or simply a little thought will show that some lovely-looking feature cannot be made to work, and had better be discarded before it becomes integral to the plot. Fantasy fiction has requirements not much different—as do historicals, mysteries, "mainstream," and every other category.

Research is essential. What you don't know is less dangerous than what you do know that isn't true, or what you take for granted must be the way things are. Writers copy from each other instead of going back to the sources, and so myths get perpetuated generation after generation. Look, friends, the fact is that the Romans did not employ slaves to row their galleys, giant stars do not last long enough to have planets suitable for life through billions of years, the work of J. B. Rhine and other psionicists is scientifically worthless, downloading a vast amount of data from a computer takes a correspondingly long time, etc., for an enormous list. Then there are the exciting, important discoveries and ideas continually coming forth in science. As a rule, they take years to reach science fiction. How much mention, let alone use, of the news about chaos, oceanography, and planetary geology (to name only three cutting edges at random) have we seen so far?

Keeping up completely is impossible, but I recommend subscriptions to *Science News* for up-to-date reports, brief but responsibly written; *Scientific American* for thoroughgoing articles; and *New Scientist* for lively, wide-ranging coverage. Several other magazines are as good in their different ways. All will call your attention to books you should read. Bear in mind, these publications don't simply keep you somewhat informed, they are rich lodes of story material, both plots and background.

Whether or not your writing is concerned with science and technology, you have need for research. The eleventh edition of the *Encyclopedia Britannica* is a treasure, and not too hard or expensive to acquire. I also have a modern encyclopedia, the current *World Almanac,* various atlases, etc., as well as subscriptions to a variety of nonscientific periodicals.

Texts on every science are more than useful. So is the *Merck Manual;* from time to time, doubtless every writer needs to know about some or other medical matter. I have amassed a fair-sized collection of books on assorted aspects of history, archeology, and anthropology, updated as new ones come forth; dictionaries of foreign languages; and, to be sure, the standard literary stuff, dictionaries of quotations, and the like. I especially recommend the *American Heritage Dictionary* and the transistorized *OED,* together with the fourth edition of Roget's Thesaurus as revised by Robert L. Chapman.

Often it is necessary to go elsewhere. Public and university libraries are a magnificent resource. Librarians are glad to help track something down. Professionals in any field are usually willing to discuss it. In such cases, naturally, one should make an appointment in advance and arrive well prepared, able to ask intelligent questions.

Direct rather than vicarious experience is almost always more enlightening. A writer does well to try as many things as are possible and legal, including travel. But some direct experience (of events in the past or on Mars) cannot be had; so we're forced back to research, and to our imaginations.

Imagination does not build on factual information; not quite. The two interact. A fact will suggest something for a story, an idea for a story will demand a factual check to see whether it's valid. In the end, though, it's the writer's mind that puts everything together. Thus we return to the general business of preparing to write.

Speaking for myself, perhaps not for others, I can only write halfway convincingly about things I know. This includes my own inventions. Whether the setting is the suburb where I live, medieval London, an imaginary planet, or anywhere else, I have to know my way around in it, the layout, how it works. This can involve a large amount of thinking, especially for an unreal place. Far from constricting the imagination, facts and logic are apt to stimulate it. Things are much more interesting when you understand what can and cannot be done with a sword than when Ugtrid the Amazon tirelessly skewers the villains she doesn't decapitate. A well-planned extrasolar world has a lot more color and surprises in it than a mere copy of Earth or one more decayed civilization along the canals of a planet turned to desert. Every world wants its own unique physical parameters, biology, sociologies, languages, histories. Besides any calculations that may be required and thought about what kind of environments the postulated conditions may produce, I draw maps, write descriptions, and, in general, dream up as many as possible of those features that do *not* follow inexorably from the assumptions.

Then we get to the characters. For a novel, and often for something shorter, I set down a physical description of each individual who will be important, usually accompanied by a sketch. If nothing else, this keeps eyes from changing color in mid-narrative, and it makes him or her a bit more real to me. Far more significant, of course, is the inner person. I write a biography of each, sometimes several pages long, including background, likes, dislikes, beliefs, and other idiosyncrasies. This is not a mechanical matter of taking parts off the shelf and sticking them together. For all of us, surely character creation is an organic and rather mysterious process. It's just that I find that writing things down as they come to me facilitates their coming, and helps me see my people as

182

wholes. Probably many of my colleagues don't need to do this, but some may find it worth trying.

Plotting isn't mechanical either. People and circumstances affect each other. The better I know them, the more clear and plausible—to me, at any rate—this interplay, the course of the story, is. Not that its development is free-form. Apparently some writers sit down with no preconceptions and watch their yarns unroll; and these can be great yarns, too. Experience has taught me that I am not among them. If the whole thing isn't to fall apart, I must figure out in advance where it's going. This helps select the characters, who will normally be the sort of people who might well get into that particular situation. But then, as said, they become an integral part of it, and to a considerable extent, how it comes out will depend on them.

Having reached this stage, some writers then outline everything section by section, and stick to the scheme. That's fine for them, but it doesn't work for me. You see, although by the time I begin writing I know how the story will end, and more or less what will happen before, I also know there will be surprises along the way. Some are pleasant, stuff I really like that hadn't occurred to me until I got to that point; I see something in the setup I hadn't noticed earlier, or a character does something unexpected but believable. Other surprises are less welcome, sudden awareness of a bad factual error or a gaping hole in the logic of events. Fortunately, thus far it's never been anything that can't be repaired; that is, it hasn't been since I went to intensive preplanning. Occasionally, though, it's necessary to do some fairly drastic revision of parts already written. A detailed outline would inhibit me in this task.

I can't produce satisfactory prose the first time around, either. Instead, I must go over the pages repeatedly, striking this out, scrawling a change in that, and then haul the whole thing through the machine again, from end to end. That calls my attention to still more flaws, and suggests new bits of business. This isn't as tedious as it might seem, being indeed a rather enjoyable, narcissistic time, quite unlike the groping, floor-pacing toil of the first draft. Generally the last couple of read-throughs turn up only a handful of words in obvious need of emendation.

If the foregoing looks laborious, well, mostly it is, though the planning is fun and the final stage pretty relaxed. It's not for every writer. We all have our own ways of trying for a good story. Quite likely the geniuses among us achieve it on sheer instinct. However, those of us who are not geniuses need methods, and perhaps one or two of you can use a little of what I have described. If so, you're welcome.

About characters, specifically human characters. First, unless they are historical figures, characters should never bear the names of real people. That is apt to prove embarrassing, and in an extreme case may bring on a lawsuit. Exceptions to this rule are so few as not to be worth discussing. Granted, coincidences are inevitable, but the writer should make every reasonable effort to avoid them. I check the phone directories of my home area, and if I find a duplicate name, change that of the character. If the character is supposed to live in a distant city, especially in the present day, I go to a library and examine that directory.

Second, readers are easily confused, and blame the author for it. Unless there is some strong reason for people in a story to bear the same name, such as their being siblings, names should be unmistakably different. Ideally, no two should even have the same initial letters.

Third, in real life names have nothing to do with personality (one of the most dashing heroes of World War II was John Glubb), but the reader of fiction will be brought up short by what seems an incongruity, whereas the sound and connotation of a well-chosen name reinforce the impression of a character's personality. Naturally, you don't want to dub a hairy-chested hero "Steele Hammer"—but don't "Kimball Kinnison" or "Robert Hedrock" suggest strength and masculinity? So does "Lazarus Long," as well as recalling this man's origin in the Bible Belt; and the "Woodrow Wilson Smith" that he originally was tells us still more about his background. "Harold Shea" is memorable without being so assertive, well suited to a fellow who is neither all bold adventurer nor all klutz, but a very human blend of both. As for women, well, "Wyoming Knott" is obviously a strong, independent sort, while "Maire ni Donnall," although no wimp herself, is one to die for.

Fourth, these examples happen to be of North European origin, but we have a whole worldful of languages to draw on, adding color, individuation, and a sense of rich background. A good source of fresh names is the encyclopedia, in its mention of long-obscure foreign figures. Another is the citations in professional journals like *Science*. A third is the phone book of any large American city. Needless to say,

184

given names should be altered, and no surname borrowed that belongs to somebody prominent.

Sorry for not having any marvelous secrets or inspirational visions, only stuff about grubby detail work. Yet doesn't the glamour often arise from this, along with the satisfaction of a job honestly done?

41

MEANWHILE, BACK AT THE RANCH . . .

BY WARREN KIEFER

A FULL-SCALE NOVEL ABOUT THE WEST is as different from a formula Western as a satellite view of the Great Plains is from a county roadmap. Although elements of "formula" writing may be used in both, the dynamics are significantly altered. But it is the formula Western and its perpetuation of the Western myth that people generally mean when they speak of Western fiction.

A "formula" Western is as structured as a sonnet, and as stately as a minuet, and any writer who breaks the rules does so at his peril. Simplicity and violent action are what matter. Humor and sex are rarely allowed, and only on the periphery of the story.

One theme, justice, is central to the plot, although there are endless variations on the righting of wrongs which include certain classic, immutable elements readers of the genre have come to expect and rely on.

Most of us are familiar with these elements, if not from the books themselves, from films and television screenplays that follow similar patterns. Good and evil, black and white, right and wrong must be clear from the start.

The hero must be single, rootless, and reluctant to be drawn into conflict. He is embarrassed about his deadly skills and tries to hide them, while the villain can brag or show off as long as he is absolutely villainous. His greed, sadism, lust or avarice should be as obvious as a sandwich board.

At the beginning, the reader of the formula Western only has to know who wants what and why he can't get it, while evil must appear to be winning. By the middle of the story, reader interest may shift to the question of who's doing what to whom, and how long can they stand it.

186

Everyone knows what must happen at the end, but nobody knows exactly how it will happen; this is the kind of suspense that invites the reader to gallop along behind.

The climax comes only after the clamor for the hero's services has peaked, and not one page earlier, when even his friends are beginning to doubt his courage. He then shows us what we suspected all along, that heroes shoot only when provoked, but are fearless, tough, and implacable even when outnumbered.

Other characters adhere to certain rules or standards, too. Wives and daughters are chaste and virtuous while dance hall girls can be "loose," but not mean or vindictive. The town drunk, gambler, or any other non-combatant can betray the hero, but only out of fear or weakness. Never for money, which only interests villains.

In the past, if blacks appeared at all, they were cast as servants, Chinese were cooks or laundrymen, and the Native American Indian passed successively from his original role as Bloodthirsty Savage to Noble Redman to Tragic Victim, all of which have mercifully bitten the dust over recent years.

But with the elimination of old racial (and racist) stereotypes, Native Americans have become as invisible as blacks in the formula Western. Action, not opinion, moves this kind of story, and dialogue works only when it complements that action. The format is visual and visceral rather than verbal, with images as precisely circumscribed as those of a fairy tale.

The prose must be lean, fast and sinewy as the hero, but with more obvious direction and control. Stylistic no-nos include such avoidable sins as intransitive or compound verbs, the passive voice, and un-wieldy dependent clauses; a list that would find a place in any chapter on clear, concise writing.

Above all, the formula Western is a commentary on universal justice and on the time-honored principle of virtue triumphant as wrongs are redressed. Although its tested structure is fairly rigid and unforgiving, it is not necessarily confining.

This may sound a little like painting by the numbers, but it doesn't have to be. Within limits, one may write anything. But to tamper with those limits is to court disaster.

How does a writer go about it then, if he wants to break the pattern? How can he write about a kindly cattle thief, an Indian policeman, a black cowboy or a near-sighted hero who drinks too much? How does he escape the old restrictive clichés to write what he believes to be a story closer to historic truth?

He abandons the formula Western entirely and writes a novel about the historic West. Only in that way is he free to create a gallery of offbeat, even eccentric characters who would never be allowed inside the Western myth. Here he can deal with sex as well as violence, and may even attempt the subtlest nuances of character without necessarily losing his reader.

Such unlimited creative freedom, however, like the wide open spaces the writer writes about, is attended by high risk. What he is attempting flies in the face of the Western myth, and he will not be easily forgiven if he fails. He must be very good and extraordinarily careful not to fall between two stools.

Verisimilitude is the hallmark of the Western novel, and a sloppily researched fact or an off-pitch line of dialogue can shatter a reader's trust. The novelist who abandons all pretense of formula writing is saying, "I will not lie." The West was a challenge, and maybe some men did fight for justice, but mainly it was a hostile, desolate place, full of danger, dirt, and disease, with greed, violence, and corruption as common as they are today. Spectacular scenery abounded, but little civilized comfort reached people except where the railroads passed, in themselves a mixed blessing. The Great Plains swarmed with buffalo, and the forests teemed with deer, but few towns boasted potable water, plumbing, street lights, or any reliable public transportation.

The historic West, as opposed to the mythic West, is exciting territory for the novelist. By abandoning the safe confines of the traditional form, he gains plenty of creative elbow room. He can be funny, bawdy, original, and clever, as well as historically accurate. But in order to make it to the end of his chosen literary trail, he will probably need as much stamina and luck as the best of his characters.

Unlike the familiar terrain of the formula Western, this strange and difficult frontier must be explored with no maps. The writer is now free to gallop ahead of a prairie fire, cross the Rockies in winter, and shoot the rapids in the Grand Canyon. But he must never forget that in his special private wilderness he is the only guide the reader can follow.

What is often the hardest task for the writer—research in depth—begins long before he starts to write. For example, when I chose turn-of-the century New Mexico for *Outlaw,* I already knew a lot about the people and politics of the place, having gone to school there. But twenty more years of research were needed for a cumulative laying up of facts.

A general interest in the period gave me a working knowledge of everything from railroad timetables and sexual mores, to the state of the art in medicine and mining. I learned about horses and jails and military meals, about oil, wars, and tropical diseases. About trolley lines and rodeos, and women's skirt hems and Gatling guns.

I read or studied hundreds of books, documents, letters, diaries, military manuals, court records, and newspapers. I pored over old photographs and even looked up a few surviving people who had been young in those days, and who remembered.

To avoid historical anomalies, every writer should acquire a feel for the workaday lives of ordinary people, the tensions between competing groups, the dreams and scams and prejudices of the time. And once he's done all that, he must find the best voice to use in telling his story.

Mark Twain once said, "I only write about what I know and then blame it on somebody else in case they catch me out." He was being facetious, but what I'm sure he meant was that every author has to find the right voice, one that is both authoritative and unique, and which the reader implicitly trusts.

For *Outlaw,* I invented eighty-nine-year-old Lee Oliver Garland, a cowboy with scant education and total recall, who began life as an orphan, became successively a cattle rustler, soldier, banker, oil millionaire, and ambassador to Mexico.

Lee Garland's story is the story of New Mexico, our third youngest state, and much of 20th-century America as well. Shards of the mythic West survive in his tale, but he soon takes it far beyond anything in formula fiction. Lee is a decent man who is faster than most with a gun. He is bigger than life, as a Western hero should be, but he is also truer to life, as no mythic hero can ever be.

Lee's own view of his exploits and crimes is succinct. He tells us:

"I wasn't no hero, even if the army did give me a medal, and I wasn't no villain, even though I did commit a murder."

I knew all about the mythic West and formula writing before I began *Outlaw,* having written scripts for Western films and television. But my involvement with Garland was an entirely new experience. I knew his was the right voice, yet two or three hundred pages into the story, I nearly abandoned it, thinking I had been too ambitious. But Garland was no quitter and gave me no sleep until I resumed the writing. Since then, the critical and commercial success of the book more than justified his persistence.

As fast with his tongue as with his Colt, Garland could never have been squeezed into any kind of formula fiction, and I was glad I had not tried to do it. But he tells it better than I do. Trying to reassure a frightened woman during an attack by Pancho Villa's bandits, he brags about his marksmanship:

"Where are you from, ma'am?"
"P-p-port Huron, Michigan."
"Back there, maybe my name ain't a household word yet, but around these parts it is. You heard of Kit Carson? Jesse James? Billy the Kid?"
She nods, tiny tears of fear watering her eyes.
"You might say I'm in the same category."
"But they're all dead," she says, with that stubborn kind of logic some females got a talent for.

His view of his own actions is summed up thus:

"Sometimes there's principles more important than the law . . . It ain't easy for a man to know where he stands anymore. Today everything's more complicated, watered down, lacks salt."

On blacks:

"A colored man's got as much right to be what he wants as me, but nobody admits that. If he's lazy like me, they call him no-account and say what do you expect? If he's smart and hardworking and educated, they say he don't know his place."

On Indians:

"We pass some Apache . . . poor as mice, walking along barefoot . . . they don't go near the ranches or towns because some folks will shoot an Apache same as a coyote. . . . It's hard to believe these was the people gave the white man the hardest run for his money. They never surrendered, never signed no treaty and never stayed put on no reservation. The poor devils kept their pride, but they sure didn't keep much else . . . you got no right to expect gratitude from an Indian."

190

And on love for his wife:

"As many years as we was together, we never got everything said we had to say to each other . . . She showed me when you love somebody enough, you never really lose them."

This is the same Lee Garland who earlier in the story hunts down the man who has murdered his friend Cody, wounds him and stands over him with a gun, thinking:

"I feel no pity for him . . . mocking my weakness, so goddamn cocksure I lack the guts to shoot him. . . . Who cares about Cody, he says? . . . There's only one answer to that and I got it . . . I fire the last shot into Sorenson's face while he's looking at me, and pull the trigger on the empty chambers until Mountain takes the gun away."

I did not plan to have Garland fight in the Battle of San Juan Hill, but after he joined Roosevelt's Rough Riders to avoid jail, I could not keep him off the battlefield:

"Our infantry starts up the other slope, their blue shirts against the green grass in the sun. Little pinpoints of fire pick at them from the Spanish trenches, and they look pitiful and disorganized, scrambling around, spread out, holding their rifles across their chests, slipping in the grass. There don't seem to be very many, not nearly enough for what they're trying to do.

"I'm thinking there's been a terrible mistake here. Somebody gave the wrong order and the poor dumb bastards don't know it. It ain't heroic or gallant or brave, just pathetic. The only thing you can admire is the stubborn way they keep going, slipping and sliding and falling. I want to call out to them to come back, not even try it."

He says about our victory in the Spanish American War:

"As wars go, it wasn't much. A couple of battles and the surrender of a third-rate power to an army of scarecrows. There was more mistakes than glory and more misery than action. None of us asks if it was worth it. Wars never are, I guess, to the men that fight them."

On his son's death during the 1918 influenza epidemic:

"I couldn't deal with it, just plain couldn't. Couldn't believe it, couldn't accept it and couldn't understand it . . . Like he forgot his manners and just left us. Like he didn't know how much we loved him and how much our own happiness depended on his staying around. . . . I spent days locked in the library with my Colt in my lap, drunk a lot and feeling sorry for myself, cocking and uncocking

191

that old revolver as I tapped the barrel against my teeth. Until one day I looked up and saw how Caroline was suffering, and realized I was the only one could help her."

In that way, Lee told his own story for me, as surely as if he had elbowed me aside while I wrote. It is a Western all the way, but as far removed from traditional mythology and formula writing as a story can be.

His was not an easy voice to catch at the beginning, and I was never sure I could sustain him throughout a rambling account of his long and exciting life. But I did not have to, really. He helped me get away with it. Like a lot of fascinating old geezers I've known, once I got him talking it was hard to shut him up.

42

GRILLING ED McBAIN

BY EVAN HUNTER

Evan Hunter: I'm often asked why I chose to use the name Ed McBain on my crime fiction. I always respond that when I first started writing the 87th Precinct novels . . .

Ed McBain: I thought *I* was the one who wrote the 87th Precinct novels.

EH: The point is . . .

McB: The point is, *we* chose the McBain pseudonym because we didn't want to mislead people.

EH: Mislead them how?

McB: Into believing they were buying a mainstream novel, and then opening the book to find a man with an ax sticking out of his head.

EH: Yes. But in addition to that, mysteries back then were considered the stepchildren of literature, and . . .

McB: They still are, in many respects.

EH: You surely don't believe that.

McB: I believe that a grudging amount of respect is given to a good mystery writer. But if you want to win either the Pulitzer Prize or the National Book Award, stay far away from corpses among the petunias.

EH: You've been writing about corpses among the petunias . . .

McB: Other places, too. Not only in flower beds.

EH: For thirty-three years now. You've remarked that you begin work at nine in the morning and quit at five in the . . .

McB: Don't you?

193

EH: Exactly.

McB: Just like an *honest* job.

EH: But I wonder if you can share with us how you manage such a regimen. It must require a great deal of discipline.

McB: No. Discipline has nothing whatever to do with it. Discipline implies someone standing over you with a whip, *forcing* you to do the job. If you have to be *forced* to write, then it's time to look for another job. If you don't *love* every minute of it, even the donkey work of endless revisions, then quit.

EH: Do you make endless revisions?

McB: Not endless, no. One of the most important things about writing is to know when something is finished.

EH: When is it finished?

McB: When it works.

EH: But how many revisions *do* you make?

McB: As many as are required to make the thing *work*. A good piece of fiction *works*. You can read it backward and forward, or from the middle toward both ends, and it will *work*. If a scene isn't working, if a passage of dialogue isn't working . . .

EH: What do you mean by working?

McB: Serving the purpose for which it was intended. Is it supposed to make my hair stand on end? If my hair isn't standing on end, the scene isn't working. Is it supposed to make me cry? Then there had better be tears on my cheeks when I finish it.

EH: Do you make these revisions as you go along, or do you save them all up for the end?

McB: I usually spend the first few hours each morning rewriting what I wrote the day before. Then, every five chapters or so, I'll reread from the beginning and rewrite where necessary. Happily, nothing is engraved in stone until the book is published. You can go back over it again and again until it works.

194

EH: There's that word again.

McB: It's a word I like.

EH: How do you start a mystery novel?

McB: How do *you* start a mainstream novel?

EH: With a theme, usually.

McB: I start with a corpse, usually. Or with someone about to become a corpse.

EH: Actually, though, that's starting with a theme, isn't it?

McB: Yes, in that murder is the theme of most mysteries. Even mysteries that start out with blackmail as the theme, or kidnapping, or arson, eventually get around to murder.

EH: How do you mean?

McB: Well, take a Private Eye novel, for example. When you're writing this sort of book, it's not necessary to discover a body on page one. In fact, most private eyes—in fiction *and* in real life—aren't hired to investigate murders.

EH: Why are they hired?

McB: Oh, for any number of reasons. Someone is missing, someone is unfaithful, someone is stealing, someone is preparing a will, or inheriting money, or settling his son's gambling debts, or what-have-you. But hardly any of these reasons for employment have anything to do with murder. In fact, the odd thing about private-eye fiction is that the presence of the p.i. on the scene is usually what *causes* a murder. Had the p.i. not been hired, there'd have been no body.

EH: What about other categories of mystery fiction?

McB: Such as?

EH: Well, Man on the Run, for example. Is it necessary to start with a body in this type of story?

McB: That depends on why the guy is running, doesn't it?

195

EH: Why *would* he be running?

McB: Because he did something.

EH: Like what?

McB: Anything but murder. If he's done murder, you can hardly ever recover this guy; he's already beyond the pale, so forget him as a hero. I would also forget rape, kidnapping, terrorism, child abuse, and arson as crimes to consider for your hero. But if he's committed a less serious crime—such as running off with a few thousand dollars of the bank's money—then the police are after him, and he must run. And running, he meets a lot of different people, one of whom he usually falls in love with, and experiences a great many things that influence his life and cause him to change—for the better, we hope.

EH: That's what fiction is all about, isn't it? Change?

McB: I like to think so.

EH: But surely there are dead bodies in a Man-on-the-Run novel.

McB: Oh, sure. Along the way. I'm merely saying that in this sub-genre of Man on the Run, it isn't essential to *start* with a corpse.

EH: Are there other sub-genres?

McB: Of Man on the Run? Sure. We were talking about a man who'd actually *done* something. But we can also have a man who'd done absolutely *nothing.*

EH: Then why would he be running?

McB: Because the something he didn't do is usually murder. And that's where we *do* need a corpse. Immediately. For the police to find. So that they can accuse our man and come looking for him, which prompts him to flee, fly, *flew* in order to solve the murder and clear his name while of course falling in love with someone along the way.

EH: A Man on the Run can also be a person who *knows* something, isn't that so?

McB: Yes. Where the body is buried, or who caused the body to become a body, or even who's about to *become* a body. Dangerous

196

knowledge of this sort can cause a person to become a man who knows too much and who must flee north by northwest in order to escape becoming a body himself.

EH: On the other hand, it isn't necessary that he *really* be in possession of dangerous knowledge, is it?

McB: No. As a matter of fact, he can know absolutely nothing. In which case, he merely *appears* to know something which the bad guys think he actually *does* know.

EH: And this semblance of knowledge becomes even more dangerous to him than the knowledge itself would have been because he doesn't even know *why* someone wants him dead.

McB: In either case, a body is the essential element that sets the plot spinning.

EH: A body, or a substitute for one. The body doesn't have to be an *actual* stiff, does it?

McB: No, it can be what Alfred Hitchcock called the MacGuffin. I prefer the real thing, but there are many successful thrillers that utilize to great effect a substitute corpse.

EH: Can you give us some examples?

McB: Well, the classic Woman-in-Jeopardy story, for example, may very well be *Wait Until Dark,* where a *blind* woman unknowingly carries through customs a doll in which the bad guys have planted dope. They want the dope back. So they come after her.

EH: That's a woman in jeopardy, all right.

McB: In spades.

EH: A gender reversal of Man on the Run.

McB: Which all Woman-in-Jeopardy stories are. In this case, the substitute corpse is a doll—a graven lifeless image of a human being. The woman doesn't *know* where the body is buried, but they think she does. Without the doll—that is, without the corpse—there'd be no reason to stalk and terrify this woman, and there'd be no thriller.

EH: And in much the same way that our Man on the Run learns and changes from *his* hair-raising escapes, so does our Woman in Jeopardy become stronger and wiser by the end of *her* ordeal.

McB: Leaving the reader or the viewer feeling immensely satisfied.

EH: Let's get back to the way you begin one of your mysteries.

McB: With a corpse, yes. Well, actually, before the corpse, there's a title.

EH: I find titles difficult.

McB: I find them easy. I look for resonance. A title that suggests many different things. For example, the title *Ice* seemed to offer limitless possibilities for development. Ice, of course, is what water becomes when it freezes. So the title dictated that the novel be set during the wintertime, when there is ice and snow . . . ah. Snow. Snow is another name for cocaine. So, all right, there'll be cocaine in the plot. But in underworld jargon, to ice someone means to kill him. And ice also means diamonds. And, further, ice is the name for a box-office scam in which tickets to hit shows are sold for exorbitant prices. The title had resonance.

EH: A lot of people had trouble with one of my titles.

McB: Which one?

EH: *Love, Dad.*

McB: That's because it's a terrible title, very difficult to say. You have to say "My new book is called Love Comma Dad." Otherwise, no one will know what you're talking about.

EH: Most people thought the title was *Dear Dad.*

McB: Why?

EH: I don't know why. Actually, I thought *Love, Dad* was a wonderful title.

McB: You should have called it *No Drums, No Bugles.*

EH: Why?

McB: Were there any drums or bugles in it?

198

EH: No.

McB: There you go.

EH: Tell me where *you* go after you've got your title and your corpse.

McB: I write the first chapter. Or the first two or three chapters. As far as my imagination will carry me until it gives out.

EH: Then what?

McB: I'll outline the next few chapters ahead.

EH: Not the whole book?

McB: No.

EH: Why not?

McB: Because in mystery fiction, the reader never knows what's going to happen next. It helps if the *writer* doesn't quite know, either. If what happens is as much a surprise to him as it is to the reader.

EH: Isn't that dangerous?

McB: *If it doesn't work, you can always go back and change it.*

EH: As I understand it, then, you keep outlining as you go along.

McB: Yes. Whenever I feel a need to move things along in a certain direction. Which, by the way, may change the moment the characters *get* there and discover things I didn't know they'd discover.

EH: I always love the moment.

McB: Which moment?

EH: When the characters do just what the hell they *want* to do.

McB: When they come alive, yes.

EH: That's when you know you've got a book. That's when you know these aren't just words on paper.

McB: A lot of writers talk about how *awful* it is to be a writer. All the suffering, all the pain. Doesn't anyone find *joy* in it?

199

EH: I do.

McB: So do I.

EH: You once said . . . or *we* once said . . .

McB: *We* once said . . .

EH: . . . when asked which qualities we considered essential for a writer of fiction today . . .

McB: Yes, I remember.

EH: We said . . . a head and a heart.

McB: Yes. The head to give the work direction, the heart to give it feeling.

EH: Would you change that in any way now?

McB: I would say only please, please, please don't forget the heart.

43

RECREATING THE PAST IN HISTORICAL NOVELS

BY ROSALIND LAKER

EVEN AS A CHILD, I HAD A SENSE OF HISTORY. Without doubt it came from my close association with my grandmother, who was a thirteenth child and able to relate family tales that had been handed down to her from forebears long since gone. My grandfather was her equal in encouraging my interest in the historical events that had taken place within the county where we lived. All this fired my imagination and paved the way for me in my adult years to write as easily about past centuries as the present.

My ancestors have slipped into several of my novels, and I have based incidents on their experiences. In my most recent book, *To Dance With Kings*, I introduced my forebear, Pierre Oinville, who fled from France to England at the time of the Huguenot persecution under Louis XIV. But it is not just a personal link with the past that helps me to develop my characters. Any beginner at writing has only to remember that whereas customs and costumes change with time, standards of living rise, and more and more knowledge is acquired, people themselves are the same now as they were hundreds of years ago. They love and hate and hope and despair just as they always have. To us, drugs are the great scourge of our day, just as in the past people agonized over the plague and other pestilences. Each generation has had its joys and its sorrows, and when placing a story in an historical setting, I never forget that the characters have to live within the boundaries of their time. Everything they do has to be governed by the traditions and manners and the laws of their era or else reality is lost.

Maybe the reason readers find my characters "so real" is that to me they are real people. I usually live and work with them for a full year, and it is impossible not to be concerned for them when they suffer misfortunes and to breathe an inward sigh of relief if the hero and heroine are lucky enough to have a happy future stretching out before them.

As I have explained, to me the past is only a breath away, and therefore it is immaterial to me whether they live in one century or another. I know their emotions are the same as those experienced by everyone throughout the ages. After writing about Thomas Chippendale, Hester Bateman, and Christopher Wren, I never hear their names without remembering how I lived with them through their struggles and illnesses and their joys. So to believe in one's characters is to make them come alive, and for that the writer must know how they looked and what they ate and where they lived, whether they be fictional or historical personages. Without that bond between the writer and the characters, they will not spring from the pages to grip the readers' interest.

Even if an historical personage is not going to hold the center of the stage in your story, you should do some research into that person's life. It is all too obvious to the reader when no thought has been given as to how that person really looked—books of portraits enable a writer to give a very personal description of appearance—or how that person would have reacted in certain situations. I recently read a book in which two historical personages drifted in and out of the story like ghosts, having no substance, and it was obvious that the writer had skipped what should have been an integral part of the research. In contrast, there is the writer who feels everything that has been researched must be put in, but the golden rule is never to pad. Put in what is necessary and leave out all the rest.

I do all my own research for two important reasons. First, I like to become absorbed in the background and setting of my story, and second, I frequently come across something else in the process that gives me an idea for another book. It was while doing some research a few years ago that I came across an interesting snippet that bore no relation to what I was looking for. It said that when Queen Victoria's Prince Consort fell ill, an entrepreneur bought up all the black material that he could lay hands on. As a result, when the Prince died two weeks later and the country went into mourning, the entrepreneur made a fortune overnight. This scrap of information formed the nucleus of *Banners of Silk,* in which my heroine was able to recoup her husband's fortune by a similar action.

The idea for *To Dance With Kings* came from a chance question. My editor had returned from a trip to France and asked me how long it was since I had been to Versailles. I replied that it was many years and that it had been a bleak and empty place then, although the fountains had been beautiful. She then described the extensive restoration work that is in progress to make the Palace once again exactly as it was in Louis XIV's day. "You should see his bedroom," she said enthusiastically. "It is all red and gold with a wonderful bed draped in glorious silks and with huge white ostrich plumes rising up from the canopy." I knew immediately that I had to write about those plumes! Thus the idea was born to tell the story of the Palace of Versailles through the eyes of four generations of women from 1664, when Louis decided to enlarge his late father's hunting lodge into a great residence, until its downfall in the Revolution.

I chose December for my research. Wintertime is always good for visiting places of historical interest, for visitors are few and guides have plenty of time to answer questions. I had many of the beautiful rooms all to myself, and several times I walked the length of the regilded Hall of Mirrors with its dazzling chandeliers without meeting anyone else. One of the guides, informed I would be setting a story at Versailles, went out of her way to show me where exclusive stalls and little shops had been located near the Queen's Staircase and costly goods sold to the courtiers. I had chosen a theme of fan-making to link my four generations of women and had been wondering where the first of them would sell her fans. Here was the solution.

I had guessed the Palace would have a good number of visitors at weekends and so I kept Saturdays and Sundays to explore the many acres of park and locate the sites of the open-air ballrooms, theaters, and supper areas that had been such a feature of Court life. I found lovely little fountains and groves hidden away that rarely saw a visitor, for as yet only the vast main section is kept in pristine condition. Most fascinating to me was the little hamlet, still just as it was, where Marie Antoinette played at being a country maid with her children, trying to forget that she was a queen. I could almost see her tying blue bows on the sheep and milking the cows into a bucket of Sevres porcelain, some of which are still to be seen on the dairy shelves. Most poignant of all is the secret grove where she was told that the mob was marching on Versailles from Paris and shouting for her blood.

My visit to Versailles was only the beginning of my research. It had to cover every stage of the building, its subsequent alteration in three reigns and also the lives and customs of those who had lived there. Yet I enjoyed it all, not least to discover that the lovely and much maligned Marie Antoinette did not say "let them eat cake!" My research brought to light the fact that two French queens before her had had that remark attributed to them.

I am fortunate in being able to do research at the great British Library and the London Library, but my local library is most helpful in getting books for me, and from what I have seen of American libraries, I am sure it is the same in the States.

I am most careful to check details in my research, and then to check again if there is the slightest doubt in my mind. The importance of this was brought home to me when I gave some talks in the States that coincided with the publication of *To Dance With Kings*. A member of the Fan Association of America who was in one of the audiences told me afterwards that she and fellow members were reading the book as much for what I had written about the history and making of fans as for the story itself. This should be a guideline for all new writers choosing a special background or theme, whether it be weaving or lace-making or railway trains or anything else. If the facts are correct, a whole range of readers will be drawn to a writer's work, knowing that if the research is trustworthy in their particular field then they can be sure it will be the same in other spheres about which they have less knowledge.

For writers who cannot visit a foreign country or historical place in which they want to set a story, the answer is to read everything available about it, especially the topography. To be able to say what trees were throwing shade or how a certain range of hills looked on the skyline is far better than writing in a vacuum or making glaring mistakes. But it is better still to write about places that can be visited if the writer wishes to be truly authentic. It may seem obvious to point out that museums are a rich source of inspiration as well as information, but I visit them whenever possible. In the United States, there are many wonderful museums where the past has been recreated with perfect accuracy. Never shall I forget the eighteenth-century gentleman who addressed me with a courtly bow in Williamsburg, Virginia. "Which part of the colony are you from, my lady?" Then there are those charming ladies at the Colonel's house at Old Sturbridge Village in Massachusetts, who look as if they have stepped from the pages of a Jane Austen novel.

When starting an historical novel, I always have a framework of events of that period—battles, wars, coronations, plagues, etc.—and interweave my story through it. In this way nothing gets out of sequence, and keeping a file of these dates on hand makes easy reference. Sometimes it is very inconvenient that a particular event in history did not take place a little earlier, or later, or even nearer a fictional character's home, but ways can always be found to involve one's character and keep the story flowing smoothly at the same time. In my new book, *Circle of Pearls,* I had to find a way to bring home the wounded Cavalier son of the family, who lived many miles from the site of the battle, while the Roundheads were set on tracking him down. So the kitchen boy from his home ran away to join the Cavalier forces and proved instrumental in arranging the young man's escape, taking in a special development of the plot at the same time.

New writers often find subplots difficult, but frequently a minor character will provide the answer. Just think about those individuals and the lives they would lead and suddenly they are falling in love or seeking advancement, invariably influencing the major characters by their actions. The kitchen boy is an example, for although he did not inspire my subplot, he was a person in his own right and was not dropped from the story.

I become fond of my characters, and when the last page of a book is written I feel I have said farewell to friends. It is always my hope that readers will feel the same.

44

FREE-FORM PLOTTING THE MYSTERY NOVEL

BY MARCIA MULLER

PLOTTING THE MODERN MYSTERY NOVEL is a complex task that bears as little resemblance to so-called formula writing as Miss Jane Marple does to Lew Archer. One of the questions most often asked by aspiring mystery writers (frequently in tones of frustration, after being outfoxed by one of their favorite authors) is, "How on earth do you complicate your plots and still get them to hang together?"

Unhappily for those who seek instant solutions, there is no one sure-fire method of plotting. The techniques vary from writer to writer along a continuum that stretches from detailed, extensive outlining to what I call winging it (writing with no planning whatsoever). Writers adopt the type of plotting that best suits their working styles and personalities. Some hit on the appropriate type immediately, others gradually make their way toward it through experimentation—plus hard work and practice. There are no major shortcuts, but there are *little* shortcuts. Tiny ones, actually. What I'm about to tell you about plotting is only my highly individualized technique; all, some, or none of my suggestions may help.

I've learned my craft the hard way. In the past fifteen years I've made every attempt to "reinvent the wheel," especially where plotting is concerned. I began by making detailed character sketches, outlines, and time charts, a method distilled down to a lengthy storyline synopsis. I've tried winging it, with unsatisfying results. What I've finally settled into is a technique that I call "free-form plotting"; as the term implies, its key ingredient is flexibility.

Before we go on, however, let's discuss the concept of plot. If someone were to ask you what a novel's plot is, you'd probably say "the story." But if you examine a given *plot,* you'll see it's somewhat different from the *story.* The story is linear; it is the events that happen,

206

both on and off scene. The plot is the *structure* you impose on those events. You select which to include, in what order, and how to tell each one. You shape your plot from the raw material—the story.

Here's an example of a crime story, simplified for our purposes:

1. Killer meets victim; they interact.
2. Killer murders victim.
3. Murder is discovered; detective enters case.
4. Detective investigates.
5. Detective solves murder; killer is apprehended.

Taking the raw material of this particular story, you could plot in a number of ways. You could tell it in a linear fashion, from step one to step five (although that's not likely to be surprising or dramatic). You could start with the discovery of the murder, continue through to the killer's apprehension, explaining in flashback or dialogue what went on in steps one and two. You could start with the actual murder, masking the identity of the killer. The steps may be ordered any whichway, depending on what kind of book you want to write. It is up to you to decide how this simple story is told; the question we are addressing here is how you make and follow through on your decision.

What I like about free-form plotting is that it allows me to defer the decision, feeling my way as I write. It saves me from becoming locked into an inflexible plot outline that may, in the end, not suit my purposes. I can start a novel with a minimal idea of where I'm going, develop some ideas and characters, experiment with them, keep what fits, discard what doesn't. An example of this is how I plotted my most recent Sharon McCone novel, *There's Something in a Sunday.*

When I started I had in mind a beginning situation, a few characters, a background, a theme, and a hazy idea of the ending. The situation has Sharon McCone being hired to follow a man who came to San Francisco every Saturday night and stayed through the early morning hours on Monday. The characters were the man, Frank Wilkonson; Sharon's client; a woman the man was looking for; and a married couple who were friends of the woman's. The background was dual: neighborhood activism and the plight of San Francisco's homeless people. The theme was the relationships between men and women, and how they go awry. And the ending—well, I won't reveal everything.

When I start a mystery novel, I like to set the situation in the first one or two chapters. In this case, it was Sharon following Wilkonson, observing his eccentric Sunday activities, and wondering if the client had told her the entire truth about his interest in Wilkonson. Because she observed Wilkonson's movements closely for nearly twenty-four hours, she feels that she knows him—and so did I, although he had not as yet uttered a single word of dialogue. In these two chapters, I had developed his character in some depth, and had begun to consider him a real person. As he developed, I began to think differently about Wilkonson and what I intended to do with him later on.

I employed the rule of flexibility very early. When I read my first two chapters, I found something was wrong: Taken together, they moved too slowly. So I broke them up, inserting a flashback chapter between them, in which I introduced the client, Rudy Goldring, and showed how Sharon had come to spend her Sunday tailing Wilkonson. By the time I finished the scene, both Goldring and the derelict who served as "doorman" at his office building had come alive for me, and I began to see new ways they could be used in the plot.

My next step was to introduce the supporting characters: the people at All Souls Legal Cooperative, where Sharon works. Again, something was wrong with the scene I'd planned. I was tired of writing about the co-op in the same old way. If I had to write the scene with Sharon sitting in her boss's office discussing the case one more time. . . . My solution was to introduce a new attorney and an assistant for Sharon, to give more prominence to an old character, the secretary, and to create personal problems for the boss, whose previous life had been placid. Now I had a situation that I was eager to write about, and a fast-developing personal subplot that (because the life of Sharon and the people at All Souls is an ongoing story from novel to novel) didn't necessarily have to be wrapped up at the end.

Of course, what happened in the scene at All Souls required going back and making minor adjustments in the first three chapters; the new attorney, for instance, was now the person who had handed Sharon the Goldring assignment, rather than her boss. This is a time-consuming necessity of free-form plotting but, as we'll see later, it has its advantages.

At this point I was ready to establish my other characters. And, while a lot had happened and a number of questions about Wilkonson and Goldring had been raised, I needed something more dramatic—the murder.

At the scene of the crime I was able to introduce another of the main characters, an unnamed woman who appeared suddenly and then vanished. In the next few chapters, as Sharon followed up on the case for reasons of personal satisfaction, I brought in the other characters who would figure prominently: the married couple, Wilkonson's wife, and his employer.

Most of these characters had turned out differently from what I'd first envisioned. A character "taking over" the story is a phenomenon that writers often discuss. No one knows exactly why or how this happens, but I suspect it has to do with the writer's being relaxed and "into" the story. As you sit at the keyboard, new ideas start to flow. Characters take on fuller identities as you allow them to speak and act and interact with one another. When this happens to me, I simply go along with whatever is developing; often I write pages and pages of dialogue or action, then pare them down or toss them out entirely. It's easier to cut or eliminate your prose than to go back and add material later. By setting down these free-flowing scenes on paper, you will avail yourself of the opportunity to create something that may vastly improve your novel. And (impossible in real life) you can always rip up the pages or hit the delete key.

One example of this phenomenon is the development of the married couple that I've mentioned—Vicky and Gerry Cushman. Originally, I'd seen them in a strictly functional sense, as friends of the woman who appears at the murder scene and then vanishes—the pivotal character in the plot. But, as Vicky began to take shape, what emerged was not the coolly efficient neighborhood activist I'd planned, but a woman with severe emotional problems. And in response to this development, her husband Gerry emerged as a selfish man who exacerbated her problems. I had created an unexpected conflict that wove nicely into the theme of the novel—and I was able to use it to further complicate my plot.

At this point—the end of your primary development stage—you can take full advantage of free-form plotting. You have your characters in all their individuality and richness; you have a situation that is ripe for additional complication; you have an idea of where you're going. Now is the time to find out exactly where that is—and how you're going to get there.

The way I accomplish this is to read what I have on paper. Then I play the game of "what if." The game is a question-and-answer process: "What if such-and-such happened? How would that work?"

In *Sunday*, I reached this point just as Frank Wilkonson disappeared. He had gone to an abandoned windmill in Golden Gate Park; Sharon was following him, but lost him in the darkness and fog; Wilkonson never returned to his car. This was an unplanned development; the setting of the windmill had occurred to me while driving by it one day, and it seemed a perfect place for an eerie, late-night scene. The scene wrote easily, but at its conclusion I had to admit I had no idea why Wilkonson had gone there or where he'd gone afterwards. Time for "what if. . . ."

Why did he? I asked myself. The obvious answer was that he planned to meet someone there. Sometimes the obvious choice is the best. But who? I could think of one character who would have reason to be there, but no reason to meet Wilkonson. But what if he was asked to contact Frank? By whom? I knew who that might be. But then, why hadn't Sharon seen Frank meet the other person? What if Wilkonson had. . .?

By the end of this question-and-answer session I found myself in possession of a new plot twist: an eventual second murder and a killer who hadn't even been on my list of primary suspects. Because of my accidental choice of a setting and the manner in which I wrote the scene, my plot had taken on greater complication—and greater mystery.

A few chapters later I was faced with another situation calling for "what if." Sharon had finally located the woman from the murder scene. The woman had ties to all the major characters, but they were as yet nebulous. In a few cases, they were nebulous even to *me*. So I considered the connections among all six of these people. What if the client was an old friend of the woman? What if they had once been lovers? No, friends was better. But what if she had had a lover? What if it was Frank? Or Gerry? Or Frank's boss? Or. . .? Because the characters were well established at this time, I was able to come up with a logical answer.

As I've said, free-form plotting requires constant readjustments of scenes and details to make them consistent with one another. This is laborious at times, often necessitating extensive rewriting. But I'm convinced that it is also extremely beneficial. As you rewrite, you are forced to pay great attention to detail, to polish your prose, to reexamine your logic.

Logic is crucial to a mystery novel. If it is flawed, the whole plot—no matter how original your premise, fascinating your characters, or vivid your settings—simply falls apart. I advise frequent rewriting and rereading. Check every detail; make sure every place is described properly, especially if the action depends on the lay of the land. As I was preparing the final draft of an earlier McCone novel, *Eye of the Storm*, I found that I'd handled a description of a boathouse in two different ways. In the early chapters, it had been a building on pilings over the water; later on, it had a concrete foundation and boat wells. Since near the end something happened in one of those wells, the initial description made no sense whatsoever!

This may sound like an incredible error, but, believe me, things like this happen to professionals, too. When I discovered it, I had read the manuscript numerous times. A friend and frequent collaborator had read it twice. Neither of us had caught the discrepancy. So check your copy. Recheck. Publishing houses have copyeditors to catch the little things, but the big things are your responsibility.

There you have the basics of free-form plotting. Develop a general situation, background, theme, characters, and ending. Set the situation. Allow your characters to act and interact with one another. When the primary development stage is complete, complicate by playing "what if." Write some more. Be flexible; play "what if" again and again. Rewrite, reread. Check, recheck. And as you write, take advantage of the surprising things that develop—they will often point the way to a truly baffling plot!

45

TECHNIQUES THAT TERRIFY

BY JOHN EDWARD AMES

IF IT SENDS A COLD SHIVER DOWN ONE'S SPINE," Edith Wharton said of the horror tale, "it has done its job and done it well." For centuries savvy horror writers have passed this visceral test by relying on proven techniques that elicit shuddering, bristling, and terror. But horror writers do not claim eminent domain over the realm of fear, an emotion integral to every genre. Some conventions of dark fantasy offer a rich mother lode of fear-inducing techniques valuable to *all* fiction writers.

Exploit the power of suggestion. Subtle doesn't always sell. Nonetheless, discerning writers often evoke the fear response through the power of suggestion rather than with graphic descriptions. Granted, modern authors have broken new ground in the art of vivid, cinematic imagery, and this modern, aggressive style has often enriched their genres. But reader interest can be blunted by any stylistic overkill. H. P. Lovecraft made his horrors convincing simply by pretending they were too horrible to describe. Used judiciously, such deliberate restraint by the writer can be more chilling than explicit realism.

Instead of docudrama-style description of a mad slasher at work, for example, skip the "slice-and-dice" approach by shifting reader attention away from the violent act itself; suggest the savagery indirectly through the spontaneous reaction of a character who happens upon the aftermath of the attack. Remember that shock is initially an intensely physical experience—"a flash of ice, a flash of fire, a bursting gush of blood," as Robert Louis Stevenson described it. Use vivid sensory images that let inner intensity suggest outer atrocities.

Another effective technique is to use a jarringly inappropriate response—hysterical laughter, say, at the moment of terror—to suggest fear or grief so powerful it challenges the character's sanity. Sixteen-year-old Johnny is being dismembered by a group of rabid playmates who are under the spell of an evil mojo fetish. His dying thought is not focused on the terror at what's happening to him or the diorama of his life passing before his eyes. Instead, he dies in mortal shame, wondering what his mother will say about his dirty underwear.

Forestall the moment of terrifying revelation. The subtle touch can also improve your plot when you use it to slow down narrative time and thus heighten suspense. "The most chilling moment of any horror film," notes director Roger Corman, "usually relates to a scene in which some character is seen in a long corridor, running away from or approaching some unspecified object of unparalleled horror. The moment *before* this revelation of the nature of that 'thing' holds the fear." Stephen King echoes this advice in *Danse Macabre,* noting that a closed door is a continuous source of fearful suspense only so long as it remains closed. Once it's opened, and the Unknown Thing—no matter how horrible—confronted, suspense is resolved.

One key to forestalling the critical moment of revelation is cinematic pacing: delaying or freezing narrative time by backpedaling point of view to another character. Unlike the flashback, which can clumsily *interrupt* narrative time, backpedaling is merely retelling the same scene or sequence of events from another character's point of view, thus attenuating or repeatedly "freeze-framing" narrative time.

John Fowles used this strategy effectively to structure his psycho-thriller *The Collector.* The first half is narrated by a deranged kidnapper; the second half covers the exact same sequence of events from his victim's point of view. Only then is the denouement finally reached. Not only does this twice-told technique extend suspense, it allows the reader to consider frightening new perspectives and possibilities missed the first time around.

Use ongoing hooks. Fear is "a feeling of anxiety and agitation caused by the presence or nearness of danger, evil, or pain." It is thus inextricably linked to the broader feeling of suspense, "a state of usually anxious uncertainty." And another way to heighten suspense, that important prerequisite of fear, is through timely placing of hooks.

Most aspiring writers dutifully provide opening or closing chapter hooks. But they should also pay attention to subtly telegraphed teasers throughout chapters and scenes—less dramatic ongoing hooks intended to answer that nagging question that plagues most professional writers during composition: *Why* should my readers want to keep reading? One answer is to supply irrestible minihooks between the mega-grabbers. These minihooks should unobtrusively promise more to come just around the narrative corner.

One of my all-time favorites is not found in the horror genre but in Owen Wister's classic western *The Virginian:* "They strolled into the saloon of a friend, where, unfortunately, sat some foolish people." This understated teaser occurs in the middle of a long scene and hardly produces *frissons* down the spine. Contrast its reduced intensity to the taut opening sentence of Robert Bloch's "The Closer of the Way": "To this day I don't know how they got me to the asylum." Yet both hooks serve the same basic narrative function: They contribute to a sense of menace and promise more to come, compelling the reader forward to find out what that "more" is.

Appeal to universal fears. Clinical psychology is replete with verbal labels for almost any conceivable fear. If, for example, you're diagnosed as triskaidekaphobic, you're badly frightened by the number 13. Some people are deathly afraid of certain colors or days of the week or foods; others have sought help because they irrationally believe their knees will suddenly collapse. While such real but relatively rare phobias may be fascinating to ponder, they don't usually underpin the most gripping fiction. But successful writers understand that archetypal fears, because of their universality, help ensure more reader identification with the characters.

Exploit traditional fears rooted in the "blood consciousness" of most of us: fear of someone or something lurking under the bed, closed (or partially opened) doors, hallways or tunnels that lead to two or more unknown fates, cramped spaces, basements, attics, heights, crowds, darkness, disease, doomsday, death. Don't neglect what may be man's most potent and ancient bête noire: fear of ostracism from society, a "phobic pressure point" that Stephen King touches so well in best sellers such as *The Dead Zone* and *Firestarter,* featuring heroes too weirdly different to fit in.

Modern writers may substitute shopping malls and high-rise apartment buildings for moors and Gothic castles. But they are still most effective when they appeal to traditional, universal fears.

Tease your readers. Dyed-in-the-wool horror fans—whose loyalty accounts for the steady sales—present a challenging paradox for writ-

214

ers: Such readers expect certain conventions, yet they rightly scorn too much predictability. Thus writers, especially in the horror, mystery, and private-eye fields, have learned to "tease" their readers, to *disrupt* expectations without disappointing them. One venerable technique for accomplishing this delicate balancing act is the strategic combination of the "fake scare" and the "fake release."

The fake scare can be any scene in which a character is startled, surprised, or shocked through a mistaken interpretation of a harmless event. Your heroine, stalked at night by a psychotic killer, is frantically rummaging through her purse for her house key; suddenly she cries out in fright at an abrupt skittering noise on the sidewalk behind her. It turns out to be only a discarded Milky Way wrapper propelled by a vagrant breeze.

But such a fake scare is in fact only the writer's equivalent of the set-shot in volleyball: a nasty "spike" may soon follow. The subsequent emotional relief experienced by character *and* reader is sometimes also a "fake release" of dramatic tension: The writer chooses this moment or one soon after, when the readers' psychological guards are down, to let the killer fling the door open from inside and leap at the heroine, his Sheffield boning knife glinting cruelly in a stray shaft of moonlight.

Readers expect these little tricks, so writers have to tease them a bit: Sometimes the harmless scare really *is* harmless, throwing readers off and providing the character (but not the uneasy reader, who *loves* this stuff) a genuine release of tension. And sometimes the skittering noise is neither harmless nor just a setup for a later zinger—the Horrible Thing really *is* there when the heroine spins around. Good writers somehow stay one step ahead of their readers, coming up with new and effective twists on the combination of fake scare and fake release. The pros know it's *technique* that delivers the scares required for almost every story.

46

THE POLICE PROCEDURAL

BY ERIC WRIGHT

IF YOU WRITE THE KIND OF NOVELS that are called "police procedurals," one of the comments you will get most frequently is "You must do a lot of research." It is a natural assumption that you cannot write about the inside of a police station without being thoroughly soaked in the day-to-day routines of the cops. It isn't true, but before I talk about my experience in this area, let me deal with the general question of research or my own attitude toward it.

One of the pieces of advice I have developed since I started writing crime novels is this: Do your research last.

I am against spending a minute longer than necessary on research, and if you do all your research before you start you will probably do ten times as much as you need, because you do not know what is necessary until you have finished the book. So let me say it again: Leave your research to the end.

If this sounds bizarre (and I've had screams of outrage from research addicts on this one), remember you are writing a novel, not a documentary, and you are not accountable for the absolute accuracy or completeness of your factual information so much as for its plausibility. Write it so that it sounds right—then check the facts. And this is the place to restate the old maxim that if the truth is implausible, you can't use it.

The important thing is that you don't become a bag-lady (of either sex), a bag-lady of literature. We've all met them. I came across them first in graduate school where they carried shopping bags and small suitcases full of notes they were accumulating for a thesis. If you said anything remotely touching on their interests, they made a little note and popped the card into the shopping bag for the day they would begin writing. Sadly, in too many cases, that day never came.

When I started to publish and as a consequence was invited to speak in public, I always saw one of these bag-ladies in the audience, usually

216

in the back row. They were the ones with the questions about how much research I had to undertake to write a book. They themselves had been "researching" a mystery novel for three years and were wondering when they should plan to begin the next stage.

Of course, if you are setting your novel in Ulan Bator in February, say, you will need to know the temperature and how much daylight there is. But chances are you already know these things or why would you set it there? Almost certainly, you have done the bare minimum of research necessary to get going, long before you started to plan. Georges Simenon is said to have set a novel in Cambridge, England, because he changed trains there one afternoon and did not wish to waste the experience. Too many people would not dream of writing about Cambridge without at least a year's study.

I want to apply this point about research to all fiction before I speak about police procedurals. I think if I were writing a novel about eighteenth-century England, I would write it out of my hazy notion of what life was like before the Industrial Revolution; then, if the fiction worked, I would "research" it. I have just finished a novel that takes place on a film set. I have never been on a film set, and in this case, I deliberately resisted all offers to visit a set until I had the book done. When I was finished, I asked a friend, a film producer, to check it, not for accuracy, but for plausibility. I didn't want to know if he would advise making a film my way, but, rather, if it was conceivable that a film might be made something like this. He said it was.

Of course, there were a number of technical points I had no idea about, things that were crucial to the plot: What happens to the exposed film at the end of the day? Who keeps the record of script changes on the set? (My ignorance was total.) But these things I guessed at, or made up, and he corrected them in a few minutes. The point is, if I had tried to research them ahead of time, I might have spent weeks doing it, and most of all, I would have wasted most of the research because I didn't know what I would need until all the details of the plot emerged. By doing the research afterward, I do only as much as I need. I could guess or make up the technical points because I have seen them or something like them in hundreds of movies and dozens of books whose plots involve movie-making. And, to come to the point, exactly the same is true of police procedurals.

My decision to write a police procedural came by a process of elimination: It was the only subgenre that would allow me to do what I wanted with the characters. I am in no way fascinated by police routine. When I wrote my first novel with a police inspector as hero, I had never been inside a Toronto police station, or spoken to a senior police officer. I have now. But in the beginning I wanted to know most of all if I could write a book like that. I wanted to spend as little time as possible doing things that might be a waste of time if it turned out I had no talent for the main task. So I devised a plot that allowed me to avoid the whole question of procedure: My murder took place in Montreal, but my story is about that part of the investigation that takes place in Toronto, the victim's hometown.

When I had finished, I found an agent. A few weeks later my agent sold the book, and then I did some research. It took me about an hour down at police headquarters to ask them the dozen or so questions that I had to have answers to, questions about pay and ranks and the vacations that Toronto police are entitled to, and the book was published.

Every succeeding book has raised three or four more questions to which I have found the answers afterward, and now, seven books later, I have a fairly good idea of police procedure in Toronto, at least, but I don't think I write better as a result.

And whenever I speak in public, invariably someone in the audience comments admiringly on the enormous amount of research I must have done to get the details of police procedure straight.

Why did I choose the procedural at all, if I have such an aversion to unnecessary work? The answer is that I wanted to write a realistic novel, created as far as possible out of my own experience of people, an experience largely confined to middle-class urban Canada. I wanted to tell stories about people I have known, about situations I have experienced, and for me, the crime novel is just that, a way of telling stories (and getting them published).

One of the stories I wanted to tell was about the life and times of a typical middle-class Canadian in mid-life (no research required here), and to continue that story through a series of novels. Having decided on that, the decision to make the hero a cop was already made for me. Private eyes rarely have a domestic life that includes children.

Having decided, or better, having long known what kind of hero you want to figure in your procedural—his age, the stage of his career, his family, his habits—the next thing is to decide fairly early if you are going to have a Horatio for your Hamlet. Nicholas Freeling's hero, Van der Valk, talks to himself, but Reginald Hill now has three policemen talking to each other. The results are equally superb. My guess is that more of us than not find it convenient for the hero to have someone to talk to, and it's nice to know that police always investigate a homicide in pairs.

Think long and hard about the relationship of the hero to his (usually) junior colleague. Should the junior be younger or older? A comic figure? Will he have his own kind of savvy, or be like Dr. Watson, as thick as two planks?

My first supporting cop was a domesticated old sergeant who treats my hero (in his late forties) like the young master. This worked very well for me for four books, but then it was time for him to retire. (In my books, people age from book to book, another decision you will have to make.) I gave my hero a new assistant, a young Yugoslavian plainclothes constable from the drug squad. I wasn't sure that these two would get along because the new man was a bit puppyish, but it turned out that he admired my hero extravagantly. Then for my recent book, *A Sensitive Case,* I found yet another sidekick, another old, nearly retired sergeant. I had a story I wanted to tell, quite apart from the murder, and it was a story that could be told only through such a man. I don't believe he will be back, but my young Yugoslavian has already returned.

A word of warning here. Like most writers, I stumbled into my stories and characters, but even if I had foreseen all my problems, I do not think I would have planned much more carefully. I am pretty sure it would have been a mistake to plan a series, because it would have affected the writing of each book, not for the better. I assume that every book is going to be the last in the series, and I tell the reader everything I know about my people. There always seems to be more when I come to the next book.

Make up your mind about your hero's private life. My hero is uxorious: His wife is just as bright as he is and better educated, which may cause him some problems one day, because he takes his job home too much. His sons create their own problems, and his father is a cantankerous old misanthrope. You see what I mean? There are times when I forget that I'm writing a crime novel as I watch the stresses produced by my hero's marriage—and reviewers have chided me for it.

The most important other character is the killer. Perhaps the chief thing I have discovered is that it is both easier to write the novel and more interesting if the villain is understandable, if not likable. I have done it both ways, but if my villain is a nasty piece of work, then I have difficulty spending much time with him. Abnormal psychology doesn't fascinate me as I know it does some very good writers. I also think that if you spend much time with him and do a thorough job of bringing him to life, then it is difficult to conceal the fact that he is the villain. What I prefer is a comprehensible homicide committed by someone who has a good deal of my sympathy. Then I can give the character some weight and substance.

The important thing about minor characters, in my experience, is to treat them as if they are major, to stay with them, think them through until they could carry a major role without boring the reader. Even if they have only a dozen lines, they must speak out of a fully realized character, or their language will be generalized and uninteresting. (It surprises me how often they unexpectedly reappear in the course of the rewriting, so I like to know them well.)

Finally, something has to be said about plot. You will have to make up your mind what kind of plot you prefer. The classic British mystery relies on a brilliant puzzle and a brilliant criminal and a slightly more brilliant detective, and the effect is of a giant game. This is not my way: I never liked this kind of novel much, and I am not ingenious enough to write one. When I look over my books I see that I have generally looked for a nearly accidental murder, often concealed by a piece of luck, and my hero employs a mixture of intuition, character analysis, and a bit of luck himself to solve them. I prefer that my crimes and their solutions be as plausible, as close to what my neighbors might perpetrate, as possible.

And here the writing begins. I never plot beyond this, because I do not know what is going to happen. If I did, I might not write it, because a huge part of the pleasure for me is wondering how my hero will solve it. I know where he must end, but I have no idea how he is going to get there.

They call my novels "low-key." That suits me. I am not trying to write about the extraordinary, or even about the unusual, but to make the ordinary interesting.

47

CREATING A CREDIBLE ALIEN

BY JERRY L. STERN

AS SCIENTISTS HAVE EXPANDED OUR KNOWLEDGE of physics, biology, and astronomy, writing science fiction has become more difficult. An alien character that would have been believable fifty years ago might now be rejected as either impossible or unreasonable. Modern fans of science fiction have far more expertise in the sciences than the fans of those early years. They love searching stories for scientific errors, and they are very good at finding them!

These modern science fiction readers won't tolerate a bug-eyed monster as the bad guy from outer space. They won't watch the hero of a story be ripped to shreds by an alien character who talks like a human, stalks like a hunter, pounces like a cat, screams like a banshee, or sniffs out your hero like a bloodhound. How terrestrial. How boring. If you can't do better than that, write a werewolf story instead, and set it in London in 1880.

Building a truly alien character is difficult. It takes a lot of work, a lot of thought, to design an alien's physical characteristics, home planet environment, and language. But without taking that time, a writer may create only an alien costume, or a man in a creature suit. That alien shell would behave exactly like a human. If the alien in your story behaves like a human, then *make it a human!* Your story gains nothing by the addition of an anthropomorphic alien. Science fiction readers can tell the difference between good and bad aliens, and they will tell you quite emphatically when you've made a mistake.

Science fiction fans constantly play "the game." Their part of the game is to find all of an author's science errors. An author's job in the game is slightly more difficult. The author must decide on the basic characteristics of a story. Are the characters performing on a oddball planet? Is the hero reptilian, or is the story about the consequences of a new invention? The game will allow nearly any combination of these factors as starting points. Once that initial premise has been established, however, every other detail in that story must be consistent not only with all the details of that premise, *but also with the reasonable extrapolations of those ideas, within the limits of current scientific knowledge.*

But you can write science fiction if you don't know every last fact about the science of the nineties. There is a method. Limit your science to the minimum necessary for your plot, and the logical extrapolations of that scientific premise. It may not be necessary to use an alien in every story. If your story really *needs* an alien for plot reasons, here are some things to consider while developing the concepts needed for building a believable alien. . . .

Biochemistry

Does the alien have our basic body biochemistry? Does it use the carbon-based system of converting sugars and water and oxygen to carbon dioxide? Then it must breathe oxygen and come from a planet that has photosynthesis, or an equivalent, to cycle that process backward. That limits its livable temperature range basically to that of liquid water. A "hot" alien, from a desert planet, where the temperature is always above 250 degrees, couldn't share our body chemistry no matter how strange its anatomy. If you choose a different chemical basis for life, be sure it is theoretically possible, or the readers will say, "Ahhh! Another inconsistency! Bad science!" Bad alien, too.

Physics

Maybe you would like to write "hard" science fiction. The "hard" applies to the science involved. It's easy to determine if a piece of science fiction writing is classified as "hard." If there is a lot of mathematics involved in proving a premise, that's hard. Unless you have a lot of science background, you might want to leave such subjects to the experts. For example, the subject of living on a neutron star has been explored by the science fiction novelist Robert L. Forward, who is also a consultant on scientific matters such as solar sails, deep space exploration, and anti-matter. His novel *Dragon's Egg* speculates how life might evolve on a neutron star, and how we could communicate with it.

Without going quite to a neutron star, you can still describe a strange environment. Think about how a heavy gravity planet would affect the development of a culture. Or maybe, how would living in the zero gravity environment of an interplanetary trading ship be different from the life on a ship limited not to space, but bound to an ocean.

Anatomy

How many arms does an alien need to work on a space-faring vessel? How many joints should there be in an arm? Or should your alien have arms? Should it be he or she? Or maybe there is a realistic story reason to use three sexes, or some other system that could only evolve under conditions that would have to be scientifically explained.

These are just some of your choices in building an alien body. You are not necessarily limited to what would look familiar or reasonable on Earth. Anything that can be explained as a reasonable evolutionary development is fair play.

Say, for the sake of a thought experiment, that you've devised an alien. We'll call this one a *he,* although we suspect some quirky adaptive bits in his biology. He comes from a planet under a sun similar to our own, although his planet is just slightly warmer than the Earth, and has considerably stronger gravity. But the creatures on his planet have evolved shaped like barrels, with five double-jointed arms and matching legs and feet, each with five smaller appendages that we'll call fingers and toes for lack of better terms.

Psychology

If something that grew up on a heavy gravity planet came to Earth, and saw the skyline of New York, what would be its reaction? In three gravities, a skyscraper could not be built with the methods and materials used on Earth.

Science fiction fans will carry this analysis much further. If you jump off a building, the factor that determines how badly you will be injured is not the height of the building; it is the speed that you're traveling when you hit the ground. On Earth, that speed is always the same for a given height off the ground. The higher the gravity, the more quickly a falling object increases in speed. On a heavy gravity planet, a drop of only a few inches would be fatal. Our alien is probably afraid of heights.

If you think that's a minor point in developing the cultural codes of a civilization, take a look at Hal Clement's novel, *Mission of Gravity*. Clement's planet Mesklin is a great example of a strange planetary environment, a flattened spheroid with variable gravity and a day of seventeen and three-quarter minutes. The gravity is strongest at the poles of the planet, where the aliens each weigh over 900 pounds. At the equator of their planet, the Mesklinites have a weight of only a few pounds each, and are understandably worried about the strong winds carrying them away.

Clement's Mesklinite aliens are sailors and explorers on a sea of liquid methane. Certainly humans could not live in such cold, so the cultures of humans and Mesklinites will have very different structures.

Culture, personality, and language

Culture and personality are the most important parts of alien characterizations. Given a background of the basic premise of the story and descriptions of the environment, chemistry, and anatomy of an alien, as a science fiction author you must develop a feel for what an alien's social culture could be like. What reasonable personality could develop from these starting points? After the third chapter, creatures that merely look strange will no longer hold the attention of a science fiction reader. There must be an *alien persona* resident in an alien, matching what should reasonably have evolved in such a creature.

Next decision: Will the alien be able to learn our language fairly well, or just a pidgin dialect? It may become difficult to convince your readers of the intelligence of an alien that has only a limited vocabulary; it may become impossible to express ideas through that alien that relate to real concerns of fully developed characters.

You'll have to watch your language when talking to aliens. The verbal shortcuts that we have developed may not be understandable. Sure, we can assume that once they learn English they will understand some of our expressions, but will symbols make any sense at all? *We* may understand "dropping pennies into a piggy bank," but our five-sided alien will not understand why we place coins in livestock.

Just as some English might not be understandable to your alien, some of his language may not be translatable into English. You'll need to make up an alien language. Fortunately, you won't need an entire vocabulary and grammar, but you will need words for the basic concepts of the alien society, including names and titles of aliens. Words for those concepts that are not translatable will be useful, as will terms of respect and admiration. Don't go overboard on language, though. The more details present in a fictional language, the more likely it is for a fan to find an inconsistency and tear your work apart. So, before you throw in alien language words, decide if those concepts really cannot be said in English.

When designing your alien's language, look out for pronunciation and phonemes. If your alien has a different mouth structure from ours, the phonemes he uses, or cannot use, will be different from ours. Could an alien with a bird beak say, *"Friend or Foe"*? An alien language does not need to be verbal, but look out! A tonal or sung language, or a language based on body movement, will be difficult to convert into words; don't approach it casually. Your readers will not appreciate being unable to pronounce character names or alien terms. If necessary, invent a subtle way to sneak in an explanation of pronunciation, maybe as an aside comment of a human character.

Human body language is a set of visual codes. Our alien is five-sided. When he nods his head, does it mean yes? Think about it. Isn't nodding or shaking your head side to side the same motion to this creature? So his body language will not be based on anything we could understand easily. Any gestures he makes will have to be explained, or translated into our own visual codes, at least the first time each gesture is made.

To see how an expert creates aliens and language and social structures, read C. J. Cherryh's novel, *Cuckoo's Egg.* Cherryh does the best aliens in the science fiction genre. She has managed to incorporate enough alien concepts to make the aliens come alive and not seem to the reader like costumed humans, and yet she has not made the aliens so strange that communication is lost.

An alien and a human must have something in common if there is to be any competition or friendship or even hate beyond pure xenophobia. There must be enough jointly held concepts to keep a conversation moving, a joint exploration traveling, or a colonial trader running from planet to planet.

Just because you've created a creature that, to human eyes, appears strange, don't assume that you've created an alien being. Even a bug-eyed monster can become a believable alien. Just use some empathy, a touch of psychological strangeness, and some good extrapolation from a purely biological description of the alien to the planet, evolution, and

225

culture that created it. As a writer, build up a picture for yourself of the kinds of events that could trigger your alien character's responses, and you'll soon have an alien writing his own action and dialogue for you. Once that happens, writing science fiction is like any other fiction. Just let the characters do what they must, and hang on for the ride through space and time.

48

No Gore, Please—They're British
An Interview with P. D. James

By Marilyn Stasio

Q. *Would you care to present your series detectives and tell us how they operate?*

P.D.J.: Adam Dalgliesh is Commander of the [London] Metropolitan Police Force. I know that makes it sound as if he had a naval rank; but it is, in fact, a rank peculiar to the Metropolitan Police Force. He is a professional policeman and head of the Murder Squad, which makes him lucky in the sense that he has the entire resources of the police behind him. He has access to police computers and to the assistance of police inspectors, constables, scene-of-crime officers and, of course, to forensic pathologists at the Metropolitan Police forensic science laboratory. I hope he's a good, realistic professional cop; I certainly intend that he shall be.

Q. *You have another detective, though, who is not affiliated with the police.*

P.D.J.: Cordelia Gray, whom I introduced in *An Unsuitable Job for a Woman.* Cordelia is a private eye who inherited her very rundown, seedy agency from a man who was formerly a detective with the Metropolitan Police. He trained her in the trade and she hopes she goes about it in a very professional way. She is not licensed, however, because we have no system here for licensing our private eyes. It's one of the differences between England and the United States.

Since it isn't at all realistic for private detectives to get involved in murder, we have to involve them in cases where it *does* seem natural and logical, either because the police have written off a particular case—as a suicide, for example—or because the detective somehow has a personal interest.

Q. *Aside from the technical challenge, doesn't having a detective who works outside the law also give the hero a chance to operate beyond the law?*

P.D.J.: Cordelia respects the methods of the professional police. But they certainly don't welcome her with open arms, as they used to do the private detective in English fiction of the 1930's. In Dorothy Sayers's Lord Peter Wimsey novels, the chief constable was always saying: "Well, my Lord, how *thankful* we are that you're here!"

In the early books of Dashiell Hammett and Raymond Chandler—which I so much admire because they were very, very fine writers who influenced the novel generally, not only their own genre—the police were commonly regarded by the heroes as brutal or corrupt or incompetent. The detective was essentially a lonely man, a crusader striding the mean streets. The private war that those heroes waged was as much against the official police force and society itself as it was against the ostensible villains.

Even Hammett's hard-boiled detective Sam Spade had his own morality. He always tried to give his clients good value for their money.

Q. *What about Raymond Chandler's Philip Marlowe?*

P.D.J.: "A man who is neither tarnished nor afraid. He must be a *complete* man in his own world and a *good* enough man for any world." Chandler says at the end of that passage, I believe, that if there were enough men like Philip Marlowe, the world would be a very safe place to live in, and yet not too dull to be *worth* living in. I believe it was that same brilliant essay, *The Simple Art of Murder,* in which Chandler also attempted to demolish the genre of the English detective mystery. He said it should be taken away from the vicarage and handed over to those who understood it. He wrote that the English may not be the best writers in the world, but they are the best *dull* writers in the world.

Q. *You hear that charge of "dull" writing from readers who prefer the pace and action of hard-boiled mysteries.*

P.D.J.: Actually, Chandler was not saying that the *writing* was dull. Only that that *kind* of crime writing was dull, in the sense that it was *unrealistic,* prettifying and romanticizing murder, but having little to do with real blood-and-guts tragedy. This was very true of many books written in the so-called Golden Age of the English mystery. One simply cannot take these as realistic books about murder, about the horror of murder, the tragedy of murder, the harm that murder does.

Q. *And yet, Agatha Christie is very popular here in the United States—along with such traditionalist British writers as Ngaio Marsh, Margery Allingham, Edmund Crispin, Michael Innes.*

P.D.J.: There's been a huge resurgence of interest here in England, too. Many of the old favorites, which have been out of print, are now being reissued. They were wonderfully ingenious, all those red herrings and false clues. But in that period, readers expected the murderer to be *diabolically* clever, and everything else became subordinate to the ingenuity of the puzzle, including character and motivation. That is the real criticism made of those writers; and for many of them, it certainly is a valid criticism.

Q. *Since you admire the moral integrity of certain hard-boiled heroes, how do you account for readers' strong genre preferences?*

P.D.J.: The separate traditions, of course, are quite distinctive in their appeal. The American crime novel seems to be very much in the hard-boiled tradition that emerged in the aftermath of the First World War—the end of puritanism, the Depression, Prohibition, gangsterism and so on. Your heroes tend to be tough and sensational, reacting very instinctively to danger and absorbing more punishment. Your stories are also generally set in a more violent society.

The British detective story is gentler, more pastoral. Because it is firmly rooted in the soil of British literary tradition, it shares assumptions that are strong in our literature; for example, the assumption that we live in an intelligible and benevolent universe; the assumption that law and order, peace and tranquility are the norm; that crime and violence are the aberration; and that the proper preoccupation of man is to bring order out of chaos. Our stories are also more likely to have happy endings.

Also in English fiction they don't believe the system to be corrupt, certainly. I think that the American private eye sees the police force more as the enemy than as an ally. I think that the English private eye sees the police force more as an ally.

229

The old psychological and moral certainties have changed although in one respect that has had a positive effect on genre fiction, by moving it closer to the so-called straight novel. There's a greater emphasis on stylistic realism, and a *far* greater emphasis on the psychological realism of character.

Q. *Does that realism extend to the depiction of violence?*

P.D.J.: Well, I would hope so, speaking for my own novels, in which I use the formula of the detective story in a realistic manner in order to try to say something that is true about men and women and, in particular, about society. But although it is true that we are a very, very much more violent society than we used to be, murder is still a very uncommon crime in England. I think the total homicide figure is well below 1,000 a year.

Q. *Are there* any crimes, *then that you—or, more properly speaking, your characters—are unlikely to deal with?*

P.D.J.: Yes. I don't think I would feel very happy writing a book about the torture and murder of a child. I think that would be extremely painful to do.

Even in a lawless society, fictional crime need not escalate. Of more interest than the event is what is going on in the mind of your character, who does not need a whole series of increasingly horrific murders in order to react in a believable manner.

Q. *In an age of increasing social turmoil, why are people turning more and more for both pleasure and reassurance to crime genre forms that, however realistic in execution, still adhere to conventions established in other, less turbulent ages?*

P.D.J.: Because they do affirm the intelligibility of the universe; the moral norm; the sanctity of life. And because, at the end, there is a *solution*. I think I'm very frightened of violence. I hate it. I'm very worried by the fact that the world is a much more violent place than when I was a girl. And it may be that by writing mysteries I am able, as it were, to exorcize this fear, which may very well be the same reason why so many people enjoy reading a mystery. It seems to me that the more we live in a society in which we feel our problems—be they international problems of war and peace, racial problems, problems of drugs, problems of violence—to be literally beyond our ability to solve, it seems to me very reassuring to read a popular form of fiction which itself has a problem at the heart of it. One which the reader knows will be solved by the end of the book; and not by supernatural means or good luck, but by human intelligence, human courage, and human perseverance. That seems to me one of the reasons why the crime novel, in all its forms and varieties, does hold its place in the affections of its readers.

49

HISTORICAL DETECTION, UNLIMITED

BY ALLISON THOMPSON

YOU WAKE UP ONE MORNING with a terrific idea for an historical novel. Your heroine will be called Jennifer (Stormy? Shana?), and she will always wear her waist-length red hair loose and flowing. Your hero— Blaze? Colt? Randy?— will defy the conventions of the time and . . .

But what were the conventions of the time they lived in? And are those names really appropriate for the period? Are you in command of your facts, or will your intelligent reader groan at the historical anachronisms you use? It's time you engage in some historical detective work to keep your novel from being illogical, inconsistent, and contrary to the easily obtained historical facts.

Engaging in historical detection has two important benefits. First, increased accuracy will save you from receiving *un*-fan mail, letters that begin: "Dear Sir or Madam, It has obviously escaped your attention that . . ." Second, your work will take on a new richness. Readers won't simply skim your prose to discover exactly when the hero and heroine fall into bed together; instead, they will be transported to a different era. They'll gag when the maggots writhe in the bread that the sailors must choke down in the ship's dark hold; they'll gasp when the heroine feels faint from the tight lacing of the corset stays that squeeze her waist into a fourteen-inch circle; they'll marvel at the gaslights that so miraculously illumine the London streets already disappearing under the first smog of the early days of the Industrial Revolution. Your characters will live with all the passions and prejudices of the period. You will produce a greater richness of plot twists and developments.

So how do you begin? How and where do you start your research, and how do you organize all that information?

Begin your research with some general sources, such as the encyclopedia or one of the many well-written, illustrated books that encapsulate the social history of a given period. Skim these to set the basic facts of the period in your mind. Also helpful are the "timeline" books available in most libraries that list concurrent events in politics, science, art, music, literature, and world affairs. These sources give you a sense of continuity and can also be a useful source of plot developments.

Once you've done your basic research on the period, try to avoid "secondary" sources, as they tend to be too general for the historical detective; instead, look for works that focus on a particular aspect of the period in which you are interested, such as Dorothy Hartley's study of rural life in fifteenth-century England, *Lost Country Life*. Best of all, listen to the people of the time themselves, as they speak through their letters, diaries, and journals. Reading through this material will improve your feel for the language and sentiments of the time. They may also give you useful plot developments, character motivation, and background lore on household expenses, servant problems, and social or political gossip of the day.

Period paintings, fashion plates, illustrations, photographs, and maps

Visual aids are invaluable to the historical detective. Use as many of them as you can. You might, for instance, examine any of the typical family portraits of a wealthy English family of the 1760s: the father, the mother, and two or three children. What are the people doing? Is their pose formal? Imperious? What do their gestures and facial expressions tell you? Do they carry implements such as a sketch pad, a bow and arrows, or a riding crop to indicate that they engage in certain activities? What is the background like? A great house? A gloomy mountain? A rich interior? Do you think you would like these people? Could you see your characters in this setting?

What conventions of physical beauty do the people exhibit? In the highly romantic 1830s, both men and women are portrayed with small heads, huge eyes, and tiny hands and feet, all characteristics thought at the time to exhibit refinement and gentility. By contrast, the "Gibson Girls" of the 1890s are tall, robust and almost Amazonian. Think about how the conventions of beauty affect character and action and vice versa: The droopy, romantic female of the idealistic 1830s would be ill at ease in the ebullient, athletic 1890s.

Don't forget to look for such items as political cartoons; fashion plates; amateur sketches of people, or watercolors of the interiors of houses; period illustrations in books or popular magazine articles; photographs and *cartes des visites*; craftsmen's drawings of furniture, guns or inventions; architects' renditions of houses and public buildings; and merchants' catalogues like those produced by Sears and Roebuck or Montgomery Ward.

Finally, don't forget resources such as atlases and maps, dictionaries (to verify usages of slang terms), and reference works such as *Bartlett's Quotations.*

What did they read?

Immerse yourself in the literature of the period for an appreciation of the social customs of the time and an instinctive ear for the use of the language. Take, for example, Samuel Richardson's *Pamela,* written in the restrained, rational language of 1740. In it, the servant girl heroine, who is so hotly pursued for immoral purposes by her wicked employer, expresses herself in a very different fashion from the impassioned, romantic hero Heathcliffe in Emily Brontë's *Wuthering Heights* (1847). While you might not choose to write in either style, your knowledge of the real sensibilities, speaking styles, and attitudes of the period will add flavor to your work.

For those researching the nineteenth century, periodicals such as *Harper's Magazine* or *Godeys Ladies' Book* are invaluable sources. Read them carefully for the tone of the period, the advertisements and the prices for unusual products, recipes, advice for the care of the ill; views on how to educate children, and the editor's opinions on deportment, education for women, and various political topics.

Read fiction of the periods before and after as well as during the specific period you are researching. Fashions and custom changed more slowly in the past than they do now. Read critically, asking yourself what social conventions a particular book or character exhibits. What does it say about the culture of the time? What are the standards of good and bad conduct? Would your hero or villain speak that way?

Art and music

Get records or tapes from the library and listen to some music of the period. Is it the rational, intellectual, and restrained music of J.S. Bach (1685–1750)? The passionate and romantic preludes of Chopin (1809–1849)? A lively galliard of the 16th and 17th century, or a perky polka of the late Victorian period? The skirl of the bagpipe or the scrape of the fiddle? What kind of music would your characters listen to? Some writers even like to have the music of the period playing while they write.

Look at paintings and sculpture of your period. The orderly interiors of the Dutch Renaissance painters represent a culture and perception of man and nature that is entirely different from the paintings of the French Impressionists.

Read etiquette books, cookery books

Etiquette manuals, beginning with Castiglione's *The Book of the Courtier* (1528) and moving through the precepts of Lord Chesterfield (1774), give an invaluable glimpse not only of what was considered proper behavior, but of the more common *improper* behavior the reader is exhorted to shun. You can learn from them what separated a gentleman from a commoner, and how a wise mistress managed servants, taught her children, and maintained the affections of her husband. Historical detectives of the nineteenth century will in particular want to read Isabella Beeton's book on cookery and domestic economy, published in 1861, and Catherine Beecher's *Treatise On The Domestic Economy* of 1846.

Historical Societies, Lecture Series, and Specialty Publications

Many cities and states have historical societies that can provide the historical detective with unusual local source materials. In addition to their research function, these organizations often sponsor special historical exhibits and lecture series. Your local art museum or gallery may also run lecture series to accompany traveling exhibits of historical works. Take advantage of these resources.

Visit antiquarian or used-book stores. In addition to old fiction, biographies, and histories, many also carry sheet music, cookbooks, children's books, and home furnishing books. You will also want to get on the mailing lists of specialty book dealers, such as those dealing in the Civil War or in Celtic lore.

Several publishing houses (in particular Dover Publications, 31 East 2nd Street, Mineola NY 11501) specialize in reprints of old books. Dover's list is particularly rich in nineteenth-century works, and carries books on architecture, plumbing, agricultural implements, and methods of transportation, as well as collections of photographs from the nineteenth century.

Make your research specific. Ask yourself difficult but important questions. Exactly how much can fit into a Conestoga wagon, and what beloved belongings will the heroine have to abandon? How long does it take to reload a muzzle-loader, and how many different steps does it entail? If the hero clasps his corseted mistress to him, will she really feel soft and yielding in his arms? Enlist your local librarian for help in finding answers to questions like these.

What about character and motivation? Could your gently born Regency heroine *really* deny her twenty-one years of strict upbringing to dress up as a highwayman, ride astride, and brandish a pistol?

The process

Taking a little extra time to conduct your research thoroughly will pay off, particularly if you plan to write more than one book set in the same period.

Start a bibliography file. On a separate index card for each book or source examined, write down the author, title, publisher, publication date, and your library's call number. If you use more than one library, note its name as well. You might also include the date you read the source, and what pages were particularly helpful.

Make your research notes on large file cards with only one topic point or quotation or fact per card. You can color-coordinate if you like (pink = fashion; green = political history; blue = domestic tips). Later, you'll be able to shuffle the cards around as you write. Note the source of the information by an abbreviated title or a code (also noted on the bibliography card) and include the pages cited. Careful organization and attention to detail at this stage will pay off as you begin to write.

Photocopy everything! It's more practical than having to go back to look at that crucial fashion plate or political cartoon. Remember to write a complete bibliographic citation on each photocopy that you make.

When you finally begin to write, keep in mind that you're not producing a scholarly thesis. The richness of the information that colors but does not dominate your work will make your writing live and will keep your readers coming back for more.

‖ 50

THE BIRTH OF A SERIES CHARACTER

BY GEORGE C. CHESBRO

FOR MOST WRITERS of so-called genre fiction the quest is for a successful series character—a man or woman who, already completely brought to life in the writer's and readers' minds, leaps into action at the drop of a plot to wend his or her perilous way cleverly through the twists and turns of the story to arrive finally, triumphantly at the solution. Great series characters from mystery and spy fiction immediately spring to mind; Sherlock Holmes, James Bond, Sam Spade, Lew Archer, Miss Marple, et al. These characters may simply step on stage to capture the audience's attention, with no need for the copious program notes of characterization that must usually accompany the debut of a new hero or heroine.

Almost two decades ago, when I was just beginning to enjoy some success in selling my short stories, I sat down one day to begin my search for a series character. Visions of great (and some not-so-great) detectives waltzed through my head; unfortunately, all of these dancers had already been brought to life by other people. The difficulty was compounded by the fact that I didn't want just any old character, some guy with the obligatory two fists and two guns who might end up no more than a two-dimensional plot device, a pedestrian problem solver who was but a pale imitation of the giants who had gone before and who were my inspiration. I wanted a *character,* a detective with modern sensibilities, whom readers might come to care about almost as much as they would the resolution of the mystery itself. Sitting at my desk, surrounded by a multitude of rejection slips, I quickly became not only frustrated, but intimidated. I mean, just who did I think I was?

It was a time when "handicapped" detectives were in vogue on television: Ironside solved cases from his wheelchair and van; another was Longstreet, a blind detective. Meditating on this, I suddenly found a most mischievous notion scratching, as it were, at the back door of my mind. I was a decidedly minor league manager looking to sign a player who might one day compete in the major leagues. What to do? The answer, of course, was obvious; if I couldn't hope to create a detective who could reasonably be expected to vie with the giants, then I would create a detective who was unique—a dwarf.

Believing, as I do, that it's good for the soul as well as the imagination, I always allow myself exactly one perverse notion a day (whether I need it or not). I'd had my perverse notion, and it was time to think on. What would my detective look like. What kind of gun would he carry, how big would it be, and how many bullets would it hold?

Scratch, scratch.

Would his trenchcoat be a London Fog or something bought off a pipe rack? What about women? How many pages would I have to devote in each story to descriptions of his sexual prowess?

Scratch, scratch.

The damn dwarf simply refused to go away, and his scratching was growing increasingly persistent. But what was I going to do with a dwarf private detective? Certainly not sell him, since it seemed to me well nigh impossible to make anybody (including me) believe in his existence. Who could take such a character seriously? Who, even in a time of dire need, would hire a dwarf detective? Where would his cases come from? He would *literally* be struggling to compete in a world of giants.

Scratch, scratch.

No longer able to ignore the noises in my head, I opened the door and let the Perverse Notion into the main parlor where I was trying to work. It seemed there was no way I was going to be able to exorcise this aberration, short of actually trying to write something about him.

Observing him, I saw that he was indeed a dwarf, but fairly large and powerfully built, as dwarfs go. That seemed to me a good sign. If this guy was going to be a private detective, he would have to be more than competent at his work; he would need extra dimensions, possess special talents that would at least partially compensate for his size.

Brains never hurt anyone, so he would have to be very smart. Fine. Indeed, I decided that he was not only very smart, but a veritable genius—a professor with a Ph.D. in Criminology; a psychological and spiritual outcast. His name is Dr. Robert Frederickson. Now, where could he live where people wouldn't be staring at him all the time? New York City, of course.

238

So far, so good. The exorcism was proceeding apace.

Fictional private eyes are always getting into trouble, and they have to be able to handle themselves physically. What would Dr. Robert Frederickson do when the two- and three-hundred-pound bad guys came at him? He had to be able to fight. So he'd need some kind of special physical talent.

Dwarfs. Circuses. Ah. Dr. Robert Frederickson had spent some time in the circus (in fact, that was how he had financed his education!). But he hadn't worked in any side show; he'd been a star, a headliner, a gymnast, a tumbler with a spectacular, death-defying act. Right. And he had parlayed his natural physical talents into a black belt in karate. If nothing else, he would certainly have the advantage of surprise. During his circus days he had been billed as "Mongo the Magnificent," and his friends still call him Mongo.

Mongo, naturally, tended to overcompensate, to say the least. He had a mind of a titan trapped in the body of a dwarf (I liked that), and that mind was constantly on the prowl, looking for new challenges. Not content with being a dwarf in a circus (albeit a famous one), he became a respected criminology professor; not content with being "just" a professor, he started moonlighting as a private detective.

But I was still left with the problem of where his cases were going to come from. I strongly doubted that any dwarf detective was going to get much walk-in business, so all of his cases were going to have to come from his associates, people who knew him and appreciated just how able he was, friends from his circus days, colleagues at the university where he teaches and, for good measure, from the New York Police Department, where, his *very* big brother, Garth, is a detective, a lieutenant.

I set about my task, and halfway through the novella that would become "The Drop," hamming it up, I discovered something that brought me up short: Dr. Frederickson was no joke. A major key to his character, to his drive to compete against all odds, was a quest for dignity and respect from others. He insisted on being taken seriously as a human being, and he was constantly willing to risk his life or suffer possible ridicule and humiliation in order to achieve that goal. Dr. Robert Frederickson, a.k.a. Mongo the Magnificent, was one tough cookie, psychologically and physically, and I found that I liked him very much.

And I knew then that, regardless of how he was treated by any incredulous editor, I, at least, would afford this most remarkable man the dignity and respect I felt he so richly deserved. I ended by writing "The Drop" as a straight (well, seriously skewed actually, but serious) detective story.

"The Drop" was rejected. The editor to whom I'd submitted it (he had published my short stories) wrote that sorry, Mongo was just too unbelievable. (Well, of course, he was unbelievable. What the hell did he expect of a dwarf private detective?)

That should have ended my act of exorcism of the Perverse Notion. Fat chance! On the same day "The Drop" was rejected, I sent it right out again to another editor (after all, Mongo would never have given up so easily), who eventually bought it.

The next day I sat down and started Mongo on his second adventure. Mongo was no longer the Perverse Notion; I had created a man who intrigued me enormously, a man I liked and respected, a most complex character about whom I wanted to know more, and who fired my imagination.

My Perverse Notion in that second story was to include a bit of dialogue in which Garth tells Mongo, after some particularly spectacular feat, that he's lucky he's not a fictional character, because no one would believe him. "High Wire" sold the first time out—to the first editor, and this time he never mentioned a word again about Mongo's believability. Four more Mongo novellas followed and were published. In the seventh, "Candala," it seemed I had sent Mongo out too far beyond the borders defining what a proper detective/mystery story should be, into the dank, murky realms of racial discrimination, self-hate and self-degradation. I couldn't place "Candala" anywhere, and it went into the darkness of my trunk.

But Mongo himself remained very much alive. I was still discovering all sorts of things about the Frederickson brothers, and the curious psychological and physical worlds they moved in; they needed larger quarters, which could be provided only in a novel.

Six Mongo novels later, Mongo and Garth continue to grow in my mind, and they continue to fire my imagination. In fact, that Perverse Notion proved to be an invaluable source of inspiration. Mongo has, both literally and figuratively, enriched my life, and he and Garth are the primary reasons that I was finally able to realize my own "impossible dream" of making my living as a writer.

"Candala" finally appeared in print, between hardcovers, in an anthology entitled, *An Eye for Justice*.

It is always risky business to try to extrapolate one's own feelings or experiences into the cheap currency of advice to others (especially in regard to that most painfully personal of pursuits, writing). However, the thought occurs to me that a belief in, and a respect for, even the most improbable of your characters in their delicate period of gestation is called for. That Perverse Notion you don't want to let in, because you fear you will waste time and energy feeding and nurturing it for no reward, may be the most important and helpful character, series or otherwise—you'll ever meet in your life.

51

PACING A THRILLER

BY BILL GRANGER

PACING MAKES OR BREAKS A THRILLER.

Have a good plot but slow it down with too much description, scene-setting, pointless dialogue or narrative explanation of what the hell is going on—and you've lost the novel. Good characters will be imprisoned by slow movement; it's the reason Henry James couldn't do spy novels, but Conan Doyle could.

Pacing is paring essentially, down to the point at which the landscape is still recognizable, but not to the point at which it turns out to be just desert.

It's happened to me: I've written books I'd like to whack twenty thousand words of ugly out of if I had a chance now, just to improve the pacing. I know more than I knew then.

Learn from my mistakes.

Pacing is a character in a thriller. It is the unspoken presence of something like fate or destiny rushing all the other characters to some final collision and resolution. "Rushing" is key, but like most keys, it should be turned slowly to make work.

Never let your reader know he's being rushed. You can't do it with words. Running "breathlessly" won't do it, having characters aware of "events closing in" is TV-ese, and ominous clocks striking off the minutes to midnight is nonsense better left to the cover of the *Bulletin for Atomic Scientists*.

Rush your readers along by these methods:

• *Set a deadline early on.* Forty-eight hours to resolve this; seven days to find so-and-so; et cetera. Unless you are a bad writer or your reader a great lummox (and never assume a reader is stupid—I don't), he'll pick up the initial point and respond to subtle, *sotto voce* reminders the rest of the way. Time in a novel is not a strong suit, but it can be trump if the element of time is intrinsically important to the plot.

Take James Grady's *Six Days of the Condor* (shortened, inexplicably, in the movie to "three days").

● *Change of scene.* Background is a character as well. If Character A is in Beirut, then the next chapter can show character B in London, trying to counter whatever A is doing. The reader gets the kick of being on top of events but also the rush of leaving one highlight for another. It's a little like channel-switching during NFL Sunday afternoons when strong games are being played on two channels simultaneously. Under steady control, changing the scene from chapter to chapter works well as a rush-builder. I recommend studying early Len Deighton for this. Aw, shucks, you can read it in my novel, *The Man Who Heard Too Much.*

● *Physical movement of characters.* No more compelling chapter on war has been written than Hemingway's description of the allied retreat in Italy in World War I in *A Farewell to Arms.* By the end of it, *you* have retreated, and you are as wounded, exhausted, and shell-shocked as everyone else. He did it with run-on sentences and breathless narrative that, nonetheless, was very precise, even in its hallucinatory passages. Try it.

The next step in improved pacing is to rethink the chapter.

The chapter, I now think, should begin in the middle. The reader has grown bored with old-fashioned openings describing scenery or mood or weather (though I still use these beginnings—briefly—for catch-your-breath chapters).

Unless it is necessary to set the mood, time, weather, locale, et cetera, start with action. And that doesn't mean violent action, either.

Here is something I have in mind:

After they made love again, they fell apart on the bed and thought separate things.

After they made love again establishes time, relationship, and certainly does tend to create a mood. You are suddenly in the chapter.
Another:

Tommy wasn't sure why the pistol felt heavy. He had carried a pistol before. He looked at it with curiosity. Maybe it was because he had never intended to kill anyone before.

A little melodramatic, but you get the idea. Tommy has a pistol, he is carrying it, he is thinking about why it is so heavy and—bam—we know he is on his way to kill someone. Pacing has flung the reader smack into a chapter he can't put down. Mickey Spillane—especially in the early Mike Hammer stories—and Hemingway, in his short stories, were masters of flinging the reader into a scene. Lawrence Block and Eugene Izzi are also very, very good at this aspect of the craft and will probably resent my giving away hard-won secrets.

Pacing, again, is paring. Write the way you like. But when you're done, go back over it. What was the point of that piece of description? That bit of background? Would an oral storyteller have used it to set up his punchline? If the answer is yes, good—keep it in. If no, see if it might be needed anyway. A good writer knows *when to slow down a thriller as well as speed it along.* No one can take 250 pages of bam, bam, bam. Soft passages are needed bridges in symphonies and novels. Relentlessness can destroy good pacing—but a soft bridge between highs does not have to be reed-weak with extra dialogue and phony descriptions. Let the mellow flow naturally, along with the more violent parts. Readers should not be aware of pacing manipulation by the author; they should merely smile broadly as they close your novel and say, "That was a good read."

52

PLOT AND CHARACTER IN SUSPENSE FICTION

BY JOAN AIKEN

WHICH CAME FIRST, the chicken or the egg? Does plot arise from character, or character from plot? The question is in many ways an artificial one; most writers have felt, at one time or another, the heady excitement of knowing that a whole story, or at least its basic elements—plot, character, and development all tangled together—is struggling to emerge from the dark.

But if this does not happen?

"What is character," says Henry James in *The Art of Fiction* (1884), "but the determination of incident? What is incident but the illustration of character?" And the Old Master goes on to add (several pages later), "The story and the novel, the idea and the form, are the needle and the thread, and I never heard of a guild of tailors who recommended the use of the thread without the needle, or the needle without the thread."

Perfectly true, and you have to have both before you can begin. But, suppose you have only half of the combination?

Characters are generally the problem. *Plots* come a dime a dozen, they are easy to pick up. We read them every day in the papers. A mother, even after several years, remains positive that the death of her teenage son, classified as suicide, was not so; but whenever she pushes her inquiries about it, other unexplained deaths take place. The pet poodle of a notorious Chicago mobster is stolen. The CIA sets up a spurious marine engineering firm in an effort to salvage a sunken Soviet submarine. A middle-aged woman demands a daily love poem from her browbeaten husband. A descendant of one of the twenty-one victims of the Boston Molasses Disaster is still seeking compensation. A convention of magicians plans to meet in an Indian town, but the citizens raise strong objections. . . .

Any of these incidents, all culled from the daily press, might trigger a

245

story, might produce that wonderful effervescent sensation, familiar to every writer (it really is like the working of yeast in one's mind), when different elements begin to ferment together and create something new. The best plots, of course, instantly create their own characters. That wife, that domineering wife, compelling her husband to produce a new love lyric every evening: we know at once what she would be like. And the cowardly put-upon husband, submitting to this tyranny, trudging off to the library for new rhymes and new verse forms, until the climactic moment when he rebels, and supplies you with the start of your story. Or the grieving, brooding mother, worrying on and on about her son's death, gradually acquiring little bits of information. It would be very easy to tell her story.

But if you have the plot without the characters?

There's nothing so frustrating for the reader as a potentially interesting, intricate story, full of turns and twists, in which the characters are so flat, machine-made, and lifeless that they form a total barrier to following the course of the narrative, because it is impossible to remember who is who. Is Miranda the actress or the secretary? Was it Wilmost whose car was stolen, or Harris? Is Casavecchia the gangster or the millionaire? Why *does* Kate hate Henry?

In murder mysteries and procedural detective novels, character portrayal is not so important. The reader won't expect great depth among the victims and suspects, while the detective probably has a number of well-established peculiarities, built up over a series of books: he is Spanish, wears elegant grey silk suits, and carries his exclamation point upside down; or he is very fat and drinks a pint of beer on every page; or he is a rabbi; or she is female, karate-trained, and has a huge wardrobe, which is just as well, since the vicissitudes of her job frequently reduce her clothes to tatters. We know all these and love them as old friends.

The problem of character arises most particularly—and can be a real handicap—in suspense novels.

Suspense novels are deservedly popular, but very hard to define. They are not murder mysteries. They are not just straight novels, because something nasty and frightening is bound to happen. That is the promise to the reader. They are not spy stories, and they are certainly not procedurals. One of the very best suspense novels ever written, *A Dram of Poison,* by Charlotte Armstrong, had no murder in it at all, not even any death (except a natural one in the first chapter, setting off the whole course of events), but it possesses more riveting tension than any other story I can recall.

In a suspense novel, the element of character matters very much indeed. The hero/heroine is pitted, not against organized crime or international terrorism, but against a personal enemy, a personal problem; the conflict is on an individual, adversarial level. And so, if either hero or hero's enemy is not a flesh-and-blood, fully rounded, recognizable entity, the tension slackens, the credulity drops.

In *A Dram of Poison,* all the mischief is caused in the first place by the arrival of the hero's sister, one of those terrible, self-satisfied, know-it-all characters (plainly Charlotte Armstrong wrote the story in the white heat of having recently encountered one of them) who can always interpret other people's motives and give them some disagreeable psychological twist. By her confident assertions, she soon has the heroine paralyzed with self-distrust and the hero downright suicidal. Then, in between the breathless excitement of trying to find what he did with that wretched little bottle of poison he had meant to swallow, the reader has the fearful pleasure of knowing that, in the end, odious Sister Ethel is bound to receive her comeuppance.

Charlotte Armstrong was particularly skilled at villains; the frightful parasitical pair of sisters who, in *Mask of Evil,* (originally published as *The Albatross*) come and prey on the two central characters are particularly memorable, with their sweet saintly selfishness. The sense of being *invaded,* taken over, in their own home, by repulsive aliens, was particularly well conveyed in that story.

The suspense novel is often a closed-world plot. The hero/heroine must battle it out against the adversary in a situation that, for some reason, allows for no appeal to outside help. There must be valid reasons for this. If not a snowstorm, with all phone lines down, then the villain has bruited it around that the hero is hysterical, unbalanced, alcoholic, a drug abuser, or just traumatized by recent grief so no call for help will be heeded or believed.

Ursula Curtiss had a particular gift for these enclosed-world situations, and she had a masterly touch with villains as well. It is an interesting exercise to compare some of her stories with others, for she was a very fertile creator of creepy domestic-suspense plots. Many of her ideas were brilliant, but some of them succeeded far better than others. Why? Because of the characters with which they were animated. *Voice Out of Darkness,* which has a fine snowy Connecticut setting and an excellent basic idea—harking back to the long-ago question of whether the heroine did or did not push her very unpleasant adoptive sister under the ice when they were both eleven—yet somehow fails to come off because it is peopled with rather stock characters: two handsome young men, two pretty girls, and some recognizable small-town citizens, the drunk writer, the gossipy lady. Her novel, *The Stairway,* however, is pure gold from the first page to the last. Why? Because of its villainness, the repulsive Cora. Judged dispassionately, the plot is simple and only just credible. Madeline, the heroine, is married to Stephen, an intolerable man whom she is about to divorce, a monster of tyranny who terrifies her small son. But Stephen falls downstairs and breaks his neck. Cora, the humble cousin, the poor relation, by pretending to believe that Madeline pushed him, gradually assumes more and more dominance over the household and seems all set to stay for the rest of her life. Madeline, in a bind because *she* believes that *Cora* pushed Stephen, feels that she can't betray her and is helpless. All this, given a moment's cool thought, seems hard to swallow. Why had Madeline married the horrendous Stephen in the first place? Why should she submit to Cora for a single moment? But Cora is made so *real,* with her greediness, her anxious, reproachful air, her dreadful clothes, her fondness for eating candy out of a paper bag and rustling the sheets of the newspaper, that all she does and says is instantly, completely credible.

Playwright Edward Albee once observed that the test he had for the solidity of his characters was to imagine them in some situation other than the play he had in mind and see if they would continue to behave in a real manner. The character of Cora would be credible and recognizable whether we saw her in a hospital ward, a supermarket, or a graveyard.

The Stairway was an early Curtiss novel, but one of her later ones, *The Poisoned Orchard,* contains the same terrifying claustrophobic, inturned quality, again because of its hateful and convincing villainness, the heroine's cousin Fen, and her accomplice, the cleaning lady, Mrs. List. This sinister pair have Sarah the heroine hog-tied, especially clowning, ugly, self-assured Fen, who continually manages to force her much nicer, much better-looking cousin into the unenviable role of straight man refusing to laugh at Fen's jokes. The relationship between the two is beautifully and most credibly realized, so that the reader is prepared to swallow the fact that Fen and her evil ally seem to be omniscient and omnipresent, able to anticipate Sarah's efforts to combat their plots almost before she can make a move. And what is it all about? We hardly know. A wicked deed, way back in Fen's past, that is catching up with her. And anyway, what can they *do* to Sarah? It hardly matters. The point is that they are menacing, and that she is more and more at their mercy. Fen is a wholly convincing monster, the more so because she is quick-witted and amusing, as well as being unprincipled. *Fear* is the essential ingredient of a suspense novel, and fear can be achieved only if the reader thoroughly sympathizes with the main character and thoroughly believes in the villain.

If the villain is less convincing, then the main character must be made more so.

Dick Francis, the English writer of deservedly best-selling mysteries with horse-racing backgrounds, wrote an interesting early novel, *Nerve,* in which all the jockeys on the turf were being persecuted by a well-known TV personality who secretly spread malicious gossip about them, prevented their getting to races on time, and had their horses doped. Why does he do this? Because he, son of a famous racehorse owner, is terrified of horses, and therefore psychotically jealous of all who succeed in the horsey world.

What a preposterous theme it sounds, set down in cold blood. And the villainous TV star, Maurice Kemp-Lore, somewhat sketchily depicted, only just makes his murderous obsession credible to the reader. What does give the book immediate life, great energy and plausibility, so that it moves at a rattling pace and carries the reader along, completely hooked by the story, is the treatment of the hero. As always in Dick Francis novels, the hero tells the story in the first person; in common with other Francis heroes he is an odd man out, who has fallen into the racing world by a series of accidents. Descended from a family of professional musicians, he is the only non-musical one; despised by his kin, he has had to justify himself in some other direction. The contrast between the hero's elegant relations conducting Beethoven at the London Festival Hall, while he gallops through the mud at Ascot, is bizarre enough to be convincing, so that we are passionately on the hero's side as he struggles to combat what he begins to recognize as a sinister plot against his whole *raison d'être*. The villain remains shadowy, but the hero, in this case, carries enough weight to sustain the story.

Given a satisfactory plot, it should not be too hard to equip it with characters. But what if the boot is on the other foot?

Some writers are compulsive character collectors. Wherever they go, they watch, listen, record, jot down notes and descriptions: the fat woman in the black-striped dress at the rail station with two elegant little pig-tailed girls, also in black-and white striped outfits, hanging on her arms. The lanky, unshaven six-foot male in the subway, with a shock of red hair and gold rings in his ears. The professional portrait painter, met at a party, who has produced a portrait every two months for the last twenty years, and has a photographic eye for a face. The woman who, though courteous and well-mannered, is an obsessive corrector, so that she can never hear a sentence spoken without chipping in to put the speaker right—politely, but *oh, so* firmly. . .

Character collecting is an excellent habit, because sooner or later some of these characters will start to move.

You have a whole cast of characters, but no plot. So: Make extensive notes about them—their preferences, dislikes, habits, childhood history. Like Edward Albee, set them in different environments, confront them with crises. What would the woman in the black-striped dress do if she were in charge of forty school children on a sinking cruise liner? Make them encounter each other. Suppose the portrait painter were sitting in a subway train, drawing lightning sketches, and the man with red hair and gold earrings, unaccountably angry at being drawn, grabs the sketchbook and gets out at the next stop? A character may suddenly get up and walk away, pulling a skein of plot behind him. Suppose they then meet by chance, somewhere else?

Imagine Jane Austen saying to herself, "Now, let's tell a story about a sensible practical sister and a self-indulgent, overemotional sister. What sort of men shall they fall in love with?"

Suppose in writing *Sense and Sensibility,* she turned her story the other way round. Suppose sensible Elinor had fallen in love with handsome, romantic Willoughby, and susceptible Marianne had been bowled over by reliable, prosaic Edward? But, no, it won't work. Marianne could never have fallen for Edward, not in a thousand years. Jane Austen, even at a young age (she was twenty-two), had her characters and plot inextricably twined together, one growing out of the other; there is no separating them. But it is fun to probe and investigate and reconsider; fun, after all, is what writing is all about. Jane Austen took huge pleasure in writing *Sense and Sensibility.* The fact is evident; she knew these characters entirely before she put pen to paper.

What is the best way of displaying your characters?

There are, of course, hundreds, but the worst way is to describe them flatly.

My recent novel, *Blackground,* has the theme of two characters who marry in romantic haste, and then, on a winter honeymoon in Venice where they are, as it were, suspended together in a vacuum, they discover that they had in fact met long ago and aren't at all the people each thinks the other to be. To make this as much of a shock as I intended, both of them and, hopefully, for the reader, I had to be familiar with their life stories right back to childhood. In order not to a) begin too early or b) bore the reader with too much flashback, I make Character A tell his story to Character B on the honeymoon, while hers is disclosed to the reader in snatches throughout the narrative.

Michael Gilbert, a writer of several different kinds of mysteries, whose characters are always remarkably individual and three-dimensional, adopts a very swift and vivid method of displaying his quite large cast of characters in his suspense novel *The Night of the Twelfth* (about sadistic murders in a boys' school). Sometimes a whole chapter is divided into blocks of conversation, often only about half a page—between A and B, between B and C, between C and A, between A and D—these fast-moving dialogues equally convey character and advance the action.

Sometimes you know your character *too* well; you could write volumes about his quirks and complications. But how do you get all this across to the reader without being pompous, or overexplicit?

How about portraying this person as seen through the eyes of another narrator, quite a simple soul (like Nelly Dean, the housekeeper in *Wuthering Heights,* who tells much of the story), or even a child? *What Maisie Knew,* by Henry James, can be an example to us all.

"Try to be one of those people on whom nothing is lost," said Henry James.

Perfect advice for a writer!

‖ 53

WRITING THE REALISTIC WESTERN NOVEL

BY RICHARD S. WHEELER

THE TRADITIONAL WESTERN NOVEL has always been hedged about with more conventions than any other category, with the possible exception of women's romances. The publishers of hardcover library westerns have allowed a certain freedom recently, but the mass market houses that spin out the novels that fill the paperback racks have essentially the same requirements as ever.

These conventions dictate that the story occur some time between the Civil War and the 1890s, roughly when the frontier vanished; also that those westerns be about loners in armed conflict—for example, the young rancher just starting out who must fight off the predatory cattle king. With very few exceptions over the years, the central figure in westerns had to be male, as in the gunman-type story. These male protagonists had to be of heroic and mythic stature. Their character is commanding: They rarely wonder what course of action is wisest or dither about what to do. Usually, they are hardy and strong, skilled in various martial arts, from gunmanship to brawling. As is true of all mythic characters, they don't grow or change as a result of their trials, but triumph because of their innate superiority over their antagonists.

Very few traditional western heroes are married. The women that do appear are portrayed as secondary figures. There is no substantial love interest, although love is not totally forbidden. But emotions are largely taboo: The mythic western heroes are poker-faced and stoic and avoid anything resembling rage, tears, shame, tenderness or laughter, and it's especially important that they not express gentle or poetic feelings. They are born leaders who never seem to suffer dissent or rebellion of their allies, and who enjoy the unquestioning obedience of women.

Another convention of the classic western is that characters are shown only in the depiction of action. Readers must never be made privy to the hero's private torments or doubts, or his rejoicing or dreams, lest the flow of action be interrupted. As a result, we rarely see a fully rounded western hero.

I have described here the classic Louis L'Amour western hero and story, and because of his awesome success, few publishers have ever deviated from the formula. L'Amour, who dominated the field for so many years, was both an asset and liability to the western story. At one point in the early 1980s, he was virtually the only author of single-title (not series) westerns being published, and he kept the category alive at a time when publishers had largely abandoned it. But if he was the rescuer of the category, he was also unwittingly responsible for keeping it in a straitjacket. His very success at writing the mythic, romantic western ensured that the mass market houses would not deviate from stories about a frontier west that never really existed. And sad to say, I believe his influence narrowed down the western market, driving away women readers, and especially better-educated readers who might have enjoyed a story about real, flawed mortals wrestling with the terrible dangers of a real frontier and wilderness. His influence was so profound that in his later years the type of western story accepted by publishers narrowed more than ever. As a result, gifted earlier authors who wrote of the west in broader strokes—Ernest Haycox in particular—would have found their manuscripts unwelcome. Haycox's women—the wives, sweethearts, or allies of his heroes—were much too feisty to fit into the L'Amour tradition.

As much as I have loved the western story all my life, I found these ironclad rules daunting. When I began writing westerns in the mid-seventies, I yearned to tell a more realistic story, about real people challenging the awesome difficulties posed by the wild west. A person of ordinary courage promised to be a better protagonist than the mythic type whose victory is foreordained. There seemed to me a much better possibility of suspense, or story tension, cowardice and honor, skill and clumsiness, moral certitude, and occasional weakness. Such a protagonist can fail; he could grow or shrink, but certainly not remain the same by the end of the story.

In the course of my extensive research, I discovered something else: The real historical west offers far better material, more colorful and fantastic, than the wildest imaginings of the romantic western novelists. For a brief, unique period in the 19th century, the great western expansion into unknown lands fraught with dangers captured the imagination of the country—indeed, of the world. There had never been anything like it, and never will be again. Far from being exhausted and arid as a result of innumerable western novels, films, and TV series, the *real* frontier west is virtually untouched, virginal material available to any novelist. The traditional mythic western has used this material only as backdrop, or stage setting, while focusing on its real theme, male pecking-order struggles between loners on a lawless land, where the social rules didn't apply. But the real west was rarely like that. The real stories and characters are much wilder, more violent, more astonishing than anything on the paperback racks.

When I set out to write westerns, I had one additional goal: to appeal to a more educated, literate readership. That meant doing two things: using a rich vocabulary, on a level with any serious novel, along with effective metaphors and other figures of speech. Here I butted against a style common in traditional westerns, which are written in the most basic, pedestrian language.

My second purpose was to deepen my characters, work within their heads, in a way that didn't slow the story. One way to do this is to make the characters' calculations a part of the plot itself.

I've had the good fortune to have editors who have permitted me to write nontraditional westerns and have encouraged me to reach toward literary quality. I set my two western series in the 1840s and 1850s, which I find much richer than the post-Civil War era. The result of all this has been a number of novels that are about as far removed from the usual category western as possible. In one, the hero is a Harvard-educated Boston Brahmin. In another, there's a venal sheriff too fat to ride a horse, so he covers his county in a buggy. In another, the hero is a former mountain man, now a trader to the Blackfeet, who'd been a classics professor at Amherst. In one of my series, the hero is an Irish doctor pressed temporarily into being a sheriff. In another series, Skye's West, the hero is a former British sailor who jumped ship and is now a boozy guide with an older Crow wife and younger Shoshone wife and a singularly evil horse. In one of my novels, the heroine is a clever con artist who matches wits with a rascal. In yet another, the hero is a farmer who's clawed a fortune in gold out of a Montana gulch,

254

only to lose it to road agents. Is he brave? No, he falls to the ground, weeping, but is later redeemed by other values.

One could scarcely imagine western heroes, or situations, farther removed from the L'Amour approach. And yet they are succeeding, some of them handsomely. And more important, they are being read by people who otherwise don't read westerns. I've written traditional stories, too, most recently one that reworks the *Shane* theme about the man familiar with weapons but who doesn't wish to use them again—in this case a young banker. But the nontraditional story is my joy.

All of which is to say that it is possible to market western stories that buck the category tradition. Much of the work of Elmer Kelton and Will Henry lies outside the stock category approach. Likewise, some of Jack Schaefer's work and the western stories of Doug Jones and Ben Capps, whose work has inspired and influenced me.

Change is in the air. It began, actually, with Larry McMurtry's great Pulitzer-Prize-winning novel, *Lonesome Dove,* back in 1985. That novel is a watershed in western fiction, and well worth close study; it is a model of what can be accomplished in a nontraditional western novel. Others worth study are Will Henry's *I, Tom Horn,* Jack Schaefer's *Monte Walsh,* and Elmer Kelton's *The Good Old Boys.* All of these transcend the realm of the category story. They can be considered literature, and are delightful, realistic expressions of frontier life.

In spite of the recent suspension or reduction of several western lines, the frontier story is not in danger of extinction. Both Bantam and Zebra continue publishing this category. The present turmoil is really an opportunity for writers to write and publish new forms of westerns, stories that will appeal to the broad national audiences that the old *Saturday Evening Post* attracted with serialized westerns enjoyed by people in all walks of life. A bold novelist willing to research and write about the *real* frontier, use realistic heroes and story lines instead of mythic ones, and add literary graces to the genre, can capture a new market for himself and his publishers. The historical frontier is a new frontier.

54

THINK OF THE READER

BY PIERS ANTHONY

I AM KNOWN AS A WRITER of popular fantasy and science fiction, though my output is not limited to that. Thus my view is that of a genre writer who is trying to understand more general principles.

Back when I was struggling to break into print, I took a correspondence course in writing. The instructors knew a great deal about writing, but little about science fiction. No matter, they said; the fundamentals of good writing apply to all genres, and they could help me. They were only half right: the fundamentals do apply, but you do have to know the genre—any genre—in order to write successfully for it. I studied my market on my own, and in the end I made it on my own. From this I derive a principle: There is virtue in being ornery. I continue to be ornery and continue to score in ways the critics seem unable to fathom.

A writer *should* study his market, and study general principles; both are essential. He should also forge his own way, contributing such limited originality as the market will tolerate. There is plenty of excellent instruction elsewhere on such things. I am concerned here with a more subtle yet vital aspect of writing than most: the writer's liaison with the reader. This can make or break a piece of writing, yet few seem to grasp its significance. This is one of my many differences with critics, so I will use them as a straw man to help make my point.

I picture a gathering of the elite of the genre, who are there to determine the critic's choice of the best works of science fiction and fantasy of all time. That is, the List that will be graven on granite for the edification of the lesser aspirants. In the genre these would be Samuel Delany's *Dhalgren*, Brian Aldiss' *Report on Probability A*, and Russell Hoban's *Riddley Walker*, and the finest writer of all time would be J. G. Ballard, despite his one failure with *Empire of the Sun*.

Have you read any of these? Have you even heard of them? No, except that you did like the motion picture based on the last? Well, the critics have an answer for you: You are an ignorant lout whose library card and book store privileges should be suspended until your tastes improve.

Yet any ordinary person who tries to read such books will wonder just what world such critics live in. The answer is, of course, a different world. They are like the poet Shelley's Ozymandias, whose colossal ruin lies in the barren sand. "Look on my works, ye mighty, and despair." Yet his works are completely forgotten.

I am in the world of commercial writing, which means it is readable and enjoyable, and the only accolade it is likely to receive from critics is a mock award for WHO KILLED SCIENCE FICTION? (I was in a five-way tie for runner-up on that one last year, but there's hope for the future.)

But I maintain that the essence of literature lies in its assimilation by the ordinary folk, and that readability is the first, not the last criterion for its merit. Therefore I address the subject of writing, regardless of genre, from this perspective. What makes it readable? To hell with formal rules of writing; they are guidelines in the absence of talent and should be honored only so long as they do not interfere. If it's clear and interesting and relates to the needs of the reader, it will score. I like to tell audiences that they may love or hate what I write, but they will be moved by it. Then I prove it. The only person to fall asleep during one of my recent readings was a senior editor. Well, there are limits, and even I can't squeeze much blood from a stone. I am successful in part because I make connections with my readers that bypass the editors as well as the critics.

How do I do it? Well, there are little tricks, and one big secret. All of them are so simple that it's a wonder they aren't practiced by every writer. But they are not, and indeed critics condemn them, and editors try to excise them from my manuscripts. I have had many an inter-necine battle with editors, and finally left a major publisher because of this. I understand I am known as a difficult writer to work with, though no editor says it to my face. I can't imagine why!

All the tricks can be subsumed under one guideline: *Think of the reader.* Do it at every stage. Every paragraph, every word. If you are writing fantasy, don't use a word like "subsumed" because the reader won't understand it. It's a lovely word, but unless your readership consists of intellectuals or folk interested in precise usage—such as

257

those who are presumed to read a book like this one—forgo your private pleasure, and speak more plainly. "All the tricks add up to this." I can with ease overreach the horizons of my readers, but I do my damnedest not to. Any writer who thinks he's smart when he baffles his readers, whether by using foreign phrases or obscure terminology, is the opposite.

When you refer to a character or situation that has not been mentioned for some pages, refresh the matter for the reader, so that he won't have to leaf back interminably to find out what you're talking about. Don't say, "The List is foolish." Huh? What list? Say "The List of the critics' top genre novels I parodied above is foolish." Editors seem to hate this; they blue-pencil it out as redundancy. But it enables the reader to check in with your concept without pausing, and that's what counts. Never let your reader stumble; lead him by the hand—and do it without patronizing him.

When you introduce a new character, don't just throw him at the reader unprepared. Have him introduced by a familiar character, if you possibly can. In my forthcoming mainstream novel *Firefly*, I start with one character, who later meets another, and then I follow the other character. That one meets a third, and I follow the third. In the course of 150,000 words, the only character the reader meets cold is the first one. Thus the reader can proceed smoothly throughout, never tripping. It was a job to arrange some of the handoffs, but that *is* my job as a writer: to do the busy-work for the reader. Some of the concepts in this novel are mind-stretching, but the little tricks smooth the way.

When I do a series—and I've done ten so far—I try to make each novel stand by itself, so that the reader who comes to it new does not have to struggle with an ongoing and confusing situation. Yes, this means repeating and summarizing some material, and it is a challenge to do that without boring those who have read the prior novels. But it means, for example, that a reader can start with my tenth Xanth novel and read backwards toward the first, and enjoy them all. Xanth has many readers, and this is part of the reason: It is easy to get into, and it does not demand more than the reader cares to give. Perhaps no other series shows a greater dichotomy between the contempt of critics and the devotion of readers. I do know my market, and it is not the critics. I suspect the same is true for most commercial writers.

Science fiction is fantastic stuff. Little of it is truly believable, and less is meant to be. It represents a flight of fancy for the mind, far removed from the dullness of mundane affairs. Yet even there, human values are paramount. There needs to be respect for every situation and every character, no matter how far out. Every thing is real on its own terms, and every one is alive, even when the thing is as outrageous as a night mare who is a female horse carrying bad dreams and the one is the Incarnation of Death itself, complete with scythe. Can a robot have feelings? Yes, and they are similar to those of a human being. For in the tacit symbolism of the genre as I practice it, a humanoid robot may be a man whose color, religion, or language differs from those of the culture into which he is thrust, and his feelings are those any of us would experience if similarly thrust. The essence of the genre is human, even when it is alien.

I am in an ongoing situation that illustrates the way that even the most fantastic and/or humorous fiction can relate to serious life. A twelve-year-old girl walking home from school was struck by a drunk driver and spent three months in a coma, barely responsive to any outside stimulus. At her mother's behest, I wrote her a letter, for she was one of my readers. I talked about the magic land of Xanth, and the sister realm of Elfquest by another author, and the value of children to those who love them, and I joked about the loathsome shot the nurse would give the Monster Under the Bed if she saw him. I spoke of the character with her name who would be in a future Xanth novel, an elf girl or maybe an ogre girl.

The child's mother read the letter to her, and it brought a great widening of her eyes, and her first smile since the accident. She became responsive, though able to move only her eyes, one big toe, and her fingers. She started to indicate YES or NO to verbal questions by looking to placards with those words printed on them. She made her preference emphatically clear: an elf girl, not an ogre girl!

It is my hope that she is now on the way to recovery, though there is of course a long way to go. It was fantasy that made the connection to reality, her response to my interest and my teasing. I think that fantasy needs no more justification than this. I, as writer, was able to relate to her, my reader, and she responded to me. The rest will be mostly in the province of medicine, but the human spark was vital to the turning point.

And here is the secret I am working toward: Writing and reading are

259

one on one, writer to reader and back again, and the rest of the universe doesn't matter. The writer must know his readers, not the details of their lives, which are myriad, but their hearts and dreams. He must relate. He must care.

When I write to you, it is as if we are in a privacy booth, and we are sharing things that neither of us would confess elsewhere. We love, we hurt, we laugh, we fear, we cry, we wonder, we are embarrassed—together. We *feel,* linked. We share our joy and our shame, and yes, I feel your tears on my face as you feel mine on yours. We may be of different sexes and other generations, or we may match—but we relate to each other more intimately than any two others, dream to dream, our emotions mixed and tangled—for that time while the book that is our connection is open. When it closes we are cut off from each other, and we are strangers again, and we regret that, but we remember our sharing, and we cherish it. We were true friends, for a while. How precious was that while!

❙ 55

WRITING SHORT CRIME STORIES

BY JEAN MCCONNELL

MAYBE ONE REASON THAT SO MUCH OF MY FICTION writing has been short, short stories has something to do with my having been a reporter. In my early days I was in the London office of a Belfast daily newspaper, and our pieces had to be sent across to Northern Ireland by early afternoon. Thus came the necessity of choosing the exact word, fast— not of finding just any word!

Also, at one time I was an actress and that taught me about making an instant impression. When you are playing a character in a play, quite apart from your appearance, the moment you speak you reveal so much to the audience by the dialect or accent you use, your speech patterns, the way you address those around you, in addition to what you are actually saying. On many levels a passage of dialogue is probably the quickest and most effective way of conveying information, whether it be about the situation, the people involved in it, or the possibilities in store.

So, when I approached fiction writing the immediate impact of the short length was most attractive to me and seemed to come naturally. Not for me the four-inch-thick novel with convoluted sentences roaming into long paragraphs of detailed description. Yes, I appreciate that some of the greatest literature is rich with long colorful accounts of location and character. In the opening chapter of *Little Dorrit,* for instance, Charles Dickens takes five hundred and twenty words to say it was a hot day in Marseilles. And you wouldn't want to lose a word of it. The very page seems scorched. But we all know the modern block-buster with the chunks of padding that send us skipping through the book like a kangaroo, from plot point to plot point, or more likely, from sex scene to sex scene. I can't write that way, even for ready money.

Yet who wants to read just a bare storyline? Somewhere between that and the circuitous passages of pointless detail lies the fine-honed little gem of a tale that has the reader muttering with satisfaction, "How true!" or "What a neat twist!"

The short crime story presents its own special problems. There is the need for a hint of threat from the very opening, the vital clue planted at exactly the right point and concealed so skillfully that the final resolution is both unexpected yet inevitable, and never unlikely or unbelievable. Ideally, all the relevant pointers will have been there in the text, leading to the inexorable conclusion, yet the reader will still have been taken by surprise.

A story I wrote called "Bobby Catch" opens like this:

"It was never haunted in my day," said Barbara. "At least not as far as I can remember. We only lived in the lodge."

"Don't say I've wasted my time bringing you down here," said Garside. "When they said you'd lived here at one time I felt sure you'd have something to tell us."

The reader knows at once that it is a ghost story. In a few more lines, the reader finds that Garside himself is not troubled by the ghost; it is his wife who wants to move out of the house, something he can't readily afford. Barbara regrets she can't help.

Things are low key, until Garside describes the nature of the apparition. When he tells Barbara it is a child, sitting astride the attic window ledge, her manner changes dramatically.

We are now one-fifth into the story, and this is a plot point: Barbara tells Garside about a bullying little boy she used to play with who fell to his death from the attic window. The couple begin to mount the stairs.

The reader now suspects the ghost may appear. But before that it is necessary to reveal more about Barbara herself so the reader may identify with her more closely. She describes how, as a child, she was made to play ball with the boy:

"For hours. And he would always throw it so hard. It was not so much a game as him aiming at a human target. And whenever I went to pick it up he would stamp on my hand. Grind his heels into my fingers. I must have got bruised. I must have done! Yet my mother never said anything. Just brought me up to the big house when they sent for me. Despite my tears. Why did she do that? How could she!"

Barbara is upset now, and Garside goes to get her a drink. The moment he leaves her alone in the attic, the reader fears something spooky will happen. Sure enough, the boy appears. Barbara is having total recall about the day when she threw the ball to him as he sat on the windowsill, where at this moment she can see him again. She forces herself to walk toward the specter. There is nothing there.

"I've exorcised it," thought Barbara. "Me coming back. That was all it needed. They won't be bothered again."

The story could have ended at this point. Barbara has laid the ghost to rest and wiped a terrible memory from the back of her own mind. But I had made the point that the boy was a bully for a definite purpose. And I ended it like this:

Barbara looked from the window and caught sight of Garside's wife driving up. She waved. Now her disquiet would be over and the pair could settle in properly and begin restoring the place. Barbara felt pleased with herself.

Then she heard the familiar voice behind her.

"Bobby, catch!"

Barbara turned—in time to see the ball coming at her.

Instinctively, she leapt for it as it flew through the window. Caught it. And traveled with it. Over the sill. Into the sunlight.

And down, down to the paved courtyard below. . . .

Although my heroine was dead, I think it was a satisfying ending to this 1500-word story.

My story called "Houseparty" opened as follows:

Not all the company accepted when Patrick Maine, star of stage and screen, threw out the invitation to his country house. The play had been running a long time, and when it closed, some of the cast were anxious for a break. Others were going into new shows. In the end, only Zoe, Wilfred, and Alan accepted.

"Patrick, how gorgeous! I can't wait to swim in your pool!" cried Zoe.

"I hope Sara won't mind us descending on her," said Wilfred.

"I guess Patrick's wife is used to surprises—of all sorts," murmured Alan, enjoying Zoe's sharp glance.

I think I made good use of these ninety-eight words. From them the reader learned the background and also became aware of the following:

(a) that Alan seems a mischievous man. Not fond of Zoe. Why?
(b) that Zoe seems young and gushing. Wary of Alan. Why? Has she been playing around with the married Patrick? Does she think Alan is jealous?

(c) Alan implies Patrick's wife is long-suffering and Patrick unpredict-
able. Has Patrick arranged this houseparty with some ulterior
motive?

One-fifth into the story, the following passage occurs:

"Pity about Sara," said Zoe.
"She's not a water-baby like you," said Patrick.
"How sad," said Zoe, looking at him with limpid eyes.
Patrick ran his hand down her body. Alan turned his face away. Zoe had told
him that Patrick was casting her in his new play.
Sara appeared and announced lunch. Patrick didn't bother to remove his
hand from Zoe's thigh.
A fresh breeze sprang up as they moved indoors. Patrick and Alan stayed to
roll out and secure the large plastic cover over the pool.

There are important plot points contained here:
(a) It is windy.
(b) Alan knows how the pool cover is secured.
(c) Patrick desires Zoe and has little feeling for his wife.
(d) Zoe finds Patrick both attractive and useful to her career.
(e) Alan has career aims similar to Zoe's, but with less success so far.
(f) Sara has some special reason for not wishing to swim with the
group.

Later Sara is found drowned under the pool cover. Is it suicide or
murder or an accident? The police arrive and, along with the reader,
they assess the possibilities. They hear that Sara always swam alone
because of an ugly birthmark. So, what happened to her alone in the
pool? And why? They come to the conclusion that it was an accident
caused by a freak gust of wind. It would have been possible. But the
story ends like this: Alan finds Patrick alone in his study—

"I was surprised that the cover was loose, Patrick. I could have sworn I saw
you lock it this morning when you opened the pool."
"Well, you saw it when we were there with the Sergeant. It must have broken
loose with that exceptional wind."
"I'll buy that. What I can't buy is that it would come loose a second time. I
locked it myself, firmly, after we found Sara's body. Now how would it come
loose again? Unless someone wanted to convince the police it was an accident."
"You didn't say all this to the Sergeant."
"No, and I don't intend to."

Patrick rose and moved toward Alan. His voice was low and emotional. "And I can trust you?"

"You can rely on it."

"You're a remarkable friend," said Patrick, shaking Alan's hand warmly. Then he regarded Alan thoughtfully. "And an excellent actor," he said, adding casually, "There's a splendid part for you in the new play, of course."

"Thank you," said Alan, smiling. "I think we'll work together often in the future, don't you?"

The final words imply a lifetime of blackmail for Patrick. Not for money, but for acting roles. For if the influential star does not assure the small-time actor Alan that he will be cast in his shows, then Alan will surely reveal that Patrick committed the murder.

The short story reader is always expected to use his imagination and his wits, and as long as the writer has played fair with him, he enjoys the challenge.

Another story of mine opens as follows:

Celia's eyes opened wide when she heard the sound of shattering glass, as she registered that the burglar alarm had failed to go off.

Raising herself on her elbow, she leaned over and opened the bedside drawer. She took out a small but efficient-looking gun. She listened, expecting to hear noises from below.

Obviously, this is a rich woman (burglar alarm), she is alone (she doesn't call anyone for help), and she is a cool, resourceful person. These are essential plot points. When the intruder appears, he bears a resemblance to Celia, with his red hair. He says that unless she pays him off, he means to wreck her marriage and create a scandal for her wealthy, upright politician husband by declaring that he is Celia's secret illegitimate son. He is a powerful young man, but he talks like a small-time gangster and makes weak jokes, so that the reader can accept it as credible when at the end of the story Celia ruthlessly kills him and arranges it to look like self-defense.

A key line of dialogue comes toward the end of the 1500-word story when the intruder says:

"You just pay me, and you'll never see me again. Guaranteed. I got my morals. Just like your husband's always sounding off on the telly."

And Celia replies:

"It's funny you should say that, young man, because morals happen to be a luxury I myself gave up long years ago. You checked on the wrong one of us."

Information can be imparted to the reader by the simplest actions. Consider the following:

Paula's door was open, but Frank rang the bell. "Hi, Paula!" he called, entering.

So, although Frank knows Paula, he apparently always rings the bell even if her door is open. What does this show? He's polite? He's not sure of her? (She may have someone else there.) He's not sure of himself? (He's never sure he's welcome anywhere.) He's basically a diffident person?

In those few opening words, the reader is invited to evaluate Frank's character and to speculate too on why Paula's door is open. Is she careless? Trusting? Is she lying dead inside!

It is occasionally said that the short story is a good exercise for writers aiming to be novelists. It is not so. I myself have written both. They do not relate, and the one is by no means a shortened version of the other.

When I read a piece of short fiction that propels me quickly and deftly into the heart of the matter, engages my full attention, moves, intrigues, or amuses me, then, whether it is a delicate fragment, a brilliant little thriller, or a nudge at my funny-bone, if it leaves me with a feeling of delight or fulfillment, I salute a master of that cunning and demanding craft.

56

WRITING A SUCCESSFUL SUSPENSE THRILLER

By WILLO DAVIS ROBERTS

I ASSUME THAT IF YOU WANT TO WRITE a suspense novel or thriller, you like reading them. Don't attempt to write one unless you do. You must have the *feel* for this kind of writing, a genuine sense of what it takes to send prickles down a reader's spine, or make his adrenaline level shoot up.

So how do you go about writing a suspenseful book that will lure an editor into offering a contract and induce readers to buy it?

It is possible to start writing a book with only a character and a situation firmly in mind, as opposed to making a detailed outline, but it's difficult to do a mystery/suspense novel that way unless you've had lots of experience; in that case, your unconscious is doing a lot of the work for you.

I have never done a detailed written outline (though all the basic elements are in my head), but there are advantages in being able to do this. For beginners, making an outline assures their being able to follow through and finish the book, rather than getting lost in the middle of it. It may enable you also, when you've a few published books to your credit, to sell a novel on a proposal or several chapters and outline.

A prospective writer in any genre should analyze other books in the field and figure out how the writer put the book together, what makes it succeed. When you do this, you'll find similarities in how the authors handle basic techniques. Note particularly how the writer begins and ends the book; chances are, in a suspense novel, both will be chilling and/or thrilling.

Some years ago, in a writer's workshop to which I belonged, a talented newcomer read the beginning of a Gothic novel she was working on. It had chains rattling in the attic, a terrified heroine in a strange place, all kinds of mysterious goings-on. The author had bogged down, however, not knowing where to go next, and when we asked who was rattling the chains and why, we found out: The author didn't know!

It read like a Gothic, but she hadn't figured out ahead of time exactly who was the villain or why he was threatening the heroine. She had no idea when she sat down and began to type, where the story was going. (Once she worked it out, she finished and sold the book.)

Where is the story going?

There are few rules that can never be broken under any circumstances. But here is one: Never, *never*, begin a mystery novel without knowing where you're going with it. By that I mean that you should know who the villain is, what his motivations are, and what he does to threaten someone else. These things can be a mystery to the reader as well as to the characters, but it should never be a mystery to the writer. You don't have to know exactly how the novel is going to end, but you should decide ahead of time the general direction the action will take. I almost never know the details of the climax until I get there; it's more fun for me to write if the action develops out of the characters, when I say "What would I do if I were confronted by this problem?"

What I would actually do would be to get hysterical and call the cops, but one's protagonist must have more fortitude than that. What I want is for the characters to develop to the stage where they are "real" people, and then act as sensibly or courageously as they can. If the characters are sufficiently well developed, they will be obliging enough to do this.

Once in a while I do work myself into a trap by not figuring out enough ahead of time. Having cut off all escape—because in order not to appear moronic, the protagonist has to be *unable* to walk away from the dangers—it sometimes takes considerable ingenuity to extricate the poor soul.

Knowing you'll have to do that, prepare for the ending. Don't forget that the villain needs to be just as strongly motivated as the protagonist: He's greedy, he's insane, he's protecting himself against the consequences of prior actions, he hates, he loves, etc. *All* characters, major and minor, must have credible reasons for whatever they do. The heroine who walks into the dark alley may do it, believably, to rescue someone else; she'd be stupid to do it for a less compelling reason. A hero might attempt a risky jump between roof-tops or off a bridge to escape a pursuer, but don't have him do it for a lesser reason that to save his own or someone else's life.

Don't write dramatic scenes that are suspenseful but don't make sense in the overall context of the story. Unless the character is literally insane, give him logical motivation. That goes for all the characters. The reader will suspend his disbelief in order to be entertained, but only to a point.

Before I begin a story, I make a list of characters. Their names, their physical descriptions, their likes and dislikes, their habits—whether they smoke, what they drink, what they eat, their backgrounds, etc. I leave space on my master list to add things that occur to me as I go along, so there will be no discrepancies. I once wrote a novel in which a character disguised himself with a full beard; he was eventually recognized without my saying that the beard had been shaved off. The editor, the copy-editor, and I all read and re-read that manuscript and didn't catch that, but a reader did!

I begin to write when I have the characters sketched out—a file card or a couple of typed pages for each one—and when I know the basic situation. Though I don't at that point have the specifics worked out, I know the general direction the novel will take: people dying under mysterious circumstances at a rest home, and a girl who goes to work there will join forces with an ex-cop whose uncle was one of the victims, to ferret out the truth about the deaths.

Beginnings

The opening is the most important part of the novel. This applies to almost every work of fiction, but particularly to suspense novels. These days many so-called mysteries are not mysteries at all, in the sense that you have a puzzle to solve. Often a story is told from the viewpoint of the perpetrator; the reader knows all along who is doing what and why, but he is kept holding his breath to see if the villain gets away with it, or when and how he'll be caught.

The opening has to have that narrative hook, that grabber that makes a reader turn the page and become immediately absorbed in the story. My favorite from my own novels reads:

The mercury stood at 98 degrees on the thermometer next to the kitchen door. I wondered afterward why that should have registered with me; one thin red line, when there was red all over the kitchen itself. Fresh blood. Her blood. Alison's.

269

Some of the manuscripts I've been asked to read and criticize purport to be mysteries, but the action doesn't start until page 10, or even chapter five. More than once I've suggested throwing away the first chapters, retaining some essential minor bits to be inserted later, and beginning the novel 30 to 50 pages into the manuscript, because that's where the action starts.

Begin the action, the suspense, on page 1, paragraph 1.

That's the hard part. Resist the temptation to foreshadow. The old Gothics sometimes began "If I had only known what awaited me at Castle Craig—" Today, foreshadowing is done subtly or, better yet, dispensed with altogether. The old saw about starting a book as close to the end as possible is still valid. Start with action, then work in the background as you go, or do a flashback, as I did in *Didn't Anybody Know My Wife?* After I'd set the stage for the murder of Dr. Scott's wife, I went back to the morning of the same day and then carried through on the story chronologically.

Sometimes you need go back for only a scene or two; sometimes you start with an exciting part and flash back for years, if necessary, to get in everything the reader must know that led up to the murder or whatever your opening ploy is. The important thing to remember about flashbacks is that the reader must never be confused about whether it's "now" or "then."

Usually I lead into a flashback by the use of "had." As in, *Scotty had expected her to be on time, but she'd never shown up.* Once you've established that you're *in* a flashback, drop the "hads" and tell it in simple past tense. And then when you come back to the present, be sure it's clear that you've done so. As in, *Now here he was, looking at the body of the woman who had been his wife.*

The climax is the next most important part of the novel, and that should be smashing, too. One way to kill an otherwise acceptable story is to wind up with a chapter or two of explanation after the excitement is over. To avoid that, get the explaining in before the final confrontation between protagonist and villain. Keep something exciting for the very last pages.

Dialogue that speaks for you

I've mentioned letting the characters take over the action and determine the course of the story. This can work only if the characters are truly individuals. You have to know how they will think and act in various circumstances, so that they'll be different from one another.

Ideally, the reader should be able to tell who is speaking by what he or she is saying. For instance, imagine that you are a woman who has just wrecked the family car. You come home and relate your tale of woe. Now, write down what the response would be from your mother ("Oh, Grace, were you hurt?"), your children ("Oh, gosh, Dad'll kill you!"), your best friend ("Your insurance will take care of it, won't it?" or maybe "Do you think you can get it fixed before George sees it?"), and your husband ("You did what? #$%$@!"). They would not all have the same point of view nor the same concerns—and neither would your characters—about the things that happen in your story. Some of them may express *your* opinions on capital punishment, or abortion, or other controversial subjects. There should, however, be convincing alternate viewpoints. This is not the place to overpower the reader with personal opinions.

A character with a hot temper speaks in an explosive manner, with exclamation points and possibly profanity. Show aggression, or tenderness, or timidity, in the dialogue; don't be content with letting adverbs to do it for you, or *telling* the reader a character is tough or gentle.

A note of caution on "realistic" dialogue: Leave out the small, irritating things that many people say, such as, "you know," unless this is essential to the character. If a scene takes place at a dining table, by all means mention the food, but don't put in every "please pass the salt." It's boring and it adds nothing to the story.

"Show, don't tell," also applies to action. Instead of telling us the girl is timid, have her be hesitant to act, or her lips tremble, or tears fill her eyes. Don't tell us a husband is a wife-beater. Have him hit the wife, swear at her, lose control of his temper. Every character, even the minor ones, will have some definite traits that can be conveyed both in speech and action.

Shared emotion

Create emotion. One way to hold your readers is to make them *care* what happens to the protagonist. Make them fear for her, laugh with her, cry for her. Make the reader *identify* with your characters, feel the sorrow, the pain, the fear, the thumping heart and the labored breathing.

A character not only can, but should, have flaws that make him human. There are editors who want all the women to be gorgeous, all the men handsome, everyone sexy and romantic. My own belief is that someone with warts, even figurative ones, is more interesting. Everyone can identify with the person who has a weight problem, or is trying to quit smoking, or is self-conscious about a big nose or an overbite or an inability to think of a retort in time to use it. Don't overdo this, but small defects can be engaging.

Thrillers should move along at a brisk pace. They should not be travelogues, with endless pages of description of an exotic setting, yet *brief* insertions of such color can add authenticity and needed atmosphere. Having mastered beginnings and endings—still a struggle for many of us, even after many years of working with them—all you have left to do is the middle. The long, long middle.

Keep it moving. Make every word count. If it doesn't move the story forward or add to our understanding of the character, cut it out. If it begins to drag, throw another problem or predicament at your protagonist. Eventually, he or she will solve or overcome all. Remember: it's O.K. to complicate the plot with coincidence—the earthquake, the accident, the bad luck—but don't *solve* it except through the actions of the protagonist. Make him or her figure out the answers and solutions, and keep them logical. It's all right to go back and add clues that you didn't think of in your first draft. If possible, set the finished manuscript aside for a time to let it "cool," and then read it again before you type the final draft. That will help you spot the places that need fixing, sometimes hard to see during the passion of writing it.

If you can do all this, chances are you'll find a publisher, and that's what it's all about.

57

THE SCIENCE FICTION VIRUS

BY JOHN SLADEK

WHEN I WAS A KID, what I really wanted to do was to waste my time hanging around the town pool hall. But since they wouldn't let me in, I had to waste my time hanging around the town library. Now that I think of it, the library was a lot like a pool hall; they both had the same kind of lamps with green glass shades, casting little cones of light over the broad tables. While there, I managed to read everything that came to hand, including the Oz books, the Hardy Boys mysteries, and a lot of O. Henry stories. Finally I picked up *From Earth to Moon,* by someone called Jules Verne. I opened the book. A science fiction virus leapt straight from its pages to the center of my brain, where it took root. I've never been the same since.

Actually, I'd already run across science fiction, but only on the radio. There was a terrifically frightening radio program called "Dimension X," which I never missed. Radio really is a superior medium for stimulating the infantile imagination. Someone only has to gasp, or whisper "What's that over there—in the corner—*my God, it's alive!*" and the listener's heart starts pounding. I remember one eerie program which began "The last man on Earth sat alone in a room. *(Pause)* There was a knock at the door." It never occurred to me, as I sat there covered with goose bumps, that this science fiction stuff could be found in books, too.

After Verne, I spent a couple of years reading all the SF I could get my hands on: mostly anthologies from the library and an occasional pulp magazine. Then some other interest came along—girls or model airplanes—and I stopped reading science fiction and forgot all about it.

Or so I thought. I continued reading other things and, somewhere in high school, I decided to become a writer. Naturally, I would only write Good Stuff. Or if not Good, at least Avantgarde Stuff. I scribbled my way through high school and college. There was my F. Scott Fitzgerald phase, my Dostoyevsky phase, and my unfortunate Kerouac phase. There was almost everything but a science fiction phase. I had already dismissed science fiction as a frivolous comic book genre, not for serious adults like me.

After college, I began a novel that was going to be high art indeed: a long, pretentious work-in-progress in the manner of Samuel Beckett (so I imagined). I might still be in progress with it, if a merciful fate had not permitted me take the manuscript to Europe with me and lose it on a train. What a tragedy! And hey, what a relief!

While recovering from this ordeal in New York, I stayed with a friend who was already writing and selling science fiction. By my incredibly high standards, this didn't make sense. Here was a literate, well-read guy, writing for pulp magazines with titles like *Amazing*. I grew curious enough about science fiction to start reading it again. The writing was uneven—pulp-magazine writers are not Samuel Becketts—but the ideas were mind-shattering.

For example, I was brought up short by an episode in one novel by Philip K. Dick. He describes perfectly ordinary surroundings—a beach where a man approaches a soft-drink stand to buy a drink. Suddenly, the stand, with all its wares and even its attendant, shimmers and disappears, leaving only a typewritten slip of paper. The man picks up the slip. It reads SOFT-DRINK STAND.

That did it. The goose bumps were back, and I was reinfected. Here was a popular fiction that could tackle big themes like the nature of reality, *and get away with it*. This had to be worth trying.

Not everyone catches the science fiction virus in just this way. There are probably a million ways to catch it. For some, it's a childhood disease that lingers. They keep on reading SF as they grow up. They join fan clubs, go to conventions, and eventually timidly try out their own stories in one of the thousands of small amateur SF publications, the "fanzines." (SF is deeply rooted in amateurism, with all the good or ill that amateurism implies.) A surprising number of big names in SF—including nearly all of the very biggest ones—began this way. Robert Silverberg was a fan before he published his first story at age eighteen. Frederik Pohl was a fan before he became an editor at twenty. Arthur C. Clarke was well-known in fan circles before he began to publish. In no other industry do fan clubs provide the stars.

The virus also hits grownups, sometimes without warning. This may explain why some established "straight" writers have suddenly, for obscure reasons, discovered the uses of SF. Even major literary figures have occasionally dipped into SF to handle themes too difficult for "straight" fiction. For instance, E. M. Forster wrote "The Machine Stops" to satirize our mechanistic, labor-saving world. (In his story, machines have saved us from even the labor of human relations.) Others who have taken the plunge include Saul Bellow, John Updike, Doris Lessing, Don DeLillo, and Gore Vidal.

Reading up

If you've been hit by the SF virus, you'll have already taken the first step to writing, which is to read constantly. Immerse yourself in the stuff you admire: magazines, anthologies, novels. You no doubt already have a favorite author or two. If you're like most of us, you'll probably begin writing by modeling your work on one of those favorites.

My own early favorites included Alfred Bester, Ray Bradbury, Brian Aldiss, and Frederik Pohl, among others.

But please don't stick exclusively to SF. Remember that SF is a little parish in a big forest. Read plenty of good fiction by good writers of every kind. Never rule anything out as too remote from science fiction concerns. Science fiction, like the Inquisition, concerns itself with everything.

Those "crazy ideas"

As in any profession, you have to be prepared to answer one question a thousand times. People will continually ask artists what their paintings "mean." Everyone wants to know how a prostitute got started in her business. If a man merely digs a hole in the street, someone is bound to come along and ask, "Digging it up, eh?" For science fiction writers, the question is always: "Where do you get all your crazy ideas?"

There's no good answer to this. Harlan Ellison used to reply: "From a crazy idea factory in Schenectady, dummy!" The truth is, getting ideas is seldom a problem.

First of all, there's science itself. Hardly a week goes by that I don't read or hear something astonishing. Scientific notions can come from the daily paper, or from magazines like *Scientific American*. A few recent examples (with my jotted notes in parentheses):

• Manic-depressive syndrome turns out to be genetic; in fact they've found the chromosomal location of the gene for it. (What about other mental states? Is there a gene for normality? For criminality? Is there a gene that compels people to sign their names with little smiling faces?)

• Killer bees are now in Mexico, heading north. (What other insect horrors might be on the way?)

• The Greenhouse Effect could change the shape of human society. (Would it be canceled by a nuclear winter?)

• Nanotechnology—the building of incredibly tiny machines that could sail the human bloodstream, repairing damage and maintaining health—offers a world of possibilities. (What if the tiny machines formed unions and threatened strikes?)

Not only the hard sciences come into play. SF writers use whatever interests them: Kate Wilhelm has used psychology; Ursula Le Guin, anthropology; Damon Knight, linguistics. But almost anything is grist to science fiction's mill:

• **History.** Orson Scott Card sets a series in an 1811 "alternate world." John Brunner describes a world where the Armada won, and America is a Spanish colony.

• **Crime fiction.** Isaac Asimov's robot detective is well-known, but SF detectives are common.

• **Literature.** Anthony Burgess developed an unusual theory of Shakespeare's authorship in a SF story

• **Politics.** I've recently seen SF novels advocating pacifism, militarism, technocracy, the Green Party, and the global electronic village. SF embraces all viewpoints: conservative, liberal, right-wing libertarian, and Marxist—and everyone in between.

• **Religion.** Robert Heinlein proposed exciting and disturbing societies based on new religions. There's plenty of New Age mysticism, too: Ian Watson, for one, has explored UFOs and whale telepathy.

• **War.** Lucius Shepard and Jerry Pournelle write war fiction from very different perspectives.

• **Social Theory.** Brian Aldiss created a congeries of interacting societies across a world in his *Helliconia* series, where periodic ice ages bring inexorable change.

Although scientific ideas can be important in science fiction, they're by no means primary. Good SF stories must first and last be good stories. One of the most brilliant SF stories ever is Avram Davidson's "And All the Seas with Oysters." It contains no science at all, unless you count the technology of bicycle repair, but it's unforgettable.

While I'm listing crazy ideas, let me put in a word for SF humor, especially satire. The premise of satire, like that of much SF, is that today's world is itself crazy, or at least badly made. The SF utopian may try to present an ideal world with the flaws removed. The SF satirist, by contrast, shows a world in which the flaw has grown huge and grotesque. Science fiction satire is a noble tradition, enfolding Jonathan Swift, Nathaniel Hawthorne, Samuel Butler, Mark Twain, H. G. Wells, and George Orwell.

If you're serious about writing SF, try not to become so involved in the trappings—conventions, workshops, fanzines—that you lose track of writing itself. Conventions can be fun, and they're a good way of meeting your fellow writers, prominent editors, and even your readers.

But conventions can be too much of a good thing. Indeed, there are one or two writers who engage in a continual round of public appearances, but never get around to writing anything. Remember that, though there are at least eighty conventions each year, they are primarily social occasions that have little to do with writing. No one gets any writing done during any of them. Writing is a solitary activity that, alas, has nothing to do with social life.

What about SF writer's workshops? These range from instant workshops at conventions to more serious ones set up by science fiction societies. Join one if you wish, but don't hope for magical results. At its best, a workshop can make you concentrate and put pen to paper, it can show you that other people have problems similar to yours, and it can give you a certain amount of confidence. But don't expect too much.

At its worst, a workshop can be destructive. Merciless criticism, often by the unqualified, can destroy self-confidence and make a shy person wish he or she had never thought of writing.

Finally, pay no attention whatsoever to reviews of your work. I speak as a reviewer. Remember that a review expresses only one person's opinion, shared with his readers. The best and worst that a review can do is to call the readers' attention to a book they might otherwise miss (among the 100–200 published each month).

On the other hand, it's important to keep track of the market, both magazines and book publishers. The magazines range in payment from

Omni and *Playboy,* who pay thousands for a story, down to fanzines, who pay in copies. No false modesty—send your stuff to the best market you honestly think you can sell it in.

Book publishers of science fiction abound. A new one seems to pop up (or vanish) every month, and their requirements change rapidly too, so it pays to keep close tabs on them. One good source for monthly info for the SF professional is the magazine *Locus* (copies are available in SF bookstores, subscriptions from *Locus* Publications, 34 P.O. Box 13305, Oakland, CA 94661).

The nature of the virus

I swore I wouldn't get involved in defining science fiction, but. . . . There are so many popular misconceptions about it. It isn't necessarily about space travel, or the future. Nor is it usually just a catalogue of brilliant inventions. (This answers another common question: "Aren't you worried that technology will overtake your stories and make them obsolete?" No, because I'm not writing user guides for new gadgets.)

Ideally, science fiction is fiction about humans dealing with science or technology (in the broadest sense). Some stories can be oddly unbalanced. At one extreme is the dreary high-tech novel that gives you the mass of the spaceship in kilograms, the mean temperature in degrees Kelvin, and the solar radiation in microwatts per square meter. No human beings in sight.

The other extreme eschews technology by proposing (say) an alternate universe where magic works. Alas, this quickly degenerates into a tedious tale of dragons, dwarfs, and sorcerers, remaining science fiction only by association. Neither extreme really has much to do with real human beings, and consequently neither is worth reading.

Between the extremes, there's room for plenty of vital innovation. And here I must stop defining SF. Real science fiction is undefinable—but you'll know it when you catch the virus.

‖ 58

CHARACTER: THE KEY ELEMENT IN MYSTERY NOVELS

BY JAMES COLBERT

BY DEFINITION, TO BE A MYSTERY a novel must have a murder at the beginning that is solved by the end. And by convention there must be a solution, whether or not there is an apprehension. This is the contract assumed by the reader when he or she picks up a book classified as a mystery. Yet despite this murder-solution requisite, mysteries offer the writer great freedom, a basic structure around which to work plot, setting, and most important, character.

Without doubt, character is the most important element of a mystery. A clever plot helps, certainly, as does a strong sense of place, but those elements are secondary, best used to show how the central character thinks and responds to events and environment. One writer may have a native Floridian solving murders while another may send a New York City detective to Florida. While Florida, of course, remains the same, the interesting thing for the reader is to see how the character responds, how he or she integrates the sense of the place into an overall experience. The same is true of the plot. No matter how interesting, unless uncovered by a central character readers find engaging, events take on a flat, two-dimensional quality. "Just the facts, ma'am. Just the facts" has its place, all right, but that place is in a newspaper, not a mystery.

So how does a writer go about portraying an engaging character? The answer to that is as multi-faceted and as complex as the character must be, and it is accomplished one small step at a time. Think of a police artist putting together a composite sketch of a suspect. Thin sheets of transparent plastic, each with slightly different lines are laid one over another, composing different parts of the face until a whole picture emerges. While the medium is different, the technique is not dissimilar to the one a writer uses. First sheet: How tall is the character, and how much does he weigh? How is he built? Second sheet: What color hair does he have? What are his distinguishing characteristics? Third sheet: What is the setting, and what is the character thinking? Small elements are put together, one over another, until a whole picture emerges.

Where the police artist leaves off with the physical portrait, however, the writer is just beginning because the reader wants to know, well, what's this guy really *like?* Is he threatening or non-threatening? Well-read or illiterate? Optimistic or pessimistic? What kind of car does he drive? What does he eat? The nuances, eccentricities, habits, way of thinking and quirks are what separate a description of a character from one who starts to *live*; and all those things are revealed as the character responds to his surroundings and reacts to events—in a very good mystery, dynamic events make the character *grow*.

Growth and change are intrinsic, inevitable elements of the human condition. The growing and the changing, however, usually occur very slowly, day by day, not very noticeably. Within the usually limited time frame of a novel, this change is often very difficult to portray, but the mystery has the advantage of a dynamic structure. A murder occurs at the beginning and is solved by the end. Events, feelings, new understandings are speeded up, compressed into a very short time. As a result, it is credible that the characters change fairly quickly in response. Really successful mysteries allow the reader not just to know a character but to grow with him, to learn his lessons as he did, without actually having to endure the violent crime. Observe Burke in Andrew Vachss's novel, *Blossom,* or listen to the first-person narrator in Scott Turow's *Presumed Innocent.* Notice how they change during the course of the book. Observe what they learn and how the new understandings affect them. And watch how, with the characters firmly in hand, the authors thrust them into the events that form the respective plots.

Plots are usually very simple ideas extended. Even the most complex plot can be described briefly. (Excellent examples of this can be found in your Sunday paper, in the film listings where even very involved movies are summarized in a line or two.) But unlike the step-by-step development of characters, plots appear complex at the outset and become more and more simple. Elements are stripped away rather than added. What appears confusing, even chaotic, at the start makes sense later on when other motives and actions are revealed: In retrospect, all the twists and turns make sense. The reader is left with a clear sense of order, a good sense of character, and, one hopes, a strong sense of place.

Evoking a place is stage setting in its most basic form. Remember, it is crucial to have the stage set for the central character—and not the other way round. Overlong descriptions of a place and a recitation of facts about it are best left to travel guides, which is not to say that setting is *un*important. But it *is* secondary. When successfully used, setting becomes the character and helps to reveal his or her foibles and way of life. In John D. MacDonald's Travis Magee novels, Travis Magee's houseboat, for example, is very much a part of Travis Magee, accommodating, even making possible, a way of life that is so much a part of him that when he travels, he seems to embody one *place* confronting another. Readers envy Travis the beachbum freedom of his life, and we understand how it feels to leave the beach and go, say, to New York City or to Mexico—or, for that matter, just to go to work. The setting is integral to Travis Magee and enriches the whole series; but while it may be difficult to imagine him anywhere else, the fact is, readers can. (MacDonald even tells us how to go about it whenever Travis considers his options.) For the writer, however, the single most important facet of technique, as important in its own way as making character primary, is to make use of what you know.

If presented well, there is no human experience that is uninteresting. Very good books have been written about what might, from all appearances, be very mundane lives. Yet mystery writers too often feel the need to write not what they know but what they perceive they *should* be writing about. As a result, the characters they create do not ring true, or in particular, they are tough when they should not be, or have no real sense of what violence is really like. But despite the hard-boiled school of detective fiction, it is *not* necessary for a central character in a mystery to be either tough or violent—the book can, in fact, be just as interesting when a character conveys some squeamishness or distaste for violence. Not all detectives have to be built like linebackers and display a penchant for brutal confrontation.

The simple fact is, what you know is what will ring true. Andrew Vachss writes about violence and violent people because he knows his subject; but Tony Hillerman eschews that and writes about Navajo Indians, which is what *he* knows. Scott Turow, the lawyer, writes about legal proceedings. All three have written very good books. But since Dashiell Hammett's *Continental Op,* far too many mystery writers have felt it mandatory to make their investigators tough, even when the writer has no notion of what real toughness is all about. The result is facade rather than substance—and the reader will sense it. In fiction, certainly, there is a need for imagination, but the imagination must spring from knowledge, not speculation. The most credible, most substantive books are those in which the author's grasp of his or her subject shows through. Allow your character to know what you know and do not attempt to impose on him what you feel he *should* know. Your character will appear shallow if you do, shallow, and most damning of all, contrived. With respect to that, it is important, too, that you consider your story first, *then* the genre it happens to fall into.

With my first novel, *Profit and Sheen,* I wasn't even aware that I had written a mystery until the first review came out. What makes me appear rather dense in one way worked to my advantage in another: I told my story as well as I knew how and was completely unencumbered by any feeling of restriction. The point is, tell your story as well as you know how and see how it comes out. *Then* worry about genre. If you start out with the expressed intent of writing a mystery, well and good; if you follow the rules. But if what you have in mind is a story with only some elements of a mystery, tell your story first and do not try to change it to conform to some vague idea of what a mystery should be. Your publisher will classify your book for you; genre classification is a subjective thing, nothing more than a handle, really, an easy and convenient way of breaking down different works into groups more for marketing purposes than for readers.

There are, of course, other aspects of writing a mystery to consider, but these are more difficult to pin down. Most notable among them, however, are point of view and voice. Selecting the right point of view is extremely important, because it determines what the reader will and will not learn. Voice is, really, the application of point of view to a consistent rhythm, a *voice* the reader hears. More often than not, point of view is intrinsic to the writing itself (the writer will begin "I . . ." or "He . . ."), but voice requires a certain conscious effort on the writer's part, an attempt to convey the story consistently through or around the central character—even when that central character's vision is rather limited or, to the writer, unattractive. The success of the voice is directly related to how true the writer remains to his character and how willing the writer is to remain "transparent."

If you work within the given structure, writing a mystery is not so different from writing any other kind of novel. Good mysteries do, in fact, have all the elements common to all good fiction: engaging characters, strong sense of place, compelling plot, believable voice. Allow the structure to work for you, write as honestly as you know how, and everything else will fall into place.

59

The Mysterious Art of Biography

By Patricia Bosworth

Since biography is the most popular form of nonfiction today, there is an increasing interest in learning the craft. The rules, however, change with every project. The only rule you must follow is that you cannot make up the facts about a life, but you can imagine the form they take.

Thus, Nancy Mitford's classic *Zelda* is completely different in tone and style from W. A. Swanberg's *Citizen Hearst*. And the monumental *Power Broker* by Robert Caro cannot be compared to Richard Ellman's superb biography of James Joyce, except to say they are both masterpieces.

In my month-long workshop on biography writing (far too short a time), I kept repeating a series of questions and considerations for my students to mull over. For the purposes of this article, I'll list them and try to elaborate on them.

For starters: *What makes the life you want to write about "significant"?*

Usually some sort of outstanding accomplishment, a distinct quality of mind that sets a character apart.

How does a life express itself?

In an action or actions. In writing my biography about the 1960s photographer Diane Arbus, I discovered that Arbus invariably chose terrifying worlds to record with her camera. And not just because those worlds fascinated her, but because she wanted to overcome her fears about them. She felt it was essential to take risks; she lived every day believing that.

Along with an action, the power of documentation—evidence from interviews and letters and diaries—cannot be overlooked. Nancy Mitford, who has been working on a biography of Edna St. Vincent Millay for over a decade, finally met the poet's elderly sister. That meeting led her to a huge cache of personal papers—some 56,000 documents—the biggest collection on a major American literary figure remaining in private hands.

Archival sleuthing can often result in vivid, multilayered portraits, but it's not easy; ideally, one should possess the combined skills of an historian, a psychiatrist, and a novelist. Whenever I get depressed by that thought, I quote Mark Twain's definition of biography: "Biography is the clothes and buttons of a man; but the real biography of a man is lived in his head 24 hours a day, and *that* you can never know."

If one is lucky, one comes away with the essence of a character—a version of a life. But there is always more than one version. Although Mark Twain doesn't say so, *I* say, never write about someone who doesn't interest you. You must be obsessed by the character you're exploring, because to write a good biography takes five years or more. Leon Edel spent 25 years writing his splendid study of Henry James. It can be pretty deadly if you don't like—or worse, don't respect—the character you're investigating. (For instance, under no circumstances would I tackle a biography of mass murderer Charles Manson.) I want to be inspired and enlightened and challenged; I want to learn something.

Another task to set yourself: Look for the minor characters in a life, characters who may bring your major character to life, as, say, David McCullough did with Theodore Roosevelt in *Morning on Horseback*. McCullough paid close attention to every Roosevelt sibling.

Just as important, find a "voice" or "voices" you're comfortable with. In a book I'm writing now—a memoir/biography of my father, the late Bartley C. Crum, an activist lawyer who was blacklisted in the 1950s after defending "The Hollywood Ten"—I juxtapose excerpts from his and my mother's journals, reminiscences from colleagues and friends, as well as from my own memories. Then, I am dotting the narrative with letters from my father's contemporaries, men he worked with, such as Earl Warren, Henry Cabot Lodge, and Harry Truman. Letters from historical figures such as Warren are not only "voices"; they express a lot about America in the last fifty years.

As for settings, if at all possible, visit the places you'll be writing about. While I was researching my biography of Montgomery Clift, I had the opportunity to wander through his ghostly New York brownstone. The bar he'd built remained in the spacious double living room; the birch trees he'd planted "in honor of Chekhov" still rustled in his garden. And the bedroom that he'd slept in (and died in) was exactly as he'd left it, complete with cigarette burns on the floor.

Watching out for backgrounds and settings doesn't mean neglecting themes like power or the relationships between individuals and eras. There are many kinds of power, one of the most complicated being the power within relationships as dramatized, say, by Phyllis Rose's *Parallel Lives,* a study of Victorian marriages.

Speaking of themes, I seem to repeat the same theme in every biography I write. I choose as subjects essentially decent, good people who are driven, creatively obsessed about completing one or more tasks. Always at some peak point in their lives, they suffer a terrible tragedy (an accident or a death). How they work it out, or incorporate it into their lives in order to survive, is something I never tire of exploring.

At the same time, I try to remember the responsibility I have in *revealing* the life. How much "right" do I have to interpret, to speculate, to analyze, to give away secrets?

A biographer must be selective and discreet, particularly if friends and relatives of the subject are still alive. (I hasten to add that it is easier to write about a dead subject than a live one.) But it isn't necessary to use everything—certainly not all the "dirt." Selection of detail is crucial. It can make or break a biography.

Selection of detail can set the tone and suggest character and relationship. For example, my father often referred to my mother as his "child bride"; she never corrected him, but once confided in the depths of her journal, "Oh, how I wish someone would call me 'sweet woman' just once!"

Details, incidents, anecdotes—they piece the story of a life into a narrative. And everybody's life is composed of a first, second, and third act. And in the last act many things are finally resolved.

When all is said and done, what do the facts add up to? What does a life *mean*? These are central questions every biographer asks and must answer in the writing of a successful biography. And of course, there is no one answer; the answer is different for every book.

Then there is the revision. A biographer likes to spend a great deal of time revising endless chapters and scenes and paragraphs, so I now find a sharp pleasure in rewriting. I didn't at first.

I recall when I handed in the fourth draft of my Arbus biography to

Knopf (I'd been writing the book for five years), my editor read it and then very gently told me I would have to rewrite the entire book because so far I hadn't trusted myself or the material enough: I was still too "tentative"; I needed to "throw myself into the experience." He was absolutely correct.

For me, the ultimate fascination of biography is that, like all art forms, it works in mysteries. A good biographer never stops asking questions and never stops looking for clues.

60

THE REVIEWER'S CRAFT

BY SVEN BIRKERTS

I CALL THIS SHORT REFLECTION "The Reviewer's Craft" rather than "The Reviewer's Art" because I want to confine myself to making useful rather than more philosophic kinds of observations. But as I begin, I feel an almost irresistible pressure to set down a few high-toned generalizations. I suppose that it comes with the terrain. Just as one almost never begins a review without making at least one reflective, high-altitude circle around one's prey, so do I succumb here.

First: I don't imagine that anyone actually *sets out* to become a critic or reviewer. One usually ends up there. Maybe "ends up" sounds too darkly fatalistic—the critic generally *arrives* at his vocation after exploratory travels elsewhere. Often that "elsewhere" involves other, often "nobler" and more "creative" kinds of writing. It may, however, be a very happy arrival (it was for me).

I came to reviewing out of writing fiction and working in bookstores. The change from one genre to another was enormously liberating. Reviewing allowed me to spread the word about what I perceived to be neglected works of literature; no less important, it let me see my name in print after frustrating years of rejection. This latter incentive is not to be underestimated.

Though I began reviewing with the idea that it was a temporary expedient, a way of keeping my hand in while I waited for bigger things to happen, I soon came to face certain truths: that I loved what I was doing, that it came to me naturally (indeed, I saw that it was the critical side of my character that had blocked my attempts at fiction), and, best of all, that it was by no means a trivial or ephemeral endeavor. The intellect, the creative impulse, and the linguistic urge were all engaged fully—depending, of course, on the nature of the book—and there was ample room for self-expression.

Naturally, every person's experience is different. I can report only how things fell out for me. For starters, I was lucky enough to connect straight off with a responsive and appreciative editor who liked a review I had written on speculation and asked for others. From that point on there was always a next step, a new assignment.

I have been reviewing for more than ten years now. A great deal has changed for me over this time. A peripheral concern has moved to the center of my life; I now pursue it as a vocation, with complete involvement. I look for the assignments I want; I try to publish in magazines that can pay me something for my work (I have written hundreds of pages gratis . . .); I juggle demands and schedules in such a way that I am often working on three or four pieces at once: reading for one, taking notes for another, putting final touches on yet a third. But for all this immersion—sometimes to the point of exhaustion—the pleasure is undiminished. And this I attribute to my choice of field: literature. While the work I read is serious, often difficult, it continually gives me the excitement and renewal that belong to art. I find that the thrill of starting to read a new novel or collection of poetry is as great as it was the first few times. What's more, the ambition of touching readers and influencing their responses to books only grows stronger.

This leads me to my last generality: the question of why one might want to be a reviewer. I see the evaluation and discussion of books as an indispensable part of what might be called the "conversation of culture." By taking up and sustaining the movement of ideas in print, one is siding with mind and sensibility against the forces of the blip and the byte. The more artistically, interestingly, and convincingly a reviewer can serve the cause of books, the greater his contribution.

Now, about the "craft" of reviewing. . . .

First, the bad news. It is all but impossible to make a living as a part-time reviewer. Unless you are lucky enough to get a berth as the regular reviewer at one of the more prestigious magazines or newspapers, you will be doing your work alongside your other work. You will fight hard to keep the different parts of your life separate. You will steal time from your other employer, jotting mysterious notes on memo pads, thinking about openings. You will feel a strong temptation to let the reviewing slide so that you can enjoy a bit more leisure time. Try to resist the temptation, but don't become joyless or humorless. *Never* work only out of a sense of duty; it will show in the prose. The world does not need one more scrap of dutiful, uninspired writing.

It is not for the money that one reviews—obviously. Passion is essential. Passion for reading—books, magazines, other reviews, trade journals. Passion, too, for thinking, meditating, digesting—for living through the afterlife of books. Passion, most certainly, for writing. But—no less important—for rewriting, and rewriting again. You cannot succeed as a reviewer if you cannot bear to see your sentences trimmed, your paragraphs pruned, your best metaphors scotched; if you cannot bear, in short, to hear that your finished copy is anything but finished. This is especially true when you begin reviewing. Later, with some luck, you will find your way to one or two congenial editors. They will admire your work and give you certain leeway. You will, in turn, internalize their standards and be better able to give them what they are looking for the first time around.

Most of the advice that follows is addressed to the would-be or beginning reviewer. Nothing I say has the status of being axiomatic. These are the things that my experience has taught me—period.

• Try as much as possible to follow the twists and warps of your own character; stay with the grain. This means using your experiences, interests, and particular kinds of expertise to best advantage. Make yourself conspicuous by doing a certain kind of review very well. If you have a special interest in psychology or women's issues or Latin American literature, begin there. Find the journals that address themselves to readers with those same interests and examine them as potential markets for your work. Don't worry that you will be typecast or straitjacketed. It is much easier to branch out later from a position of strength than to try to be everything to everyone.

When you have found one or more publications that you would like to write for, do some further research. Read several dozen reviews published in those journals and see if there is anything that could be called a "house style." Spend some time in bookstores to acquaint yourself with titles and authors of current books in the field to get a sense of the landscape. Then, go the library and read through some current issues of *Publishers Weekly* and *Kirkus Reviews.* Look for early reviews of books that you might be interested in proposing for review.

• The next step is to write an honest, non-pretentious (and not overlong) letter to the reviews editor of the journal in question. Identify yourself, cite your relevant interests and experiences, and ask if they would be interested in having a review of X, Y, or Z on speculation (always suggest several possibilities). Show some familiarity with the journal and the kind of material it publishes. If you have any writing samples—"clips" of other reviews—include one or two of the best ones. If you think you have an angle on the book(s) proposed, give some explanation. At this point you have done all you can. You can only hope that the editor is responsive and that the chance will be offered. (Give the editor about two weeks to respond—after that, follow up with a note or a phone call.)

● How to write a review. It should go without saying that you read the book. Not only must you read it, but you must read it better—more searchingly, more thoughtfully—than anyone else. This is your real job as a reviewer: You are the ideal intelligence sent out to greet the work; you have to introduce and explain it to others. Ideally, therefore, you will read it more than once. You will also—ideally—have read certain background material, enough to know the larger context of the book. The more you know, the better is your chance to make the kinds of interesting connections that lift a review out of the mold of unimaginative summary.

Under the best circumstances, you will have time between finishing the book and beginning your review. I find this brooding period absolutely essential. It not only helps to clarify the book's outlines, revealing more sharply what is important and what is not, but it also gives you time to locate your true response. Many books can seduce at close quarters and later prove to be second-rate. Give yourself a chance to cool from your first ardors, or your initial distaste.

I am a great believer in letting the unconscious intelligence do its share of the work. The longer I can walk around in a condition of attentive idleness, the more likely is the shape of my response to emerge on its own. There is also an art to knowing when it's time to stop mulling and start writing. For me, that time comes when I can make out the outlines of my opening paragraph, when I can feel the tone and momentum of my first pitch. Generally at this point the first sentence is ready—it sets a rhythm and indicates a direction.

● Do everything you can to keep your review within assigned word limits. Apart from writing clear, polished prose, this is the fastest way to win the love of an editor: write pieces that don't need to be cut or inflated to meet space requirements. This takes a certain amount of practice, but it does eventually become second nature. A good reviewer knows how to think 500-word thoughts, 1000-word thoughts, and so on. He knows, too, the formula for balance for any given word length—just how much description, how much quotation, and how much rendering of judgment.

- Be punctual—get the review in on time, or before deadline. Don't ever call an editor at the last possible moment to ask for an extension. If there is a problem coming, call in and give warning.

- Be ready to take the "phone edit" call. Have your piece where you can find it. Be attentive and flexible; don't waste time being defensive. A good editor is usually right about your prose—believe it or not. Editors will repeatedly ask for changes, cuts, and substitutions. Be ready to think fast—but make sure you understand the editor's suggestions. Do as much as you can to help. But never let an editor talk you into saying something you don't believe. Don't allow the piece to be printed if you are not happy with it—just because you want to see your name in print. There is nothing more dispiriting than seeing your by-line on a piece of writing that you are ashamed of; it will keep you awake nights.

- Learn to compartmentalize projects. If you are serious about becoming a reviewer, you will have to learn to keep three or four balls in the air at a time. There is no other way to produce as steadily as you need to for your name to stay alive in the public mind. Moreover, not only is it possible to have several projects going at once—at different stages—it's actually good for the work. Ideas and energies have a way of crossing project boundaries: Your thinking about structuralism will enrich your review of a biography of Charles Dickens. Also, having several projects going at once keeps you from the kind of one-track obsession that often leads to paralysis.

- The rewards? Money, no. But books . . . Jiffy bag after Jiffy bag. The mailman walks with a lighter step after he has stopped at your door. What else? A sense of daily independence. Of mental fitness: There is no better way to keep the brain in aerobic trim. And reading: What other profession allows you to read in bed in the middle of the afternoon (after you hit the big time, that is)? At some point or another every reviewer confides his secret to someone: "I can't believe I get paid to do this. . . ." Well, that feeling comes rarely. But when it comes, it makes a nice counterweight to the interminable chore of composition.

61
WRITING AND SELLING TRAVEL ARTICLES

BY JANET STEINBERG

TO THE OUTSIDE OBSERVER, that illusive magic carpet known as "Travel Writing" is glamour . . . excitement . . . adventure. It is sunrise in Bali . . . sunset in Spain; piranhas in the Amazon . . . pyramids along the Nile.

To the struggling free lancer, trying to make a living in this limited field can be instant frustration and starvation. However, if you are endowed with stamina, determination, and the financial means to get you through those first lean years, travel writing can be a most rewarding profession.

The following tips, garnered from more than a decade of travel writing experience, should be helpful to you along the way.

Write as if you are talking to your best friend: With pen in hand, pretend you've picked up the phone to tell your friend about the wonderful place you've just visited. Tell which sights are not to be missed and which are a waste of time and money. Tell where to eat—in a variety of price ranges—and what dish must absolutely be tried. Go beyond the overhyped shopping malls to the unusual boutiques that specialize in goods unique to that area.

Write to assault your readers' sense: The opening paragraph should immerse your readers in the destination and make them want to go there more than any other place in the world. Through your words they should be able to see the sun rise in Bali . . . hear the cacophony of sounds in the Casbah . . . smell the spice-laden, cow-dunged streets of India.

Anecdotes make good opening paragraphs: Quote the joke that the cab driver told you or begin with the tour guide's remark that put the entire busload of tourists into stitches.

Write to entertain: Travelers, both real and armchair, need to be entertained as well as informed. Otherwise, you will lose them after the first few paragraphs. Your facts must be current and informative but not boring. If it's in-depth research your readers want, they will turn to an encyclopedia or comprehensive guidebook.

Make your first sentence powerful: Let it paint a picture, arouse curiosity . . . or even anger. "I'm just wild about Harry," a successful travel article began. Playing upon the old song title, it compels readers to learn just who Harry is and what he is doing in the travel section.

"I love calories! I love cholesterol! I love Fauchon!" Who or what is Fauchon? Curious readers have to read beyond this award-winning opening. "Auschwitz is the flip side of Disneyworld." This first sentence of another prize-winning travel article instilled anger in some readers until they continued for the explanation. But they *did* continue.

Breathe new life into the old: Make antiquity come alive as you uncover the past. Your readers might have difficulty picturing Mark Antony and Cleopatra walking along the Arcadian Way in Ephesus, Turkey. However, a mention of Charlton Heston gliding down those ancient marble streets in his chariot will conjure up a myriad of images in the minds of millions of movie buffs.

Seek unexplored subjects and unique angles: When you visit a destination, think of all the articles you've read about that place. Then go one step farther. Skip the overdone Warsaw ghetto. Instead, write about the ghetto in Venice, Italy. Forget the tourist-trap restaurants in the old walled city of Dubrovnik. Instead, write about that secluded seafood spot, thirty minutes down the road on the Yugoslavian Riviera. A day in Rio may be hackneyed for most publications, but a day on nearby Paqueta Island is new and refreshing.

Visit the destination: If you want authenticity and credibility, let your readers know you've been to the spot about which you are writing. Describe something you ate or something you bought. Quote a local resident. Don't write from a brochure. Readers can peruse those without your help.

Timely events are a time bomb: Unless you have a regular market and are insured of immediate publication, don't write about events occurring currently or in the near future. By the time an editor gets around to reading—and using—your story, it may be dead.

Be aware of the shrinking newspaper market: Where once the free lancer was a major force in the travel sections of Sunday newspapers, today these sections are filled mostly with pieces by staff writers or articles obtained from outside news services.

Expand your markets: Forget the traditional newspaper markets and concentrate on secondary markets such as magazines targeting sports, business, art, and senior citizens.

Go behind the scenes: The kitchen at Air France . . . the flight attendants' training center at Singapore Airlines . . . the semi-annual sale at Harrods; the cockpit of the *Concorde* . . . the kennel of the *QE2* . . . the shop on the *Orient Express*. All topics not likely to be over-done.

Think ahead: Jump the gun. If your city is planning a bicentennial in two years, now is the time to query that travel magazine. If the local senior citizens club sponsors an annual motor coach tour for fall leaf-ing, query seniors' magazines, a year ahead, to see if they'd like an on-the-coach reporter.

Work with a local travel agency: Convince them of the importance of a monthly newsletter or insert to go with their regular mailings. Payment can be much better than what you'd get for a newspaper article—and much steadier.

Work with a local public relations firm: Though your byline may never see the light of day, the pay for travel-related press releases is much better than for newspaper articles. The same holds true for writing for the tourist offices of various cities or countries.

Rely on round-ups: Grouping short items on one subject or theme into a single article is a favorite of editors. The world's best: golf courses . . . tennis camps . . . adventure travel . . . honeymoons. The world's worst: restaurants . . . cruises . . . shopping, etc.

Professional travel tips: Even though you might overpack when you travel, the reading public still wants you to tell them how to travel lightly. They also want to know what type of luggage you recommend, how to deal with jet lag and what to do about nasty customs officials.

Be a photographer: Even though you may not know a shutter from a lens, learn to take your own pictures. Presenting a complete package to an editor gives you the leading edge. Smart cameras make it easy for dumb photographers.

Don't try to be what you're not: Sophisticated readers want travel articles written by sophisticated writers. Adventurers want to read about trekking the Himalayas by someone who has trekked them.

Leave golf vacations to golfers, shopping sprees to shoppers. Don't try to write for a publication that features a lifestyle totally foreign to you.

Give editors what they want: When magazines request a query, send a query; when they request an SASE (self-addressed, stamped envelope), send an SASE. Familiarize yourself with the writing style of the publication you're aiming for, noting the number of words in the average article. Editors prefer not to edit.

Be accurate: Establishing a long-term relationship with an editor is directly dependent upon the reliability of your work. Many travel writers offer readability; not as many offer credibility.

Include consumer information: An informative sidebar is a necessity with most travel articles. The reader needs to know how to get there; what documentation is required; what the local currency is and the best place to get it; what the weather's like; appropriate clothing at different times of year, etc.

Submit clean copy: No matter how enjoyable and informative your article may be, an editor will pitch out a messy manuscript rather than suffer eye strain trying to decipher it.

62

FINDING IDEAS THAT SELL ARTICLES

BY SAMM SINCLAIR BAKER

HOW CAN YOU GET WRITING IDEAS that will sell your articles? How can you tell whether an idea has sales potential or should be discarded? How can you develop the ideas fully so that they will make sales?

Through many years of rejections as well as successes, I worked out a four-step process for getting and judging ideas that would sell. I looked beyond that to seek and assess ideas for their potential as cover articles and bestselling books based on their value in attracting and serving readers.

This system has proved its worth many times to beginning and published writers whom I have taught and advised. Here are the four progressive steps that have worked repeatedly; now they are yours for the using.

Step 1. *Be alert every minute for new ideas.*

Keep all your senses alive wherever you are to spark ideas by seeing, listening, smelling, and touching. If you don't make it a habit to stay alert for the salable idea, then potential winners will pass you by. Even a minor item in a newspaper or magazine can evoke a big idea. Watching news or other programs on television can touch off the pursuit of an idea when you are consciously receptive. Here are some examples proving that lucrative new ideas can be found by using all your senses.

Look: I was reading *The New York Times Sunday Magazine* and scanning a general feature on beauty, not a subject of great interest to me. My eye caught the word "Scarsdale," a neighboring village. I read the few lines that aroused me, though they were buried in the lengthy piece.

My mind was trained to seek out anything that might contain an idea for writing, so I read on attentively. The author reported that many fashionable Scarsdale residents were reducing remarkably with a one-page diet sheet obtained from a local doctor. Furthermore, the sheet was available to readers who sent a stamped, self-addressed envelope to the doctor at his address.

I followed through by sending for a copy. I studied the details of the diet and approved basically but not fully. I wrote to the doctor (Herman Tarnower) that I saw an idea for a book in his sheet and had some specific suggestions. He invited me to meet with him. We clicked and co-authored *The Complete Scarsdale Medical Diet,* which has sold over ten million copies worldwide, becoming the best-selling diet book ever.

I told this to a friend who had written a number of published articles and books in the diet field. "My God," she exclaimed, "I saw that item and skipped right over its potential as a book idea. I missed the boat because my brain was asleep."

Watching a popular TV mystery program, I noted the subtitle of the episode, something like "Screech Owl and a Blood-Curdling Scream." I said to my wife, "Those TV titles are crazy." She agreed and added, "Isn't that an article idea?" Over the next week I collected a batch of the subtitles and wrote, "Those Crazy TV Titles." A national magazine grabbed it.

Going through your mail can produce writing ideas if you're on the lookout. Consider the possibilities before you discard anything quickly. One day, I opened an envelope and found a reprint of an article by a top copyright lawyer who wrote about movie producers losing millions of dollars through improper and inadequate copyrighting. As a result, copyrights expired without renewal. Film pirates were taking advantage of the opportunities by selling unauthorized copies of the movies to TV, cable, and videocassette merchandisers.

I wondered, was there an article idea here? I saw the possibility of interesting a national magazine because of the vast audience of readers who watched TV and movies. The same mail brought an "Idea tips" sheet from the "Office of Medical Information" at a large university, and also a similar bulletin from an area hospital.

I pulled out several items that might be researched, expanded, and used as material for fresh, salable articles. One note discussed the "Biological Basis for Couch Potatoes." It highlighted the increase in muscle energy defects that result from children and adults lounging for hours watching television instead of being physically active. The university press relations department offered writers details and interviews with staff scientists. Many universities offer such services. Your mail contains idea banks you can draw on.

Hear: Listening to a radio interview while driving, I heard a man explain his unique business. He said that from his studies of music, he developed the ability to read rough score sheets by music arrangers. He set up a special printing press in his home after he learned how to separate and print the parts for each instrument in an orchestra. I tracked him down and incorporated his fascinating explanation in an article for a newspaper magazine.

Smell: A writer friend told me, "I was cooking a pot of vegetable soup and the aroma suddenly transported me back to my mother's kitchen. That gave me an idea. I interviewed several psychologists about the relationship between odors and memories. Their dramatic explanations went into an article that was an easy sale."

Feel: As I noted and handled an unusual piece of jacquard fabric offered by a decorator, I marveled at the unusual texture of the intricate design. I tracked down the designer, interviewed him by phone and then in person, since he was an hour's drive away. I sold his profile and details about the weaving process to a leading magazine for interior decorators.

It makes profitable sense to use your senses as scouts to spot ideas you can transform into salable articles. However, it pays off only if you as a writer have trained yourself always to be on the hunt for ideas. Otherwise you're likely to miss one possibility after another. It pays to keep all your senses on the *qui vive* at all times.

Step 2: *Follow up on the slightest spark.*

You're listening to a discussion on the radio, and it arouses a glimmer of an idea—but you fail to make a note of it and it evaporates.

You're watching a TV news report, and a bulletin sparks the beginning of an idea for an article, but you're not totally aware and the idea dwindles into nothingness.

You're on vacation, and suddenly a gust of wind off the salty sea tantalizes your sense of smell. If you're alert, it may trigger an idea about collecting memorable vacation experiences of others in an article. You feel good about that, but you don't jot down the inherent idea and it blows away with the breeze.

You touch and gently rub the smooth, yielding skin of a fresh peach and it brings to mind an idea for an article on food, always a promising subject. Do you follow up and dig up fresh facts on taste and nutrition and other slants about food which would be of interest to many? Or do you let the idea get out of touch?

It's up to you to follow through and hogtie those slight beginnings, to wrestle with them and flesh them out into a series of salable pieces that might even be expanded into a book. I joined a group at a barbecue in a neighbor's yard and listened to a bright-eyed woman tell how she was helping teach English to recent immigrants in the area. Was there an article embodied there? Our hostess's reaction was, "Teaching English? Dull, dull, dull."

I chatted with the woman who had been speaking and learned that she had become involved with a volunteer organization named English-in-Action. She explained that their purpose was to help foreign new-comers learn the language and become familiar with shopping and other everyday procedures, thus speeding their way to citizenship. A visit to the English-in-Action officers provided me with printed material along with leads for interviews. As a result of digging, I wrote and sold three articles with different slants to national, regional, and local publications.

Step 3. *Track down vital facts related to the idea.*

When I was writing a book about creative thinking, a top business executive told me, "First, I cram my head full of facts—and something worthwhile always comes out." Digging for facts about creative thinking, I learned that Thomas Edison's procedure was to compile all available facts and discoveries about a subject; he would then seek previously unknown or unrecognized relationships among them. In short, search for something new, a different twist; emphasize the something new that generally makes the difference between sale or rejection.

Sir Isaac Newton talked of searching for knowledge and ideas by compiling facts "like children who pick up pebbles on the beach." I believe that if I pick up enough pebbles, I may come across a jewel. In my years of writing, I often have.

In doing research for a new book, I read a story about the great attorney Clarence Darrow, one of the most creative persons in law. Cross-examining a very able doctor during a trial, Darrow had torn

300

apart the physician's testimony, by burying him under an astonishing outpouring of facts and knowledge.

After the trial, Darrow was asked, "When did you learn medicine and get your M.D.?"

He replied, "In my study last night, from midnight to 3 A.M."

How can collecting facts, assessing them, and seeking relationships and connections in a chain of facts help you in writing? For a diet book I was writing, I filled a file cabinet with my factual findings and notes. When I analyzed the material, I found that a number of case histories gathered in my interviews and searching revealed that just three words formed the basis for successful reducing by man: "quick weight loss."

I found an experienced diet doctor—Dr. Irwin Stillman—who agreed with my conclusions. We collaborated on *The Doctor's Quick Weight Loss Diet,* which became a historic bestseller. Digging for, gathering, and assessing facts involves loads of work, but who ever said that creating and producing salable writing was easy? You'll find that the rewards are thrilling and unquestionably worthwhile.

Step 4. *Write from the reader's and editor's viewpoint.*

You have settled on the idea, and now you're ready to start writing. The main thing I had to learn and observe to flesh out my ideas into salable material is this: Scrutinize what you write with the prospective readers' eyes. The key to my success during my years as an advertising writer was that I achieved a transference to become the customer as well as the writer, myself on one side of a counter and the customer on the other. Similarly, I now try to project myself into the viewpoint of the editor. It works for the writers I've taught, for me, and it can work for you.

The step-by-step mental process makes idea-producing sense. Deliberately proceeding step by step will help you develop ideas that pay off. And the more you follow this simple *modus operandi,* the more effective it will become for you. As Oliver Wendell Holmes pointed out, *"A person's mind stretched by a new idea can never go back to its original dimension."*

63

WRITING TRUE-LIFE CRIME

BY WILLIAM K. BEAVER

THE TRUE-LIFE CRIME GENRE originated in the late 19th century and has grown in popularity ever since. After nearly forty true-life detective magazines were born and died, modern magazine and book publishers discovered that a solid audience exists for the true-life crime story. Books like *The Preppie Murder* or *The Stranger Beside Me* consistently find their way to the bestseller lists.

Writing about true-life crime is not for hack writers. Finding a fresh detective story inside a crime that has already been widely covered by the media requires the skills of a sleuth and the style of a novelist. Here are seven secrets for writing successful true-life crime articles.

1. **Find the perfect crime.** Recognizing the perfect crime for a true-life article eventually becomes an intuitive flash. Many of the detective magazines will accept a story about almost any crime, but to increase the chance of success, search for a crime with some notoriety and color to it.

Serial killings, mass murders, and terrorist-related murders are obvious choices, but smaller crimes can also provide excellent material. Consider the following:

I queried an editor concerning the murder of a bank teller during an armed robbery. The young woman's murder was of itself interesting enough for an article, but what gave it a special twist was the brutal way the crime was committed. The assailant had started for the door to make his escape when he suddenly turned, walked back to the desk under which the teller was hiding, pulled her out, and shot her.

In writing the true-life crime story, the writer must face the worst that human beings are capable of doing. Forgetting the article and its subject sometimes takes effort, especially when you must visualize the event as you write.

The perfect true-life crime article for any of the detective magazines and for most book publishers requires another element—superlative detective work on the part of investigators. The readers of true-life crime want to know how the police solved aspects of the case that had originally stumped them. Articles editorializing what the police did wrong are best left to investigative pieces.

The third aspect of the perfect crime involves knowing the conclusion of the story. Articles about unsolved crimes or ones in which the accused is found innocent usually do not satisfy or appeal to editors or readers. Most true-life crime buffs believe in law and order, so stories in which the accused were found guilty usually stand the best chance of being accepted.

2. **Develop the available information.** To begin research for an article, first unravel the basic facts of the story by finding all the information that is readily available. The best method is to photocopy newspaper or magazine articles about the particular crime and use them as your starting point.

If you failed to follow the story and keep newspaper clippings as it developed, you will need to visit libraries and possibly newspaper morgues. Depending on the library, indexes may be available in which the story is listed under the subject of homicides and murders, or under the name of the victim and/or assailant.

After you gather the available information, organize it into four categories: information about the victim; the suspects; information from the police and coroner; and details of the crime scene. Correlate all the information you have collected under one of the four columns, noting what information and details are missing.

3. **Interview other sources.** You now must find information that the press or the investigators did not reveal at the time of the crime. Start with the investigation team at the police department. Your task becomes difficult because you are trying to write about a crime on which the police have already been endlessly questioned.

You can gain the police's cooperation by emphasizing that you wish to write the article from their point of view: how did the investigators crack the case? Ask to speak with the police officer in charge of the original investigation, since he's the person with the most knowledge about the crime.

The key to a successful interview with the police, like any other interview, is to prepare carefully for it. Ask the officer to tell you about the case in his own words, recording the interview if he will permit it. As he speaks, listen for the facts you already have, and especially for new material not mentioned previously.

Don't be afraid to ask for any additional details the police have.

I have managed to obtain copies of police reports and been given access to a complete case file, which provided a wealth of information not usually given to the press.

Be sure to double-check the facts you obtained from newspaper and magazine articles. Ask the police officer about such important details as names, dates, and methods. One newspaper article about the murder of a young girl described the murder weapon as a nail file found lying on the bedroom floor, but the detective told me the actual weapon was a box-cutting knife found in the suspect's apartment.

4. Search for "color." Little details discovered during your research add immeasurably to the story. I will often go to the neighborhood of the crime scene to absorb the sights, the sounds, and the people.

If the police give you access to photographs of the crime scene, look for details like the time on the clock, the furnishings in the room, unusual photographs on the wall or table.

Ask the police if there was anything unusual about the investigation. In writing about one crime I discovered that the police tried using a psychic to find the murderer. The psychic described a scene that did not relate to the crime in question, but sounded like another crime that took place in another city.

Investigators called the police there and gave them the psychic's information. When I later wrote about the second murder, the investigators mentioned the psychic's tip (which I already knew about), and I was able to use the anecdote in my story.

The suspect is another source of color. Try to find small bits of information that show how the criminal was perceived by those around him who were unaware of his activities. These could be observations of strange behavior or awards for good behavior. In fact, once when I worked as a resumé and business writer, I found the resumé belonging to the first mass murderer I wrote about. The resumé listed four awards for exemplary performance at the hospital where he murdered seventeen patients.

5. **Use fiction techniques to develop both suspense and the characters.** Once you discover the color of the story and gather all the information, start to weave the elements into a tight, cohesive story. A good true-life crime article demands the same attention to setting, character, and pacing as a fictional story does.

As with all articles, the choice of the lead is vital. You must decide on the starting point from which to develop the story, and also how to work in all the details. The first true-life piece I tackled concerned a serial killer—a hospital orderly—who murdered more than fifty-four people. I had several options for the lead, but a thorough review of the material provided it for me. A coroner's office pathologist detected the smell of almonds while performing an autopsy on an accident victim who had died in the hospital. The smell of almonds sometimes indicates the presence of cyanide, but since the odor can be detected by only twenty per cent of the population, the pathologist ran a test for cyanide. The test came back positive, the pathologist had discovered a murder that later led to the arrest of the serial killer/orderly, and I had my lead.

Try to pace the piece by developing the setting so the reader can visualize as much as possible. Describe the scene of the crime, the actions of the investigators, and what is known about the victim. The most important detail, however, is to delay identification of the murderer until the last possible moment. Use suspense techniques, such as dead-end investigative leads, to build the story.

Use the same format as you would in writing fiction: the introduction, story buildup, the climax, and finally the resolution.

6. **Know the required format.** Most true-life crime articles use the same basic formats, but it's a good idea to write to the various magazines and request their writers' guidelines.

Ask about photographs. Does the magazine pay extra for the pictures or are they included—even expected—in the manuscript price?

Always submit the query and manuscript in professional form. Nothing will bring a rejection faster than sloppy presentation or obvious mistakes. Keep track of all source materials, including interviews and newspaper clippings. Most magazines will check your facts and will require copies of your material for their files. These will provide references in the event of a lawsuit.

7. Be on the lookout for more sources and the perfect crime. If you continue as a true-life crime writer, you must gain the confidence of your sources in the police department and the coroner's office, among others, in the same manner a newspaper journalist might. Respect their wishes.

I approached a police department for information about a crime I was writing about. Since I was unknown to them, their reception was guarded and aloof. But when they later saw how I treated the story, the next time I went back, they shared information with me that the newspaper did not have, including the film taken by a hidden camera during the bank robbery/murder.

If you are serious about writing true-life crime articles, join any legal groups in your area. I was invited to speak about the pursuit of Nazi war criminals for a discussion group that included two county coroners, several legal aides, and several investigators and attorneys, all of whom expressed a willingness to help me in the future.

The key to writing true-life crime centers on *information* and *presentation*. If you have enough information and polish your presentation, chances are you will be successful writing about the perfect crime.

64

WRITING THE PRO/CON ARTICLE

BY BARBARA MCGARRY PETERS

SKILLED WRITERS WHO TYPICALLY SAIL THROUGH FACTUAL NEWS reports or how-tos often shy away from controversial subjects. It's easy to understand why. Pro/con articles have inherent perils and pitfalls and so are tricky to do well.

Why then enter the fray? A well-written pro/con piece brings several rewards. One payoff is the insight you gain from successfully thrashing out a complex problem with no obvious answer. Another is the satisfaction of helping your readers make a difficult choice. A third is the challenge of writing an honest article that's fit to print—and getting paid for it.

Here are seven guidelines that might help you, as they've helped me, with the writing process.

1. *Choose a point of view.* This will be your story line. This doesn't mean you should come down hard on one side or the other. That would be courting rejection. Your point of view comes from an organizing principle—a point at which the two sides meet or at least brush by one another. From this unifying thread or central idea, you can move in either direction, and your article takes shape.

Without this strong theme, you may end up with a string of ideas not clearly linked to a developing story line. This happened to me when I was trying too hard to write a well-balanced piece. To the editor, my article appeared "disjointed and choppy—jumping back and forth abruptly without moving in a particular direction." Wanting to present both sides of the argument without taking sides and keep within the word limit, I had cut the connective tissue that held the article together. As a result the editor was as perplexed about the problem at the end of the article as he was at the beginning. But, thanks to his detailed rejection letter with suggestions for revision, I refashioned my article, and it appeared in print a month later.

2. *Get to the point quickly and stick to it.* Don't stumble or back your way into the article. Use punchy words and snappy, short sentences to capture your readers' interest. Your lead should announce your theme. Make it clear who your target audience is: for example, women or men of a special age group. Soon after you present the pro side, acknowledge the con position.

After you state your theme, tell readers your reason for writing the piece, and why you are writing it now. Has there been a fresh development that makes the article newsworthy? Your "angle" or "hook" could be a report from a recent conference, a political speech, a public announcement, or the publication of a scientific study.

Begin with general statements, then zoom in on details. But don't tell the readers anything they don't have to know. Irrelevant or tangential facts clutter the page and mask the story line. Scrutinize each sentence of your draft, and ask yourself: "Can my reader make a decision without knowing this?"

3. *Give evidence of thorough research.* Steep yourself in the subject, and interview experts from a wide range of disciplines. Controversies often affect people in a variety of ways: physical, emotional, social, political, and spiritual. It's important to include quotes on all aspects of a complex problem because one part of the problem might have a bearing on another. For instance, an article on the pros and cons of postmenopausal hormone treatment might include specialists in disease prevention and health promotion, gynecology, heart and bone disease, breast and uterine cancer, and genetic research. An article on the abortion controversy might include specialists in law, sociology, women's and children's health, psychology, medical research, religion, and ethics. Weave the experts' quotes into the article with smooth transitions, so that they reinforce your idea without slowing the pace.

Devote at least one paragraph to every argument. Imagine your reader asking you to clarify a point. What could you do to make the idea clearer, more understandable, persuasive?

4. *Keep your focus on general guidelines.* Don't overwhelm your reader with statistics related to the arguments, such as figures on

mortality, disease, or divorce rates or voter preferences. Statistics are virtually meaningless in a complex problem, especially one that involves more than one person. Even if risks were certain, making a choice between options would still be difficult, because there is always a trade-off between benefits and risks. And too many numbers confuse readers and slow the pace of the article.

5. *Keep your tone neutral.* A "let's reason together" tone is most likely to keep a reader's attention. Use concrete words for emotional effect. Avoid inflammatory words. If you're trying to remain objective and an angry tone slips into your writing, you'll lose most editors fast. It's tempting to use colorful, emotion-packed quotes, but your editor may become convinced you're promoting one side and will reject your article.

Avoid judgmental words or phrases; specious reasoning; unfair or weak arguments; uninformed, offensive remarks of unknown origin; questionable, simplistic, or vague accusatory comments.

6. *Save your strongest pro and con arguments for last.* It is the end of your article that will stick in your reader's mind. Don't discount the fact that many readers habitually take a peek at the end before they even finish the lead. A strong conclusion gives the reader something to think about—a clinching bit of evidence, a promising resource, a challenging question.

Wrap up your article by rephrasing your theme, and then leave readers with a new, provocative idea that invites them to weigh the implications of their decision.

7. *Ask a colleague or friend who is objective to read the manuscript for clarity,* to make sure it is not condescending, preachy, or insulting to your readers' intelligence. What questions have not been answered about the subject that should be? This step will help root out ambiguous sentences and unconvincing arguments.

Following these seven tips will greatly improve your chances of acceptance, but there still may be some frustrations along the way when you write about a controversial topic. The only writers who seem to have an easy time with it are those who refuse to consider both sides of the question.

What if you tackle a hot issue and find yourself with a pile of conflicting research, all supposedly valid arguments from leaders in the field? You must try to put things into perspective and consider the humorous aspects. As Bertrand Russell said, "The most savage controversies are those about matters . . . to which there is no good evidence either way."

❰ 65

PREPARING A NONFICTION BOOK PROPOSAL

BY NICHOLAS BAKALAR

EDITORS IN EVERY TRADE PUBLISHING HOUSE I have ever known are intensely, sometimes perhaps even desperately, searching for publishable manuscripts. It may come as a surprise to authors whose manuscripts have been rejected more than once that editors actually do not like to reject books. On the contrary, each time editors open an envelope, they are eager, eager to find an interesting book, a book they like, a book they can successfully publish, a book that is really *good*. They do not reject books casually: It is their duty, and pleasure, to read what is put before them, and to take seriously what they read.

You don't need to be told that manuscripts should be typed with a clean ribbon, double spaced, with standard grammar and punctuation. Elegant binders and high-tech laser printers add little to a good manuscript, and, to me at least, they make a bad one look even worse. So a straightforward, neat physical presentation is probably best.

But that's the easy part. What about the hard part? What is a book editor hoping to find when he or she opens those envelopes? What do editors want?

No editor I know can consistently publish books that he does not like. The idea that there are editors who can say to themselves, "well, this is a piece of absolute junk, but it will no doubt sell a million copies, so let's publish it" is a myth whose origin I do not know. The fact is that the editors who publish popular fiction, or gothic romances, or westerns, or mystery stories, or exercise books, or cartoon and humor books—enjoy those genres. They like them, they read them, they know a good one when they see it. And the editors who publish important works of nonfiction that are reviewed in the pages of the *New York*

Review of Books—often, I should add, the same editors who publish those mystery stories and westerns—enjoy those books as well.

This is not to say that editors never make decisions cynically. Occasionally, no doubt, they do. But I know of no editor who has successfully made a career of it. So the first criterion for deciding to publish is clear: First, I have to like it. Obviously, no editor likes everything, so one of the first things to do when submitting a proposal is to find the right editor to submit it to. Most trade editors have no specialty, but they do have their likes and dislikes, and these are not hard to discover. Find a good book, preferably recently published, that is comparable in style or subject or format to the book you have in mind to publish. Call the publisher and ask him who the editor is. At most houses, you will get a quick and straightforward answer to this question. Believe it or not, editors actually *do* want to receive proposals for books, and they are happy to have their names and addresses given out to writers. There is a wacky idea in certain quarters that editors consider it an imposition to be asked to read proposals. Let us dispense with this notion.

The question, "Is there a book in this?" is posed so frequently around publishing houses that it is almost a refrain, but how can editors tell if "there is a book in this" when they sit down with a proposal? Sometimes the process takes on mechanical aspects. Has this author been published before? Is he really an expert in this field, and how do we know he is? Have we ever done a book like this? How many copies did the one we did before sell? What is the sales record of this author, and do we have any authors to whom he can be compared? These are the easy questions—they have dates and numbers attached to them.

There are other practical considerations as well. Does the sales department do well with things like this? Can we get the sales force interested enough to push this book with the stores, or will it be the sort of thing that they will find easy to ignore when they go over the list with their accounts? Will the publicity department be able to use this author or this subject productively?

Nor are editors above asking some selfish questions: Will this book be easy to edit? Will the author require quantities of time and attention before he is able to complete his work? Perhaps even more crudely, will he be a nuisance during the production of the book and after it comes out? Is he "difficult"? Don't forget an editor is going to have to line edit the manuscript, argue with the author, make sure permissions are in order, write catalogue and flap copy, present the book at a sales conference, convince the publicity department to show some interest, urge the rights department to get busy selling rights, and take care of a million other details essential to successful publication. An author and an editor are going to spend a good deal of time together, in one way or another, during the eighteen months or two years it takes to produce and publish a book. The question, "Is this someone I want to spend time with?" is neither irrelevant nor ignoble.

Among editors there are always two contradictory responses to a proposal to publish a book similar to a recently successful one. The first is "There's too much competition for books like this, so we probably shouldn't do it." The second is "Everyone is having great success with books like this, so we'd better have one of our own." In the resolution of this conflict is often found, for better or worse, the publishing decision.

So you must know the competition. You must know the bibliography in your field, of course, and include it in some form in your proposal, but sometimes the easiest way to find out what's needed is to look in a bookstore—a technique that is for some reason often overlooked by even the most intelligent and astute writers. You want to write a book on repairing furniture? Fine. But you have to concede that there *are* a few books already out there on the subject. Why not go into a bookstore and have a look? How is your book going to measure up? There is a limited amount of space for furniture repair books, so one of those on the bookseller's shelf is going to have to be displaced to make room for yours. Why should he bother? That these kinds of practical questions rarely occur to authors is perhaps as it should be—after all, their preoccupation should be producing an intelligent and well-written proposal, not guessing at the commercial requirements of book retailing. Yet editors have to consider these things—and it can only be helpful for a writer to forestall at least the most obvious objections an editor can raise to a proposal for a book.

In this quick survey of what trade book editors look for in a proposal, I have not directly discussed the special case of fiction, and publishing fiction varies so greatly from house to house that I am not even sure such a discussion would be helpful in this context. But what I have said about nonfiction applies, *mutatis mutandis,* to the novel you want to see published. Find the right house, locate the right editor, present your proposal (normally a complete manuscript) intelligently, and your novel, provided it is publishable, will find a home.

Above all, don't be discouraged. Over 40,000 trade books are published every year. Your good idea for a trade book, presented properly to the right editor in the right house, will be published as well.

66

ESSAYS: AN ALTERNATIVE FOR FICTION WRITERS

BY KATHY PETERSEN CECALA

WHEN I LEFT COLLEGE, I vowed I'd devote myself entirely to the art of fiction. With idealistic (and arrogant) fervor, I decided I'd write short stories and novels only, and not waste my time and talent on mere journalism or nonfiction in any form. I was undaunted by my professors' warnings of the shrinking fiction market and the immense competition that awaited me. I was sure I'd be different.

Twelve years later, I can report that I'm still writing fiction. I've sold a single short story (about six years ago, to *McCall's*) and have amassed an impressive collection of rejection letters. The nicest ones—those praising my style and sensitivity and vision—are tacked up on my wall. But to be honest, they're no substitute for the simple thrill of being in print: seeing in hard type words and phrases that once existed only in your brain; seeing your name across the top of the page and on the table of contents; looking up your very own listing in *Readers' Guide to Periodical Literature*. I was grateful for the encouragement of editors, but I longed to be a published writer. I wanted a scrapbook full of clippings to show to dubious friends and family: "See? I *am* a writer! Really I am!"

Marketing fiction has always seemed to me a great war: You use whatever weapon you can find—talent, the recommendation of a friend, an editor's name gleaned from *Literary Market Place*—and try doggedly to advance, usually getting knocked off your horse in the process. I'd been wounded a number of times, once so badly I left the battlefield completely for a while. Rejection, no matter how brave you try to be about it, is always debilitating and dejecting.

Recently I decided to try a different battlefield. I did not give up short stories and novels, but tried some nonfiction, specifically, some short essays.

315

Essays: The very word conjures up agonizing scenes from high school and college, or it brings to mind certain adjectives: stuffy; long-winded; boring. But if you look through a variety of contemporary magazines and newspapers, you'll find numerous essays. They have other names, of course: "My Say," "My Turn," "Opinion," "Readers' Corner," and so on. They can be anything from pure opinion to rabid attack to gentle musing to impassioned argument to witty observation. I came to see that these short pieces could offer almost as much creative opportunity as my short stories did.

At first, these pieces seemed very remote from my fiction. They were based on hard facts and the real world, a world in which I felt I didn't really belong. Moreover, I felt vaguely guilty, as if I were "selling out," taking precious time away from the more worthy pursuit of fiction. Perhaps I wouldn't have spent very much more time on them if it weren't for an amazing happening—I sold them!

The first sold to our local paper—well, that *really* wasn't such a coup, was it? But friends and neighbors—who hitherto had seen little evidence of my vocation—were impressed, and I did get paid. Then I sold an essay to a big regional newspaper; then to a national magazine, then another . . . and it seemed to me this was more than coincidence. Was I to abandon fiction and become an essayist?

Not necessarily. But it does appear that the essay market is wide and receptive and a good way for frustrated fiction writers—against whom the odds of having their stories published increase depressingly—to break into print. Actually, in some magazines the essay has replaced the traditional short story. Why, I'm not sure. Perhaps modern times have become so uncertain, so harried, readers want to be told what they should be thinking, what's important and meaningful in life.

What's more, writing essays is not "selling out," but rather honest, enriching, and a good complement to fiction. My years of fiction writing, in turn, have served as a marvelous apprenticeship to essay writing. The discipline required in writing a short story is helpful in organizing an essay as well, and all those years of writing and revising do help polish one's style.

Writing essays has helped me find a voice, which at times comes through even more clearly and powerfully than in fiction. When I began to write, I wasn't aware of how raw, unformed, unpolished my work actually was (not to mention terribly derivative of whatever writer I was reading at the time). I took little time to consider what was behind my stories or my attempts at novels, or what the essential themes of my work were. Essays force you to distill important ideas and thoughts into clean, clear prose, to take a stand. And when you understand what you care most deeply about—ideas and beliefs so urgent, so compelling that you *have* to keep writing about them—it can't help but affect your fiction in a positive way. The late John Gardner, in his splendid book, *The Art of Fiction,* describes the fiction writer as a type of judge and says that the value of great fiction is ". . . not just that it entertains us, or distracts us from our troubles, not just that it broadens our knowledge of people and places, but that it helps us to know what we believe, reinforces those qualities that are noblest in us, leads us to feel uneasy about our faults and limitations."

Essays needn't be grandiose and gut-wrenching, or fraught with great meaning. I find that my best essays spring from simple, though sometimes quirky, ideas. One of my first nationally published essays was a short piece I wrote for *Commonweal* on an obscure Catholic novel I'd read as a parochial-school student. The idea came to me when I was clearing off a bookshelf and came across the book—*Mr. Blue*—and while flipping idly through it, noticed it had first been published exactly sixty years ago. I reread it, thought about it, then wrote up a little essay about my reaction to it now, and what meaning I thought the book of the late 1920s had for the late 1980s. It seemed perfect for *Commonweal,* a magazine I'd been reading for several years. Not only did this piece lead to an assignment from the magazine's editors, but it brought some enthusiastic letters from readers as well.

Before submitting an essay to a publication, it helps to do some research. If you love to read, this is no problem. You can start—as I did—with a local paper or magazine. A simple "Letter to the Editor" is a great mini-exercise in essay writing. The editors at our local paper say they are always looking for well-written, *rational* letters to print.

Try submitting something to magazines you read on a regular basis. Once a week, I make a trip to the local library to catch up on all the magazines I can't afford to subscribe to but enjoy. This approach is much more fun than scanning the market lists, trying to make your essay fit somebody else's qualifications. It also cuts down on the rejections. Sometimes, an editor will reject your piece, only because she just bought a piece on the same topic—but she'll ask for another essay. And very often, you may be asked to revise a piece. I once revised a piece three times, each time despairing over it (and almost not revising it at all), but in the end, the editor bought it. She told me later that she almost hadn't, but saw a "spark" of an idea in the first version and was pleased that I was finally able to develop it.

I often use essays to work out some moral dilemma or problem I'm facing in writing a novel or short story, and it seems now that all of my writing is connected, interrelated, with similar ideas and themes weaving in and out of each piece, published and unpublished. I feel like more of a Writer, with a capital W.

And I finally have that scrapbook. I splurged on one of those over-sized artist's portfolios, with the black, plastic-enclosed pages, and it's slowly filling up. At first I separated the fiction from the essays (and tucked the Letters to the Editor way in the back), but now they're all mixed up, each an interesting observation and comment on the other. They're in chronological order now, a real record of my development as a writer.

67

ANONYMOUS BUT PROFITABLE

BY MARTHA SHEA MCDOWELL

EARLY ON, I DISCOVERED THAT I WROTE MOST WILLINGLY when I knew there was money at the end of the typewriter ribbon. Although in the past I've sold articles to *Parents, McCall's, Your New Baby,* and a host of lesser publications, I've earned far more money writing as an *anonymous* word merchant.

To follow the path of anonymity successfully I had to put bylines in the perspective they deserve. For this I had early lessons. While still in my twenties fortune smiled, and to my own astonishment I was a feature writer for the *Chicago Daily News.* I got a byline every day; some days I got more than one. A year and one-half of bylines in a paper of at least one million readers, and you know what? I was neither rich nor famous; bylines gratify the ego, but have little lasting value . . . unless your name is Russell Baker or Mary McGrory.

I left the *Daily News* to care for my new baby, but I still needed to earn money. Fortunately, in Chicago I had contacts as a result of the newspaper job. Through them I located a publisher of educational pamphlets who wanted ghost writers to produce manuscripts or doctor the work of other writers. No byline . . . just money. I did one pamphlet; then we moved, eventually settling in Washington, D.C., a city bandaged in anonymous words.

In Washington, however, almost everyone you meet who is not a lawyer is a writer or journalist, so the competition was fierce. But the work is there, just as it is in your community, *if you're willing to be anonymous.* This anonymity further entails a graceful willingness to use your skill to make another person or institution look good. You never take credit. You only take money—a fee agreed upon before the first word is written. And if you have realistic questions about a client's financial reliability, you ask for one-quarter to one-half in advance.

Why is this market so ready for you? For those of us who have even a modest talent for writing, it is hard to understand that most men and women simply do not. I've watched bank officials and bureaucrats chew pencils and break into perspiration trying for half a day to find words for a simple letter to constituents or customers. If the problem is just a simple letter, I usually can solve it quickly. Clients often want to change a word here or there, or switch a paragraph, and unless there's a good legal or public relations reason *not* to change, that's fine. Sometimes the client's change improves the copy, because he or she knows the subject better than you possibly can know it.

Let me be specific about the kinds of clients I've written for—anonymously. Unless you live on a remote mountain top, someone in your community wants something written and is willing to pay for it.

• Every town has charitable, non-profit organizations that are totally dependent on donations. Such groups need: letters of solicitation, brochures of their service to the community told in specific, vivid prose, and thank-you letters for volunteers and donors. I have written a zillion of these, and been well paid for my efforts. After all, if your letter raises $50,000, you deserve payment.

• Small banks and financial institutions need: brochures telling of their customer services, annual reports, sales letters, thank-you letters, and sometimes employee newsletters. Big financial institutions hire advertising agencies to do these things. Small institutions are your market. Annual reports are a little tricky: accountants do the figures, graphic artists do the bar graphs. I have written only the narrative, such as a letter from the chairman of the board, or a description of a new building or service, and explanations of the graphs.

• Governmental bodies have a continuing need for the written word. Every town, city or county must inform citizens of services: a brochure for welfare; another describing services for senior citizens or children; still another about a bond issue coming up for a vote. Someone must write these. Often such brochures are put out to bid, so your first approach to this market may be through the purchasing department of your town or county. Usually written proposal specifications will tell you how to bid on the writing portion of the project.

In metropolitan areas often several small jurisdictions cluster around the central city; a writer could work for several of these jurisdictions. In Washington this is a limitless market. Cities, towns and counties surround the federal city, and all need the services of writers. I have written pamphlets for federal agencies, and even a series of recruiting ads for the Navy.

• Newsletters offer vast potential. Organizations, clubs and various groups use newsletters to inform members; often they will pay for them. Your chamber of commerce should have a quarterly newsletter for the businesses it serves. If it doesn't, convince the chamber that it needs one, and that you should do it. Factories or sizable businesses in your area may use different newsletters for circulation to their employees, stockholders, and community leaders. Travel agencies and insurance agencies should all have customer newsletters as sales tools. So should hospitals. This market may be yours for the asking.

• My favorite kind of anonymous writing is for politicians. I have never written for candidates for national office, but I have written for a number of candidates for state and local office. One caveat: If you don't know the candidate, or can't be certain of the campaign's financial soundness, get at least half your money up front. Politicians by law must pay for print, radio and television ads in advance. Many printers demand advance payment from campaigns. So the campaign won't be surprised by your request for early payment.

Politicians need brochures that will fit inside a #10 envelope, or can be used as self-mailers. They need fund-raising and thank-you letters. They need publicity releases and speeches. Speech writing, however, takes practice and special skills. Since you do not write to be read, but to be heard, the speeches should be in the language and cadence of the candidate. So unless you have experience or a natural talent for this, it may not be in the cards for you.

Nothing in this anonymous writing I've described does much for your ego. Most people don't know that you did the job. Other people take credit for your words. You can't show your friends your bylined article or story. It's even hard to describe to people what you do.

The surprise is that such writing does help develop your skill. Remember, you do not have to give up your other, perhaps more creative writing life when you do anonymous writing. In essence, it is writing to sell something: a product, a service, an idea, or a candidate. The buying public wants the facts . . . just the facts, and has little patience with empty, idle words. Each word must work; verbs used in the active voice move copy along and make it sparkle.

The writer learns word economy, and when he or she turns to fiction or an article these lessons serve well. No matter what you write you must compete for the reader's attention. Every day a mountain of material beckons the reader: newspapers, how-to manuals, professional reports, billboards, even STOP signs, and at last in a moment of leisure a serious novel. Your words must GRAB that reader's attention, preferably in the first sentence, and commercial writing can help you do that.

There are other advantages:

Most often, you are writing on some kind of deadline. There is no time for writer's block. You *must* produce.

You learn a lot, quickly, since you must understand a subject before you can write about it. This means asking a lot of questions that help focus the client's thinking and enrich your knowledge. I think it is an advantage *not* to know too much about a subject when you approach it. Often the public you write for is also uninformed, and would probably want to ask the same questions you will ask.

How much should the anonymous writer charge? To some degree that depends on where you live, and whether it's a one-shot job, or a long-term project, such as a continuing chamber of commerce newsletter.

On a one-shot job I charge by the hour, and I include time spent in conference, on the telephone, and in writing. On a project such as a regular chamber of commerce newsletter, I would set an annual fee to be paid to me on a monthly basis. On all projects I write a letter of agreement and ask the client to countersign it, with a copy for each of us. This helps clarify terms on both sides.

Where you live will determine how much you and your competition may charge. In New York or Los Angeles where living is more costly, writers will charge more than they might in Wichita, Kansas. However, I can't imagine any professional writer in the United States charging less than $25 an hour, plus expenses, including long-distance phone calls or necessary travel. (This is the kind of detail you will cover in your letter of agreement.)

On hearing about the profitability of anonymity, poets and novelists may shake heads in pity, wondering at the crassness of it all. You could devote your life to serious "creative" writing and still be anonymous *and* poor. Trading in your byline for a month's rent is not a bad deal. You might come to enjoy it.

68

Writing Biographies: The Problems and the Process

By Katherine Ramsland

Biographers are fixed on their heroes in a very peculiar manner," said Sigmund Freud. By that he meant that writing a biography is motivated by some psychological preoccupation. It is difficult for biographers to sustain such demanding work without intense emotional involvement with their subjects. Biographers must be prepared to make a major commitment, to immerse themselves totally in the point of view of another person so they can recreate that person's life with accuracy.

Choosing the subject

Most biographers write about their subjects because they know them, admire them, or believe a biography will make a contribution. Some biographers rework old material in new ways, and much of the "detective work" is already done. Those who introduce the subject for the first time must spend considerable effort collecting data. Writers of "authorized" biographies have access to private papers, while others have to struggle along without such cooperation. If the subject is living, the biographer faces problems not a factor when the subject is dead.

The choice of subject is also dictated by publishers' criteria. An academic publisher may want a scholarly book on an existing body of information, emphasizing literary criticism, while a commercial biography must demonstrate its market value, i.e., its readability and appeal to the general reader.

Dealing with research

Basically, there are two methods for dealing with facts. One is to collect them first, and organize them later. This prevents premature interpretations from highlighting some facts over others. The second method involves collecting just enough facts to set up a general guide for future directions. Your own personality will dictate which one you choose.

Both methods benefit from an active and passive phase. After a flurry of fact-gathering, allow your unconscious mind to go to work to reveal meaningful patterns as well as gaps in research. To be understood, facts must be absorbed and digested in the context of other information.

Inevitably you will be faced with an inordinate amount of data that needs careful organization and interpretation. Facts are malleable; they can be magnified out of proportion, interpreted out of context, minimized or suppressed. The first rule is to resist the impulse to appear omniscient. No person's life can be known completely. At best, a biography is a *perspective* based on the biographer's vision. Undocumented conjecture, while sometimes necessary, should be so acknowledged. The point is to create from raw data an organic portrait that reveals the significance of the subject's life or work. Not all of the facts will contribute to this goal. However, an abundance of facts must still be gathered to pinpoint those that give shape to how the subject's life was lived. There are many sources for locating that material.

1. Information may already be written in archives, letters, diaries, media profiles, unpublished manuscripts, and in earlier biographies.

2. Interviewing people who had personal acquaintance with the subject is essential. If the subject is living, he or she may give you a list. Otherwise, surviving family members can be helpful. Friends and relatives provide perspectives that can corroborate or broaden your understanding. Sometimes these contacts will be made over the phone or by mail, but often they will be face-to-face. Some people will be eager to cooperate; others may be reluctant. Friends will seek to protect, enemies to malign. You need tact, patience, persistence and discernment to obtain as many perspectives as possible. Prepare questions ahead of time. In the immediacy of an interview it is easy to forget points you wanted to raise.

All comments should be recorded, if possible. Do not count on being able to reconstruct a conversation later, especially as you begin to accumulate data. Biographies evolve. Your first impressions may not correspond to later insights. I am constantly surprised as I read over transcripts how items jump out at me that I had earlier overlooked. Had I just taken notes, those items would have been lost to me. Always ask permission to record, even over the phone. Be prepared to take notes if they say no.

3. Visit places that have meaning for the subject. Anne Rice lived in New Orleans. In writing her biography, I walked the streets she walked, and experiencing some of the same sensory impressions as she did—the smell of magnolias, the noise of rattling streetcars—gave me a perspective on her childhood.

4. You should have some grasp of the social and cultural influences that affected the subject.

5. General reference books on relevant subjects are helpful. I read books on psychology, sociology, alcoholism, and creativity to enhance understanding. Also, reading short profiles of other personalities can suggest new directions and help the writer create vivid impressions.

6. Reading books that influenced your subject can yield surprising insights.

7. Your own intuition is important. Note your emotional connections. You may have to make reasonable guesses about the subject's motivations, and using the facts you *do* have along with your intuition can help you make logical associations.

8. Photographs can reveal a great deal about a person's character and emotional development.

The idea of research is to find unifying themes among seemingly contradictory events or actions. Keep your eyes open for ideas or events that changed the person's *perspective* so you can monitor his or her emotional pulse. The points at which subjects' lives are most vivid to them are the points with which readers will identify most.

There is no end to the amount of factual data you can accumulate. One way you can organize and focus this research is to make an outline that provides logical progression and continuity. And you can structure your outline by choosing a biographical model.

Choosing a model

Biography involves both content and form. The form is like the plot of a novel: it makes the diverse elements work together to serve the purpose of the whole. Facts and quotes must be accurate, and critical interpretations interesting, but there is a consensus among contemporary biographers that there be enough flexibility of form to allow a biographer to make a work unique. In other words, biographers are free to give their books an *aesthetic* unity and to interpret the stages of this subject. The choice of a model is important to this process.

1. Interpretive models guide readers, typically through psychological explanations, to reveal the motives that make sense of the subject's choices.

2. Objective models use all the known facts to document how the subject lived. This method is viewed more as historical than artistic.

3. Dramatic models *show* the subject through fictional devices, telling the life story through a series of vignettes and events. Virginia Woolf first coined the term "creative fact" to describe a fact that suggests or creates mood and character, even as it provides information. In such biographies, the "facts" are interpreted by the writer's imagination, thus replacing objectivity with intimacy. These biographies read more like novels than factual nonfiction.

The strength of a biography lies in creating the moments that reveal the most profound psychological truths—the motivations, transformations, and points of conflict—in the life of the subject. Biographers make choices in their writing as did the subjects in their lives. The writer's goal is to enable readers to *see* the subjects and to grasp how they acted and reacted, intentionally and unconsciously.

Many biographers make use of fictional devices, constructing their books with "plots," and paying special attention to creating tone and mood. Chapter endings may be "cliff-hangers," and using anecdotes with dialogue can provide details.

Ask yourself how closely you should stick to "just the facts." Dramatic styles take more license than objective styles. However, even the most fact-oriented biography can utilize fictional devices to create tension, advance the story, give information and reveal character.

For example, dialogue and physical impressions can be constructed from memory or from recordings to create scenes at important moments in the lives of the subjects. You can write dialogue by quoting from an exchange of letters, or if the subject is living, use what he or she recalls in dialogue.

Short chapters can give the feeling of tension, impatience, and urgency, as does Gerald Clarke's *Capote*. Metaphors and imagery deliver powerful impressions. The idea is to reveal the essence of the person, and to accomplish this, figurative language is sometimes superior to facts.

Uncomfortable discoveries

You may be confronted with information about your subject that gives you pause: sexual misconduct, cruelty, bigotry or marital discord. Perhaps the subject has even created a false picture of his or her life to manipulate public opinion. If the subject is still alive, and especially if he or she is cooperative, such information will raise important questions. How much must be revealed to facilitate an understanding of the person's life and how much is really just gratuitous gossip?

Arguments can be made for either side. Advocates of full revelation might consider one of the following points:

1. On the "objective" model, suppressing anything is an interpretation; to achieve objectivity, *all* facts must be revealed.

2. The dramatic model feeds on personal information—the more personal the better—to make the work truly vivid.

3. Some biographers idealize their subjects and justify avoiding the "dark" areas as unimportant in order to keep to their view of the person. For example, it was once thought that biographies of women should not disclose (for the "higher purposes" of society) information that detracted from their femininity. Carol Heilbrun, in *Writing a Woman's Life,* disagrees. She urges biographers of women to include "unfeminine" anger, dissatisfaction with roles, and quests for sensuality and power. Presenting the *whole* person takes priority.

Yet there are also arguments *against* full disclosure. For example:

1. People still alive may be harmed by the revelations.

2. Gossip detracts from scholarship. If the biographer reveals the information only to play up scandal, then he or she is not playing fair—(though including this type of information often adds to the readability of the book).

There are no easy answers to writing biography, and authors must decide for themselves what information will best serve their purpose. The purpose of biography is not to "spill the beans," but to deliver an interesting and comprehensive portrait guided by principles, imposed partly by the author and partly by the need for continuity, accuracy, depth, and focus.

69

THE LIBRARY: A RESEARCHER'S BEST FRIEND

BY MARGARET G. BIGGER

WOULDN'T IT BE GREAT TO HAVE A NETWORK of friends to help you with research and even contact other resource people for you? You do. In virtually every county in every state, the library stands ready to offer assistance not just from 9 to 5 weekdays, but often at night and on weekends, too. And, like true friends, libraries rarely charge for their services.

Reference department workers at most public libraries will reply to questions by phone about census statistics, national organizations, famous people, and an enormous variety of other topics easily found in their reference books. I ask only one question per call and only something that would likely be found in a book on the main floor in the reference area (not in the stacks or other remote sections). Recently, I called a reference librarian to find out the attendance at the 1989 Rose Bowl game; though she could tell me the number of seats in the stadium, she could not immediately locate the exact information I needed. She took down my name and phone number, and at noon the next day, she called to say she was still looking; by evening she called in triumph with the answer: "101,668!"

To do more involved research, you will have to go to a library, preferably the main library. A telephone call first, however, will determine whether a particular library or branch has material on your topic. Card catalogues, the *Readers' Guide to Periodical Literature,* and encyclopedias are handy tools, but the experienced librarian can help you find resources you may not think of. Be specific when you explain your needs.

World almanacs and atlases may be the best quick-fact books, but you should also consider these: *The Book of Answers* explores topics from the calendar to medicine, and from inventions to defense. *The Lincoln Library of Essential Information* has facts about major subjects, plus 3,600 brief biographies of noteworthy people who lived during 4,000 years of recorded history. To find out about well-known personalities, try biographical dictionaries, *Who's Who* and *Who Was Who* volumes, for which there are indexes.

If you want quotes from an important person, *Names & Numbers (A Journalist's Guide to the Most Needed Information Sources & Contacts)* has more than 20,000 listings arranged in such categories as the media, government, emergency agencies, business, sports, consumers, economics, education, religion, science and technology, politics, most newsworthy Americans, recreation-arts-entertainment, sports, and weather. Also, under "world," you will find international organizations, U.N. agencies, foreign embassies, U.S. embassies and the desks or country offices in the State Department. *Names and Numbers* will tell you whether your library is a regional depository for U.S. government documents.

Similar reference books include *The New Address Book: How to Reach Anyone Who's Anyone,* listing over 3,500 celebrities, corporate executives and other VIP's; *Information USA* (U.S. government experts); *Encyclopedia of Associations* (contact persons for national organizations, associations, and fraternities); and *Dial an Expert,* a consumer's sourcebook of free and low-cost information available by phone.

Of course, many of the people you wish to reach will be listed in current phone books. Many public libraries (or business branches) have not only phone books from towns and cities throughout that state, but microfiche of both white and yellow pages of the nation's largest cities. Catalogues from colleges across the country, manufacturers' directories, corporate annual reports, government documents, and recent magazines are also available on microfiche.

At the main library in my city, old city directories, census records, and back issues of local newspapers since the turn of the century and earlier are on microfilm. I found old newspapers invaluable in my research for a book about the 1920s and 1930s; they gave me a "feel" for the times. Later, they provided clues to finding living relatives of people I named in the book, to whom my publisher sent pre-publication brochures. Obituaries, social columns, news stories, and even ads for local businesses were great sources. I made extensive use of out-of-town telephone book microfiche to locate current home or business addresses.

While working on a biography, I found information in old city directories about the subject's relatives who were unknown by living descendants. Those directories listed all the adults living in the household at the time, as well as their occupations.

The New York Times, The Wall Street Journal, and *The Christian Science Monitor* are also available on microfilm at many regional libraries. Indexes for these are in book form, and many have on-line data bases for newspapers. Vu/Text indexes major Knight-Ridder newspapers and a few magazines. Dialogue provides the largest data base for periodicals and journals. If your library has one of these or a similar index service, you can do a "global" or a regional search for even a narrow topic. A bibliography will flash on the computer screen; you choose the article you need, and the entire article will be printed out.

For listings of markets for your work, you may want to consult *Ulrich's International Periodicals Directory, Gale Directory of Publications, The Writer's Handbook, The Literary Market Place, Standard Periodical Directory, Magazine Industry Market Place, International Writers' & Artists' Yearbook, Editor & Publisher International Yearbook,* and *Editor & Publisher Syndicate Directory.*

Make use of your library's photocopier. At small cost, you can reproduce pages to read later at your own desk. Some microfiche reading machines and microfilm machines will photocopy a specific page for as little as ten cents.

Through the Interlibrary Loan system, you can borrow material not available in your hometown library. Many major libraries have an on-line data base that can locate particular books, and for a minimal fee, you can get photocopies of magazine or newspaper articles from another library. A book or microfilm can be transferred to your library within about two weeks, usually at no charge or for a small insurance fee. You may borrow the book for a couple of weeks, but the microfilm must be viewed in the local library.

If you find that a certain town has source material you want, address a letter to the head librarian or reference librarian there, explaining what you are looking for and where you think that information might be found. Always provide a self-addressed, stamped envelope. If appropriate, leave space after each question, so the librarian can fill in the answers without having to write a separate letter. Allow several weeks for a response. You can try phoning for quick reference data, or you might say in your letter that you will call on a certain day for the answers.

While checking old tales about a specific area in Oklahoma, I asked small-town librarians there to help me locate people who might have been present at a particular event. As a result, I got first-person accounts—far more valuable than newspaper versions. In one instance, a librarian posted my letter on the Town Hall bulletin board, and an elderly woman validated information about a murder that had been deliberately expunged from public records!

Although I don't know the names of many of the librarians who have helped me over the years—they often prefer to remain anonymous—in one of my books, I acknowledged thirty-three "for their continued personal interest in seeking answers to a cascade of obscure questions."

70

How to Write a Profile

By Lou Ann Walker

ONE OF THE FIRST PROFILES I EVER READ was of Candice Bergen. I remember every detail vividly: what her room looked like, how she was dressed, the ideas she found frivolous, what mattered to her. As a teenager, I thought young Bergen was a wonderful role model. She believed in hard work and challenge, and ignoring her detractors. Not long ago, *New York Woman* magazine asked me to write a cover story on Bergen. I became very nervous. She was too glamorous to talk to, I thought. After the reams of copy that had been written about her, how could I make her come alive on paper? And then I reminded myself that I was curious about how she had developed over the years. I realized the challenge was to capture her essence, to rediscover what had enthralled me before, and to present Bergen in a new way.

To write a profile, you don't have the muss or fuss of figuring out what your topic is. You have a finite number of facts, and you can't get lost in too many subplots. Your job is to make the reader think that he or she has had a long, candlelit dinner full of shared intimacies and revelations. And, yes, usually laughs. Using your interview and research materials can be a far more creative and enriching process than writing most journalistic stories. After all, you're a detective, a psychologist, and a sage all rolled into one. The more talents you have, the better. Getting a *good* interview is 75% of the battle. Here are some tactics for making a profile come alive.

Getting the interview right

The interview, I've come to realize, is really a skillfully crafted performance, a *pas de deux*. Here are some tips for making the "dance" work.

1. Be creative in setting up an interview. Sometimes, particularly

with celebrities, I'll have an intermediary, a press agent, or a magazine editor tell me some of the activities the subject likes. Then, if I call the subject directly, I'm armed with a notion of the kind of article I'll do, and some of the topics I'll focus on. Usually home turf for the person is best. An office is all right, but often people are stiffer in that setting. Hollywood child star and comedienne Jane Withers taught me that if you're going to a restaurant, call ahead and ask the maitre d' for the quietest table.

One of the best tactics is to stay with a person all day, particularly on a movie set. Academy Award winning actress Marlee Matlin allowed me to tag along on a free day, and we had a most illuminating time. I let her drive me all over Los Angeles. (Frankly, it was a death-defying stunt. She's so excitable that when she uses her hands to sign, she often takes both of them off the steering wheel.) She took me to visit her elderly grandmother in a nursing home, and I could see the family affection. We went to a Beverly Hills restaurant where she used her TTY (telecommunications device for the deaf) on the phone at our table to have a conversation with her boyfriend, an actor on location in Canada. It was these small moments that made our interview memorable.

2. Become friendly with the people who work with the person you're interviewing. Charming a secretary who is snooty can lead to important revelations. One such secretary confided in me that the actress I was interviewing was just breaking up with a man and dating someone new. I never would have found that out if I hadn't done a little buttering up.

3. Research, research, research. *Before* you meet the person, you need to know everything you can. There is a warmth, a relaxation, that subjects undergo when writers have done their homework. Knowing background can help you read deeper meanings into answers.

4. Make a list of questions. For days before an interview, I ask myself what I want to know about the subject. Why does this politician care so much about drug task forces? Was someone in his family mugged? I think up questions while I'm driving around, or jogging. I rarely look at my list during the interview, but it's there just in case there's an awkward silence or the subject freezes up.

5. Don't be afraid to ask dumb questions. I've gotten many of my best answers that way. Keep a few stock questions in reserve for dry spells. "What are your best qualities? What are your worst?" might not

seem to have Pulitzer-winning potential, yet you'd be surprised where they may lead. Don't be afraid of silences, by the way. People often free associate in riveting ways. My favorite question is: "Why?"

6. Go with the conversational flow. If someone starts opening up about the worst day of his or her life, don't suddenly say, "What year were you born?"

7. The number one worst sin of interviewers: Talking too much. Many interviewers are really more interested in talking about themselves than they are in the subject. Your time with a person is precious. Use it to find out what you need for your profile. Being a bit forthcoming is useful, but Joe DiMaggio would probably not be terribly interested in your son's Little League score.

8. Play poker. In other words, don't pounce on perceived indiscretions on your subject's part. Stay cool, and later on bring up that name your subject dropped to find out what response you get. Don't get testy if there are interruptions. You might get revealing material from an overheard phone conversation.

9. Be compulsive. I use a tape recorder and write notes at the same time. I know of too many instances when batteries died, and I've also discovered that background noise drowns out a person's voice. It's better to have notes than nothing at all. But develop the technique of writing while looking your subject square in the eye as much as possible. Also, at some point, you must be compulsive about facts; you have to figure out if the explorer moved to New Zealand before or after he lived in Timbuktu.

10. Don't waste time. The best interviews aren't necessarily the longest. Use your judgment. Several shorter interviews are probably better for the subject than one marathon. Too much information can be hard to sift through. And you'll repeat yourself. But don't be shortchanged. Before leaving an interview, ask the person for a number where he or she can be reached if you have more questions or need to check some facts.

11. Ask about friends or acquaintances you can talk to. It's useful to interview other well-known people about a celebrity, but they'll probably give you pat answers. An old high school pal or college roommate will often provide more illuminating material. Ask to look at photo albums. Or places where certain events took place.

12. Never be intimidated. Remember, the subject, no matter how

important, had traumas and defeats as well as successes. And whether it was good or bad, most people like talking about their childhood. You don't have to be ingratiating. Sometimes winning a subject's trust means shaking the person up a bit or disagreeing with a point. As an interviewer, you're like a psychologist, figuring out what makes that person tick. Use your knowledge of human nature every way you can. There are times when you need to be confrontational, say with a senator who has been stripped of his congressional seat. But you don't need to be argumentative while interviewing a puppeteer for the local paper. Have a good understanding of what your editor wants.

13. Some time ago *The New Yorker* ran a two-part article by Janet Malcolm about the relationship between a writer and his subject. Malcolm's premise is that an interviewer is a seducer, then betrays the subject with what is written. Certainly there's an element of that in a story. But it's also true that many subjects are seducing writers, trying to manipulate the portrait. Be prepared for such seduction. If someone says: "You're going to write a nice article, aren't you?" don't dissemble. Be ready to say: "I'm going to write a fair piece."

14. Get people to be specific. Ask for examples. Most people talk in generalities to reporters. They think they sound more intelligent when, in actuality, it just makes for a dry story. You need anecdotes and details. If someone says, "I'm a very poor storyteller," your retort should be, "Give me an example." That, surprisingly enough, can turn out to be, "Well, when I met Winston Churchill . . ."

15. Observe and make notes about everything. Jot down the person's eye color, what photos are on the desk, the type of decor. After I walk out the door I usually stand in the hallway or sit in my car writing down impressions while they're still fresh.

Capturing the person on paper

1. Get reacquainted with the person. I generally type out all my notes, even if it takes a lot of time, as a way of imagining myself with the subject again. Usually when I'm typing, lines or images stand out, and I can tell immediately what the beginning and end of the piece will be.

2. Play around with structure. You're telling a story. Make it entertaining. Read other profiles for techniques for weaving together background with the present. It's just plain boring to write: "So-and-so was born in 1946. . . ." You want bounce and verve in your writing, even if

your subject was dry as dust. Make a dateline for the person. Or a chart to show the ups and downs of someone's career. Or maybe make a list of memorable quotations. I recently interviewed a 91-year-old woman doctor who still sees patients every day. She had so many crusty quotes, I couldn't possibly fit them all in. So I settled on a box with her "prescriptions" for modern man. It worked wonderfully well.

3. Make associations. Do some free-floating thinking about figures in history whose careers parallel your subject's. Or that your character looks like Meryl Streep but acts like Madonna. Push your creative buttons. Otherwise, you're a quotation box.

4. Examine the text closely. Throw out the canned responses immediately—unless you're making the point that someone is in a rut. Having read published articles about your subject, you know what is really fresh. Scan the answers for themes. For example, a television producer I recently interviewed used the word "control" over and over again. Having won a battle with cancer, she was re-establishing dominion over her own life. From the opening sentence, I built the piece around this producer's tug-of-war with life.

5. Give your analysis. The reader wants you to explain how or why the subject said what he or she said. You are the guide in this expedition. So lead.

6. Vary the tone. No life is all happy or sad. No profile should sound the same note again and again.

7. An infallible rule: You can never, ever tell how people are going to react to what you write. I did a tough portrait of a well-known actress. It was not a puff piece, but I was absolutely scrupulous in telling the truth about her failures and successes. She later wrote me it was the best article ever written about her. Her husband thought so, too. Intelligent subjects don't want to come off sounding like Milquetoasts. They want you to come up with original angles, not press release rehashes. It's balance you're after.

Finally, advice no one else will give you: Don't be afraid to turn down an assignment if you have negative feelings about the subject. I'm not saying you have to like the person you're interviewing. Tension can be good. But if you have no respect for the person's work or beliefs, then the interview will suffer.

The best way to be true to an interview subject is to be true to yourself. An editor I often write for recently told me that she realized my secret. I'm wide-eyed and non-judgmental, so people just open up to me. It can be a curse in a supermarket line or on a long plane trip, but I've come to realize it's one of my strong suits. If you're an enthusiastic person, there's no sense trying to mask that with a somber demeanor. If you're serious, don't try for the jollies. Just channel your interests and your behavior to get and write the best story you can.

Over the course of time, the people who write the best profiles are the ones who are, quite simply, captivated by others: That's what makes almost all wonderful writers. Simple fascination with humankind.

71

HOW TO WRITE A HOW-TO THAT SELLS

BY GAIL LUTTMAN

ANY ACTIVITY THAT INTERESTS YOU—from canoeing to cooking to collecting Civil War relics to cutting your own hair—is a potential how-to article. And whether you are an expert or a novice, you are qualified to write about it.

Where to start

The most successful introductions to how-to pieces state a problem and then propose one or more possible solutions, perferably those relating to the seven basic human motivators.

Ego—Does your solution to the problem improve the way you look, the way you feel about yourself, your ability to relate to others?

Economy—Does it save money, protect the environment, improve quality without increasing cost?

Health—Does it give you more energy, promote safety practices, increase your psychological well-being?

Romance—Does it enhance sex appeal, create a cozy atmosphere, improve personal relationships?

Family—Does it entertain children, foster loyalty, help research family history?

Leisure—Does it enliven holiday activities, provide an engrossing hobby, help plan exciting vacations?

Individuality—Does the activity appeal to the universal desire for uniqueness by offering something new, different or better?

These motivators often overlap. A hobby may bring in income. Dieting may improve both health and self-image. An inexpensive bungalow of unusual construction may serve as a romantic retreat. The more motivators you appeal to, the greater interest you will generate in your how-to.

Moving on

After piquing the reader's interest, offer a brief explanation of what the activity involves, couched in enthusiastic words that inspire confidence. Can the skill be learned in five easy steps? Fifteen minutes a day? Does it require a special setting, or will a corner of the garage do? What special tools or materials are needed?

Rather than barrage readers at the beginning with a large number of tools or materials required, you may want to list them in a sidebar, a separate boxed-off article that accompanies the main story. Sidebars are a great way to include data or lengthy explanations without interrupting the narrative flow. Some editors favor articles with one, two, or even three sidebars if the article is very long or complex.

Definitions of unfamiliar terms might go into a vocabulary sidebar, especially when they are numerous; on the other hand, if special words are few or are easy to define, it is better to explain their meanings as you go along.

Whenever possible, describe new concepts by drawing a comparison with something familiar. In a piece about building stone walls, for example, a description of the proper consistency of mortar as "buttery" sparks instant recognition.

Complicated procedures don't seem quite as confusing when written up in short, uncomplicated sentences of the sort found in cookbooks. Explicitness also ensures clarity. Vague directions such as "measure out six to eight cups of water" or "cut two to three yards of string" leave the reader wondering which of the two stated amounts to use.

Clarity is also improved by separating general principles from specific procedures. If you are writing about how to build a chicken coop, for example, after the introductory remarks, explain how the layout and dimensions are established, then include some specific plans. In a how-to about cooking a Christmas goose, first describe how to roast the goose, then offer some favorite recipes. In that way you'll satisfy both the creative reader who likes to improvise and the less adventuresome reader who feels more comfortable with step-by-step instructions.

The final and best way to ensure clarity is with illustrations. The less commonplace the subject, the more important photographs and sketches become, and they are essential when dimensions are involved. In addition, the market is more receptive to illustrated how-tos. But

339

don't despair if you are not an accomplished photographer or artist; many how-to magazines have illustrators who will enhance your article with clear, easy-to-follow illustrations.

Organization

The subject of a how-to usually dictates whether to organize the steps chronologically or to start with simple procedures and work toward difficult ones. If two steps are to be taken at the same time, it is important to make that clear. In bread baking, for instance, point out that yeast should be softening in warm water while the other ingredients are being measured.

Repetition can help or hinder reader understanding. Too much repetition causes readers to lose interest. In a short article, a brief reference to the original explanation is usually all that's needed. But if the article is very long or complex and the explanation is relatively short, repetition is better than asking readers to flip pages back to find the required information.

Include a timetable for each step to help readers gauge their progress. How long does concrete take to set? Eggs to hatch? Wine to ferment? Do varying conditions influence timing? Can or should any deliberate measures be taken to speed things up or slow them down? What specific signs might the reader watch for as the project nears completion?

Finally, what can go wrong? Think twice before including a separate how-not-to section or a trouble-shooting sidebar. Faced with a long list of things that can go wrong, a reader might understandably wonder whether the whole thing is worth the bother. But, in general, as long as a how-to is clearly written and well organized, it doesn't hurt to point out danger spots along the way.

Research, including interviews with appropriate experts, supplies background that adds depth and authority to how-tos, thereby increasing reader interest and credibility. It also helps a writer discover whether his experiences are typical or not. If not, avoid making sweeping or questionable generalizations.

When consulting authoritative sources, watch out for regional variations in the terms and methods you plan to describe, especially when you're writing for a national magazine. Mention chicken wire and a southerner is likely to picture what the westerner calls lifestock fencing. Talk about reupholstering a divan or davenport, and there are readers who won't realize you are discussing a couch or a sofa. Before you write your article, look up alternative terminology from other areas.

Voice

Of course, the target audience determines how to approach your subject. If you are describing a new weaving technique to experienced weavers, you may use standard terms freely without defining them. But you should define any words that are specific to the new technique and you should definitely explain why the new technique is worth learning.

It is your job as a how-to writer to make certain that all readers achieve the same level of information by the time they reach the heart of your piece, and to do it without talking down. You can manage this by pretending you are writing a detailed letter to an interested friend.

You will find your most effective how-to voice by writing your article as if you were addressing a particular person who engages you in especially lively conversation. If you can't think of anyone suitable, invent someone. By writing expressly for that single reader, real or fictitious, you will delight all your readers with the personal tone of your how-to.

72

WRITING FOR THE ANTIQUES AND COLLECTIBLES MARKET

BY DAWN E. RENO

EVERYONE IN THE WORLD COLLECTS SOMETHING. Your Aunt Mildred may collect porcelain teacups, Uncle Charley has a dusty group of model cars on his mantle, and your niece Jill has more Barbie dolls than you can count. As a writer, you could take advantage of the wonderful and strange objects people collect by writing about them for a wide variety of newspapers and magazines in a number of different ways.

In my ten years as a writer on the antiques world, I have submitted articles on collections ranging from fine art and antiques to my own collection of Marilyn Monroe posters, books, and photographs. These articles were submitted to a wide variety of markets, including newspapers published for dealers in antiques, as well as to in-flight magazines. Writing for these publications often seems difficult to free-lance writers until they realize how few writers cover the antiques and collectibles field and how hungry the trade papers, in-flight magazines, women's magazines, and many other general periodicals are for such material.

You do not need to be an expert in the art or antiques world, nor do you need to know the face of each player printed on baseball cards, to write a knowledgeable and interesting article for those interested in these fields. All that's necessary is that you do some research on the subject, discover some little known or unusual facts, and present the article in a clear, concise fashion.

The first step is to find a collectible or an antique that interests you. Perhaps you know someone who collects old fountain pens. By engaging that person in a conversation about his/her collection, you are tapping into a wealth of information. Most collectors have devoted their lives to learning all they can about what they collect. They can direct you to books on the subject, articles on the value of these items, and they may even be able to tell you about auctions or sales where certain examples of their collection have been or will be sold.

One of the biggest stories in the antiques world in the last couple of years was the sale of Andy Warhol's extensive collections. During his lifetime, he had accumulated Indian rugs and jewelry, fine furniture and porcelains, pop art and Mickey Mouse watches. Boxes upon boxes of collections were unearthed and the antiques world was abuzz as to how much the auction would bring. Needless to say, millions of dollars were paid for Warhol's collections, much more than he had paid for the items originally, and the story made not only the antiques trade papers, but the national newspapers and magazines as well.

Second, distill the information the collector has given you into a few pertinent facts so that you may tempt a publication to buy your idea.

Write a strong query letter to the editor of an antiques magazine or newspaper or to a general-interest magazine that runs a column of this type, detailing your fascination for the subject and how you intend to go about researching the item. Make sure to drop a tidbit, such as how much was paid for an item of this type at a recent Sotheby's auction.

It is always a good idea to outline your qualifications for writing such an article. A person with an interest in the subject, an enthusiasm for what he or she writes about, will be able to translate that fervor into a query letter, and the editor will recognize it immediately.

Third, while you're waiting for the answer to your letter, immerse yourself in more research.

Copies of auction reports and antiques newspapers are available at a good public library. Some, like *Antiques and the Arts Weekly*, are, as the name implies, on a weekly basis; others, like *Maine Antique Digest*, are published monthly. Not only will these papers give you information about local auctions and sales, but they may have featured an article about your subject within the last couple of years that will provide you with background information or valuable contacts.

By studying these papers, you will also be able to note which dealers specialize in the item you are researching. Clip their ads for reference because dealers are always a good source of information. They have to be knowledgeable about what they sell, as well as about the intricacies of the trade. They are usually willing to share their information and know-how, as long as you say you will mention their names in the article or quote them.

Keep your eyes open for ads of auctions that may feature your chosen subject. If you can't attend the auction, call the auctioneer to find out what he expects the item you are interested in to bring; how much interest it has generated; and whether or not he can keep you informed of the final knockdown prices. The promise of a quote from a knowledgeable auctioneer used in your story will make the auctioneer more eager to share his or her secrets of the trade.

Then, it's back to the books in the reference section of the library. If you are researching teacups, you may want to find out when the major porcelain factories were in business, where they were located, and how long they produced that particular product. If your subject is baseball cards, uncovering some statistics about a particular player will give some added color to your article. One recent article in an in-flight magazine included a report on a carousel that had been in operation since the late 1800s and about the carver who made the beautiful animals the children rode on.

Not all articles published in the antiques and collectibles field need to be researched feature pieces. Antiques and collectibles publications are always interested in the people who amass important collections, and features about these individuals sell well, as long as the individuals are as interesting as their collection.

Consider, also, the reporting aspect of the field. Antiques auctions and shows take place almost every day of the year. Should you attend one, take notes on the most unusual or valuable items, remembering that size and condition are important, as well as the price for which they sold. Include a profile of the auctioneer, the weather, and the attendance at the sale.

It is a good idea to map out your schedule of attending these events ahead of time, query the editor, then receive a go-ahead. This was the way I graduated from covering shows and auctions to writing feature articles for a number of publications, then on to magazines and full-length nonfiction books on subjects I discovered during my apprenticeship.

Even the decorating magazines, which abound on newsstands and supermarket racks, have columns devoted to collectibles that can enhance the home. A recent proposal of mine for an article on Indian pottery resulted in a piece for *Country Living* magazine. Another, about the art of illumination and one of the last master illuminators in the world, was sold to *USAir* Magazine.

An editor will consider it a bonus if you indicate in your cover letter that photos will be made available.

Newspapers generally use black-and-white prints, but some of the monthlies are now using color on their covers. Good, clear shots of the objects you are writing about are essential for good reproduction. Take your pictures against a plain background under good lighting. Be sure the items are attractively displayed, and always include caption information. If you are asked for color photos, slides are the most common. Along with your article, send a selection of six to twelve shots of representative items in the collection.

The pay range for articles in the antiques and collectibles field varies as much as the subject matter and depends largely on the publication. Smaller ones pay $25 for a reporting article, but $50–75 is the norm. A feature article will bring you $50–$250, again depending on the size and importance of the publication. Magazines pay much better rates, but also require a polished writing style, excellent photos, and a thorough knowledge of the subject; $250–$1200 is the range for articles of this type.

Whatever avenue you try in the wide field of antiques and collectibles, you will certainly never run out of subject matter, for people collect the strangest things!

73

READ MY QUIPS!

BY SELMA GLASSER

THE KIND OF WRITING I DO OFFERS READERS playful relaxation for serious material. It's entertaining and recreational. What fun I have!

I pull out an arsenal of pizzazz to create powerful word play or witticisms. I give simple words or phrases new sparkle, variety, energy, and meaning. Timely subjects act as dynamic idea generators, recognizable because of their relevance to topics of the day. Just being alert and observant can pay off.

The best part is that it's almost "instant income" with a minimal number of words or time invested, from idea to submission. The rate of pay can range from $10–$1,000 or more, trips all over the world, to bylines in major publications.

For example, on a car stopped in front of me in heavy traffic, I noticed a bumper sticker that read, ANSWER MY PRAYERS. PLEASE STEAL THIS CAR. I sold it to *Reader's Digest*. Recently, I received $60 for a three-word cartoon idea for "Dennis, the Menace." In studying Hank Ketchum's work, I noted that each cartoon depicted a young boy's actions with adult phraseology. Mine showed Dennis using his crayons, asking his mother: "Need anything colorized?!"

It's a good idea to get the slant before submitting any cartoon, filler, or contest entry. Always avoid the obvious.

When the Netherlands offered a trip to Holland, instead of writing about windmills and tulips, my entry declared: IT'S TIME I GOT IN DUTCH!

This brought me a prize of ten days as guest of Queen Beatrix, and yes, I did get to meet her at a social event in honor of the prize winners.

An idea for light verse presented itself when I overheard a discussion about *problem drinkers*. I paraphrased those two words and sold this verse:

PROBLEM THINKERS

Advice on marriage, love or sex, our columnists provide,
They're clever, sensible and wise and very qualified;
But surely, problems cross their path, at home, where they reside,
I wonder, where they turn for help, in whom do they confide?

Taking a traditional Christmas song and changing the season, I wrote a poem for *Good Housekeeping* entitled: "On the Twelfth Day of August." It was a take-off showing a mother's plight when youngsters are on vacation.

In a national grocery competition, I parodied another famous poem by starting off:

How do I love thee? Let me count the ways:
I love thee on big (double) coupon days . . .

and ended with:

I love thee for trying so hard to please,
And for making my shopping a breeze!

In keeping with the summer season (after a severe sunburn), I wrote and sold:

BURNING TO RETURN

Vacationing is pretty sound,
For those who want to get unwound,
But truthfully, here's what I found:
I'm happiest when homeward browned.

The popular phrase "remedial reading" was reworked on another summer theme in this way:

WHAT GOES DOWN MUST COME UP

Though I spend weeks of spading, top soiling and pleading,
My plot's a sad lot, which is surely not leading . . .
I'm thinking of taking remedial weeding!

Naturally, the seasonal verses were submitted six to eight months prior to the summertime. In mid-July when visitors flocked to my vacation home, I thought of this verse about Christmas:

LET's ENACT THE SANTA "CLAUS"

The constant stream of people here,
To wish us Yuletide cheer,
Proves Santa has the right idea:
Visit people once a year!

Ordinary words or phrases in their literal meaning can help you invent a funny filler. For example, I put together a few that sold to *Saturday Evening Post*, with the title, "Fun Facts":

A GET-WELL CARD	What you would send someone prospecting for oil
VIRUS	What the electric company does for us
MINNEHAHA	Short laugh
CARTOON	Auto song
UNMANNED VEHICLE	Car driven by a female

I wrote a similar filler for *Good Housekeeping* called, "Two-Way Brain Teaser":

What do boys do when they see a fence?	CLIMATE
What's fear of relatives?	KINDRED
What's an oversized hairpiece?	BIGWIG
What do you do when you give up spinach?	SCRAP IRON
Where should folks take their automobiles swimming?	IN CAR POOLS

Following the same line of pun-fun, I took the word "Friday" and gave it the double entendre treatment in this epigram sold to *Good Housekeeping:*

The only person who got all his work done by Friday was Robinson Crusoe.

Clichés and proverbs reworked can be another easy way to get published. How about the expression "little things count"? Here's how I sold that one:

A kindergarten teacher is a woman who knows how to make little things count.

I reread some old proverbs and adapted a few for this feature:

348

Still water causes ecology problems.
Absence makes the heart grow fonder, but presents get better results.
All work and no play makes jack.
Cleanliness is next to impossible.
As you sow so shall you mow.
Every cloud has a silver airliner.

Occasionally, a filler published in one magazine can be reprinted in *Reader's Digest*. In that case, the writer gets paid twice. Using my word-storming formula (analogy), this epigram sold first to *Good Housekeeping* and later to *Reader's Digest:*

Remarks that are uncalled for are usually delivered. (Postal analogs: uncalled for . . . delivered)

Playboy has been known to use analogies. Here are a few sold to them:

A man with money to burn usually meets his match . . . (analogy here is burn-match)
Alimony: disinterest compounded annually (note financial analogs)

A TV booklet distributed free at supermarkets each month offers lots of cash and groceries with an annual Grand Slam Prize for the Best of the Year. I hit the jackpot using an analogy to write about the advertisers in musical terminology:

It takes genius to arrange a harmonious medley of merchants who offer scores of services . . . It's the easiest way to shop and get Bach in no time flat, and that beats the band!

(Note also the use of puns and alliteration.)
This analogy technique is the easiest device you can use to coax words onto the page. When asked to review a play called *Angry House-wives,* presented by a local theater group, I started this way:

The percolating plot starts on a low burner but boils over with bubbling talent. It's a well-done show cooking with gags.

(It never hurts to insert a pun for extra punch.)
Another fun game I play is "terse verse," which calls for a rhymed

349

definition for a given word. I've written columns called "Rime Time" and "Phraze Craze." One picked up and reprinted by *Reader's Digest* read:

A fat cat is a flabby tabby.

A few others:

An animal doctor is a pet vet.
A royal court jester is a crown clown.
A matchmaker is a knotter plotter.
An unwed Santa is a single Kringle.
A hot house is a swelter shelter.

Reader's Digest reprinted my list of definitions of ordinary words. This time, the meanings were defined in colors. For example:

Nudist—come azure
Economist—cost of living rose
Psychologist—Freudian gilt
Politician—bipartisan slate
Gangster—come and get me copper

For *Catholic Digest,* I rhymed a shortie like this:

Outdoor theater sign: "Closed for the season. Reason? Freezin'."

Rhyme, parody, or pun wherever you can. Once you get your mind working along these lines, you'll see how much fun it is. Just today, I heard a western song called: "I'm a Legend in my Time." Immediately, I thought of the late Richard Armour (my mentor) as "a legend in his rhyme." Listening to Bob Hope sing his theme song, "Thanks for the Memories," made me think of "franks for the memories." As soon as some ad agency or contest needs a slogan for hot dogs, I'm ready! The TV game show called "The Phrase That Pays" brought to mind that "The Re-Phrase That Pays" is what this article is all about.

⑈74

WRITING ARTICLES FROM PERSONAL EXPERIENCE

BY RACHEL POLLACK

I WRITE, I ONCE TOLD SOME FRIENDS, BECAUSE that is what I love best. Occasionally, I paraphrase Monet: "Words are my daily and nightly obsession, my joy and my torment." But several years ago, I paced the floor, caught in that unhappy space, the limbo between magazine writing assignments.

I went for a walk; I considered my life, my work, and the beautiful spring day in New York. I thought about my recent move to the city, the birth of my first grandchild some months before, a forthcoming trip to Cape Cod. I listened to the intonations and accents of people talking. There in the midst of the ever-changing city, I discovered what I had been resisting as a free-lance writer: writing about my own life. The idea was somewhat daunting; my thoughts were there in abundance, but would words be there when I needed them?

I raced back to my apartment, looked through my journal and made a list of my favorite things, which, I discovered, were mainly people close to me. I then made another list of favorite times: birthday parties, holidays, reading with a flashlight under the covers when I was young, working in political campaigns, helping in a soup kitchen, walking alone on the beach, holding my little grandchild close.

I looked through family photographs. Was it possible that what made me smile in remembrance might move others? I thought about people who had made a difference in my life: a favorite uncle who took me to fine restaurants where he always knew the owner or the maitre d'; the first teacher who expanded my horizons by introducing me to Shakespeare; my father, who gave me the gift of love for nature. I thought about myself in several roles: mother, daughter, writer, sister. And my lists grew, haphazardly at first, but that didn't matter. It was a beginning.

The sights and sounds of life are everywhere. Look into your own life, the extraordinary as well as the mundane. Perhaps especially the mundane, which is not banal when you give it your particular point of view. From beached whales to moving from one house to another; from childhood friendships to holding fast to scraps of the past—the first early drawings of our children, perhaps—all take on a special meaning as you discover your sense of wonder and give it your special voice.

My first personal essay—like all such pieces, written from the heart and filtered through the mind—was about the summer my whole family, four generations, spent time together at Cape Cod. It was a time captured in memory that could not be again. I sold it three times, updating it after the death of my father. Memory plays an important part in the personal essay and in finding a voice that is uniquely one's own. Regular writing evokes memories, allows us to ask questions and discover answers.

At first, in my most serious essays, I hoped to emulate columnist Ellen Goodman, but she does not speak in my voice, nor I in hers. Later, when I discovered quite by accident that I could make people laugh, I attempted to follow the path Erma Bombeck had climbed so successfully. That wasn't my voice either. My first humorous piece concerned letting my gray hair grow out after years of coloring it. I called the article, "Back to My Roots." It sold to a national magazine, a second time to a newspaper, and later, was syndicated. Friends around the country told me they had read it and laughed. Humor, it seems, has its own rewards.

At one point, actor friends in New York casually asked if I wanted to be an extra in a movie. I jumped at the chance, not for any latent thespian urge, but because I believed it would be something I could write an amusing essay about. It was. I did. And I sold it.

Do I write about these experiences because I've had them, or do I seek them in order to write about them? Imagination *might* have sufficed had I not "mastered" the technique of losing the last of my inhibitions under klieg lights! Whatever the answer, in this case I had a lot of fun, made doubly enjoyable by writing about it.

Write a descriptive phrase about a few items on your list of favorite people, places, things, times. Decide if you want to try your hand at humor. Has something funny or outrageous happened to you recently? Or to any of your favorite people? Can you describe it succinctly and then expand upon it, using exaggeration, irony, a fanciful phrase, a heightened sense of the ridiculous or the absurd? Is there a sly elf in you, creating mischief and mayhem, making the pedestrian seem clever, witty, and original? When you read what you've written, do people chuckle and not just out of politeness? Can you see things through other people's eyes—perhaps a driver with a flat tire, a teen-age boy on his first date, a child catching his or her first fish, learning to ice skate? What about a woman cleaning the attic who cannot bear to part with anything in spite of good intentions. Try it. Take a notebook everywhere you go. Conversations and discussions you hear, especially funny ones, on busses, trains, in offices and restaurants can be subjects for humor articles.

Of course, not everything is funny. A brush with the possible diagnosis of melanoma (the type of skin cancer that caused my father's death) sent me frightened and vulnerable to my journal. From this experience came a personal essay, "A Little Piece of Skin." Some tragic experiences are too painful to write about.

Some writers believe that writing about their favorite things in personal essays makes them more vulnerable to editors' whims and fancies. This may be true because in general personal essays must be completed before they are submitted, rather than simply proposed in a few paragraphs of a query letter to see whether an editor would be interested. But vulnerability and openness are the essence of personal writing, and there is no way of avoiding that kind of exposure.

Know your markets, read every magazine and newspaper you can, and find out which hometown publications accept personal essays. If one magazine rejects your work, send it off to the next one on the list. Don't watch your mailbox! If you receive a kind note from an editor (but not an acceptance), take it as encouragement and write something else for that magazine immediately.

What is important is to love what you do, to begin each day excited about its possibilities, to write honestly. And in your own voice. Writing about your favorites, whether people, places, or things, can strike a responsive chord in editors and readers.

75

HOW TO WRITE AND SELL HEALTH AND FITNESS ARTICLES

BY RICHARD D. ROTHSCHILD

YOU DON'T HAVE TO PUMP IRON, run in the Boston Marathon, be an aerobic dance instructor or nutritionist to write and sell articles in the burgeoning health, fitness, and nutrition market. In fact, being a medical, fitness or nutrition professional can be a handicap. What you do need is an active interest in health, fitness, or nutrition and the persistence to get to the bottom of things.

The market is large and growing, providing opportunities for newcomers. Articles are being sought by general interest, men's, women's, in-flight, and other special interest publications as well as health, fitness and nutrition magazines.

What editors want is information wrapped in a brief, entertaining narrative, free of technical gobbledygook.

What are you going to write about? Things that are happening to you, your family and friends often provide the best subjects.

But if nothing comes to mind, national newspapers are excellent "primers." Read *The New York Times, The Washington Post, The Los Angeles Times,* and *The Wall Street Journal,* as well as some of the smaller papers (often available in the periodical room of the public library) for article ideas. There is often a health or fitness angle in straight news reports that can be developed into an article. Or, you may find the idea for an article in a press release from an academic institution or organization, or even from a public relations agency, promoting a new product, medication, a new service or a story about a person in the health and nutrition field.

But the best articles are likely to come out of your own experience or the experiences of someone you know. When researching such an idea, try to think of how you can make the personal more universal. John Grossman, contributing editor of *Health Magazine* who has also written articles for *The New York Times, McCall's, American Way,* and *Hippocrates,* gives this example: "An article I am writing now about the health of returning Peace Corps Volunteers suggested itself when my brother, a former Peace Corps Volunteer, began to develop service-related health problems."

For ideas for more "newsy" articles, browse through medical and health journals such as *The New England Journal of Medicine, The Journal of the American Medical Association, Lancet, The Physician and Sports Medicine, The Journal of Infectious Diseases, Health, Diversion, The Walking Magazine,* and newsletters like those put out by various medical schools and hospitals—for example, *The Harvard Medical School Health Letter.*

Don't ignore your local paper. There's bound to be a report about a local personality, athletic, medical or food event in which there is a health, fitness or nutrition angle for you to discover.

Local health and fitness professionals are good sources for article material. What do local hospital or school dieticians have to say about recent changes in nutrition programs? How does the physical education director compare the fitness of today's graduating high school class with graduates five years ago?

Articles in health and fitness periodicals should not be ignored. The time may be ripe for a follow-up on last year's story—updating developments, revealing new or conflicting findings.

Before you start querying editors, do enough preliminary research to enable you to write the piece you have in mind. Make sure the information you will need is available and that you can find suitable and willing experts to be interviewed. The amount and depth of such research depends on the publication you are targeting, but usually it is worthwhile to exhaust print sources before querying the editors.

If your library has a computerized Info Track system, you should be able to locate appropriate newspaper and periodical articles in minutes. If not, you may have to rely on two old standbys, *The Readers' Guide to Periodical Literature* and the *Newspaper Index.*

Once you've noted articles that might be useful, try to locate them in the library's back issues or microfilm. Photocopy those with names, information, and quotations you are likely to need. If your story hinges on particular interviewees, confirm their willingness to be interviewed before querying.

Having settled on your slant, devise a working title. Suppose you've decided to write about quick, vitamin-rich dishes that can be prepared in a pressure cooker, and your angle is that they are more healthful and better-tasting than those from the microwave.

Your first attempt at a working title yields, "All Steamed Up." Test it by putting yourself in the place of the reader. Does the title suggest what your article is about? Would it induce you to read the article? If the answer is no to either of these questions, try again. A second try might bring forth "Steaming at Mealtime." This title might grab attention, but it could be misleading. Think about other steam applications— steam engines, steam heat—and suddenly a catchy title and a subhead leap to mind, "Steam Eat—A quick way to healthy meals, rediscovered."

With the subject, slant, and a working title pinned down, identify your most likely markets. Start by making a preliminary market list, using such sources as *The Writer* Magazine and *The Writer's Handbook* (both published by The Writer, Inc.). You will find extensive listings of health, fitness, men's, women's, general interest, inflight, and other publications that use health and fitness articles. For more complete magazine listings (about 800 health entries), consult *The Standard Periodical Directory* (published by Oxbridge Communications, Inc.). It covers 70,000 periodicals in the United States and Canada. For newspaper markets see Editor and Publisher's *The International Yearbook,* which lists daily, weekly, national, tabloid, and special interest newspapers by county, state and city. These reference volumes may be found in the reference department of most good public libraries.

From your initial list of possible markets, prune those that never carry articles on your subject, have covered the subject you have in mind in the past three months (and are therefore unlikely to want another soon), and those in which the health and fitness articles are written regularly by editors or staff writers. (You can do this by checking bylines against the names on the masthead.) If the last article on your chosen subject appeared over a year ago, you may have a good prospect. It is important to study back issues of magazines, either in the library or by writing for sample copies, usually available for a modest fee.

Query letters are your important first contacts with health and fitness publication editors. This one landed an assignment for an article on Lyme disease:

Dear Ms. Gallagher:

Lyme disease has spread into 43 states, reaching near-epidemic proportions in some. Is it any wonder that *American Health* readers are concerned as summer, the season of the infectious deer tick, approaches?

A new defense is proving its effectiveness, just in time. Informed readers will be able to use it to lower the risk of contracting this potentially devastating disease.

Under the working title, *The Magic Bullet Is A Cotton Ball,* my article will report on the new weaponry, Damminix, with which residents in the Northeast already have begun to win decisive battles against Lyme disease.

Readers will share the excitement of the island investigation in which the mystery of Lyme disease transmission was solved, as told to me by entymologist/professor Andrew Spielman of Harvard's School of Public Health. And it will explain how the resulting new defense method can be used most effectively. Practical tips on how to enjoy the outdoors more safely will be shared by Rick Apgar, jovial, suspendered proprietor of Mill River Supply, a highly regarded local expert on Lyme disease control.

Three weeks after I receive your o.k. I can deliver this lively, authoritative article. If you wish, it can include a sidebar on recognizable early symptoms of Lyme disease. Are you interested? Please let me know, and thanks.

Most successful query letters start with a shocking statement, a provocative question, an intriguing problem, or an engaging anecdote. My opening paragraph combined the first two.

The second paragraph should expand the topic and begin to explain what the article will be about.

In the third paragraph, mention your working title, expand on how you will develop the article, and include a list of the experts you will be interviewing.

Credentials of interviewees are important if the subject is technical or controversial. Here's how I handled this aspect in a query that brought a go-ahead phone call from the editor:

Does stair-climbing really work? To prove it does, the article will quote such authorities as Dr. Ralph Paffenberger, Jr., of Stanford, Kelly Brownell, Ph.D. at the University of Pennsylvania, Dr. Leonore Zohman of Montefiore Hospital, and others.

Where did I locate these experts? They were mentioned and quoted in material I found in my preliminary research. Since anecdotes and humor were welcome in the publication I was querying, I added—

Humorous anecdotes about some highly unorthodox stair-climbers will be included.

Your fourth paragraph should demonstrate that you are qualified to write the proposed article. Mention writing credits and enclose relevant clips. Conclude by giving the length of the article and when you can deliver it. Ask for a reply, and thank the editor for considering your proposal. Don't forget to enclose an SASE.

Once you have received a go-ahead from the editor, start to set up your interviews, using the in-between time for final research of written material.

You are unlikely to find many medical journals in general libraries. Locate your nearest medical library. Often it is housed in or near a hospital. I found it was necessary only to identify myself and explain my purpose, to gain admittance. Make photocopies of any written material you will cite or from which you plan to quote, as the publication will request them later to check facts and avoid legal hassles.

An outline is the skeleton of the article. Later, you will flesh it out and clothe it attractively. My typical outline includes a working title, introductory statement, anecdote, or other exposition of the theme, a list of points to be covered in the body of the article, a summary statement, an anecdote or quotation confirming the theme, and a conclusion.

When I start writing the first draft, I try to keep the tone lively. If I find myself getting bored, I know the reader will be, too. Once you have completed your first draft, take off your writer's hat, put on a tough editor's green eyeshade, and read what you have written. Eliminate the extraneous, rearrange the awkward, compress, and polish, while listening intently to your inner voice to alert you to style and accuracy problems. Joan Lippert, whose health and fitness articles have appeared in *Health, Reader's Digest, U.S.Air, New Woman,* and *Ladies' Home Journal,* puts it this way: "When you read over your story, you will often hear an inner voice saying, 'Better check that' or 'this doesn't sound quite right.' Even though you are in a hurry and want to avoid more work, you must always listen to that voice."

She also finds it helpful to put a piece aside for a few days, then reread it from the point of view of an editor or reader.

Health and fitness writers often find their inspiration for articles in personal experiences, and those of family and friends. Few are professionals in the fields they write about. All are vitally interested in fitness and health.

If you share these qualities, you may have the makings of a successful health and fitness writer.

76

WHERE TO GET A START: THE COMMUNITY NEWSPAPER

BY JEAN CUMMINGS

AN EAGER MARKET FOR YOUR ARTICLES may be just down the street from where you live: Community newspapers, weeklies, and small-town dailies are always looking for local material.

There are about 9,000 small newspapers with circulations of 10,000 or less in the United States. These community newspapers have a total circulation estimated to be from 38 million to 150 million readers. Most community newspapers leave world, national, and even statewide news to the metropolitan dailies, but are open to all sorts of article ideas from writers, as long as they have something to do with the immediate locality. The community newspaper for which I am Assistant and Contributing Editor concentrates on printing local and personal news. Our readers want articles about people they can identify with—familiar people and places.

Beginning writers living in a small town or rural area often feel they are at a disadvantage because they live off the beaten path. But their own community newspaper is an especially attractive market for them, one where they won't be competing with experienced writers. Since community newspapers can't afford to pay high rates for contributions, they do not appeal to experienced professional writers. Most small papers pay approximately 50¢ per column inch, and some can't pay anything at all. But, wait! Don't turn your back on this market because of the low rates. By submitting your articles and seeing how they are individually edited, you will get an education in writing. Your submissions to national markets are probably returned with form rejections that tell you nothing about why your submission was rejected.

At the community newspaper, you will be able to discuss your submissions with an editor or editorial assistant. In most instances, their suggestions for changes will be helpful to you. By writing for your small hometown paper, you will be learning your craft while writing about your friends and neighbors. As you contribute articles more frequently and the newspaper begins to depend upon you as a source of articles, your rate of pay will likely increase. If it doesn't, ask the editor about it.

Beginning writers living in metropolitan areas served by large daily newspapers should search out the small suburban weeklies, which cover their town's local news in much the same way as small-town newspapers do.

What sort of material do community newspapers want?

- **A local angle to a national or worldwide event**

A local connection to a nationally newsworthy event will pique an editor's interest. My paper has carried an article about a hometown boy, now a paratrooper, who parachuted into Honduras with the 82nd Airborne. While the large dailies and television were covering this news as a national problem with intervention in Central American affairs, we published the local angle—concerned parents worried about their son, a local high school graduate, who is far off in jungles and perhaps facing danger.

After the invasion of Panama we carried an article about a paratrooper who had been severely wounded in the knee. The feature showed him visiting a local sixth-grade class that was studying Panama. The wide-eyed students blinked at the bolted-together leg bone and learned a lesson about the human cost of our nation's involvement. Seeing him as a true local hero, they lined up for his autograph.

- **Meetings and activities**

Consider various local activities you are interested in and check with the editor about which need covering. If you have children in school, you might want to report on school board meetings or PTA meetings. Are your children involved in Scouting or 4-H activities? School sports and other events make good subjects for local newspaper stories.

- **An inside story to a local event**

The small daily in my locality reported on the long traffic jam which resulted from a drawbridge being stuck open: "Problems with a frozen switch and a circuit breaker caused the U.S. 31 drawbridge to be stuck open for an hour Monday afternoon, backing up traffic in all directions."

Several days after the drawbridge incident, our community newspaper published an article telling about the young mother-to-be in labor, who was heading for the hospital when caught in the traffic jam. This article only briefly mentioned the facts about the malfunctioning bridge. It described the feelings of this frightened young woman and her equally terrified husband, whose nerves already were jangled from having quit smoking.

- **Local people with interesting hobbies or occupations, past or present**

We carried a feature about a local woman who was a WASP (female pilot) in World War II, including her war stories of engine failures and emergency landings. The feature was tinged with romance, since in the service she met and married her husband, also a military pilot.

Another popular article told about two sisters who were reunited after being separated for 50 years. Though the older sister had been looking for the younger for years, the younger sister hadn't been aware of her older sister's existence. Over the years their paths had crossed, but without recognition by either of them.

A young man who has just earned his Eagle Scout badge would make an ideal subject for a feature story for a community newspaper. Get him to tell about the fun and hardships of earning this rank. Add to it a little research about Eagle Scouting in general, what famous men have been Eagle Scouts, and you have a perfect story for a community-oriented newspaper.

Our paper is waiting for an article about the local man who bought a Sherman tank and keeps it in his backyard, and a story about a huge Italianate mansion being constructed in a cornfield, miles from anywhere.

There are many fascinating people in your community who have stories to share. Devotion, hard work, persistence, and sometimes eccentricity are all around us.

- **Local history**

Our readers love articles dealing with local history—stories about what it was like before roads were black-topped; walking three miles to school each day; and when the passenger trains chugged into the local depot.

The "historic" information doesn't have to be about events happening 50 or 100 years ago. We carried a series of reminiscences about a totem pole that was constructed by a 4th-grade class about 20 years ago. Those youngsters are now approaching 30. They and their parents loved seeing old photos and reading students' recollections of how they accomplished that task.

● **Exchange students at the local high school**

An article about a foreign exchange student always makes an interesting article. Readers are eager to learn about similarities and differences of the various countries.

Teachers and principals are good sources of ideas about students' accomplishments. They are eager to put their school in a good light, and they will welcome your requests for information about interesting and talented students.

● **Seasonal material**

Think ahead to special holidays coming up. For small newspapers you don't have to plan as far ahead as for national magazines. If you can get something about Christmas together in early December, it probably would be soon enough for a Christmas edition.

Easter: One year we carried an article about two children who raised lop-eared rabbits. Another possibility would be an article about a local person who raises chickens to produce eggs. Service organizations often put on Easter egg hunts for children and there has to be a story there. How long have they been doing it? How many eggs do they buy? Who is the most clever hider and finder of eggs?

Halloween: If you ask around, you can usually hear about a giant pumpkin, and the grower will be delighted to tell you how he or she managed to grow it. This accomplished gardener may give you ideas about growing vegetables or flowers that would make a good gardening article for a spring edition.

Any holiday or special event: Of interest are families who decorate their homes in unusual ways for Halloween, Christmas, Easter, Independence Day. What is distinctive about their decorations? Why do they do this, and how did the custom start?

363

- **Are there guidelines for writing for the small community newspaper?**

In general, most small newspapers are looking for:

1) Information telling something positive or interesting that has been done by a local person.

2) Useful information about happenings of interest to people in the newspaper's locality.

You will find that there are many benefits of writing for your small local paper.

First, you will increase your mastery of the writing craft through the helpful criticism of the local editor, a one-on-one review and evaluation of how your article can be improved.

Second, as more articles with your byline are published, you will find the community growing closer to you. Readers of small-town papers feel they know the writers for their paper on a first-name basis. They will begin to stop you on the street or in the store and give you a tidbit that "might make a story." And often it does. This will just make your job of digging out stories easier for you.

77

NINE STEPS FOR OUTLINING NONFICTION

BY SHIRLEY BARTLEY

BOOKS PILED HIGH ON THE FLOOR; manila folders, magazines, and mounds of paper yellowing with age on dusty shelves; desk drawers filled to overflowing with notecards, notebooks, and newspaper clippings. These are a few of the telltale signs of creative disorder. As long as the mess clutters just an office, the only one who complains is the writer. But if this state of disarray transfers itself to one's work then you have a real problem.

Trouble presenting ideas in an orderly manner can be your biggest obstacle to nonfiction sales. Your manuscripts are disorganized if your written ideas seem thrown together like pieces of a jigsaw puzzle. Outlining will help you find the pattern for those pieces. It can be a creative part of planning and writing nonfiction. The following nine-step process will help you organize both nonfiction articles and books; only length and scope differentiate the two.

1. *Narrow your topic statement*
Like an artist's sketch, an outline is a preliminary picture. However, using an outline is not like painting by number; rather, the process produces complex and original portraits.

As an example, let's say that I begin my work week by searching my files for an intriguing topic. I pull out a thick folder on gems as I fantasize about the ones I would buy with the money I make from writing.

After flipping through my research file, I limit the topic to the pros and cons of investing in genuine gem stones. Next, I remind myself that I should slant my piece toward the consumer. I list specific slants that have recently appeared in print. What's missing? I jot down several ideas. I conclude that what is needed is an article on the dangers of telephone sales of flawed gems.

2. *Invent new ideas about your topic*

Explore new patterns of thought. Within your chosen slant, try to get beyond empty generalities and banal observations. Write down as many variations on your focus as possible.

You should experience no dearth of creative ideas. If you do, you need to rethink your original slant and possibly start over with a new angle.

Suppose, as I brainstorm, I come up with several new ideas, including the history of the gem-scam operators, likely customers, types of gems telephone con artists typically sell, and so on.

3. *List ideas under general headings*

Use notecards to catalogue your ideas and data. Cards can be labeled with general headings such as history, present problems, extent and significance of problem, definition of key terms, solutions, and so on.

4. *Arrange ideas into a logical pattern.* What matters most is the organizing principle that lies behind the selection and arrangement of material.

There are numerous options from which to choose. Standard ways of organizing material include a *chronological* arrangement—*past, present,* and *future;* a *spatial* arrangement, in which the topics are connected by their relation to each other in space; *cause and effect; step-by-step;* an *inductive* pattern, in which you move from specifics to a conclusion; a *deductive* pattern, where you move from generalizations to conclusions, citing specific cases; a *hierarchical* pattern, which goes from least important to most important, or vice versa; *problem and solution;* and even a *random* pattern, which can be used if the main headings are of equal importance.

Returning to my gem-selling example, I organize my ideas chronologically. This is one of the easiest arrangements to master, while still preserving a readily identifiable logic. As the following sample outline illustrates, each main heading is a short, declarative sentence, which emphasizes one critical idea. Evidence is relegated to the sub-subheadings.

Title: Buying gems by phone is a risky business.

Introduction: Higher prices, a weakened dollar, and a nervous stock market are causing consumers to experiment with nontraditional investments such as gems. Con men are preying on investors.

Body:

I. **In the past, con men have pitched gems by phone.**
    A. Scams started in the late 1970s when the price of diamonds soared.
        1. Inflation was over ten percent and nervous investors looked for new money-making strategies.
        2. According to a New York appraiser, in 1977 a 1-carat diamond was worth $11,000. By 1980, same diamond sold for up to $60,000. By 1982, same diamond was worth less than $15,000.
    B. Hungry for fast profits, armchair investors got scalped by professional con men.
        1. Example of Texas huckster who targeted only oil-rich investors who had money to burn.
            a. Specialty of "Diamond Jim" was phoning only "serious" investors such as those with over $25,000 to invest in a single stone.
            b. By the time consumers caught on to the scam, "Diamond Jim" had vanished without a trace.
        2. Example of how *Fair Credit Billing Act of 1974* protected one consumer who bought flawed stones using a credit card. Law states that consumer is protected from having to pay for flawed merchandise when it is charged.
            a. This case was a rare one since most consumers paid with personal checks, cashier's checks or money orders.
            b. This law was not sufficient to stop con men.

II. **At present, gem-scam operators are bilking consumers out of hundreds of millions of dollars.**
    A. Hucksters are selling flawed colored gems.
        1. Florida state attorney general's office reports that sapphires, rubies, topazes, and emeralds are being sold over the phone.
            a. Stones are genuine but flawed.
            b. Colored stones are assessed on a purely subjective basis. No standards for clarity and color as there are for diamonds.
        2. Example of one investor who bought a Thai ruby over the phone for $24,000. Since it is imperfect and doesn't reflect the light, the stone is worth only $4,000.
    B. Anyone can be a victim.
        1. Florida state attorney general's office reports that hucksters get mailing lists of periodicals or the clientele of a brokerage house.
        2. Example of how a consumer gets hooked during a two-call process. First call offers gems for sale. Second call from a "different" firm offers to buy back same gems at a higher price. Therefore, the consumer gets hooked by the bait of fast and easy profits.
    C. Problem is significant on a national basis.
        1. Federal Trade Commission reports that individual scam operators are taking in millions of dollars.
        2. Jewelry-industry analysts report that thousands of people have been victimized and don't even know it.

3. According to the California state attorney general's office, problem is getting worse since scam operators set up their phone banks in one state and then flee to another.

III. **In the future, consumers would be safer if the following recommendations are followed.**

A. Protecting consumers against any type of telephone fraud should be a national priority.

    1. Federal watchdog agency which would work with state authorities should be created. Purpose would be to stop all phone scams.

        a. Consumers would be able to call and report suspicious phone offers.

        b. Program would not be prohibitively costly.

    2. State agencies would work in tandem with federal.

B. Protect consumers by establishing objective standards for colored stones.

    1. Gemologist in Tulsa reports on advantages of verifiable and objective standards for colored stones.

    2. Jewelry appraised in Houston recommends the type of standards that can be used.

    3. Widely publicized standards would reduce marketability of huckster's stones.

Conclusion: Consumers should protect themselves from gem-scam operators by refusing to buy any gems over the phone. Purchases should be made only from reputable dealers. Consumers should invest in gems that have been appraised by experts, and remember the Latin motto: *Caveat emptor.*

5. *Accumulate data*

Check your outline for any holes. Is it heavy on factual data but short on authoritative testimony?

Fearing rejection, most writers err on the side of over-researching a topic. An outline can save you time and quell your anxieties, since it tells you exactly how much data you need and where it goes.

6. *Rethink the logic of your outline*

An outline establishes logical connections between ideas. Delete material that interferes with the logical sequence of your ideas. A good outline will help you catch errors of thought, language, or data.

I originally used a chronological pattern for my gem-selling example, but after rethinking my outline, I decided that the slant would be much stronger for consumers if I used a problem-and-solution pattern. Accordingly, I quickly reorganized my ideas and data.

368

7. *Ask your outline questions*

With a clean copy of your outline in hand, try to find out what you have left out or overlooked.

My favorite question is: "So what?" I use this question as a test for provocativeness. Asking a question such as this helps to delete fallacies of reasoning or boring bits of data.

8. *Do more research*

While it is easy to do too much research, it is also easy to do too little. An outline shows if you have made statements that you cannot prove. A short phone call or a brief trip to the library can do the trick.

9. *Transform your outline into a final manuscript*

An effective outline is the bare bones of the article. It must be fleshed out with lively style and, of course, convincing material. Outlining is one of the nuts and bolts of the writing trade that can make the difference between rejection and acceptance.

78

SPORTSWRITING IS ABOUT PEOPLE

BY DEBORAH FOWLER O'MELIA

WHEN GIVEN THE OPPORTUNITY TO WRITE a monthly sports column, I realized for the first time how different this is from reporting a basketball game play by play, which is written from the point of view of the spectator. Sportswriting, on the other hand, whether it involves the world-class athlete or the neighborhood volleyball team, is about *people* who have worked very hard to get where they are.

I know of no other category of writing that offers a wider range of topics. There's a sport for everyone, whether it's running, aerobics, weight lifting, camping, fishing, hunting, target shooting, rock climbing, bicycling, or horseback riding, to mention only a few. And sportswriting frequently offers a story within a story; related topics like training techniques, fitness, athletic clothing, and sports medicine provide additional article ideas.

Finding people to interview is simple. While some celebrities resist interviews, I've found that athletes generally love to talk about what they do. If you want to do a story on rock climbers but don't know any, just call mountaineering stores and schools. I found a climbing instructor who seemed pleased to demonstrate a difficult ascent and who allowed me to take some photos and record a brief interview. Athletic organizations usually will refer you to some of their members. Try the Yellow Pages and the advertisements and announcements in the magazine for which you'd like to write. Your friends, relatives, and co-workers are also good sources of information.

Look at yourself. Do you go to aerobics classes or participate in "fun runs"? Use your expertise; you know more than you think you do. From all of this you will come up with a national champion, a unique athletic club, or a great behind-the-scenes story. Start with sports that interest you most, and you will find that you become interested in others.

Press releases and media kits, which are information packets that provide background information on sports celebrities and sometimes offer personal interview appointments, are available to the free-lance sportswriter. To place yourself on lists to receive this information, you will have to do some telephone work. You do need to locate your own sources, because they vary from one area to another. Look in the Yellow Pages under "Public Relations." Call every one of the PR firms, explain that you are a free-lance writer and would like to receive press releases for any events featuring sports celebrities.

Generally, PR people are pleased to add writers to their list of contacts. Get the name of the person to whom you've spoken and follow up in writing! Include writing samples if they request them. Sports organizations are often eager to work with you in the same manner, so look under "Associations" and "Athletic Associations" that you can add to your telephone list.

The value of these sources will become evident when you suddenly find yourself receiving detailed media kits, being invited to exclusive press conferences, and personally interviewing famous athletes.

Endless publishing opportunities await the sportswriter. *The Writer's Handbook*'s 2,500 listings include a healthy sports section. Dozens of sports magazines are on display at good newsstands. Take a pen and pad of paper and write down the names and addresses of several. Purchase a magazine or two so the owner of the shop or newsstand won't mind your browsing. Analyze the contents, style, ads, etc. It will be worth it. You'll also find sports magazines in sporting equipment stores, particularly those specializing in such sports as mountaineering, skiing, fly fishing, etc. And keep in mind that most large libraries have a good selection of sports publications. Many non-sports, general magazines publish sports articles, too.

It's to every free lancer's benefit to find out what sports editors like (and don't like). All sports and athletic magazines (and others that publish sports articles, features, or sections) have specific requirements, and submitting blindly is like trying to win the state lottery. Send for the sample copy first. It will be worth the small fee. Request the writer's guidelines, too.

Editors are understandably annoyed by a writer who has not bothered to read an issue of their publication but submits a query or manuscript. Pat Shea, editor of *Rocky Mountain Sports & Fitness,* says his pet peeve is a writer "who calls me on the phone and asks, 'What's your magazine like, anyway?' " Any writer should become familiar with the style, tone, and focus of a publication to which he plans to send material.

Study the "Market News" in *The Writer* and the special lists of sports magazines and those that are looking for sports articles. If you focus on the person or persons you want to interview, you may be able to turn the basic information you have gathered into a piece for a general audience publication. Consider local magazines and newspapers that use feature articles, especially if the person or subject has a local background or connection, or if, for instance, a local athlete has become famous, or a local sporting event has some unusual or special significance.

If you land an interview with the latest winner of the Boston Marathon, don't ask him questions only about the race. Find out why he runs, how he got started, what other aspects of his life are like, where he plans to be six months or a year from now. Who is his coach, and what other runners has his coach trained? Are there some ways in which this runner applies his sport to his business life? Statistics must be accurate. Many sports readers are well informed and follow the sport of their choice with great attention. Double-check your facts.

Photographs are nearly always essential. If you don't already own a quality, 35mm camera, consider purchasing one. This is no place to skimp; all 35mm cameras are not equal. Shop around and get advice from reputable dealers! If the expense is out of the question, try to find a shutter-happy friend who will accompany you out to the runner's track. Some professional photographers will do photos gratis for the credit. Professional athletes often provide press photos.

The most attention-getting sales tool is a "query package" that includes the following:

Query letter. Sports editors are usually most attracted by upbeat, straightforward query letters of no more than one single-spaced page. Begin your letter as you would the proposed article. Don't bother with, "I wonder if you're interested . . ." or "Enclosed please find . . ." Instead, start with, "The first American woman to reach Mt. Everest's summit was Stacy Allison," or "Boulder, Colorado, has been named the Number One town by *Outside* magazine." Next, include a paragraph of your proposed article (possibly the opening). Then describe your article. Use a "one-line description" that will appeal to the editor and make him want to publish *your* article! Add three or four other sentences to describe your approach. Then wrap it up with a closing paragraph that says you've enclosed sample published clips, a brief resume, and SASE. Also, inform the editor that quality photos or slides are available (as they usually are) and sign off.

Resume. When I query an editor, I always include a short resume, with relevant aspects of my experience and a list of my writing credits (without dates of publication). The format looks like this:

- Free-lance sales to *Outside, Backpacker,* and *The Writer.*
- Completed novel in submission; lead character is based on World Cup Marathon winner.
- Ran the Bolder Boulder and Governor's Cup.

Entries like these demonstrate your writing skills as well as your interest in sports.

Writing samples. Your letter is the "writing sample" the editor will see first; if you've baited him into looking beyond that cover page, be ready to supply clips of your published work, if the editor requests them. Although they don't have to be sports-related, they should be similar in tone and style to your proposed piece. Keep high-quality photocopies on hand. If you don't have published clips, use an unpublished manuscript as a sample.

Submission: When you get the go-ahead from an editor, submit the complete manuscript. Your manuscript should shout professionalism. Use strong manila envelopes and SASE's, with sufficient postage on the return envelope in case the manuscript is not accepted.

Sportswriting has not only earned me bylines and brought me invitations to query major magazines, but has boosted my confidence as a writer.

79

WRITING POETRY: THE MAGIC AND THE POWER

By T. Alan Broughton

SPRING—WHICH IN VERMONT is a form of late winter. My four-year-old son and I are taking advantage of a pocket of sunshine to blow bubbles on the front lawn. He likes to wave the wand, then see if he can recapture one of the larger bubbles, perching it on the tip where he can watch it make oily, transparent shifts through the colors of the rainbow. Sometimes, with a wave of generosity, he will free the bubble again to rise into its ultimate journey. Today an uncertain breeze is blowing whatever he makes straight up, or sideways, or into our faces.

He holds out his wand, stares at me through the soapy hole that will become a bubble, and says, "I am magic even though the bubbles have the power."

"What?"

But like any professional oracle he does not repeat or explain. The hand waves, the bubbles coalesce out of air, he dips again and runs across the lawn, trailing a cloud behind him.

I have begun to write down such statements when I can, although I swear I will try not to embarrass him with them when he is older, if he finds them so. An only child has enough self-consciousness to deal with. But this statement won't let go. It snags me the way an image, a word, an incident—glimpsed through my own eyes or vicariously—will when they demand to become a poem. But this time I'm going to blow it off in prose, here, in a brief essay about the making of bubbles that are poems.

Write a poem. That is the first, terrifying instruction I often give my students in a writing class. Ninety percent, if not more, of the instruction in such a course is concerned with revision. Skill, technique, examples of fine poems and some of their drafts, assignments based on specific objectives—these are matters that can be taught consciously with the hope that they will become so well learned that they are innate. But that first assignment, its terror and, if it works, its joy, is directed toward that other part of the process—the unknown, the constantly new, the unlearned that can be learned only in the moment of doing. I give the assignment not to discourage or crush a shaky talent, but to let each of those writers know what every writer feels like, no matter how experienced, when sitting down to make a new poem.

I read poetry not only to find out more of its secrets, even if I cannot use them, but also to remind myself that poems can be written. In the silence of one's mind, no matter how many stacks of books have been filed there, no matter how much knowledge about line-lengths or figures of speech has been stored away, the image of the blank page or screen is fitting metaphor for the fearful ignorance of beginning. By now I have written thousands of poems, only a handful of which I would want anyone to read, although, sometimes to my embarrassment, more than a handful have been published. But no one *wants* to write the same poem again and again, even if some of us are doomed by the limits of talent to do so. The resistance writers so often describe as being present each morning (or evening if they are night-writers) is inevitable. "Momentum" is perhaps an appropriate term to use in sports where a team is melding into a tribe rather than being a mere gathering of disparate individuals, but for the single writer in the solitude of study or park bench, each poem is discovering again that poems can be written.

Which is where the joy resides, and probably also where the need to do it again and again, even for a whole lifetime, originates. Words begin to happen. Perhaps the first few are brutally and impatiently crossed out, the pen for a moment thrown down in impatience. Try again. The next few stick like burrs—at least through this first version. Later one may delete them without regret. But it is happening, whether line by line, image by image, sound by sound, or all together. Each writer will do it in her or his own way—out loud, standing up, lying down, in notebooks, on scraps of paper, on the greenish glow of a screen.

It is a moment that no one can take away from the writer, no matter how fiercely some critic will respond later to the object made. At least my premise is that this is what makes the difference between the writer who persists and the one who gives it a try and goes on to prefer real estate or engineering or the teaching of literature. It is not just the hope that the next poem will be the best poem that keeps the poet going, but also the simple surprise that more poems are there and that the magic is available.

Which is not to say that the process is without its practical side. The distortion in my description so far is that even if "momentum" is not the right term, there is some accumulation of experience. Those students who find the first assignment so daunting that they return with deep circles under their eyes and one of those poems about "how I am trying to write a poem and not succeeding and this is it" can be helped along. Such help can be only tentative and personal, but like any talisman, once used to enter the next level in the cave, it can be thrown away and that person can find his or her own better means.

1. For the moment, forget what any other poet has written about. Write out of your own experience. Despite the anxiety that we are just like everyone else, the fear that we are lost in the *pluribus* rather than standing out as *unum,* the miracle of existence is that each one of us is uncloned, comes piled with genes never before accumulated in quite the same pattern. Enjoy. Now. Because the price for that, of course, is that you must die. What you have done, seen, reacted to, absorbed, dreamed, imagined is not exactly like anyone else's experience. Because you are a member of the human species, the larger patterns are similar—which does enable you to hope that what you write sufficiently incarnates those patterns to be accessible to others. But the intensity will come from those fine, small differences that make you and your poem an-other.

2. So the corollary is be concrete, be specific, sing out of the sensuous facts of your own body. Large abstract terms are the voice of the herd lowing to itself—Love, Hope, Joy, Defeat. We need them—the smoothed objects of ritual naming that help us believe we know what we have done and seen. But to journey into them, we need a map of their huge domains as detailed as the description of their hedges and weeds, the sound a specific woman's voice makes when it calls from the window of a particular house. Perhaps the sound will add up to Loneliness or Loss, but your reader will believe that only when he is tricked into hearing the voice, and he will believe what he has heard is much richer and more complex than the single term.

3. And that complexity is what the words poems use can give us—

especially in Metaphor, that yoking of the disparate or opposite, the comparison that is known but often unacknowledged until the poet shows it to us.

Translated loosely, and for a New England readership, Moritake's haiku could be "A fallen leaf returning to the branch." It is meaningless without its title: "Butterfly." Two utterly known, utterly common objects. A leaf, a butterfly. They are superimposed. The delight may be small—a leaf seen as a butterfly, a butterfly seen as a leaf. The basis of comparison is motion—that faltering, fluttering, seemingly indeterminate flight of both. The poet's ability to defy gravity is the surprise. Small effect. But is it so small if, after having read the poem, one always sees the two objects in their flights differently from before?

The yoking of disparate elements is a larger pattern of poems, that incorporation of the Yin and Yang of the world. In writing through the first drafts, part of the struggle is in keeping the mind open to illogic, to prevent all the training we have had since childhood in being "reasonable" from taking over. At the moment of writing, the mind is not so much concentrating on belief as admitting that whatever the poem has started to say, is saying at this very moment I am putting down words, it may be about something else, a something else I could never have imagined without doing what I am doing now—writing it into existence. Perhaps in the first draft that "otherness" will show only in glints, and then revision will be in sleuthing, trying to find those unexpected moments.

Bear in mind that metaphor does not reside in images alone, but in situations also. I remember once trying to write a poem that I thought was a story about a boy falling from a flagpole. He had come to a place with his father to fix the pole. The narrator was a man watching, describing the event that happened to virtual strangers even if he had hired them. What I discovered was a poem that was really about the man and his marriage, the terrible descent he and his wife and his own small son were going through. The foreground remained the death of the boy climber, but the foreground was the way to present the other descents. In another instance, a poem I thought was to be about stopping by the side of the road and hearing Mozart coming through the air from the open window of someone's truck becomes yoked with a death in the nearby woods, a suicide and its investigation that might seem to be as far removed from a Mozart Serenade as possible.

Serenade for Winds

We know life so little that it is very little in our power to distinguish right from wrong, just from unjust, and to say that one is unfortunate because one suffers, which has not been proved. (Van Gogh, to his brother Theo and sister-in-law Jo.)

Clustered beside the road are a van,
pick-up, two sedans. In another season
we might imagine hunters tracking deer
or lugging sixpacks away from their wives.
But the Seal of State on one door warns
a new fact has burned its brand on the landscape.

From the vacant truck a radio plays
Mozart into the summer breeze.
Now an oboe floats above
the bass of bassoon, a clarinet
lures the horn to join
this conversation on the waves.

We have stopped to check the map
but might believe that only this
was why we drove for hours—
leaves lifted in a freshet,
all else forgotten and offstage
when air and music are one.

In the forest a trooper stops
a witness from cutting the rope
with his knife. Procedures require
cameras and tape, a careful report.
A man's body, halted by noose
and gravity, slowly swings
from the maple's limb.
In an hour or two a wife
and elder son will try
through taut jaw to say
they're not surprised, blame him,
the State, or bank, or all.

Only a few bars remain.
Cut him down. Let him drop
on the layered leaves.
The notes rise into the silence of air
through which the body must descend.

That's enough for starters, at least for me when I sit down to try to find a new poem. Everyone who knows poets intimately has to learn to forgive them for their metaphor-hounding. Any little act or word can be snatched up and transformed by poems. I hope my son, if he sees this years from now, will forgive my plagiarizing. But I couldn't have found a better way to say it—that moment of sharing between poet and poem when the day's last word announces itself, when that bubble called a poem begins to take its translucent form. "I am magic, even though the bubbles have the power."

80

How to Write a Funny Poem

By Jack Prelutsky

WRITING HUMOROUS VERSE is hard work. For the humor to succeed, every part of the poem must be just right: It requires delicacy. If the poet uses too heavy a hand, the poem goes beyond being funny and turns into something disquieting or even grotesque. Conversely, if the poet doesn't push the idea far enough, the incongruities that are supposed to make the poem funny bypass the reader.

Humorous poetry is often highly underrated. The reader responds easily to humor with laughter, often unaware of the mental and technical gymnastics that the poet has performed to elicit this response. Physiological studies have shown that the body has a much easier time laughing than getting angry. Since humor is such a facile emotion, the reader assumes that the funny poem is also a simple poem—about as complicated as slipping on a banana peel.

How do I make a poem funny? Exactly what are these gymnastics? I'll start with one that is a favorite, and then continue with several others that should be standard in any humorist's repertoire.

I love the technique of asking serious questions about a silly idea. You can make almost anything funny by starting with an absolutely nonsensical premise, and asking common sense questions about it. I once was in a supermarket selecting some boneless chicken breasts for dinner, and it suddenly occurred to me to ask the question, "What about the rest of the chicken—was that boneless, too?" And if so, where did it live, what did it do, and what did the other chickens think of it? When I'd finished answering my "serious" questions, I had the groundwork for a poem, "Ballad of a Boneless Chicken," which appears in *The New Kid on the Block*.

While I was writing the poem, one last question occurred to me: Exactly what sort of egg does a boneless chicken lay? The answer provided me with a surprising, yet somehow logical conclusion.

Ballad of a Boneless Chicken

I'm a basic boneless chicken,
yes, I have no bones inside,
I'm without a trace of rib cage,
yet I hold myself with pride,
other hens appear offended
by my total lack of bones,
they discuss me impolitely
in derogatory tones.

I am absolutely boneless,
I am boneless through and through,
I have neither neck nor thighbones,
and my back is boneless too,
and I haven't got a wishbone,
not a bone within my breast,
so I rarely care to travel
from the comfort of my nest.

I have feathers fine and fluffy,
I have lovely little wings,
but I lack the superstructure
to support these splendid things.
Since a chicken finds it tricky
to parade on boneless legs,
I stick closely to the hen house,
laying little scrambled eggs.

Another of my tricks is to find that one small special something in the ordinary, or to add something unexpected to the apparently mundane. For example, in *The New Kid on the Block,* I have a poem called, "Euphonica Jarre." Euphonica would be unexceptional, were it not for one preposterous talent—she's the world's worst singer. In this poem, I applied another device, one familiar to all humorists—*exaggeration!* To make Euphonica outlandishly funny, I decided that her vocalizing should cause unlikely events, such as ships running aground, trees defoliating themselves, and the onset of avalanches.

Euphonica Jarre

Euphonica Jarre has a voice that's bizarre,
but Euphonica warbles all day,
as windowpanes shatter and chefs spoil the batter
and mannequins moan with dismay.

Mighty ships run aground at her horrible sound,
pretty pictures fall out of their frames,
trees drop off their branches,
rocks start avalanches,
and flower beds burst into flames.

When she opens her mouth, even eagles head south,
little fish truly wish they could drown,
the buzzards all hover, as tigers take cover,
and rats pack their bags and leave town.

Milk turns into butter and butterflies mutter
and bees look for something to sting,
pigs peel off their skins, a tornado begins
when Euphonica Jarre starts to sing.

In *The New Kid on the Block,* there's another poem called, "Forty Performing Bananas," which illustrates the tactic of making something extraordinary out of the ordinary. On the surface, there's nothing unusual about bananas. They're found in every food market, and we take them for granted when we slice them over our breakfast cereal. However, they become uniquely foolish when imbued with the skill to sing and dance. Some inanimate objects are just naturally amusing when they're anthropomorphized. Performing bananas are among them; airborne hot dogs, which appear in my newest book, *Something Big Has Been Here,* are another.

By the way, I use a lot of wordplay in the banana poem: their features are "appealing" and their fans "drive here in bunches." It's probably already occurred to you, but I'd like to mention that I routinely combine several techniques in a poem and can wind up with some complex results. Another way to find humor in the ordinary is to take this item or idea and keep amplifying it until it reaches a totally absurd conclusion. When I was writing *Something Big Has Been Here,* I was struck with the notion of an uncuttable meat loaf. It's an old joke, and there are dozens of examples on TV and film. I searched for an approach that would allow the reader to experience that old joke in a new way. In this case, the meat loaf in question resists all attempts to slice, hammer, drill or chisel it. The implements become more and more exotic, the speaker resorts to bows and arrows, a blowtorch, a power saw, and finally a hippopotamus to trample it. Nevertheless, the meat loaf remains intact. Though I could have ended the whole business here, I decided to employ an additional tactic, that of combining two different ideas that normally don't belong together, further stretching credulity. I conclude the poem by accepting the meat loaf for what it is (indestructible) and reveal that additional meat loaves are now being manufactured as building materials. Of course, no builder would use meat loaves to erect a house, but by making such an absurd leap, I made the poem even funnier.

I'd like to touch on a rather obvious resource for any poet who writes humor: letting the humor grow out of the words themselves. There are numerous kinds of wordplay: puns, anagrams, spoonerisms, and malapropisms. I love puns, and in *Something Big Has Been Here,* I expanded on the sayings that children write to each other in their autograph books when I composed the poem, "I Wave Good-bye When Butter Flies." In this list of puns, you can watch a pillow fight, sew on a cabbage patch, dance at a basket ball, etc.

I Wave Good-bye When Butter Flies

I wave good-bye when butter flies
and cheer a boxing match,
I've often watched my pillow fight,
I've sewn a cabbage patch,
I like to dance at basket balls
or lead a rubber band,
I've marveled at a spelling bee,
I've helped a peanut stand.

It's possible a pencil points,
but does a lemon drop?
Does coffee break or chocolate kiss,
and will a soda pop?
I share my milk with drinking straws,
my meals with chewing gum,
and should I see my pocket change,
I'll hear my kettle drum.

It makes me sad when lettuce leaves,
I laugh when dinner rolls,
I wonder if the kitchen sinks
and if a salad bowls,
I've listened to a diamond ring,
I've waved a football fan,
and if a chimney sweeps the floor,
I'm sure the garbage can.

Another common technique to achieve humor is the surprise ending. My use of this device is the result of being so astounded and delighted by the O. Henry stories I read as a child. One of my most successful uses of a surprise ending is in the title poem of my book, *The New Kid on the Block*. I recite a complaint about a neighborhood bully, the new kid who punches, tweaks my arm, pulls my hair, likes to fight, is twice my size, and just at the point when everyone has conjured up an image of some big, loutish boy, I end the poem with the following lines:

". . . that new kid's really bad, I don't care for her at all."

I admit that the punch line's humor depends heavily on the shameless use of one of contemporary society's most common stereotypes, but it has never failed to draw laughter whenever I've recited the poem to an audience. This is a good place to remind everyone that much of our humor is culture bound. Very often, what may be hilarious to an American audience may draw blank looks from residents of the Himalayas. Actually, I don't have to go as far as Tibet to make an apt comparison; there are many moments on the British "Benny Hill" television show that draw blank looks from me.

One last device I'll mention is irony. It can be as simple as in my poem, "My Dog, He is an Ugly Dog" (from *The New Kid on the Block*), where I list all the things wrong with my dog: He's oddly built, sometimes has an offensive aroma, has fleas, is noisy, stupid, and greedy. Nevertheless, despite this litany of his drawbacks, I declare that he's the only dog for me.

In my poem, "I Met a Rat of Culture" (from *Something Big Has Been Here*), the irony becomes a bit more sophisticated when I describe a learned and highly skilled rodent; he's handsomely attired, recites poetry (a bit of irony within irony), speaks many languages, is knowledgeable about all the arts and sciences, and so on, but at the end of the poem, he reveals his true nature: ". . .but he squealed and promptly vanished at the entrance of my cat, for despite his erudition, he was nothing but a rat."

There are several other methods I incorporate, but I'll leave them to some desperate graduate student to uncover. A few involve simple observation and focusing on incongruities. That's what happened when I was squirrel-watching, and noticed that their tails looked like question marks. I wrote a poem in which I concluded that it's pointless for them to wear question marks, inasmuch as "there's little squirrels care to know." ("Squirrels," from *Something Big Has Been Here*.) And there's always the riddle trick, when you start with the punch line and work backward, as I did in "A Wolf is at the Laundromat" from *The New Kid on the Block*. You learn in the last line that the unusually polite wolf doing its laundry is not to be feared, since it is nothing more than a "wash-and-wear-wolf."

So much for the mechanics of making a poem humorous. What do you do when you're stuck for a really funny idea? Watch an "I Love Lucy" rerun—it hasn't failed me yet.

❙ 81

INSIDE A POEM

BY EVE MERRIAM

INSIDE A POEM are the feelings that we all have but usually don't put into words. The feeling of being happy for some special reason or perhaps for no reason at all. The feeling of sadness at the end of summer or just feeling lonely even with family or friends around. For like nature, human nature changes from one mood to another: from sunshiny to stormy, from raging wind to calm and serene, and then blowing up a storm once again. It is the purpose—and the pleasure—of poetry to express these emotions out in the open.

When something is too beautiful or too terrible or even too funny for words: then it is time for poetry.

Although written on the printed page, poetry is always meant to be heard aloud as a conversation between the writer and reader. And yet, it takes many forms, some that may even seem to be like prose. It may tell a story, as fiction does, or it may present facts, as nonfiction does. It may have no rhyming scheme, because a poem doesn't always have to rhyme; nor does it always have to have a regular beat or meter to the line; nor are there always capital letters at the beginning of each line. And some free verse seems to have no formal rhythmic pattern at all. Yet there is a difference between prose and poetry, and it can always be clearly seen.

The difference is this: that poetry speaks directly to and for our emotions. There is no middle ground; nothing standing in between to run interference for us, to soften the blow or reduce the impact. In a novel, we generally takes sides: We may sympathize with one group against another, and we may come to identify with one particular character. But in a poem, there is only one central character and it is always the same person. It is the "I" of the poet who is really you the reader.

It is possible to be a spectator at many things, to sit back as an observer and watch what is going on. Not in poetry. Here you are always on center stage, directly involved in the action every moment. And so whether a poem is written about some emotion that was felt long ago, or whether it springs from a more immediate source, the time inside a poem always seems to be in the present tense. Another reason a poem seems so immediate is that the language is highly concentrated: All non-essential words have been left out so that the essence of the emotion can come through.

When a poem succeeds in untangling our feelings and putting them into words, two interesting things happen—and they happen at the same moment. It is a little like the intermingling of hot and cold currents in a lake when you are swimming. First, it is a relief to be taken out of ourselves and to have our mood expressed—whether it is a joyful or sad one, serious or comic. We find that we are not alone in our emotions; the poet feels as we do. At the same time, our feelings are made more sharply individual for us as our vivid emotions are relived again in the life of the poem. A paradox takes place as we read: A double feeling that we are the same as others and yet we are unique— that is the inner message of a poem. "Yes," we may think as we read a verse describing a parent, "that is how I sometimes feel about my father, too, and yet—" and our mind goes leaping from the poet's images to images of our own.

Reading prose once is usually enough. We follow the story through to the end, for we want to find out what happens; then we are satisfied to be finished with the experience. But reading a poem once is only the beginning. For a poem is written like a surprise package: There are always more layers to unwrap. Prose *is* what it is; a poem suggests. The music and the meaning will shine through more clearly the second time around—or perhaps the third, or even the thirteenth. Do not expect it to be crystal-clear at once; remember that a crystal has many facets. As a crystal can be turned in the sunlight to reveal all the colors of the rainbow, so a poem can be turned over and over in your mind and new meanings and new music will radiate. For a good poem contains both meaning and music. Even nonsense verse contains a certain sense of logic, ridiculous as it may sound. And without song in its syllables, the most lofty verse will fall flat on its prosy face. Why so? Again because a poem, unlike prose, appeals directly to the emotions; and in order to do so effectively the words have to be chosen not only for what they express, but also for how they sound. Music is an emotional experience, and when music is added to the meaning of words there is a double force. And so the poet learns to use language as an orchestra. Word-music can be a velvet lullaby or a rough-booted march, depending on what effect one wishes to create.

Poets use many tools and tricks. It is their job to play with words, to juggle and toss the words until they are arranged in the most satisfactory pattern. Awareness of the tools and tricks available may increase our pleasure in reading as well as writing poetry. Poets may use established verse forms like the couplet, the quatrain, the limerick, the sonnet, among others, and surely will use such figures of speech as metaphor and simile. They may also use alliteration, assonance, and onomatopoeia as subtle kinds of music, less obvious and sometimes more haunting than rhyme.

As we learn how the poet makes the wheels go round, we may come to enjoy poetry all the more. And along the way, we may learn such useful things as how to avoid clichés in our own poetry writing and speech, and how to increase our vocabulary. But most useful of all is learning how to enjoy reading a poem for its own sake—that is to say, for our own.

▌ 82

MAKING A NAME IN POETRY

BY X. J. KENNEDY

AS POETS KNOW only too well, trying to sell poetry to paying magazines and book publishers is a rough task, often impossible. Even giving away poems may be difficult: Some little magazines that pay in free copies can be choosey. And as John Ciardi once observed, it is hard for poets to prostitute their talents. There just aren't that many buyers around.

It would be hypocritical for me to claim that for a poet to see print shouldn't matter. Of course it matters. If you write poems, having them accepted helps convince you that you are right to believe in yourself. Disappointments notwithstanding, just being published once in a while encourages a poet to stick to what William Butler Yeats glumly called "this sedentary trade."

That poems are hard to peddle isn't terribly depressing—to poets who live for the pleasure of making poems. "Well, so Editor X has bounced my sublime ode," they'll tell themselves. "The benighted creep." But to writers who aren't yet widely published and who fiercely crave to be, writers who live not necessarily to write good poems but to see their names in print, this difficulty leads to chagrin.

Writing poetry is radically different from writing articles, stories, or fillers. Most moneymaking writers—that is, writers who aren't poets—scout for a likely market. Then, they often shrewdly adapt their product to suit that market's needs. Their lives make sense: They can supply a demand. Poets, however, if they are serious about writing good poems, have to think differently.

Poetry is probably the one field of writing in which it is a mistake to try to psych out editors. In fact, specific marketing advice can sometimes harm the novice poet by enticing him to pursue fashions. The poet's best hope is to sound like *nobody* else: The finest, most enduring poetry constructs a new marketplace of it own.

Excellent poems are like better mousetraps: Build one, said Emer-

389

ago, so there is no longer much point in a poet's trying for celebrity. The celebrity that a poet may attain isn't the tenth part of one percent of the celebrity that a rock songwriter can attain from a single video. If you are going into the poetry writing business, you might as well forget about fame and fortune and seek other rewards.

Some writers think that bringing out that first collection of poems will be an experience far superior to beholding the beatific vision. This view is distorted. Publishing a book can be a lot of fun, but it may not transform your life. Having published a volume of poetry, you, unlike Michael Jackson or Madonna, can walk the streets and not be over-whelmed by autograph-seekers. Moreover, you can publish a book of poems and continue to suffer from any ailment or lacks that afflicted you.

Poetic fame, like sea water, isn't worth thirsting for. Poets, if they are any good, compete for space in books not only with their peers but with the giants of the ages. They race not only with John Ashbery and Tess Gallagher, to name two deservedly admired contemporaries, but with John Milton and Emily Dickinson. Let them not imitate the plumage of any currently acclaimed poet. Let them discover their own natures, however disappointing the discovery, and stay faithful to whoever they may be.

At the risk of appearing to hold myself up as a sterling example, I shall recall that as a whitehat in the Navy back in the early fifties, just beginning to fool around writing poems, I made plenty of mistakes. (One mistake was trying to write like Dylan Thomas, an attempt that rendered my work thick, fruitcake-like, and impenetrable.) One mistake I didn't make was to crave premature publication. I resigned myself to just writing, piling up poems, not showing them to anybody. Pigheadedly, I believed that one day an editor would print my work, or some of it. At least that attitude kept up my morale: I didn't have to cope with the rejection slips I would certainly have received. And when I finally started licking stamps and getting poems rejected, I was a little (but not a whole lot) more competent.

For a poet, there can be no greater luxury than to work as a complete unknown. When you are an undiscovered gem, there isn't the least bit of pressure on you to publish, to become better and better and stun your critics, to win prizes, and all that debilitating responsibility. All you need care about is writing good poems. Too many college sophomores and also a few grandparents who have never read any poetry other than Hallmark greeting card verse assume that if their first stumbling efforts don't get published, they have failed miserably. But that Sylvia Plath won a noteworthy prize when she was a college student, that Amy Clampitt published her first book in middle age and won immediate accolades, doesn't mean that they should feel any grim duty to succeed. America is full of excellent poets who have had their poems published for years, despite the fact that they receive little notice. Luckily for our poetry, they persist.

Nowadays, lust for hasty fame takes root early. The other day I was talking with a bunch of fourth-graders in a public library in Quincy, Massachusetts, and a lad of ten asked me again and again—insistently rephrasing the question—how you get poems published. I wanted to tell him, Kid, forget it. I'll bet your stuff at the moment, while it may show flickers of something good, is not much good yet; you will be smart to shelve your ambition for another ten or fifteen years. But, too craven to hit him with the hard truth, I pointed out how rare it is to publish poems in nationwide places when you are ten. Myra Cohn Livingston in her wonderful book *The Child as Poet* tells some horror stories about fledgling poets whose parents goaded them into print at an early age.

All right, call me a sourpuss. I'm trying to dash a little cold water on the notion, so dear to many unpublished writers, that publication is the be-all and end-all of existence. This attitude makes such people push-overs for racketeers: for contests that charge forty-dollar entrance fees, accept everything, then try to sell the contestants a bound volume containing their supposedly winning work for $38.95, or $62.95 for the gold-edged edition. It makes them suckers for vanity publishers who, appealing to their pride and frustration, urge them to subsidize an edition of their own poems, which will sell to nobody, or to practically nobody, unless they themselves sell the copies, and which no reviewer in a national magazine would touch with a thirty-foot flagpole.

Letting oneself be the victim of such con games is all right if seeing your name in print is your one aim. And with any luck, sheer, tireless stamp-licking will result in *some* kind of publication. But sometimes, if viewed as fortresses to be stormed and overpowered, poetry magazines tend to resist. I can recall when, as poetry editor for the *Paris Review,* I kept getting a tide of manuscripts from a poet who had published little but whose name must have been known to every poetry editor. His son, and the world will beat a path to your door. It always amazes me how quickly a good, original book of poetry becomes known: W. D. Snodgrass's *Heart's Needle,* for instance, a book acclaimed soon after publication and laden with a Pulitzer, despite the fact that its author had published relatively little before.

Evidently, it is much simpler to chase after fashions than to transform yourself into a fine poet, the likes of whom the world hasn't seen before. It is easy to advise anyone whose poetic ambition goes no further than to achieve publication. To such a person, I'd suggest the following strategies:

1. Center your poem on your experience, your family, your everyday concerns—however drab. If you write a poem about your cousin's case of AIDS, you will surely find an editor who will accept it, no matter how bad it may be, for he fears that if he doesn't, you will think him a coarse, unfeeling swine who won't sympathize with your cousin. I'm serious!

2. Write in the first person, in the present tense. Not long ago, Peter Davison, poetry editor for *The Atlantic,* remarked that most of the poems he currently receives are like that. Some other, less discriminating editors mistakenly believe that the present tense lends everything a kind of immediacy.

3. Brainstorm, force your unconscious to yoke together disparate things. In the midst of a dull poem on your grandfather's old antimacassar, throw in a mention of something completely far-out and unexpected, such as a fur-lined frying pan.

4. Include a dash of violent realism, preferably straight out of current news. If you can relate your workaday world to, say, war-torn Nicaragua, you've got it made.

5. Give your poem a snappy title to catch an editor's eye. With a little more brainstorming, you can readily invent titles of poems for which many editors, the dolts, will be pushovers: "Contracting Chicken-pox in a First Kiss," "A Lesbian Mother Tells Her Daughter the Facts of Life." Titles like that either promise something interesting, or else reek of Significance with a capital S.

6. Don't, whatever you do, write in traditional forms. To do so will only slow your rate of production. Even worse, you might reveal your

lack of skill. Traditional forms, such as sonnets and blank verse, which held sway over English-speaking poetry for five centuries (up until about 1960), can still nourish wonderful poems—as witness recent work by Seamus Heaney, Derek Walcott, Gjertrud Schnackenberg, and Timothy Steele. But remember, I'm not talking about quality. If you write in traditional forms, you had better be good. In rhymed metrical stanzas, mediocre poetry tends to look shoddy in an obvious way, while bad poetry looks really horrible. On the other hand, bad poems in open forms (or "free verse") tend to seem passable. And—I hate to say this, but it's true—mediocre poems in open forms look like most poems appearing nowadays in respectable places.

7. Study an annual that lists poetry markets such as the *International Directory of Little Magazines and Small Presses* (found in the reference section of many libraries). Then zero in on the less competitive markets, like *Superintendent's Profile & Pocket Equipment Directory,* a monthly for highway superintendents and directors of departments of public works. Although it uses only poems about snowplowing and road repairing, the magazine prints two out of every three poems it receives.

If indeed all you care about is becoming a widely published poet, those hints may be as good as any. What I hope, of course, is that you will ignore all those suggestions.

For a poet who cares about the art of poetry, merely to be published isn't enough. The first time you see your name in print, it may seem to scintillate on the page like a Fourth of July sparkler. Karl Shapiro once recalled the joy of seeing rows of his own book on a shelf, "saying my golden name from end to end." But after you see it a few times, your own name may not prove especially interesting. At the moment, the problem for a poet in this country isn't to get published. A couple of thousand markets now publish poetry, some of whose editors have no taste. And anyone who can't get published can, for $200, start his own little magazine and generously heap his own work with acceptances. Unfortunately, the problem, in this time of dwindling attention spans, is to find attentive readers.

Poets whose work is widely published may still be widely ignored. The poetry star system that produced household names like Robert Frost, Dylan Thomas, and E.E. Cummings passed away twenty years manuscripts came in *daily* showing the wrinkles of many previous rejections. Always folded and refolded sixteen times, sometimes looking as if they'd been given a fresh press with a steam iron, always in envelopes saying Biltmore and Statler and Hilton (pilfered, it seemed, from writing desks in hotel lobbies). If only the contributor had devoted as much time to learning to write as he spent stuffing envelopes!

Why is it that hundreds of thousands of people want to be poets? I don't know, but I have a hunch. In this anonymous society in which we feel like zip codes or social security numbers, writing a poem and publishing it is one way to stand up on your hind legs and sass the universe. A printed poem proclaims, "I exist." There is something powerfully appealing in the thought that you can seize paper and pencil in an odd moment and scrawl a few lines that might make you immortal in anthologies. Immortality is all very well, but it is more interesting to think about the problems of writing good poetry. You don't need to publish a thousand poems in order to become immortal; you need publish only one poem, if it is good enough.

Literary history is full of cases of great poets who garnered no fame or praise or significant publication in their lifetimes. Gerard Manley Hopkins, whose strange masterpiece "The Wreck of the Deutschland" was rejected by a small Jesuit magazine, showed his poems to only a tiny handful of correspondents. Emily Dickinson, after local newspaper editors rewrote the few items she submitted to them, evidently said the hell with them and stitched her poems into little packets that she stashed away in her attic, as is well known. Hopkins and Dickinson, to be sure, were superb poets whose work refused to die. But my point is that they placed quality first and bravely turned their backs upon celebrity.

Sometimes, when I look at the current spate of forgettable poems, I think it would be a great idea if literary magazines were to declare a moratorium on by-lines for a few years. Just suppose every poem were printed anonymously. By and by, of course, the real original poets would be recognized by the character of their work, as surely as "The Pearl" poet of the Middle Ages. But the great mass of poems, undistinguished and forgettable, would slip into oblivion. And there would be fewer of them, since people who now publish poems in order to boost their egos would have no reason to.

I think it is a good idea for young poets to start having their poems published in the very smallest magazines, those read by few people. If in later years they should decide that their maiden works were poor, they can comfort themselves with the knowledge that practically nobody will have read them. Most poets I have known have come to regard their first works as pretty embarrassing. John Ciardi, who won a prize in a student writing contest at the University of Michigan, once told me he longed to burgle his found manuscript from the library and burn it.

Those poets willing to try the most onerous route of all—growing in depth and in skill—might cultivate an aloof coolness toward publication. No formula, no market tip, no advice from me or anybody else will help you write a great poem. But you can take action. You can try reading. Most poets do too little of that. Talk to any editor of a poetry magazine, and you will learn that the would-be contributors usually outnumber paying subscribers by at least five to one. Many poets want to heap their outpourings upon the world, expecting the world to take them gladly. Too impatient to read other poets, they never find out how poetry is written, and they keep repeating things that have already been done well, and so do not need redoing.

If you haven't been published and deserve to be, you might make a personal anthology of poems you admire—the dozen or twenty poems you'd swear by. This task will concentrate your attention, make you aware of your own standards, and reveal your nature to you. I made such a anthology once and learned to my surprise that the poems I most cherish in all of literature are religious ones. You might also try writing a lot—and throwing most of it away. Delmore Schwartz said that a poet is wise to write as much, and to publish as little, as possible.

Keats put it beautifully in a letter to a friend: "I should write for the mere yearning and fondness I have for the beautiful, even if my night's labors should be burnt every morning and no eye shine upon them." That is, I think, a noble attitude. Rejections—or critical attacks—could not thwart a Keats; they simply had no great power over him. For a poet, the only sure reward is the joy of making a poem. Any reward besides—fame, prizes, publication—is like money found in the street. If you see a silver dollar gleaming on the sidewalk, you pick it up. But you need not roam the streets desperately looking for that gleam.

83

THE POET WITHIN YOU

BY DAVID KIRBY

I FIGURE POETRY is a way of beating the odds. The world is never going to give you everything you want, so why not look elsewhere? In a wonderful book called *The Crisis of Creativity* (now regrettably out of print) by George Seidel, it is stated that the artist will always have one thing no one else can have: a life within a life.

And that's only the start. If you have talent and luck and you work like a son of a gun, you might even end up, as the poet John Berryman says, adding to "the store of available reality."

But at least you can have a life within a life, no matter who you are. Not all of us can be great poets. If that were so, the Nobel Prize would be in every box of breakfast cereal—you'd get up, write your poem for the day, and collect your prize. But every literate person has it in him- or herself to be a good poet. Indeed, I have wonderful news for you— each of us is a poet already, or at least we used to be. It's just that most of us have gone into early retirement.

Seriously, when interviewers ask the marvelously gifted William Stafford when he started to write poetry, Stafford often replies, "When did you stop?" All children put words together imaginatively; just talk to one and you'll see what I mean. But then they grow up and enter the world of bills and backaches. They start chasing that dollar, and suddenly their time is limited. Poetry is usually the first thing to go. People get so busy with their lives that they forget to have a life within a life. But you have a life anyway, right? So forget about it for a minute—it'll still be there when you come back—and let's talk about the poet within you.

The first thing you need to do is forget that all poets are supposed to be erratic or unstable. Flaubert was quite clear on this point. He said, "Be regular and orderly in your life, like a bourgeois, so that you may be violent and original in your work." In other words, there's no point in sapping your resources by pursuing some phony "artistic" lifestyle. First, the outer person has to be calm and self-disciplined; only then can the inner one be truly spontaneous.

And that means getting organized. Here are a few rules I use to make my life as orderly and bourgeois as possible, so that the poet within me can be as wild as he wants to be.

1) *Start small.* Most beginning writers tackle the big themes: love, death, the meaning of life. But don't we already know everything there is to know about these subjects? Love is wonderful, death is terrible, life is mysterious. So start small and work your way up. Take a phrase you overheard, a snippet of memory, a dream fragment, and make a poem of that. Once the details are in place, the big theme (whatever it is) will follow, but the details have to come first.

2) *Write about what you remember.* It is a commonplace that you should write about what you know, but usually the present is too close for us to see it clearly. We have to move away from the events in our lives before we can see them in such a way that we can write about them engagingly. Don't waste time on the guy you saw talking to his dog this morning; take a few notes, if you like, but if he's memorable, he'll pop into your mind later, when you really need him. Instead, why not write a poem about the girl in your third-grade class who could throw a baseball better than any of the boys and all the problems that caused? By putting these memories down on paper and shaping them, you're enriching not only your own life but also the lives of others.

3) *Be a sponge.* Shakespeare was. His plays are based on historical accounts and on lesser plays by earlier playwrights. So what are you, better than Shakespeare? I once wrote a poem called "The Last Song on the Jukebox" that was published in a magazine and then in a collection of my poetry and now in an anthology that is widely used on college campuses; people seem to like it pretty well. Looking back at the poem, I can hear in it echoes of two country songs that I used to be able to sing in their entireties but have since forgotten. Somebody says something in my poem that is a variation on something a character says in a novel called *Ray,* by the talented Barry Hannah. And the overall tone of "The Last Song on the Jukebox" owes much to a poet I heard reading his own work one night. His voice was perfect—it had just the right twang to it—so I used it for the speaker in my poem. Now that I

397

think about it, I realize that I didn't like the guy's poetry that much. That didn't stop me from adapting his twang to my purpose.

4) *Play dumb.* Just about anything can be turned into a poem if you play dumb about it, because when you're smart, everything makes sense to you and you go about your business, whereas when you're dumb, you have to slow down, stop, figure things out. Recently, in Chicago, I saw a man being arrested. The police had cuffed him and were hauling him away while an elderly woman shook with rage and screamed after them as they all climbed into the paddywagon. "Liar!" she shouted, "liar!" You mean you can get arrested just for lying, I said to myself? Is that only in Chicago, or does the law apply everywhere? Now if I were a smart person, I might have figured out what really happened: Probably the guy grabbed her purse, and she called the cops, and he said he didn't do it, and she said he *did* do it, and so on. But by being dumb, I got a flying start on a poem. I haven't finished the poem yet, but as you can see, I have already given myself a lot to work with, thanks to my astonishingly low IQ.

5) *Reverse your field.* When you catch yourself on the verge of saying something obvious, don't just stop; instead, say the opposite of what you were going to say in the first place. Listen to the poet within you. If you want to eat a chocolate bar, that's not poetry; everybody likes chocolate. But suppose the chocolate bar wanted to eat you? Now that's a poem. Here's another example: I'm thinking of ending my liar-in-Chicago poem with something about husbands and wives and how they have to be truthful to each other, and I can see myself heading toward a stanza in which the speaker wonders what his wife really means when she says (and this would be the last line of the poem), "I love you." The problem is that that's too pat for a last line, too cloying, too sentimental, an easy out. Instead, since people who are really crazy about each other sometimes kid around in a mock-hostile way, why not have the speaker wonder whether the wife is telling the truth or not when she laughs and hits him on the arm and says, "I hate you, you big lug!" Such an unexpected statement would come as a surprise to the reader, although first it will have come as a surprise to me, who was heading in the opposite direction before I realized that I needed to reverse my field.

6) *Work on several poems at once.* For one thing, you won't end up giving too much attention to a poem that doesn't need it—like children, some poems do better if you don't breathe down their necks all the time. For another, if you're working on just one poem and it isn't going anywhere, you're likely to feel terribly frustrated, whereas if one poem is dying on the vine and three others are doing pretty well, you'll feel as though you are ahead of the game (because you will be). Also, sometimes our poems are smarter than we are, and a word or a line or a stanza that isn't right for one poem will often migrate to another and find a home for itself there. Poems are happiest in the company of other poems, so don't try to create them in a vacuum. You probably wouldn't try to write four novels at once, but there's no reason why you shouldn't take advantage of poetry's brevity and get several poems going simultaneously.

7) *Give yourself time.* This is actually related to the preceding rule, since you wouldn't tend to rush a poem if you were working on several of them at once. I have a friend whose daughter is learning how to cook. But she's a little impatient, so when she has a recipe that says you should bake the cake at 350 degrees for thirty minutes, she doesn't see why you can't cook it at 700 degrees for fifteen minutes. If you take this approach to poetry, your poems are going to end up like my friend's daughter's cakes, charred on the outside and raw in the middle. If you saw a stunningly handsome stranger walking down the street, would you run up to him and shout, "Marry me"? Of course not—he might say yes! Poems are the same way, and if you try to make them yours too soon, you won't be happy with the results, I promise you. Be coy, be flirtatious; draw the poem out a little and see what it's really about. There's no hurry, because you've got all those other poems you're working on, remember?

8) *Find a perfect reader.* A perfect reader is like a perfect tennis partner, someone who is a little better than you are (so you feel challenged), but not that much better (so you don't get demoralized). And like an ideal tennis partner, a good reader is going to be hard to find. You don't play tennis with your mother, so don't expect her to critique your writing.

Anyway, what kind of mother would tell her own child that his poetry is terrible? That's what friends are for. So no parents. And no room-mates, either: people are always saying to me, "You're going to love this poem; my roommate says it's the best thing I've ever written." What else would a roommate say? You can hardly go on living with someone after you've told him to throw his notebook away and take up basket-weaving. Just as you would play tennis with a couple of dozen people before you pick the one you want to play with every Saturday, so too should you pass your poems around until you find the one person who can show you their strengths and weaknesses without inflating or deflating your ego too much. If you're lucky, you'll then do what I did when I found my perfect reader—you'll marry her (or him).

If you have a knack for language and you follow these rules and you get a break from time to time and you look both ways whenever you cross the street, after a while you will find you have created for yourself a life within a life. You will have awakened—reawakened, actually—the poet within you. And even if this isn't your year to win the Nobel Prize, I have to say that I never met anybody who didn't break out into a big happy smile when I introduced myself as a poet. I don't know what it is; maybe people associate me with Homer or Milton. At any rate, every-one seems happy to know there is a poet in the neighborhood.

Well, not everybody. Once I was negotiating with a man to buy his house, and I was getting the better of him. So the man lost his temper and said I didn't know what I was doing, I *couldn't* know, because I was a poet and I ought to go back to my poems and leave business affairs to men like him, practical, level-headed men. For a couple of days, I felt pretty rotten, although the whole thing turned out spledidly for me, since I later found another house I liked even better than his. Mean-while, the practical level-headed fellow had lost a great buyer; like Flaubert, I believe in paying my bills on time.

And I got my revenge: I wrote a poem about him.

‖ 84

WHAT MAKES A POET? WHAT MAKES A POEM?

BY PHYLLIS HOGE THOMPSON

HOW CAN YOU TELL if you really are a poet? *Can* you tell?

I think there are three clear signs: One is that poets love poetry. They read a lot of it. When I open a magazine, I turn first to the poems. In my personal library, hundreds of slender volumes of poetry cram every other kind of book off the shelves.

The second sign is that the poet loves the sound, the *sounds,* of language—the "feel" of words on the tongue, the rhythms words fall into, and those pleasurable echoes called alliteration, assonance, consonance, and rhyme. (Not all poets agree that sound and meaning are equally important. I think they are.)

Love of the sound of language cannot be altogether separated from love of language itself. A poet delights in words, their meanings, and the ways the meanings of words have changed, and the bones of the language—grammar and syntax. A poet gets a kick out of syntax, is not put off by grammar, and is probably interested in the history of language, which is, after all, the poet's instrument, as the violin is the instrument of the violinist. I call the general love of language the third sign.

These identifying characteristics are not all there is to it, naturally, but I think that almost everyone who takes the game seriously has at least these three.

I am intentionally leaving out what the world in general quite probably thinks of as the poet's stock in trade, that is, an artistic and sensitive temperament. I don't believe in it.

Depth of feeling is what the poet shares with every human being. It is what makes poetry important in the lives of those who do not write it. But it is mastery of craftsmanship that distinguishes the poet. Achieving such mastery takes years. It's hard work, but it's not a burden. Poets need to know how poems are constructed. Otherwise the poet is not in control of the poem.

If a poet can figure out what's going on grammatically in his or her poem, he can figure out what's happening in another poet's work and what techniques are being used. Poets read poetry for pleasure, but also to discover new tools to help them with their own poetry writing.

Almost (*almost*) everything else the poet has to learn depends on practicing technique. I think poets should be so thoroughly versed in all forms and meters that they can easily use them in writing their poems. In this way, the poet can be "ready" whenever a poem turns up, ready to give it whatever form is right for it, able to feel what fits a particular idea—a rhymed quatrain or blank verse or free, unmetered lines. Though it is useful to learn the descriptive names and definitions for various poetic forms, it is not essential. Learning through practice to use all of the forms, traditional and contemporary, is hard but essential, and for me surpasses all other entertainments. For one thing, the more one practices writing poetry in various forms, the more the poet gets a very reliable feel for where a line should end.

By learning how to make a rhymed thought draw to a close, or move along naturally into the next line, a poet even learns how to end a line of free verse. Practicing poets confront hundreds of problems during practice, and what's more important, they learn how to solve them in their own individual, even idiosyncratic way, under the critical eye of the sternest of teachers—themselves.

When the poet has achieved a certain mastery of the craft, enough to have some control of it, the next critical step is to recognize a poem when it comes along. A peculiar excitement tells me when a poem is coming. Something breathes energy into me, gathers my emotions around a center. They come together, coalesce into a poem.

The excitement is started off by a particular experience or event or sound—say, a name, a word, a bowl of blue flowers, or even an old blanket. But the difference between simply noticing blanket or flowers and the poetic moment is that at the same time I am experiencing a significant feeling, a feeling that may have to do with someone else, say love or praise or sadness, and also with a whole range of similar moments in my past, a group of memories. My poetic response is to try to recreate that present moment in a poem, and to gather into the moment whatever from the past illuminates that single feeling. The precise thing that initiated the feeling may disappear from the final poem; that doesn't matter. It has done its work. It has inspired the feeling.

Here is the instance I was reminded of by an old blanket, together with a print of a Madonna and Child. The print had disappeared from the poem by the time it was finished.

A Childhood

First snow had fallen.
Inside, cross-legged on the bare wood floor,
We faced one another.
Wrapped in warm blankets,
We talked all night.
There was no lamp. The moon
Filled the window and flooded the cold room
Moving slowly around the walls
And away by daybreak.

In half a century
I have been equally happy maybe five times.

You turned twelve in December.

I did not know why I wept all spring
Or what I longed for.

From *The Ghosts of Who We Were,* University of Illinois Press, 1986.

After you've convinced yourself that you're a poet, all you have to do for the rest of your life is to follow your natural bent: You write poems and you soak in everything you come across in the language you make poems from. Much of it comes easily—origins of words, for instance, or the way one word is related to a word in another language. And since poets are addicted to dictionaries, these fascinating discoveries are exciting and stimulating.

Writing poetry takes time. If life—business, family, illness, study—presses in, demanding all the time a person has, there may be no time then for the poems to get written. But that doesn't mean they're not still there, waiting. Years may pass before the time comes. It's never too late, if the poems are really there.

Afterword

I can't recommend practice too strongly. Through all the years I didn't have enough hours in a day to write real poems, but I did have time to practice, until rhythms and forms pulsed in my veins.

Ten suggestions for practice in iambic pentameter
1. Write ten lines of blank verse.
2. Write ten lines of end-stopped blank verse.
3. Write ten lines of runover blank verse.
4. Change the position of the caesura in each line.
5. Add one syllable to each line.
6. Add two syllables to each line in different feet.
7. Rhyme the lines *abba*.
8. Rhyme the lines *abab*.
9. Rhyme the lines *ababcdcdefefgg* (sonnet).
10. Go through the same processes for iambic tetrameter (to get a feel for how pentameter differs).

If you can't think of anything to write about, take any—and I mean *any*—prose your eye lights on and use it as a basis for the exercise. For example, I took this totally at random from a book ad and reworked it:

"These brief, radiant essays discuss sixty key books that are basic documents in the history of the imagination."

> These brief and shining essays now discuss
> The sixty basic books that are for us,
> And for the world, the documental key
> Of the imagination's history.

85

THE WRITER AS STARLING: ADVICE TO A YOUNG POET

BY ROBERT DANA

It is always a matter, my darling,
Of life or death, as I had forgotten. I wish
What I wished you before, but harder.

"The Writer," by Richard Wilbur

IN HIS POEM "The Writer," Richard Wilbur re-experiences, as he listens to his young daughter typing, the urgency we all felt as young writers to express our feelings toward experience. These feelings are, he suggests, "the great cargo" of our first poems. Wilbur also recalls the difficulty of trying to write well. Words, the poem goes on to say, come "Like a chain hauled over a gunwale." The image is that of drawing up by hand a heavy anchor from very deep water, a few iron links at a time, phrase by phrase, across a threshold.

But the images of the heavy cargo and hauled anchor in Wilbur's poem are very quickly replaced by the image of the writer as a bird, a common starling which has flown mistakenly into a room and must keep trying, failure after failure, until it finally makes a "smooth course for the right window/And . . . the world."

". . . I wish/What I wished you before, but harder," he says finally. What he's wished for his daughter earlier in the poem is "a lucky passage." A phrase that means, as I read it, both a stretch of writing so good it could not have been written without the cooperation of chance, and a writing life marked by fame and good fortune.

Most of the young poets I encounter around the country seem to have started out for a life of fame and good fortune pretty much like Wilbur's daughter, like most of us for that matter, equipped with little more than luck and a precious cargo of feelings. Many are genuinely talented. And most of them are in the process of finding out that the work of a professional poet is both more difficult and more mysterious than they had supposed. Like the trapped starling in Wilbur's poem, they find themselves "humped and bloody" with battering the glass of the wrong windows, looking for a clear "passage."

There is, of course, a limit to what I, or anyone else, can do to help them. If you set up shop as a teacher of poetry writing, it does help to be a poet. Then you know firsthand what it is to batter against glass, to see a world you cannot reach, to grow desperate. You know that learning to write consistently well is, for most of us, a long process, marked by many failures. You know that talent is not enough.

Knowledge and skill are qualities young poets begin to acquire when luck falters and feelings prove common to everyone. Even our experiences prove, alas, to be not entirely unique—frost on the tall grass, the ride down the mountain, love in a burning building. A real knowledge of subject, and skill with the language, we come to see if we stick it out long enough, are exactly the qualities that create the "lucky passage," the poetry that stuns the reader into wakefulness.

In my experience as a teacher, I am always astonished by the fact that young poets don't seem to have read much, if any, poetry. They often seem to think, oddly enough, that being a writer means to be exempt from reading. But how can young writers become poets without knowing what poetry is? And how can they know what poetry is without experiencing, many times over, the work of the best poets in the language: Shakespeare, Keats, Wordsworth, Whitman, Dickinson, Yeats, and all the rest?

Poetry at its highest levels is an art akin to magic. But at its basic level it's a craft, skills passed on from master craftsman to journeyman to apprentice. From Whitman to Frost to Sylvia Plath and Gerald Stern and Robert Dana. I doubt that these same young poets think that being able to pound a nail in the wall so that they can hang up their coat makes them a carpenter, but they will try to write poetry without really knowing quite what it is.

On the other hand, those who generally know "a hawk from a hand-saw" where poetry is concerned often don't know the names of the trees they walk under every day, or the names of birds, or the slightest thing about string-theory or cellular biology or Fabian socialism. They know a great deal about Chaucer and Whitman but nothing about solar winds or limestone or tender offers. The kind of knowledge they lack is not so much the knowledge of craft, as knowledge of a working world. Information.

In fact, the kind of information I'm talking about—precise, accurate, and concrete—is the basis of all good writing, whether poetry or prose. It's exactly the kind of information Robert Lowell refers to in his poem, "Epilogue": "Pray for the grace of accuracy/ . . . give/ to each figure in the photograph/ his living name." But, of course, to do this means to take the time to learn the names of the figures in the photograph, or the things of this world. And not only the names, but the nature of things, whether flowers or political movements, business deals or pathological states.

This means, probably, not only reading but studying. Studying not only those subjects we like, but those we think we dislike and avoid: sciences and mathematics; political science and history. It means collecting names and dates and stories. And when I speak of "study," I certainly don't mean to imply that school is the only place where these things can be learned. They can be learned anywhere. From a *National Geographic* magazine, or a book on nuclear war. As one of my favorite students used to say, "Hell, you can get an education free if you want one. It's called a library card." And much of what any writer knows, he or she learns from careful, repeated, firsthand observation.

The only thing perhaps more important to a writer than subject matter is language. "A poem is a machine made of words," William Carlos Williams liked to say. I think Williams knew that people would find the notion of the poem-as-machine not only unglamorous, but shocking and offensive. But he also knew that the act of writing poetry had to be de-frilled and demystified, had to be seen as an efficient and practical aspect of everyday life, if it were to have any place in modern, industrial America. Secondly, I think Williams is talking about language as a tool. Poems are machines; words, parts of the machine, each with its specific function; clutch, drive shaft, fan belt, air filter, turn signals. Some poems, like some machines, are poorly made. On its way to the final draft, the poem often breaks down. The poet's job is to fix it. Or build a better poem. For this he or she needs a vocabulary adequate to the needs of the poem, and command of grammar (in some cases even of *un*grammar).

It would be wonderful to be able to say, "Poems break down for the following three reasons: . . ." But poems, in fact, break down for every conceivable reason: The poet doesn't know and can't find out what his poem is about; his or her language is inadequate or inappropriate to the experience; the poet has failed to think through the necessary transitions from one part of the poem to another—one could go on almost endlessly. "A poem is never finished; it's just abandoned," Paul Valéry said. That's certainly been my experience. But the poem is revised many times before we call it finished or simply leave it behind.

"Revision is the name of the game," I tell young poets. "If you can't revise, you'll never become a good writer." James Dickey used to talk about revising a poem as many as 150 times, working on it sometimes just "to get that worked-on quality out of it," to get that feeling of inevitability into the language. For good poetry always bears that impress of "rightness" in its language, that sense that the words for this specific experience must be these words and no other.

Sometimes those words come to you freely in a moment of perfect and intense perception. I remember driving from Gainesville, Florida, to Saint Augustine one day in 1974, "a thin, viral mist fizzing the windshield." I suppose I'd been listening to this particular kind of rain making its particular kind of sound for several months by then. It was not the kind of rain you get in the Midwest or the Northeast or the West, and it did not beat on the windshield or even fog it. It "fizzed." And it was thin and raw, the kind that brings on sickness if you're exposed to it very long, the kind of rain common to the malarial tropics. And when the words came, I knew they were exactly right. What I did not know was that it would be seven years, and I would be far from Florida, before the poem would show up in which I would use them in a stanza in "Everything Else You Can Get You Take":

> No place we ever imagined
> we'd be. No sea's edge
> where a low wave sputters,
> ignites like a fuse, and races
> hissing along the shore.
> No thin, viral mist fizzing
> the windshield, gorges rising
> grey as China in the rain.

On the other hand, how many years had I been watching lightning before I saw that it wasn't all one color, that besides white and yellow, some of it cracked red, some green, and some violet, an observation I made use of in the opening lines of "Getting It Right":

> Lightning cracks its red
> and green and violet whips,
> or sets its white hooks
> deep into your soundest sleep,
> and you wake.

And I suppose there are many things and feelings for which I will never find the word that is the perfect match. But as a poet, as a writer, it is my job to keep searching for it.

In my experience, we rarely get many of the words right in a first draft or even the second. The machine coughs and sputters, and its turn signals don't work. It takes days, even weeks, and when we're young, sometimes months, maybe a year even, to get one poem right. For a while, maybe we just abandon poem after poem. But we either believe in the value of what we are doing enough to work, really work at it, acquiring all the necessary knowledge and skills, including the ability to revise, or we don't. If we do, we sometimes come through, finally, to the "lucky passage," the one Ezra Pound used to call a "vortex," the passage that draws into its center everything we know, and all our skill with the language and more, to produce a breathtaking, a dazzling literary moment. Perhaps something we didn't even know we knew.

This is the point at which poetry ceases to be an exercise of will and skill and approaches the condition of genuine magic, or what Wilbur in his poem calls luck. Teachers can teach, and students can learn subject matter and techniques of language. They can even invent them. And it's probably true that the more you know about something—sailing, daylilies, Nicaragua—the more authority your language will have. But no one can teach you how to transform a merely very good passage into an inspired one.

It's popular among writers and critics to say things like "this poet has earned his distinctive voice," or "her poem has not earned its difficult and brilliant conclusion." My quarrel is not with these statements as value judgments, necessarily, but with the word "earned." It has the effect of reducing the act of writing to a business transaction. As if by investing time and effort, the writer, like the banker or broker, were guaranteed the reward of profit or interest. As if writing a poem word by

409

word, and line by line, were an act akin to saving coins in a piggy bank, and when you got enough of them you changed them into a five-dollar bill.

Do I need to say that good writing is not a matter of earnings in this sense even if it is a matter of work? Good writing is its own pleasure. And great writing stops our breath, perhaps precisely because it seems to leap effortlessly the boundaries marked by the sweaty hand, the chewed pencil, or the word processor. I'm with Wilbur, gentle reader. ". . . I wish/What I wished you before, but harder."

86

POETIC DEVICES

BY WILLIAM PACKARD

THERE is a good story about Walter Johnson, who had one of the most natural fast balls in the history of baseball. No one knows how "The Big Train" developed such speed on the mound, but there it was. From his first year of pitching in the majors, 1907, for Washington, Walter Johnson hurtled the ball like a flash of lightning across the plate. And as often as not, the opposing batter would be left watching empty air, as the catcher gloved the ball.

Well, the story goes that after a few seasons, almost all the opposing batters knew exactly what to expect from Walter Johnson—his famous fast ball. And even though the pitch was just as difficult to hit as ever, still, it can be a very dangerous thing for any pitcher to become that predictable. And besides, there were also some fears on the Washington bench that if he kept on hurtling only that famous fast ball over the plate, in a few more seasons Walter Johnson might burn his arm out entirely.

So, Walter Johnson set out to learn how to throw a curve ball. Now, one can just imagine the difficulty of doing this: here is a great pitcher in his mid-career in the major leagues, and he is trying to learn an entirely new pitch. One can imagine all the painful self-consciousness of the beginner, as Johnson tried to train his arm into some totally new reflexes—a new way of fingering the ball, a new arc of the elbow as he went into the wind-up, a new release of the wrist, and a completely new follow-through for the body.

But after awhile, the story goes, the curve ball became as natural for Walter Johnson as the famous fast-ball pitch, and as a consequence, Johnson became even more difficult to hit.

When Walter Johnson retired in 1927, he held the record for total strike-outs in a lifetime career (3409), and he held the record for total pitching of shut-out games in a lifetime career (110)—records which have never been equaled in baseball. And Walter Johnson is second only to the mighty Cy Young for total games won in a lifetime career.

Any artist can identify with this story about Walter Johnson. The determination to persist in one's art or craft is a characteristic of a great artist and a great athlete. But one also realizes that this practice of one's craft is almost always painstakingly difficult, and usually entails periods of extreme self-consciousness, as one trains oneself into a pattern of totally new reflexes. It is what Robert Frost called "the pleasure of taking pains."

The odd thing is that this practice and mastery of a craft is sometimes seen as an infringement on one's own natural gifts. Poets will sometimes comment that they do not want to be bothered with all that stuff about metrics and assonance and craft, because it doesn't come "naturally." Of course it doesn't come naturally, if one hasn't worked to make it natural. But once one's craft becomes second nature, it is not an infringement on one's natural gifts—if anything, it is an enlargement of them, and an enhancement and a reinforcement of one's own intuitive talents.

In almost all the other arts, an artist has to learn the techniques of his craft as a matter of course.

The painter takes delight in exploring the possibilities of his palette, and perhaps he may even move through periods which are dominated by different color tones, such as viridian or Prussian blue or ochre. He will also be concerned, as a matter of course, with various textural considerations such as brushing and pigmentation and the surface virtue of his work.

The composer who wants to write orchestra music has to begin by learning how to score in the musical notation system—and he will play with the meaning of whole notes, half notes, quarter notes, eighth notes, and the significance of such tempo designations as *lento, andante, adagio,* and *prestissimo.* He will also want to explore the different possibilities of the instruments of the orchestra, to discover the totality of tone he wants to achieve in his own work.

Even so—I have heard student poets complain that they don't want to be held back by a lot of technical considerations in the craft of poetry.

That raises a very interesting question: Why do poets seem to resist learning the practice and mastery of their own craft? Why do they protest that technique *per se* is an infringement on their own intuitive gifts, and a destructive self-consciousness that inhibits their natural and magical genius?

I think a part of the answer to these questions may lie in our own modern Romantic era of poetry, where poets as diverse as Walt Whitman and Dylan Thomas and Allen Ginsberg seem to achieve their best effects with little or no technical effort. Like Athena, the poem seems to spring full blown out of the forehead of Zeus, and that is a large part of its charm for us. Whitman pretends he is just "talking" to us, in the "Song of Myself." So does Dylan Thomas in "Fern Hill" and "Poem in October." So does Allen Ginsberg in "Howl" and "Kaddish."

But of course when we think about it, we realize it is no such thing. And we realize also, in admiration, that any poet who is so skillful in concealing his art from us may be achieving one of the highest technical feats of all.

What are the technical skills of poetry, that all poets have worked at who wanted to achieve the practice and mastery of their craft?

We could begin by saying that poetry itself is language which is used in a specific way to convey a specific effect. And the specific ways that language can be used are expressed through all of the various poetic devices. In "The ABC of Reading," Ezra Pound summarized these devices and divided them into three categories—phonopoeia (sight), melopoeia (sound), and logopoeia (voice).

SIGHT

The image is the heart and soul of poetry. In our own psychic lives, we dream in images, although there may be words superimposed onto these images. In our social communication, we indicate complete understanding of something when we say, "I get the picture"— indicating that imagistic understanding is the most basic and primal of all communications. In some languages, like Chinese and Japanese, words began as pictures, or ideograms, which embodied the image representation of what the word was indicating.

It is not accidental that our earliest record of human civilization is in the form of pure pictures—images of bison in the paleolithic caves at Altamira in Northern Spain, from the Magdalenian culture, some 16,000 years B.C. And there are other records of stone statues as pure

413

images of horses and deer and mammoths, in Czechoslovakia, from as far back as 30,000 years B.C.

Aristotle wrote in the "Poetics" that metaphor—the conjunction of one image with another image—is the soul of poetry, and is the surest sign of genius. He also said it was the one thing that could not be taught, since the genius for metaphor was unaccountable, being the ability to see similarities in dissimilar things.

Following are the principal poetic devices which use image, or the picture aspect of poetry:

image—a simple picture, a mental representation. "That which presents an intellectual and emotional complex in an instant of time." (Pound)

metaphor—a direct comparison. "A mighty fortress is our God." An equation, or an equivalence: A = B. "It is the east and Juliet is the sun."

simile—an indirect comparison, using "like" or "as." "Why, man, he doth bestride the narrow world/Like a Colossus..." "My love's like a red, red rose."

figure—an image and an idea. "Ship of state." "A sea of troubles." "This bud of love."

conceit—an extended figure, as in some metaphysical poetry of John Donne, or in the following lines of Shakespeare's Juliet:

> Sweet, good-night!
> This bud of love, by summer's ripening breath,
> May prove a beauteous flower when next we meet...

SOUND

Rhythm has its source and origin in our own bloodstream pulse. At a normal pace, the heart beats at a casual iambic beat. But when it is excited, it may trip and skip rhythm through extended anapests or hard dactyls or firm trochees. It may even pound with a relentless spondee beat.

In dance, rhythm is accented by a drumbeat, in parades, by the cadence of marching feet, and in the night air, by churchbell tolling.

These simple rhythms may be taken as figures of the other rhythms of the universe—the tidal ebb and flow, the rising and setting of the sun, the female menstrual cycles, the four seasons of the year.

Rhythm is notated as metrics, but may also be seen in such poetic devices as rhyme and assonance and alliteration. Following are the poetic devices for sound:

414

assonance—rhyme of vowel sounds. "O that this too too solid flesh would melt..."

alliteration—repetition of consonants. "We might have met them dareful, beard to beard, And beat them backward home."

rhyme—the sense of resonance that comes when a word echoes the sound of another word—in end rhyme, internal rhyme, perfect rhyme, slant or imperfect rhyme, masculine rhyme, or feminine rhyme.

metrics—the simplest notation system for scansion of rhythm. The most commonly used metrics in English are:

iamb $(\breve{}\,{}')$

trochee $({}'\,\breve{})$

anapest $(\breve{}\,\breve{}\,{}')$

dactyl $({}'\,\breve{}\,\breve{})$

spondee $({}'\,{}')$

VOICE

Voice is the sum total of cognitive content of the words in a poem. Voice can also be seen as the signature of the poet on his poem—his own unmistakable way of saying something. "Only Yeats could have said it that way," one feels, in reading a line like:

That is no country for old men...

Similarly, Frost was able to endow his poems with a "voice" in lines like:

Something there is that doesn't love a wall...

Following are the poetic devices for voice:

denotation—literal, dictionary meaning of a word.

connotation—indirect or associative meaning of a word. "Mother" means one thing denotatively, but may have a host of other connotative associations.

personification—humanizing an object.

diction—word choice, the peculiar combination of words used in any given poem.

syntax—the peculiar arrangement of words in their sentence structures.

rhetoric—"Any adornment or inflation of speech which is not done for a particular effect but for a general impressiveness..." (Eliot)

persona—a mask, an assumed voice, a speaker pretending to be someone other than who he really is.

415

So far these are only words on a page, like diagrams in a baseball book showing you how to throw a curve ball. The only way there can be any real learning of any of these devices is to do endless exercises in notebooks, trying to master the craft of assonance, of diction shifts, of persona effects, of successful conceits, of metrical variations.

Any practice of these craft devices may lead one into a period of extreme self-consciousness, as one explores totally new reflexes of language. But one can trust that with enough practice they can become "second nature," and an enhancement and reinforcement of one's own intuitive talents as a poet.

87

FINDING THE SUBJECT FOR YOUR POEM

BY JOYCE PESEROFF

POEMS EVOLVE IN MANY WAYS. Sometimes they spring from a striking image preserved in a notebook, sometimes from a bit of overheard conversation that teases and intrigues, or a story that demands to be told. A poem may arise, full of energy, driven by the propulsive rhythm of a sentence or a phrase. I have written from all of these possibilities, but most often I begin with the desire to write about a subject—spring, a Maine landscape, or a birthday party; or my aging uncle, or my aerobic exercise class. All of these subjects—whether ancient as a classic text or commonplace and contemporary—offer prospects for a poet writing today. Yet in half of these poems, the topic was not immediately obvious to me; in fact, I began by writing about some other subject entirely.

Because poetry involves unconscious as well as conscious processes—like an iceberg, nine-tenths of a poet's work may lie below the surface of the mind—a poem's true subject may not reveal itself at once. I begin a poem with real interest and excitement, only to bog down around the third stanza. Energy that first generated line after enjambed line packed with vivid language evaporates; the urgency with which I began the poem later eludes me. I file the drafts in a "wait" folder and, grumbling, turn to other work.

When this happens, I know that I need to give my psyche time, as well as space, to discover what the poem is really about. Rather than abandon such promising starts, I go back, willing to cut and rewrite. With patience and openness to new directions, I find the poem's true subject—perhaps a difficult or uncomfortable one, perhaps merely more complex than first imagined—revealed. Let me give three examples of how such rewriting—and rethinking—works.

The first problem is common to novice poets, but more experienced ones also need to recognize what I call the "runway" problem. These

417

poems start with a long, often expository, foreground before they really take off. Example: A baby, at six months, has her final DPT shot; she's furious with the nurse who administers the needle. I begin a poem about her infant rage and go on to write about the mass immunizations begun in the 1950s with Salk's discovery of the polio vaccine. As I continue, trying to link this bit of history to the baby, I realize that it is *my* childhood I want to write about: the mysteriousness of grownups invading that world of children; the second-grader who cried invisibly behind a screen set up by the public health nurse. Soon I realize that although the baby's response was the key to my memories, it doesn't belong in the poem. It was the "runway" for my own experiences to emerge, brought forward by images of shots and nurses common to both scenarios.

Perhaps I will use the discarded material somewhere else. Often enough, in order to preserve the integrity of a poem, a writer must cut the line or stanza that pleases her most, even—and sometimes especially—if it was the sentence that started her writing in the first place.

My second example involves a poem I had been thinking about for a long time. I wanted to describe an incident my mother had mentioned when we were both looking through a box of family photographs: When I was four years old, my friends' parents had threatened to boycott a birthday party because my mother had invited the son of our apartment building's only black family. After hearing a poet I esteem read new work about her upbringing in the old *de jure* segregated South, I was moved to write about this incident in New York City's *de facto* segregated housing projects.

I got stuck while describing the room full of children—the hats, the cake, the furniture too large for them. I decided to look more closely at the *characters* I had introduced, possibly adding some, while exploring their family relationships. Although I did use material about the black boy's sisters, this did not lead to a satisfying resolution to the poem.

After character, I examined the poem's *setting*. Was there more to say about the place where I grew up? I had written about that subject before and didn't want to repeat myself; images and the emotion arising from them must be freshly discovered, not ready-made. Otherwise, a poet finds what Yeats called "rhetoric" doing the work of the imagination.

Finally, I returned to the source of the poem—the box of photographs. When I *dramatized* this scene between me and my mother, I found I could use it to frame the poem. The party became a flashback, which I rewrote in the past tense.

What else was in that box of photographs? I developed a new series of *images:*

Julian

Halloween—a sulky gypsy pines
for her sister's store-bought costume,
disdaining yards of Mother's precious scarves
and clinking necklaces . . .
      two women

rigged in a tight suit and lacy tablecloth
(bridegroom and pregnant bride)
who knocked door to door for drinks,
   demanded bread,
upset our cupboard for two cans of soup . . .

The images forced me to recall my mother's fury at these begging women, the same vulgar parents who nearly ruined a child's party because they felt superior to blacks. More and more of the poem's emotion seemed to center not on the boy, Julian, but on my mother.

I added her presence to the poem's first lines and concluded with images of my mother alone, drinking coffee and working a crossword puzzle. The birthday party—original impulse for the poem—shrank from two stanzas to four lines. The theme of "Julian," I discovered through rewriting, was not segregation but isolation, and its subject not, after all, the title character.

This last example began as two separate poems, one about fall and the onset of winter, the other about my grandmother's death. A careful reader might immediately notice the affinity between these subjects, since the first is often used as a metaphor for the second:

October

September cooling to October
stops the throat with a doughy phlegm—
a hundred years ago "lung fever"
killed thousands, left the rest
to cabin fever—then, for whoever emerged
from that white chrysalis: spring.
Dying, my grandmother became a student
of migration, tallying species

419

at the hospital feeder. I almost believed
the evening grosbeak put on earth
to soothe her, and the V of geese a sign
of direction in adversity.

It was the image of "fever" in the first half of "October" that alerted me to its connection with the untitled poem about my grandmother. I cut all description from my "fall into winter" poem that didn't share references to disease. From the second poem, I eliminated all details of hospital routine except the ones that involved the natural world: the feeder and the flying birds. I linked these two poems through their shared imagery and in the process noticed that my subject had shifted subtly: Instead of an elegy, I had written a testament to a living woman's courage in the face of death.

These are three examples I was able to salvage from the "wait" file and place, when completed, in a manuscript. I have many more poems that still need work as I approach their true subject. It may take months for a poem's subject to become clear to me. Often, I have to distract my conscious mind so that the unconscious might do the work of association and identification. Here are some suggestions that may help both with their proper tasks:

1) Save all drafts; throw nothing out. The image you discarded ten pages ago may give you the one necessary clue to your subject. The way you broke a line may suggest new connections as it shifts the emphasis of your poem from one word to another. This is the reason word processors are not useful to poets, at least during composition: You'd have to stop and print each version as you write it, in order not to lose anything.

2) Don't hurry. A poem may take months, or years, to complete. And even then, you may have to put it aside for another month or year before you're sure it's finished.

3) Look carefully at any two poems you begin at the same time. They may hold themes in common and point to concerns below the surface of your words. Look for images that recur, or a turn of phrase you repeat. As in "October," sometimes what begins as two poems may end as one.

4) Be ruthless with cuts. The loveliest, vowel-filled line does a poem no good if it distracts from what playwrights call the "through-line"— the inevitable chain of action leading to a satisfying conclusion. Be sure

And under the first star,
Gather cedar for a fire.

Phase two begins when the first glow has faded, or has begun to. *Then* there is the shock of recognition, as you encounter the text you have produced. It is not necessarily disappointing. You may be happily surprised by the electricity in some phrases. You may also note lapses, stretches of dead language, redundancy. Now, with the text in hand, you apply maximum pressure. The poem won't be inhibited. It already exists. *Always* keep the first draft. You aren't a painter who loses the early version in revision. Be as self-critical as you can be. Call everything into question. Go from self-love to self-hate. But avoid extremes. A *balanced* appreciation, an objective appraisal of weaknesses and failings in your own writing is needed. It is essential for you to recognize excellence as well as to admit fault.

You want to see the poem clearly, as it is, and for many poets (including myself), this requires part of phase two to be a revision that questions everything, that entertains the possibility that the whole poem may be a failure. I tend to over-revise at this point, possibly to over-rationalize, and perhaps to make the poetic statement artificially complete, too explicit. Since I seem to need to do this, I allow it to happen, knowing that it is part of phase two: critically confronting the poem.

Phase three emphasizes the fact that the "real poem" knows more than "I" do, that ideally it combines the phase-one spontaneity and the phase-two appraisal. Thinking too much about it, trying all possible combinations of key words in troublesome phrases, is only another effort on your part to see the essence of the poem clearly. Thus, phase three involves a kind of "forgetting" of this highly conscious, trial-and-error revision. I let the text rest, like dough between kneadings. This may be for weeks or months. Then something will reawaken interest. I will recall the true poem, the real poem, from the confusion of various versions. Sometimes I literally recall the poem by writing it out afresh as I remember it at this point, perhaps with help from earlier drafts, especially the first. Often I find that the revision has helped pare away the nonessential, and to prepare a place for what in the first draft was really final. I cherish the sense that for each real poem there is some absolute, inevitable form toward which I have been fumbling through successive drafts. This is in part an illusion, for even "final" texts get

425

revised. You should never turn down what you consider better insight. The real poem seems to gather up into itself the many competing glimpses scattered through various versions. I think of prose as linear, a link through time, but a poem is more a circle, which, when completed, does not end. It looks forward and backward, resisting the erosion of more revisions.

I am myself a runner, and *River Writing: An Eno Journal* was largely composed while I was running along the Eno River in all seasons, all weathers. It started accidentally, but once begun, my premise came to be that the poem would be founded on whatever I saw or thought during the run. The river is over the ridge behind my house, so I could go out and return without interruption. (By the way, *shield* yourself from interruption during the time you set aside to write. If writing is as important to you as you think it is, treat it as such. Give it that central importance in your life.)

The finished version of "Clear Winter" is four lines shorter than the first draft, and words have been cut or substituted in a number of lines that remain. These changes help allow the rhythm of lines to fuse one into the other, so that the whole seems a single movement. For example, "chill limbs against chill air" becomes "chill limbs high in chill air." The first draft let the word *death* appear twice at the ends of lines, and the word *star* appears twice. It also allows the word *corpses* to come in too soon. It was as if my first impulse had known generally what it wanted, but had had to move toward that goal by trial and error. But notice that except for a change in tense, the ending stands as first imagined and drafted.

Here is the published version of "Clear Winter":

Clear Winter

(Published in *River Writing: An Eno Journal,*
Princeton University Press, 1988)

Confusion of seasons is over.
Today was clear winter.
Light that on trunks seemed warm
Looked bleak and bare
On chill limbs high in chill air.
I saw bodies of trees
Piled mercilessly by past
High water, crotch-chunk

Of one upon trunk of another.
Angular cedars, their crowns
Thinned of needles by drought,
Seemed a desert tribe
Overtaken by an angel of death.
Finally I climbed clear
Of the valley which memory
Stocked with its proxy
Corpses. I saw air
In its isolation now pure.
We are unable to endure
This light the cold whets to steel.
I stood above river land
And hypothesized the being
We cannot understand, who
Begins things with flame of a star,
Who is the zero far dark.
I sniffed for scent of some smoke,
For coffee, leaf-smolder or
Cigarette odor. All unendurably
Absent. I turned toward home,
Alone as a pane of ice
The keen sun shines through.
I kissed my warm wife
And under the first star
Gathered cedar for a fire.

Here is the lesson I learned from the poems in *River Writing*. It is good sometimes to let the cadences and larger structures of your poetry and its emotional momentum build. Learn to write with ease, with relaxation. You can't really run faster or farther over the long haul simply by bearing down harder. You have to raise the level of your effort, then relax, and trust that preparation. Then perfect the draft later. With joy. As Fred Astaire said to a new partner, "Don't be nervous, but don't make a mistake." Learning not to be nervous, not to make yourself nervous, because of your relaxation and confidence in revision, will help you prevent making a mistake. And remember that the only real mistake in poetry is not ever to get the poem written.

But the key element for most poets who are learning the process is knowing when and how to apply the pressure. Writing poetry is like training for athletic competition. Performance in the event—the writing of the poem—is largely a product of conditioning, associated with analysis of form and technique. But you don't perform that analysis in the act of writing. You somewhat analyze the problem before you, but finally you have to get in there and perform. You don't sit there anxiously wondering whether the last word was really the right one. You don't sit there worrying whether the poem will finally be any good. Time will tell.

89

Is It Good Enough for Children?

By Madeleine L'Engle

A WHILE AGO WHEN I WAS TEACHING A COURSE on techniques of fiction, a young woman came up to me and said, "I do hope you're going to teach us something about writing for children, because that's why I'm taking this course."

"What have I been teaching you?" I asked her.

"Well—writing."

"Don't you write when you write for children?"

"Yes, but—isn't it different?"

No, I assured her, it isn't different. The techniques of fiction are the techniques of fiction, and they hold as true for Beatrix Potter as they do for Dostoevsky.

But the idea that writing for children isn't the same as writing for adults is prevalent indeed, and usually goes along with the conviction that it isn't quite as good. If you're a good enough writer for adults, the implication is, of course, you don't write for children. You write for children only when you can't make it in the real world, because writing for children is easier.

Wrong, wrong, wrong!

I had written several regular trade novels before a publisher asked me to write about my Swiss boarding school experiences. Nobody had told me that you write differently when you write for children, so I didn't. I just wrote the best book I possibly could; it was called *And Both Were Young*. After that I wrote *Camilla*, which has been reissued as a young adult novel, and then *Meet the Austins*. It's hard today for me to understand that this simple little book had a very hard time finding a publisher because it's about a death and how an ordinary family reacts to that death. Death at that time was taboo. Children weren't supposed to know about it. I had a couple of offers of publication if I'd take the death out. But the reaction of the family—children as well as the parents—to the death was the core of the book.

Nowadays what we offer children makes *Meet the Austins* seem pale, and on the whole, I think that's just as well, because children know a lot more than most grown-ups give them credit for. *Meet the Austins* came out of my own family's experience with several deaths. To have tried to hide those deaths from our children would have been blind stupidity. All hiding does is confuse children and add to their fears. It is not subject matter that should be taboo, but the way it is handled.

A number of years ago—the first year I was actually making reasonable money from my writing—my sister-in-law was visiting us, and when my husband told her how much I had earned that year, she was impressed and commented, "And to think most people would have had to word so hard for that!"

Well, it is work, it's most certainly work; wonderful work, but work. Revision, revision, revision. Long hours spent not only in the actual writing, but in research. I think the best thing I learned in college was how to do research, so that I could go right on studying after I had graduated.

Of course, it is not *only* work; it is work that makes the incomprehensible comprehensible. Leonard Bernstein says that for him music is cosmos in chaos. That is true for writing a story, too. Aristotle says that what is plausible and impossible is better than what is possible and implausible.

That means that story must be *true*, not necessarily *factual*, but true. This is not easy for a lot of people to understand. When I was a school child, one of my teachers accused me of telling a story. She was not complimenting me on my fertile imagination; she was accusing me of telling a lie.

Facts are fine; we need facts. But story takes us to a world that is beyond facts, out on the other side of facts. And there is considerable fear of this world.

The writer Keith Miller told me of a young woman who was determined that her three preschool children were going to grow up in the real world. She was not, she vowed, going to sully their minds with myth, fantasy, fairy tales. They were going to know the truth—and for truth, read fact—and the truth would make them free.

One Saturday, after a week of rain and sniffles, the sun came out, so she piled the children into her little red VW bug and took them to the Animal Farm. The parking lot was crowded, but a VW bug is small, and she managed to find a place for it. She and the children had a wonderful day, petting the animals, going on rides, enjoying the sunshine. Suddenly, she looked at her watch and found it was far later than she realized. She and the children ran to where the VW bug was parked, and to their horror, found the whole front end was bashed in.

Outraged, she took herself off to the ranger's office. As he saw her approach, he laughed and said, "I'll bet you're the lady with the red VW bug."

"It isn't funny," she snapped.

"Now, calm down, lady, and let me tell you what happened. You know the elephant your children had such fun riding? She's a circus-trained elephant, and she was trained to sit on a red bucket. When she saw your car, she just did what she was trained to do and sat on it. Your engine's in the back, so you can drive it home without any trouble. And don't worry. Our insurance will take care of it. Just go on home, and we'll get back to you on Monday."

Slightly mollified, she and the kids got into the car and took off. But she was later than ever, so when she saw what looked like a very minor accident on the road, she didn't stop, but drove on.

Shortly, the flashing light and the siren came along, and she was pulled over. "Lady, don't you know that in this state it's a crime to leave the scene of an accident?" the trooper asked.

"But I wasn't in an accident," she protested.

"I suppose your car came that way," she said, pointing to the bashed-in front.

"No. An elephant sat on it."

"Lady, would you mind blowing into this little balloon?"

That taught her that facts alone are not enough; that facts, indeed, do not make up the whole truth. After that she read fairy tales to her children and encouraged them in their games of Make Believe and Let's Pretend.

I learned very early that if I wanted to find out the truth, to find out why people did terrible things to each other, or sometimes wonderful things—why there was war, why children are abused—I was more likely to find the truth in story than in the encyclopedia. Again and again I read *Emily of the New Moon,* by Lucy Maud Montgomery, because

Emily's father was dying of diseased lungs, and so was mine. Emily had a difficult time at school, and so did I. Emily wanted to be a writer, and so did I. Emily knew that there was more to the world than provable fact, and so did I. I read fairy tales, the myths of all nations, science fiction, the fantasies and family stories of E. Nesbit. I read Jules Verne and H. G. Wells. And I read my parents' books, particularly those with lots of conversation in them. What was not in my frame of reference went right over my head.

We tend to find what we look for. If we look for dirt, we'll find dirt, whether it's there or not. A very nice letter I received from a reader said that she found *A Ring of Endless Light* very helpful to her in coming to terms with the death of a friend, but that another friend had asked her how it was that I used dirty words. I wrote back saying that I was not going to reread my book looking for dirty words, but that as far as I could remember, the only word in the book that could possibly be construed as dirty was *zuggy,* which I'd made up to avoid using dirty words. And wasn't looking for dirty words an ugly way to read a book?

One of my favorite books is Frances Hodgson Burnett's *The Secret Garden.* I read it one rainy weekend to a group of little girls, and a generation later to my granddaughters up in an old brass bed in the attic. Mary Lennox is a self-centered, spoiled-rotten little heroine, and I think we all recognize at least a little of ourselves in her. The secret garden is as much the garden of Mary's heart as it is the physical walled garden. By the end of the book, warmth and love and concern for others have come to Mary's heart, when Colin, the sick boy, is able to walk and run again. And Dickon, the gardener's boy, looks at the beauty of the restored garden and says, "It's magic!" But "magic" is one of the key words that has become taboo to today's self-appointed censors, so, with complete disregard of content, they would add *The Secret Garden* to the pyre. I shudder. This attitude is extreme. It is also dangerous.

It comes down to the old question of separate standards, separate for adults and children. The only standard to be used in judging a children's book is: *Is it a good book?* Is it good enough for me? Because if a children's book is not good enough for all of us, it is not good enough for children.

90

THINK PICTURE BOOK

BY EVE BUNTING

THE BAD NEWS IS THAT NO, picture books are not easy to write. The good news is that there are some useful guidelines in picture book writing, and although they will never guarantee a sale, they will at least put you on course if writing a beautiful picture book is your heart's desire. So let's think picture book.

Most obviously, *think pictures*. Perceive your story as a moving slide show, vivid, arresting, and dramatic. Give the illustrator something to work with. If you are both author and illustrator you will be doing yourself the same favor. Incidentally, it is not necessary for you to provide the pictures. The publisher will take care of that for you.

Remember, static scenes without variety do not make a good slide presentation.

I once had a friend show me a picture book manuscript she'd written.

"It's so cute," she said. "But I've sent it out and sent it out, and no one wants to buy it. Why?"

In the book, a cat stands before a mirror, trying on hats—a cowboy hat, a fireman's helmet, a baseball cap, etc. One character, one scene, one action, repeated over and over.

"He could be a very cute cat," I said. "But nothing happens."

My friend looked puzzled and a little irritated by my lack of perception.

"Something does happen," she said. "He changes hats."

I amended my words. "Not enough happens."

That cat in the mirror would make a dull slide show and a dull picture book.

An art director in a major publishing house once told me: "The words in a picture book should be a gift to the illustrator."

I had always believed that the illustrator's paintings were gifts to the writers, adding dimensions often undreamed of. And that is true. But it

433

has to work the other way around, too. What the art director meant was that if the scenes in the text are varied, imaginative, plentiful, the illustrator doesn't have to struggle and the book is what it should be, a happy collaboration. To achieve this, keep in mind that the scenes should roll forward in an ever-moving diversity of character and action. This does not always happen naturally for me. I have to work at it. You can, too.

When you've finished your manuscript, divide it by drawing lines across the text to mark what you see as the natural ending of a page. Or set up a dummy by taking eight sheets of blank paper and folding them horizontally to make a 32-page book (32 pages is the usual picture book length, less three or four for front matter: title page, copyright, and dedication). Write your text on each dummy page. Do you have enough pictures? Do you have too many words? Look for balance. Visualize your little reader, or listener, impatient to get on with it, to turn the page to find out what happens next.

If I see an ungainly chunk of text in my own work, I deliberately set out to "break" it up with picture possibilities.

For instance, in *The Mother's Day Mice*, there is a scene in which the three little mice are watching Honeysuckle Cottage, waiting and hoping that the cat on the porch will go away. It is important here that I give the impression of time passing, since Little Mouse needs to hear many repeats of the song being played on the piano inside the cottage. When I read what I'd written, I realized I had a static scene. So I added:

(Middle Mouse) set his strawberry on the ground and a beetle came on the run. Middle picked it up again and shooed the beetle away.
Little Mouse began creeping toward the cottage on his belly.
Biggest yanked him back by his tail.

These few lines add action and a little humor. They use all three mouse characters and a new peripheral character, the beetle, is placed on the scene. But better, better, better, they add two picture possibilities. And Jan Brett, the illustrator, used both charmingly.

Adding scenes is not that difficult. But it is harder because of the second unbreakable law of the picture book—*think short*. Think 1,000 words, or less. Think concise. Say what you need to say in the most economical way possible that makes sense and that sounds poetic, because a poetic telling is the essence of the picture book.

A few weeks ago I visited a school where examples of "pretty sentences from picture books" were pinned on the wall of the library.

"We talk about them," the librarian told me. "We ask: 'Why did the author say it this way instead of another way?' We listen to the sounds of the words and the cadence of the sentence and look for images."

So "pretty" sentences are a must, if we want to make it on the wall. Not overblown, though. Not gushy or sentimentally sweet.

Isn't it more breathtaking to read, "The air hissed to the beat of wings" *(The Man Who Could Call Down Owls)* than, "There was the sound of wings in the air"? Try to use the actual "sound" word. The air *hissed;* the bus *wheezed;* the leaves *flurried* in the wind.

Long passages of undiluted description are out in the picture book. But I believe short descriptions add immeasurably to the texture of the story and enhance the word awareness of even the youngest reader. A line or two can set the scene:

Milk bottles stood on front steps, waiting to be let in. The sky was the color of his mother's pearl brooch. The one she wore on Sundays. *(St. Patrick's Day in the Morning)*

Crows cawed in the white air. The arms of the trees scratched at the sky. *(The Valentine Bears)*

Our table seemed monstrously big. Chairs, hump-backed, clawed and crouched around it. *(Ghost's Hour, Spook's Hour)*

Enough description, but not too much.

A picture book, then, must be short, not abrupt. It must be pure, not sterile. There is room for a story and for a few beautiful word pictures, too.

There is also room to say something valuable. A picture book that does not has no value of itself. Heavy or deeply moralistic, no. Worthwhile, yes. The treasure is well hidden, but it's there for the child to feel and understand. In *Ghost's Hour, Spook's Hour,* I am saying: "No need to be afraid of the dark. The scary things can be explained away. See? No need to be afraid." Those actual words never appear in the text. They are self-evident as Jake and his trusty dog, Biff, search the dark house for Mom and Dad while in the hallway the big clock strikes midnight—ghost's hour, spook's hour.

On a trip to mainland China a few years ago, I spent some time browsing in a bookstore and brought back with me a picture book entitled *A Boy and His Kitten* (for children from 4 to 8). The story is about Maomao who will not go to bed. He and his kitten play through the night hours, disturbing his good little sister.

"How troublesome are those children who do not go to bed," the text says.

In the morning, little sister, who presumably got some sleep, is up at dawn doing her morning exercises. Alas for Maomao and his kitten who are now sleeping the day away:

> For them, it is too late
> To breathe the fresh morning air,
> Or hear their teacher's interesting stories.
> Oh, what a great pity it is
> for Maomao and his kitten!
>
> Our little friends,
> Be not like these two.
> Early to bed,
> And early to rise,
> Keeps you fit and wise.

One has to hope that the story lost a little something in the translation!

You must try not to do this in the picture books you write. In fact, I venture to say, do this and you'll never have a picture book. So *think subtle*. The worthwhile thing you have to say will come across just as clearly and much more palatably.

The picture book writer, perhaps more than writers in any other genre, must *think original*. The field is overflowing with books about cats and dogs, horses and ponies, dinosaurs, rabbits, ducks, mice; boys who are having terrible, awful days, girls who can be anything they want to be; moms, dads, pesky little sisters—all subjects that interest little kids. But writers need to find the *new* angle. As in Carol and Donald Carrick's book: *What Happened to Patrick's Dinosaurs?* The dinosaurs, Patrick says, liked helping people to build houses and lay roads. But after a while the people were willing to sit back and let the dinosaurs do it. They didn't help themselves. So the dinosaurs, for the sake of the people and still helping them, took off in space ships. And *that's* what happened! A nice, original touch and a theme that is there without being belabored.

When I wrote *Scary, Scary Halloween*, I knew of the numerous picture books about this popular holiday. What was there to say that hadn't already been said? So I did trick or treating from a cat's point of view, a mama cat, hiding under the house with her baby kittens, waiting fearfully for the monsters, who are the children in costume, to leave. When they do—

> It's quiet now, the monsters gone
> The streets are ours until the dawn.
> We're out, we prowlers of the night
> Who snap and snarl and claw and bite.
> We stalk the shadows, dark, unseen . . .
> Goodbye 'til next year, Halloween.

A different angle? I think so, and the editor agreed.

When you think picture book, think lasting and forever, because that is what the best picture books are. How many children have been frightened and reassured by *Where the Wild Things Are* (Maurice Sendak)? How many have learned to read for pleasure through the good graces of Dr. Seuss and *The Cat in the Hat* or *Green Eggs and Ham*? How many have gone to sleep to the lullaby lull of *Goodnight Moon*? How many will? A picture book is not temporary, it is not ephemeral. It is as lasting as truth itself and should, said Arnold Lobel, "Rise out of the lives and passions of its creators." It should be unique and ageless and seemingly effortless in its smooth, easy flow.

For all the effort involved, the pruning and shaping and sculpting of words, you will be rewarded with joy as you hold in your hand this small polished jewel that is *your* picture book.

91

CALLING IT QUITS

BY LOIS LOWRY

"You put <u>what</u> in it?" my son asked, his fork halfway to his mouth.

"Ginger snaps," I repeated. "Crushed ginger snaps."

"I thought that's what you said." I watched while he put his fork back down on his plate and then pushed the plate away from him. It was clear to me that my son, normally a good sport, was not going to eat my innovative beef stew.

It was clear to me, after I tasted it myself, that he had made the right decision.

SOMETIMES IN THE PROCESS OF CREATING, it is very difficult to know when to quit adding things.

Some years back, I received in the mail the first foreign edition of my first young adult book, *A Summer to Die*. Fortunately it was French. Later I would receive, with a gulp of astonishment, the Finnish, the Afrikaans, the Catalan; but this first one was French. French I can read.

And so I leafed through the pages, savoring the odd, startling sense of recognition that I had, seeing my own words translated into another language.

On the last page, I read the line of dialogue with which I had concluded the book. " 'Meg,' he laughed, putting one arm over my shoulders, 'you were beautiful all along.' " There it was, in French.

But there was something else, as well. I blinked in surprise, seeing it. In French, the book concluded: "They walked on."

They walked on? Of course they *had* walked on, those two characters, Meg and Will. I knew they had, and I had trusted the reader to know that they had. But I hadn't written that line. The translator had.

I don't know why. I can only guess that the translator simply couldn't resist that urge that makes all of us throw a crushed ginger snap into the stew now and then.

438

Knowing when to stop is one of the toughest tasks a writer faces.

Is there a rule that one can follow? Probably not. But there is, I think, a test against which the writer can measure his ending, his stopping place.

When something more is going to take place, but the characters have been so fully drawn, and the preceding events so carefully shaped that the reader, on reflection, knows what more will happen, and is satisfied by it—then the book ends.

In essence, you, as writer, will have successfully taught the reader to continue writing the book in his mind.

What about the concept of resolution, then? Isn't the writer supposed to tie up the loose ends of the story neatly at the conclusion? And if everything is neatly packaged and tied, then how on earth can something more take place?

Your story—your plot—your theme— is only a portion of the lives of the characters you have created. Their lives, if you have made them real to the reader, are going to continue in the reader's mind.

Your role is only a part of that process. And you need to know when and how to get out when your role is finished. As author, you tie up and resolve the piece of a life you have chosen to examine. Then you leave, gracefully. The life continues, but you are no longer looking at it.

You have engaged and directed the imagination of the reader; and then you have turned the reader loose.

Writing this, I looked at the endings of some of my own books, to see if they followed any kind of pattern.

In one, *Anastasia on Her Own,* a mother and daughter are laughing and tap-dancing together up a flight of stairs.

In *Find a Stranger, Say Goodbye,* a young girl is packing to go away; she is deciding what to take and what to leave behind.

The narrator and her mother in *Rabble Starkey* are together in a car, heading into a somewhat uncertain future. (Not coincidentally, that book is published in Great Britain under the title *The Road Ahead.*)

The forms of these endings are different. Some are descriptive, some consist of dialogue. Some are lighthearted, others more introspective.

But they do seem to have a few elements in common:

They all include the main character—sometimes more than one—in the final scene.

Each of them, in various forms, reflects a sense of motion, of flow, of moving forward.

And each in its own way contains a kind of conclusive statement.

Anastasia fell in behind her mother and tried to follow the complicated hops, turns, and shuffles her mother was doing. Together they tap-danced down the hall and up the stairs. It was silly, she thought; but it was fun. And it sure felt good, having her mother back in charge.

—Anastasia on Her Own

It was the throwing away that was the hardest. But she did it, until the trunk was packed, the trash can was filled, and the room was bare of everything except the memories; those would always be there, Natalie knew.

—Find a Stranger, Say Goodbye

She sped up a little, driving real careful, and when we went around the curve I looked, and it was all a blur. But there was nothing there. There was only Sweet Hosanna and me, and outside the whole world, quiet in the early morning, green and strewn with brand new blossoms, like the ones on my very best dress.

—Rabble Starkey

The common elements that you can see and hear in those ending paragraphs are a little like the basics in a good stew; maybe you could equate them to a garlic clove, a bay leaf, and a dollop of wine.

As for the crushed ginger snap? The ingredient that qualifies as overkill and makes the whole thing just a little nauseating?

Well, I confess that those three passages have one more thing in common. Each one was tough to end. Like the translator who added another sentence to my book, I wanted to go on, too. I wanted to add crushed ginger snaps: more sentences, more images, embellishments, explanations, embroidery.

And if I had? Take a look:

She sped up a little, driving real careful, and when we went around the curve I looked, and it was all a blur. But there was nothing there. There was only Sweet Hosanna and me, and outside the whole world, quiet in the early morning, green and strewn with brand new blossoms, like the ones on my very best dress.

What would the future hold for us? I had no way of knowing. But I remembered how, in the past years, my mother had worked and saved to bring us this far. I looked at her now, her eyes intent on the road, and I could see the determination . . .

Et cetera. You can't read it—I couldn't *write* it—without a feeling of wanting to push your plate away. It's too much. It's unnecessary. It is, in a word, sickening.

The letters I get so often from kids provide me, unintentionally, with a reminder of the impact of a good ending. Boy, if anyone in the world knows how to *end,* it's a kid writing a letter.

"Well," they say, "I have to quit now."

92

WRITING NONFICTION BOOKS FOR YOUNG READERS

BY JAMES CROSS GIBLIN

WHERE do you get the ideas for your nonfiction books?" is often the first thing I'm asked when I speak to writers. My usual reply is, "From anywhere and everywhere."

I've found a good place to start in the search for ideas is with your own interests and enthusiasms. It also helps if you can make use of personal experience. For example, the idea for my *The Skyscraper Book* (Crowell) really had its beginnings when I was a child, and loved to be taken up to the observation deck of the Terminal Tower, the tallest building in my home city of Cleveland.

Years later, after I moved to New York, I rented an apartment that was just a few blocks away from the Flatiron Building, one of the city's earliest and most striking skyscrapers. No matter how many times I passed the building, I always saw something new when I looked up at the carved decorations on its surface.

Although I had edited many books for children, I'd never thought of writing for a young audience until I was invited to contribute a 500-word essay to *The New York Kid's Book*. I chose the Flatiron Building as my topic because I wanted to find out more about it myself.

That piece led to an expanded magazine article (for *Cricket*) called "Buildings That Scrape the Sky," and then to *The Skyscraper Book*. In the latter I was finally able to tell the story behind Cleveland's Terminal Tower, the skyscraper that had fascinated me forty years earlier.

Besides looking first to your own interests and knowledge, you should also be open to ideas that may come your way by luck or chance. The idea of *Chimney Sweeps* (Crowell) literally came to me out of the blue when I was flying to Oklahoma City on business.

The plane stopped in Chicago and a tall, rangy young man carrying what I thought was a musical instrument case took the seat next to me. We started to talk, and I discovered that the man—whose name was Christopher Curtis—was a chimney sweep, and his case contained samples of the brushes he manufactured at his own small factory in Vermont. He was on his way to Oklahoma City to conduct a seminar for local sweeps on how to clean chimneys more efficiently.

Chris went on to tell me a little about the history of chimney sweeping and its revival as a profession in the last decade, because of the energy crisis. In turn, I told him I was a writer of children's books, and that he'd fired my interest in chimney sweeps as a possible subject.

We exchanged business cards, and a month or so later I wrote to tell him that I'd followed up on the idea and had started researching the book on chimney sweeps. I asked him if he'd be willing to read the manuscript for accuracy. He agreed to do so and volunteered to supply photographs of present-day sweeps that could be used (and were) as illustrations in the book.

According to an old English superstition, it's lucky to meet a chimney sweep. Well, meeting Christopher Curtis was certainly lucky for me!

Evaluating an idea

Once you have an idea for a book, the next step is to decide whether or not it's worth pursuing. The first thing I do is check R. R. Bowker's annual *Subject Guide to Children's Books in Print*, available in the reference department of most libraries, to see what else has been written on the subject. With *Chimney Sweeps*, there was nothing at all. In the case of *The Skyscraper Book*, I discovered that there were several books about *how* skyscrapers are constructed, but none with a focus on *why* and *by whom* they're constructed, which was the angle of the book I wanted to write. There may be many books on a given subject, but if you find a fresh or different slant, there'll probably be room in the market for yours, too.

Another thing to weigh when evaluating an idea is the matter of levels: A subject worth treating in a book usually has more than one. For instance, when I began researching *Chimney Sweeps*, I soon realized that besides the obvious human and social history, the subject also touched on economic and technological history. Weaving those different levels together made the book more interesting to write—and I believe it makes it more interesting for readers also.

A third important factor to consider is what age group to write the book for. That decision has to be based on two things: the nature of the subject and a knowledge of the market for children's books. I aimed *Chimney Sweeps* at an older audience, because I felt that the subject required more of a sense of history than younger readers would have. At the same time, I kept the text as simple and compact as possible, because I knew that there's a much greater demand today for children's nonfiction geared to the upper elementary grades than there is for Young Adult nonfiction.

After you've checked out your idea and decided what slant to take with it, and what age group to write for, it's time to begin the research. An entire article could be devoted to research methods alone. The one thing I feel it's safe to say after writing seven books is that each project requires its own approach, and you have to discover it as you go along.

When I was researching *The Scarecrow Book* (Crown, 1980), I came up against one stone wall after another. It seemed no one had ever bothered to write anything about scarecrows. Research became a matter of following up on the skimpiest of clues. For example, a brief mention in a magazine article that the Japanese had a scarecrow god led me to the Orientalia Division of the Library of Congress, where a staff member kindly translated a passage from a Japanese encyclopedia describing the god and its relation to Japanese scarecrows.

The Skyscraper Book presented the opposite problem. There was so much background material available on skyscrapers that I could easily have spent ten years researching the subject and never come to the end. Choices had to be made early on. I settled on the eight or ten New York skyscrapers I wanted to discuss and sought detailed information only on those. I did the same thing with skyscrapers in Chicago and other cities around the country.

Chimney Sweeps opened up the exciting area of primary source material. On a visit to the Economics Division of the New York Public Library, I discovered the yellowing transcripts of early 19th-century British investigations into the deplorable living and working conditions of child sweeps.

Fireworks, Picnics, and Flags: The Story of The Fourth of July Symbols (Clarion) introduced me to the pleasures of on-site research. I had spent two days at beautiful Independence National Historical Park in Philadelphia. I toured Independence Hall, visited the rented rooms nearby where Thomas Jefferson drafted the Declaration of Independence, and watched a group of third-grade youngsters touch the Liberty Bell in its pavilion. I won't soon forget the looks of awe on their faces.

Whenever I go out on a research expedition, I always take along a supply of 4 × 6-inch cards. At the top of each one, I write the subject for handy reference when I file the cards alphabetically in a metal box. I also write the title, author, publisher, and date of the book I'm reading so that I'll have all that information on hand when I compile the bibliography for my book. Then I go on to jot down the facts I think I might be able to use.

I try to check each fact against at least two other sources before including it in the text. Such double-checking can turn up myths that have long passed as truths. For instance, while researching *Fireworks, Picnics, and Flags,* I read two books that said an old bell-ringer sat in the tower of Independence Hall almost all day on July 4, 1776. He was waiting for word that independence had been declared so that he could ring the Liberty Bell.

At last, in late afternoon, a small boy ran up the steps of the tower and shouted, "Ring, Grandfather! Ring for Liberty!" The old man did so at once, letting all of Philadelphia know that America was no longer a British colony. It makes a fine story—but according to the third source I checked, it simply isn't true.

By no means will all of the facts I find appear in the finished book. Only a small part of any author's research shows up in the final manuscript. But I think a reader can feel the presence of the rest beneath the surface, lending substance and authority to the writing.

Picture research

With most of my books, I've gathered the illustrations as well as written the text, and this has led me into the fascinating area of picture research. On *The Scarecrow Book,* for example, I discovered the resources of the Prints and Photographs Division of the Library of Congress, where I located several stunning photographs of Southern scarecrows taken during the 1930s. Later, in a back issue of *Time* magazine, I came across a story about Senji Kataoka, a public relations officer with the Ministry of Agriculture in Tokyo, whose hobby was taking pictures of scarecrows. Over the years, the article said, Mr.

Kataoka had photographed more than 2000 examples in the countryside around Tokyo.

I decided to follow up on this lead, remote as it might prove to be. From the Japanese consulate in New York I obtained the address of the Ministry of Agriculture in Tokyo, and wrote Mr. Kataoka there. Six weeks later his answer arrived in neatly printed English, along with eight beautiful color snapshots of scarecrows. I wrote back saying I needed black-and-white photos for the book and Mr. Kataoka immediately mailed me a dozen, four of which were used in the chapter on Japanese scarecrows. Another appeared on the jacket. When I asked Mr. Kataoka how much he wanted for his photos, he said just a copy of the book.

Experiences such as these have taught me several important things about doing picture research. The first is: Never start with commercial photographic agencies. They charge high reproduction fees which are likely to put you in the red if your contract states that you are responsible for paying such costs.

Instead, try non-profit sources like U.S. government agencies, which provide photographs for just the cost of the prints; art and natural history museums, which charge modest fees; and national tourist offices, which will usually give you photographs free of charge, asking only that you credit them as the source.

Other good sources of free photos are the manufacturers of various products. Their public relations departments will be happy to send you high quality photographs of everything from tractors to inflatable vinyl scarecrows in return for an acknowledgment in your book.

Selling

Writers often ask me if they should complete all the research for a nonfiction book before trying to sell the idea to a publisher. That's usually not necessary. However, if you're a beginner you should do enough research to make sure there's sufficient material for a book. Then you'll need to write a full outline and draft one or two sample chapters. After that, you can send query letters to publishers and ask if they'd like to look at your material.

If a publisher is interested, you should be prepared to rewrite your sample chapters several times before being offered a contract. That happened to me with my first book, *The Scarecrow Book,* and looking back now I'm glad it did. For it helped me and my collaborator, Dale Ferguson, to sharpen the focus of that book.

Of course it's different after you become an established author. Then both you and your editors know what you can do, and generally a two- or three-page proposal describing your new book idea will be enough for the publisher to make a decision.

Once you have your contract for the book in hand, you can proceed with the writing of the manuscript. Some authors use electric type-writers, others have turned to word processors. I write longhand in a spiral notebook and mark in the margins the date each passage was drafted. That encourages me as I inch through the notebook, working mainly on Saturdays and Sundays and during vacations from my full-time editorial job.

Achieving a consistent personal voice in a nonfiction book takes me at least three drafts. In the first, I get down the basic material of the paragraph or section. In the second, I make certain the organization is logical and interesting, and I then begin to smooth out those spots where the style of the original research source may be too clearly in evidence. In the third draft, I polish the section until the tone and voice are entirely mine.

After I deliver to the editor the completed manuscript and the il-lustrations I've gathered, I may heave a sigh of relief. But chances are my work won't be over. The editor may feel that extensive revisions are necessary; sections of the manuscript may have to be reorganized, others rewritten. Perhaps the editor will want me to compile a bibliogra-phy, or a glossary of unfamiliar words used in the text.

At last everything is in place, and a year or so later—during which time the manuscript has been copyedited, designed, and set in type— the finished book arrives in the mail. That's an exciting moment, fol-lowed by a few anxious weeks as you wait for the first reviews to appear. The verdict of the critics isn't the final one, though. There's yet another stage in the life of any children's book: the reaction of young readers.

Perhaps a boy will come up to me after a library talk and tell me that he was inspired to find out more about the skyscrapers in his city after reading *The Skyscraper Book.* Or a girl will write to say that the chapter on a day in the life of a climbing boy in *Chimney Sweeps* made her cry. It's only then that I know I'm on the way toward achieving my goal—to write lively, accurate, and entertaining books for young people.

447

93

FANTASY: LET THE READER BELIEVE

BY BEATRICE GORMLEY

REALISTIC FICTION IS HARD ENOUGH TO WRITE CONVINCINGLY. Isn't fantasy that much more difficult? Wouldn't it help to give the reader elaborate explanations of how the magic works, reams of corroborating evidence?

No! The more you explain, the less believable it gets. The more you go on about how plausible it is—for instance, that a fairy godmother agency is operating in our world—the more the reader is bound to think you protest too much.

The main thing to remember about fantasy readers is that they *want* to believe. Why do you think they'll pick up your book, with the tell-tale word "magic" in its title or a picture of a mythical creature on its cover, in the first place? They *like* fantasy. They're ready and willing to experience it—all the writer has to do is help a little.

What does make fantasy convincing? Exactly the same thing that makes any fiction convincing: the illusion of experience.

How do you make your readers experience a story? You help them see it, hear it, smell it, taste it, feel it. In E. Nesbit's *Five Children and It,* the brothers and sisters first hear the fantasy creature's "dry, husky voice" from the sand pit and then see "something brown and furry and fat . . . rubbing the ends of its eyes." The *ends* of its eyes? At this point we suspect we have been led down the garden path and across the line into fantasy. But we believe, because we have seen the fat, furry shape of the Psammead's body and heard its dry voice.

In Mary Norton's *The Borrowers,* the reader is led toward these tiny people through their territory under the floor:

There were yards of dark and dusty passageway, with wooden doors between the joists and metal gates against the mice. Pod used all kinds of things for these gates—a flat leaf of a folding cheese grater, the hinged lid of a small cash-box, squares of pierced zinc from an old meat-safe, a wire fly-swatter . . .

The revealing detail of the mouse-gates, together with the list of items Pod has borrowed from humans to use for the gates, pull us immediately down into the Borrowers' world beneath the floorboards.

The catch in presenting the reader with those convincing details is that you the writer have to experience them first. You have to find out just how a good witch and a bad witch would look and act, as L. Frank Baum did in *The Wizard of Oz* and John Bellairs did in *The House with a Clock in Its Walls*. Or you have to find out how it would feel to change bodies with someone else, as I did in writing *Fifth Grade Magic*.

In my early drafts, I had glossed over that experience, having Gretchen, my main character, simply wake up to find herself in Amy's body. But then I realized I was fudging. Who would believe Gretchen could change bodies with Amy, if I didn't describe what the changeover was like? Besides, it was important for the story to make Gretchen feel every frightening and uncomfortable moment of the body change. After all, she was fooling around with magic she didn't understand, and she (and the reader) had to be warned that events were spiraling out of her control.

So as I sat at my typewriter, I concentrated: I imagined my skin feeling tighter and tighter. I imagined pressure growing inside my head, as if it were "inflating like a beach ball." I felt the panicky desire—too late—to stop the changeover process, and then I felt myself slipping helplessly away from my body, like "a grape spurting out of its skin." I felt the terror of existing, for an instant, between my body and someone else's, hanging in "black, soundless emptiness." And then I experienced the relief of being back in a body again, with the skin "loose and comfortable."

This was a lot to imagine. There *is* a lot to imagine, in any fantasy. But don't be intimidated by the prospect of having to manufacture all this fantasy detail. If you feel a pull to write about a magic tuba, then the details about it—who made it, what it feels like to play it, what the effects of its music are—must already lie in the murky depths of your unconscious. You just need to develop techniques for fishing them out.

So make friends with your unconscious. Try sitting down with a pad of paper and scribbling, "The magic tuba was first seen by . . ." Keep on writing. Or start, "When Louise blew into the magic tuba, people in the audience began to . . ." Again, keep on writing, without stopping to think or edit out silly ideas. You can't sort out the good ideas from the silly ones until you've pumped them all up from the bottom of your mind.

Often, the fantasy element that comes up resembles something in real life. If so, it will help you to study the real-life aspect for authentic details. When I decided, in writing *Fifth Grade Magic,* that modern fairy godmothers should wear uniforms, I went to the post office to see what the employees were actually wearing. Similarly, I can imagine Mary Norton wandering around her house, picking up items and muttering:

Mouse-gates have to be metal. This cheese-grater would work, if he could pry it off the hinge. Cash box lid—would have to be *small* cash box, not this big.

There is one kind of realistic detail about a fantasy that at first seems simply wrong to use: the *unbelievability* of it. But surprisingly, having one of your characters question it makes the fantasy element *more* believable. Confront the impossibility directly by having someone in the story say or think, "There aren't any fairy godmothers," or, "Witchcraft doesn't really work." By doing this, you relieve the reader of the burden of having to question the fantasy. In fact, this technique actually encourages the readers to root for the fantasy and gives them the pleasant feeling of being one up on the characters.

In writing the first version of my first fantasy novel, *Mail-Order Wings,* I was greatly concerned about convincing the reader that my heroine could actually get off the ground. This concern showed in the story—Andrea herself acted worried and tentative about using her wings. "She should be beside herself with excitement!" advised my editor.

Of course she should! I then realized that my anxiety about making the flying believable was keeping the story earthbound. So I voiced my doubts in the thoughts of the natural unbeliever in the story—Andrea's teenage brother Jim. "Did you ever hear that people can't fly?" he jeers, as he examines the wings Andrea has put together and stuck onto her back. While Jim expresses the vast superiority a sixteen-year-old feels over a nine-year-old, the reader knows that the joke will be on Jim. In fact, Andrea flies for the first time that very night.

A neat example of how to confront the incredible element in a story occurs in C. S. Lewis's science fiction/fantasy novel, *Out of the Silent*

Planet. Ransom, the hero, has been shanghaied onto a spaceship to Mars. When he questions the unscrupulous physicist Weston about how the spaceship works, Weston answers curtly, "By exploiting the less observed properties of solar radiation."

In order to come up with this dialogue, C. S. Lewis did *not* have to imagine how an interplanetary spaceship would work. He only had to imagine what he already had a very good idea of—how a contemptuous physicist would respond to a medievalist scholar. Yet, the exchange has the effect of convincing the reader that Weston does know exactly how the ship works, and that it is bearing them swiftly toward Mars.

Sometimes the best way to lure the reader down the rabbit hole is indirectly, through some kind of tantalizing, secondhand evidence. For instance, in *Lizard Music* by Daniel Pinkwater, a boy sees a lizard quintet playing on a late-night TV show. He (and the reader) feel sure there are real reptilian musicians around, and can't wait to find them.

In writing the first version of my novel *Richard and the Vratch*, I began with Richard's finding the vratch (a small descendant of the dinosaur Ornithomimus) right away. It turns up in the Havheart trap, intended to catch a raccoon, out by the trash barrels. That version, as my editor described it in her letter of rejection, was "inherently dull and slow-moving."

I was crushed. I knew my editor was right, but how had I managed to turn such an exciting idea as a boy discovering an unknown animal into a boring story? One thing that was wrong, I decided, was revealing the vratch too early. Better for this astonishing creature to be in disguise when Richard first meets it. Let the reader suspect, long before Richard does, that the dog he gets from the animal shelter is no dog at all. Let the reader deduce that the mad scientist Dr. MacNary, who claims a colony of "ornithoids" is living in the hills behind Richard's house, is not so crazy. Besides increasing the suspense in the story (always a good idea), this reworking of the fantasy element makes the reader more and more eager to see the vratch. When the climax of the story comes and Richard and the reader are finally allowed to see the undisguised creature, disbelief is no longer a problem.

Similarly, in *The House with a Clock in Its Walls*, one of the first clues Lewis, the main character, has that his uncle is someone out of the ordinary is his pack of playing cards:

451

On each faded blue back was a round golden seal with an Aladdin's lamp in the middle. Above and below the seal were the words: CAPHARNAUM COUNTY MAGICIANS SOCIETY.

Lewis's uncle hasn't pulled a rabbit out of a hat, but the readers are well on their way to believing that he is a magician. And if *you* can tell your fantasy story with this kind of seeable, touchable detail, your reader will gladly join you in the magician's parlor, or under the floor with the little people, or in the night sky in which Andrea flies south with the geese. You will have turned fantasy into reality, by letting the reader believe.

94

CREATING SUSPENSE IN THE YOUNG ADULT MYSTERY

BY JOAN LOWERY NIXON

CREATING SUSPENSE in the young adult mystery novel is not just a matter of keeping the reader guessing: Suspense calls for all the nail-biting emotional responses of anxiety, excitement, and fear, as readers live through the viewpoint of the main character.

Young adult readers are impatient. They'll often read the first few lines of a book, and if it doesn't intrigue them, they'll put the book down and reach for another; so suspense must begin in the first few paragraphs, as in my book *The Kidnapping of Christina Lattimore:*

> I don't like the way he's looking at me.
> It's a kind of creepy look as though the two of us shared some kind of secret, and it's making me uncomfortable.

The story might begin with an immediate, fully written scene of terror, as in *The Dark and Deadly Pool:*

> Moonlight drizzled down the wide glass wall that touched the surface of the hotel swimming pool, dividing it into two parts. The wind-flicked waters of the outer pool glittered with reflected pin-lights from the moon and stars, but the silent water in the indoor section had been sucked into the blackness of the room.
> I blinked, trying to adjust my eyes to the darkness, trying to see the edge of the pool that curved near my feet. I pressed my back against the wall and forced myself to breathe evenly. I whispered aloud, "Mary Elizabeth Rafferty, there is nothing to be afraid of here! Nothing!" But even the sound of my own wobbly words terrified me.

It's not enough just to capture the attention and interest of young adult readers; the author has to keep them in suspense throughout the entire story, and there are a number of ways in which this can be done.

1. *Challenge readers with a situation that is completely new and different.* Many of us fondly remember stories from our childhood that involved buried treasure, trunks in attics, and secret passages. But those stories are familiar to today's adolescent mystery fans, too, and unless you can come up with an original, unusual twist, you'd better develop a plot based on your own ideas. Ask yourself an intriguing question and challenge yourself to find the answer.

What if a thirteen-year-old girl, who has been shot during a robbery, wakes from a semi-comatose state four years later to find that she is the only eyewitness to the unsolved crime? (*The Other Side of Dark*)

What if a girl with a serious illness has given up hope and decides not to fight for her life? Suppose her life were in danger from an unexpected direction—wouldn't she instinctively, automatically fight to live? (*The Specter*)

2. *Take a sudden, unexpected turn, making good use of the element of surprise.* In *The Seance,* another of my mysteries, the girls' nervousness during the seance builds to terror, resulting in a scene of panic, in which the candles—the only light in the house—are extinguished. During those few minutes of darkness, before a lamp is plugged in and turned on, one of the girls—Sara—disappears. It's a "locked room mystery" until readers are led to suspect that one of the other girls present must have been involved in Sara's disappearance. When it's revealed that the main character, Lauren, is the one who is responsible, it comes as a total surprise. From this point, the story shifts, and Lauren becomes a potential murder victim.

3. *Throw suspicion on someone whom the main character has trusted.* In *The Ghost of Now,* Angie's brother has been struck by a hit-and-run driver. She tries to unravel the events of that night and comes to suspect that her brother's accident had really been attempted murder. As Angie uncovers information that may lead to the identity of the killer, she confides in Del, a boy she's begun to care for. Then one night Del says something that arouses Angie's suspicions, and she begins to be afraid that Del might be the one who tried to kill her brother.

4. *Let readers know something that the main character hasn't found out yet.* In the novel of detection, a crime has been committed, and the

454

identity of the criminal must be discovered by both the main character and the readers. In the novel of suspense, someone is out to do away with the main character—who may or may not know the identity of this person—but readers know what is planned and watch the main character head into danger, ignorant of what awaits.

I combined these two forms in *The Stalker.* Every odd-numbered chapter is written in the form of *detection,* from the viewpoint of Jennifer, whose best friend's mother has been murdered. Circumstantial evidence points to the friend, but Jennifer enlists the help of a retired police detective to help her prove Bobbie's innocence. Every even-numbered chapter is written in the form of *suspense,* in the mind of the murderer. The murderer's identity is unknown to both Jennifer and to readers, but readers are aware that he presents an ever-growing danger to Jennifer.

5. *Let the main character become aware of some information but keep it from the reader for a while.* While you must play fair with readers by eventually giving them every clue, there is no reason you can't heighten suspense by showing your reader that your main character knows something but is not yet ready to divulge it. In Chapter One of *The Stalker,* Jennifer, still in shock with news of the murder, questions her grandmother.

> "Where is Bobbie? Did they say?"
> "Good question. Police don't know where she is. Looks like she up and run away. Nobody on God's earth knows where that girl's gone off to."
> Jennifer clutched the (freshly ironed) shirts to her chest, ducking into the smell of starch and scorch so that Grannie couldn't see her face. "I'll start supper," she mumbled, and hurried from the room.
> Where was Bobbie? Suddenly, surely, Jennifer knew.

The chapter ends as the police question Jennifer, who is so angry that she keeps her knowledge from them, too.

> There was a pause. The detective with the pad and pen leaned toward her just a fraction. The other one did, too. It was coming—the question Jennifer had expected, had been afraid of.
> "Jennifer," he said, "do you know where Bobbie Trax is now?"
> Jennifer looked at him without blinking, as steadily as she could manage. She gripped the arms of her chair so tightly that her fingers ached as she answered, "No, I don't."

455

It is not until Chapter Three, when Jennifer is on her way to join Bobbie, that readers are made aware of what Jennifer has known all along.

6. *Tantalize readers by hinting at other kinds of secrets that are up to them to uncover.* In *A Deadly Game of Magic*, Lisa and three companions seek refuge from a storm in a nearby house. From the beginning, Lisa, who is intuitive, feels uncomfortable in this house, sensing that though they thought they were alone, there is some other presence in the house with them; her fear zeros in on a room at the end of the bedroom wing—the only room in which the door stands open. Throughout the story an unseen person again and again attempts to lure them toward that room, but each time they manage to avoid entering it. While readers begin to suspect what might be in that room, the final clue isn't given until the last paragraph in the book, and readers must figure out the answer themselves.

7. *Let readers see your main character make a mistake, or choose a totally wrong course of action, as a result of a personality flaw.* In *The Stalker*, Jennifer has been characterized as loyal and loving, but impulsive and stubborn, too. Readers are well aware that she should stay away from the scene of the crime, but her impatient single-mindedness causes her to make the wrong choice. Without telling her detective-partner, Jennifer goes alone to the scene, placing herself in immediate danger.

8. *Description of the setting can help to create and maintain suspense.* Highly visual writing through active picturesque verbs is the essential tool here. In *The Ghosts of Now*, an empty house holds such an important place in the story that it deserves the detailed description which begins:

The Andrews place squats alone at the end of an empty, quiet street. Maybe it's because of the overlarge lot that surrounds it; maybe it's because the house looks like an unkempt, yellowed old man who badly needs a barber, but I feel that the other houses on the block have cringed away from this place, tucking in their tidy porches and neat walkways and dropping filmy curtains over blank eyes. . . .
Someone once lived in this house and loved it, and for a few moments I feel sad that it should be so neglected, left alone to die.
But the house is not dead.

There are small rustlings, creakings, and sounds barely loud enough to be heard as the house moves and breathes with the midday heat. I feel that it's watching me, waiting to see what I'll do. Or could someone be watching, listening, just as I listen?

9. *Sub-mysteries can aid suspense.* A sudden shadow on the porch, which is accounted for in the next chapter; a character whose actions are so peculiar that they frighten your main character; an aunt who is frantic to keep something hidden—such sub-mysteries tie in with the central mystery to be solved and heighten suspense. Sometimes they can do double duty by serving as red herrings. In *The Kidnapping of Christina Lattimore,* Christina, upstairs in bed and doing her homework, thinks she is alone in the house, until:

Maybe there was the click of a doorknob downstairs. If there was, I didn't notice it. I hold my breath and listen as I become aware that softly, very softly, through the thick plush carpeting on the stairway, footsteps are padding, patting, like little slaps with a power puff. And they are coming up the stairs!

Christina, preparing to defend herself, discovers it's only her father's secretary, Rosella, and relaxes. But as they talk, Rosella's inconsistent, nervous behavior arouses Christina's suspicions.

10. *A peculiar character can add suspense whenever he or she appears.* In *The Seance,* the daily life of Ila Hughes, grandmother of one of Lauren's friends, is built around superstitions, some of them creepy, such as the cat she has buried inside the walls of her house to keep the devil away. And her hobby?

My glance fell on something that made me automatically step back. On the mantel, on a level with my eyes, was a row of little gray skulls!
There was a chuckle close to my ear, and Mrs. Hughes touched my shoulders, moving me forward again. "Those are my little birds," she said, laughing. "Aren't they precious? Little bird skulls. I began finding them in the Thicket years ago."

11. *Old tricks can still be used.* We're all familiar with the *time is running out* technique, but it can still be effective. And so can the technique of *making the readers—but not the main characters—aware that someone is sneaking toward the house or slowly turning the knob on the bedroom door.* Pull out all the stops. Readers of young adult mysteries love it.

12. *Each chapter ending should be so intriguing that readers can't close the book.* These last sentences can whet curiosity or be downright terrifying, but their job is to lead readers from one chapter into the next, nonstop:

From *The Other Side of Dark:*

If I shot Jarrod, wouldn't it be self-defense? And wouldn't it end the trials and the questions and the badgering and the harassment and the nightmares and the worries and the years and years of fear?
Carefully I aim the gun.

From *A Deadly Game of Magic:*

I would have liked to comfort her. I would have loved it if someone had tried to comfort me. All I could do was lean against the door, hoping it would hold me. My legs were wobbly. My mind seemed to tremble as much as my body, but one thought came through clearly. "Whatever Sam saw," I said, "is still in this house. And like it or not, we're trapped in here with it."

To keep readers from becoming exhausted, you must have the suspense in your mystery build and peak, drop and build again. The valleys are a good place for humor, for development of the relationships between the main character and her family and friends, for her moments of introspection and attempts to handle the non-mystery problems that are part of her life.

But it's those peaks of suspense that will cause your readers to write, "I just couldn't put your book down. When is your next mystery coming out?"

458

95

DOUBLE VISION: A SPECIAL TOOL FOR YOUNG ADULT WRITERS

BY CHERYL ZACH

WRITING A YOUNG ADULT NOVEL with an authentic teen voice requires the author to see the world with double vision—both as the child he was and the adult he is now. We have all lived through adolescence, endured its pains, joys, and frustrations. Delving into your own teenage memories will enable you to relive those strong, sometimes overwhelming emotions and recreate them in your fiction, producing the immediacy and validity that the genre demands.

Do you remember your first date? (Could you ever forget it?) The first time someone asked you out? The first time that special person kissed you? The sweating palms, the rumbling stomach, the anguished attempts at achieving a poise that often failed you at the most crucial moments—these feelings are universal and timeless. Attributing such emotions to your characters will give them depth and reality, propel them off the page and into full dimension.

Adolescence involves a series of stages, changing year by year. Think back to the summer you were thirteen—what were your most pressing concerns? Girls with developing figures who snubbed you unmercifully? The low velocity in your fast ball that might keep you off the team?

Now jump to your sixteenth birthday! How have you changed? Have you achieved a reputation for being "cool" that makes you the envy of all the other guys, but might be lost if you reveal your attraction for the girl who smiles at you in chemistry class—a girl that not everyone admires? Or, from the feminine perspective, have you had your first date, your first kiss, and then—horrors—lost your first love to an older, more sophisticated girl? How will you ever recover, and who wants to? Has an essay you've written or a unique science project you've prepared drawn praise from your favorite teacher, causing you to dream for the first time of attending college—even though you know your parents can't afford to send you? Remember—and put it all into the characters you create.

Then, returning to your adult perspective, examine these characters. Reliving your own emotions will give your characters validity and elicit the essential reader sympathy. As the writer, you must add the exterior polish. Emotions do not change, nor do many of the "first" experiences—first date, first kiss, first car, etc. But the outer trappings—clothes, fads, slang—do.

To make your teen characters ring true to your young adult readers, now you must substitute observation for nostalgia. Watch today's teenagers in their natural settings—schools, restaurants, movies, malls, beaches, among others. Notice that they wear Reeboks or Nikes, not saddle shoes; acid-washed denim, not poodle skirts. Note the music coming from a teenager's Walkman, the activities that attract them as participants or observers. And if you don't enjoy spending time with teens, beware: writing YA novels may not be for you. Immersing yourself in the lives of your teenage characters as you write your novel will be difficult unless you have a genuine liking for this age group.

After creating strong, believable characters, you must grapple with the related question of conflict and plot. What is your character's problem, and how will he or she solve it? Looking at this from your perspective as a teenager will help you avoid a common pitfall among would-be YA authors: an adult-centered plot rather than one that is teen-centered. Again, think back to your own teen years. What was your biggest problem and how did you handle it? Did your older sister steal your boyfriends? What did you do about it? Were you and your best friend in love with the same person? How did you work it out? Allowing your character to cope with his or her problem in a manner consistent with the character's age shapes your plot outline.

Reverting to your adult viewpoint allows you to check your plot for possible flaws. Most of all, remember that the conflict must be solvable by your teen protagonist. Having an adult, friendly or not, step in to deal with your young hero's problem is a fatal mistake. When my shy, teenaged protagonist in *The Frog Princess* is elected class president because of a cruel joke, no adult can be allowed to solve her dilemma for her. Kelly has to solve her problem by herself, gaining self-confidence as well as the respect of her classmates in the process.

Having looked at your conflict through your young protagonist's eyes

460

should also protect you from another common pitfall—the condescension that creeps in when the writer's "adult" side has not been effectively exorcised. The problems you faced at thirteen or fifteen or seventeen were real and vital and soul-shaking: they mattered. The fact that getting a date for the big dance or outshining your older brother seems a minor worry now does not lessen its original importance. Remembering this should deter you from talking down to your teen readers, or, even worse, preaching to them. Problem-solving and moments of revelation can come only through your teen protagonist, and cannot be superimposed by an intrusive author. At the end of *The Frog Princess,* Kelly receives a compliment from Tony, the good-looking classmate she has secretly admired, despite the dirty trick he played on her earlier. But by now she has realized that "Tony would smile only for party-pretty girls in new dresses," and decides this guy is not worth any heartache.

Having believable characters, a strong but age-appropriate conflict and logical plotting, what next? Dialogue is just as crucial in teen fiction as in adult novels, with an added twist—challenge of "current" teen slang. Your child's eye will remind you of basic interests—friends, school, family problems—but dialogue is one element of your novel that may benefit most from your adult/detached writer's perspective.

Sit on a park bench, on a bus, at the beach or amusement park, and listen to teenagers talk. Write down what you hear. Will this give you good dialogue? Only if you cut the inconsequential chatting that forms a large part of real conversation. Good dialogue is not the same as real speech; it only sounds that way. Listen to how teenagers really speak—using lots of monosyllables and elliptical phrases, as in the following:

> "Butt out," Pete told me, his voice thick with anger. "What's it to you?"
> "She's my sister," I said.
> "So?"
> "So she's coming home, right now."

What about current slang—often a double-edged sword? Watch out for outdated expressions. An anachronistic slang word will alert readers—and editors—that the author isn't paying attention. Teen catchwords change quickly. The expression you hear today may be "out" by the time your book gets into print. So use even the most up-to-date slang judiciously, to add flavor but not overpower the other essentials.

What about setting? Unless your book takes place during a holiday period, school will probably be part of your background. In some ways, schools are unchanging, but in others, they may have altered greatly since your own school days. Take a look at the schools in your neighborhood. What are the kids studying, what are they doing for extra-curricular activities? Read student newspapers; they will inform you about student opinions, issues that concern them, their opinions, and interests.

Remember the first rule, however: Look at the school scene through the eyes of a teenager, not those of a curious adult. To a fourteen-year-old, the essential part of the school day will most likely take place before, between and after classes.

And when you return to your adult viewpoint, consider other, more novel settings. Editors sometimes complain about overused lunchroom scenes. This doesn't necessitate moving your story to exotic locales. My YA novel, *Too Many Cooks,* in which the action centers around a small catering business, won critical praise for its "vivid and unusual setting."

Last, point of view. Most YA novels are written either from first person—the "I" viewpoint—or third person limited—looking inside one or two main characters. Both have advantages and pitfalls. First person can lend an impression of immediacy and help the writer focus strongly on the protagonist. It can also be limiting, presenting only what your main character witnesses. Also, some Young Adult editors have grown tired of first-person viewpoint and are less likely to be impressed with a novel using it.

Using third person lets you present more than one viewpoint, widening the scope of your novel. But switching viewpoints must be done skillfully and not too often, or your book will sound choppy and confuse your reader. Accidental switches in points of view are one of the most obvious signs of a beginning writer and throw up a red flag to editors. While viewing the situation through your eyes as an adolescent will enable you to make the point of view authentic, you must go over your manuscript carefully from your perspective as an adult.

When you have brought your YA novel to a satisfying and believable conclusion and have rewritten, polished, and proofread it, how do you market it? With the same care that you would use for an adult novel, studying the marketplace and individual publishers' requirements.

The YA market changes just as the adult market does. Currently, series using continuing characters are "hot." While this may make it harder to sell your individual title, a strong novel may be adapted to a series concept. Why not sell four or six book ideas instead of one? And series do offer opportunities for beginning writers to break into the field, gaining valuable experience.

YA romance novels, which once occupied much of the bookstore shelf space, have lost ground to books in which romance is only one of many concerns facing teenage protagonists. Recent popular series titles reveal this diversity: *Sweet Valley High, Sisters, Sorority Girls, Roommates* all cover the full spectrum of teen life. Problem novels, dealing with darker conflicts of drugs, suicide, abortion, etc., are not presently being sought; humor, on the other hand, is very popular with readers and editors. YA hardcover sales have dropped, but the market for original YA paperbacks continues to grow.

The most essential requirement doesn't vary: a good manuscript with strong, believable characters and an authentic teen voice. Your double vision will aid you in crafting a satisfying and special YA novel.

❚ 96

AN OBJECT LESSON FOR PLAYWRIGHTS

BY JEFFREY SWEET

THE EXPERIMENT GOES SOMETHING LIKE THIS: You place a sheet of paper over a magnet. Then you pour iron filings onto the paper. Almost instantly, the filings arrange themselves into a pattern. The pattern indicates the outline of the magnetic field.

You don't *see* the field. You see the *pattern* the filings make because of the *presence* of the field.

And yes, this does have something to do with writing plays.

By way of demonstration, here's a short scene that takes place in a suburban living room between a man and a teenage boy. As it begins, the boy is heading out the door when the man stops him by saying—

MAN: What's that in your hand?
BOY: Nothing.
MAN: Open it, please.
BOY: Dad—
MAN (*Firmly*): Open your hand. (*The boy opens it to reveal a key.*) Well?
BOY: I'm only going out for an hour.
MAN: Give it to me.
BOY: There's someplace I have to be.
MAN: You give that key to me now or I'll ground you another week. (*The man opens his hand. The boy hesitates, then puts the key into the man's hand.*)

Not a lot of dialogue. But look at how much we learn in this short passage: The man and boy are father and son. The father wields his authority with a firm hand. The son is not above trying to pull a fast one to get around his father's orders. The son wants to go out for an hour and he needs the key to do so, leading to a reasonable guess that the key is for the family car, which he is not supposed to be using. Additionally, from the father's threat to extend the son's grounding, we gather the son is currently being punished.

Just as the pattern the iron filings form indicates the magnetic field acting upon them, so the contest over the car key indicates the dramatic field in existence between the father and son.

To rephrase this into a general principle: You can often dramatize what is going on between your characters through the way they negotiate over an object.

This technique is particularly useful because it allows the audience to figure a good deal out for themselves, obviating the writer from having to go through tedious explanations. Notice, for instance, that in the scene above, the father doesn't say anything like, "I'm very disappointed in your behavior." Nor does the son say, "I'm upset about the way you restrict my movements." Both of these statements indeed would be accurate expressions of their feelings, but how much more effective it is to allow the viewer, by analyzing the negotiation over the key, to arrive at his or her own conclusions as to the nature of the relationship between the characters.

The great plays are filled with brilliant negotiations over objects. Whenever Shakespeare introduces an object onstage, you can be sure it will be used to strong dramatic effect. In fact, according to chroniclers of the time, it was with a scene containing the resourceful use of objects that Shakespeare first established his reputation as a hot young playwright.

Act I, Scene 4 of *Henry VI, Part 3*. The Duke of York, who with his sons has led a revolt against Henry VI, has been captured by Margaret, Henry VI's bloodthirsty queen. Margaret steps forward to taunt York. She shows him a handkerchief with a red stain on it, and informs him in a casual way that it was dipped in the blood of his youngest and much-beloved son Rutland, whom one of her followers has just killed. "And if thine eyes can water for his death," she says, "I give thee this to dry thy cheeks withal," and does indeed offer it to him. (In one particularly effective production I saw, York refused to take the handkerchief, so she draped it over his shoulder.) Continuing with her cruel sport, Margaret goes on to say, in essence, "So you want to be a king, hunh? Well, let's see how you'd look in a crown." And she makes a paper crown and puts it onto his head and remarks sarcastically, "Ay, marry, sir, now looks he like a king!"

Powerful stuff, the power of which derives largely from the *physicalization* of York's downfall and Margaret's sadism by the introduction of two imaginatively chosen objects. The paper crown is a particularly strong choice. Being paper, of course it doesn't have the value of the real crown, an adroit way of conveying the contempt with which Margaret views York's aspirations for the throne.

This use of objects is a technique Shakespeare employed to great advantage in his other plays. Think of Hamlet holding Yorick's skull. Think of the way Iago uses Desdemona's handkerchief (another handkerchief!) to goad Othello. Think of the counterfeit letter used to beguile Malvolio in *Twelfth Night*.

It is a technique that modern playwrights have also employed to great effect. Much of the action in Lillian Hellman's *The Little Foxes* revolves around a safe deposit box and bonds stolen from it. In Frederick Knott's *Wait Until Dark,* the villains' actions are motivated by the desire to get their hands on a doll stuffed with drugs. In William Gibson's *The Miracle Worker,* Annie Sullivan and Helen Keller go head to head over a variety of objects—a key, a plate of food, a pile of silverware and so on.

What's more, the *transformation* or *destruction* of an object introduced onstage can give a scene even greater impact.

At the beginning of the third act of Neil Simon's *The Odd Couple,* Oscar and Felix are feuding. Oscar sees that Felix is eating a plate of pasta and decides to spoil it by spraying it with an aerosol. Oscar makes a derisive remark about Felix's spaghetti. Felix laughs at Oscar's ignorance. "It's not spaghetti. It's linguini!" Whereupon, Oscar picks up the plate, goes to the kitchen door, hurls the food at an unseen wall and announces, "Now it's garbage!" The transformation of the food to garbage graphically dramatizes the disintegration of Felix and Oscar's relationship.

In Tennessee Williams's *The Glass Menagerie,* the shy Laura shows Jim, the gentleman caller, her favorite piece of a collection of glass figures, a unicorn. In an effort to raise her spirits, Jim begins to waltz with Laura, but, during the dance, they bump into the table on which the unicorn is sitting. It falls to the floor and its horn breaks off. Later, when she realizes that Jim's visit will not be the beginning of the relationship between them for which she had hoped (during the scene, he reveals he has recently become engaged), Laura gives him the damaged unicorn as a souvenir. The shattering of the unicorn gives particular emphasis to a scene concerned with the shattering of Laura's illusions.

466

This technique—the negotiation over objects—may be extended to the negotiation over things that are not physical objects. In *A Streetcar Named Desire*, Tennessee Williams has his principals clash memorably over a variety of props (Blanche's trunk, clothes and letters, the deed to Belle Reve, etc.), but they also contest other elements.

At one point, for instance, Blanche turns on the radio. Stanley, in the middle of a poker game with friends, finds the music distracting and orders Blanche to turn it off. A little later, when she turns it on again, Stanley grabs the radio and tosses it out the window. Clearly, then, one can negotiate over sound. (Certainly, as anyone who has had to endure the sound of a boom box on the street, one can negotiate over volume.)

Shortly after she arrives, Blanche covers the naked lightbulbs in Stanley and Stella's apartment with Chinese lanterns. Late in the play, when Mitch confronts her with the truth about her past, he yanks off the lanterns so as to be able to see her clearly. A negotiation over light. (See also the battles between the father and sons over the use of light in Eugene O'Neill's *Long Day's Journey Into Night*.)

In the climactic confrontation, Blanche, feeling threatened by Stanley, wants to walk past him and asks him to move out of her way. He insists she has plenty of room to get by and then backs her into the bedroom. A negotiation over space. (Much of *The Odd Couple,* too, is about the negotiation over space, as two men of different habits and natures try to share one apartment.)

So, characters may negotiate over objects, over sound, over light and over space. Also over time, over temperature, over elevation—over anything, in fact, to which a character might attach value.

Including *people.* Returning to *Streetcar,* notice that Blanche and Stanley carry on a play-long struggle over Stella, and Stanley wins. For that matter, *any* play concerning a triangle, romantic or otherwise, inevitably involves two parties negotiating over the third.

On a more abstract level, the negotiation may be over ideas. Much of David Mamet's *American Buffalo* concerns Teach and Donny arguing over how to steal a set of rare coins from an apartment. Their differing approaches to the plan go a long way toward establishing the differences in their characters and highlighting the ethical issues which are the heart of this remarkable work. And so, too, virtually anything George Bernard Shaw wrote. He almost always defines his characters on the basis of their conflicting opinions on intellectual matters.

Yes, what I'm describing is a technical device. But it's no artificial trick. One of the reasons this technique works so well onstage is that it reflects the way people behave in real life.

For we are constantly negotiating with each other. When two people on a date debate whether to see a kung fu movie or a revival of *Singing in the Rain,* they're revealing their differing tastes through the arguments they advance in support of their respective choices. When children fight over who's going to sleep in the upper bunk, the resolution of their controversy tells a great deal about which child has what powers and prerogatives. When a wife upbraids her husband for constantly leaving the cap off the tube of toothpaste, one may quickly glean something of the health of their marriage.

To bring such negotiations to the stage is to reveal to the audience the ways people use whatever tools are at hand to pursue their objectives with each other. It is to show how, in contests over such seemingly mundane objects as a key, a credit card, a handkerchief, or an alarm clock, human beings often inadvertently reveal the deeper issues between them.

97

PLAYWRITING AS ARCHITECTURE

BY GRAM SLATON

THERE'S A MAN WHO WANTS TO TELL A STORY," my father would often tell me, with heavy significance, "and there's a man who has a story to *tell.*"

It's rather conventional wisdom. It's also why my father never wrote a word in his life. Who could write with joy in his heart while hand-cuffed with the burden of imparting an unassailable, all-encompassing *truth?*

The fact is, everyone has a story to tell. Anyone who has ever related a two-minute postmortem of his or her workday is part of that. The difference between a storyteller and a *good* storyteller is primarily a matter of craft, an understanding of basic tools, and an open mind toward how best to tell each individual story. And forget hiding behind the shield of historical fact, because the flip side of the old "this really happened" excuse is the equally old saw of "well, I guess you had to be there . . ."

I teach a beginning course in playwriting that approaches the craft from an architectural perspective, not only because it demystifies the process through thorough analysis of the individual building compo-nents—the monologue, the protagonist, the arc of a scene—but because it allows a way of seeing an idea through from first germ to final draft without the defensiveness associated with more "navel-staring" ap-proaches. Its success is dependent on three givens: that the students allow themselves a sense of wonder; that they not be wedded to any single idea; and that they dare to fail, and fail often. This last is a rather subversive concept in a success-driven world, but, as Lillian Hellman said, "Nothing you write, if you hope to be any good, will ever come out as you first hoped." Embracing the right to fail is the key that unlocks the handcuffs; after that, the rest is easy.

We begin by imagining that each of us has just inherited a thousand acres of land and the means to build a dream home on it. This land offers a little of everything—fields, forests, streams, hillside, lake-shore—but where is the ideal site for this home we have yet to design? To this end I offer an exercise in "discovering" a concept: Name a stand-out event that's happened to you or a friend in the past six weeks. What are the dramatic possibilities of that event? What are its limitations? In the best of all possible worlds, where would this event take place, and when? What would this place look like? What would the world immediately beyond this place look like? By the end of the exercise, a tentative concept has been arrived at. Architecturally, a building site has been explored. And emotionally, the first deadly hurdle a new writer faces—OH LORD WHAT AM I GONNA FIND TO WRITE ABOUT—has possibly been cleared.

Because the sad truth of writing is this: After you cope with the awful solitude of the art, the discipline it demands, the immense odds of achieving popular success—after you address all the things you can *do something* about—you still ram against the stone wall of there being only 27 plots in the universe. Mix and match or cut and paste, there are only 27, and no matter what you write, it will remind somebody of something from somewhere else.

Invariably, I get a student who's determined to flush out the 28th plot, to whom I say good luck and pack a lunch. But to those accepting the cruel reality of the 27 plots *and* the right to fail, a creative breakthrough is suddenly imminent. What becomes clear in a flash is that the only thing that separates one comfortably familiar story from another is the teller's own unique spin. And all spins are *created* equal. It's what you *do* with yours that counts.

This leads to the two vital "surveying" tools a writer possesses: The Great Why and The Great What If. They do the significant work of stripping away the arbitrary underbrush and replacing it with specific choices. Clichés are inevitable; your job is to retool them with your own personal stamp. The Great Why forces you to explore the realm of personal choice and how you got there; The Great What If helps to break those choices open and probe other, usually until then uncon-sidered possibilities.

Let's say your idea, like many first ideas, is a coming-of-age story, and you want to set it in a bar. Skillions of these plays exist—how are you going to help yours make an impact? Why a bar? You like the space, you like its attraction to a broad spectrum of humanity. Why? Because the collisions possible through alcohol consumption and a confluence of pathways intrigue you. Why? Because you want someone to lose and find himself and have it abated and abetted by strangers. Ah-h-h. Now we're getting somewhere. Well, what if instead of a bar, your situation moved to a bus station? A laundromat? A city park? A bowling alley? The quarterdeck of the QE2? The idea is opening up. What time were you thinking of? Oh, nighttime, summer. Why? Because it's relaxed, open, a time to measure events of the day. Why? Because it's a watermark, a daily milestone. Why? Because people have regrets. Ah-h-h. Well, how about a *specific* nighttime, say near a holiday like Christmas or Thanksgiving when families gather, or an important birthday, like 30 or 65 or 18, or an anniversary of a personal or shared event, like the loss of a loved one or the anniversary of a flood? And on and on and on.

Now you have your idea and you're burrowing through a first, exploratory draft. Failure is O.K., so you veer off willy-nilly in this direction and that, chasing possibilities, running up a few blind alleys, finally turning the corner into a new dimension that makes all the pieces suddenly go *click*. Congratulations. And up pops the age-old riddle: Now that I've got the idea, how long should a play be?

Again, architecture to the rescue. The riddle has a simple, if elusive, answer: As long as it needs to be, and no longer. Playwriting, like architecture, is one long exercise in economy and control. You've groped this play in the dark for a while; listen to it now, and let it tell you its size. If you're aiming for a cozy cottage in the woods, you don't throw in grand staircases and a ballroom. Conversely, if you have Versailles-sized aspirations, you don't cram them in three tiny rooms. Let the idea give you your cue. If you're tackling the decline of western civilization, a one-act won't cut it. If you're dramatizing an incident from your morning bus ride, chances are you don't need three acts and a prologue.

Determination of size boils down to two questions: What does the play/act/scene need to accomplish, and what impediments stand in its way? If, in reviewing your early drafts, you uncover an exchange or scene or series of scenes that are witty, insightful, and dynamite stuff but do nothing substantive in furthering the idea, then you should consider removing that "room" from your next draft. A young writer will often unconsciously pack two or three different plays into a single outing. That's great, because it gives you material to explore, *next time*. Airlift those additions out now, and set them someplace else on your thousand acres. Plenty of good building sites left.

Obviously, for this article I've ignored the individual components and haven't begun to do justice to the above ideas. What I hope the reader is left with is a sense that playwriting need not be dogged enslavement to a single, tyrannical *whole*. Plays are never whole; they never tell you all their secrets. One blind alley The Great Why may seem to drive you up is a panicked, defensive "I don't know!" But don't despair—implied in every "I don't know" is the tag word "yet." You as writer don't know *yet*. But you have the freedom to keep digging until you uncover what's right, even if sometimes you don't know why. Yet. One thing you *will* know: It's easier to do without handcuffs.

98

TEN GOLDEN RULES FOR PLAYWRIGHTS

BY MARSHA NORMAN

Budding playwrights often write to ask me advice on getting started—and succeeding—in writing plays. The following are a few basics that I hope aspiring playwrights will find helpful.—M.N.

1. Read at least four hours every day, and don't let anybody ask you what you're doing just sitting there reading.

2. Don't write about your present life. You don't have a clue what it's about yet. Write about your past. Write about something that terrified you, something you *still* think is unfair, something that you have not been able to forget in all the time that's passed since it happened.

3. Don't write in order to tell the audience how smart you are. The audience is not the least bit interested in the playwright. The audience only wants to know about the characters. If the audience begins to suspect that the thing onstage was actually written by some other person, they're going to quit listening. So keep yourself out of it!

4. If you have characters you cannot write fairly, cut them out. Grudges have no place in the theatre. Nobody cares about your grudges but you, and you are not enough to fill a house.

5. There must be one central character. One. Everybody write that down. Just one. And he or she must want something. And by the end of the play, he or she must either get it or not. Period. No exceptions.

6. You must tell the audience right away what is at stake in the evening, i.e. how they know when they can go home. They are, in a sense, the jury. You present the evidence, and then they say whether it seems true to them. If it does, it will run, because they will tell all their friends to come see this true thing, God bless them. If it does not seem true to them, try to find out why and don't do it any more.

7. If, while you are writing, thoughts of critics, audience members or family members occur to you, stop writing and go read until you have successfully forgotten them.

8. Don't talk about your play while you are writing it. Good plays are always the product of a single vision, a single point of view. Your friends will be helpful later, after the play's direction is established. A play is one thing you can get too much help with. If you must break this rule, try not to say what you have learned by talking. Or just let other people talk and you listen. Don't talk the play away.

9. Keep pads of paper near all your chairs. You will be in your chairs a good bit (see Rule 1), and you will have thoughts for your play. Write them down. But don't get up from reading to do it. Go right back to the reading once the thoughts are on the paper.

10. Never go to your typewriter until you know what the first sentence is that day. It is definitely unhealthy to sit in front of a silent typewriter for any length of time. If, after you have typed the first sentence, you can't think of a second one, go read. There is only one good reason to write a play, and that is that there is no other way to take care of it, whatever it is. There are too many made-up plays being written these days. So if it doesn't spill out faster than you can write it, don't write it at all. Or write about something that does spill out. Spilling out is what the theatre is about. Writing is for novels.

❙ 99

CONFLICT: THE HEARTBEAT OF A PLAY

BY D. R. ANDERSEN

EVERY PLAYWRIGHT is a Dr. Frankenstein trying to breathe life into a page for the stage. In a good play, the heartbeat must be thundering. And the heartbeat of a play is conflict.

Simply put, conflict exists when a character wants something and can't get it. Conflict may sometimes be internal—as when a character struggles to choose between or among opposing desires. For example, Alma in Tennessee Williams's *Summer and Smoke* longs to yield to her sexual yearnings but is prevented by the repressed and conventional side of her nature.

Conflict in drama may also be external—as when a character struggles against another *character* (Oscar and Felix in Neil Simon's *The Odd Couple*); against *society* (Nora in Ibsen's *A Doll's House*); against *nature* (the mountain climbers in Patrick Meyers' *K2*); or against *fate* (Sophocles' *Oedipus*).

In most plays, the conflict is a combination of internal and external struggles. In fact, internal conflict is often externalized for dramatic impact. In Philip Barry's *Holiday,* for instance, the hero's inner dilemma is outwardly expressed in his attraction to two sisters—one who represents the safe but boring world of convention, and the other who is a symbol of the uncertain but exciting life of adventure.

Granted that a conflict may be internal or external; that a character may be in conflict with another character, society, nature or fate; and that most plays are a combination of internal and external conflict, many plays that have these basic elements of conflict do not have a thundering heartbeat. Why? These plays lack one, some, or all of the five magic ingredients of rousing, attention-grabbing-and-holding conflict.

475

The five magic ingredients

I. *Never let your audience forget what your protagonist wants.*

You can achieve this in a number of ways. Often the protagonist or another character states and periodically restates in dialogue what is at stake. Or in some plays, he explains what he wants directly to the audience in the form of a monologue. As you read or watch plays you admire, take note of the obvious and ingenious techniques playwrights use to tell the reader or audience what the characters' goals are.

Sometimes the method used to keep your audience alerted to your protagonist's goal/concern/need is a direct reflection of the protagonist's personality. In the following three short passages from my play *Graduation Day,*[1] a mother and father with very traditional values have a conversation while waiting to meet their rebellious daughter, who has told them she has a big surprise. Notice how the protagonist—Mrs. Whittaker—nervously and comically manipulates the conversation, reminding her husband and the audience of her concern for her daughter Jane:

MRS. WHITTAKER
(Knocking on the door)
Jane. Jane. It's Mom and Dad.
(Pause)
No answer. What should we do, Tom?
MR. WHITTAKER
Let's go in.
MRS. WHITTAKER
Suppose we find Jane in a compromising situation?
MR. WHITTAKER
Nobody at Smith College has ever been found in a compromising situation.

* * *

MRS. WHITTAKER
Tom, you know, this was my freshman room.
MR. WHITTAKER
Of course, I know.
MRS. WHITTAKER
And Jane's. It was Jane's freshman room too, Tom. Remember?

* * *

MR. WHITTAKER
Mary, you get in the craziest moods at these reunions. I may never bring you back again.

---

1. First produced by Playwrights Horizons in New York, starring Polly Holliday.

MRS. WHITTAKER

Do you know why you fell in love with me, Tom?

MR. WHITTAKER

I fell in love with you the minute I saw you eat pancakes.

MRS. WHITTAKER

That's a sound basis for a relationship. Tom, where do you suppose Jane is? And more frightening, what do you suppose she wants to tell us? She said just enough on the phone to suggest that she's going to be bringing a boy here for us to meet.

MR. WHITTAKER

A man, Mary, a man.

MRS. WHITTAKER

Oh, God. I never even considered that possibility. Suppose Jane brings a fiancé—our age—like Pia Zadora did.

MR. WHITTAKER

Don't you want Jane to live her own life?

MRS. WHITTAKER

No. Especially not her own life. Practically anyone else's. But not her own.

MR. WHITTAKER

What *do* you want for Jane?

MRS. WHITTAKER

I don't see why Jane can't fall in love with a plain Harvard Business School student, let's say. Someone who'll be steady and dependable.

And so it goes. The protagonist discusses a number of topics, but she inevitably leads the conversation back to her overriding concern. Mrs. Whittaker's desire to see her daughter do the right thing and marry wisely is always uppermost in the mind and conversation of the character.

In this one act, a comic effect is achieved by having Mrs. Whittaker insistently remind the audience what she wants. Once you have clearly established what a character wants, you can then write powerful and often hilarious scenes in which the audience, already knowing the character's point of view, is able to anticipate his reaction.

II. *Show your protagonist struggling to achieve what he wants.*

This principle is, of course, the basic writing advice to *show,* not tell, and it was a major concern for me when I was writing *The House Where I Was Born.*[2]

The plot: A young man, Leo, has returned from the Vietnam War, a psychosomatic mute because of the atrocities he witnessed. He comes back to a crumbling old house in a decaying suburb, a home populated

_____

2. First produced by Playwrights Horizons in New York.

by a callous stepfather; a mother who survives on aphorisms and by bending reality to diminish her despair; a half-crazy aunt; and a grandfather who refuses to buckle under to the pressures from his family to sell the home.

I set out to dramatize Leo's painful battle to free himself of memories of the war and to begin a new life. However, each time I worked on the scene in the play when Leo first comes home, his dialogue seemed to trivialize his emotions.

Then it occurred to me that Leo should not speak at all during the first act; that his inability to speak would *show* an audience his suffering and pain far better than his words could.

At the end of the third act, when Leo regains some hope, some strength to go on, every speech I wrote for him also rang false. The problem, I eventually realized, was that as playwright, I was *telling* the audience that a change had taken place, instead of *showing* the change as it took place.

In the final draft, I solved this dramatic problem by having Leo, who had loved music all his life, sit down at the piano and begin playing and singing Christmas carols while his surprised and relieved family joined in.

First silence, then singing, served my play better than mere telling.

III. *Create honest, understandable, and striking obstacles against which your protagonist must struggle.*

Many plays fail because their characters' problems seem too easily solved. I wrestled with this issue when I was writing *Oh Promise Me!*[3] a play that takes place in a private boarding house for the elderly. The play's original title was *Mr. Farner Wants a Double Bed*. The plot involved the attempt of an elderly man and woman—an unmarried couple—to share a double bed in a rooming house run by a repressed and oppressive owner. I wanted to explore contemporary attitudes toward the elderly, particularly as they concerned sexuality.

The more I played with the idea, the more I repeatedly heard an inner voice saying, "Chances are the couple could find some place to live where nobody cared if they were married or not." This voice—like the

---

3. Winner of the Jane Chambers Memorial Playwriting Award.

audience watching a play without an honest, understandable, convincing obstacle for the protagonist—kept saying, "So what?"

The writer's response: "Suppose, instead of a man and a woman, the couple is two men." Here was a real obstacle: Two elderly, gay men, growing feeble, want to sleep together in a double bed under the roof of an unsympathetic and unyielding landlord.

Suddenly, the play was off and running.

IV. *In the final scene or scenes, make sure your protagonist achieves what he wants; comes to understand that there is something* else *he wants; or accepts (defiantly, humbly, etc.) that he cannot have what he wants.*

If we spend time in the theater watching a character battle for something, we want to know the outcome—whatever it may be.

In my psychological thriller *Trick or Treat*,[4] Kate, a writer in her forties, has been badly burned in a love affair and is unable to decide whether to accept or reject a new relationship. She is involved at present with Toby, a younger man, but—as the following dialogue reveals—she insists on keeping him at a cool distance.

KATE
That does it, Toby. We're getting out of this place.
TOBY
Okay. Tomorrow we'll check into the local Howard Johnson's.
KATE
I want to go home—to New York—to my own apartment.
TOBY
Okay. Okay. If you insist. Besides, Howard Johnson's is not to be entered into lightly.
KATE
Huh?
TOBY
It's an old college rule. You'd never shell out for a room at Howard Johnson's—unless you were *very* serious about the girl.
KATE
I'll remember that. The day I agree to check into a Howard Johnson's—you'll know I've made a serious commitment to our relationship.

In the course of the play, Kate faces a number of trials—including a threat to her life—as she tries to expose the fraudulent leader of a

---

4. First produced by the Main Street Theater, New York, New York.

religious cult. Through these trials—with Toby by her side—Kate comes to realize that she's ready to forget the past and give herself over to a new relationship. This critical decision is humorously expressed in the last seconds of the play:

KATE

Do you love me, Toby?

TOBY

Yes, I do. I found that out tonight . . . when I thought I might be losing you forever. Do you love me?

KATE

Yes. And I can prove it.

TOBY

How?

KATE

Take me to Howard Johnson's—please! Take me to Howard Johnson's!

The curtain falls and the audience knows that the heroine has made an unequivocal decision.

V. *Make sure that the audience ultimately sympathizes with the protagonist's yearning to achieve his goal, however outlandish his behavior.*

This may be the most important of the five magic ingredients of conflict. It may also be the most elusive. To oversimplify, in a good play, the protagonist must be very likable and/or have a goal that is universal.

In the plays I've had produced, one character seems to win the sympathy of the audience hands down. In my romantic comedy *Funny Valentines,*[5] Andy Robbins, a writer of children's books, is that character. Andy is sloppy, disorganized, and easily distracted, and—this is his likable trait—he's painfully aware of his shortcomings and admits them openly. Here's Andy speaking for himself:

ANDY

Judging by my appearance, you might take me to be a complete physical and emotional wreck. Well, I can't deny it. And it's gotten worse—much worse—since Ellen left. You know that's true.

---

5. Published by Samuel French; winner of the Cummings/Taylor Playwriting Award; produced in Canada under the title *Drôles de Valentins.*

Andy is willing to admit his failings to old friends and strangers alike. Here he's talking to an attractive young woman he's just met.

ANDY

You don't have to be consoling just because I haven't finished a book lately. I won't burst into tears or create a scene. No. I lied. I might burst into tears—I'm warning you.

ZAN

I didn't mean to imply . . . (*She laughs.*)·

ANDY

Why are you laughing?

ZAN

You stapled your shirt.

ANDY

What's so odd about that? Millions of derelicts do it every day.

ZAN

And your glasses are wired together with a pipe cleaner.

ANDY

I didn't think twine would be as attractive.

In addition to liking Andy, audiences seem to sympathize with his goal of wanting to grow up and get back together with his collaborator and ex-wife, Ellen.

Whether you're wondering where to find an idea for a one-act play or beginning to refine the rough draft of a new full-length work or starting rehearsals of one of your plays, take your cue from the five magic ingredients of conflict. Whatever your experience as a playwright and whatever your current project, understanding the nature of dramatic conflict and how to achieve it will prove invaluable at every point in the writing and staging process.

* * *

Five exercises for creating dramatic conflict

Try these exercises to develop your skill in handling conflict.

1. Choose five plays you like. Summarize each in one sentence, stating what the protagonist wants. For example, Hamlet wants to avenge his father's murder.
2. Write one page of dialogue in which character A asks character B to do something that character B doesn't want to do. Have character A

make a request in three different ways, each showing a different emotion—guilt, enthusiasm, humility, anger.

3. Write a speech in which a character talks to another character and conveys what he wants without explicitly stating his goal.

4. Choose a famous play you enjoy. Rewrite the last page or two so that the outcome of the conflict for the protagonist is entirely different from the original.

5. Flip through today's newspaper until you find a story about a person—famous or unknown—who interests you. Then summarize the story in one sentence, stating what the person wants. For example: X wants to save an endangered species of bird. Next list the obstacles the person is facing in trying to get what he wants:

   • A developer wants to build a shopping mall where the remaining members of the endangered species live.

   • Pollution from a nearby factory is threatening the birds' food supply.

Finally, write several short scenes in which X (the protagonist) confronts the people (the antagonists) who represent the cause of each obstacle. (In this example, the antagonist would be the developer or the owner of the factory.) Decide which of the scenes you've written is the most dramatically satisfying. Identify the reasons you think it is the best scene.

▌100

PLAYS THAT JUMP OUT OF THE PILE

BY DAVID COPELIN

SCENE: *The script department of a major West Coast regional theater, 1977. The* LITERARY MANAGER *reads a new play. With mounting excitement, he runs up the stairs and into the office of the theater's* ARTISTIC DIRECTOR.

LITERARY MANAGER
We have to do this play, and you have to direct it!

ARTISTIC DIRECTOR
(laughing)
We *have* to do this play? You never say things like that.

LITERARY MANAGER
I'm saying it now. This one's special!
(*The* ARTISTIC DIRECTOR *reads the script and agrees with the* LITERARY MANAGER *that it is eminently suitable for the theater. The West Coast premiere of Ted Tally's* Terra Nova *is a notable success.*)

I was that literary manager.
["Literary managers" serve as script readers in the American not-for-profit theater. They are generally experts on theatrical texts who advise other theater artists on the dramatic merits of classical, modern and contemporary plays. Many also write extensive program notes, and moderate pre- or post-performance discussions with audiences. "Dramaturgs" often have similar functions, but go beyond script reading by helping producers decide which plays to include in their seasons. They may also contribute research services to playwrights and directors, and many offer an "objective eye" in rehearsals. Both literary managers and

dramaturgs have been known to function as gadflies, sounding-boards, and general artistic resources for their theaters. Some also write, translate, adapt, direct and/or act in plays.]

When I was asked to give some advice to aspiring playwrights, I started thinking about the plays that have persuaded me to recommend them strongly to the producers I've worked for. What made them special? What authorial choices and techniques elicit enthusiasm from this professional script reader? Though I respect many of the new plays I read, I fight hard for very few. But those plays that inspire me and give me energy make me want to work hard to get them produced. Let's examine a few of these to see what general principles underlie their effectiveness.

Five such plays come to mind: *Terra Nova* by Ted Tally. *The Conduct of Life* by Maria Irene Fornes. *Ashes* by David Rudkin. *A Knife in the Heart* by Susan Yankowitz. And—no, I think I'll let the fifth play remain a secret for now.

*   *   *

Terra Nova struck me so forcefully because it creates a unique world—the tragic Antarctica of Robert F. Scott—and because the conflict between Scott's doomed idealism and Roald Amundsen's more successful pragmatism is viscerally embodied in the struggle of Scott and his teammates to survive their own mistakes. The play's visual, verbal, thematic, and emotional elements combine in a strong, dramatically clear fashion. I was persuaded of the importance of the story by its romantic, mythical qualities, which gave it "size" and resonance. The play is very much about Scott and his men. It is also very much about two different ways of looking at life, and about the gains and losses that each vision entails.

Principle #1: *Make sure that both your story and your theme are vivid and pungent.* The theme should derive complexly from the story. Plays that merely illustrate platitudes are reductive and bland.

Principle #2: *Give both sides of your conflict approximately equal weight for as long as you can.* If one side is too obviously the side you want the audience to take, they'll be bored. Boring is not good.

Terra Nova was ideal for the theater I was working for because that theater is well known for producing plays of social import. Moreover, the artistic director's directing talents were extremely well suited to the play. A script that engages the gifts of a theater's resident artists obviously has an easier time getting produced there than one that does not. Furthermore, the play's physical demands fit right into the theater's performance space.

Principle #3: *Learn as much as possible about a theater's history, taste, resident artists and performance spaces before submitting your play.* You'll save time and money, and you'll minimize rejection.

* * *

I saw Maria Irene Fornes's production of *The Conduct of Life* in New York in 1985. Her writing is mysterious, enormously affecting and quite unlike anyone else's. This play tells a simple story about events in the household of a member of a military junta that governs an unnamed Latin American country. A domestic tale, it focuses on the women of the house, how they behave when the man is at home, and how they behave when he is elsewhere. Irene deals with the repetitive activities of daily life, with characters, actions and objects that look familiar to us. In Irene's hands, though, that familiarity is deceptive.

The Conduct of Life showed me something crucial about the relationship between public *machismo* and the private brutality, shame, and hypocrisy that are often concealed within homes that supposedly believe in "family values." Not because the playwright makes this relationship obvious; in fact, it's never mentioned. Her delicacy and her indirect way of giving information combine with her painterly sense of the stage to make her subtle insights emotionally and dramatically effective.

Principle #4: *Plays of indirect action can be as affecting as plays of direct action.* But you need a poetic sensibility to write them well.

Principle #5: *Metaphors are generally more powerful than statements.* At the time, I was working for a theater in Washington, D.C. I gave copies of the Fornes play to my superiors there, but they did not respond to it with enthusiasm. That's something else that's out of a playwright's hands: A literary manager may believe in your work and fight for it, but sometimes lose the battle. A theater may feel that your play, however well written, may not interest audiences in sufficient numbers to justify the expense of production. It's a judgment call. Since theaters' resources are limited, a kind of artistic triage is inevitable. When a theater rejects your scripts, it doesn't mean that there's anything wrong with it—or even that the readers think there is.

Principle #6: *If a theater doesn't feel compelled to produce your play, it's better for you if it doesn't produce it.*

When a play I like is rejected by a theater I'm working for, I try to find a home for it elsewhere. My efforts have occasionally helped secure productions for writers whose work I think deserves an audience. Besides, producers can change their minds about a new play once another theater has risked that crucial first staging and been successful. That's why literary managers keep an "I told you so" list.

Principle #7: *You never know.* A theater that initially rejects your script may be more receptive to it after it's been produced elsewhere. Many producers base their programming decisions on reviews rather than on scripts. And sometimes, scripts improve during the rehearsal process. On the other hand, some theaters still suffer from the "virgin play" syndrome—if it's been done, it's been undone, and they don't want it.

I didn't have to fight very hard for British playwright David Rudkin's *Ashes*. It had been produced in England before the artistic director of that same West Coast theater read it, in 1975. He passed it on to me without comment. I found it a magnificent piece of work.

Ashes is about a couple determined to have a child. Slowly, however, they come to terms with the fact that they cannot do so and will not be allowed to adopt one. Clinical, occasionally vulgar, even brutal, the play nevertheless has its own knotty poetry and a refreshing lack of sentimentality. I found its characters intelligent and sensitive, its structure highly theatrical, its understanding of the connection between private agony and public conflict profound. I thought it was an admirable, difficult, beautiful play that would be controversial.

My artistic director thought so, too. Then he asked, "And can it fill our 742 seats for eight performances a week for six weeks?" We both doubted it. But we agreed that somehow, we had to do this play, that our theater was *about* just such turbulent, adult, rewarding material. If we passed up the chance to mount the American premiere of *Ashes,* we'd regret it.

Ashes became part of a four-play repertory package that filled an extended production slot. The play engendered fierce arguments, with audiences and critics strongly divided about its merits. I was proud to work for a theater that could recognize the play's quality, then alter its usual producing structure to bring that play before the public.

Principle #8: *A truly unusual and provocative treatment of a subject close to people's hearts will get a theater's full attention.*

I read Susan Yankowitz's *A Knife in the Heart* when I was between dramaturgical gigs. Not having a boss to recommend it to, I mentioned it to every literary manager and artistic director I knew. This play is one of the scariest, saddest, most honest scripts I've ever read.

It's about a murderer, a gifted, twisted boy who is driven by some inexplicable urge to kill the governor of his state. His father is limp and ineffectual, and his mother dotes on him, but this is true of many people who do not become killers. The horror of the play, in fact, is that no explanation for the boy's action makes any sense. Neighbors, psychiatrists, clergymen, and others offer reasons, but all sound glib, facile and self-serving. What happens, happens, and both his family and the audience must adjust to the cold facts of random, irrational violence. This is hard enough to do in real life, but it is especially difficult to confront the notion of inexplicability in the theater—the place where so many of us come to be enlightened, helped to understand the world, shown the way to a better tomorrow. This play dares to say that some things cannot be understood. They must be endured.

Principle #9: *Be patient.* Plays with difficult themes and non-mainstream points of view may take longer to receive stagings than more immediately accessible or crowd-pleasing work. Remember, Ibsen, Brecht, Shepard, and others eventually found their public. So may you.

A Knife in the Heart eventually was produced—in circumstances practically guaranteed to sink the play without a trace. The artistic director of a major summer theater decided to stage the play himself, but neither his largely tourist audience nor his own skills as a director served the text properly. The production was a disaster. This did nothing to make the play attractive to other theater managements.

Principle #10: *Be very careful about who premieres your play.* A wretched first production may make it nearly impossible to find another.

As for the fifth play I've been excited by: It's *The Foreigner,* by the late Larry Shue. What, you ask, is a popular farce doing on my otherwise highfalutin list?

In 1981, when I first read *The Foreigner,* the play had been commissioned and produced by the Milwaukee Repertory Theatre, but was not yet the international box-office success that it has since become. I read it for New York's Phoenix Theatre (now defunct), and my response to the play was highly unusual. Normally, I despise ramshackle cornpone comedies, which *The Foreigner* surely is—but it made me laugh my head off. I could have suppressed my reaction on theoretical grounds, or because of simple embarrassment, but instead I passed the play to my artistic director with a strong recommendation. Alas, the play was under option to producers whose plans did not include the Phoenix.

My problem with genre plays is that so few of them are of more than routine interest. Somehow, *The Foreigner* got past all my customary defenses, and this fact alone made me pay attention to it. Then, too, it's truly funny. The playwright had brought new life to tired conventions with his wit, his actor's sensibility, and his instinctive command of stagecraft. He also had a wonderful way with words, and rarest of rarities, he could write plays that are silly without being stupid. On the surface, *The Foreigner* seems merely entertaining, yet it appeals as much to intellectuals as it does to average theatergoers.

Principle #11: *If you write a genre play, transcend the genre!*

In one way or another, my five plays grabbed me by the throat, forced me to listen to what they had to say, and reminded me why I work in theater in the first place. Every script reader, literary manager, and dramaturg can come up with a similar list of plays that have impressed him or her, though many of us would disagree with each other's choices. That's fortunate; the more variety in theaters' programming, the more chance that your script may find a sympathetic response somewhere. It's a big country with lots of theaters. But you have to find a way to make your play "jump out of the pile" that is on every script reader's desk. Not by using fancy binding or odd-colored paper, not by writing overly detailed stage directions, and certainly not by trying to imitate the style of some currently popular playwright. We already have an August Wilson, a Harold Pinter, a Caryl Churchill, a David Mamet, a Wendy Wasserstein. What we want is *you*.

Where to Sell

This year's edition of *The Writer's Handbook* includes a completely revised and updated list of free-lance markets, and writers at all levels of experience should be encouraged by the number and wide variety of opportunities available to them. Editors, publishers, and producers rely on free lancers for a wide range of material, from articles and fiction to play scripts, op-ed pieces, how-tos, and children's books, and they are very receptive to the work of newcomers.

The field of specialized publications, including travel, city and regional magazines, and those covering such areas as health, science, consumer issues, sports, and hobbies and crafts, remains one of the best markets for beginning free lancers. Editors of these magazines are in constant need of authoritative articles (for which the payment is usually quite high), and writers with experience in and enthusiasm for a particular field, whether it's gardening, woodworking, bicycling, stamp collecting, bridge, or car repair, will find their knowledge particularly helpful, as there is usually at least one publication devoted to every one of these areas. Such interests and activities can generate more than one article if a different angle is used for each magazine and the writer keeps the audience and editorial content firmly in mind.

The market for technical, computer, health, and personal finance writing is also very strong, with articles on these topics appearing in almost every publication on the newsstands today. For these subjects, editors are looking for writers who can translate technical material into lively, readable prose, often the most important factor in determining a sale.

While some of the more established markets may seem difficult to break into, especially for the beginner, there are thousands of lesser-known publications where editors will consider submissions from first-time free lancers. City and regional publications offer some of the best opportunities, since these editors generally like to work with local writers and often use a wide variety of material, from features to fillers. Many newspapers accept op-ed pieces, and are most receptive to pieces on topics not covered by syndicated columnists (politics, economics, and foreign affairs); pieces with a regional slant are particularly welcome here.

It is important for writers to keep in mind the number of opportunities that exist for nonfiction, because the paying markets for fiction are somewhat limited. Many general-interest and women's magazines do publish short stories; however, beginners will find these markets extremely competitive, with their work being judged against that of experienced professionals. We highly recommend that new writers look into the small, literary, and college publications, which always welcome the work of talented beginners. Payment usually is made only in copies, but publication in literary journals can lead to recognition by editors of larger circulation magazines, who often look to the smaller publications for new talent. A growing number of regional, specialized, and Sunday magazines use short stories and are particularly interested in local writers.

The market for poetry in general-interest magazines continues to be tight, and the advice for poets, as for fiction writers, is to try to get established and build up a list of publishing credits by submitting material to literary journals. Poets should look also to local newspapers, which often use verse, especially if it is related to holidays or other special occasions.

Community, regional, and civic theaters and college dramatic groups offer new playwrights the best opportunities for staged production in this competitive market. Indeed, many of today's well-known playwrights received their first recognition in regional theaters, and aspiring writers who can get their work produced by one of these have taken a significant step toward breaking into this field. In addition to producing plays and giving dramatic readings, many theaters also sponsor competitions or new play festivals.

As for the television market, unfortunately it is inaccessible without an agent, and most writers break into it only after a careful study of the medium and a long apprenticeship.

While the book publishing field remains competitive, beginners should be especially encouraged by the many first novels published over the past few years, with more editors than ever before seeking out new works of fiction. An increasing number of publishers are broadening their nonfiction lines as well, and editors at many hardcover and paperback houses are on the lookout for new authors, especially those with a knowledge of or training in a particular field. Writers of juvenile and young adult books will be pleased to hear that in response to a growing audience of young readers and increased sales, many publishers are greatly expanding their lists of children's books.

Small presses across the country continue to flourish—in fact, they are currently publishing more books by name authors and more books on mainstream subjects, than at any other time in recent years—offering writers an attractive alternative for their manuscripts.

All information in these lists concerning the needs and requirements of magazines, book publishing companies, and theaters comes directly from the editors, publishers, and directors, but editors move and addresses change, as do requirements. No published listing can give as clear a picture of editorial needs and tastes as a careful study of several issues of a magazine, and writers should never submit material without first thoroughly researching the prospective market. If a magazine is not available in the local library, write directly to the editor for a sample copy (often sent free or at a small cost). Contact the publicity department of a book publisher for an up-to-date catalogue or a theater for a current schedule. Many companies also offer a formal set of writers guidelines, available for an SASE upon request.

ARTICLE MARKETS

The magazines in the following list are in the market for free-lance articles of many types. Unless otherwise stated in these listings, a writer should submit a query first, including a brief description of the proposed article and any relevant qualifications or credits. A few editors want to see samples of published work, if available. Manuscripts must be typed double-space on good white bond paper (8½ × 11), with name, address, and telephone number at the top left- or right-hand corner of the paper. Do not use erasable or onion skin paper, since it is difficult to work with, and always keep a copy of the manuscript, in case it is lost in the mail. Submit photos or slides *only* if the editor has specifically requested them. A self-addressed envelope with sufficient postage to cover the return of the manuscript or the answer to a query should accompany all submissions. Response time may vary from two to eight weeks, depending on the size of the magazine and the volume of mail it receives. If an editor doesn't respond within what seems to be a reasonable amount of time, it's perfectly acceptable to send a polite inquiry. Many publications have writers guidelines, outlining their editorial requirements and submission procedures; these can be obtained by sending a self-addressed, stamped envelope (SASE) to the editor. Also, be sure to ask for a sample copy: Editors indicate the most consistent mistake free lancers make is failing to study several issues of the magazine to which they are submitting material.

GENERAL-INTEREST PUBLICATIONS

ACCENT—P.O. Box 10010, Ogden, UT 84409. Caroll Shreeve, Pub. Articles, 1,200 words, about destinations in the U.S. and Canada. Must include tranparencies. Query. Pays 15¢ a word and $35 to $50 for photos, on acceptance.

AMERICAN HERITAGE—60 Fifth Ave., New York, NY 10011. Byron Dobell, Ed. Articles, 750 to 5,000 words, on U.S. history and background of American life and culture from the beginning to recent times. No fiction. Pays from $300 to $1,500, on acceptance. Query. SASE.

AMERICAN HISTORY ILLUSTRATED—2245 Kohn Rd., P.O. Box 8200, Harrisburg, PA 17105. Articles, 3,000 to 5,000 words, well researched. Style should be popular, not scholarly. No travelogues, fiction, or puzzles. Pays $200 to $1,000, on acceptance. Query.

THE AMERICAN LEGION MAGAZINE—Box 1055, Indianapolis, IN 46206. Daniel S. Wheeler, Ed.-in-Chief. Articles, 750 to 1,800 words, on current world affairs, public policy, and subjects of contemporary interest. Pays $100 to $1,000, on acceptance. Query.

AMERICAN VISIONS, THE MAGAZINE OF AFRO AMERICAN CULTURE—The Carter G. Woodson House, 1538 9th St. N.W., Washington, DC 20001. Joanne Harris, Ed. Articles, 1,500 to 4,000 words, and columns, 750 to 2,000 words, on people and events that contribute significantly to black culture and heritage. Pays from $100 to $1,000, on publication. Query first.

AMERICAS—OAS, 19th and Constitution Ave. N.W., Washington, DC 20006. Rebecca Read Medrano, Ed. Features, 2,500 to 5,000 words, on Latin America and the Caribbean. Wide focus: anthropology, the arts, travel, science, and development, etc. No political material. Query. Pays from $250, on publication.

AMTRAK EXPRESS—140 E. Main St., Suite 11, Huntington, NY 11743. Christopher Podgus, Ed. General-interest articles on business, health, books, sports, personal finance, lifestyle, entertainment, travel (within Amtrak territory), science for Amtrak travelers. Submit seasonal material three to six months in advance. Pays on publication, $300 to $700 for 1,500- to 2,000-word manuscript. Query with published clips.

THE ATLANTIC—745 Boylston St., Boston, MA 02116. William Whitworth, Ed. In-depth articles on public issues, politics, social sciences, education, business, literature, and the arts. Ideal length: 3,000 to 6,000 words, though short pieces (1,000 to 2,000 words) are also welcome. Pays excellent rates.

BETTER HOMES AND GARDENS—1716 Locust St., Des Moines, IA 50336. David Jordan, Ed. Articles, to 2,000 words, on home and family entertainment, building, decorating, food, money management, health, travel, pets, environment, and cars. Pays top rates, on acceptance. Query.

BON APPETIT—5900 Wilshire Blvd., Los Angeles, CA 90036. Barbara Fairchild, Exec. Ed. Articles on fine cooking (menu format or single focus), cooking classes, and gastronomically-focused travel. Query with samples of published work. Pays varying rates, on acceptance.

CAPPER'S—616 Jefferson St., Topeka, KS 66607. Nancy Peavler, Ed. Articles, 300 to 500 words: human-interest, personal experience for women's section, historical. Pays varying rates, on publication.

CAPSTONE JOURNAL OF EDUCATION—P.O. Box 870231, Tuscaloosa, AL 35487–0231. Alexia M. Kartis, Asst. Ed. Articles, to 5,000 words, on contemporary ideas in education. Guidelines.

CHATELAINE—MacLean Hunter Bldg., 777 Bay St., Toronto, Ont., Canada M5W 1A7. Elizabeth Parr, Sr. Ed. Articles, 1,500 to 3,500 words, for Canadian women, on current issues, personalities, medicine, psychology, etc., covering all aspects of Canadian life. "Upfront" columns, 500 words, on relationships, health, nutrition, fitness, parenting. Pays from $350 for columns, from $1,250 for features, on acceptance.

THE CHRISTIAN SCIENCE MONITOR—One Norway St., Boston, MA 02115. David Holmstrom, Feature Ed. Articles, 800 words, on arts, education, food, sports, science, and lifestyle; interviews, literary essays for "Home Forum" page; guest columns for "Opinion Page." Pay varies, on acceptance. Original material only.

COLUMBIA—1 Columbus Plaza, New Haven, CT 06507–0901. Richard McMunn, Ed. Journal of the Knights of Columbus. Articles, 500 to 1,500 words, on a wide variety of topics of interest to K. of C. members, their families, and the Catholic layman: current events, religion, education, art, etc. Must include substantial quotes from a variety of sources and must be illustrated with color transparencies. Pays $250 to $500, inclusive of art, on acceptance.

THE COMPASS—Grand Central Towers, 230 E. 44th St., Suite 14B, New York, NY 10017. J.A. Randall, Ed. True stories, to 2,500 words, on the sea, sea trades, and aviation. Pays to $600, on acceptance. Query.

CONSUMERS DIGEST—5705 N. Lincoln Ave., Chicago, IL 60659. John Manos, Ed. Articles, 500 to 3,000 words, on subjects of interest to consumers: products and services, automobiles, health, fitness, consumer legal affairs, and personal money management. Photos. Pays from 35¢ to 50¢ a word, extra for photos, on publication. Buys all rights. Query with resumé and published clips.

COSMOPOLITAN—224 W. 57th St., New York, NY 10019. Helen Gurley Brown, Ed. Guy Flatley, Man. Ed. Articles, to 3,500 words, and features, 500 to 2,500 words, on issues affecting young career women. Query.

COUNTRY—5400 S. 60th, Greendale, WI 53129. Deb Mulvey, Assoc. Ed. People-centered articles, 500 to 1,000 words, for a rural audience. (No articles on production techniques.) Fillers, 50 to 200 words. Taboos: tobacco, liquor, and sex. Pays $125 to $200, on acceptance. Query.

COUNTRY JOURNAL—P.O. Box 8200, 2245 Kohn Rd., Harrisburg, PA 17105. Peter V. Fossel, Ed. Articles, 2,500 to 3,000 words, for country and small town residents; practical, informative pieces, essays, humor, and reports on contemporary rural life. Pays $500 to $1,500, on acceptance. Query with SASE.

DALLAS LIFE MAGAZINE—*The Dallas Morning News*, Communications Center, Dallas, TX 75265. Melissa Houtte, Ed. Well-researched articles and profiles, 1,000 to 3,000 words, on contemporary issues, personalities, on subjects of strictly Dallas-related interest. Pays 20¢ and up a word, on acceptance. Query.

DAWN—628 N. Eutaw, Baltimore, MD 21201. Charles Brown, Ed. Illustrated feature articles, 750 to 1,000 words, on subjects of interest to black families. Pays $100, on publication. Query.

DIVERSION MAGAZINE—60 E. 42nd St., Suite 2424, New York, NY 10165. Stephen Birnbaum, Ed. Dir. Articles, 1,200 to 2,500 words, on travel, sports, hobbies, entertainment, food, etc., of interest to physicians at leisure. Photos. Pays from $400, on acceptance. Query.

EBONY—820 S. Michigan, Chicago, IL 60603. Lerone Bennett, Jr., Exec. Ed. Articles, with photos, on blacks: achievements, civil rights, etc. Pays from $150, on publication. Query.

THE ELKS MAGAZINE—425 W. Diversey Parkway, Chicago, IL 60614. Fred D. Oakes, Ed. Articles, 3,000 words, on business, sports, and topics of current interest, for non-urban audience with above-average income. Informative or humorous pieces, to 2,500 words. Pays $150 to $500 for articles, on acceptance. Query.

ESQUIRE—1790 Broadway, New York, NY 10019. David Hirshey, Articles Ed. Lisa Grunwald, Features Ed. Articles, 2,500 to 4,000 words, for intelligent adult audience. Pay varies, on acceptance. Query with published clips; complete manuscripts from unpublished writers. SASE required.

ESSENCE—1500 Broadway, New York, NY 10036. Susan L. Taylor, Ed.-in-Chief. Provocative articles, 1,500 to 2,500 words, about black women in America today: self-help, how-to pieces, business and finance, health, celebrity profiles, and political issues. Short items, 300 to 750 words, on work, parenting, and health. Query required; send complete manuscript for "Brothers," "Interiors," and "Back Talk" departments. Pays varying rates, on acceptance.

FAMILY CIRCLE—110 Fifth Ave., New York, NY 10011. Susan Ungaro, Exec. Ed. Ellen Stoianoff, Sr. Ed., Nancy Josephson, Health Ed. Articles, to 2,500 words, on "women who have made a difference," marriage, family, and child-rearing issues; consumer affairs, health and fitness, humor and personal opinion essays. Query required. Pays $1 a word, on acceptance.

FORD TIMES—One Illinois Center, 111 E. Wacker Dr., Suite 1700, Chicago, IL 60601. Scott Powers, Ed. Articles for a family audience, particularly geared to ages 18 to 35: topical pieces (trends, lifestyles); profiles; first-person accounts of unusual vacation trips or real-life adventures; unusual sporting events or outdoor activities; food and cooking; humor. Bright, lively photos desired. Travel and dining anecdotes for "Road Show"; pays $50, on publication. Payment for articles, 1,200 to 1,700 words, is $550 to $800; $400 for 800 to 1,200 words; and $250 for short pieces (500 to 800 words), on acceptance. Query with SASE required for all but humor.

GLAMOUR—350 Madison Ave., New York, NY 10017. Ruth Whitney, Ed.-in-Chief. Lisa Bain, Art. Ed. Articles on careers, health, psychology, interpersonal relationships, etc. Editorial approach is "how-to" for women, 18 to 35. Fashion, health, and beauty material staff written. Pays from $1,000 for 1,500- to 2,000-word articles, from $1,500 for longer pieces, on acceptance.

GLOBE—5401 N.W. Broken Sound Blvd., Boca Raton, FL 33487. Charlie Montgomery, Exec. Ed. Factual articles, 500 to 1,000 words, with photos: exposés, celebrity interviews, consumer and human-interest pieces. Pays $50 to $1,500.

GOLDEN YEARS—233 E. New Haven Ave., Melbourne, FL 32902–0537. Carol Brenner Hittner, Ed. Bimonthly for people over the age of 50. Pieces on unique hobbies, beauty and fashion, sports, and travel, 500 words. Pays 10¢ a word, on publication.

GOOD HOUSEKEEPING—959 Eighth Ave., New York, NY 10019. Joan Thursh, Articles Ed. Personal-experience articles, 2,500 words, on a unique or trend-setting event; family relationships; personal medical pieces dealing with an unusual illness, treatment, and result; personal problems and how they were solved. Short essays, 750 to 1,000 words, on family life or relationships. Pays top rates, on acceptance. Queries preferred. Guidelines.

GOOD READING MAGAZINE—Litchfield, IL 62056. Peggy Kuethe, Assoc. Ed. Articles, 500 to 1,000 words, with B&W photos, on current subjects of general interest; travel, business, personal experiences, relationships. Pays $10 to $100.

GRIT—208 W. Third St., Williamsport, PA 17701. Alvin Elmer, Assoc. Ed. Articles, to 800 words, with photos, on interesting people, communities, jobs, recreation, families, and coping. Pays 15¢ a word, extra for photos, on acceptance.

HARPER'S BAZAAR—1700 Broadway, New York, NY 10019. Anthony Mazzola, Ed.-in-Chief. Articles, 1,500 to 2,000 words, for active, sophisticated women. Topics include the arts, world affairs, food, wine, travel, families, education, personal finance, careers, health, and sexuality. No unsolicited manuscripts; query first with SASE. Payment varies, on acceptance.

HARPER'S MAGAZINE—666 Broadway, New York, NY 10012. Address Managing Editor. Articles, 2,000 to 5,000 words. Query first for nonfiction.

HISTORIC PRESERVATION—1785 Massachusetts Ave. N.W., Washington, DC 20036. Anne Elizabeth Powell, Ed. Lively feature articles from published writers, 1,500 to 4,000 words, on residential restoration, preservation issues, and people involved in preserving America's heritage. High-quality photos. Pays $300 to $1,000, extra for photos, on acceptance. Query.

HOUSE BEAUTIFUL—1700 Broadway, New York, NY 10019. Elaine Greene, Ed. Service articles related to the home. Pieces on architecture, design, travel, and gardening; mostly staff-written. Pays varying rates, on acceptance. Query with detailed outline. Guidelines.

INQUIRER MAGAZINE—*Philadelphia Inquirer*, P.O. Box 8263, 400 N. Broad St., Philadelphia, PA 19101. Fred Mann, Ed. Local-interest features, 500 to 7,000 words. Profiles of national figures in politics, entertainment, etc. Pays varying rates, on publication. Query.

INSIDE MAGAZINE—226 S. 16th St., Philadelphia, PA 19102. Jane Biberman, Ed. Articles, 1,000 to 3,000 words, on Jewish issues and the arts. Queries required; send clips if available. Pays $75 to $600, within 4 weeks of acceptance.

KIWANIS—3636 Woodview Trace, Indianapolis, IN 46268. Chuck Jonak, Exec. Ed. Articles, 2,500 to 3,000 words, on home; family; international issues; the social, health, and emotional needs of youth (especially under 6-years-old); career and community concerns of business and professional people. No travel pieces, interviews, profiles. Pays $400 to $1,000, on acceptance. Query.

LADIES' HOME JOURNAL—100 Park Ave., New York, NY 10017. Lynn Langway, Exec. Ed. Jane Farrell, Articles Ed. Articles on contemporary subjects of interest to women. Personal-experience and regional pieces. Query required. Not responsible for unsolicited manuscripts.

LISTEN MAGAZINE—12501 Old Columbia Pike, Silver Spring, MD 20904. Gary B. Swanson, Ed. Articles, 1,200 to 1,500 words, on problems of alcohol and drug abuse, for teenagers; personality profiles. Photos. Pays 5¢ to 7¢ a word, extra for photos, on acceptance. Query. Guidelines.

MCCALL'S—230 Park Ave., New York, NY 10169. Anne Mollegen Smith, Ed.-in-Chief. Andrea Thompson, Articles Ed. Interesting, unusual, and topical narratives, reports on social trends relating to women of all ages, 1,000 to 3,000 words. Mothers' experiences. Human interest stories. Pays top rates, on acceptance.

MADEMOISELLE—350 Madison Ave., New York, NY 10017. Liz Logan, Articles Ed. Articles, 1,500 to 2,000 words, on subjects of interest to single, working women in ther 20s. Pays from $1,750 for full-length articles, on acceptance. Query.

MAGAZINE OF THE MIDLANDS—*The Omaha World-Herald*, World Herald Sq., Omaha, NE 68102. David Hendee, Ed. Regional-interest articles and profiles, 400 to 2,000 words, with tie-in to Omaha and the Midwest. Pays $40 to $150, on publication. Query.

MARRIAGE & FAMILY —Abbey Press Publishing Div., St. Meinrad, IN 47577. Kass Dotterweich, Man. Ed. Articles, 1,500 to 1,700 words, on husband-wife and parent-child relationships; faith dimension essential. Pays 7¢ a word, on acceptance. Query.

MD MAGAZINE—10 Astor Pl., New York, NY 10003. Richard J. Litell, Ed. Articles, 750 to 2,500 words, for doctors, on the arts, history, other aspects of culture; fresh angle required. Pays 50¢ to $1 per word, on acceptance. Query by mail only.

METROPOLITAN HOME—750 Third Ave., New York, NY 10017. Service and informational articles for residents of houses, co-ops, lofts, and condominiums, on real estate, equity, wine and spirits, collecting, trends, travel, etc. Interior design and home furnishing articles with emphasis on lifestyle. Pay varies. Query.

MODERN MATURITY—3200 East Carson St., Lakewood, CA 90712. Ian Ledgerwood, Ed. Articles on careers, workplace, human interest, living, finance, relationships, and consumerism, for persons over 50 years, to 2,000 words. Photos. Pays $500 to $2,500, extra for photos, on acceptance. Query first.

THE MOTHER EARTH NEWS—80 Fifth Ave., New York, NY 10011. Alfred Meyer, Ed. Articles, with photos, for rural and urban readers: home improvements, how-tos, indoor and outdoor gardening, family pastimes, etc. Also, self-help, health, food-related, ecology, energy, and consumerism pieces. Pays varying rates, on acceptance. Guidelines.

MOTHER JONES—1663 Mission St., San Francisco, CA 94103. Doug Foster, Ed. Investigative articles, political essays, cultural analyses. "OutFront" pieces, 250 words, about change, "either good, bad, or strange." Pays $750 to $2,000, after acceptance. Query in writing only; do not FAX.

MS.—One Times Square, New York, NY 10036. Address Manuscript Ed. Articles relating to feminism, women's roles, and societal change; reporting, profiles, essays, theory, and analysis. Pays market rates. Query with SASE required.

NATIONAL ENQUIRER—Lantana, FL 33464. Articles, of any length, for mass audience: topical news, the occult, how-to, scientific discoveries, human drama, adventure, personalities. Photos. Pays from $325. Query; no unsolicited manuscripts accepted.

NATIONAL EXAMINER—5401 N.W. Broken Sound Blvd., Boca Raton, FL 33431. Cliff Linedecker, Exec. Ed. Celebrity interviews and human-interest pieces, 500 to 1,000 words. Must be well documented. Pays varying rates, on acceptance. Query required.

NEW WOMAN—215 Lexington Ave., New York, NY 10016. Gay Bryant, Ed. "Read the magazine in order to become familiar with our needs before querying." Articles on self discovery, work, building a business, marriage, relationships, surviving divorce, health and diets, adventure. Pays varying rates, on acceptance. Query with SASE.

NEW YORK—755 Second Ave., New York, NY 10017. Edward Kosner, Ed. Laurie Jones, Man. Ed. Feature articles of interest to New Yorkers. The magazine focuses on current events in the metropolitan New York area. Pays from $850 to $3,500, on acceptance. Query required; not responsible for unsolicited material.

THE NEW YORK ANTIQUE ALMANAC—Box 335, Lawrence, NY 11559. Carol Nadel, Ed. Articles on antiques, shows, shops, art, investments, collectibles, collecting suggestions, nostalgia, related humor. Photos. Pays $5 to $75, extra for photos, on publication.

THE NEW YORK TIMES MAGAZINE—229 W. 43rd St., New York, NY 10036. Address Articles Ed. Timely articles approximately 4,000 words, on news items, forthcoming events, trends, culture, entertainment, etc. Pays $350 to $500 for short pieces, $1,000 to $2,500 for major articles, on acceptance. Query with clips.

THE NEW YORKER—25 W. 43rd St., New York, NY 10036. Address the Editors. Factual and biographical articles for "Profiles," "Reporter at Large," etc. Pays good rates, on acceptance. Query.

NEWSWEEK—444 Madison Ave., New York, NY 10022. Original opinion essays, 1,000 to 1,100 words, for "My Turn" column: must contain verifiable facts. Submit manuscript with SASE. Pays $1,000, on publication.

OMNI—1965 Broadway, New York, NY 10023–5965. Patrice Adcroft, Ed. Articles, 2,500 to 3,000 words, on scientific aspects of the future: space, machine intelligence, ESP, origin of life, future arts, lifestyles, etc. Pays $750 to $4,000, less for short features, on acceptance. Query.

PARADE—750 Third Ave., New York, NY 10017. Fran Carpentier, Sr. Articles Ed. National Sunday newspaper supplement. Factual and authoritative articles, 1,000 to 1,500 words, on subjects of national interest: health, education, consumer and environmental issues, science, the family, sports, etc. Profiles of well-known personalities and service pieces. No fiction, poetry, games, or puzzles. Photos with captions. Pays from $1,000. Query.

PENTHOUSE—1965 Broadway, New York, NY 10023–5965. Peter Bloch, Ed. Robert Sabat, Man. Ed. General-interest or controversial articles, to 5,000 words. Pays from 20¢ a word, on acceptance.

PEOPLE IN ACTION—Box 10010, Ogden, UT 84409. Caroll Shreve, Pub. Features, 1,200 words, on nationally noted individuals in the fine arts, literature, entertainment, communications, business, sports, education, etc. Must exemplify positive values. Manuscripts should be accompanied by high-quality color transparencies. Query. Pays 15¢ a word and $35 to $50 for photos, on acceptance.

PEOPLE WEEKLY—Time-Life Bldg., Rockefeller Ctr., New York, NY 10020. Hal Wingo, Asst. Man. Ed. Considers article proposals only, 3 to 4 paragraphs, on timely, entertaining, and topical personalities. Pays good rates, on acceptance. Most material staff written.

PHILIP MORRIS MAGAZINE—153 Waverly Pl., 3rd Floor, New York, NY 10014. Frank Gannon, Ed. Profiles of American innovators, entertainers, sports figures, animal conservationists. Also U.S. travel destinations, food. Pays on publication.

PLAYBOY—680 N. Lakeshore Dr., Chicago, IL 60611. John Rezek, Articles Ed. Sophisticated articles, 4,000 to 6,000 words, of interest to urban men. Humor: satire. Pays to $3,000, on acceptance. Query.

PRIME TIMES—2802 International Ln., Suite 120, Madison, WI 53704. Rod Clark, Assignment Ed. Articles, 500 to 1,800 words, for dynamic, creative mid-lifers. Departments, 850 to 1,000 words. Pays $125 to $750, on publication. Query. Guidelines with SASE.

PSYCHOLOGY TODAY—80 Fifth Ave., New York, NY 10011. Talley Sue Hohlfeld, Man. Ed. Lively articles, 2,500 to 3,000 words, and short news items about timely subjects and people, not limited to research findings of social scientists and the insights of psychotherapists; jargon free. Department pieces, 1,200 to 1,500 words, on health, work, relationships, the brain, etc. Pays good rates, on publication.

READER'S DIGEST—Pleasantville, NY 10570. Kenneth O. Gilmore, Ed.-in-Chief. Unsolicited manuscripts will not be read or returned. General-interest articles already in print and well-developed story proposals will be considered. Send reprint or query to any editor on the masthead.

REDBOOK—224 W. 57th St., New York, NY 10019. Annette Capone, Ed.-in-Chief. Diane Salvatore, Sr. Ed. Toni Gerber Hope, Articles Ed. Articles, 1,000 to 3,500 words, on subjects related to relationships, sex, current issues, marriage, the family, and parenting. Pays from $750, on acceptance. Query.

ROLLING STONE—745 Fifth Ave., New York, NY 10151. Magazine of modern American culture, politics, and art. No fiction. Query; "rarely accepts free-lance material."

THE ROTARIAN—1560 Sherman Ave., Evanston, IL 60201. Willmon L. White, Ed. Articles, 1,200 to 2,000 words, on international social and economic issues, business and management, human relationships, travel, sports, environment, science and technology; humor. Pays good rates, on acceptance. Query.

SATELLITE ORBIT—8330 Boone Blvd., Suite 600, Vienna, VA 22182. Mike Doan, Ed. Television-related articles, 750 to 2,500 words; personality profiles; and articles of interest to the satellite and cable TV viewer. Query with clips. Pay varies, on acceptance.

THE SATURDAY EVENING POST—1100 Waterway Blvd., Indianapolis, IN 46202. Ted Kreiter, Exec. Ed. Family-oriented articles, 1,500 to 3,000 words: humor, preventive medicine, destination-oriented travel pieces (not personal experience), celebrity profile, the arts, and sciences. Pieces on sports and home repair (with photos). Pays varying rates, on publication. Queries preferred.

SAVVY WOMAN—3 Park Ave., New York, NY 10016. Analyn Swan, Ed. Profiles of successful women in all fields, and articles that relate to women, 3,000 words. Payment varies. Query.

SELF—350 Madison Ave., New York, NY 10017. Alexandra Penney, Ed.-in-Chief. Articles for young women with a particular interest in health, nutrition, fitness, relationships, fashion and beauty, and related lifestyle subjects. Pays from $1 a word. Query.

SOAP OPERA DIGEST—45 W. 25th St., New York, NY 10010. Lynn Davey, Man. Ed. Investigative reports and profiles, to 1,500 words, about New York- or Los Angeles-based soaps. Pays from $250, on acceptance. Query.

SOAP OPERA UPDATE—158 Linwood Plaza, Ft. Lee, NJ 07024. Allison J. Waldman, Ed. Soap-opera oriented articles, 750 to 1,250 words; fillers to 500 words. Pays $100 to $175, on publication. Queries preferred.

SPORTS ILLUSTRATED—1271 Ave. of the Americas, New York, NY 10020. No unsolicited material.

STAR—660 White Plains Rd., Tarrytown, NY 10591. Topical articles, 50 to 800 words, on human-interest subjects, show business, lifestyles, the sciences, etc., for family audience. Pays varying rates.

SUCCESS—342 Madison Ave., New York, NY 10173. Scott Degarmo, Pub./Ed.-in-Chief. Profiles of successful executives, entrepreneurs; management science, psychology, behavior, and motivation articles, 500 to 3,500 words. Query.

SUNDAY JOURNAL MAGAZINE—*Providence Sunday Journal*, 75 Fountain St., Providence, RI 02902. Elliot Krieger, Ed. Features on some aspect of life in New England, especially Rhode Island and S.E. Massachusetts. Pays $100 to $500, on publication.

TDC: THE DISCOVERY CHANNEL—8201 Corporate Dr., Suite 1200, Landover, MD 20785. Rebecca Farwell, Ed. Monthly read by viewers of cable TV's "Discovery" channel. Articles on travel, politics, science, history, sociology, and anthropology. "All submissions will be used to familiarize us with writers, since we assign all material. Writers should specify any areas of expertise; we will accept manuscripts or clips for review."

THE TOASTMASTER—P.O. Box 9052, Mission Viejo, CA 92690–7052. Suzanne Frey, Ed. Member-supported monthly. Articles, 1,500 to 2,500 words, on decision making, speech outlining, introducing speakers, leadership development, speaking techniques, etc. Pays $100 to $250, on acceptance.

TOWN & COUNTRY—1700 Broadway, New York, NY 10019. Address Features Dept. Considers one page proposals for articles. Rarely buys unsolicited manuscripts.

TRAVEL & LEISURE—1120 Ave. of the Americas, New York, NY 10036. Ila Stanger, Ed.-in-Chief. Articles, 800 to 3,000 words, on destinations and leisure-time activities. Regional pieces for regional editions. Pays $600 to $3,000, on acceptance. Query.

TROPIC—*The Miami Herald*, One Herald Plaza, Miami, FL 33132. Tom Shroder, Ed. Essays and articles on current trends and issues, light or heavy, 1,000 to 4,000 words, for sophisticated audience. No fiction or poetry. Limited humor. Pays $200 to $1,000, on publication. SASE. Allow 4 to 6 weeks for response.

TV GUIDE—Radnor, PA 19088. Andrew Mills, Asst. Man. Ed. Short, light, brightly-written pieces about humorous or offbeat angles of television. Pays on acceptance. Query.

UNIQUE—P.O. Box 1224, Bridgeview, IL 60455. Hugh M. Cook, Ed. Bimonthly. Articles, 3,500 to 5,000 words, on politics, social issues, and personalities, and topical essays, 1,000 to 2,500 words, on pop culture. Pays 10¢ a word, on acceptance. Guidelines.

US MAGAZINE—One Dag Hammarskjold Plaza, New York, NY 10017. Carol Wallace, Ed. Helen F. Rubinstein, Man. Ed. Articles, 750 to 3,500 words, on celebrities and entertainment-related topics. Pays from $500, on publication. Query with published clips required.

VILLAGE VOICE—842 Broadway, New York, NY 10003. Sarah Jewler, Man. Ed. Articles, 500 to 2,000 words, on current or controversial topics. Pays $75 to $450, on acceptance. Query or send manuscript with SASE.

VISTA—999 Ponce, Suite 600, Coral Gables, FL 33134. Renato Perez, Sr. Ed. Articles, to 1,500 words, for English-speaking Hispanic Americans, on job advancement, bilingualism, immigration, the media, fashion, education, medicine, sports, and food. Profiles, 100 words, of Hispanic Americans in unusual jobs; photos welcome. Pays 20¢ a word, on acceptance. Query required.

VOGUE—350 Madison Ave., New York, NY 10017. Address Features Ed. Articles, to 1,500 words, on women, entertainment and the arts, travel, medicine, and health. General features. Query.

VOLKSWAGEN WORLD—Volkswagen of America, Troy, MI 48099. Marlene Goldsmith, Ed. Articles, 600 to 1,000 words, for Volkswagen owners: profiles of well-known personalities; inspirational or human-interest pieces; travel; humor; high-tech German product pieces; German travel. Photos. Pays $150 per printed page, on acceptance. Query. Guidelines.

WASHINGTON JOURNALISM REVIEW—2233 Wisconsin Ave. N.W., Washington, DC 20007. Bill Monroe, Ed. Articles, 500 to 3,000 words, on print or electronic journalism. Pays 20¢ a word, on publication. Query.

WASHINGTON POST MAGAZINE—*The Washington Post*, 1150 15th St. N.W., Washington, DC 20071. Linton Weeks, Man. Ed. Essays, profiles, and general-interest pieces, to 5,000 words, on business, arts and culture, politics, science, sports, education, children, relationships, behavior, etc. Pays from $1,000, after acceptance.

WEEKLY WORLD NEWS—600 S. East Coast Ave., Lantana, FL 33462. Edward Clontz, Ed. Bizarre news pieces, about 500 to 1,000 words. Query first. Pays $125 to $500, on publication.

502

WIGWAG—73 Spring St., New York, NY 10012. Claudia Rowe, Submissions Ed. Elizabeth Macklin, Poetry Ed. Published monthly except January and July. Fiction, articles, and poetry of varying lengths. "Readership includes educated people who like to read. Celebrity gossip is the only taboo." Submit photos and illustrations to Paul Davis. Payment varies, on publication.

WISCONSIN—*The Milwaukee Journal Magazine*, P.O. Box 661, Milwaukee, WI 53201. Alan Borsuk, Ed. Trend stories, essays, humor, personal-experience pieces, profiles, 500 to 2,000 words, with strong Wisconsin emphasis. Pays $75 to $500, after publication.

WOMAN'S DAY—1633 Broadway, New York, NY 10019. Rebecca Greer, Articles Ed. Articles, 500 to 2,500 words, on subjects of interest to women: marriage, education, family health, child rearing, money management, interpersonal relationships, changing lifestyles, etc. Dramatic first-person narratives about women who have experienced medical miracles or other triumphs, or have overcome common problems, such as alcoholism. Query first. Pays top rates for articles, on acceptance.

WOMAN'S WORLD—270 Sylvan Ave., Englewood Cliffs, NJ 07632. Articles, 600 to 1,800 words, of interest to middle-income women between the ages of 18 and 60, on love, romance, careers, medicine, health, psychology, family life, travel, dramatic stories of adventure or crisis, investigative reports. Pays $300 to $750, on acceptance. Query.

WORKING WOMAN—342 Madison Ave., New York, NY 10173. Kate White, Ed. Articles, 1,000 to 2,500 words, on business and personal aspects of working women's lives. Pays from $400, on acceptance.

YANKEE—Dublin, NH 03444. Judson D. Hale, Ed. Articles, to 3,000 words, with New England angle. Photos. Pays $150 to $1,000 (average $750), on acceptance.

YOUR HOME/INDOORS & OUT—Box 10010, Ogden, UT 84409. Caroll Shreeve, Pub. Articles, 1,200 words, with fresh ideas for home decor, construction, management, ownership, and working with a realtor. No do-it-yourself articles. Prefer color transparencies. Pays 15¢ a word, $35 to $50 for pictures, on acceptance. Query.

CURRENT EVENTS, POLITICS

AFRICA REPORT—833 U.N. Pl., New York, NY 10017. Margaret A. Novicki, Ed. Well-researched articles by specialists, 1,000 to 2,500 words, with photos, on current African affairs. Pays $150 to $250, on publication.

THE AMERICAN LEGION MAGAZINE—Box 1055, Indianapolis, IN 46206. Daniel S. Wheeler, Ed.-in-Chief. Articles, 750 to 1,800 words, on current world affairs, public policy, and subjects of contemporary interest. Pays $500 to $1,000, on acceptance. Query.

THE AMERICAN SCHOLAR—1811 Q St. N.W., Washington, DC 20009. Joseph Epstein, Ed. Non-technical articles and essays, 3,500 to 4,000 words, on current affairs, the American cultural scene, politics, arts, religion, and science. Pays $450, on acceptance.

THE AMICUS JOURNAL—Natural Resources Defense Council, 40 W. 20th St., New York, NY 10011. Peter Borrelli, Ed. Investigative articles, book reviews, and poetry related to national and international environmental policy. Pays varying rates, on acceptance. Queries required.

THE ATLANTIC—745 Boylston St., Boston, MA 02116. William Whitworth, Ed. In-depth articles on public issues, politics, social sciences, education, business, literature, and the arts, with emphasis on information rather than opinion. Ideal length: 3,000 to 6,000 words, though short pieces (1,000 to 2,000 words) are also welcome. Pays excellent rates, on acceptance.

COMMENTARY—165 E. 56th St., New York, NY 10022. Norman Podhoretz, Ed. Articles, 5,000 to 7,000 words, on contemporary issues, Jewish affairs, social sciences, community life, religious thought, culture. Serious fiction; book reviews. Pays on publication.

COMMONWEAL—15 Dutch St., New York, NY 10038. Margaret O'Brien Steinfels, Ed. Articles, to 3,000 words, on political, social, religious, and literary subjects for Catholic audience. Pays 3¢ a word, on acceptance.

THE CRISIS—4017 24th St., #8, San Francisco, CA 94114. Fred Beauford, Ed. Articles, to 1,500 words, on the arts, civil rights, and problems and achievements of blacks and other minorities. Pays $75 to $500, on acceptance.

ENVIRONMENT—4000 Albemarle St. N.W., Washington, DC 20016. Barbara T. Richman, Man. Ed. Articles, 2,500 to 5,000 words, on environmental, scientific, and technological policy and decision-making issues. Pays $100 to $300, on publication. Query.

FOREIGN POLICY JOURNAL—11 Dupont Circle N.W., Washington, DC 20036. Charles William Maynes, Ed. Articles, 3,000 to 5,000 words, on international affairs. Honorarium, on publication. Query.

FOREIGN SERVICE JOURNAL—2101 E St. N. W., Washington, D.C. 20037. Articles on American diplomacy, foreign affairs, and subjects of interest to Americans representing U.S. abroad. Query.

THE FREEMAN—Foundation for Economic Education, Irvington-on-Hudson, NY 10533. Brian Summers, Sr. Ed. Articles, to 3,500 words, on economic, political, and moral implications of private property, voluntary exchange, and individual choice. Pays 10¢ a word, on publication.

INQUIRER MAGAZINE—*Philadelphia Inquirer*, P.O. Box 8263, 400 N. Broad St., Philadelphia, PA 19101. Fred Mann, Ed. Local-interest features, 500 to 7,000 words. Profiles of national figures in politics, entertainment, etc. Pays varying rates, on publication. Query.

IRISH AMERICA—432 Park Ave. S., Suite 1000, New York, NY 10016. Sean O'Murchu, Ed. Articles, 1,500 to 2,000 words, of interest to Irish-American audience; preferred topics include history, sports, the arts, and politics. Pays 10¢ a word, after publication. Query.

LABOR'S HERITAGE—10000 New Hampshire Ave., Silver Spring, MD 20903. Stuart Kaufman, Ed. Quarterly journal of The George Meany Memorial Archives. Publishes 15- to 30-page articles to be read by labor scholars, labor union members, and the general public. Pays in copies.

MIDSTREAM—515 Park Ave., New York, NY 10022. Murray Zuckoff, Ed. Jewish-interest articles and book reviews. Pays 5¢ a word, after publication.

MOMENT—3000 Connecticut Ave., Suite 300, Washington, DC 20008. Charlotte Anker, Man. Ed. Sophisticated articles and some fiction, 2,500 to 5,000 words, on Jewish topics. Pays $150 to $400, on publication.

MOTHER JONES—1663 Mission St., San Francisco, CA 94103. Doug Foster, Ed. Investigative articles, political essays, cultural analyses. "OutFront" pieces,

50 to 200 words, about change, "either good, bad, or strange." Pays $750 to $2,000, after acceptance. Query in writing only.

THE NATION—72 Fifth Ave., New York, NY 10011. Victor Navasky, Ed. Articles, 1,500 to 2,500 words, on politics and culture from a liberal/left perspective. Pays $75 per published page, to $300, on publication. Query.

THE NEW YORK TIMES MAGAZINE—229 W. 43rd St., New York, NY 10036. Address Articles Ed. Timely articles, approximately 4,000 words, on news items, trends, culture, etc. Pays $350 to $500 for short pieces, $1,000 to $2,500 for major articles, on acceptance. Query with clips.

THE NEW YORKER—25 W. 43rd St., New York, NY 10036. Address the Editors. Factual and biographical articles, for "Profiles," "Reporter at Large," "Annals of Crime," "Onward and Upward with the Arts," etc. Pays good rates, on acceptance. Query.

NEWSWEEK—444 Madison Ave., New York, NY 10022. Original opinion essays, 1,000 to 1,100 words, for "My Turn" column: must contain verifiable facts. Submit manuscript with SASE. Pays $1,000, on publication.

NUCLEAR TIMES: ISSUES & ACTIVISM FOR GLOBAL SURVIVAL—P.O. Box 351, Kenmore Station, Boston, MA 02215. Leslie Fraser, Ed. News and feature articles, 500 to 4,000 words, on peace, justice, the enviroment, nuclear disarmament, military policy, and militarization of American culture. Pays from 25¢ a word, on publication.

THE PROGRESSIVE—409 E. Main St., Madison, WI 53703. Erwin Knoll, Ed. Articles, 1,000 to 3,500 words, on political, social problems. Light features. Pays $75 to $300, on publication.

PUBLIC CITIZEN MAGAZINE—2000 P St. N.W., Suite 610, Washington, DC 20036. Ana Radelat, Ed. Investigative reports and articles of timely political interest, for members of Public Citizen: consumer rights, health and safety, environmental protection, safe energy, tax reform, and government and corporate accountability. Photos, illustrations. Pays to $500.

REGARDIE'S—1010 Wisconsin Ave. N.W., Suite 600, Washington, DC 20007. Brian Kelly, Ed. Profiles and investigations of the "high and mighty" in the DC area: "We require aggressive reporting and imaginative, entertaining writing." Pays 50¢ a word, on publication. Queries required.

ROLL CALL: THE NEWSPAPER OF CAPITOL HILL—900 2nd St. N.E., Washington, DC 20002. James K. Glassman, Ed.-in-Chief. Factual, breezy articles with political or Congressional angle: Congressional historical and human-interest subjects, political lore, etc. Political satire and humor. Pays on publication.

THE ROTARIAN—1560 Sherman Ave., Evanston, IL 60201. Willmon L. White, Ed. Articles, 1,200 to 2,000 words, on international social and economic issues, business and management, environment, science and technology. "No direct political or religious slants." Pays good rates, on acceptance. Query.

SATURDAY NIGHT—36 Toronto St., Suite 1160, Toronto, Ont., Canada M5C 2C5. John Fraser, Ed. Canada's oldest magazine of politics, social issues, culture, and business. Features, 1,000 to 3,000 words, and columns, 800 to 1,000 words; fiction, to 3,000 words. Must have Canadian tie-in. Payment varies, on acceptance.

TROPIC—*The Miami Herald*, One Herald Plaza, Miami, FL 33132. Tom Shroder, Ed. Essays and articles on current trends and issues, light or heavy, 1,000 to 4,000 words, for sophisticated audience. Pays $200 to $1,000, on publication. Query with SASE; 4 to 6 weeks for response.

VFW MAGAZINE—406 West 34th St., Kansas City, MO 64111. Richard K. Kolb, Ed. Magazine for Veterans of Foreign Wars and their families. Articles, 1,000 words, on current issues and history, with veteran angle. Photos. Pays from $400, extra for photos, on acceptance. Guidelines.

VILLAGE VOICE—842 Broadway, New York, NY 10003. Michael Caruso, Features Ed. Articles, 500 to 2,000 words, on current or controversial topics. Pays $75 to $450, on acceptance. Query or send manuscript with SASE.

THE WASHINGTON MONTHLY—1611 Connecticut Ave. N.W., Washington, DC 20009. Charles Peters, Ed. Investigative articles, 1,500 to 5,000 words, on politics, government and the political culture. Pays 10¢ a word, on publication. Query.

WASHINGTON POST MAGAZINE—*The Washington Post*, 1150 15th St. N.W., Washington, DC 20071. Linton Weeks, Man. Ed. Essays, profiles, and general-interest pieces, to 5,000 words, on politics and related issues. Pays from $1,000, after acceptance. SASE required.

REGIONAL AND CITY PUBLICATIONS

ADIRONDACK LIFE—P.O. Box 97, Jay, NY 12941. Tom Hughes, Ed. Features, to 3,000 words, on outdoor and environmental activities and issues, arts, wilderness, profiles, history, and fiction; focus is on the Adirondack region and north country of New York State. Pays to 25¢ a word, on acceptance. Query.

ALASKA—808 E St., Suite 200, Anchorage, AK 99501. Ron Dalby, Ed. Articles, 2,000 words, on life in Alaska and northwestern Canada. Pays varying rates, on acceptance. Guidelines.

ALOHA, THE MAGAZINE OF HAWAII—49 South Hotel St., #309, Honolulu, HI 96801. Cheryl Chee Tsutsumi, Ed. Articles, 1,500 to 4,000 words, on the life, customs, and people of Hawaii and the Pacific. Poetry. Fiction. Pays $150 to $400 for full-length features, on publication. Query first.

AMERICAN WEST—7000 E. Tanque Verde Rd., Tucson, AZ 85715. Marjory Vals Maud, Exec. Ed. Articles, 2,500 to 3,000 words, and department pieces, 900 to 1,000 words, that celebrate the West, past and present; emphasis on travel. Pays $200 to $800, on acceptance. Query required.

ANGELES—11601 Wilshire Blvd., Los Angeles, CA 90025. Joanne Jaffe, Ed. Features on design, art, architecture, food, and fashion aimed at Los Angeles' Westside population. Pays good rates, on acceptance.

ARIZONA HIGHWAYS—2039 W. Lewis Ave., Phoenix, AZ 85009. Merrill Windsor, Ed. Articles, 1,500 to 2,000 words, on travel in Arizona; pieces on adventure, humor, lifestyles, nostalgia, history, archaeology, nature, etc. Pays 30¢ to 45¢ a word, on acceptance. Query first.

ARKANSAS TIMES—Box 34010, Little Rock, AR 72203. Mel White, Ed. Articles, to 6,000 words, on Arkansas history, people, travel, politics. All articles must have strong AR orientation. Pays to $500, on acceptance.

ATLANTA—1360 Peachtree St., Suite 1800, Atlanta, GA 30309. Lee Walburn, Ed. Articles, 1,500 to 5,000 words, on Atlanta subjects or personalities. Pays $600 to $1,200, on publication. Query.

THE ATLANTIC ADVOCATE—P.O. Box 3370, Gleaner Bldg., Prospect St., Fredericton, N.B., Canada E3B 5A2. Marilee Little, Ed. Well-researched articles on Atlantic Canada and general-interest subjects; fiction, to 1,500 words. Pays to 8¢ a word, on publication.

ATLANTIC CITY MAGAZINE—1270 W. Washington Ave., Suite 100, Cardiff, NJ 08232. Tom McGrath, Ed. Lively articles, 500 to 4,000 words, on Atlantic City and southern New Jersey, for locals and tourists: entertainment, casinos, business, personalities, environment, local color, crime. Pays $100 to $700, on acceptance. Query.

BALTIMORE MAGAZINE—16 S. Calvert St., Suite 1000, Baltimore, MD 21202. Stan Heuisler, Ed. Articles, 500 to 3,000 words, on people, places, and things in the Baltimore metropolitan area. Consumer advice, investigative pieces, profiles, humor, and personal experience pieces. Payment varies, on publication. Query required.

THE BIG APPLE PARENTS' PAPER—928 Broadway, Suite 709, New York, NY 10010. Helen Rosengren Freedman, Ed. Articles, 600 to 750 words, for New York City parents. Pays $50 to $75, within 60 days of acceptance, plus $25 cover bonus. Buys first NY area rights.

BIRMINGHAM—2027 First Ave. N., Birmingham, AL 35203. Joe O'Donnell, Ed. Personality profiles, features, business, and nostalgia pieces (to 2,500 words) with Birmingham tie-in. Pays $50 to $175, on publication.

BOCA RATON—JES Publishing, Amtec Center, Suite 100, 6413 Congress Ave., Boca Raton, FL 33487. Christina Houlihan, Ed. Articles, 800 to 3,000 words, on Florida topics, personalities, and travel. Pays $50 to $500, on publication. Query with clips required.

THE BOSTON GLOBE MAGAZINE—*The Boston Globe*, Boston, MA 02107. Ande Zellman, Ed. General-interest articles on local, national, and international topics and profiles, 2,500 to 5,000 words. Query and SASE required.

BOSTON MAGAZINE—300 Massachusetts Ave., Boston, MA 02115. David Rosenbaum, Ed. Informative, entertaining features, 1,000 to 4,000 words, on Boston area personalities, institutions, and phenomena. Pays $250 to $2,000, on publication. Query Betsy Buffington, Man. Ed.

BOSTONIA—10 Lenox St., Brookline, MA 02146. Keith Botsford, Ed. Articles (1,800 words) on politics, the arts, travel, food, and wine; lifestyle essays (1,200 words) with regional tie-in. Pays $150 to $800, on publication. Queries required.

BOUNDARY WATERS JOURNAL—Route 1, Box 1740, Ely, MN 55731. Stuart Osthoff, Ed. Articles, 2,000 to 3,000 words, on recreation and natural resources in Minnesota's Boundary Waters region, including canoe routes, fishing, wildlife, history, and lifestyles of residents. Pays $200 to $400, on publication.

BUFFALO SPREE MAGAZINE—Box 38, Buffalo, NY 14226. Johanna Shotell, Ed. Articles, to 1,800 words. Pays $75 to $100, $25 for poetry, on publication.

BUSINESS DIGEST OF GREATER NEW HAVEN—20 Grand Ave., New Haven, CT 06513. Jean McAndrews, Ed. Feature articles, 1,500 to 2,000 words, on New Haven area businesses. Pays $2.75 per published inch, $10 per photo, on publication. Query required.

BUSINESS IN BROWARD—2455 E. Sunrise Blvd., Suite 300, Ft. Lauderdale, FL 33304. T. Constance Coyne, Ed. Small business regional bimonthly; 2,500-word articles for eastern Florida county. Pay varies, on acceptance.

CALIFORNIA—11601 Wilshire Blvd., Los Angeles, CA 90025. Rebecca Levy, Man. Ed. Features with a California focus, on politics, business, environmental issues, ethnic diversity, travel, style, fashions, restaurants, the arts, and sports. Service pieces, profiles, and well-researched investigative articles. Pays $500 to $2,500 for features, $250 to $500 for shorter articles, on acceptance. Query first.

CALIFORNIA BUSINESS—4221 Wilshire Blvd., Suite 400, Los Angeles, CA 90010. Christopher Bergonzi, Ed. Articles, 500 to 3,500 words, on Los Angeles-based businesses. Payment varies, on acceptance. Query.

CAPE COD LIFE—P.O. Box 222, Osterville, MA 02655. Brian F. Shortsleeve, Pub. Articles on Cape Cod current events, business, art, history, gardening, and lifestyle, 2,000 words. Pays 10¢ a word, 30 days after publication. Queries preferred.

CAPITAL MAGAZINE—(formerly *Capital Region Magazine*) 4 Central Ave., Albany, NY 12210. Dardis McNamee, Ed.-in-Chief/Pub. News, features, and profiles angled to the Albany, New York, region (1,000 to 5,000 words); anecdotes, vignettes, short profiles, and humor (250 to 500 words). Pays 10¢ a word, within 90 days of acceptance. Query required.

CARIBBEAN TRAVEL AND LIFE—8403 Colesville Rd., Silver Spring, MD 20910. Veronica Gould Stoddart, Ed. Articles, 500 to 3,000 words, on all aspects of travel, recreation, leisure, and culture in the Caribbean, Bahamas, and Bermuda. Pays $75 to $550, on publication. Query with published clips.

CHESAPEAKE BAY MAGAZINE—1819 Bay Ridge Ave., Annapolis, MD 21403. Jean Waller, Ed. Articles, 8 to 10 typed pages, related to the Chesapeake Bay area. Profiles. Photos. Pays on publication. Query first.

CHICAGO HISTORY—Clark St. at North Ave., Chicago, IL 60614. Russell Lewis, Ed. Articles, to 4,500 words, on Chicago's urban, political, social, and cultural history. Pays to $250, on publication. Query.

CHICAGO TRIBUNE MAGAZINE—*Chicago Tribune*, 435 N. Michigan Ave., Rm. 532, Chicago, IL 60611. Ruby Scott, Man. Ed. Profiles and articles, to 6,000 words, on public and social issues on the personal, local, or national level. Prefer regional slant. Query. Pays $250 to $1,500, on publication.

CINCINNATI MAGAZINE—409 Broadway, Cincinnati, OH 45202. Laura Pulfer, Ed./Pub. Articles, 1,000 to 3,000 words, on Cincinnati people and issues. Pays $75 to $100 for 1,000 words, on acceptance. Query with writing sample.

CITY SPORTS—P.O. Box 193693, San Francisco, CA 94119. Susanna Levin, Ed. Articles, 500 to 2,000 words, on participant sports, family recreation, travel, and the active lifestyle. Pays $100 to $650, on publication. Query.

CLINTON STREET—Box 3588, Portland, OR 97208. David Milholland, Ed. Articles (to 15 pages) and creative fiction (2 to 20 pages). "Eclectic blend of politics, culture, humor, and art." Compelling first-person accounts welcome. Pays $50 to $200, on publication.

COLORADO BUSINESS—5951 S. Middlefield Rd., Littleton, CO 80123. Jeff Rundles, Ed. Articles, varying length, on business and economic trends in Colorado. Pays on publication. Query.

COLORADO HOMES & LIFESTYLES—5951 S. Middlefield Rd., Littleton, CO 80123. Darla J. Worden, Pub. Articles on topics related to Colorado: travel, fashion, design and decorating, gardening, luxury real estate, art, celebrity lifestyles, people, food, and entertaining. Pays to 20¢ a word, on acceptance.

CONNECTICUT—789 Reservoir Ave., Bridgeport, CT 06606. Charles Monagan, Ed. Articles, 1,500 to 3,500 words, on Connecticut topics, issues, people, and lifestyles. Pays $500 to $1,000, on publication.

CRAIN'S DETROIT BUSINESS—1400 Woodbridge, Detroit, MI 48207. Mary Kramer, Ed. Business articles, 500 to 1,000 words, about Detroit, for Detroit business readers. Pays $100 to $200, on publication. Query required.

CREATING EXCELLENCE—New World Publishing, P.O. Box 2084, S. Burlington, VT 05403. David Robinson, Ed. Inspirational and practical business-oriented articles, profiles, and essays related to Vermont. Pays $50 to $250, on publication.

D—3988 N. Central Expressway, Suite 1200, Dallas, TX 75204. Ruth Fitzgibbons, Ed. In-depth investigative pieces on current trends and problems, personality profiles, and general-interest articles on the arts, travel, and business, for upper-class residents of Dallas. Pays $350 to $500 for departments, $800 to $1,200 for features. Written queries only.

DALLAS LIFE MAGAZINE—*The Dallas Morning News*, Communications Center, Dallas, TX 75265. Melissa Houtte, Ed. Well-researched articles and profiles, 1,000 to 3,000 words, on contemporary issues, personalities, or subjects of strictly Dallas-related interest. Pays from 25¢ a word, on acceptance. Query required.

DALLAS MAGAZINE—2301 N. Akard, Suite 400, Dallas, TX 75201. Jeff Hampton, Ed. Features, 2,500 words, on business and businesses in Dallas. Department pieces, 1,500 words. Pays $100 to $600, on acceptance. Query required.

DELAWARE TODAY—P.O. Box 4440, Wilmington, DE 19807. Lise Monty, Ed. Service articles, profiles, news, etc., on topics of local interest. Pays $75 to $125 for department pieces, $125 to $300 for features, on publication. Queries with clips required.

DETROIT FREE PRESS MAGAZINE—*Detroit Free Press*, 321 W. Lafayette Blvd., Detroit, MI 48231. Articles, to 5,000 words, on issues, lifestyles. Personality profiles; essays; humor. Pays from $150. Query appreciated.

DETROIT MONTHLY—1400 Woodbridge, Detroit, MI 48207. Diane Brozek, Ed. Articles on Detroit-area people, issues, lifestyles, and business. Payment varies. Query required.

DOMAIN—P.O. Box 1569, Austin, TX 78767. Catherine Chadwick, Ed. Bimonthly lifestyle supplement to *Texas Monthly*. Articles on Texas architecture, art, home design, gardens, travel, and cuisine. Features (750 to 2,500 words) and department pieces (2,500 words or less). Payment varies, on acceptance. Query.

DOWN EAST—Camden, ME 04843. Davis Thomas, Ed. Articles, 1,500 to 2,500 words, on all aspects of life in Maine. Photos. Pays to 20¢ a word, extra for photos, on acceptance. Query.

ERIE & CHAUTAUQUA MAGAZINE—Charles H. Strong Bldg., 1250 Tower La., Erie, PA 16505. Kim Kalvelage, Man. Ed. Feature articles, to 2,500 words, on issues of interest to upscale readers in the Erie, Warren, and Crawford counties (PA), and Chautauqua (NY) county. Pieces with regional relevance. Pays after publication. Query preferred, with writing samples. Buys all rights. Guidelines available.

FLORIDA HOME & GARDEN—600 Brickell Ave., Suite 207, Miami, FL

33131. Kathryn Howard, Ed. Features,1,000 to 2,000 words, and department pieces, 1,000 words, about Florida interior design, architecture, landscape architecture, gardening, cuisine, trendy new products, art, travel (Florida and Caribbean), and home entertaining. Pays $200 to $400, photos extra.

FLORIDA KEYS MAGAZINE—505 Duval St., Upper Suite, Key West, FL 33040. David Ethridge, Ed. Articles, 1,000 to 2,000 words, on the Florida Keys: history, environment, natural history, profiles, etc. Fillers, humor. Photos. Pays varying rates, on publication. Query preferred.

FLORIDA TREND—Box 611, St. Petersburg, FL 33731. Tom Billitteri, Man. Ed. Articles on Florida business and businesspersons. Query letter required.

FLORIDA WILDLIFE—620 S. Meridian St., Tallahassee, FL 32399–1600. Andrea H. Blount, Ed. Bimonthly of the Florida Game and Fresh Water Fish Commission. Articles, 800 to 1,200 words, that promote native wildlife (flora and fauna), hunting, fishing in Florida's fresh waters, outdoor ethics, and conservation of Florida's natural resources. Pays $50 to $200, on publication.

'GBH MAGAZINE—420 Boylston St., Boston, MA 02116. Jack Curtis, Man. Ed. Member magazine for WGBH, Boston's public TV and radio stations. Articles, 700 to 1,000 words, based on WGBH programming, written in first- or third-person. Pays from $500 to $850, on acceptance. Query required.

GEORGIA JOURNAL—Grimes Publications, P.O. Box 27, Athens, GA 30603–0027. Millard B. Grimes, Ed. and Pub. Articles, 1,200 words, on people, history, events, travel, etc., in and around GA. Poetry, to 20 lines. Pays $50 to $150, on publication.

GRAND RAPIDS—40 Pearl St. N.W., #1040, Grand Rapids, MI 49503. Carole Valade Smith, Ed. Service articles (dining guide, travel, personal finance, humor) and issue-oriented pieces related to Grand Rapids, Michigan. Pays $35 to $100, on publication. Query.

GREAT LAKES SAILOR—572 W. Market St., Suite 6, P.O. Box 951, Akron, OH 44309. Drew Shippy, Ed. Department pieces: "Destinations" (2,500 to 3,000 words, on cruises); "Trailer Sailor" (trips for day sailors, to 1,500 words); and "First Person" (profiles, 2,500 to 3,000 words). How-to pieces on sailing and navigational techniques, human-interest stories. Photos. Pays to 20¢ a word, on publication. Queries required. Guidelines.

GULF COAST GOLFER—See *North Texas Golfer*.

GULFSHORE LIFE—2975 S. Horseshoe Dr., Naples, FL 33942. Janis Lyn Johnson, Ed. Articles, 800 to 3,000 words, on southwest Florida personalities, travel, sports, business, interior design, arts, history, and nature. Pays $150 to $300. Query.

HAWAII—Box 6050, Mission Viejo, CA 92690. Dennis Shattuck, Ed. Bimonthly. Articles, 1,000 to 5,000 words, related to Hawaii. Pays 10¢ a word, on publication. Query.

HIGH COUNTRY NEWS—Box 1090, Paonia, CO 81428. Betsy Marston, Ed. Articles on environmental issues, public lands management, energy, and natural resource issues; profiles of western innovators; pieces on western politics. Poetry. B&W photos. Pays $2 to $4 per column inch, on publication, for 750-word roundups and 2,000-word features. Query first.

HONOLULU—36 Merchant St., Honolulu, HI 96813. Brian Nicol, Ed. Features highlighting life in the Hawaiian islands: politics, sports, history, people, events are all subjects of interest. Pays $500, on acceptance. Columns and department pieces are mostly staff-written. Queries are required.

HOUSTON METROPOLITAN MAGAZINE—P.O. Box 25386, Houston, TX 77265. Mike Peters, Man. Ed. Gabrielle Cosgriff, Ed. Dir. Articles with strong Houston-area angles. Issue-oriented features, profiles, lifestyle pieces. Also gardening and design pieces; department columns ("City Insight," "Art Beat," "Metropolitan Marketplace"). Pays $50 to $500 for columns; $600 to $1,000 for features.

ILLINOIS ENTERTAINER—2250 E. Devon, Suite 150, Des Plaines, IL 60018. Michael C. Harris, Ed. Articles, 500 to 1,500 words, on local and national entertainment (emphasis on alternative music) in the greater Chicago area. Personality profiles; interviews; reviews. Photos. Pays varying rates on publication. Query preferred.

ILLINOIS TIMES—Box 3524, Springfield, IL 62708. Fletcher Farrar, Jr., Ed. Articles, 1,000 to 2,500 words, on people, places, and activities of Illinois, outside the Chicago metropolitan area. Pays 4¢ a word, on publication. Query required.

INDIANAPOLIS MONTHLY—8425 Keystone Crossing, Indianapolis, IN 46240. Deborah Paul, Ed./Pub. Sam Stall, Man. Ed. Articles, 1,000 words, on health, sports, politics, business, interior design, travel, and Indiana personalities. All material must have a regional focus. Pays varying rates, on publication.

INDUSTRY MAGAZINE—441 Stuart St., Boston, MA 02116. Alan R. Earls, Ed./Pub. Articles, 500 to 1,500 words, related to business and industry in Massachusetts. Pays negotiable rates, on acceptance. Queries required.

INLAND—Inland Steel Co., 18 South Home Ave., Park Ridge, IL 60068. Sheldon A. Mix, Man. Ed. Articles, varying lengths, about the Middle West. History, folklore, commentaries, nature, humor. Send completed manuscripts. Pays on acceptance.

INQUIRER MAGAZINE—*Philadelphia Inquirer*, 400 N. Broad St., Philadelphia, PA 19101. Fred Mann, Ed. Articles, 1,500 to 2,000 words, and 3,000 to 7,000 words, on politics, science, arts and culture, business, lifestyles and entertainment, sports, health, psychology, education, religion, and humor. Short pieces, 850 words, for "Up Front" department. Pays varying rates. Query.

INSIDE CHICAGO—2501 W. Peterson Ave., Chicago, IL 60659. Barbara Young, Man. Ed. Features, to 3,000 words, on Chicago-related trends, profiles of Chicagoans, entrepreneuring, architecture (to 1,500 words). Short reports, 200 to 400 words. Department pieces, 900 to 1,000 words. Pays varying rates. Query.

THE IOWAN MAGAZINE—108 Third St., Suite 350, Des Moines, IA 50309. Charles W. Roberts, Ed. Articles, 1,000 to 3,000 words, on business, arts, people, and history of Iowa. Photos a plus. Pays $200 to $600, on publication. Query required.

ISLAND LIFE—P.O. Box 929, Sanibel Island, FL 33957. Joan Hooper, Ed. Articles, 500 to 1,200 words, with photos, on unique or historical places in Florida, wildlife, architecture, fashions, home decor, cuisine, people on barrier islands off Florida's southwest. Gulf Coast (Sanibel, Captiva, Marco). Pays on publication. SASE.

JACKSONVILLE TODAY—White Publishing Co., 1325 San Marco Blvd., Suite 900, Jacksonville, FL 32207. Dale Dermott, Ed. Features, 2,000 to 3,000 words, relating to Jacksonville and North Florida personalities. Pays $200 to $350, on publication. Query required.

511

KANSAS!—Kansas Dept. of Commerce, 400 W. Eighth Ave., 5th Fl., Topeka, KS 66603–3957. Andrea Glenn, Ed. Quarterly. Articles of 5 to 7 typed pages on the people, places, history, and events of Kansas. Color slides. Pays to $250, on acceptance. Query.

L/A TODAY—P.O. Box 3163, Lewiston, ME 04243–3163. John C. Turner, Pub. Articles, 500 to 2,000 words, on Maine-related topics, for readers in Lewiston/Auburn area: personalities, profiles, places, and activities (contemporary or historical). Pays 10¢ a word, on publication.

L.A. WEST—919 Santa Monica Blvd., Santa Monica, CA 90401. Mary Daily, Ed. Features, 850 to 1,200 words, relating to western Los Angeles; humorous essays on current lifestyles; profiles, 350 to 500 words, on westside professionals; travel pieces, 800 words, on foreign and domestic destinations. Pays $75 to $600, photos extra, on acceptance. Queries preferred. Guidelines.

LAKE SUPERIOR MAGAZINE—P.O. Box 16417, Duluth, MN 55816–0417. Paul Hayden, Ed. Articles with unusual twists on regional subjects: historical pieces that highlight the people, places, and events that affect the Lake Superior region. Pictorial essays; humor and occasional poetry. Photos a plus. "Writers must have a thorough knowledge of the subject and how it relates to our region." Pays to $400, after publication. Photos: $20 to $30, more for covers. Query first.

LOS ANGELES MAGAZINE—1888 Century Park E., Los Angeles, CA 90067. Lew Harris, Exec. Ed. Articles, to 3,000 words, of interest to sophisticated, affluent southern Californians, preferably with local focus on a lifestyle topic. Pays from 10¢ a word, on acceptance. Query.

LOS ANGELES READER—5550 Wilshire Blvd., Suite 301, Los Angeles, CA 90036. James Vowell, Ed. Articles, 750 to 5,000 words, on subjects relating to the Los Angeles area; special emphasis on feature journalism, entertainment, and the arts. Pays $25 to $300, on publication. Query preferred.

LOS ANGELES TIMES MAGAZINE—Times Mirror Sq., Los Angeles, CA 90053. Linda Mathews, Ed. General-interest news features, photo spreads, profiles, and interviews focusing on people and events of interest in Southern California, to 3,500 words. Pays to $2,500, on acceptance. Query required.

LOUISVILLE—One Riverfront Plaza, Louisville, KY 40202. James Oppel, Jr., Ed. Articles, 1,000 to 2,000 words, on community issues, personalities, and entertainment in the Louisville area. Photos. Pays from $50, on acceptance. Query; articles on assignment only. Limited free-lance market.

MAGAZINE OF THE MIDLANDS—*Omaha World-Herald*, World Herald Sq., Omaha, NE 68102. David Hendee, Ed. Articles, 400 to 2,000 words, that focus on people and places of the greater Midwest. Photos. Pays $40 to $150, on publication. Query.

MAGNETIC NORTH—Thorn Books, Inc., Franconia, NH 03580. Jim McIntosh, Ed. Well-researched, offbeat articles, 500 to 1,500 words, for visitors to New Hampshire's White Mountains. Pays $50 to $150, on publication. Query with SASE.

MARYLAND—c/o Dept. of Economic and Employment Development, 217 E. Redwood St., 9th Fl., Baltimore, MD 21202. D. Patrick Hornbercer, Ed. Dir. Bonnie Joe Ayers, Ed. Articles, 800 to 2,200 words, on Maryland subjects. Pay varies, on acceptance. Query preferred. Guidelines.

MEMPHIS—MM Corp., Box 256, Memphis, TN 38101. Larry Conley, Ed. Articles, 1,500 to 4,000 words, on a wide variety of topics related to Memphis and

512

the Mid-South region: politics, education, sports, business, etc. Profiles; investigative pieces. Pays $75 to $1,000, on publication. Query. Guidelines available.

MICHIGAN BUSINESS—26111 Evergreen, Suite 303, Southfield, MI 48076. Ron Garbinski, Ed. Business news features on Michigan businesses. Query. Pay varies, on publication.

MICHIGAN LIVING—17000 Executive Plaza Dr., Dearborn, MI 48126. Len Barnes, Ed. Travel articles, 500 to 1,500 words, on tourist attractions and recreational opportunities in the U.S. and Canada, with emphasis on Michigan: places to go, things to do, costs, etc. Color photos. Pays $100 to $350, extra for photos, on acceptance.

MIDWEST LIVING—1912 Grand Ave., Des Moines, IA 50309. Barbara Humeston, Ed. Bimonthly. Lifestyle articles relating to any or all of the 12 Midwest states; town, neighborhood, and personality profiles. Humorous essays occasionally used. Pays varying rates, on acceptance; buys all rights.

MID-WEST OUTDOORS—111 Shore Dr., Hinsdale, IL 60521. Gene Laulunen, Ed. Articles, 1,500 words, with photos, on where, when, and how to fish, within 500 miles of Chicago. Pays $25, on publication.

MILWAUKEE—312 E. Buffalo, Milwaukee, WI 53202. Judith Woodburn, Ed. Profiles, investigative articles, and historical pieces, 3,000 to 4,000 words; local tie-in a must. Some regional fiction. Pays from $600, on publication. Query required.

MPLS. ST. PAUL—12 S. 6th St., Suite 400, Minneapolis, MN 55402. Claude Peck, Man. Ed. In-depth articles, features, profiles, and service pieces, 400 to 3,000 words, with Minneapolis-St. Paul focus. Pays to $600.

MINNESOTA MONTHLY—15 S. Ninth St., Suite 320, Minneapolis, MN 55402. Amy Gage, Man. Ed. Articles, to 4,000 words, on the people, places, events, and issues in Minnesota; fiction, to 3,000 words; poetry, to 50 lines. Pays $50 to $800, on acceptance. Query for nonfiction only.

MONTANA MAGAZINE—P.O. Box 5630, Helena, MT 59604. Carolyn Cunningham, Ed. Where-to-go items, regional profiles, photo essays. Montana-oriented only. B&W prints, color slides. Pays $75 to $350, on publication.

NEVADA—1800 East Hwy. 50, Suite 200, Carson City, NV 89710. Kirk Whisler, Ed. Articles, 500 to 700 or 1,500 to 1,800 words, on topics related to Nevada: travel, history, profiles, humor, and place. Photos. Pay varies, on publication.

NEVADAN—*The Las Vegas Review-Journal*, Box 70, Las Vegas, NV 89125–0070. A.D. Hopkins, Ed. Feature articles, 1,500 to 5,000 words, on social trends, people, and history. All articles must have regional angle: Nevada, southwest Utah, northeast Arizona, and Death Valley area of California. Photos a plus. Pays $200 to $650 for articles, $20 to $25 per photo, on publication. Queries required.

NEW ALASKAN—Rt. 1, Box 677, Ketchikan, AK 99901. R.W. Pickrell, Ed. Articles, 1,000 to 5,000 words, and fiction must be related to southeastern Alaska. Pays 1½¢ a word, on publication.

NEW DOMINION—2000 N. 14th St., Suite 750, Arlington, VA 22201. Philip Hayward, Ed. "The Magazine for and about Northern Virginia." Articles, 600 to 2,000 words, on regional business and lifestyles. Query with writing samples. Pays $5.50 per column inch, on publication.

NEW ENGLAND TRAVEL—(formerly *New England Getaways*) 215 Newbury St., Peabody, MA 01960. Features, 1,500 to 2,500 words, "designed to lure travelers to specific regions of New England. We are looking for specific, informational articles that will motivate the reader to explore New England and will supply the tools (addresses, phone numbers, hours of business) to make the trip easy." Pays $150 to $250, on publication.

NEW JERSEY FOCUS—490 S. Riverview, Totowa, NJ 07512. Charles Jacobs, Ed. Sunday supplement on such themes as health, science, education, travel, and real estate; New Jersey tie-in essential. Articles 1,300 words. Query for topics. Pays $100 to $200 per printed page, on acceptance.

NEW JERSEY MONTHLY—P.O. Box 920, Morristown, NJ 07963–0920. Patrick Sarver, Exec. Ed. Articles, profiles, and service pieces, 2,000 to 3,000 words; department pieces on health, business, education, travel, sports, local politics, and arts, 1,200 to 1,800 words, with New Jersey tie-in. Pays $35 to $100 for shorts, $450 to $1,500 for features, on acceptance. Query with SASE and clips. Guidelines.

NEW JERSEY REPORTER—The Center for Analysis of Public Issues, 16 Vandeventer Ave., Princeton, NJ 08542. Rick Sinding, Ed. Alice Chasan, Man. Ed. In-depth articles, 2,000 to 6,000 words, on New Jersey politics and public affairs. Pays $100 to $250, on publication. Query required.

NEW MEXICO MAGAZINE—Joseph M. Montoya Bldg., 1100 St. Francis Dr., Santa Fe, NM 87503. Address Ed. Articles, 250 to 2,000 words, on New Mexico subjects. Pays about 22¢ a word, on acceptance.

NEW ORLEANS MAGAZINE—111 Veterans Blvd., Metairie, LA 70005. Errol Laborde, Ed. Articles, 3 to 15 triple-spaced pages, on New Orleans area people and issues. Photos. Pays $15 to $500, extra for photos, on publication. Query.

NEW YORK—755 Second Ave., New York, NY 10017. Edward Kosner, Ed. Laurie Jones, Man. Ed. Feature articles on subjects of interest to New Yorkers. Payment negotiated, made on acceptance. Query required.

NEW YORK ALIVE—152 Washington Ave., Albany, NY 12210. Mary Grates Stoll, Ed. Articles aimed at developing knowledge of and appreciation for New York State. Features, 3,000 words maximum, on lifestyle, sports, travel and leisure, history, and the arts. Department pieces for regular columns, including "Great Escapes" (travel ideas) and "Expressly New York" (unusual places, products, or events in New York). Pays $200 to $350 for features, $50 to $150 for departments. Query preferred.

NORTH DAKOTA HORIZONS—P.O. Box 2467, Fargo, ND 58108. Sheldon Green, Ed. Quarterly. Articles, about 3,000 words, on the people, places, and events that affect life in North Dakota. Photos. Pays $75 to $300, on publication.

NORTH GEORGIA JOURNAL—110 Hunters Mill, Woodstock, GA 30188. Olin Jackson, Pub./Ed. History, travel, and lifestyle features, 2,000 to 3,000 words, on North Georgia. History features need human-interest approach written in first person, include interviews. Photos a plus. Pays $75 to $350, extra for photos, on acceptance. Query.

NORTH TEXAS GOLFER—9182 Old Katy Rd., Suite 212, Irving, TX 77055. Bob Gray, Ed. Articles, 800 to 1,500 words, involving local golfers or related directly to north Texas. Pays from $50 to $250, on publication. Query. Same requirements for *Gulf Coast Golfer* (related to south Texas).

NORTHEAST MAGAZINE—*The Hartford Courant*, 285 Broad St., Hartford, CT 06115. Lary Bloom, Ed. Articles and short essays that reflect the concerns of Connecticut residents, 750 to 3,000 words. Pays $250 to $1,000, on acceptance.

514

NORTHERN LIGHTS—Box 8084, Missoula, MT 59807–8084. Address Editor. Thoughtful articles, 500 to 3,000 words, about the contemporary West. Occasional fiction. "We're open to virtually any subject as long as it deals with our region (the Rocky Mountains) in some way." Pays to 10¢ a word, on publication.

NORTHWEST—1320 S.W. Broadway, Portland, OR 97201. Ellen E. Heltzel, Ed. Sunday magazine of *The Sunday Oregonian*. Articles, to 3,000 words, on Pacific Northwest issues and personalities: regional travel, science and business, outdoor recreation, and lifestyle trends. Personal essays. Local angle essential. Pays $75 to $1,000. Query first.

NORTHWEST LIVING!—130 Second Ave. S., Edmonds, WA 98020–3512. Terry W. Sheely, Ed. Lively, informative articles, 400 to 1,000 words, on the natural resources of the Northwest: homes, gardens, people, travel, history, etc. Color photos essential. Shorts, 100 to 400 words. Pays $50 to $400, on acceptance. Query with SASE.

NORTHWEST PRIME TIMES—10829 N.E. 68th St., Kirkland, WA 98033. Neil Strother, Pub./Ed. News and features aimed at 50 and up audience. Pays $25 to $50 on publication. Limited market.

OH! IDAHO—Peak Media, Box 925, Hailey, ID 83333. Colleen Daly, Ed. "Articulate, image-oriented" features, 1,500 to 2,000 words, on Idaho's residents, recreation, and other Idaho topics. Department pieces, 1,200 words, on a wide variety of subjects including food and travel in Idaho. Pays from 10¢ a word, on publication. Query. Guidelines.

OHIO MAGAZINE—40 S. Third St., Columbus, OH 43215. Ellen Stein Burbach, Ed. Profiles of people, cities, and towns of Ohio; pieces on historic sites, tourist attractions, little-known spots. Lengths and payment vary. Query.

OKLAHOMA TODAY—Box 53384, Oklahoma City, OK 73152. Sue Carter, Ed. Travel articles; profiles, history, nature and outdoor recreation, and arts articles. All material must have regional tie-in. Queries for 1,000- to 2,000-word articles preferred. Pays $100 to $300, on acceptance. SASE for guidelines.

ORANGE COAST—245-D Fisher, Suite 8, Costa Mesa, CA 92626. Palmer Jones, Ed. Articles of interest to educated, affluent Southern Californians. Pieces, 1,000 to 1,500 words, for regular departments: "Profile," "Coasting" (op-ed), "Media," "Business" (hard news about the regional business community). Feature articles, 1,500 to 2,500 words: investigative, lifestyle, business trends in the area, and issue-oriented topics. Query. Pays $150 for features, $100 for columns, on acceptance. Guidelines.

ORLANDO MAGAZINE—P.O. Box 2207, Orlando, FL 32802. Michael Candelaria, Ed. Articles and profiles, 1,000 to 1,500 words, related to growth, development, and business central Florida. Photos a plus. Pays $100 to $200, on publication. Query required.

PALM SPRINGS LIFE—Desert Publications, 303 N. Indian Ave., Palm Springs, CA 92262. Jamie Lee Pricer, Ed. Articles, 1,000 to 2,000 words, of interest to "wealthy, upscale people who live and/or play in the desert": food, interior design, luxury cars, shopping, sports, homes, personalities, arts, and culture. Pays $150 to $200 for features, $30 for short profiles, on publication. Query required.

PARENTGUIDE NEWS—2 Park Ave., Suite 2012, New York, NY 10016. Leslie Elgort, Ed. Monthly. Articles, 1,000 to 1,500 words, related to New York families and parenting: trends, profiles, special programs and products, etc. Humor, jokes, puzzles, and photos also considered. Payment varies, on publication.

PENNSYLVANIA HERITAGE—P.O. Box 1026, Harrisburg, PA 17108–1026. Michael J. O'Malley III, Ed. Quarterly of the Pennsylvania Historical Museum Commission. Articles, 3,000 to 4,000 words, on fine and decorative arts, architecture, archaeology, oral history, exhibits, industry and technology, travel, and folklore, written with an eye toward illustration. Photographic essays. Pieces should "introduce readers to the state's rich culture and historic legacy." Pays $300 to $500 for articles; up to $100 for photos and drawings, on acceptance.

PENNSYLVANIA MAGAZINE—Box 576, Camp Hill, PA 17011. Albert E. Holliday, Ed. General-interest features with a Pennsylvania flavor. All articles must be illustrated. Send photocopies of possible illustrations. Photos. Guidelines.

PHILADELPHIA—1500 Walnut St., Philadelphia, PA 19102. Laurence Stams, Articles Ed. Articles, 1,000 to 5,000 words, for sophisticated audience, relating to Philadelphia area. No fiction or poetry. Pays on acceptance. Query.

PHOENIX MAGAZINE—(formerly *Phoenix Metro Magazine*) 4707 N. 12th St., Phoenix, AZ 85014. Richard Vonier, Ed. Articles, 1,000 to 3,000 words, on topics of interest to Phoenix-area residents. Pays $300 to $1,500, on publication. Written queries preferred.

PITTSBURGH—4802 Fifth Ave., Pittsburgh, PA 15213. Bruce VanWyngarden, Ed. Articles, 850 to 3,000 words, with western Pennsylvania slant, 2- to 4-month lead time. Pays on publication.

PORTLAND MAGAZINE—578 Congress St., Portland, ME 04101. Colin Sargent, Ed. Articles on local people, fashion, culture, trends, commercial and residential real estate. Fiction, to 1,000 words. Pays on publication. Query preferred.

REGARDIE'S—1010 Wisconsin Ave. N.W., Suite 600, Washington, DC 20007. Brian Kelly, Ed. Profiles and investigations of the "high and mighty" in the DC area: "We require aggressive reporting and imaginative, entertaining writing." Pays 50¢ a word, on publication. Queries required.

RHODE ISLAND MONTHLY—60 Branch Ave., Providence, RI 02904. Vicki Sanders, Man. Ed. Features, 1,000 to 4,000 words, ranging from investigative reporting and in-depth profiles to service pieces and visual stories, on Rhode Island and southeastern Massachusetts. Seasonal material, 1,000 to 2,000 words. Fillers, 150 to 250 words, on places, customs, people, events, products and services, restaurants and food. Pays $250 to $900 for features; $25 to $50 for shorts, on publication. Query.

ROCKFORD MAGAZINE—331 E. State St., Box 678, Rockford, IL 61105. John Harris, Ed. Lively regional magazine covering northern Illinois and southern Wisconsin. Feature articles 3,000 words, and columns, 1,000 to 2,000 words, on area personalities, events, arts, business, nostalgia, family, and more. Pays from 10¢ a word, on publication. Query with samples.

RURAL LIVING—4201 Dominion Blvd., Suite 101, Glen Allen, VA 23060. Richard G. Johnstone, Jr., Ed. Features, 1,000 to 1,500 words, on people, places, historic sites in Virginia and Maryland's Eastern Shore. Queries preferred. Pays $100 to $150 for articles, on publication.

RURALITE—P.O. Box 558, Forest Grove, OR 97116. Address Ed. or Feature Ed. Articles, 800 to 1,000 words, of interest to a primarily rural and small-town audience in Oregon, Washington, Idaho, Nevada, northern California, and Alaska. Upbeat articles, biographies, local history and celebrations, self-help, etc. Humorous articles and animal pieces. No fiction or poetry. No sentimental nostalgia. Pays $30 to $130, on acceptance. Queries preferred. Guidelines.

SACRAMENTO MAGAZINE—P.O. Box 2424, Sacramento, CA 95811. Ann McSisemore, Man. Ed. Features, 2,500 words, on a broad range of topics related to the region. Department pieces, 1,200 to 1,500 words, and short pieces, 400 words, for "City Lights" column. Pays $150 to $300, on acceptance. Query first.

SAN DIEGO MAGAZINE—4206 W. Point Loma Blvd., P.O. Box 85409, San Diego, CA 92138. Virginia Butterfield, Assoc. Ed. Articles, 1,500 to 3,000 words, on local personalities, politics, lifestyles, business, history, etc., relating to San Diego area. Photos. Pays $250 to $600, on publication. Query with clips.

SAN DIEGO READER—P.O. Box 80803, San Diego, CA 92138. Jim Holman, Ed. Articles, 2,500 to 10,000 words, on the San Diego region. Literate nonfiction. Pays $500 to $2,000, on publication.

SAN FRANCISCO FOCUS—680 Eighth St., San Francisco, CA 94103. Mark Powelson, Ed. Service features, profiles of local newsmakers, and investigative pieces of local issues, 2,500 to 3,000 words. Short stories, 1,500 to 5,000 words. Pays $250 to $750, on acceptance. Query required.

SEATTLE HOME AND GARDEN—222 Dexter Ave. N., Seattle, WA 98109. Jo Brown, Man. Ed. Quarterly addition to *Pacific Northwest* Magazine. Home and garden articles, 500 to 2,000 words, relating directly to the Northwest. Pays $100 to $800, on publication. Guidelines.

SEATTLE'S CHILD—P.O. Box 22578, Seattle, WA 98122. Ann Bergman, Ed. Articles (400 to 2,500 words) of interest to parents, educators, and childcare providers of children under 12, plus investigative reports and consumer tips on issues affecting families in the Puget Sound region. Pays $75 to $400, on publication. Query required.

SENIOR MAGAZINE—3565 S. Higuera St., San Luis Obispo, CA 93401. Personality profiles and health articles, 600 to 900 words, and book reviews (of new books or outstanding older titles) of interest to senior citizens of California. Pays $1.50 per inch, $10 to $25 for B&W photos, on publication.

SILENT SPORTS—717 10th St., P.O. Box 152, Waupaca, WI 54981. Upper Midwest monthly on bicycling, cross country skiing, running, canoeing, hiking, backpacking, and other "silent" sports; articles, 1,000 to 2,000 words. Pays $40 to $100 for features; $20 to $50 for fillers, on publication. Query.

SKYLINE—857 Carroll St., Brooklyn, NY 11215. William J. Lawrence, Ed.-in-Chief. Articles and fiction, 2,000 to 4,000 words, that focus on the positive aspects of New York City's past and present. Also, poetry, fillers, humor, photographs, and illustrations. Payment varies, on acceptance.

SOUTH CAROLINA WILDLIFE—P.O. Box 167, Columbia, SC 29202. Address Man. Ed. Articles, 1,000 to 3,000 words, with regional outdoors focus: conservation, natural history and wildlife, recreation. Profiles, natural history. Pays from 10¢ a word. Query.

SOUTH FLORIDA HOMEBUYER'S GUIDE—2151 W. Hillsboro Blvd., Suite 300, Deerfield Beach, FL 33442. Diana Tafel, Ed. Articles on developments in the housing industry, home improvements, security, decorating, energy efficiency, etc.; advice on finding, buying, and maintaining a home or condominium in south Florida. Pays 10¢ a word, on acceptance. Query.

SOUTH FLORIDA MAGAZINE—600 Brickell Ave., Suite 207, Miami, FL 33131. Marilyn Moore, Ed. Features, 2,000 to 3,500 words, and department pieces, 900 to 1,300 words, on a variety of subjects related to south Florida. Short, bright items, 200 to 400 words, for the "Undercurrents" section. Pays $75 to $900, 15 days after acceptance.

SOUTHERN OUTDOORS—N. 1, Bell Rd., Montgomery, AL 36141. Larry Teague, Ed. How-to articles, 200 to 600 words or 1,500 to 2,000 words, on hunting and fishing, for fishermen and hunters in the 16 southern states. Pays 15¢ a word, on acceptance. Query.

SOUTHWEST ART—Franklin Tower, 5444 Westheimer, Suite 1440, Houston, TX 77056. Susan McGarry, Ed. Articles, 1,800 to 2,200 words, on the artists, museums, galleries, history, and art trends west of the Mississippi River. Particularly interested in representational or figurative arts. Pays from $300, on acceptance. Query with slides of artwork to be featured.

THE STATE: DOWN HOME IN NORTH CAROLINA—128 S. Tryon St., Suite 2200, Charlotte, NC 28202. Jim Duff, Ed. Articles, 600 to 2,000 words, on people, history, and places in North Carolina. Photos. Pays on publication.

SUNDAY MAGAZINE—*Providence Sunday Journal*, 75 Fountain St., Providence, RI 02902. Elliot Krieger, Ed. Nonfiction, 1,000 to 3,000 words, with a New England focus. Pays $100 to $500, on publication.

SUNSET MAGAZINE—80 Willow Rd., Menlo Park, CA 94025. William Marken, Ed. Western regional. Queries not encouraged.

SUNSHINE: THE MAGAZINE OF SOUTH FLORIDA—*The Sun-Sentinel*, 101 N. New River Dr., Ft. Lauderdale, FL 33301–2293. John Parkyn, Ed. Articles, 1,000 to 3,000 words, on topics of interest to south Floridians. Pays $250 to $1,000, on acceptance. Query first. Guidelines.

SUSQUEHANNA MONTHLY MAGAZINE—Box 75A, RD1, Marietta, PA 17547. Richard S. Bromer, Ed. Well-documented articles, 1,000 to 4,000 words, on regional (PA, DE, MD, DC) biographical history. Pays to $75, on publication. Query with SASE required. No fiction, poetry, opinion, or travel.

TALLAHASSEE MAGAZINE—2365 Centerville Rd., Tallahassee, FL 32308. Marion McDanield, Ed. Articles, 800 to 1,100 words, with a positive outlook on the life, people, and history of the north Florida area. Pays 12¢ a word, on publication. Query.

TAMPA BAY LIFE—Bayport Plaza, Suite 990, 6200 Courtney Campbell Causeway, Tampa, FL 33607–1458. David J. Wilson, Ed. Articles, 1,000 to 2,500 words, on the people, events, and issues shaping the region's future. Pays $125 to $300 for department pieces; $400 to $600 for features, on acceptance.

TEXAS HIGHWAYS MAGAZINE—State Dept. of Highways and Public Transportation, P.O. Box 141009, Austin, TX 78714–1009. Frank Lively, Ed. Texas travel, history, and scenic features, 200 to 1,800 words. Pays 40¢ to 60¢ a word, $80 to $500 per photo, on acceptance. Guidelines for writers and photographers.

TEXAS MONTHLY—P.O. Box 1569, Austin, TX 78767. Gregory Curtis, Ed. Features (2,500 to 5,000 words) and departments (under 2,500 words) on art, architecture, food, education, business, politics, etc. "We like solidly researched pieces that uncover issues of public concern, reveal offbeat and previously unreported topics, or use a novel approach to familiar topics." Pays varying rates, on acceptance. Queries required.

TIMELINE—1982 Velma Ave., Columbus, OH 43211–2497. Christopher S. Duckworth, Ed. Articles, 1,000 to 6,000 words, on history of Ohio (politics, economics, social, and natural history) for lay readers in the Midwest. Pays $100 to $900, on acceptance. Queries preferred.

TOLEDO MAGAZINE—*The Blade*, Toledo, OH 43660. Sue Stankey, Ed. Articles, to 5,000 words, on Toledo area personalities, events, etc. Pays $50 to $500, on publication. Query with SASE.

TROPIC—*The Miami Herald*, One Herald Plaza, Miami, FL 33132. Gene Weingarten, Exec. Ed. Tom Shroder, Ed. General-interest articles, 750 to 3,000 words, for south Florida readers. Pays $200 to $1,000, on acceptance. Send SASE.

TUCSON LIFESTYLE—Old Pueblo Press, 7000 E. Tanque Verde, Tucson, AZ 85715. Sue Giles, Ed.-in-Chief. Features on local businesses, lifestyles, the arts, homes, and fashion. Payment varies, on acceptance. Query preferred.

TWIN CITIES READER—5500 Wayzata Blvd., Minneapolis, MN 55416. D.J. Tice, Ed.-in-Chief. Articles, 2 to 4 printed pages, on cultural phenomena, city politics, and general-interest subjects, for local readers aged 25 to 44. Pays to $5 to $8 per inch, on publication.

VALLEY MAGAZINE—16800 Devonshire, Suite 275, Granada Hills, CA 91344. Barbara Wernik, Ed. Articles, 1,000 to 1,500 words, on celebrities, issues, education, health, business, dining, and entertaining, etc., in the San Fernando Valley. Pays $100 to $350, within 8 weeks of acceptance.

VENTURA COUNTY & COAST REPORTER—1583 Spinnaker Dr., Suite 213, Ventura, CA 93001. Nancy Cloutier, Ed. Articles, 3 to 5 pages, on any locally slanted topic. Pays $10, on publication.

VERMONT LIFE—61 Elm St., Montpelier, VT 05602. Tom Slayton, Ed.-in-Chief. Articles, 500 to 3,000 words, about Vermont subjects only. Pays 20¢ a word, extra for photos. Query preferred.

VIRGINIA BUSINESS—411 E. Franklin St., Suite 105, Richmond, VA 23219. James Bacon, Ed. Articles, 1,000 to 2,500 words, related to the business scene in Virginia. Pays varying rates, on acceptance. Query required.

VIRGINIA WILDLIFE—P.O. Box 11104, Richmond, VA 23230–1104. Monthly of the Commission of Game and Inland Fisheries. Articles, 1,500 to 2,500 words, with Virginia tie-in, on conservation and related topics, including fishing, hunting, wildlife management, outdoor safety and ethics, etc. Articles must be accompanied by color photos. Query with SASE. Pays 10¢ a word, extra for photos, on acceptance.

WASHINGTON—200 W. Thomas, Suite 300, Seattle, WA 98119. Larry Shook, Ed. Articles (500 to 4,000 words) on the people, places, and issues of Washington state. Pays from 15¢ to 25¢ a word, on acceptance. Query required.

WASHINGTON POST MAGAZINE—*The Washington Post*, 1150 15th St. N.W., Washington, DC 20071. Linton Weeks, Man. Ed. Personal-experience essays, profiles, and general-interest pieces, to 6,000 words, on business, arts and culture, politics, science, sports, education, children, relationships, behavior, etc. Articles should be of interest to people living in Washington, D.C. Pays from $300, on acceptance. Limited market.

THE WASHINGTONIAN—1828 L St. N.W., Suite 200, Washington, DC 20036. John Limpert, Ed. Helpful, informative articles, 1,000 to 4,000 words, on Washington-related topics. Pays 30¢ a word. Query or completed manuscript.

WE ALASKANS MAGAZINE—*Anchorage Daily News*, Box 149001, Anchorage, AK 99514–9001. George Bryson, Ed. Articles, 2,000 words, and features, 3,000 to 4,000 words, on Alaska topics only. Profiles, narratives, fiction, and humor. Pays $75 to $125 for articles, $300 for features, on publication.

THE WEEKLY, SEATTLE'S NEWS MAGAZINE—1931 Second Ave., Seattle, WA 98101. David Brewster, Ed. Articles, 700 to 4,000 words, with a Northwest perspective. Pays $75 to $800, on publication. Query. Guidelines.

WEST—*San Jose Mercury News*, 750 Ridder Park Dr., San Jose, CA 05190. Charles Matthews, Man. Ed. Sunday magazine. Pieces related to San Francisco Bay, Monterey Bay, and northern California, including personalities, places, and events. Pays $150, on acceptance.

WESTERN SPORTSMAN—P.O. Box 737, Regina, Sask., Canada S4P 3A8. Roger Francis, Ed. Informative articles, to 2,500 words, on hunting, fishing, and outdoor experiences in Alberta and Saskatchewan. How-tos, humor, cartoons. Photos. Pays $75 to $400, on publication.

WESTWAYS—Box 2890, Terminal Annex, Los Angeles, CA 90051. Mary Ann Fisher, Ed. Articles, 1,000 to 1,500 words, and photo essays, on western U.S., Canada, and Mexico: history, contemporary living, travel, personalities, etc. Photos. Pays from 20¢ a word, extra for photos, 30 days before publication. Query.

WISCONSIN—*The Milwaukee Journal Magazine*, Journal/Sentinel, Inc., Box 661, Milwaukee, WI 53201. Alan Borsuk, Ed. Articles, 500 to 2,000 words, on business, politics, arts, science with strong Wisconsin emphasis. Personal-experience essays, profiles and investigative articles. Pays $75 to $500, on publication. Query.

WISCONSIN TRAILS—P.O. Box 5650, Madison, WI 53705. Geri Nixon, Man. Ed. Articles, 1,500 to 3,000 words, on regional topics: outdoors, lifestyle, events, adventure, travel; profiles of artists, craftspeople, and regional personalities. Fiction, with regional slant. Fillers. Pays $100 to $450, on acceptance and on publication. Query.

WISCONSIN WEST MAGAZINE—P.O. Box 381, Eau Claire, WI 54702–0381. Articles on contemporary issues for residents of western Wisconsin; profiles of towns, neighborhoods, families in the region; and historical pieces. Short humor. Payment varies, on publication.

WORCESTER MONTHLY—One Exchange Pl., Worcester, MA 01608. Michael Warshaw, Ed. Articles, to 3,000 words, on the arts, entertainment, fashion, events, and issues specific to central Massachusetts. Pays to $200, on publication. Query required.

YANKEE—Yankee Publishing Co., Dublin, NH 03444. Judson D. Hale, Ed. Articles and fiction, about 2,500 words, on New England and residents. Pays about $600 for features, $1,000 for fiction, on acceptance.

YANKEE MAGAZINE'S TRAVEL GUIDE TO NEW ENGLAND AND ITS NEIGHBORS—Main St., Dublin, NH 03444. Janice Brand, Ed. Articles, 500 to 2,000 words, on activities, attractions, places to visit in New England, New York State, and Atlantic Canada. Photos. Pays $50 to $300, on acceptance. Query with outline and writing samples required.

TRAVEL ARTICLES

AAA WORLD—1000 AAA Dr., Heathrow, FL 32746–5063. Douglas Damerst, Ed. Articles, 600 to 1,500 words, on consumer automotive and travel concerns. Pays $200 to $800, on acceptance. Query with writing samples required.

ACCENT—Box 10010, Ogden, UT 84409. Bryan Larsen and June Krannbule, Eds. Articles, 1,200 words, on travel destinations, ways to travel, and travel tips. Pays 15¢ a word, $35 for color photos, on acceptance. Query first.

AIRFARE INTERLINE MAGAZINE—4 Park Ave., New York, NY 10016. Ratu Kamlani, Ed. Travel articles, 1,000 to 2,500 words, with photos, on shopping, sightseeing, dining, and night life for airline employees. Prices, discount information, and addresses must be included. Pays $75, after publication.

ARIZONA HIGHWAYS—2039 W. Lewis Ave., Phoenix, AZ 85009. Richard G. Stahl, Man. Ed. Informal, well-researched travel articles, 2,000 to 2,500 words, focusing on a specific city or region in Arizona and environs. Also articles dealing with nature, environment, flora and fauna, history, anthropology, archaeology, hiking, boating, industry. Pays 30¢ to 45¢ a word, on acceptance. Query with published clips. Guidelines.

BRITISH HERITAGE—P.O. Box 8200, Harrisburg, PA 17105–8200. Gail Huganir, Ed. Travel articles on places to visit in the British Isles, 800 to 1,000 words. Include detailed historical information with a "For the Visitor" sidebar. Pays $100 to $200, on acceptance.

CALIFORNIA HIGHWAY PATROLMAN—2030 V St., Sacramento, CA 95818. Carol Perri, Ed. Travel articles, to 2,000 words, focusing on places in California and the west coast. "We prefer out-of-the-way stops instead of regular tourist destinations." Query or send completed manuscript. SASE required. Pays 2½¢ a word, extra for B&W photos, on publication.

THE CAMPER TIMES—See *RV Times Magazine*.

CARIBBEAN TRAVEL AND LIFE—8403 Colesville Rd., Suite 830, Silver Spring, MD 20910. Veronica Gould Stoddart, Ed. Lively, informative articles, 500 to 2,500 words, on all aspects of travel, leisure, recreation, and culture in the Caribbean, Bahamas, and Bermuda, for up-scale, sophisticated readers. Photos. Pays $75 to $550, on publication. Query.

COLORADO HOMES & LIFESTYLES—5951 S. Middlefield Rd., Littleton, CO 80123. Darla Worden, Pub. Travel articles on cities, regions, establishments in Colorado; roundups and travel pieces with unusual angles; 1,000 to 1,500 words. Pays 10¢ to 15¢ a word, on acceptance. Query.

CRUISE TRAVEL—990 Grove St., Evanston, IL 60201. Charles Doherty, Man. Ed. Features, 800 to 2,000 words, on the ship-, port-, and cruise-of-the-month; interviews with ship crew members; cruise company profiles; travel suggestions for one-day port stops. Color photos. Payment varies, on acceptance. Query.

DISCOVERY—One Illinois Center, 111 E. Wacker Dr., Suite 1700, Chicago, IL 60601. Scott Powers, Ed. Articles, 1,000 to 2,500 words, on travel topics that explore the world and its people; pieces should be geared to the automotive traveler. Photos on assignment only. Pays from $800, on acceptance. Query with published clips required.

EARLY AMERICAN LIFE—Box 8200, Harrisburg, PA 17105. Frances Carnahan, Ed. Travel features about historic sites and country inns, 1,000 to 3,000 words. Pays $50 to $500, on acceptance. Query.

FAMILY CIRCLE—110 Fifth Ave., New York, NY 10011. Sylvia Barsotti, Regional Ed. Dir. Travel articles, to 2,000 words. Concept travel pieces should appeal to a national audience and focus on both luxury and affordable activities for families; prefer service-filled, theme-oriented travel pieces or first-person family vacation stories. Pay rates vary, on acceptance. Query first.

FRIENDLY EXCHANGE—Locust at 17th, Des Moines, IA 50336. Adele Malott, Ed. Articles, 1,000 to 1,800 words, of interest to active midwestern and western families, on travel and leisure. Photos. Pays $300 to $800, extra for photos. Query preferred. Send SASE for guidelines.

GREAT EXPEDITIONS—Box 8000–411, Sumas, WA 98295–8000. Craig Henderson, Ed. Articles, 700 to 2,500 words on independent, adventurous, budget-conscious travel and unusual destinations. Pays $30 to $65, on publication. Guidelines.

GUIDE TO LIVING OVERSEAS—See *Transitions Abroad*.

GULFSHORE LIFE—Collier Park of Commerce, 2975 S. Horseshoe Dr., Naples, FL 33942. Janis Lyn Johnson, Ed. Florida travel articles focusing on the unusual and unique, 1,800 to 2,400 words. Don't want "typical" sunshine state destinations. Pay negotiable, on publication. Queries required.

INNSIDER—821 Wanda, Ferndale, MI 48220. Cynthia La Ferle, Ed. Bimonthly "for travelers actively seeking quality accommodations in country inns, bed-and-breakfast inns, and other historic lodgings." Inn profiles (1,500 words; 1,800 to 3,000 words for profiles of two or more inns); book reviews (300 words); and sidebars (to 400 words). Color photos welcome; mention availability when querying. Pays within 60 days of acceptance: $375 to $650 for inn profiles; $65 for book reviews; $70 to $90 for sidebars; $75 per photo. Guidelines.

INTERNATIONAL LIVING—824 E. Baltimore St., Baltimore, MD 21202. Kathleen Peddicold, Ed. Newsletter. Short pieces and features, 200 to 2,000 words, with useful information on investing, shopping, travel, employment, education, real estate, and lifestyles overseas. Pays $100 to $400 after publication.

ISLANDS—3886 State St., Santa Barbara, CA 93105. Destination features, 1,000 to 3,000 words, on islands as well as department pieces and front-of-the-book items on island-related topics. Pays about 50¢ a word, on publication. Query required. Guidelines.

MICHIGAN LIVING—Automobile Club of Michigan, 17000 Executive Plaza Dr., Dearborn, MI 48126. Len Barnes, Ed. Informative travel articles, 500 to 1,500 words, on U.S. & Canadian tourist attractions and recreational opportunities; special interest in Michigan.

THE MIDWEST MOTORIST—12901 N. Forty Dr., St. Louis, MO 63141. Michael Right, Ed. Articles 1,000 to 1,500 words, with color slides, on domestic and foreign travel. Pays from $150, on acceptance.

MODERN BRIDE—475 Park Ave. S., New York, NY 10016. Geri Bain, Travel Ed. Articles, 1,800 to 2,000 words, on honeymoon travel, covering the U.S., Caribbean, Bahamas, Bermuda, Canada, Mexico, South Pacific, and Europe. Queries with clips required. Pays $600 to $1,200, on acceptance.

NATIONAL GEOGRAPHIC—17th and M Sts. N.W., Washington, DC 20036. William P.E. Graves, Ed. First-person articles on geography, exploration, natural history, archeology, and science. Half staff written; half written by recognized authorities and published authors. Does not review manuscripts.

NATIONAL GEOGRAPHIC TRAVELER—National Geographic Society, 17th and M Sts. N.W., Washington, DC 20036. Richard Busch, Ed. Dir. Articles 1,500 to 4,000 words, that highlight specific places. "Most articles are assigned to people who have proven their travel-writing excellence with us before, and chances of breaking in with a feature are slight." Query with 1- to 2-page proposal, resumé, and published clips required. Pays $1 a word, on acceptance.

NATIONAL MOTORIST—Bayside Plaza, 188 The Embarcadero, San Francisco, CA 94105. Jane Offers, Ed. Illustrated articles, 500 to 1,100 words, for California motorists, on motoring in the West, car care, roads, personalities, places, etc. Photos from transparencies only. Pays from 10¢ a word, on acceptance. Photos paid on publication. SASE required.

NEW ENGLAND TRAVEL—215 Newbury St., Peabody, MA 01960. Features, 1,000 to 2,500 words, designed to lure travelers to New England; include specific information such as addresses, phone numbers, hours of business, etc. Pays $100 to $250, after publication.

NEW WOMAN—215 Lexington Ave., New York, NY 10016. Gay Bryant, Ed. Armchair travel pieces; women's personal experience and "what I learned from this experience" pieces, 1,000 to 2,000 words. Pays $500 to $2,000, on acceptance. Query required.

THE NEW YORK TIMES—229 W. 43rd St., New York, NY 10036. Nancy Newhouse, Travel Ed. Considers queries only; include writer's background, description of proposed article. No unsolicited manuscripts or photos. Pays on acceptance.

NORTHWEST—*The Sunday Oregonian*, 1320 S.W. Broadway, Portland, OR 97201. Travel articles, 1,000 to 1,500 words, third-person perspective. All material must pertain to the Northwest (OR, WA, ID, and MT). Include details about where to go, what to see, plans to make, with specific information about reservations, ticket reservations, purchases, etc. Pays $150 to $250, on acceptance. Query with clips. Experienced writers only.

NORTHWEST LIVING!—130 Second Ave. S., Edmonds, WA 98020–3512. Terry W. Sheely, Ed. Articles, 400 to 1,500 words, on regional travel and natural resources. Color slides or B&W prints. Query with SASE required.

OFF DUTY MAGAZINE—3303 Harbor Blvd., Suite C-2, Costa Mesa, CA 92626. Gary Burch, U.S. Ed. Travel articles, 1,800 to 2,000 words, for active duty military Americans (age 20 to 40) and their families, on U.S. regions or cities. Must have wide scope; no out-of-the-way places. Military angle essential. Photos. Pays from 16¢ a word, extra for photos, on acceptance. Query required. Guidelines. Limited market.

RV TIMES MAGAZINE—(formerly *The Camper Times*) Royal Productions, Inc., Box 6294, Richmond, VA 23230. Julie Posner, Ed. Articles and fiction, 500 to 2,000 words, related to outdoor or leisure activities, travel attractions in the MD, VA, NJ, NY, DE, and PA areas. Pays 7¢ a word (to $90), on publication. Queries preferred.

SACRAMENTO MAGAZINE—P.O. Box 2424, Sacramento, CA 95812–2424. Jan Haag, Ed. Destination-oriented articles within a 6-hour drive of Sacramento, 1,000 to 1,500 words. Pay varies, on acceptance. Query.

TEXAS HIGHWAYS MAGAZINE—State Dept. of Highways and Public Transportation, P.O. Box 141009, Austin, TX 78714–1009. Frank Lively, Ed. Travel, historical, cultural, scenic features on Texas, 200 to 1,800 words. Pays 40¢ to 50¢, on acceptance; photos $80 to $500. Guidelines.

TOURS & RESORTS—World Publishing Co., 990 Grove St., Evanston, IL 60201–4370. Ray Gudas, Man. Ed. Features on international vacation destinations and resorts, 1,500 words; also essays, nostalgia, humor, tour company profiles, travel tips, and service articles, 800 to 1,500 words. Pays up to $350, on acceptance. Top-quality color slides a must. Query.

TRANSITIONS ABROAD—18 Hulst Rd., Box 344, Amherst, MA 01004. Dr. Clayton A. Hubbs, Ed. Articles for travelers overseas who seek an in-depth experience of the culture: work, study, travel, budget tips. Include practical, first-hand information. Emphasis on establishing meaningful contact with people and socially responsible, ecology-minded travel. "Eager to work with inexperienced writers who travel to learn and want to share information." B&W photos a plus. Pays $1.50 per column inch, after publication. Same requirements for *Guide to Living Overseas*, for nontourist (educational, cultural, vocational) travel abroad. Guidelines.

TRAVEL AGE WEST—100 Grant Ave., San Francisco, CA 94108. Robert Carlsen, Man. Ed. Articles, 800 to 1,000 words, with photos, on any aspect of travel useful to travel agents, including names, addresses, prices, etc.; news or trend angle preferred. Pays $2 per column inch, after publication.

TRAVEL & LEISURE—1120 Ave. of the Americas, New York, NY 10036. Ila Stanger, Ed.-in-Chief. Articles, 800 to 3,000 words, on destinations and travel related activities. Regional pieces for regional editions. Pays $600 to $3,000, on acceptance. Query; articles on assignment.

TRAVEL SMART—Dobbs Ferry, NY 10522. Short pieces, 250 to 1,000 words, about interesting, unusual and/or economical places. Give specific details on hotels, restaurants, transportation, and costs. Pays on publication.

VIAJANDO/TRAVELING—6355 N.W. 36th St., Virginia Gardens, FL 33166. Cristina Juri Arencibia, Ed. Inflight magazine of AeroPeru, published in Spanish and English. General-interest articles, 1,500 words, on travel, art, science, technology, food, lifestyles, etc., with Peruvian and/or Floridian destinations. No political or controversial topics. Photos. Pays $100 for articles, $150 if photos are included, on publication.

VISTA/USA—Box 161, Convent Station, NJ 07961. Kathleen M. Caccavale, Ed. Travel articles, 1,200 to 2,000 words, on U.S., Canada, Mexico, and the Caribbean. Plus, general interest, hobby/collecting, culture, and Americana. "Flavor of the area, not service oriented." Shorts, 500 to 1,000 words, on "Minitrips," "CloseFocus," "American Vignettes." Pays from $500, for features, from $150 for shorts, on acceptance. Query with writing sample and outline. Limited market.

VOLKSWAGEN WORLD—Volkswagen of America, Inc., P.O. Box 3951, 888 W. Big Beaver, Troy, MI 48007–3951. Marlene Goldsmith, Ed. Travel articles on unique places or with a unique angle, to 750 words. Pays $150 per printed page, on acceptance. Query.

WESTWAYS—P.O. Box 2890, Terminal Annex, Los Angeles, CA 90051. Mary Ann Fisher, Exec. Ed. Travel articles on where to go, what to see, and how to get there, 1,300 to 1,500 words. Domestic travel articles are limited to western U.S., Canada, and Hawaii; foreign travel articles are also of interest. Quality color transparencies should be available. Pays 25¢ a word, 30 days before publication.

YACHT VACATIONS MAGAZINE—P.O. Box 1657, Palm Harbor, FL 34682–1657. Charity Cicardo, Ed. Articles and photography on chartered yacht, resort, and dive vacations worldwide, 1,200 words. Pays varying rates, on publication. Query first.

YANKEE MAGAZINE'S TRAVEL GUIDE TO NEW ENGLAND AND ITS NEIGHBORS—Main St., Dublin, NH 03444. Janice Brand, Ed. Articles 500 to 2,000 words, on unusual activities, restaurants, places to visit in New England, New York, and Atlantic Canada. Photos. Pays $50 to $300, on acceptance. Query with outline and writing samples.

INFLIGHT MAGAZINES

ABOARD—North-South Net, Inc., 100 Almeria Ave., Suite 220, Coral Gables, FL 33134. Georgina Fernandez, Ed. Inflight magazine of eight Latin American international airlines. Articles, with photos, on Chile, Dominican Republic, Ecuador, Guatemala, El Salvador, Bolivia, Venezuela, and Honduras. Pieces on science, sports, home, fashion, and gastronomy, 1,200 to 1,500 words. Pays $150, with photos, on acceptance and on publication. Query required.

ALASKA AIRLINES MAGAZINE—2701 First Ave., Suite 250, Seattle, WA 98121. Giselle Smith, Man. Ed. Articles, 800 to 2,500 words, on lifestyle topics, business, travel, and profiles of regional personalities for West Coast business travelers. Query. Payment varies, on publication.

AMERICAN WAY—4200 American Blvd., MD 2G23, Fort Worth, TX 76155. Doug Crichton, Ed. American Airline's inflight magazine. Features of interest to the business traveler, emphasizing travel, adventure, business, and the arts/culture. Pays from $750, on acceptance. Query.

AMERICANA WEST AIRLINES MAGAZINE—Skyword Marketing, Inc., 7500 N. Dreamy Draw Dr., Suite 240, Phoenix, AZ 85020. Michael Derr, Ed. Articles celebrating creativity, 750 to 2,000 words; regional angle helpful. Pays from $250 to $750, on publication. Query required. Guidelines.

HORIZON—See *Midway*.

MIDWAY—Skies Publishing Co., Plaza West, 9600 S.W. Oak St., Suite 310, Portland, OR 97223. Terri Wallo, Ed. Articles, 1,000 to 1,300 words; and columns, 500 to 700 words, of interest to business travelers. Pays $200 to $400 for features, $50 to $100 for columns, on publication. Query letters preferred. Same requirements for *United Express* and *Horizon*.

SKY—12955 Biscayne Blvd., North Miami, FL 33181. Lidia de Leon, Ed. Delta Air Lines' inflight magazine. Articles on business, lifestyle, high tech, sports, the arts, etc. Color slides. Pays varying rates, on acceptance. Query.

UNITED EXPRESS—See *Midway*.

USAIR—1301 Carolina St., Greensboro, NC 27401. Maggie Oman, Ed. Articles, 1,500 to 3,000 words, on travel, business, sports, entertainment, food, health, and other general-interest topics. No downbeat or extremely controversial subjects. Pays $350 to $800, before publication. Query first.

VIS A VIS—East/West Network, 34 E. 51st St., New York, NY 10022. Susan C. Shipman, Ed. First-person articles, 600 to 700 words, on profiles, resorts, and luxury vacations. Pays varying rates, on acceptance. No photos. Queries required. Guidelines.

WOMEN'S PUBLICATIONS

BBW: BIG BEAUTIFUL WOMAN—9171 Wilshire Blvd., Suite 300, Beverly Hills, CA 90210. Carole Shaw, Ed.-in-Chief. Articles, 2,500 words, of interest to women ages 25 to 50, especially large-size women, including interviews with successful large-size women and personal accounts of how to cope with difficult situations. Tips on restaurants, airlines, stores, etc., that treat large women with respect. Payment varies, on publication. Query.

BEAUTY—(formerly *Beauty Digest*) 404 Park Ave. S., New York, NY 10016.

Trisha McMahon Drain, Ed.-in-Chief. Innovative angles for pieces on beauty, health, fitness, emotional self-help for women. Submit queries with published clips. Pay varies.

BLACK ELEGANCE—475 Park Ave. S., New York, NY 10016. Sharyn J. Skeeter, Ed. Articles, 1,000 to 2,000 words, on fashion, beauty, relationships, home design, careers, personal finance, and personalities, for black women age 25 to 45. Short interviews. Include photos if available. Pays $150 to $225, on publication. Query. Guidelines.

BRIDAL GUIDE—Globe Communications Corp., 441 Lexington Ave., New York, NY 10017. Deborah Harding, Ed. Bimonthly covering wedding planning, fashion, beauty, contemporary relationships, honeymoon travel, and plans for the first home. Regular departments include: finance, sex, remarriage, and advice for the groom. Prefers queries for articles 800 to 1,600 words. Pays $200 to $600, on acceptance.

BRIDE'S—350 Madison Ave., New York, NY 10017. Andrea Feld, Man. Ed. Articles, 800 to 3,000 words, for engaged couples or newlyweds, on communication, sex, housing, finances, careers, remarriage, step-parenting, health, birth control, pregnancy, babies, religion, in-laws, relationships, and wedding planning. Pays $300 to $1,000, on acceptance.

CAPPER'S—616 Jefferson St., Topeka, KS 66607. Nancy Peavler, Ed. Human interest, personal experience, historical articles, 300 to 700 words. Poetry, to 15 lines, on nature, home, family. Novel-length fiction for serialization. Letters on women's interests, recipes, hints, for "Heart of the Home." Jokes. Children's writing and art section. Pays varying rates, on publication.

CHATELAINE—Maclean Hunter Bldg., 777 Bay St., Toronto, Ont., Canada M5W 1A7. Elizabeth Parr, Sr. Ed. Articles, 2,500 words, on current issues and personalities of interest to Canadian women. Pays from $1,200 for 1,500 to 3,000 words; from $350 for 500-word "Up-front" columns (relationships, health, parents/kids), on acceptance. Send query with outline or manuscript with international reply coupon.

COMPLETE WOMAN—1165 N. Clark, Chicago, IL 60610. Susan Handy, Sr. Ed. Articles, 1,500 to 2,000 words, with how-to sidebars, giving practical advice to women on careers, health, personal relationships, etc. Inspirational profiles of successful women. Pays varying rates, on publication. Send manuscript or query with SASE.

COSMOPOLITAN—224 W. 57th St., New York, NY 10019. Helen Gurley Brown, Ed. Betty Nichols Kelly, Fiction and Books Ed. Articles, to 3,500 words, and features, 500 to 2,500 words, on issues affecting young career women. Fiction on male-female relationships: short shorts, 1,500 to 3,000 words; short stories, 3,000 to 4,000 words; condensed published novels, 25,000 words.

COUNTRY WOMAN—P.O. Box 643, Milwaukee, WI 53201. Kathy Pohl, Man. Ed. Profiles of country women (photo/feature packages), inspirational, reflective pieces. Personal-experience, nostalgia, humor, service-oriented articles, original crafts, and how-to features, to 1,000 words, of interest to country women. Pays $40 to $150, on acceptance.

ELLE—551 Fifth Ave., New York, NY 10176. Joan Harting, Sr. Ed. Articles, varying lengths, for fashion-conscious women, ages 20 to 50. Subjects include beauty, health, careers, fitness, travel, and lifestyles. Pays top rates, on publication. Query required.

526

ESSENCE—1500 Broadway, New York, NY 10036. Harriette Cole, Contemporary Living Ed. Provocative articles, 800 to 2,500 words, about black women in America today: self-help, how-to pieces, business and finance, health, celebrity profiles, art, travel, and political issues. Short items, 500 to 750 words, on work, parenting, and health. Features and fiction, 800 to 2,500 words. Pays varying rates, on acceptance. Query for articles.

EXECUTIVE FEMALE—127 W. 24th St., New York, NY 10011. Diane Burley, Ed. Features, 6 to 12 pages, on managing people, time, and careers, for women in business. Articles, 4 to 6 pages, for "More Money," "Profiles," and "Viewpoint." Pays varying rates, on publication. Limited market.

FAMILY CIRCLE—110 Fifth Ave., New York, NY 10011. Susan Ungaro, Exec. Ed. Articles, 2,000 words, on "women who have made a difference," marriage, family, and child-care and elder-care issues; consumer affairs, travel, humor, health, nutrition and fitness, personal opinion essays. Query required. Pays top rates, on acceptance.

FIRST FOR WOMEN—P.O. Box 1649, Englewood Cliffs, NJ 07632. Dennis Neeld, Ed. Bibi Wein, Fiction Ed. Query first for articles. Send manuscript for fiction. Mainstream stories, 3,500 to 4,500 words, reflecting the concerns of contemporary women; no formula or experimental fiction. Short-shorts, 850 to 1,000 words. "A humorous twist is welcome in fiction." Pay varies, on acceptance. Allow 8 to 12 weeks for response.

GLAMOUR—350 Madison Ave., New York, NY 10017. Ruth Whitney, Ed.-in-Chief. Barbara Coffey, Man. Ed. How-to articles, from 1,500 words, on careers, health, psychology, interpersonal relationships, etc., for women ages 18 to 35. Fashion and beauty pieces staff written. Submit queries to Lisa Bain, Articles Ed. Pays from $500.

GOOD HOUSEKEEPING—959 Eighth Ave., New York, NY 10019. Joan Thursh, Articles Ed. Lee Quarfoot, Fiction Ed. In-depth articles and features on controversial problems, topical social issues; dramatic personal narratives with unusual experiences of average families; new or unusual medical information, personal medical stories. No submissions on food, beauty, needlework, or crafts. Short stories, 2,000 to 5,000 words, with strong identification for women, by published writers and "beginners with demonstrable talent." Unsolicited fiction will not be returned. "If you receive no response within 6 weeks, assume work was unsuitable for us." Pays top rates, on acceptance.

HARPER'S BAZAAR—1700 Broadway, New York, NY 10019. Anthony Mazzola, Ed.-in-Chief. Articles, 1,500 to 2,000 words, for active, sophisticated women. Topics include the arts, world affairs, food, wine, travel, families, education, personal finance, careers, health, and sexuality. No unsolicited manuscripts; query first with SASE. Payment varies, on acceptance.

IDEALS—P.O. Box 140300, Nashville, TN 37214–0300. Nancy Skarmeas, Assoc. Ed. Articles, 600 to 800 words; poetry, 12 to 50 lines, no free verse. Light, reminiscent pieces of interest to women. Pays $10 for poems. Send SASE for guidelines.

LADIES' HOME JOURNAL—100 Park Ave., New York, NY 10017. Myrna Blyth, Pub. Dir./Ed.-in-Chief. Articles of interest to women. Send queries with outlines to: Lynn Langway, Exec. Ed. (news/general interest); Jane Farrell, Articles Ed. (news/human interest); Nelly Edmondson Gupta (health/medical); Jill Rachlin (celebrity/entertainment); Pamela Guthrie O'Brien (psychology); Lois

Johnson (beauty/fashion/fitness); Lauren Payne (decorating); Jan Hazard (food); Shana Aborn (personal experience); Mary Mohler, Man. Ed. (children and families). Fiction accepted through literary agents only; humorous poetry accepted for "Last Laughs" column. Guidelines, for SASE.

LADY'S CIRCLE—111 E. 35th St., New York, NY 10016. Mary F. Bemis, Ed. How-to, food, and crafts articles for homemakers. "Upbeat" pieces for over-50 audience. Pays $125 for articles, $10 for pet peeves, $5 for recipes or helpful hints, on publication.

LEAR'S—655 Madison Ave., New York, NY 10021. Audreen Ballard, Exec. Ed. "Literate, lively, and compelling" articles, 800 to 1,200 words, for women, on health, finance, contemporary issues, personalities, and leisure. Query with clips and SASE. Pays $1 a word, on acceptance.

MCCALL'S—230 Park Ave., New York, NY 10169. Andrea Thompson, Articles Ed. Articles, 1,000 to 3,000 words, on current issues, human interest, family relationships. Pieces, 800 to 1,000 words, that "describe a problem and solution in a way of interest to parents everywhere," for "The Mothers' Page." Pays top rates ($750 for "The Mothers' Page"), on acceptance.

MADEMOISELLE—350 Madison Ave., New York, NY 10017. Liz Logan, Articles Ed. Eileen Schnurr, Fiction Ed. Pays $800 to $1,000 for short articles, from $1,500 for full-length features; $1,000 for short-short stories; from $2,000 for short stories, on acceptance.

MODERN BRIDE—475 Park Ave. South, New York, NY 10016. Mary Ann Cavlin, Man. Ed. Articles, 1,800 to 2,000 words, for bride and groom, on wedding planning, financial planning, juggling career and home, etc. Query Travel Editor Geri Bain with articles on honeymoon travel. Pays $600 to $1,200, on acceptance.

MS.—One Times Sq., New York, NY 10036. Address Manuscript Editor with SASE. Articles relating to feminism, women's roles, and societal change; reporting, profiles, essays, theory, and analysis. Query with SASE required.

NA'AMAT WOMAN—200 Madison Ave., Suite 2120, New York, NY 10016. Judith Sokoloff, Ed. Articles on Jewish culture, women's issues, social and political topics, and Israel, 1,500 to 2,500 words. Short stories with a Jewish theme. Pays 8¢ a word, on publication. Query or send manuscript.

NEW WOMAN—215 Lexington Ave., New York, NY 10016. Gay Bryant, Ed. Self-help/inspirational articles, on psychology, sex, relationships, money, careers. Travel features, with personal discovery angle. Lifestyle, health, and fitness features. Profiles of celebrities, business women. Pays to $1 a word, on acceptance. Query with SASE.

NEW YORK WOMAN—1120 Sixth Ave., 9th Fl., New York, NY 10036. Betsy Carter, Ed. Articles, 500 to 3,000 words, for women age 25 to 45, living in the New York metropolitan area. Pays $1 a word, on publication. Queries with SASE required.

PLAYGIRL—801 Second Ave., New York, NY 10017. Nancie S. Martin, Ed.-in-Chief. In-depth articles for contemporary women. Fiction, 2,500 words. Humor, celebrity interviews. Pays varying rates. Query first with clips. Guidelines.

QUARANTE—P.O. Box 2875, Arlington, VA 22202. Michele Linden, Articles Ed. The Magazine of Style and Substance for the Woman Who Has Arrived. Features (800 to 1,500 words) and fiction (to 3,000 words), poetry (3 to 18 lines), and short profiles for "Women of Substance" column. Topics include fashion, politics, health, cuisine, and finance geared to women over 35. Pays to $150, on publication. SASE required. Guidelines. "Study magazine before submitting."

RADIANCE—P.O. Box 31703, Oakland, CA 94604. Alice Ansfield, Ed./Pub. Quarterly. Articles, 1,500 to 2,500 words, that provide information, inspiration, and resources for women who wear size 16 or over: profiles, interviews with designers/manufacturers of plus-size clothing; occasional fiction and poetry. Pays to $100, on publication.

REDBOOK—224 W. 57th St., New York, NY 10019. Dawn Raffel, Fiction Ed. Lisa Couturier, Articles Ed. Fiction and articles for women ages 25 to 40. Pays from $1,000 for short stories to 25 typed pages; to $850 for short shorts, to 9 typed pages; $750 for personal-experience pieces, 1,000 to 2,000 words, on solving problems in marriage, family life, or community, for "Young Mother's Story." Query for articles only. SASE required.

SAVVY WOMAN—3 Park Ave., New York, NY 10016. Martha Nelson, Ed.-in-Chief. Sophisticated articles on careers, for successful women; topical features and profiles of interesting women, 2,000 to 2,500 words. Payment varies.

SELF—350 Madison Ave., New York, NY 10017. Alexandra Penney, Ed.-in-Chief. Query for articles on current women's issues. No poetry. Payment varies. Include SASE.

VOGUE—350 Madison Ave., New York, NY 10017. Address Features Ed. Articles, to 1,500 words, on women, entertainment and the arts, travel, medicine, and health. General features. No unsolicited manuscripts. Query first. Pays good rates, on acceptance.

WOMAN'S DAY—1633 Broadway, New York, NY 10019. Rebecca Greer, Articles Ed. Human-interest or helpful articles, to 2,500 words, on marriage, child-rearing, health, careers, relationships, money management. Dramatic first-person narratives of medical miracles, rescues, women's experiences, etc. Pays top rates, on acceptance. Query.

WOMEN IN BUSINESS—American Business Women's Assn., 9100 Ward Pkwy., Box 8728, Kansas City, MO 64114–0728. Wendy S. Myers, Ed. Features, 1,000 to 1,500 words, for working women between 35 and 55 years. No profiles. Pays on acceptance. Written query required.

WOMEN'S CIRCLE—P.O. Box 299, Lynnfield, MA 01940. Marjorie Pearl, Ed. Success stories on home-based female entrepreneurs. How-to articles on contemporary craft and needlework projects. Unique money-saving ideas and recipes. Pays varying rates, on acceptance.

WOMEN'S HOUSEHOLD—306 E. Parr Rd., Berne, IL 46711. Allison Ballard, Ed. Profiles, 2,500 words, of women in history, crafts and food articles, and pieces on relationships. Romance stories, 1,500 words. Pieces on pen pals (arranging meetings, reunions, etc.). Pays $40 to $250, on publication.

WORKING MOTHER—Lang Communication, 230 Park Ave., New York, NY 10169. Address Editorial Dept. Articles, to 1,000 words, that help women in their task of juggling job, home, and family. "We like humorous pieces that solve or illuminate a problem unique to our readers." Payment varies, on acceptance.

WORKING WOMAN—342 Madison Ave., New York, NY 10173. Kate White, Ed.-in-Chief. Articles, 1,000 to 2,500 words, on business and personal aspects of the lives of working women. Pays from $400, on acceptance.

HOME AND LIFESTYLE PUBLICATIONS

THE AMERICAN ROSE MAGAZINE—P.O. Box 30,000, Shreveport, LA 71130. Kris McKnight, Exec. Dir. Articles on home rose gardens: varieties, products, etc. Pays in copies.

BETTER HOMES AND GARDENS—1716 Locust St., Des Moines, IA 50336. David Jordan, Ed. Articles, to 2,000 words, on home and family entertainment, money management, health, travel, pets, and cars. Pays top rates, on acceptance. Query.

CHILD—110 Fifth Ave., New York, NY 10011. Freddi Greenberg, Ed. Articles on the lifestyles of children and families. Departments: "Fashion," "Home Environment," "Baby Best," and "Travel." Pays from $750. Query.

CHOCOLATIER—Haymarket, Ltd., 45 W. 34th St., New York, NY 10001. Barbara Albright, Ed. Articles related to chocolate and desserts, cooking and baking techniques, lifestyle and travel. Pays varying rates, on acceptance. Query required. Guidelines.

THE CHRISTIAN SCIENCE MONITOR—One Norway St., Boston, MA 02115. David Holmstrom, Features Ed. Newspaper. Articles on lifestyle trends, women's rights, family, parenting, and consumerism. Pays varying rates, on acceptance.

CONCEIVE—P.O. Box 2047, Danville, CA 94526. Catherine C. Knipper, Ed. Articles, 400 to 4,000 words, written in lay terms about current medical technologies and advances for infertile individuals. Pieces addressing the emotional side of infertility and lifestyle alternatives (adoption, child-free living). Pays on publication: $50 to $175; $1 per line of poetry (4 to 30 lines); $10 per 100 words of filler (do not exceed 250 words).

CONSUMERS DIGEST—5705 N. Lincoln Ave., Chicago, IL 60659. John Manos, Ed. Articles, 500 to 3,000 words, on subjects of interest to consumers: products and services, automobiles, health, fitness, consumer legal affairs, and personal money management. Photos. Pays from 30¢ a word, extra for photos, on publication. Buys all rights. Query with resumé and published clips.

THE COOK'S MAGAZINE—2710 North Ave., Bridgeport, CT 06604. Deborah Hartz, Ed.-in-Chief. Articles on trends in home and restaurant food and cooking. Query with brief outline, published clips, and sample recipe (for writing and recipe style). Pays $200 to $1,000, on acceptance. SASE required.

COUNTRY—5400 S. 60th St., Greendale, WI 53129. Address Deb Mulvey. Pieces on interesting rural and country people who have unusual hobbies or businesses, 500 to 1,500 words; liberal use of direct quotes. Good, candid, color photos required. Pays on acceptance. Queries preferred.

DECORATING REMODELING—110 Fifth Ave., New York, NY 10011. Olivia Bell Buehl, Ed. Columns on finance and collecting. Articles on home decorating, remodeling, architecture, and gardening. Query first. Payment varies, on acceptance.

ELLE DECOR—1633 Broadway, New York, NY 10019. Mitchell Owens, Articles Ed. "Personality profiles (500 to 2,000 words) of new artists, designers, and craftspeople are a good way to catch our attention." Query. Pays $1 a word, on acceptance.

FARM AND RANCH LIVING—5400 S. 60th St., Greendale, WI 53129. Bob Ottum, Ed. Articles, 2,000 words, on rural people and situations; nostalgia pieces, profiles of interesting farms and farmers, ranches and ranchers. Poetry. Pays $15 to $400, on acceptance and on publication.

FLORIDA HOME & GARDEN—600 Brickell Ave., Suite 207, Miami, FL 33131. Kathryn Howard, Ed. Features, 800 to 1,000 words, and department pieces, 500 to 750 words, about Florida interior design, architecture, landscape architecture, gardening, trendy new products, art, travel (Florida, Caribbean, and Mexico's gulf coast), and home entertaining. Pays $200 to $400, extra for photos.

FLOWER & GARDEN MAGAZINE—4251 Pennsylvania, Kansas City, MO 64111. How-to articles, to 1,200 words, with photos, on indoor and outdoor home gardening. Pays varying rates, on acceptance. Query preferred.

FOOD & WINE—1120 Ave. of the Americas, New York, NY 10036. Carole Lalli, Ed.-in-Chief. Warren Picower, Man. Ed. Current culinary or beverage ideas for dining and entertaining at home and out. Submit detailed proposal.

GARDEN—The Garden Society, Botanical Garden, Bronx, NY 10458. Karen Polyak, Ed. Articles, 1,000 to 2,500 words, on botany, horticulture, ecology, agriculture. Photos. Pays to $300, on publication. Query.

GARDEN DESIGN—4401 Connecticut Ave. N.W., Fifth Fl., Washington, DC 20008. Karen D. Fishler, Ed. Articles, 1,000 to 1,500 words, on classic and contemporary examples of residential landscape design, garden art, and garden history. Pays $350 for features, $250 for departments, on publication. Query.

GROWING CHILD/GROWING PARENT—22 N. Second St., Lafayette, IN 47902. Nancy Kleckner, Ed. Articles, to 1,500 words, on subjects of interest to parents of children under 6. No personal experience pieces or poetry. Guidelines.

HARROWSMITH COUNTRY LIFE—Ferry Rd., Charlotte, VT 05445. Tom Rawls, Ed. Investigative pieces, 4,000 to 5,000 words, on issues of ecology and the environment, rural life, gardening, energy-efficient housing, and healthful food. Short pieces for "Screed" (opinions) and "Gazette" (news briefs). Pays $500 to $1,500 for features, from $50 to $600 for department pieces, on acceptance. Query required. Send SASE for guidelines.

HEALTHY KIDS—Cahners Publishing, 475 Park Ave. S., New York, NY 10016. Phyllis Steinberg, Ed. Published three times yearly in two editions: *Birth-3* and *4–10 Years*. Articles, 1,500 to 2,000 words, addressing the elements of raising a healthy, happy child (basic care, nutrition, analysis of the growing mind, behavior patterns, emergencies, etc.). "All articles should be written by experts or include interviews with appropriate pediatricians and other health-care professionals." Query. Pays $500 to $1,000, on acceptance.

THE HERB QUARTERLY—P. O. Box 548, Boiling Springs, PA 17007. Linda Sparrowe, Ed. Articles, 2,000 to 4,000 words, on herbs: practical uses, cultivation, gourmet cooking, landscaping, herb tradition, medicinal herbs, crafts ideas, unique garden designs, profiles of herb garden experts, practical how-tos for the herb businessperson. Include garden design when possible. Pays on publication. Guidelines.

HG: HOUSE & GARDEN—350 Madison Ave., New York, NY 10017. Nancy Novogrod, Ed.-in-Chief. Dana Cowin, Man. Ed. Articles on decorating, style, design, architecture, and the arts. No unsolicited articles.

HOME MAGAZINE—5900 Wilshire Blvd., 15th Fl., Los Angeles, CA 90036. Joseph Ruggiero, Ed. Articles of interest to homeowners: architecture, remodeling, decorating, how-tos, project ideas, landscaping, taxes, insurance, conservation, and solar energy. Pays varying rates, on acceptance. Query, with 50- to 200-word summary.

HOMEOWNER—3 Park Ave., New York, NY 10016. Joe Carter, Ed. Articles, 500 to 1,500 words, with photos, on home improvement, remodeling, landscaping, and do-it-yourself projects. Pays $400 to $1,000 for feature stories, on acceptance. Query.

HORTICULTURE—Statler Bldg., 20 Park Plaza, Suite 1220, Boston, MA 02116. Deborah Starr, Articles Ed. Authoritative, well-written articles, 500 to 2,500 words, on all aspects of gardening. Pays competitive rates. Query first.

HOUSE BEAUTIFUL—1700 Broadway, New York, NY 10019. Elaine Greene, Ed. Service articles related to the home. Pieces on design, travel, and gardening; mostly staff-written. Send for writer's guidelines. Query with detailed outline. SASE required.

HOUSTON METROPOLITAN MAGAZINE—5615 Kirby, Suite 600, P.O. Box 25386, Houston, TX 77265. Gabrielle Cosgriff, Ed. Dir. Mike Peters, Man. Ed. Articles on political and social issues, home design and gardening, real estate, arts, lifestyles, health, travel; profiles. All material must have a strong Houston-area angle. Pays $50 to $500 for columns; $600 to $1,000 for feature articles. Query.

INDEPENDENT LIVING—44 Broadway, Greenlawn, NY 11740. Anne Kelly, Ed. Articles, 1,000 to 2,000 words, addressing lifestyles of persons who have disabilities. Possible topics: home health care, travel, sports, cooking, hobbies, family life, and sexuality. Pays 10¢ a word, on publication. Query.

LIFE IN THE TIMES—The Times Journal Co., Springfield, VA 22159–0200. Barry Robinson, Ed. Travel articles, 900 words; features on food, 500 to 1,000 words; and short, personal-experience pieces, 750 words, of interest to military people and their families around the world. Pays from $25 to $150 for short pieces, to $350 for general-interest features up to 2,000 words, on acceptance.

LOG HOME GUIDE FOR BUILDERS & BUYERS—Rt. 2, Box 581, Cosby, TN 37722. Articles, 500 to 1,500 words, on building new, or restoring old, log homes, especially with solar or alternative heating systems, as well as pieces on decorating or profiles of interesting builders of log homes. Pays 20¢ a word, extra for photos, on publication. Limited market. Query first.

LOG HOME LIVING—610 Herndon Pkwy., Suite 500, Herndon, VA 22070. Roland Sweet, Man. Ed. Articles, 1,000 to 1,500 words, on modern manufactured and handcrafted kit log homes: home owner profiles, design and decor features, home producer profiles, historical features, technical articles. Pays $200 to $600, on acceptance.

MARRIAGE & FAMILY—Abbey Press Publishing Div., St. Meinrad, IN 47577. Kass Dotterweich, Man. Ed. Expert advice, some personal-experience articles, with moral, religious, or spiritual slant, to 2,500 words, on husband-wife and parent-child relationships. Pays 7¢ a word, on acceptance.

MATURE OUTLOOK—Meredith Corp., 1716 Locust, Des Moines, IA 50336. Marjorie P. Groves, Ed. Articles, 500 to 2,000 words, for "energetic" readers over the age of 50: covers travel and leisure topics, health, food, gardening, and personalities. Pays $200 to $1,500, on acceptance.

METROPOLITAN HOME—750 Third Ave., New York, NY 10017. Barbara Graustark, Articles Ed. Service and informational articles on apartments for young, professional, urban audience. Pay varies. Query.

MIDWEST LIVING—1912 Grand Ave., Des Moines, IA 50309. Barbara Humeston, Ed. Bimonthly. Lifestyle articles relating to any or all of the 12 midwest states; town, neighborhood, and personality profiles. Humorous essays used occasionally. Pays varying rates, on acceptance; buys all rights.

MILITARY LIFESTYLE MAGAZINE—1732 Wisconsin Ave. N.W., Washington, DC 20007-2313. Hope Daniels, Ed. Articles, 1,000 to 2,000 words, for military families in the U.S. and overseas; pieces on child raising, marriage, health, fitness, food, and issues concerning young military families; home decor and "portable" or "instant" gardening articles; fiction. Pays $300 to $700, on publication. Query first.

THE MOTHER EARTH NEWS—80 Fifth Ave., New York, NY 10011. Alfred Meyer, Ed. Articles on country living: home improvement and construction, how-tos, indoor and outdoor gardening, crafts and projects, etc. Also self-help, health, food-related, ecology, energy, and consumerism pieces; profiles. Pays from $100 per published page, on acceptance. Address Submissions Ed.

NATIONAL GARDENING MAGAZINE—180 Flynn Ave., Burlington, VT 05401. Warren Schultz, Ed. Articles, 300 to 3,000 words: seed-to-table profiles of major crops; firsthand reports from experienced gardeners in this country's many growing regions; easy-to-follow gardening techniques; garden food recipes; coverage of fruits, vegetables, and ornamentals. Pays $75 to $450, extra for photos, on acceptance. Query preferred.

NEW AGE JOURNAL—342 Western Ave., Brighton, MA 02135. Phillip Whitten, Ed. Features, 2,000 to 4,000 words; columns, 750 to 1,500 words; short news items, 500 words; and first-person narratives, 750 to 1,500 words, for readers who take an active interest in holistic health, personal and spiritual growth, environmentalism, social responsibility, and contemporary social issues. Pays varying rates. Query or send completed manuscript.

NEW CHOICES FOR THE BEST YEARS—28 W. 23rd St., New York, NY 10010. Carol Mauro, Exec. Ed. Lifestyle/service magazine for people ages 45 to 65. Articles on careers, health/fitness, travel, gardening, relationships, entertaining, and finance. Columns on "Generations," "Collecting," nostalgia, the new volunteerism, pets, cars. Send complete manuscript with SASE. Payment varies, on acceptance.

NEW HOME—P.O. Box 2008, Laconia, NH 03247. Steven Maviglio, Man. Ed. Articles, 250 to 2,500 words, "that give upscale new homeowners whatever they need to make their home more comfortable, practical, and personal." Department pieces on landscaping, security, and interviews with professionals in their homes. Pays $200 to $1,000, on acceptance. Query required.

NEW YORK FAMILY—420 E. 79th St., New York, NY 10021. Felice Shapiro, Susan Ross, Eds. Articles related to family life in New York City and general parenting topics. Pays $50 to $100. Same requirements for *Westchester Family*.

1001 HOME IDEAS—3 Park Ave., New York, NY 10016. Ellen Frankel, Ed. General-interest articles, 500 to 2,000 words, on home decorating, remodeling, building, furnishings, food, household tips, gardening, crafts. How-to and problem-solving pieces. Pays varying rates, on acceptance. Query.

PALM SPRINGS LIFE—Desert Publications, 303 N. Indian Ave., Palm Springs, CA 92262. Jamie Pricer, Ed. Articles (1,000 to 3,000 words) of interest to "wealthy, upscale people who live and/or play in the desert." Pays $150 to $400 for features, $30 for short profiles, on publication. Query required.

533

PARENTING—501 Second St., San Francisco, CA 94107. David Markus, Ed. Articles, 500 to 3,500 words, on education, health, fitness, nutrition, child development, psychology, and social issues, for parents of young children. Pays to $2,000. Query.

PARENTS—685 Third Ave., New York, NY 10017. Ann Pleshette Murphy, Ed. Articles, 1,500 to 3,000 words, on parenting, family, women's and community issues, etc. Informal style with quotes from experts. Pays from $1,000, on acceptance. Query.

PARENTS AND TEENAGERS—289 N. Monroe Ave., Box 481, Loveland, CO 80539. Joani Schultz, Ed. Dir. Articles, 200 to 1,400 words, with Christian focus, on the parenting of teenagers; include quotes of experts, practical tips, and anecdotes. Pays $25 to $100, on acceptance. Query.

SEATTLE HOME AND GARDEN—222 Dexter Ave. N., Seattle, WA 98109. Jo Brown, Man. Ed. Quarterly addition to *Pacific Northwest Magazine*. Home and garden articles, 500 to 2,000 words, relating directly to the northwest. Pays $100 to $800, on publication. Guidelines.

SELECT HOMES—50 Holly St., Toronto, Canada M4S 3B3. Diane McDougall, Ed. How-to articles, profiles of Canadian homes, humor essays, 750 to 1,200 words. Pays from $250 to $700 (Canadian), on acceptance. Query with international reply coupons. Send SAE with international reply coupons for guidelines.

VIRTUE—P. O. Box 850, Sisters, OR 97759. Marlee Alex, Ed. Articles, 1,000 to 1,500 words, on the family, marriage, self-esteem, working mothers, opinions, food, crafts. Fiction. Pays 15¢ to 25¢ a word, on acceptance. Query required.

WEIGHT WATCHERS MAGAZINE—360 Lexington Ave., New York, NY 10017. Ruth Papazian, Articles Ed. Articles on nutrition and health. Pays from $350, on acceptance. Query with clips required. Guidelines.

WESTCHESTER FAMILY—See *New York Family*.

WORKBENCH—4251 Pennsylvania, Kansas City, MO 64111. Robert N. Hoffman, Ed. Illustrated how-to articles on home improvement and woodworking, with detailed instructions. Pays from $150 per printed page, on acceptance. Send SASE for writers' guidelines.

SPORTS, OUTDOORS, RECREATION

THE AMERICAN FIELD—542 S. Dearborn, Chicago, IL 60605. B.J. Matthys, Man. Ed. Yarns about hunting trips, bird-shooting; articles to 1,500 words, on dogs and field trials, emphasizing conservation of game resources. Pays varying rates, on acceptance.

AMERICAN HANDGUNNER—591 Camino de la Reina, Suite 200, San Diego, CA 92108. Cameron Hopkins, Ed. Semi-technical articles on shooting sports, gun repair and alteration, handgun matches and tournaments, for lay readers. Pays $100 to $500, on publication. Query.

AMERICAN HUNTER—470 Spring Park Place, Suite 1000, Herndon, VA 22070. Tom Fulgham, Ed. Articles, 1,400 to 2,500 words, on hunting. Photos. Pays on acceptance. Guidelines.

THE AMERICAN RIFLEMAN—470 Spring Park Place, Suite 1000, Herndon, VA 22070. Bill Parkerson, Ed. Factual articles on use and enjoyment of sporting firearms. Pays on acceptance.

AMERICAN SQUAREDANCE MAGAZINE—216 Williams St., P.O. Box 488, Huron, OH 44839. Cathie Burdick, Co-Ed. Articles and fiction, 1,000 to 1,500 words, related to square dancing. Poetry. Fillers to 100 words. Pays $2 per column inch.

THE ATLANTIC SALMON JOURNAL—1435 St. Alexandre, Suite 1030, Montreal, Quebec, Canada H3A 2G4. Terry Davis, Ed. Material related to Atlantic salmon: fishing, conservation, ecology, travel, politics, biology, how-tos, anecdotes, cuisine. Articles, 1,500 to 3,000 words. Pays $100 to $350, on publication.

BACKPACKER MAGAZINE—Rodale Press, 33 Minor St., Emmaus, PA 18049. John Viehman, Exec. Ed. Articles, 250 to 3,000 words, on self-propelled backcountry travel: backpacking, technique, kayaking/canoeing, mountaineering, nordic skiing, health, natural science. Photos. Pays varying rates. Query.

THE BACKSTRETCH—19899 W. 9 Mile Rd., Southfield, MI 48075. Harriet Randall, Ed. United Thoroughbred Trainers of America. Feature articles, with photos, on subjects involved with thoroughbred horse racing. Pays after publication.

BASEBALL ILLUSTRATED—See *Hockey Illustrated*.

BASSIN'—15115 S. 76th E. Ave., Bixby, OK 74008. Gordon Sprouse, Man. Ed. Articles, 1,500 to 1,800 words, on how to and where to bass fish, for the amateur fisherman. Pays $275 to $400, on acceptance.

BASSMASTER MAGAZINE—B.A.S.S. Publications, P.O. Box 17900, Montgomery, AL 36141. Dave Precht, Ed. Articles, 1,500 to 2,000 words, with photos, on freshwater black bass and striped bass. "Short Casts" pieces, 400 to 800 words, on news, views, and items of interest. Pays $200 to $400, on acceptance. Query.

BAY & DELTA YACHTSMAN—2019 Clement Ave., Alameda, CA 94501. Bill Parks, Ed. Cruising stories and features. Must have northern California tie-in. Photos and illustrations. Pays varying rates.

BC OUTDOORS—1132 Hamilton St., #202, Vancouver, B.C., Canada V6B 2S2. George Will, Ed. Articles, to 2,000 words, on fishing, hunting, conservation, and all forms of non-competitive outdoor recreation in British Columbia and Yukon. Photos. Pays from 15¢ to 25¢ a word, on acceptance.

BICYCLE GUIDE—711 Boylston St., Boston, MA 02116. Theodore Costantino, Ed. "Our magazine covers all aspects of cycling from an enthusiast's perspective: racing, touring, sport riding, product reviews, and technical information. We depend on free lancers for touring articles, personality profiles, and race coverage." Queries are preferred. Pays varying rates, on publication.

BICYCLING—33 E. Minor St., Emmaus, PA 18098. James C. McCullagh, Ed. Articles, 500 to 2,500 words, on recreational riding, fitness training, nutrition, bike maintenance, equipment, racing and touring, for serious cyclists. Photos, illustrations. Pays $25 to $1000, on acceptance. Guidelines.

BIRD WATCHER'S DIGEST—P.O Box 110, Marietta, OH 45750. Mary B. Bowers, Ed. Articles, 600 to 2,500 words, for bird watchers: first-person accounts; how-tos; pieces on endangered species; profiles. Cartoons. Pays from $50, on publication.

BLACK BELT—P.O. Box 7728, 1813 Victory Pl., Burbank, CA 91510–7728. Articles related to self-defense: how-tos on fitness and technique; historical, travel, philosophical subjects. Pays $100 to $200, on publication. Query required. Guidelines.

BOAT PENNSYLVANIA—Pennsylvania Fish Commission, P.O. Box 1673, Harrisburg, PA 17105–1673. Art Michaels, Ed. Articles, 200 to 2,500 words, with photos, on boating in Pennsylvania: motorboating, sailing, waterskiing, canoeing, kayaking, and rafting. No pieces on fishing. Pays $50 to $250, on acceptance. Query. Guidelines.

BOUNDARY WATERS JOURNAL—9396 Rocky Ledge Rd., Ely, MN 55731. Stuart Osthoff, Ed. Articles, 2,000 to 3,000 words, on recreation and natural resources in Minnesota's Boundary Waters Canoe Area Wilderness and Ontario's Quetico Provincial Park. Regular features include canoe route journals, fishing, camping, hiking, cross-country skiing, wildlife and nature, regional lifestyles, history, and events. Pays $200 to $400, on publication; $50 to $150 for photos.

BOW & ARROW HUNTING—Box HH, 34249 Camino Capistrano, Capistrano Beach, CA 92624. Roger Combs, Ed. Dir. Articles, 1,200 to 2,500 words, with B&W photos, on bowhunting; profiles and technical pieces. Pays $50 to $300, on acceptance. Same address and mechanical requirements for *Gun World*.

BOWHUNTER MAGAZINE—2245 Kohn Rd., Box 8200, Harrisburg, PA 17105–8200. M.R. James, Ed. Informative, entertaining features, 500 to 2,000 words, on bow and arrow hunting. Fillers. Photos. Pays $25 to $300, on acceptance. Study magazine first.

BOWHUNTING WORLD—319 Barry Ave. S., Suite 101, Wayzata, MN 55391. Tim Dehn, Ed. Articles, 1,800 to 3,000 words, on all aspects of bowhunting and competitive archery, with photos. Pays from $200, on acceptance, with premium for features available on 5¼ disks.

BOWLERS JOURNAL—101 E. Erie St., Chicago, IL 60611. Mort Luby, Ed. Trade and consumer articles, 1,200 to 2,200 words, with photos, on bowling. Pays $75 to $200, on acceptance.

BOWLING—5301 S. 76th St., Greendale, WI 53129. Dan Matel, Ed. Articles, to 1,500 words, on amateur league and tournament bowling. Profiles. Pays varying rates, on publication.

CALIFORNIA HORSE REVIEW—P.O. Box 2437, Fair Oaks, CA 95628. Articles, 750 to 2,500 words, on horse training, for professional horsemen; profiles of prominent west coast horses and riders. Pays $35 to $125, on publication.

CANOE—P.O. Box 3146, Kirkland, WA 98083. David F. Harrison, Ed.-in-Chief. Features, 2,000 to 4,000 words; department pieces, 500 to 2,000 words. Topics include canoeing or kayaking adventures, destinations, boat and equipment reviews, technique and how-tos, short essays, camping, environment, humor, health, history, etc. Pays $5 per column inch, on publication. Query or send complete manuscript.

CAR AND DRIVER—2002 Hogback Rd., Ann Arbor, MI 48105. William Jeanes, Ed. Articles, to 2,500 words, for enthusiasts, on car manufacturers, new developments in cars, etc. Pays to $2,000, on acceptance. Query with clips.

CAR CRAFT—8490 Sunset Blvd., Los Angeles, CA 90069. Jim McGowan, Ed. Articles and photofeatures on unusual street machines, drag cars, racing events; technical pieces; action photos. Pays from $150 per page, on publication.

CASCADES EAST—716 N.E. Fourth St., P.O. Box 5784, Bend, OR 97708. Geoff Hill, Ed./Pub. Articles, 1,000 to 2,000 words, on outdoor activities (fishing, hunting, golfing, backpacking, rafting, skiing, snowmobiling, etc.), history, special events, and scenic tours in Cascades region. Photos. Pays 3¢ to 10¢ a word, extra for photos, on publication.

536

CHESAPEAKE BAY MAGAZINE—1819 Bay Ridge Ave., Annapolis, MD 21403. Jean Waller, Ed. Technical and how-to articles, to 1,500 words, on boating, fishing, conservation, in Chesapeake Bay. Photos. Pays $85 to $125, on publication.

CHEVY OUTDOORS—3221 W. Big Beaver, Suite 110, Troy, MI 48084. Michael Brudenell, Ed. Published five times yearly. Articles (800 to 1,200 words) on unusual travel destinations, activities, and personality profiles relating to recreational vehicles, of interest to outdoors enthusiasts. Pays $600 to $800, on publication. Guidelines.

CITY SPORTS —P.O Box 193693, San Francisco, CA 94119. Sue Levin, Ed. Articles, 200 to 2,000 words, on the active lifestyle, including service pieces, trend pieces, profiles, and nutrition. Pays $50 to $650, on publication. Query editor.

CROSS COUNTRY SKIER—819 Barry Ave. S., Wayzata, MN 55391. Jim Chase, Ed. Articles, to 3,000 words, on all aspects of cross-country skiing. Departments, 1,000 to 1,500 words, on ski maintenance, skiing techniques, health and fitness. Published October through February. Pays $300 to $700 for features, $100 to $350 for departments, on publication. Query.

CRUISING WORLD—524 Thames St., Newport, RI 02840. Bernadette Brennan, Ed. Articles on sailing, 1,000 to 2,500 words: technical and personal narratives. No fiction, poetry, or logbook transcripts. 35mm slides. Pays $100 to $600, on acceptance. Query preferred.

CYCLE WORLD—853 W. 17th St., Costa Mesa, CA 92627. David Edwards, Ed. Technical and feature articles, 1,500 to 2,500 words, for motorcycle enthusiasts. Photos. Pays $100 to $200 per page, on publication. Query.

CYCLING U.S.A.—U.S. Cycling Federation, 1750 E. Boulder St., Colorado Springs, CO 80909. Kyle Woodleif, Ed. Articles, 500 to 1,500 words, on bicycle racing. Pays 15¢ a word, on publication. Query first.

THE DIVER—P.O. Box 313, Portland, CT 06480. Bob Taylor, Ed. Articles on divers, coaches, officials, springboard and platform techniques, training tips, etc. Pays $15 to $75, extra for photos ($5 to $25 for cartoons), on publication.

EQUUS—Fleet Street Corp., 656 Quince Orchard Rd., Gaithersburg, MD 20878. Emily Kilby, Ed. 1,000- to 3,000-word articles on all breeds of horses, covering their health, care, the latest advances in equine medicine and research, and horse-world events. "Attempt to speak as one horse-person to another." Pays $100 to $400, on acceptance.

FIELD & STREAM—2 Park Ave., New York, NY 10016. Duncan Barnes, Ed. Articles, 1,500 to 2,500 words, with photos, on hunting, fishing. Fillers, 250 to 1000 words. Cartoons. Pays from $800 for feature articles with photos, $250 to $450 for fillers, $100 for cartoons, on acceptance. Query for articles.

FISHING WORLD—51 Atlantic Ave., Floral Park, NY 11001. Keith Gardner, Ed. Features, to 2,500 words, with color transparencies, on fishing sites, technique, equipment. Pays to $500 for major features, $250 for shorter destination articles. Query preferred.

THE FLORIDA HORSE—P.O. Box 2106, Ocala, FL 32678. Bernie Dickman, Ed. Articles, 1,500 words, on Florida Thoroughbred breeding and racing. Pays $100 to $200, on publication.

FLY FISHERMAN—2245 Kohn Rd., Box 8200, Harrisburg, PA 17105. John Randolph, Ed. Articles, to 3,000 words, on how to and where to fly fish. Fillers, to 100 words. Pays from $50 to $500, on acceptance. Query.

FLY ROD & REEL—P.O. Box 370, Camden, ME 04843. James E. Butler, Man. Ed. Fly fishing pieces, 2,000 to 2,500 words, and occasional fiction; articles on the culture and history of the areas being fished. Pays on publication. Query.

THE FLYFISHER—1387 Cambridge, Idaho Falls, ID 83401. Dennis G. Bitton, Ed. Articles, 500 to 3,000 words, on techniques, lore, history, and flyfishing personalities; how-pieces. Serious or humorous short stories related to flyfishing. Pays from $50 to $200, after publication. Queries are preferred. Guidelines.

FLYFISHING NEWS, VIEWS AND REVIEWS—1387 Cambridge, Idaho Falls, ID 83401. Dennis G. Bitton, Ed. Articles 500–3,500 words on flyfishing, fiction, humor, nonfiction reports, or where tos/ how tos. Guest opinion articles and letters to the editor. Pays $50 to $150 for articles, $25 to $50 for prints or drawings. Queries preferred.

FOOTBALL DIGEST—Century Publishing Co., 990 Grove St., Evanston, IL 60201. Michael K. Herbert, Ed.-in-Chief. Profiles of pro stars, "think" pieces, 1,500 words, aimed at the pro football fan. Pays on publication.

FOOTBALL FORECAST—See *Hockey Illustrated*.

FUR-FISH-GAME—2878 E. Main St., Columbus, OH 43209. Mitch Cox, Ed. Illustrated articles, 800 to 2,500 words, preferably with how-to angle, on hunting, fishing, trapping, dogs, camping, or other outdoor topics. Some humorous or where-to articles. Pays $40 to $150, on acceptance.

GAME AND FISH PUBLICATIONS—P.O. Box 741, Marietta, GA 30061. Publishes 31 monthly outdoors magazines for 48 states. Articles, 1,500 to 2,500 words, on hunting and fishing. How-tos, where-tos, and adventure pieces. Profiles of successful hunters and fishermen. No hiking, canoeing, camping, or backpacking pieces. Pays $125 to $175 for state-specific articles, $200 to $300 for multi-state articles, before publication. Pays, $25 to $75 for photos.

GOAL—650 Fifth Ave., 33rd Fl., New York, NY 10019. Michael A. Berger, Ed. Official magazine of the National Hockey League. Player profiles and trend stories, 1,000 to 1,800 words, for hockey fans with knowledge of the game and players, by writers with understanding of the sport. Pays $150 to $300, on acceptance. Query.

GOLF DIGEST—5520 Park Ave., Trumbull, CT 06611. Jerry Tarde, Ed. Instructional articles, tournament reports, and features on players, to 2,500 words. Fiction, 1,000 to 2,000 words. Poetry, fillers, humor, photos. Pays varying rates, on acceptance. Query preferred.

GOLF FOR WOMEN—2130 Jackson Ave. W., Oxford, MS 38655. George Kehoe, Ed.-in-Chief. Golf-related articles of interest to women; fillers and humor. Instructional pieces staff written. Pays from 40¢ a word, on publication. Query first.

GOLF ILLUSTRATED—3 Park Ave., New York, NY 10016. Al Barkow, Ed. Hal Goodman, Man. Ed. Golf-related features, 1,000 to 2,000 words: instruction, profiles, photo essays, travel, technique, nostalgia, opinion. Pays $750 to $1,500, on acceptance. Query preferred.

GOLF JOURNAL—Golf House, Far Hills, NJ 07931. Robert Sommers, Ed. U.S. Golf Assn. Articles on golf personalities, history, travel. Humor. Photos. Pays varying rates, on publication.

GOLF MAGAZINE—2 Park Ave., New York, NY 10016. Jim Frank, Ed. Articles, 1,000 words with photos, on golf history and travel (places to play around the world); profiles of professional tour players. Shorts, to 500 words. Pays 75¢ a word, on acceptance. Queries preferred.

THE GREYHOUND REVIEW—National Greyhound Association, Box 543, Abilene, KS 67410. Tim Horan, Man. Ed. Articles, 1,000 to 10,000 words, pertaining to the greyhound racing industry: how-to, historical nostalgia, interviews. Pays $85 to $150, on publication.

GULF COAST GOLFER—See *North Texas Golfer*.

GUN DIGEST—4092 Commercial Ave., Northbrook, IL 60062. Ken Warner, Ed. Well-researched articles, to 5,000 words, on guns and shooting, equipment, etc. Photos. Pays from 10¢ a word, on acceptance. Query.

GUN DOG—P.O. Box 35098, Des Moines, IA 50315. Bob Wilbanks, Man. Ed. Features, 1,000 to 2,500 words, with photos, on bird hunting: how-tos, wheretos, dog training, canine medicine, breeding strategy. Fiction. Humor. Pays $50 to $150 for fillers and short articles, $150 to $350 for features, on acceptance.

GUN WORLD—See *Bow & Arrow Hunting*.

GUNS & AMMO—8490 Sunset Blvd., Los Angeles, CA 90069. E. G. Bell, Jr., Ed. Technical and general articles, 1,500 to 3,000 words, on guns, ammunition, and target shooting. Photos, fillers. Pays from $150, on acceptance.

HANG GLIDING—U.S. Hang Gliding Assn., P.O. Box 8300, Colorado Springs, CO 80933. Gilbert Dodgen, Ed. Articles, 2 to 3 pages, on hang gliding. Pays to $50, on publication. Query.

HOCKEY ILLUSTRATED—Lexington Library, Inc., 355 Lexington Ave., New York, NY 10017. Stephen Ciacciarelli, Ed. Articles, 2,500 words, on hockey players, teams. Pays $125, on publication. Query. Same address and requirements for *Baseball Illustrated*, *Wrestling World*, *Pro Basketball Illustrated*, *Pro Football Illustrated*, *Basketball Annual* (college), *Baseball Preview*, *Baseball Forecast*, *Pro Football Preview*, *Football Forecast*, and *Basketball Forecast*.

HORSE & RIDER—P.O. Box 72001, San Clemente, CA 92672. Sue M. Copeland, Ed. Articles, 500 to 1,700 words, with photos, on Western riding and general horse care geared to the performance horse: training, feeding, grooming, etc. Pays varying rates, on publication. Buys all rights. Guidelines.

HORSEMEN'S YANKEE PEDLAR—785 Southbridge St., Auburn, MA 01501. Nancy L. Khoury, Pub. News and feature-length articles, about horses and horsemen in the Northeast. Photos. Pays $2 per published inch, on publication. Query.

HORSEPLAY—P.O. Box 130, Gaithersburg, MD 20884. Cordelia Doucet, Ed. Articles, 1,500 to 3,000 words, on eventing, show jumping, horse shows, dressage, driving, and fox hunting, for horse enthusiasts. Pays 10¢ a word for all rights, 9¢ a word for 1st American rights, after publication. Query. SASE required.

HOT BIKE—2145 W. La Palma, Anaheim, CA 92801. Buck Lovell, Ed. Articles, 250 to 2,500 words, with photos, on motorcycles (contemporary and antique). Event coverage on high performance street and track and sport touring motorcycles, with emphasis on Harley Davidsons. Pays $50 to $100 per printed page, on publication.

HOT ROD—8490 Sunset Blvd., Los Angeles, CA 90069. Jeff Smith, Ed. How-to pieces and articles, 500 to 5,000 words, on auto mechanics, hot rods, track and drag racing. Photo-features on custom or performance-modified cars. Pays to $250 per page, on publication.

HUNTING—8490 Sunset Blvd., Los Angeles, CA 90069. Craig Boddington, Ed. How-to articles on practical aspects of hunting. At least 15 photos required with articles. Pays $250 to $400 for articles with B&W photos, extra for color photos, on publication.

THE IN-FISHERMAN—Box 999, Brainerd, MN 56401–0999. Doug Stange, Ed. Published seven times yearly. How-to articles, 1,500 to 4,500 words, on all aspects of freshwater fishing. Humor, 1,000 to 1,500 words, for "Reflections" column. Pays $250 to $650, on acceptance.

INSIDE TEXAS RUNNING—9514 Bristlebrook Dr., Houston, TX 77083. Joanne Schmidt, Ed. Articles and fillers on running, cycling, and triathlons in Texas. Pays $35 to $100, $10 for photos, on acceptance.

KEEPIN' TRACK OF VETTES—P.O. Box 48, Spring Valley, NY 10977. Shelli Finkel, Ed. Articles of any length, with photos, relating to Corvettes. Pays $25 to $200, on publication.

KITPLANES—P.O. Box 6050, Mission Viejo, CA 92690. Dave Martin, Ed. Articles geared to the growing market of aircraft built from kits and plans by home craftsmen, on all aspects of design, construction, and performance, 1,000 to 4,000 words. Pays $150 to $350, on publication.

LAKELAND BOATING—1600 Orrington Ave., Suite 500, Evanston, IL 60201. Douglas Seibold, Ed. Articles for boat owners on the Great Lakes and other area waterways, on long distance cruising, short trips, maintenance, equipment, history, regional personalities and events, and environment. Photos. Pays on acceptance. Query first. Guidelines.

MEN'S FITNESS—21100 Erwin St., Woodland Hills, CA 91367. Jim Rosenthal, Features Ed. Features, 1,500 to 2,500 words, and department pieces, 1,000 to 1,500 words: "authoritative and practical articles dealing with fitness, health, and men's lifestyles." Pays $400 to $600, on acceptance.

MEN'S HEALTH—Rodale Press, 33 E. Minor Dr., Emmaus, PA 18098. Michael Lafavore, Exec. Ed. Articles, 1,000 to 2,500 words, on fitness, diet, health, relationships, sports, and travel, for men ages 25 to 55. Pays from 50¢ a word, on acceptance. Query first.

MICHIGAN OUT-OF-DOORS—P.O. Box 30235, Lansing, MI 48909. Kenneth S. Lowe, Ed. Features, 1,500 to 2,500 words, on hunting, fishing, camping, and conservation in Michigan. Pays $75 to $150, on acceptance.

MID-WEST OUTDOORS—111 Shore Dr., Hinsdale, IL 60521. Gene Laulunen, Ed. Articles, 1,500 words, with photos, on where, when, and how to fish and hunt in the Midwest. Pays $15 to $35, on publication.

MOTOR TREND—8490 Sunset Blvd., Los Angeles, CA 90069. Jack Nerad, Ed. Articles, 250 to 2,000 words, on autos, racing, events, and profiles. Photos. Pay varies, on acceptance. Query.

MOTORCYCLIST—8490 Sunset Blvd., Los Angeles, CA 90069. Art Friedman, Ed. Articles, 1,000 to 3,000 words. Action photos. Pays $75 to $100 per published page, on publication.

MOTORHOME MAGAZINE—29901 Agoura Rd., Agoura, CA 91301. Bob Livingston, Ed. Articles, to 2,000 words, with color slides, on motorhomes; travel and how-to pieces. Pays to $600, on acceptance.

MOUNTAIN BIKE—Rodale Press, 33 E. Minor St., Emmaus, PA 18098. Ed Pavelka, Ed. Dir. Articles, 1,200 to 2,000 words, on mountain bike touring; major off-road events; political, sport, or land-access issues; riding techniques; fitness and training tips. Pays $200 to $1,600, on publication. Query first.

MUSCULAR DEVELOPMENT—351 W. 54th St., New York, NY 10019. Alan Paul, Ed. Articles, 1,000 to 2,500 words, personality profiles, training features, and diet and nutrition pieces. Photos. Pays $100 to $300 for articles; $35 for color photos, $20 for B&W, and $300 to $500 for cover photos.

MUSHING—P.O. Box 149, Ester, AK 99725. Todd Hoener, Ed. How-tos, profiles, and features (1,500 to 2,000 words) and department pieces (500 to 1,000 words) for competitive and recreational dog drivers and skijorers. International audience. Photos. Pays $25 to $250, after acceptance. Queries preferred. Guidelines.

NATIONAL PARKS MAGAZINE—1015 31st St., N.W., Washington, DC 20007. Michele Strutin, Ed. Articles, 1,000 to 2,000 words, on natural history, wildlife, outdoors activities, travel and conservation as they relate to national parks: illustrated features on the natural, historic, and cultural resources of the National Park System. Pieces about legislation and other issues and events related to the parks. Pays $100 to $1,000, on acceptance. Query. Send for guidelines.

THE NEW ENGLAND SKIERS GUIDE—Box 1125, Waitsfield, VT 05673. Andrew Bigford, Ed. Annual (August closing). Articles on alpine and nordic skiing, equipment, and winter vacations at New England resorts. Rates vary.

NISSAN DISCOVERY—2401 E. Katella Ave., Suite 600, Anaheim, CA 92806. Wayne Thoms, Ed. Controlled-circulation magazine for owners of Nissan vehicles. Articles, from 1,500 words, on travel, lifestyle, show business, humor, and food. Top quality color photos. Query. Pays $300 to $1,000, on acceptance.

NORTH TEXAS GOLFER—9182 Old Katy Rd., Suite 212, Houston, TX 77055. Bob Gray, Ed. Articles, 800 to 1,500 words, of interest to golfers in North Texas. Pays $50 to $250, on publication. Queries required. Same requirements for *Gulf Coast Golfer*.

NORTHEAST OUTDOORS—P.O. Box 2180, Waterbury, CT 06722–2180. Jean Wertz, Ed. Articles, 500 to 1,800 words, preferably with B&W photos, on camping in Northeast U.S.: recommended private campgrounds, camp cookery, recreational vehicle hints. Stress how-to, where-to. Cartoons. Pays $20 to $80, on publication. Guidelines.

OFFSHORE—220 Reservoir St., Needham Heights, MA 02194. Martha Lostrom, Ed. Articles, 1,200 to 2,500 words, on boats, people, and places along the New England, New York, and New Jersey coasts. Writers should be knowledgeable boaters. Photos a plus. Pays $100 to $300.

ON TRACK—17165 Newhope St., "M," Fountain Valley, CA 92708. Andrew Crask and Craig Fisher, Eds. Features and race reports, 500 to 2,500 words. Pays $4 per column inch, on publication.

OPEN WHEEL—P.O. Box 715, Ipswich, MA 01938. Dick Berggren, Ed. Articles, to 6,000 words, on open wheel drivers, races, and vehicles. Photos. Pays to $400 on publication.

OUTDOOR AMERICA—1401 Wilson Blvd., Level B, Arlington, VA 22209. Quarterly publication of the Izaak Walton League of America. Articles, 1,500 to 2,000 words, on natural resource conservation issues and outdoor recreation; especially fishing, hunting, and camping. Pays 20¢ a word for features. Query Articles Ed. with published clips.

OUTDOOR LIFE—2 Park Ave., New York, NY 10016. Clare Conley, Ed.-in-Chief. Articles on hunting, fishing, and related subjects. Pays top rates, on acceptance.

OUTSIDE—1165 N. Clark, Chicago, IL 60610. High-quality articles, with photos, on sports, environmental issues, wilderness travel, adventure, etc. Pays varying rates. Query.

PENNSYLVANIA ANGLER—Pennsylvania Fish Commission, P.O. Box 1673, Harrisburg, PA 17105–1673. Address Art Michaels, Ed. Articles, 250 to 2,500 words, with photos, on freshwater fishing in Pennsylvania. Pays $50 to $250, on acceptance. Must send SASE with all material. Query. Guidelines.

PENNSYLVANIA GAME NEWS—Game Commission, 2001 Elmerton Ave., Harrisburg, PA 17110–9797. Bob Mitchell, Ed. Articles, to 2,500 words, with photos, on outdoor subjects, except fishing and boating. Photos. Pays from 6¢ a word, extra for photos, on acceptance.

PERFORMANCE HORSEMAN—Gum Tree Corner, Unionville, PA 19375. Joanne Tobey, Articles Ed. Factual how-to pieces for the serious western rider, on training, improving riding skills, all aspects of care and management, etc. Pays from $300, on acceptance.

PETERSEN'S FISHING—8490 Sunset Blvd., Los Angeles, CA 90069. Robert Robb, Ed. "We're interested primarily in how-to articles (2,000 to 2,500 words), though pieces on where to fish, unusual techniques and equipment, and profiles of successful fisherman will also be considered. Photos must accompany all manuscripts, and we prefer to be queried first." Pays $300 to $400, on acceptance.

PETERSEN'S HUNTING—8490 Sunset Blvd., Los Angeles, CA 90069. Craig Boddington, Ed. How-to articles, 2,500 words, on all aspects of sport hunting. B&W photos; color slides. Pays $300 to $500, on acceptance. Query.

PGA MAGAZINE—The Quartron Group, 2155 Butterfield, Suite 200, Troy, MI 48084. Articles, 1,500 to 2,500 words, on golf-related subjects. Pays $300 to $500, on acceptance. Query.

PLEASURE BOATING—1995 N.E. 150th St., North Miami, FL 33181. Don Zern, Exec. Ed. Articles, 1,000 to 2,500 words, on fishing, cuising, recreational boating, travel, offshore racing, covering Florida, Bahamas, and Caribbean. Special sections on Florida Keys, Bahamas, Jamaica, Cayman Islands, and Puerto Rico. Pays varying rates, on publication. Query first. Study sample copies. Guidelines.

POWERBOAT—15917 Strathern St., Van Nuys, CA 91406. Lisa Nordskog, Man. Ed. Articles, to 1,500 words, with photos, for powerboat owners, on outstanding achievements, water-skiing, competitions; technical articles on hull and engine developments; how-to pieces. Pays $300 to $700, on acceptance. Query.

PRACTICAL HORSEMAN—Gum Tree Corner, Unionville, PA 19375. Joanne Tobey, Articles Ed. How-to articles on English riding, training, and horse care. Pays on acceptance. Query.

PRIVATE PILOT—P.O. Box 6050, Mission Viejo, CA 92690. Mary F. Silitch, Ed. Technically based aviation articles for general aviation pilots and aircraft owners, 1,000 to 4,000 words, for aviation enthusiasts. Photos. Pays $75 to $250, on publication. Query.

PRO BASKETBALL ILLUSTRATED—See *Hockey Illustrated*.

PRO FOOTBALL ILLUSTRATED—See *Hockey Illustrated*.

PURE BRED DOGS/AMERICAN KENNEL GAZETTE—51 Madison Ave., New York, NY 10010. Marion Lane, Exec. Ed. Judy Hartop, Sen. Ed. Articles, 1,000 to 2,500 words, relating to pure-bred dogs. Pays from $100 to $300, on acceptance. Queries preferred.

RESTORATION—3153 E. Lincoln, Tucson, AZ 85714–2017. W.R. Haessner, Ed. Articles, 1,200 to 1,800 words, on restoration of autos, trucks, planes, trains, etc., and related building (bridges and structures). Photos. Pays varying rates —from $50 per page—on publication. Queries required.

RIDER—29901Agoura Rd., Agoura Hills, CA 91301. Mark Tuttle, Jr., Ed. Articles, with slides, to 3,000 words, with emphasis on travel, touring, commuting, and camping motorcyclists. Pays $100 to $500, on publication. Query.

RUNNER'S WORLD—Rodale Press, 33 E. Minor St., Emmaus, PA 18098. Bob Wischnia, Sr. Ed. Articles for "Human Race" (submit to Eileen Shovlin), "Finish Line" (to Cristina Negron), and "Health Watch" (to Kate Delhagen) columns. Send feature articles or queries to Bob Wischnia. Payment varies, on acceptance. Query.

SAIL—Charlestown Navy Yard, 100 First Ave., Charlestown, MA 02129. Patience Wales, Ed. Articles, 1,500 to 3,500 words, features, 1,000 to 1,500 words, with photos, on sailboats, equipment, racing, and cruising. How-tos on navigation, sail trim, etc. Pays $75 to $1,000 on publication. Guidelines sent on request.

SALT WATER SPORTSMAN—280 Summer St., Boston, MA 02210. Barry Gibson, Ed. Articles, 1,200 to 1,500 words, on how anglers can improve their skills, and on new places to fish off the coast of U.S. and Canada, Central America, the Caribbean, and Bermuda. Photos a plus. Pays $350 to $700, on acceptance. Query.

SCORE, CANADA'S GOLF MAGAZINE—287 MacPherson Ave., Toronto, Ont., Canada M4V 1A7. John Gordon, Man. Ed. Articles, 800 to 2,000 words, on travel, golf equipment, golf history, personality profiles, or prominent professionals. (Canadian content only.) Pays $125 to $600 for features, on assignment and publication. Query with published clips.

SEA KAYAKER—6327 Seaview Ave. N.W., Seattle, WA 98107. Christopher Cunningham, Ed. Articles, 400 to 4,500 words, on ocean kayaking. Fiction. Pays 5¢ to 10¢ a word, on publication. Query with clips and international reply coupons.

SEA, THE MAGAZINE OF WESTERN BOATING—17782 Cowan, Irvine, CA 92714. Linda Yuskaitis, Exec. Ed. Features, 800 to 2,000 words, and news articles, 200 to 400 words, of interest to West Coast boating enthusiasts: profiles of boating personalities, cruise destinations, analyses of marine environmental issues, technical pieces on navigation and seamanship, news from Western harbors. No fiction, first-person, poetry, or cartoons. Pays varying rates, on publication.

SHOTGUN SPORTS—P.O. Box 6810, Auburn, CA 95604. Frank Kodl, Ed. Official publication of The United States Sporting Clays Assoc. Articles with photos, on trap and skeet shooting, sporting clays, hunting with shotguns, reloading, gun tests, and instructional shooting. Pays $25 to $200, on publication.

SILENT SPORTS—717 10th St., P.O. Box 152, Waupaca, WI 54981. Upper Midwest monthly on bicycling, cross country skiing, running, canoeing, hiking, backpacking, and other "silent" sports; articles, 1,000 to 2,000 words. Pays $50 to $100 for features; $20 to $50 for fillers, on publication. Query.

SKI MAGAZINE—2 Park Ave., New York, NY 10016. Dick Needham, Ed. Articles, 1,300 to 2,000 words, for experienced skiers: profiles, humor, "it-happened-to me" stories, and destination articles. Short, 100- to 300- word, news items for "Ski

Life" column. Equipment and racing articles are staff written. Query first (with clips) for articles. Pays from $200, on acceptance.

SKI RACING—Box 1125, Rt. 100, Waitsfield, VT 05673. Articles on alpine and nordic racing, training, personalities. Photos. Rates vary.

SKIN DIVER MAGAZINE—8490 Sunset Blvd., Los Angeles, CA 90069. Bill Gleason, Pub./Ed. Illustrated articles, 500 to 2,000 words, on scuba diving activities, equipment, and dive sites. Pays $50 per published page, on publication.

SKYDIVING MAGAZINE—P. O. Box 1520, DeLand, FL 32721. Michael Truffer, Ed. Timely news articles, 300 to 800 words, relating to sport and military parachuting. Fillers. Photos. Pays $25 to $200, extra for photos, on publication.

SNOWBOARDER—P.O. Box 1028, Dana Point, CA 92629. Steve Casimiro, Man. Ed. Published four times yearly from Sept. to Jan. Articles, 1,000 to 1,500 words, on snowboarding personalities, techniques, and events; four-color transparencies or black-and-white prints. Occasional fiction, 1,000 to 1,500 words. Pays $150 to $800, on acceptance and on publication.

SNOWMOBILE—319 Barry Ave., S., Suite. 101, Wayzata, MN 55391. Dick Hendricks, Ed. Articles, 700 to 2,000 words, with color or B&W photos, related to snowmobiling: races and rallies, trail rides, personalities, travel. How-tos, humor; cartoons. Pays to $450, on publication. Query.

SOCCER AMERICA MAGAZINE—P. O. Box 23704, Oakland, CA 94623. Paul Kenned, Ed. Articles, to 500 words, on soccer: news, profiles, coaching tips. Pays $25 to $50, for features, within 60 days of publication.

SOUTH CAROLINA WILDLIFE—P. O. Box 167, Columbia , SC 29202. John E. Davis, Ed. Articles, 1,000 to 3,000 words, with regional outdoor focus: conservation, natural history, wildlife, and recreation. Profiles, how-tos. Pays on acceptance.

SOUTHERN GAMEPLAN—701 S. 37th St., Suite 9, Birmingham, AL 35222. Ben Cook, Ed. Sports articles, 1,200 to 1,500 words, with a "southern flair." Queries are preferred. Pay varies, on publication. Guidelines.

SOUTHERN OUTDOORS—1 Bell Rd., Montgomery, AL 35117. Larry Teague, Ed. Essays, 1,200 to 1,500 words, related to the outdoors. Pays 15¢ to 20¢ a word, on acceptance.

SPORT MAGAZINE—8490 Sunset Blvd., Los Angeles, CA 90069. Kelly Garrett, Ed. Query with clips. No fiction, poetry, or first person.

THE SPORTING NEWS—1212 N. Lindbergh Blvd., St. Louis, MO 63132. John D. Rawlings, Ed. Articles, 1,000 to 1,500 words, on baseball, football, basketball, hockey, and other sports. Pays $150 to $500, on publication.

SPORTS ILLUSTRATED—1271 Avenue of the Americas, New York, NY 10020. Chris Hunt, Articles Ed. No unsolicited material.

SPUR MAGAZINE—P. O. Box 85, Middleburg, VA 22117. Address Editorial Dept. Articles, 300 to 5,000 words, on Thoroughbred racing, breeding, polo, show jumping, eventing, and steeplechasing. Profiles of people and farms. Historical and nostalgia pieces. Pays $50 to $400, on publication. Query.

STOCK CAR RACING—P. O. Box 715, Ipswich, MA 01938. Dick Berggren, Feature Ed. Articles, to 6,000 words, on stock car drivers, races, and vehicles. Photos. Pays to $400, on publication.

SURFING—P. O. Box 3010, San Clemente, CA 92672. Bill Sharp, Ed. Eric

Fairbanks, Man. Ed. Short newsy and humorous articles, 200 to 500 words. No first person travel articles; knowledge of sport essential. Pays varying rates, on publication.

SWIMSUIT INTERNATIONAL—Swimsuit Publishers, 801 Second Ave., New York, NY 10017. Nicole Dorsey, Ed.-in-Chief. Articles, 1,000–2,000 words, on swimwear-related topics. Pays varies. Query.

TENNIS—5520 Park Ave., P. O. Box 0395, Trumbull, CT 06611–0395. Donna Doherty, Ed. Instructional articles, features, profiles of tennis stars, 500 to 2,000 words. Photos. Pays from $100 to $750, on publication. Query.

TENNIS WEEK—124 E. 40th St., Suite 1101, New York, NY 10016. Eugene L. Scott, Pub. Steven Sheer, Ed. In-depth, researched articles, from 1,000 words, on current issues and personalities in the game. Pays $125, on publication.

TRAILER BOATS—20700 Belshaw Ave., P. O. Box 5427, Carson, CA 90249–5427. Wiley Poole, Ed. Technical and how-to articles, 500 to 2,000 words, on boat, trailer, or tow vehicle maintenance and operation; skiing, fishing, and cruising. Fillers, humor. Pays 10¢ to 15¢ a word, on publication.

TRAILER LIFE—29901 Agoura Rd., Agoura, CA 91301. Bill Estes, Ed. Articles, to 2,500 words, with photos, on trailering, truck campers, motorhomes, hobbies, and RV lifestyles. How-to pieces. Pays to $600, on acceptance. Send for guidelines.

TRAILS-A-WAY—Compass Publishing Group, 6489 Parkland Dr., Sarasota, FL 34243. Martha Higbie, Ed. RV-related travel articles, 1,000 to 1,200 words, for "the monthly magazine dedicated to Midwest camping families." Pay varies, on publication.

TREASURE DIVER—P.O. Drawer 7419, Van Nuys, CA 91409. Stanford Nielsen, Ed. Bimonthly. Articles (1,000 to 2,500 words) on or related to underwater adventure. Color slides or B&W photos must accompany submissions. Pays $1.50 per column inch, including photos; $75 per cover photo; made on publication.

TRIATHLETE—1415 Third St., Suite 303, Santa Monica, CA 90401. Richard Graham, Ed. Published 10 times yearly. Articles, varying lengths, pertaining to the sport of triathlon. "We can't use articles about marathons, long-distance cycling events, or rough-water swimming." Color slides. Pays 10¢ to 30¢ a word, on publication.

VELONEWS—5595 Arapahoe, Suite G, Boulder, CO 80303. John Wilcockson, Ed. Articles, 500 to 1,500 words, on competitive cycling, profiles, training, nutrition, interviews. No how-to or touring articles. "We focus on the elite of the sport." Pay varies, on publication.

VOLKSWAGEN WORLD—Volkswagen of America, Troy, MI 28007. Marlene Goldsmith, Ed. Articles, 750 to 1,000 words, accompanied by color slides. Pays $150 to $325 per printed page, on acceptance. Query required. Guidelines.

THE WALKING MAGAZINE—9–11 Harcourt, Boston, MA 02116. Bradford Ketchum, Ed. Articles, 1,500 to 2,000 words, on fitness, health, equipment, nutrition, travel, and adventure, famous walkers, and other walking-related topics. Shorter pieces, 500 to 1,500 words, and essays for "Ramblings" page. Photos welcome. Pays $750 to $2,500 for features, $100 to $600 for department pieces. Guidelines.

WASHINGTON FISHING HOLES—P.O. Box 32, Sedro Wolley, WA 98284. Detailed articles, with specific maps, 800 to 1,500 words, on fishing in

Washington. Local Washington fishing how-tos. Photos. Pays on publication. Query. Send SASE for guidelines.

THE WATER SKIER—799 Overlook Dr., Winter Haven, FL 33884. John Baker, Ed. Offbeat articles on waterskiing. Pays varying rates, on acceptance.

THE WESTERN HORSEMAN—P.O. Box 7980, Colorado Springs, CO 80933. Pat Close, Ed. Articles, around 1,500 words, with photos, on care and training of horses. Pays to $250, on acceptance.

WESTERN OUTDOORS—3197-E Airport Loop, Costa Mesa, CA 92626. Timely, factual articles on fishing and hunting, 1,200 to 1,500 words, of interest to western sportsmen. Pays $400 to $500, on acceptance. Query. Guidelines.

WESTERN SPORTSMAN—P.O. Box 737, Regina, Sask., Canada S4P 3A8. Roger Francis, Ed. Articles, to 2,500 words, on outdoor experiences in Alberta and Saskatchewan; how-to pieces. Photos. Pays $75 to $325, on publication.

WINDRIDER—P.O. Box 2456, Winter Park, FL 32790. Debbie Snow, Ed. Features, instructional pieces, and tips, by experienced boardsailors. Fast action photos. Pays $50 to $75 for tips, $250 to $300 for features, extra for photos. Send guidelines first.

WOMAN BOWLER—5301 S. 76th St., Greendale, WI 53129–1191. Karen Sytsma, Ed. Profiles, interviews, and news articles, to 1,000 words, for women bowlers. Pays varying rates, on acceptance. Query with outline.

WOMEN'S SPORTS & FITNESS—1919 14th St., Suite 421, Boulder, CO 80302. Jane McConnell, Ed. How-tos, profiles, active travel, and controversial issues in women's sports, 500 to 3,000 words. Fitness, nutrition, and health pieces also considered. Pays on publication.

WORLD TENNIS—Family Media, Inc., 3 Park Ave., New York, NY 10016. Peter Coan, Man. Ed. Articles, 750 to 1,500 words, on tournaments, technique, celebrities, equipment, player profiles, tennis resorts, and related subjects. Payment varies, on acceptance. Query.

WRESTLING WORLD—See *Hockey Illustrated*.

YACHTING—2 Park Ave., New York, NY 10016. Charles Barthold, Exec. Ed. Articles, 1,500 words, on recreational power and sail boating. How-to and personal-experience pieces. Photos. Pays $350 to $1,000, on acceptance. Queries preferred.

AUTOMOTIVE MAGAZINES

AAA WORLD—AAA Headquarters, 1000 AAA Dr., Heathrow, FL 32746–5063. Douglas Damerst, Ed. Automobile and travel concerns, including automotive travel, maintenance, and upkeep, 750 to 1,500 words. Pays $300 to $600, on acceptance. Query with clips preferred.

AMERICAN MOTORCYCLIST—American Motorcyclist Assn., Box 6114, Westerville, OH 43081–6114. Greg Harrison, Ed. Articles and fiction, to 3,000 words, on motorcycling: news coverage, personalities, tours. Photos. Pays varying rates, on publication. Query with SASE.

CAR AND DRIVER—2002 Hogback Rd., Ann Arbor, MI 48105. William Jeanes, Ed. Articles, to 2,500 words, for enthusiasts, on car manufacturers, new developments in cars, etc. Pays to $2,000, on acceptance. Query with clips.

CAR AUDIO AND ELECTRONICS—21700 Oxnard St., Woodland Hills,

CA 91367. Bill Neill, Ed. "We want articles that cover complicated topics simply." Features (1,000 to 2,000 words) on electronic products for the car: audio, cellular telephones, security systems, CBs, radar detectives, etc.; how to buy them; how they work; how to use them. Pays $300 to $1,000, on acceptance. Send manuscript or query.

CAR CRAFT—8490 Sunset Blvd., Los Angeles, CA 90069. Jim McGowan, Ed. Articles and photo features on unusual street machines, drag cars, racing events; technical pieces; action photos. Pays from $150 per page, on publication.

CHEVY OUTDOORS—3221 W. Big Beaver, Suite 100, Troy, MI 68084. Michael Brudenell, Ed. Published five times yearly. Articles (800 to 1,200 words) on unusual travel destinations, activities, and personality profiles relating to recreational vehicles and of interest to outdoors enthusiasts. Query. Pays $600 to $800, on publication. Guidelines.

CYCLE WORLD—853 W. 17th St., Costa Mesa, CA 92627. David Edwards, Ed. Technical and feature articles, 1,500 to 2,500 words, for motorcycle enthusiasts. Photos. Pays $100 to $200 per page, on publication. Query.

HOT BIKE—2145 W. La Palma, Anaheim, CA 92801. Buck Lovell, Ed. Articles, 250 to 2,500 words, with photos, on motorcycles (contemporary and antique). Event coverage on high performance street and track and sport touring motorcycles, with emphasis on Harley Davidsons. Pays $50 to $100 per printed page, on publication.

HOT ROD—8490 Sunset Blvd., Los Angeles, CA 90069. Jeff Smith, Ed. How-to pieces and articles, 500 to 5,000 words, on auto mechanics, hot rods, track and drag racing. Photo features on custom or performance-modified cars. Pays $250 per page, on publication.

KEEPIN' TRACK OF VETTES—P.O. Box 48, Spring Valley, NY 10977. Articles of any length, with photos, relating to Corvettes. Pays $25 to $200, on publication.

MOTOR TREND—8490 Sunset Blvd., Los Angeles, CA 90069. Jack Nerad, Ed. Articles, 250 to 2,000 words, on autos, racing, events, and profiles. Photos. Pay varies, on acceptance. Query.

MOTORCYCLIST—8490 Sunset Blvd., Los Angeles, CA 90069. Art Friedman, Ed. Articles, 1,000 to 3,000 words. Action photos. Pays $75 to $100 per published page, on publication.

OPEN WHEEL—See *Stock Car Racing*.

RESTORATION—3153 E. Lincoln, Tucson, AZ 85714-2017. W.R. Haessner, Ed. Articles, 1,200 to 1,800 words, on restoration of autos, trucks, planes, trains, etc., and related building (bridges, structures, etc.). Photos. Pays varying rates (from $50 per page) on publication. Queries required.

RIDER—29901 Agoura Rd., Agoura Hills, CA 91301. Mark Tuttle, Jr., Ed. Articles, with slides, to 3,000 words, with emphasis on travel, touring, commuting, and camping motorcyclists. Pays $100 to $500, on publication. Query.

ROAD & TRACK—1499 Monrovia Ave., Newport Beach, CA 92663. Ellida Maki, Man. Ed. Monthly for knowledgeable car enthusiasts. Short automotive articles (to 450 words) of "timeless nature." Pays on acceptance. Query.

STOCK CAR RACING—P.O. Box 715, Ipswich, MA 01938. Dick Berggren, Ed. Features, technical automotive pieces, up to ten typed pages, for oval track racing enthusiasts. Fillers. Pays $75 to $350, on publication. Same requirements for *Open Wheel*.

VOLKSWAGEN WORLD—Volkswagen of America, Troy, MI 28007. Marlene Goldsmith, Ed. Articles, 750 to 1,000 words, accompanied by color slides. Pays $150 to $325 per printed page, on acceptance. Query required. Guidelines.

FITNESS MAGAZINES

AMERICAN FITNESS—15250 Ventura Blvd., Suite 310, Sherman Oaks, CA 91403. Peg Jordan, Ed. Rhonda Wilson, Man. Ed. Articles, 500 to 1,500 words, on exercise, health, sports, nutrition, etc. Illustrations, photos, cartoons.

EAST WEST: THE JOURNAL OF NATURAL HEALTH & LIVING—17 Station St., Box 1200, Brookline, MA 02147. Features, 1,500 to 2,500 words, on holistic health, natural foods, gardening, etc. Material for "Body," "Healing," "In the Kitchen," and "Beauty and Fitness." Interviews. Photos. Pays 10¢ to 15¢ a word, extra for photos, on publication.

HEALTH—3 Park Ave., New York, NY 10016. Articles, 800 to 2,500 words, on fitness and nutrition. Pays up to $2,000 on acceptance. Query.

IDEA TODAY—6190 Cornerstone Ct. East, Suite 204, San Diego, CA 92121–3773. Patricia Tyan, Ed. Practical articles, 1,000 to 3,000 words, on new exercise programs, business management, nutrition, sports medicine, and dance-exercise and one-to-one training techniques. Articles must be geared toward the aerobics instructor, exercise studio owner or manager, or personal trainer; no consumer or general health articles. Payment is negotiable, on acceptance. Query preferred.

INSIDE TEXAS RUNNING—9514 Bristlebrook Dr., Houston, TX 77083. Joanne Schmidt, Ed. Articles and fillers on running, cycling, and triathlons in Texas. Pays $35 to $100, $10 for photos, on acceptance.

MEN'S FITNESS—21100 Erwin St., Woodland Hills, CA 91367. Jim Rosenthal, Features Ed. Features, 1,500 to 2,500 words, and department pieces, 1,000 to 1,500 words: "authoritative and practical articles dealing with fitness, health, and men's lifestyles." Pays $200 to $400, on acceptance.

MEN'S HEALTH—Rodale Press, 33 E. Minor Dr., Emmaus, PA 18098. Michael Lafavore, Exec. Ed. Articles, 1,000 to 2,500 words, on fitness, diet, health, relationships, sports, and travel, for men ages 25 to 55. Pays from 50¢ a word, on acceptance. Query first.

MUSCULAR DEVELOPMENT—351 W. 54th St., New York, NY 10019. Alan Paul, Ed. Articles, 1,000 to 2,500 words, on competitive bodybuilding, power lifting, sports, and nutrition for serious weight training athletes: personality profiles, training features, and diet and nutrition pieces. Photos. Pays $100 to $300 for articles; $35 for color photos, $20 for B&W, and $300 to $500 for cover photos.

NEW BODY—1700 Broadway, New York, NY 10019. Nayda Rondon, Ed. Lively, readable service-oriented articles, 800 to 1,500 words, on exercise, nutrition, lifestyle, diet, and health for women aged 18 to 35. Writers should have some background in or knowledge of the health field. Pays $100 to $300, on publication. Query.

THE PHYSICIAN AND SPORTSMEDICINE—4530 W. 77th St., Minneapolis, MN 55435. Lauren Pacelli, Acquisitions Ed. News and feature articles, 500 to 3,000 words, on fitness, sports, and exercise. Medical angle necessary. Pays $150 to $900, on acceptance. Guidelines.

VEGETARIAN TIMES—P.O. Box 570, Oak Park, IL 60603. Paul Obis, Pub. Articles, 750 to 2,500 words, on health, nutrition, exercise and fitness, meatless meals, etc. Personal-experience and historical pieces, profiles. Pays $25 to $500, on publication.

VIM & VIGOR—8805 N. 23rd Ave., Suite 11, Phoenix, AZ 85021. Leo Calderella, Ed. Positive articles, with accurate medical facts, on health and fitness, 1,200 to 2,000 words, by assignment only. Pays $350 to $450, on publication. Query.

THE WALKING MAGAZINE—9–11 Harcourt, Boston, MA 02116. Bradford Ketchum, Ed. Articles, 1,500 to 2,500 words, on fitness, health, equipment, nutrition, travel and adventure, famous walkers, and other walking-related topics. Shorter pieces, 150 to 800 words, and essays for "Ramblings" page. Photos welcome. Pays $750 to $1,800 for features, $100 to $500 for department pieces. Guidelines.

WEIGHT WATCHERS MAGAZINE—360 Lexington Ave., New York, NY 10017. Ruth Papazian, Articles Ed. Articles on nutrition and health. Pays from $350, on acceptance. Query with clips required. Guidelines.

WOMEN'S SPORTS & FITNESS—1919 14th St., Suite 421, Boulder, CO 80302. Lewis Rothlein, Ed. How-tos, profiles, active travel, and controversial issues in women's sports, 500 to 3,000 words. Fitness, nutrition, and health pieces also considered. Pays on publication.

YOGA JOURNAL—2054 University Ave., Berkeley, CA 94704. Stephan Bodian, Ed. Articles, 1,200 to 4,000 words, on holistic health, meditation, consciousness, spirituality, and yoga. Pays $50 to $350, on publication.

CONSUMER/PERSONAL FINANCE

BETTER HOMES AND GARDENS—1716 Locust St., Des Moines, IA 50336. Articles, 750 to 1,000 words, on "any and all topics that would be of interest to family-oriented, middle-income people." Address Margaret V. Daly, Executive Features Editor, *Better Homes and Gardens*, 750 Third Ave., New York, NY 10017.

BLACK ENTERPRISE—130 Fifth Ave., New York, NY 10011. Earl G. Graves, Ed. Articles on money management, careers, political issues, entrepreneurship, high technology, and lifestyles for black professionals. Profiles. Pays on acceptance. Query.

CHANGING TIMES—1729 H St. N.W., Washington, DC 20006. Articles on personal finance (i.e., buying a stereo, mutual funds). Length and payment vary. Query required. Pays on acceptance.

CONSUMERS DIGEST—5705 N. Lincoln Ave., Chicago, IL 60659. John Manos, Ed. Articles, 500 to 3,000 words, on subjects of interest to consumers: products and services, automobiles, travel, health, fitness, consumer legal affairs, and personal money management. Photos. Pays from 35¢ to 50¢ a word, extra for photos, on acceptance. Query with resumé and clips.

FAMILY CIRCLE—110 Fifth Ave., New York, NY 10011. Susan Ungaro, Exec. Ed. Susan Sherry, Sr. Ed. Enterprising, creative, and practical articles (1,000 to 1,500 words) on investing, starting your own business, secrets of successful entrepreneurs, and consumer news that helps one be a smarter shopper. Query first with clips. Pays $1 a word, on acceptance.

GOLDEN YEARS—233 E. New Haven Ave., Melbourne, FL 32902–0537.

Carol Brenner Hittner, Ed. "We consider articles (to 600 words) on preretirement, retirement planning, real estate, travel, celebrity profiles, humor, and contemporary issues of particular interest to affluent people over 50." Pays on publication.

KIWANIS—3636 Woodview Trace, Indianapolis, IN 46468. Chuck Jonak, Exec. Ed. Articles (2,500 to 3,000 words) on financial planning for younger families in a variety of areas; pieces on financial planning for retirees and small business owners. Pays $400 to $1,000, on acceptance. Query required.

MODERN MATURITY—3200 E. Carson St., Lakewood, CA 90712. Ian Ledgerwood, Ed. Articles, 1,000 to 2,000 words, on a wide range of financial topics of interest to people over 50. Pays to $2,500. Queries required.

MONEY MAKER—5705 N. Lincoln Ave., Chicago, IL 60659. Dennis Fertig, Ed. Informative, jargon-free articles, to 2,500 words, for beginning-to-sophisticated investors, on investment opportunities, personal finance, and low-priced investments. Pays 25¢ a word, on acceptance. Query with clips for assignment.

THE MONEYPAPER—1010 Mamaroneck Ave., Mamaroneck, NY 10543. Vita Nelson, Ed. Financial news and money-saving ideas. Brief, well-researched articles on personal finance, money management: saving, earning, investing, taxes, insurance, and related subjects. Pays $75 for articles, on publication. Query with resumé and writing sample.

SELF—350 Madison Ave., New York, NY 10017. Marie D'Amico, Money/ Careers Ed. Articles, 1,200 to 1,500 words, on money matters for career women in their 20s and 30s. Pays from $1,000, on acceptance. Query first.

WOMAN'S DAY—1633 Broadway, New York, NY 10019. Rebecca Greer, Articles Ed. Articles, to 2,500 words, on financial matters of interest to a broad range of women. Pays top rates, on acceptance. Query first.

PROFESSIONAL/TRADE PUBLICATIONS

ABA JOURNAL—American Bar Association, 750 N. Lake Shore Dr., Chicago, IL 60611. Gary A. Hengstler, Ed./Pub. Articles, to 3,000 words, on law-related topics: current events in the law and ideas that will help lawyers practice better and more efficiently. Writing should be in an informal, journalistic style. Pays $750 to $950, on acceptance; buys all rights.

ACCESS CONTROL—6255 Barfield Rd., Atlanta, GA 30328. Steven Lasky, Ed./Assoc. Pub. Comprehensive case studies, from 3,000 words, on large-scale access control installations in industrial, commercial, governmental, retail, and transportational environments: door and card entry, gates and operators, turnstiles and portals, perimeter security fencing and its accessories, perimeter and interior sensors, CCTV technology, system design strategies, integration of hardware, and guard services. Photos. Pays from 20¢ a word, extra for photos, on publication. Query.

ACCESSORIES MAGAZINE—50 Day St., Norwalk, CT 06854. Reenie Brown, Ed. Dir. Articles, with photos, for women's fashion accessories buyers and manufacturers. Profiles of retailers, designers, manufacturers; articles on merchandising and marketing. Pays $75 to $100 for short articles, from $100 to $300 for features, on publication. Query.

ACROSS THE BOARD—845 Third Ave., New York, NY 10022. Justine Martin, Asst. Ed. Articles, to 5,000 words, on a variety of topics of interest to business executives; straight business angle not required. Pays $100 to $750, on publication.

ALTERNATIVE ENERGY RETAILER—P.O. Box 2180, Waterbury, CT 06722. John Florian, Ed. Feature articles, 1,000 words, for retailers of alternative energy products: wood, coal, and fireplace products and services. Interviews with successful retailers, stressing the how-to. B&W photos. Pays $200, extra for photos, on publication. Query first.

AMERICAN BANKER—One State Street Plaza, New York, NY 10004. Frederick R. Bleakley, Ed., Patricia Stunza, Features Ed. Articles, 1,000 to 3,000 words, on banking and financial services, technology in banking, consumer financial services, human resources, management techniques. Pays varying rates, on publication. Query preferred.

AMERICAN COIN-OP—500 N. Dearborn St., Chicago, IL 60610. Ben Russell, Ed. Articles, to 2,500 words, with photos, on successful coin-operated laundries: management, promotion, decor, maintenance, etc. Pays from 8¢ a word, $8 per B&W photo, two weeks prior to publication. Query. Send SASE for guidelines.

AMERICAN DEMOGRAPHICS—P.O. Box 68, Ithaca, NY 14851. Caroline Arthur, Man. Ed. Articles, 3,000 to 5,000 words, on demographic trends and business demographics for strategists in industry, government, and education. Pays $300, on publication. Query.

AMERICAN FARRIERS JOURNAL—63 Great Rd., Maynard, MA 01754. Susan G. Philbrick, Ed. Articles, 800 to 5,000 words, on general farrier issues, hoof care, tool selection, equine lameness, and horse handling. Pays 30¢ per published line, $10 per published illustration or photo, on publication. Query.

AMERICAN MEDICAL NEWS—535 N. Dearborn St., Chicago, IL 60610. Ronni Scheier, Asst. Exec. Ed. Features, 1,000 to 3,000 words, of interest to physicians across the country. No pieces on health, clinical treatments, or research. Query required. Pays $50 to $1,000, on acceptance. Guidelines.

THE AMERICAN SALESMAN—424 N. Third St., Burlington, IA 52601–5224. Barbara Boeding, Ed. Articles, 900 to 1,200 words, on techniques for increasing sales. Author photos requested on article acceptance. Buys all rights. (No advertising.) Pays 3¢ a word, on publication. Guidelines.

AMERICAN SALON—7500 Old Oak Blvd., Cleveland, OH 44130. Jayne Morehouse, Ed. Official publication of the National Cosmetology Assoc. Business and fashion articles of varying lengths for salon professionals. Payment varies, on publication. Query.

AMERICAN SCHOOL & UNIVERSITY—401 N. Broad St., Philadelphia, PA 19108. Joe Agron, Ed. Articles and case studies, 1,200 to 1,500 words, on design, construction, operation, and management of school and college facilities.

ARCHITECTURE—1130 Connecticut Ave. N.W., Suite 625, Washington, DC 20036. Deborah Dietsch, Ed. Articles, to 3,000 words, on architecture, urban design. Book reviews. Pays $100 to $500, extra for photos. Query.

AREA DEVELOPMENT MAGAZINE—400 Post Ave., Westbury, NY 11590. Tom Bergeron, Ed. Articles for top executives of manufacturing companies, on industrial and office facility planning. Pays $40 per manuscript page. Query.

ART BUSINESS NEWS—777 Summer St., P.O. Box 3837, Stamford, CT 06905. Jo Yanow-Schwartz, Ed. Articles, 1,000 words, for art dealers and framers, on trends and events of national importance to the art industry, and relevant business subjects. Pays from $75, on publication. Query preferred.

ART MATERIAL TRADE NEWS—6255 Barfield Rd., Atlanta, GA 30328. Tim Cooper, Ed. Articles, from 800 words, for dealers, wholesalers, and manufacturers of artist materials; must be specific to trade. Pays to 15¢ a word, on publication. Query.

AUTOMATED BUILDER—P.O. Box 120, Carpinteria, CA 93014. Don Carlson, Ed. Articles, 500 to 750 words, on various types of home manufacturers and dealers. Query required. Pays $350, on acceptance, for articles with slides.

AUTOMOTIVE EXECUTIVE—8400 Westpark Dr., McLean, VA 22102. Joe Phillips, Man. Ed. National Automobile Dealers Assn. Articles, 1,500 to 2,500 words, on management of automobile and heavy-duty truck dealerships and general business management and automotive issues. Color photos. Pays on publication. Query.

BARRISTER—American Bar Assn., 750 N. Lake Shore Dr., Chicago, IL 60611. Anthony Monahan, Ed. Articles, to 3,500 words, on legal and social affairs, for young lawyers. Pays to $700, on acceptance.

BARRON'S—200 Liberty St., New York, NY 10281. Alan Abelson, Ed. National-interest articles, 1,200 to 2,500 words, on business and finance. Query.

BETTER BUSINESS—235 East 42nd St., New York, NY 10017. John F. Robinson, Pub. Articles, 10 to 12 double-spaced pages, for the small business/minority business markets and for businesses owned by women. Query. SASE required.

BOATING INDUSTRY—390 Fifth Ave., New York, NY 10018. Paul C. Larsen, Ed. Articles, 1,000 to 1,500 words, on marine management, merchandising and selling, for boat dealers. Photos. Pays varying rates, on publication. Query.

BUILDER—Hanley-Wood, Inc., 655 15th St. N.W., Suite 475, Washington, DC 20005. Mitchell B. Rouda, Ed. Articles, to 1,500 words, on trends and news in home building: design, marketing, new products, etc. Pays negotiable rates, on acceptance. Query.

BUSINESS DIGEST OF GREATER NEW HAVEN—20 Grand Ave., New Haven, CT 06513. Jean McAndrews, Ed. Feature articles, 1,500 to 2,000 words, on successful New Haven-area businesses and owners. Pays $2.75 per published inch, on publication. Query required.

BUSINESS MARKETING—220 E. 42nd St., New York, NY 10017. Bob Donath, Ed. Articles on selling, advertising, and promoting products and services to business buyers. Pays competitive rates, on acceptance. Queries are required.

BUSINESS TIMES—8 Glastonbury Ave., Rocky Hill, CT 06067. Ann Hansen, Man. Ed. Articles on Connecticut-based businesses and corporations. Query.

BUSINESS TODAY—P.O. Box 10010, 1720 Washington Blvd., Ogden, UT 84409. Caroll Shreeve, Pub./Ed.-in-Chief. Informative articles, 1,200 words, on business concerns of the businessperson/entrepreneur in the US and Canada. Pays 15¢ a word, $35 for color photos, on acceptance. Query. Guidelines.

BUSINESS VIEW—See *Florida Business/Southwest*.

CALIFORNIA LAWYER—1390 Market St., Suite 1016, San Francisco, CA 94102. Thomas Brom, Man. Ed. Articles, 2,500 to 3,000 words, for attorneys in California, on legal subjects (or the legal aspects of a given political or social issue); how-tos on improving legal skills and law office technology. Pays $300 to $1,200, on acceptance. Query.

CAMPGROUND MANAGEMENT—P.O. Box 5000, Lake Forest, IL 60045–5000. Mike Byrnes, Ed. Detailed articles, 500 to 2,000 words, on managing recreational vehicle campgrounds. Photos. Pays $50 to $200, after publication. Overstocked until 1991.

CAR AUDIO AND ELECTRONICS—21700 Oxnard St., Woodland Hills, CA 91367. Bill Neill, Ed. Features, 1,000 to 2,000 words, on electronic products for the car: audio systems, security systems, CBs, radar detectors, cellular telephones, etc. Pays $300 to $1,000, on acceptance.

CERAMIC SCOPE—3632 Ashworth N., Seattle, WA 98103. Michael Scott, Ed. Articles, 800 to 1,500 words, on retail or wholesale business operations of hobby ceramic studios. Photos. Pays 10¢ a word, extra for photos, on publication. Query.

CHEESE MARKET NEWS—See *Dairy Foods Magazine*.

CHIEF EXECUTIVE—233 Park Ave. S., New York, NY 10003. J.P. Donlon, Ed. CEO bylines. Articles, 2,500 to 3,000 words, on management, financial, or business strategy. Departments on investments, amenities, and travel, 1,200 to 1,500 words. Features on CEOs at leisure, Q&A's with CEOs, other topics. Pays varying rates, on acceptance. Query required.

CHINA, GLASS & TABLEWARE—P.O. Box 2147, Clifton, NJ 07015. Amy Stavis, Ed. Case histories and interviews, 1,500 to 2,500 words, with photos, on merchandising of china and glassware. Pays $50 per page, on publication. Query.

CHRISTIAN RETAILING—600 Rinehart Rd., Lake Mary, FL 32746. Brian Peterson, Ed. Articles, 850 to 1,200 words, on new products, industry news, or topics related to running a profitable Christian retail store. Pays $50 to $150, on publication.

CLEANING MANAGEMENT—15550-D Rockfield, Irvine, CA 92718. R. Daniel Harris, Jr., Pub. Articles, 1,000 to 1,500 words, on managing efficient cleaning and maintenance operations. Photos. Pays 10¢ a word, extra for photos, on publication.

CMAA—16 Forest St., New Canaan, CT 06840. John Delves, III, Ed. The official magazine of the Club Managers Assoc. of America. News items from 100 words, features to 2,000 words, on management, budget, cuisine, personnel, government regulations, etc., for executives who run private clubs. "Writing should be tight and conversational, with liberal use of quotes." Color photos usually required with manuscript. Query preferred. Pays $25 for short news items; to $200 per page for features, on publication. Guidelines.

COLLEGE STORE EXECUTIVE—P.O. Box 1500, Westbury, NY 11590. Janice A. Costa, Ed. Articles, 1,000 words, for college store industry only; news; profiles. No general business or how-to articles. Photos. Pays $4 to $5 a column inch, extra for photos, on publication. Query.

COMMERCIAL CARRIER JOURNAL—Chilton Way, Radnor, PA 19089. Jerry Standley, Ed. Factual articles on private fleets and for-hire trucking operations. Pays from $50, on acceptance. Queries required.

COMPUTER GRAPHICS WORLD—One Technology Park Dr., Westford, MA 01886. Stephen Porter, Man. Ed. Articles, 1,000 to 3,000 words, on computer graphics technology and its use in science, engineering, architecture, film and broadcast, and graphic arts areas. Photos. Pays $600 to $1,200 per article, on acceptance. Query.

CONCRETE INTERNATIONAL—Box 19150, 22400 W. Seven Mile Rd., Detroit, MI 48219. William J. Semioli, Assoc. Pub. & Ed. Articles, 6 to 12 double-spaced pages, on concrete construction and design, with drawings and/or photos. Pays $100 per printed page, on publication. Query.

THE CONSTRUCTION SPECIFIER—Construction Specifications Institute, 601 Madison St., Alexandria, VA 22314. Kimberly Young, Ed. Technical articles, 1,000 to 3,000 words, on the "nuts and bolts" of commercial construction, for architects, engineers, specifiers, contractors, and manufacturers. Pays 15¢ per word, on publication.

CONTRACTORS MARKET CENTER—See *Equipment World*.

CONVENIENCE STORE NEWS—7 Penn Plaza, New York, NY 10001. Barbara Grondin, Ed. Features and news items, 500 to 750 words, for convenience store owners, operators, and suppliers. Photos, with captions. Pays $3 per column inch or negotiated price for features; extra for photos, on publication. Query.

COOKING FOR PROFIT—P.O. Box 267, Fond du Lac, WI 54936–0267. Colleen Phalen, Ed. Practical how-to articles, 1,000 words, on commercial food preparation, energy management; case studies, etc. Pays $75 to $250, on publication.

CORPORATE CASHFLOW—6255 Barfield Rd., Atlanta, GA 30328. Richard Gamble, Ed. Articles, 1,250 to 2,500 words, for treasury managers in public and private institutions: cash management; investments; domestic and international financing; credit and collection management; developments in law, economics, and tax. Pays $125 per published page, on publication. Query.

CORPORATE HEALTH—5700 Old Orchard Rd., First Fl., Skokie, IL 60077. Lisbeth Maxwell, Ed. Articles, 2,800 to 4,200 words, and columns, 1,400 to 2,800 words, on employee benefits, cost containment, fitness, health, and safety, of interest to CEOs and benefits managers. Payment varies, on publication. Query preferred.

CRAIN'S CHICAGO BUSINESS—740 Rush St., Chicago, IL 60611. Mark Miller, Ed. Business articles about the Midwest exclusively. Pays $11.50 per column inch, on acceptance.

CREATING EXCELLENCE—New World Publishing, P.O. Box 2084, S. Burlington, VT 05407. David Robinson, Ed. Self-help and inspirational articles: profiles and essays related to business success. "Purpose is to inform and inspire people to be their best, personally and professionally." Pays $75 to $250, on acceptance. Queries preferred.

CREDIT AND COLLECTION MANAGEMENT BULLETIN—Bureau of Business Practice, 24 Rope Ferry Rd., Waterford, CT 06386. Russell Case, Ed. Interviews, 500 to 1,250 words, for commercial and consumer credit managers, on innovations, successes, and problem solving. Query.

D&B REPORTS—299 Park Ave., New York, NY 10171. Patricia W. Hamilton, Ed. Articles, 1,500 to 2,000 words, for top management of smaller businesses: government regulations, export opportunities, employee relations; how-tos on cash management, sales, productivity; profiles; etc. Pays on acceptance.

DAIRY FOODS MAGAZINE —Gorman Publishing Co., 8750 W. Bryn Mawr, Chicago, IL 60631. Mike Pehanich, Ed. Articles, to 2,500 words, on innovative dairies, dairy processing operations, marketing successes, new products, for milk handlers and makers of dairy products. Fillers, 25 to 150 words. Pays $25 to $300, $5 to $25 for fillers, on publication. Same requirements for *Cheese Market News*.

DAIRY HERD MANAGEMENT—P.O. Box 2400, Minnetonka, MN 55343. Edward Clark, Ed. Articles, 500 to 2,000 words, with photos, on dairy finance, production, and marketing. Pays on acceptance. Query.

DEALERSCOPE MERCHANDISING—North American Publishing Co., 401 N. Broad St., Philadelphia, PA 19108. Murray Slovick, Ed. Articles, 750 to 3,000 words, for dealers and distributors of audio, video, personal computers for the home, office; satellite TV systems for the home; major appliances on sales, marketing, and finance. How-tos for retailers. Pays varying rates, on publication. Query with clips.

DENTAL ECONOMICS—P.O. Box 3408, Tulsa, OK 74101. Dick Hale, Ed. Articles, 1,200 to 3,500 words, on business side of dental practice, patient and staff communication, personal investments, etc. Pays $100 to $400, on acceptance.

DRAPERIES & WINDOW COVERINGS—450 Skokie Blvd., Suite 507, Northbrook, IL 60062. Katie Renckens, Ed. Articles, 1,000 to 2,000 words, for retailers, wholesalers, designers, and manufacturers of draperies and window coverings. Profiles, with photos, of successful businesses in the industry. Pays $150 to $250, after acceptance. Query.

DRUG TOPICS—680 Kinderkamack Rd., Oradell, NJ 07649. Valentine A. Cardinale, Ed. News items, 500 words, with photos, on drug retailers and associations. Merchandising features, 1,000 to 1,500 words. Pays $100 to $150 for news, $200 to $400 for features, on acceptance. Query for features.

EARNSHAW'S INFANT'S & CHILDREN'S REVIEW—393 Seventh Ave., New York, NY 10001. Christina Gruber, Ed. Articles on retailers, retail promotions, and statistics for children's wear industry. Pays $50 to $200, on publication. Query. Limited market.

ELECTRICAL CONTRACTOR—7315 Wisconsin Ave., Bethesda, MD 20814. Larry C. Osius, Ed. Articles, 1,000 to 1,500 words, with photos, on construction or management techniques for electrical contractors. Pays $110 per printed page, before publication. Query.

ELECTRONIC MANUFACTURING NEWS—1350 E. Touhy Ave., Box 5080, Des Plaines, IL 60018. Diane Pirocanac, Man. Ed. Articles, 500 to 750 words, of interest to engineers and managers in the electronic manufacturing industry. Payment varies, on acceptance. Query required.

EMERGENCY—6300 Yarrow Dr., Carlsbad, CA 92009. Rhonda Foster, Ed. Features (to 3,000 words) and department pieces (to 2,000 words) of interest to paramedics, emergency medical technicians, flight nurses, and other pre-hospital personnel: disaster management, advanced and basic life support, assessment, treatment. Pays $100 to $400 for features, $50 to $250 for departments. Photos are a plus. Guidelines and editorial calendar available.

EMPLOYEE SERVICES MANAGEMENT—NESRA, 2400 S. Downing, Westchester, IL 60154. Elizabeth Martinet, Ed. Articles, 1,200 to 2,500 words, for human resource, fitness, and employee service professionals.

ENGINEERED SYSTEMS—7314 Hart St., Mentor, OH 44060. Robert L. Schwed, Ed. Articles, case histories, and product information related to engineered hvac systems in commercial, industrial, or institutional buildings. Pays $4.75 per column inch, $12 per illustration, on publication. Query.

THE ENGRAVERS JOURNAL—26 Summit St., Box 318, Brighton, MI 48116. Michael J. Davis, Man. Ed. Articles, of varying lengths, on topics related to the engraving industry or small business. Pays $60 to $175, on acceptance. Query.

ENTREPRENEUR—2392 Morse Ave., Irvine, CA 92714. Rieva Lesonsky, Ed. Articles for established and aspiring independent business owners, on all aspects of running a business. Pay varies, on acceptance. Queries required.

ENTREPRENEURIAL WOMAN—2392 Morse Ave., Irvine, CA 92714. Rieva Lesonsky, Ed. Profiles, 1,800 words, of female entrepreneurs; how-tos on running a business, and pieces on coping as a woman owning a business. Payment varies, on acceptance.

EQUIPMENT WORLD—(formerly *Contractors Market Center*) P.O. Box 2029, Tuscaloosa, AL 35403. Marcia Gruver, Ed. Features, 500 to 1,500 words, for contractors who buy, sell, and use heavy equipment; stories offering information on equipment selection, application, maintenance, and replacement. Pay varies, on acceptance.

EXPORT MAGAZINE—386 Park Ave. South, New York, NY 10016. Jack Dobson, Ed. Articles, 1,000 to 1,200 words. From U.S.-based free lancers: articles on developments in hardware and appliances, air conditioning and refrigeration, sporting goods and leisure products. From overseas-based free lancers: articles on merchandising techniques of foreign retailers who import above-described items from U.S. Pays $300 to $400 with photos, on acceptance. Query required.

FARM JOURNAL—230 W. Washington Sq., Philadelphia, PA 19105. Practical business articles on growing crops and producing livestock. Pays $50 to $500, on acceptance. Query required.

FARM STORE—P.O. Box 2400, 12400 Whitewater Dr., Suite 160, Minnetonka, MN 55343. Jan Johnson, Ed. Articles, 500 to 1,500 words, of interest to farm store owners and managers. Payment varies, on publication. Query.

FINANCIAL WORLD—1328 Broadway, New York, NY 10001. Douglas A. McIntyre, Pub. Features and profiles of large companies and financial institutions and the people who run them. Pays varying rates, on publication. Queries are required.

FITNESS MANAGEMENT—P.O. Box 1198, Solana Beach, CA 92075. Edward H. Pitts, Ed. Authoritative features, 750 to 2,500 words, and news shorts, 100 to 750 words, for owners, managers, and program directors of fitness centers. Content must be in keeping with current medical practice; no fads. Pays 8¢ a word, on publication. Query.

FLORIDA BUSINESS/SOUTHWEST—(formerly *Business View*) P.O. Box 9859, Naples, FL 33941. Eleanor K. Somer, Pub. Ken Gooderham, Ed. Innovative articles and columns, 750 to 2,000 words, on business, economics, finance; profiles of business leaders; new trends in technology and advances in management techniques. Real estate and banking trends. Southwest Florida regional angle required. Pays $50 to $300, on publication. Query.

FLORIST—29200 Northwestern Hwy., P.O. Box 2227, Southfield, MI 48037. Susan Nicholas, Man. Ed. Articles, to 2,000 words, with photos, on retail florist business improvement. Photos. Pays 8¢ a word.

FLOWERS &—Teleflora Plaza, Suite 260, 12233 W. Olympic Blvd., Los Angeles, CA 90064. Marie Moneysmith, Ed.-in-Chief. Articles, 1,000 to 3,500 words, with how-to information for retail florists. Pays from $500, on acceptance. Query with clips.

FOOD MANAGEMENT—747 Third Ave., New York, NY 10017. Donna Boss, Ed. Articles on food service in hospitals, nursing homes, schools, colleges, prisons, businesses, and industrial sites. Trends and how-to pieces, with management tie-in. Query.

FOREIGN TRADE—8208 W. Franklin, Minneapolis, MN 55426. John Freivalds, Ed. Articles and interviews, 1,700 to 2,100 words, on topics related to international trade that examine problems managers have faced, and how they solved them. Pays $400, on publication. Guidelines.

THE FOREMAN'S LETTER—24 Rope Ferry Rd., Waterford, CT 06386. Carl Thunberg, Ed. Interviews with top-notch supervisors and foremen. Photos required. Pays 10¢ to 14¢ a word, extra for photos, on acceptance.

FREQUENT FLYER—1775 Broadway, New York, NY 10019. Jane L. Levere, Man. Ed. Articles, 1,000 to 3,000 words, on all aspects of frequent business travel, international trade, aviation, etc. Few pleasure travel articles; no personal experience pieces. Pays up to $500, on acceptance. Query required.

GARDEN DESIGN—4401 Connecticut Ave. N.W., Fifth Fl., Washington, DC 20008. Karen Fishler, Ed. Society of American Landscape Architects. Articles, 1,500 to 2,000 words, on classic and contemporary examples of residential landscaping, garden art, history, and design. Interviews. Pays $350, on publication. Query.

GENETIC ENGINEERING NEWS—1651 Third Ave., New York, NY 10128. John Sterling, Man. Ed. Features and news articles. on all aspects of biotechnology. Pays varying rates, on acceptance. Query.

GLASS DIGEST—310 Madison Ave., New York, NY 10017. Charles Cumpston, Ed. Articles, 1,200 to 1,500 words, on building projects and glass/metal dealers, distributors, storefront and glazing contractors. Pays varying rates, on publication.

GOLF COURSE NEWS—38 Lafayette St., P.O. Box 997, Yarmouth, ME 04096. Mark Leslie, Man. Ed. Features, 500 to 1,500 words, and news stories of any length, on all aspects of golf course maintenance, design, building, and management. Pays $300 to $500, on acceptance.

GOLF SHOP OPERATIONS—5520 Park Ave., Box 395, Trumbull, CT 06611–0395. Michael Schwanz, Ed. Articles, 200 to 800 words, with photos, on successful golf shop operations; new ideas for merchandising, display, bookkeeping. Short pieces on golf professionals and retailers. Pays $250 to $350, on publication. Query with outline.

GOVERNMENT EXECUTIVE—1730 M St. N.W., Suite 1100, Washington, DC 20036. Timothy Clark, Ed. Articles, 1,500 to 3,000 words, for civilian and military government workers at the management level.

GREENHOUSE MANAGER—P.O. Box 1868, Fort Worth, TX 76101. David Kuack, Ed. How-to articles, success stories, 500 to 1,800 words, accompanied by color slides, of interest to professional greenhouse growers. Profiles. Pays $50 to $300, on acceptance. Query required.

HARDWARE AGE—Chilton Way, Radnor, PA 19089. Terrence V. Gallagher, Chief Ed. Articles on merchandising methods in hardware outlets. Photos. Pays on acceptance.

HARDWARE TRADE—2965 Broadmoor Valley Rd., Suite B, Colorado Springs, CO 80906. Linda Marqueses, Ed. Articles, 800 to 1,000 words, on unusual hardware and home center stores and promotions in the Northwest and Midwest. Photos. Pays 8¢ a word, extra for photos, on publication. Query.

HARVARD BUSINESS REVIEW—Harvard Graduate School of Business Administration, Boston, MA 02163. Query editors on new ideas about management of interest to senior executives. Pays on publication.

HEALTH FOODS BUSINESS—567 Morris Ave., Elizabeth, NJ 07208. Gina Geslewitz, Ed. Articles, 1,200 words, with photos, profiling health food stores. Shorter pieces on trends, research findings, preventive medicine, alternative therapies. Interviews with doctors and nutritionists. Pays on publication. Query. Send for guidelines.

HEARTH & HOME—P.O. Box 2008, Laconia, NH 03247. Kenneth E. Daggett, Pub./Ed. Profiles and interviews, 1,000 to 1,800 words, with specialty retailers selling both casual furniture and hearth products (fireplaces, woodstoves, accessories, etc.). Pays $150 to $250, on acceptance.

HEATING/PIPING/AIR CONDITIONING—2 Illinois Center, Chicago, IL 60601. Robert T. Korte, Ed. Articles, to 5,000 words, on heating, piping, and air conditioning systems in industrial plants and large buildings; engineering information. Pays $60 per printed page, on publication. Query.

HOSPITAL SUPERVISOR'S BULLETIN—24 Rope Ferry Rd., Waterford, CT 06386. Michele Dunaj, Ed. Interviews, articles with non-medical hospital supervisors on departmental problem solving. Pays 12¢ to 15¢ a word. Query.

HOSPITALS—211 E. Chicago Ave., Suite 700, Chicago, IL 60611. Mary Grayson, Ed. Articles, 800 to 3,200 words, for hospital administrators. Pays varying rates, on acceptance. Query.

HUMAN RESOURCE EXECUTIVE—Axon Group, 1035 Camphill Rd., Fort Washington, PA 19034. David Shadovitz, Ed. Profiles, case stories, and opinion pieces (1,800 to 2,200 words) of interest to people in the personnel profession. Pays varying rates, on acceptance. Queries required.

INC.—38 Commercial Wharf, Boston, MA 02110. George Gendron, Ed. No free-lance material.

INCENTIVE MAGAZINE—633 Third Ave., New York, NY 10017. Regina Eisman, Sr. Ed. Articles on marketing, managing incentive travel, and product categories; motivation and incentive sales and merchandising strategies. Pays $125 to $800, on acceptance.

INCOME OPPORTUNITIES—380 Lexington Ave., New York, NY 10017. Stephen Wagner, Ed. Helpful articles, 1,000 to 2,500 words, on how to make money full- or part-time; how to run a successful small business, improve sales, etc. Pays varying rates, on acceptance.

INCOME PLUS—6 N. Michigan Ave., Chicago, IL 60602. Roxane Farmanfarmaian, Ed. How-to articles on starting a small business, franchise, or mail-order operation. Pays 5¢ a word, on acceptance. Query.

INDEPENDENT BUSINESS—875 S. Westlake Blvd., Suite 211, Westlake Village, CA 91361. Daniel Kehrer, Ed. Articles (500 to 2,000 words) of practical interest and value to small business owners. Pays $200 to $1,500, on acceptance. Query.

INSTANT & SMALL COMMERCIAL PRINTER—P.O. Box 1387, Northbrook, IL 60065. Catherine Bazzon, Ed. Articles, 3 to 6 typed pages, for operators and employees of printing businesses specializing in retail printing and/or small commercial printing: case histories, how-tos, technical pieces. Opinion pieces, 1 to 2 typed pages. Photos. Pays $150 to $250 ($25 to $50 for opinion pieces), extra for photos, on publication. Query.

INSTITUTIONAL RESEARCH—See *Research Magazine*.

INTERNATIONAL DESIGN—330 W. 42nd St., New York, NY 10036. Annetta Hanna, Ed. Articles to 2,000 words, on product development, design management, graphic design, design history, fashion, art, and environments for designers and marketing executives. Profiles of designers and corporations that use design effectively. Pays $250 to $600, on publication.

INTV JOURNAL—49 E. 21st St., New York, NY 10010. William Dunlap, Ed. Features and short pieces on trends in independent television. Pays to $650, after publication. Query.

JEMS, JOURNAL OF EMERGENCY MEDICAL SERVICES—P.O. Box 1026, Solana Beach, CA 92075. Nancy Peterson, Man. Ed. Articles (1,500 to 3,000 words) of interest to emergency medical providers (from EMTs to paramedics to nurses and physicians) who work in the EMS industry worldwide.

LLAMAS—P.O. Box 1038, Dublin, OH 43017. Susan Ley, Asst. Ed. "The International Camelid Journal," published 8 times yearly. Articles, 300 to 3,000 words, of interest to llama and alpaca owners. Pays $25 to $300, extra for photos, on acceptance. Query.

LOTUS—P.O. Box 9123, Cambridge, MA 02139. Larry Marion, Ed.-in-Chief. Articles, 1,500 to 2,000 words, for business and professional people using electronic spreadsheets. Query with outline required. Pay varies, on final approval.

LP-GAS MAGAZINE—131 W. First St., Duluth, MN 55802. Zane Chastain, Ed. Articles, 1,500 to 2,500 words, with photos, on LP-gas dealer operations: marketing, management, etc. Photos. Pays to 15¢ a word, extra for photos, on acceptance. Query.

MACHINE DESIGN—Penton Publications, 1100 Superior Ave., Cleveland, OH 44114. Richard Beercheck, Exec. Ed. Articles, to 10 typed pages, on design-related topics for engineers. Pays varying rates, on publication. Submit outline or brief description.

MAGAZINE DESIGN & PRODUCTION—8340 Mission Rd., Suite 106, Prairie Village, KS 66206. Maureen Waters, Man. Ed. Articles, 6 to 10 typed pages, on magazine design and production: printing, typesetting, design, computers, layout, etc. Pays $100 to $200, on acceptance. Query required.

MAINTENANCE TECHNOLOGY—1300 S. Grove Ave., Barrington, IL 60010. Robert C. Baldwin, Ed. Articles with how-to information on maintenance of electrical and electronic systems, mechanical systems and equipment, and plant facilities. Readers are maintenance managers, supervisors, and engineers in industrial plants and hospitals. Payment varies, on acceptance. Query required.

MANAGE—2210 Arbor Blvd., Dayton, OH 45439. Doug Shaw, Ed. Articles, 1,500 to 2,200 words, on management and supervision for first-line and middle managers. Pays 5¢ a word.

MANUFACTURING SYSTEMS—191 S. Gary, Carol Stream, IL 60188. Tom Inglesby, Ed. Articles, 500 to 2,000 words, on computer and information systems for industry executives seeking to increase productivity in manufacturing firms. Pays 10¢ to 20¢ a word, on acceptance. Query required.

MEMPHIS BUSINESS JOURNAL—88 Union, Suite 102, Memphis, TN 38103. Barney DuBois, Ed. Articles, to 2,000 words, on business, industry trade, agri-business and finance in the mid-south trade area. Pays $80 to $200, on acceptance.

MINIATURES DEALER—21027 Crossroads Cir., P.O. Box 1612, Waukesha, WI 53187. Geraldine Willems, Ed. Articles, 1,000 to 1,500 words, on advertising, promotion, merchandising of miniatures and other small business concerns. Interviews with miniatures dealers. Pays to $175, on publication.

MIX MAGAZINE—6400 Hollis St., Suite 12, Emeryville, CA 94608. David Schwartz, Ed. Articles, varying lengths, for professionals, on audio, video, and music entertainment technology. Pays varies, on publication. Query required.

MODERN HEALTHCARE—740 N. Rush St., Chicago, IL 60611. Clark Bell, Ed. Features on management, finance, building design and construction, and new technology for hospitals, health maintenance organizations, nursing homes, and other health care institutions. Pays $200 to $400, on publication. Very limited free-lance market.

MODERN OFFICE TECHNOLOGY—1100 Superior Ave., Cleveland, OH 44114. Lura Romei, Ed. Articles (3 to 4 double-spaced, typed pages) on new concepts, management techniques, technologies, and applications for management executives. Payment varies, on acceptance. Query preferred.

MODERN TIRE DEALER—P.O. Box 8391, 341 White Pond Dr., Akron, OH 44320. Lloyd Stoyor, Ed. Tire retailing and automotive service articles, 1,000 to 1,500 words, with photos, on independent tire dealers and retreaders. Pays $300 to $350, on publication.

NANNY TIMES—P.O. Box 31, Rutherford, NJ 07070. Gillian Gordon, Ed./Pub. How-to articles, 1,000 to 1,500 words, on childcare or anything related to the business of being or employing a nanny: safety, first aid, entertainment, nutrition, psychology, etc. Pays $5 to $75 for features, $5 to $15 for fillers, on publication. Buys all rights. Guidelines.

NATIONAL FISHERMAN—120 Tillson Ave., Rockland, ME 04841. James W. Fullilove, Ed. Articles, 200 to 2,000 words, aimed at commercial fishermen and boat builders. Pays $4 to $6 per inch, extra for photos, on publication. Query preferred.

NATION'S BUSINESS—1615 H St. N.W., Washington, DC 20062. Articles on business-related topics, including management advice and success stories aimed at small- to medium-sized businesses. Pays negotiable rates, after acceptance. Guidelines available.

NEPHROLOGY NEWS & ISSUES—13901 N. 73rd St., Suite 214, Scottsdale, AZ 85260. Mark E. Neumann, Ed. "We publish news articles, human-interest features, and opinion essays on dialysis, kidney transplantations, and kidney disease." Pays varying rates, on publication. Photos a plus. Queries required.

NEVADA BUSINESS JOURNAL—3800 Howard Hughes Pkwy, Suite 120, Las Vegas, NV 89109. Lyle Brennan, Ed. Business articles, 1,000 to 3,000 words, of interest to Nevada readers; profiles, how-to articles. Pays $150 to $250 on publication. Query. Guidelines.

560

NEW CAREER WAYS NEWSLETTER—67 Melrose Ave., Haverhill, MA 01830. William J. Bond, Ed. How-to articles, 1,500 to 2,000 words, on new ways to succeed in business careers. Pays varying rates, on publication. Query with outline.

NORTH AMERICAN INTERNATIONAL BUSINESS—(formerly *Northeast International Business*) 401 Theodore Fremd Ave., Rye, NY 10580. David E. Moore, Exec. Ed. Articles, 1,000 to 1,500 words, on global marketing strategies, and short (500 words) pieces with tips on operating abroad. Profiles, 750 to 3,000 words, on individuals or companies. Pays 50¢ a word, on acceptance and on publication. Query required.

NORTHEAST INTERNATIONAL BUSINESS—See *North American International Business*.

NSGA RETAIL FOCUS—National Sporting Goods Assoc., 1699 Wall St., Suite 700, Mt. Prospect, IL 60056. Larry Weindruch, Ed. Members magazine. Articles, 700 to 1,000 words, on sporting goods industry news and trends, the latest in new product information, and management and store operations. Payment varies, on publication. Query.

NURSINGWORLD JOURNAL—470 Boston Post Rd., Weston, MA 02193. Shirley Copithorne, Ed. Articles, 800 to 1,500 words, for nurses, nurse educators, and students of nursing, etc., on all aspects of nursing. B&W photos. Pays from 25¢ per column inch, on publication.

OPPORTUNITY MAGAZINE—6 N. Michigan Ave., Suite 1405, Chicago, IL 60602. Jack Weissman, Ed. Articles, 900 to 1,500 words, on sales psychology, sales techniques, successful small business careers, self-improvement. Pays $40 to $50, on publication.

PC WEEK—800 Boylston St., Boston, MA 02119. Jennifer DeJong, Exec. Ed. No free-lance submissions.

PET BUSINESS—5728 Major Blvd., Suite 200, Orlando, FL 32819. Karen Payne, Ed. Brief documented articles on animals and products found in pet stores; research findings; legislative/regulatory actions. Pays $4 per column inch, on publication. Photos, $10 to $20.

PETS/SUPPLIES/MARKETING—One E. First St., Duluth, MN 55802. David D. Kowalski, Ed. Articles, 1,000 to 1,200 words, with photos, on pet shops, and pet and product merchandising. Pays 10¢ a word, extra for photos. No fiction or news clippings. Query.

PHOTO MARKETING—3000 Picture Pl., Jackson, MI 49201. Margaret Hooks, Man. Ed. Business articles, 1,000 to 3,500 words, for owners and managers of camera/video stores or photo processing labs. Pays $150 to $500, extra for photos, on publication.

PHYSICAL THERAPY/OCCUPATIONAL THERAPY JOB NEWS—470 Boston Post Rd., Weston, MA 02193. John C. Hinds, Jr. Articles, case studies, and profiles (1,500 to 2,500 words) of interest to professional and student physical therapists. Guidelines available. Pays on publication.

PHYSICIANS FINANCIAL NEWS—McGraw-Hill Health Care Group, 800 Second Ave., New York, NY 10017. Noreen Perrotta, Ed. Articles (1,000 words) on investment and personal finance and non-clinical medical economic subjects. Pays $400, after acceptance. Queries required.

PHYSICIAN'S MANAGEMENT—7500 Old Oak Blvd., Cleveland, OH

44130. Bob Feigenbaum, Ed. Articles, about 2,500 words, on finance, investments, malpractice, and office management for primary care physicians. No clinical pieces. Pays $125 per printed page, on acceptance. Query with SASE.

PIZZA TODAY—P.O. Box 114, Santa Claus, IN 47579. Paula Werne, Ed. Pizza business management articles, to 2,500 words, of use to pizza entrepreneurs. Pizza business profiles. Pays $75 to $150 per published page, on publication.

P.O.B.—5820 Lilley Rd., Suite 5, Canton, MI 48187. Victoria L. Dickinson, Ed. Technical and business articles, 1,000 to 4,000 words, for professionals and technicians in the surveying and mapping fields. Technical tips on field and office procedures and equipment maintenance. Pays $150 to $400, on acceptance.

POLICE MAGAZINE—6300 Yarrow Dr., Carlsbad, CA 92009. Sean T. Hilferty, Ed. Articles and profiles (1,000 to 3,000 words) on specialized groups, equipment, issues, and trends of interest to people in the law enforcement profession. Pays $100 to $400, on acceptance.

POOL & SPA NEWS—3923 W. Sixth St., Los Angeles, CA 90020. News articles for the swimming pool, spa, and hot tub industry. Pays from 10¢ to 15¢ a word, extra for photos, on publication. Query first.

PRIVATE PRACTICE—Box 12489, Oklahoma City, OK 73157. Brian Sherman, Ed. Articles, 1,500 to 2,000 words, on state or local legislation affecting medical field. Pays $150 to $300, on publication.

PRO—1233 Janesville Ave., Fort Atkinson, WI 53538. Rod Dickens, Ed. Articles, 1,000 to 1,500 words, on business management for owners of lawn maintenance firms. Pays $150 to $300, on publication. Query.

PROFESSIONAL OFFICE DESIGN—111 Eighth Ave., New York, NY 10011. Muriel Chess, Ed. Articles, to 1,500 words, on space planning and design for offices in the fields of law, medicine, finance, accounting, advertising, and architecture/design. Pays competitive rates, on publication. Query required.

PROGRESSIVE GROCER—Four Stamford Forum, Stamford, CT 06901. Michael J. Sansolo, Man. Ed. Articles related to retail food operations; ideas for successful merchandising, promotions, and displays. Short pieces preferred. Cartoons and photos. Pay varies, on acceptance.

THE QUALITY REVIEW—253 W. 73rd St., New York, NY 10023. Brenda Niemand, Man. Ed. Articles, 2,000 to 4,000 words, on "relationship of quality to public policy, global business, and growing concerns about competitiveness." Pieces should be nontechnical; include case studies for illustration. Pay varies, on acceptance.

QUICK PRINTING—1680 S. W. Bayshore Blvd., Port St. Lucie, FL 34984. Bob Hall, Ed. Articles, 1,500 to 3,000 words, of interest to owners and operators of quick print shops, copy shops, and small commercial printers, on how to make their businesses more profitable; include figures. Pays from $100, on acceptance.

REAL ESTATE TODAY—National Association of Realtors, 430 N. Michigan Ave., Chicago, IL 60611. Educational, how-to articles on all aspects of residential, finance, commercial-investment, and brokerage-management real estate, to 2,000 words. Query required. Pays in copies.

REMODELING—Hanley-Wood, Inc., 655 15th St., Suite 475, Washington, DC 20005. Wendy A. Jordan, Ed. Articles, 250 to 1,700 words, on remodeling and industry news for residential and light commercial remodelers. Pays 20¢ a word, on acceptance. Query.

RESEARCH MAGAZINE—2201 Third St., P.O. Box 77905, San Francisco, CA 94107. Anne Evers, Ed. Articles of interest to stockbrokers, 1,000 to 3,000 words, on financial products, selling, how-tos, and financial trends. Pays from $300 to $900, on publication. Same requirements for *Institutional Research*, for institutional investors. Query.

RESTAURANTS USA—1200 17th St. N.W., Washington, DC 20036-3097. Sylvia Rivchun-Somerville, Ed. Publication of the National Restaurant Association. Articles, 1,500 to 3,500 words, on the food service and restaurant business. Pays $350 to $750, on acceptance. Query.

ROOFER MAGAZINE—10990 Metro Pkwy., Ft. Myers, FL 33912. Mr. Shawn Holiday, Ed. Technical and non-technical articles, human-interest pieces, 500 to 1,500 words, on roofing-related topics: new roofing concepts, energy savings, pertinent issues, industry concern. No general business or computer articles. Pays negotiable rates, on publication. Guidelines.

RV BUSINESS—29901 Agoura Rd., Agoura, CA 91301. Katherine Sharma, Exec. Ed. Articles, 1,500 to 2,500 words, on manufacturing, financing, selling, and servicing recreational vehicles. Articles on legislative matters affecting the industry. Pays varying rates.

THE SAFETY COMPLIANCE LETTER—24 Rope Ferry Rd., Waterford, CT 06386. Margot Loomis, Ed. Interview-based articles, 800 to 1,250 words, for safety professionals, on solving OSHA-related safety and health problems. Pays to 15¢ a word, on acceptance. Query.

SAFETY MANAGEMENT—24 Rope Ferry Rd., Waterford, CT 06386. Margot Loomis, Ed. Interview-based articles, 1,100 to 1,500 words, for safety professionals, on improving workplace safety and health. Pays to 15¢ a word, on acceptance. Query.

SALES & MARKETING MANAGEMENT—Bill Communications, Inc., 633 Third Ave., New York, NY 10017. A.J. Vogl, Ed. Short and feature articles of interest to sales and marketing executives. Looking for practical "news you can use." Pays varying rates, on acceptance. Queries preferred.

SALON BIZ—2416 Wilshire Blvd., Santa Monica, CA 90403. Cynthia Weinstein, Assoc. Ed. Monthly. General-interest pieces, 500 to 1,000 words, on hair, beauty, and fashion of interest to hairdressers. Payment varies, on publication.

SALTWATER DEALER—One Bell Rd., Montgomery, AL 36117. Dave Ellison, Ed. Articles (300 to 1,250 words) for merchants who carry saltwater tackle and marine equipment: business focus is required, and writers should provide practical information for improving management and merchandising. Pays varying rates, on acceptance.

SECURITY MANAGEMENT—1655 N. Ft. Myer Dr., Suite 1200, Arlington, VA 22209. Mary Alice Crawford, Pub. Articles, 2,500 to 3,000 words, on legislative issues related to security; case studies of innovative security applications; management topics: employee relations, training programs, etc. Query.

SIGN BUSINESS—P.O. Box 1416, Broomfield, CO 80038. Emerson Schwartzkopf, Ed. Articles specifically targeted to the sign business. Pays $50 to $200, on publication.

SNACK FOOD MAGAZINE—131 W. First St., Duluth, MN 55802. Jerry Hess, Ed. Articles, 600 to 1,500 words, on trade news, personalities, promotions, production in snack food manufacturing industry. Short pieces; photos. Pays 12¢ to 15¢ a word, $15 for photos, on acceptance. Query.

SOFTWARE MAGAZINE—1900 W. Park Dr., Westborough, MA 01581. John Desmond, Ed. Technical features, 1,000 to 1,200 words, for computer-literate audience, on how software products can be used. Pays about $500 to $750, on publication. Query required. Calendar of scheduled editorial features available.

SOUTHERN LUMBERMAN—P.O. Box 1627, Franklin, TN 37064. Nanci P. Gregg, Man. Ed. Articles on sawmill operations, interviews with industry leaders, how-to technical pieces with an emphasis on increasing sawmill production and efficiency. Pays $100 to $250 for articles with B&W photos. Queries preferred.

SOUVENIRS AND NOVELTIES—7000 Terminal Square, Suite 210, Upper Darby, PA 19082. Articles, 1,500 words, quoting souvenir shop managers on items that sell, display ideas, problems in selling, industry trends. Photos. Pays from $1 per column inch, extra for photos, on publication.

SPECIALTY STORE SERVICE BULLETIN—6604 W. Saginaw Hwy., Lansing, MI 48917. Ralph D. Ward, Ed. Articles on how to run a business: promotions, fashion trends, sales training, etc., for women's clothing store owners and managers. Payment varies, on acceptance. Query.

SUCCESSFUL FARMING—1716 Locust St., Des Moines, IA 50336. Gene Johnston, Man. Ed. Articles, to 2,000 words, for farming families, on all areas of business farming: money management, marketing, machinery, soils and crops, livestock, and buildings; profiles. Pays from $300, on acceptance. Query required.

TAVERN SPORTS INTERNATIONAL—101 E. Erie St., Suite 850, Chicago, IL 60611. Jocelyn Hathaway, Man. Ed. Personality profiles and news features, 1,000 to 2,000 words, with color photos if possible, on organized amateur sports (darts, pool, shuffleboard, etc.) and issues concerning the coin-operated game industry. Payment varies, on publication.

TEA & COFFEE TRADE JOURNAL—130 W. 42nd St., New York, NY 10036. Jane P. McCabe, Ed. Articles, 3 to 5 pages, on trade issues reflecting the tea and coffee industry. Query first. Pays $5 per published inch, on publication.

TEXTILE WORLD—4170 Ashford-Dunwoody Rd. N.E., Suite 420, Atlanta, GA 30319. L.A. Christiansen, Ed. Articles, 500 to 2,000 words, with photos, on manufacturing and finishing textiles. Pays varying rates, on acceptance.

TILE WORLD/STONE WORLD—485 Kinderkamack Rd., Oradell, NJ 07649–1502. John Sailer, Man. Ed. Articles, 750 to 1,500 words, on new trends in installing and designing with tile and stone. For architects, interior designers, and design professionals. Pays $80 per printed page, on publication. Query.

TODAY'S OR NURSE—6900 Grove Rd., Thorofare, NJ 08086. John Bond, Ed. Clinical or general articles, from 2,000 words, of direct interest to operating room nurses. Pays $200 honorarium, on acceptance.

TOP SHELF—199 Ethan Allen Hwy., Ridgefield, CT 06877. Jane Tougas, Ed. Dir. Trade news and advice (1,000 to 2,500 words) for bar owners and managers. "The emphasis is on personalities; taboos include irresponsible marketing of alcohol and promotion of overconsumption." Pays $300 to $600, on acceptance. Query.

TOURIST ATTRACTIONS AND PARKS—7000 Terminal Square, Suite 210, Upper Darby, PA 19082. Articles, 1,500 words, on successful management of parks and leisure attractions. News items, 250 and 500 words. Pays 7¢ a word, on publication. Query.

TRAILER/BODY BUILDERS—P.O. Box 66010, Houston, TX 77266. Paul

Schenck, Ed. Articles on engineering, sales, and management ideas for truck body and truck trailer manufacturers. Pays from $100 per printed page, on acceptance.

TRAINING, THE MAGAZINE OF HUMAN RESOURCES DEVELOPMENT—50 S. Ninth St., Minneapolis, MN 55402. Jack Gordon, Ed. Articles, 1,000 to 2,500 words, for managers of training and development activities in corporations, government, etc. Pays to 20¢ a word, on acceptance. Query.

TRAVEL PEOPLE—CMP Publications, 600 Community Dr., Manhassett, NY 11030. Linda Ball, Ed. Personality profiles, 1,000 to 1,500 words, of successful travel industry workers. Pay varies, on acceptance.

VENDING TIMES—545 Eighth Ave., New York, NY 10018. Arthur E. Yohalem, Ed. Features and news articles, with photos, on vending machines. Pays varying rates, on acceptance. Query.

VIEW—80 Fifth Ave., Suite 501, New York, NY 10011. Peter Caranicas, Ed. Dir. Features and short pieces on trends in the business of television programming (network, syndication, cable, and pay). Profiles. Pays to $600, after publication.

WESTERN INVESTOR—400 S.W. Sixth Ave., Suite 1115, Portland, OR 97204. Business and investment articles, 800 to 1,200 words, about companies and their leaders listed in the "Western Investor" data section. Pays from $50, on publication. Query first.

WINES & VINES—1800 Lincoln Ave., San Rafael, CA 94901. Philip E. Hiaring, Ed. Articles, 1,000 words, on grape and wine industry, emphasizing marketing and production. Pays 5¢ a word, on acceptance.

WOMAN'S ENTERPRISE—28210 Dorothy Dr., Agoura Hills, CA 91301. Caryne Brown, Ed.-in-Chief. Articles, 1,500 to 2,000 words, on the management of businesses owned by women; features on specific businesses and all aspects of their operation, including success factors, pitfalls, income expenditure, and profit figures. Pays 20¢ a word, on acceptance. SASE required.

WOMEN IN BUSINESS—9100 Ward Parkway, Box 8728, Kansas City, MO 64114–0728. Wendy Myers, Ed. Publication of the American Business Women's Association. Features, 1,000 to 2,000 words, for career women from 25 to 55 years old; no profiles. Pays 15¢ per published word, on acceptance. Query.

WOODSHOP NEWS—Pratt St., Essex, CT 06426–1185. Ian C. Bowen, Ed. Features (1 to 3 typed pages) for and about people who work with wood: business stories, profiles, news. Pays from $3 per column inch, on publication. Queries preferred.

THE WORK BOAT—P.O. Box 1348, Mandeville, LA 70470. Marilyn Barrett, Assoc. Ed. Features (to 2,000 words) and shorts (500 to 1,000 words) providing current, lively information for work boat employees, suppliers, and regulators: topics include construction and conversion; politics and industry; new products; and profiles. Payment varies, on acceptance and on publication. Queries preferred.

WORLD OIL—Gulf Publishing Co., P.O. Box 2608, Houston, TX 77252. T.R. Wright, Jr., Ed. Engineering and operations articles, 3,000 to 4,000 words, on petroleum industry exploration, drilling, or producing. Photos. Pays from $50 per printed page, on acceptance. Query.

WORLD SCREEN NEWS—49 E. 21st St., 11th Fl., New York, NY 10010. Gregory P. Fagan, Ed. Features and short pieces on trends in the business of international television programming (network, syndication, cable, and pay). Pays to $750, after publication.

WORLD WASTES—6255 Barfield Rd., Atlanta, GA 30328. Bill Wolpin, Ed./Pub. Allison Baer, Assoc. Ed. Case studies, 1,000 to 2,000 words, with photos, of refuse haulers, landfill operators, resource recovery operations, and transfer stations, with solutions to problems in field. Pays from $125 per printed page, on publication. Query preferred.

YOUNG FASHIONS—119 Fifth Ave., New York, NY 10003. Articles, 1,500 to 3,000 words, that help store owners and department store buyers of children's clothes with merchandising, fashion issues, or operations; how-to pieces. Pays $300 per article, on publication. Query required.

IN-HOUSE MAGAZINES

Publications circulated to company employees (sometimes called house magazines or house organs) and to members of associations and organizations are excellent, well-paying markets for writers at all levels of experience. Large corporations publish these magazines to promote good will, familiarize readers with the company's services and products, and interest customers in their products. And, many organizations publish house magazines designed to keep their members abreast of the issues and events concerning a particular cause or industry. Always read an in-house magazine before submitting an article; write to the editor for a sample copy (offering to pay for it) and the editorial guidelines. Stamped, self-addressed envelopes should be enclosed with any query or manuscript. The following list includes only a sampling of publications in this large market.

CALIFORNIA HIGHWAY PATROLMAN—2030 V St., Sacramento, CA 95818. Carol Perri, Ed. Articles, on transportation safety, California history, travel, consumerism, past and present vehicles, humor, general items, etc. Photos a plus. Pays 2½¢ a word, $5 for B&W photos, on publication. Guidelines with SASE.

CATHOLIC FORESTER—P.O. Box 3012, 425 W. Shuman Blvd., Naperville, IL 60566–7012. Barbara Cunningham, Ed. Official publication of the Catholic Order of Foresters, a fraternal life insurance company for Catholics. Articles, to 2,000 words, of general interest. Fiction, to 3,000 words, (prefer shorter) that deals with contemporary issues; no moralizing, explicit sex or violence. Pays from 5¢ a word, on acceptance.

COLUMBIA—1 Columbus Plaza, New Haven, CT 06507–0901. Richard McMunn, Ed. Journal of the Knights of Columbus. Articles, 1,500 words, for Catholic families. Must be accompanied by color photos or transparencies. No fiction. Pays to $500 for articles and photos, on acceptance.

THE COMPASS—Grand Central Towers 230 E. 44th St., Suite 14B, New York, NY 10017. J.A. Randall, Ed. Articles, to 2,500 words, on the sea and deep sea trade; also articles on aviation. Photos. Pays to $600, on acceptance. Query with SASE.

THE ELKS MAGAZINE—425 W. Diversey Pkwy., Chicago, IL 60614. Judith L. Keogh, Man. Ed. Articles, to 2,500 words, on business, sports, and topics of current interest; for non-urban audience with above-average income. Informative or humorous pieces, to 2,500 words. Pays $150 to $500 for articles, on acceptance. Query.

FIREHOUSE—PTN Publishing Company, 445 Broad Hollow Rd., Melville, NY 11747. Thomas J. Rahilly, Exec. Ed. Articles, 500 to 2,000 words: on-the-scene accounts of fires, trends in firefighting equipment, controversial fire service issues, and lifestyles of firefighters. Pays $100 per typeset page. Also pays for photos. Query.

FOCUS—Turnkey Publications, 4807 Spicewood Springs Rd., Suite 3150, Austin, TX 78759. Robin Perry, Ed. Magazine of the North American Data General Users Group. Articles, 700 to 4,000 words, on Data General computers. Photos a plus. Pays to $100, on publication. Query required.

FORD NEW HOLLAND NEWS—Ford New Holland, Inc., New Holland, PA 17557. Gary Martin, Ed. Articles, to 1,500 words, with strong color photo support, on production, agriculture, research, and rural living. Pays on acceptance. Query.

FRIENDS, THE CHEVY OWNERS' MAGAZINE—3221 W. Big Beaver Rd., Suite 110, Troy, MI 48084. Claire Hinsberg, Ed. Feature articles, 800 to 1,200 words, auto-travel related with specific focus; outdoor/adventure oriented; lifestyle; celebrity profiles; entertainment. Pays varying rates, extra for photos, on acceptance. Query.

THE FURROW—Deere & Company, John Deere Rd., Moline, IL 61265. George R. Sollenberger, Exec. Ed. Specialized, illustrated articles on farming. Pays to $1,000, on acceptance.

GEOBYTE—P.O. Box 979, Tulsa, OK 74101. Ken Milam, Man. Ed. Publication of the American Association of Petroleum Geologists. Articles, 20 typed pages, on computer applications in exploration and production of oil, gas, and energy minerals for geophysicists, geologists, and petroleum engineers. Pay varies, on acceptance. Queries preferred.

INLAND—Inland Steel Flat Products Co., 18 South Home Ave., Park Ridge, IL 60068. Sheldon A. Mix, Man. Ed. Articles, varying lengths, of interest to midwestern readers. History, folklore, commentaries, nature, humor. Send completed manuscripts. Pays on acceptance. Sample copies available but no guidelines.

KIWANIS—3636 Woodview Trace, Indianapolis, IN 46268. Chuck Jonak, Exec. Ed. Articles, 2,500 words (sidebars, 250 to 350 words) on lifestyle, relationships, world view, education, trends, small business, religion, health, etc. No travel pieces, interviews, profiles. Pays $400 to $1,000, on acceptance. Query.

THE LION—300 22nd St., Oak Brook, IL 60521. Robert Kleinfelder, Sr. Ed. Official publication of Lions Clubs International. Articles, 800 to 2,000 words, and photo essays, on club activities. Pays from $50 to $500, including photos, on acceptance. Query.

THE MODERN WOODMEN—Modern Woodmen of America, 1701 1st Ave., Rock Island, IL 61201. Gloria Bergh, Manager, Public Relations. Member publication for fraternal life insurance society. Family- and community-oriented, general-interest articles; some quality fiction. Color photos. Pays from $50, on acceptance. Publication not copyrighted.

OPTIMIST MAGAZINE—4494 Lindell Blvd., St. Louis, MO 63108. Gary S. Bradley, Ed. Articles, to 1,500 words, on activities of local Optimist Club, and techniques for personal and club success; also articles of general interest to the membership. Pays from $100, on acceptance. Query.

RESTAURANTS USA—1200 17th St. N.W., Washington, DC 20036–3097. Sylvia Rivchun-Somerville, Ed. Publication of the National Restaurant Association. Articles, 2,500 to 3,500 words, on the food service and restaurant business. Pays $350 to $750, on acceptance. Query.

THE RETIRED OFFICER MAGAZINE—201 N. Washington St., Alexandria, VA 22314. Articles, 800 to 2,000 words, of interest to military retirees and their families. Current military/political affairs: recent military history, humor, travel, hobbies, military family lifestyles, health, and second-career job opportunities. Photos a plus. Pays to $500, on acceptance. Query Manuscripts Ed. Guidelines.

THE ROTARIAN—1560 Sherman Ave., Evanston, IL 60201. Willmon L. White, Ed. Publication of Rotary International, world service organization of business and professional men and women. Articles, 1,200 to 2,000 words, on international social and economic issues, business and management, human relationships, travel, sports, environment, science and technology; humor. Pays good rates, on acceptance. Query.

SILVER CIRCLE—1001 Commerce Dr., Irwindale, CA 91706. Jay Binkly, Ed. Quarterly for members of Home Savings of America. Consumer service articles, 800 to 2,000 words, on money, health, home, gardening, etc. Query. Pays $250 to $1,000 (20% kill fee), on acceptance.

VFW MAGAZINE—406 West 34th St., Kansas City, MO 64111. Richard K. Kolb, Ed. Magazine for Veterans of Foreign Wars and their families. Articles, to 1,500 words, on current issues and military history, with veteran angle. Photos. Pays to $400, extra for photos, on acceptance. Guidelines.

WOODMEN OF THE WORLD MAGAZINE—1700 Farnam St., Omaha, NE 68102. George M. Herriott, Ed. Articles on history, travel, sports, do-it-yourself projects, health, science, etc. Photos. Pays 10¢ a word, extra for photos, on acceptance.

RELIGIOUS AND DENOMINATIONAL

ADVANCE—1445 Boonville Ave., Springfield, MO 65802. Harris Jansen, Ed. Articles, 1,200 words, slanted to ministers, on preaching, doctrine, practice; how-to features. Pays to 5¢ a word, on acceptance.

AGLOW MAGAZINE—P.O. Box 1548, Lynnwood, WA 98046–1557. Articles and testimonials, 1,000 to 2,000 words, that encourage, instruct, inform, or entertain Christian women of all ages, and relate to the work of the Holy Spirit. Should deal with contemporary issues. Pays 8¢ to 10¢ a word, on acceptance. Queries required.

AMERICA—106 W. 56th St., New York, NY 10019. George W. Hunt, S.J., Ed. Articles, 1,000 to 2,500 words, on current affairs, family life, literary trends. Pays $75 to $150, on acceptance.

AMERICAN BIBLE SOCIETY RECORD—1865 Broadway, New York, NY 10023. Clifford P. Macdonald, Man. Ed. Material related to work of American Bible Society: translating, publishing, distributing. Pays on acceptance. Query.

AMIT WOMAN—817 Broadway, New York, NY 10003. Micheline Ratzersdorfer, Ed. Articles, 1,000 to 2,000 words, of interest to Jewish women: Middle East, Israel, history, holidays, travel. Pays to $75, on publication.

ANNALS OF ST. ANNE DE BEAUPRÉ—P.O. Box 1000, St. Anne de Beaupré, Quebec, Canada G0A 3C0. Roch Achard, C.Ss.R., Ed. Articles, 1,100 to 1,200 words, on Catholic subjects and on St. Anne. Pays 2¢ to 4¢ a word, on acceptance.

BAPTIST LEADER—American Baptist Churches-USA, P.O. Box 851, Valley Forge, PA 19482–0851. L. Isham, Ed. Practical how-to or thought-provoking articles, 1,200 to 1,600 words, for local church lay leaders and teachers.

THE B'NAI B'RITH INTERNATIONAL JEWISH MONTHLY—1640 Rhode Island Ave. N.W., Washington, DC 20036. Jeff Rubin, Ed. Original, lively articles, 500 to 3,000 words, on trends, politics, personalities, and culture of the Jewish community. Fiction, 1,000 to 4,000 words. Pays 10¢ to 25¢ a word, on publication. Query.

BREAD—6401 The Paseo, Kansas City, MO 64131. Karen De Sollar, Ed. Church of the Nazarene. Devotional, Bible study, and Christian guidance articles, to 1,200 words, for teenagers. Religious short stories, to 1,500 words. Pays from 4¢ a word for first rights, 3½¢ a word for reprints, on acceptance. SASE for guidelines.

BRIGADE LEADER—Box 150, Wheaton, IL 60189. Paul Heidebrecht, Man. Ed. Inspirational articles, 1,000 to 1,800 words, for Christian men who lead boys, with an emphasis on fathering. Pays $60 to $150. Query only.

CATECHIST—2451 E. River Rd., Dayton, OH 45439. Patricia Fischer, Ed. Informational and how-to articles, 1,200 to 1,500 words, for Catholic teachers, coordinators, and administrators in religious education programs. Pays $25 to $75, on publication.

CATHOLIC DIGEST—P.O. Box 64090, St. Paul, MN 55164. Address Articles Ed. Articles, 2,000 to 2,500 words, on Catholic and general subjects. Fillers, to 300 words, on instances of kindness rewarded, for "Hearts Are Trumps"; accounts of good deeds, for "People Are Like That." Pays from $200 for original articles, $100 for reprints, on acceptance; $4 to $50 for fillers, on publication.

CATHOLIC LIFE—35750 Moravian Dr., Fraser, MI 48026. Rev. John J. Majka, Ed. Articles, 600 to 1,200 words, on Catholic missionary work in Hong Kong, India, Latin America, Africa. Photos. No fiction or poetry. Pays 6¢ a word, extra for photos, on publication.

CATHOLIC NEAR EAST MAGAZINE—1011 First Ave., New York, NY 10022–4195. Thomas McHugh, Ed. Michael La Civit, Ed. Asst. A quarterly publication of Catholic Near East Welfare Assoc., a papal agency for humanitarian and pastoral support. Articles 1,500 to 2,000 words, on people of the Balkans, Eastern Europe, Egypt, Ethiopia, Middle East, and India; their religious affairs, heritage, culture, and current state of affairs. Special interest in Eastern Christian churches. Color photos for all articles. Query with SASE. Pays 15¢ a word, on publication.

CATHOLIC TWIN CIRCLE—12700 Ventura Blvd., Suite 200, Studio City, CA 91604. Mary Louise Frawley, Ed. Articles and interviews of interest to Catholics, 1,000 to 2,000 words, with photos. Strict attention to Catholic doctrine required. Enclose SASE. Pays 10¢ a word, on publication.

CHARISMA & CHRISTIAN LIFE—600 Rinehart Rd., Lake Mary, FL 32746. Nancy Brett, Ed. Mgr. Charismatic/evangelical Christian articles, 1,500 to 2,500 words, for developing the spiritual life. Photos. Pays varying rates, on publication.

THE CHRISTIAN CENTURY—407 S. Dearborn St., Chicago, IL 60605. James M. Wall, Ed. Ecumenical. Articles, 1,500 to 2,500 words, with a religious angle, on political and social issues, international affairs, culture, the arts. Poetry, to 20 lines. Photos. Pays about $25 per printed page, extra for photos, on publication.

CHRISTIAN HERALD—40 Overlook Dr., Chappaqua, NY 10514. Bob Chuvala, Ed. Evangelical. Articles, personal-experience pieces, to 1,200 words, on biblically oriented topics. Pays from 10¢ a word for full-length features, from $25 for short pieces, after acceptance. Query or send complete manuscript. No poetry.

CHRISTIAN SINGLE—127 Ninth Ave. N., Nashville, TN 37234. Cliff Allbritton, Ed. Articles, 600 or 1,200 words, on leisure activities, inspiring personal experiences, for single Christian adults. Humor. Pays 5¢ a word, on acceptance. Query. Send 9x12 SASE with 85¢ postage for guidelines and sample issue.

CHRISTIAN SOCIAL ACTION—100 Maryland Ave. N.E., Washington, DC 20002. Lee Ranck, Ed. Articles, 1,500 to 2,000 words, on social issues for concerned persons of faith. Pays $75 to $100, on publication.

CHRISTIANITY TODAY—465 Gundersen Dr., Carol Stream, IL 60188. Lyn Cryderan, Ed. David Neff, Man. Ed. Doctrinal social issues and interpretive essays, 1,500 to 3,000 words, from evangelical Protestant perspective. Pays $300 to $500, on acceptance. Query required.

CHURCH & STATE—8120 Fenton St., Silver Spring, MD 20910. Joseph L. Conn, Man. Ed. Articles, 600 to 2,600 words, on religious liberty and church-state relations issues. Pays varying rates, on acceptance. Query.

CHURCH ADMINISTRATION—127 Ninth Ave. N., Nashville, TN 37234. Gary Hardin, Ed. Southern Baptist. How-to articles, 1,500 to 1,800 words, on administrative planning, staffing, pastoral ministry, organization, and financing. Pays 5½¢ a word, on acceptance. Query.

CHURCH EDUCATOR—Educational Ministries, Inc., 2861-C Saturn St., Brea, CA 92621. Robert G. Davidson, Ed. How-to articles, to 1,750 words, on Christian education: activity projects, crafts, learning centers, games, bulletin boards, etc., for church school, junior and high school programs, and adult study group ideas. Allow 3 months for response. Pays 3¢ a word, on publication.

THE CHURCH HERALD—6157 28th St. S.E., Grand Rapids, MI 49546–6999. John Stapert, Ed. Reformed Church in America. Articles, 500 to 1,500 words, on Christianity and culture, politics, marriage, and home. Pays $40 to $125, on acceptance. Query required.

THE CHURCH MUSICIAN—127 Ninth Ave. N., Nashville, TN 37234. W. M. Anderson, Ed. Articles for spiritual enrichment, testimonials, human-interest pieces, and other subjects of interest to music directors, pastors, organists, pianists, choir coordinators, and members of the music council in local churches. Pays to 5¢ a word, on acceptance. Same address and requirements for *Glory Songs* (for adults), and *The Senior Musician* (for senior adults).

THE CIRCUIT RIDER—P.O. Box 801, Nashville, TN 37202. Keith Pohl, Ed. Articles for United Methodist pastors, 800 to 1,600 words. Pays $25 to $100, on acceptance. Query, with SASE, preferred.

COLUMBIA—1 Columbus Plaza, New Haven, CT 06507–0901. Richard McMunn, Ed. Knights of Columbus. Articles, 1,500 words, for Catholic families. Must be accompanied by color photos or transparencies. No fiction. Pays to $500 for articles with photos, on acceptance.

COMMENTARY—165 E. 56th St., New York, NY 10022. Norman Podhoretz, Ed. Articles, 5,000 to 7,000 words, on contemporary issues, Jewish affairs, social sciences, religious thought, culture. Serious fiction; book reviews. Pays on publication.

COMMONWEAL—15 Dutch St., New York, NY 10038. Margaret O'Brien Steinfels, Ed. Catholic. Articles, to 3,000 words, on political, religious, social, and literary subjects. Pays 3¢ a word, on acceptance.

CONFIDENT LIVING—Box 82808, Lincoln, NE 68501. Jan Reeser, Man. Ed. Articles, to 1,500 words, on relating biblical truths to daily living. Photos. Pays 7¢ to 15¢ a word, on acceptance. No simultaneous submissions. SASE required. Photos paid on publication.

DAILY MEDITATION—Box 2710, San Antonio, TX 78299. Ruth S. Paterson, Ed. Inspirational nonsectarian articles, 650 to 2,000 words. Fillers, to 350 words; verse, to 20 lines. Pays ½¢ to 2¢ a word for prose; 14¢ a line for verse, on acceptance. SASE required.

DECISION—Billy Graham Evangelistic Association, 1300 Harmon Pl., Minneapolis, MN 55403. Roger C. Palms, Ed. Articles, Christian testimonials, 1,800 to 2,000 words. Vignettes, 500 to 1,000 words. Pays varying rates, on publication.

DISCOVERIES—6401 The Paseo, Kansas City, MO 64131. Molly Mitchell, Ed. Fiction for children (grades 3 to 6) 400 to 900 words, defining Christian experiences and demonstrating Christian values and beliefs. Pays 3½¢ a word, on acceptance.

EVANGEL—Light and Life Press, Box 535002, Indianapolis, IN 46253–5002. Vera Bethel, Ed. Free Methodist. Personal experience articles, 1,000 words; short devotional items, 300 to 500 words; fiction, 1,200 words, showing personal faith in Christ to be instrumental in solving problems. Pays $10 to $25 for articles, $45 for fiction, $5 for poetry, on publication.

EVANGELICAL BEACON—1515 E. 66th St., Minneapolis, MN 55423. Carol Madison, Ed. Evangelical Free Church. Articles, 250 to 1,750 words, on religious topics: testimonials, pieces on current issues from an evangelical perspective, short inspirational and evangelistic devotionals. Pays 3¢ to 4¢ a word, on publication. Send SASE for writers' guidelines.

FAITH TODAY—Box 8800, Sta. B, Willowdale, Ontario, Canada M2K 2R6. Brian C. Stiller, Ed. Audrey Dorsch, Man. Ed. Articles, 1,500 words, on current issues relating to the church in Canada. Pays negotiable rates, on publication. Queries are preferred.

THE GEM—Box 926, Findlay, OH 45839. Marilyn Rayle Kern, Ed. Articles, 300 to 1,600 words, and fiction, 1,000 to 1,600 words: true-to-life experiences of God's help, of healed relationships, and of growing maturity in faith. For adolescents through senior citizens. Pays $15 for articles and fiction, $5 to $10 for fillers, after publication.

GLORY SONGS—See *The Church Musician.*

GROUP, THE YOUTH MINISTRY MAGAZINE—Box 481, Loveland, CO 80539. Joani Schultz, Ed. Dir. Interdenominational magazine for leaders of junior and senior high school Christian youth groups. Articles, 500 to 1,700 words, about practical youth ministry principles, techniques, or activities. Short how-to pieces, to 300 words, for "Try This One"; news items, to 500 words, for "News, Trends, and Tips." Pays to $150 for articles, $15 to $25 for department pieces, on acceptance. Guidelines available.

GUIDE—Review and Herald Publishing Co., 55 W. Oak Ridge Dr., Hagerstown, MD 21740. Stories and articles, to 1,200 words, for Christian youth, ages 10 to 14. Pays 3¢ to 4¢ a word, on acceptance.

HOME LIFE—127 Ninth Ave. N., Nashville, TN 37234. Charlie Warren, Ed. Mary P. Darby, Asst. Ed. Southern Baptist. Articles, preferably personal-experience, and fiction, to 1,500 words, on Christian marriage, parenthood, and family relationships. Human-interest pieces, 200 to 500 words; cartoons and short verse. Pays to 5¢ a word, on acceptance.

INSIDE MAGAZINE—226 S. 16th St., Philadelphia, PA 19102. Jane Biberman, Ed. Articles, 1,500 to 3,000 words, and fiction, 2,000 to 3,000 words, of interest to Jewish adults. Pays $100 to $500, on acceptance. Query.

INSIGHT—55 West Oak Ridge Dr., Hagerstown, MD 21740. Christopher Blake, Ed. Seventh-day Adventist. Personal-experience narratives, articles, and humor, to 1,500 words, for high school students. Parables; shorts; poetry. Pays 10¢ to 15¢ a word, extra for photos, on acceptance. Same requirements for *Insight/Out*, for Christian non-denominational readers.

THE JEWISH MONTHLY—B'nai B'rith International, 1640 Rhode Island Ave. N.W., Washington, DC 20036. Marc Silver, Ed. Articles, 500 to 2,000 words, on politics, religion, current events, history, culture, and social issues of Jewish concern with an emphasis on people. Pays $50 to $300, on publication.

JOURNEY—Christian Board of Publication, Box 179, St. Louis, MO 63166. Michael E. Dixon, Ed. Fiction, 100 to 1,200 words; articles, 600 to 1,000 words; and poetry, to 20 lines. Accepts material for 12- to 16-year-olds. Pays 3¢ a word for prose, from $3 for poetry, on acceptance. Guidelines available.

KEY TO CHRISTIAN EDUCATION—8121 Hamilton Ave., Cincinnati, OH 45231. Marjorie Miller, Ed. Articles, on teaching methods, and success stories for workers in Christian education. Pays varying rates, on acceptance.

LIBERTY MAGAZINE—12501 Old Columbia Pike, Silver Spring, MD 20904-1608. Roland R. Hegstad, Ed. Timely articles, to 2,500 words, and photo essays, on religious freedom and church-state relations. Pays 6¢ to 8¢ a word, on acceptance. Query.

LIGHT AND LIFE—P.O. Box 535002, Indianapolis, IN 46253. Robert Haslam, Ed. Fresh, lively articles about practical Christian living, and sound treatments of vital issues facing the Evangelical in contemporary society. Pays 4¢ a word, on publication.

LIGUORIAN—Liguori, MO 63057. Rev. Allan Weinert, Ed. Francine O'Connor, Man. Ed. Catholic. Articles and short stories, 1,500 to 2,000 words, on Christian values in modern life. Pays 10¢ to 12¢ a word, on acceptance.

LIVE—Gospel Publishing House, 1445 Boonville Ave., Springfield, MO 65802. Lorraine Mastrorio, Ed. Weekly story-paper of practical Christian living for adults (18 to 65+). True stories and fiction, 500 to 2,000 words; fillers, 200 to 700 words; and poetry, 12 to 25 lines. Payment is 3¢ a word for first rights, 2¢ a word for second rights, on acceptance. Send SASE for guidelines.

THE LIVING LIGHT—U.S. Catholic Conference, Dept. of Education, 3211 4th St. N.W., Washington, DC 20017-1194. Berard L. Marthaler, Exec. Ed. Theoretical and practical articles, 1,500 to 4,000 words, on religious education, catechesis, and pastoral ministry.

LIVING WITH CHILDREN—127 Ninth Ave. N., Nashville, TN 37234. Articles, 800 to 1,450 words, on parent-child relationships, told from a Christian perspective. Pays 5¢ a word, after acceptance.

LIVING WITH PRESCHOOLERS—127 Ninth Ave. N., Nashville, TN 37234. Articles, 800 to 1,450 words, and anecdotes, for Christian families. Pays 5¢ a word, on acceptance.

LIVING WITH TEENAGERS—127 Ninth Ave. N., Nashville, TN 37234. Articles told from a Christian perspective for parents of teenagers; first-person approach preferred. Poetry, 4 to 16 lines. Pays 5½¢ a word, on acceptance.

THE LOOKOUT—8121 Hamilton Ave., Cincinnati, OH 45231. Simon J. Dahlman, Ed. Articles, 1,000 to 2,000 words, on families and people overcoming problems by applying Christian principles. Inspirational or humorous shorts, 500 to 800 words; fiction, to 2,000 words. Pays 4¢ to 7¢ a word, on acceptance.

THE LUTHERAN—8765 W. Higgins Rd., Chicago, IL 60631. Edgar R. Trexler, Ed. Articles, to 2,000 words, on Christian ideology, personal religious experiences, social and ethical issues, family life, church, and community. Pays $100 to $600, on acceptance. Query.

MARRIAGE & FAMILY—Division of Abbey Press, St. Meinrad, IN 47577. Kass Dotterweich, Man. Ed. Expert advice, personal-experience articles with moral, religious, or spiritual slant, to 1,900 words, on marriage and family relationships. Pays 7¢ a word, on acceptance.

MATURE LIVING—127 Ninth Ave. N., Nashville, TN 37234. General-interest and travel articles, nostalgia and fiction, 900 words, for Christians, 60 years and older. Profiles, 25 lines; must include a B&W action photo. Brief, humorous items for "Cracker Barrel." Pays 5¢ a word, $25 for profile and photo, $5 for humor on acceptance. Buys all rights.

MATURE YEARS—201 Eighth Ave. S., P.O. Box 801, Nashville, TN 37202. Donn Downall, Ed. United Methodist. Articles on retirement or related subjects, 1,500 to 2,000 words. Humorous and serious fiction, 1,500 to 1,800 words, for adults. Poetry, to 14 lines. Include Social Security no. with manuscript. Buys all rights.

MESSENGER OF THE SACRED HEART—661 Greenwood Ave., Toronto, Ont., Canada M4J 4B3. Articles and short stories, about 1,500 words, for American and Canadian Catholics. Pays from 4¢ a word, on acceptance.

MIDSTREAM—515 Park Ave., New York, NY 10022. Jewish-interest articles and book reviews. Fiction, to 3,000 words, and poetry. Pays 5¢ a word, after publication.

THE MIRACULOUS MEDAL—475 E. Chelten Ave., Philadelphia, PA 19144. Robert P. Cawley, C.M. Ed. Dir. Catholic. Fiction, to 2,400 words. Religious verse, to 20 lines. Pays from 2¢ a word for fiction, from 50¢ a line for poetry, on acceptance.

MOMENT—3000 Connecticut Ave., Suite 300, Washington, DC 20008. Charlotte Anker, Man. Ed. Sophisticated articles and some fiction, 2,500 to 5,000 words, on Jewish topics. Pays $150 to $400, on publication.

MOMENTUM—National Catholic Educational Assn., 1077 30th St. N.W., Suite 100, Washington, DC 20007–3852. Patricia Feistritzer, Ed. Articles, 500 to 1,500 words, on outstanding programs, issues, and research in education. Book reviews. Pays 2¢ a word, on publication. Query.

MOODY MONTHLY—820 N. La Salle Dr., Chicago, IL 60610. Andrew Scheer, Man. Ed. Anecdotal articles, 1,200 to 1,800 words, on the evangelical Christian experience in school, the home, and the workplace. Pays 10¢ to 15¢ a word, on acceptance. Query.

THE NATIONAL CHRISTIAN REPORTER—See *The United Methodist Reporter*.

NEW ERA—50 E. North Temple, Salt Lake City, UT 84150. Richard M. Romney, Man. Ed. Articles, 150 to 2,000 words, and fiction, to 2,000 words, for young Mormons. Poetry; photos. Pays 5¢ to 10¢ a word, 25¢ a line for poetry, on acceptance. Query.

NEW WORLD OUTLOOK—475 Riverside Dr., Rm. 1351, New York, NY 10115. Susan Keirn Kester, Exec. Ed. Articles, 1,500 to 2,500 words, on Christian missions, religious issues, and public affairs. Pays on publication.

OBLATES—15 S. 59th St., Belleville, IL 62223–4694. Address Jacqueline Lowery Corn, Man. Ed. Articles, 500 to 600 words, for mature Catholics, that inspire, uplift, and motivate through positive Christian values in everyday life. Inspirational poetry, to 16 lines. Pays $75 for articles, $25 for poems, on acceptance. Send complete manuscript only. Send 45¢ SASE for guidelines and sample copy.

OUR FAMILY—Box 249, Battleford, Sask., Canada S0M 0E0. Nestor Gregoire, Ed. Articles, 1,000 to 3,000 words, for Catholic families, on modern society, family, marriage, current affairs, and spiritual topics. Humor; verse. Pays 7¢ to 10¢ a word for articles, 75¢ to $1 a line for poetry, on acceptance. SASE with international reply coupons required with all submissions. Guidelines.

OUR SUNDAY VISITOR—Huntington, IN 46750. Greg Erlandson, Ed. In-depth features, 1,000 to 1,200 words, on the Catholic church in America today. Pays $150 to $250, on acceptance

PARISH FAMILY DIGEST—200 Noll Plaza, Huntington, IN 46750. Corine B. Erlandson, Ed. Articles, 750 to 900 words, fillers and humor, for Catholic families and parishes. Pays 5¢ a word, on acceptance.

PENTECOSTAL EVANGEL—1445 Boonville Ave., Springfield, MO 65802. Richard Champion, Ed. Assemblies of God. Religious personal experience, and devotional articles, 500 to 1,200 words. Verse, 12 to 30 lines. Pays 6¢ a word, on acceptance.

PRESBYTERIAN SURVEY—100 Witherspoon, Louisville, KY 40202. Vic Jameson, Ed. Articles, 1,200 words, of interest to members of the Presbyterian Church or ecumenical individuals. Pays to $150, on acceptance.

THE PRIEST—200 Noll Plaza, Huntington, IN 46750. Robert A. Willems, Assoc. Ed. Articles, to 2,500 words, on life and ministry of priests, current theological developments, etc., for priests, permanent deacons, and seminarians. Pays $35 to $150, on acceptance.

PURPOSE—616 Walnut Ave., Scottdale, PA 15683–1999. James E. Horsch, Ed. Stories, articles, and fillers, to 1,000 words, on Christian discipleship themes, with good photos; pieces of history, biography, science, hobbies, from a Christian perspective. Fiction, to 1,000 words, on Christian problem solving. Poetry, to 12 lines. Pays to 5¢ a word, to $1 a line for poetry, on acceptance.

QUEEN—26 S. Saxon Ave., Bay Shore, NY 11706. J. Patrick Gaffney, S.M.M., Ed. Publication of Montfort Missionaries. Articles and fiction, 1,000 to 2,000 words, related to the Virgin Mary. Poetry. Pay varies, on acceptance.

THE QUIET HOUR—850 N. Grove Ave., Elgin, IL 60120. Richard Lint, Ed. Short devotionals. Pays $15, on acceptance. By assignment only; query required.

THE RECONSTRUCTIONIST—Box 1336, Roslyn Heights, NY 11577. Rabbi Joy Levitt, Ed. Articles and fiction, 2,000 to 3,000 words, relating to Judaism. Poetry. Pays $18 to $36, on publication.

ST. ANTHONY MESSENGER—1615 Republic St., Cincinnati, OH 45210. Norman Perry, O.F.M., Ed. Articles, 2,000 to 3,000 words, on personalities, major movements, education, family, religious and church issues, spiritual life, and social issues. Human interest pieces. Humor; fiction (2,000 to 3,000 words). Pays 14¢ a word, on acceptance. Articles and stories should have religious implications. Query for nonfiction.

ST. JOSEPH'S MESSENGER—P.O. Box 288, Jersey City, NJ 07303. Sister Ursula Maphet, Ed. Inspirational articles, 500 to 1,000 words, and fiction, 1,000 to 1,500 words. Verse, 4 to 40 lines.

SEEK—8121 Hamilton Ave., Cincinnati, OH 45231. Eileen H. Wilmoth, Ed. Articles and fiction, to 1,200 words, on inspirational and controversial topics and timely religious issues. Christian testimonials. Pays to 5¢ to 7¢ a word, on acceptance. Guidelines.

THE SENIOR MUSICIAN—See *The Church Musician*.

SHARING THE VICTORY—8701 Leeds Rd., Kansas City, MO 64129. John Dodderidge, Ed. Articles, interviews, and profiles, to 1,000 words, for co-ed Christian athletes and coaches in high school and college. Pays from $50, on publication. Query required.

SIGNS OF THE TIMES—P. O. Box 7000, Boise, ID 83707. Kenneth J. Holland, Ed. Seventh-day Adventists. Feature articles on Christians who have performed community services; current issues from a biblical perspective; health, home, marriage, human-interest pieces; inspirational articles, 500 to 2,000 words. Pays 13¢ to16¢ a word, on acceptance.

SISTERS TODAY—The Liturgical Press, St. John's Abbey, Collegeville, MN 56321. Articles, 500 to 3,500 words, on Roman Catholic theology, religious issues for women and the Church. Poetry, to 34 lines. Pays $5 per printed page, $10 per poem, on publication; $50 for color cover photos and $25 for B&W inside photos. Send articles to Sister Mary Anthony Wagner, O.S.B., Ed. , St. Benedict's Convent, St. Joseph, MN 56374. Send poetry to Sister Audrey Synnott, R.S.M., 1437 Blossom Rd., Rochester, NY 14610.

SOCIAL JUSTICE REVIEW—3835 Westminster Pl., St. Louis, MO 63108. Rev. John H. Miller, C.S.C., Ed. Articles 2,000 to 3.000 words, on social problems in light of Catholic teaching and current scientific studies. Pays 2¢ a word, on publication.

SPIRITUAL LIFE—2131 Lincoln Rd. N.E., Washington, DC 20002–1199. Steven Payne, O.C.D., Ed. Professional religious journal. Religious essays, 3,000 to 5,000 words, on spirituality in contemporary life. Pays from $50, on acceptance. Send 7x10 SASE with 4 first-class stamps for guidelines and sample issue.

SPIRITUALITY TODAY—3642 Lindell Blvd., St. Louis, MO 63108. Regina Siegfried, A.S.C., Ed. Quarterly. Biblical, liturgical, theological, ecumenical, historical, and biographical articles, 4,000 words, about the challenges of contemporary Christian life. Pays from 1½¢ a word, on publication. Query required, with SASE. Guidelines.

STANDARD—6401 The Paseo, Kansas City, MO 64131. Articles, 300 to 1,700 words; true experiences; poetry, to 20 lines; fiction with Christian emphasis but not overtly preachy; fillers; short articles with devotional emphasis; cartoons in good taste. Pays 3½¢ a word, on acceptance.

SUNDAY DIGEST—850 N. Grove Ave., Elgin, IL 60120. Articles, 1,000 to 1,500 words, on Christian faith in contemporary life; inspirational and how-to articles; free-verse poetry. Anecdotes, 500 words. Pays $60 to $200 (less for reprints), on acceptance.

SUNDAY SCHOOL COUNSELOR—1445 Boonville Ave., Springfield, MO 65802–1894. Sylvia Lee, Ed. Articles, 1,000 to 1,500 words, on teaching and Sunday school people, for local Sunday school teachers. Pays 3¢ to 5¢ a word, on acceptance.

SUNSHINE MAGAZINE—Sunshine Press, Litchfield, IL 62056. Peggy Kuethe, Ed. Inspirational articles, to 600 words. Short stories, 1,000 words, and juveniles, 400 words. No heavily religious material or "born again" pieces. Pays varying rates, on acceptance.

TEACHERS INTERACTION—1333 S. Kirkwood Rd., St. Louis, MO 63122. Martha S. Jander, Ed. Articles, 800 to 1,200 words; how-to pieces, to 100 words, for Lutheran volunteer church school teachers. Pays $10 to $35, on publication. Limited free-lance market.

TEENS TODAY—Church of the Nazarene, 6401 The Paseo, Kansas City, MO 64131. Karen DeSollar, Ed. Short stories that deal with teens demonstrating Christian principles, 1,200 to 1,500 words. Pays 4¢ a word for first rights, 3½¢ a word for reprints, on acceptance. Guidelines.

THEOLOGY TODAY—Box 29, Princeton, NJ 08542. Hugh T. Kerr, Ed. Articles, 1,500 to 3,500 words, on theology, religion, and related social issues. Literary criticism. Pays $75 to $100, on publication.

THE UNITED CHURCH OBSERVER—85 St. Clair Ave. E., Toronto, Ont., Canada M4T 1M8. Factual articles, 1,500 to 2,500 words, on religious trends, human problems, social issues. No poetry. Pays after publication. Query.

UNITED EVANGELICAL ACTION—P. O. Box 28, Wheaton, IL 60189. Don Brown, Ed. National Assn. of Evangelicals. News-oriented expositions and editorials, 750 to 1,000 words, on current events of concern and consequence to the evangelical church. Pays about 7¢ to 10¢ a word, on publication. Query with writing samples required.

THE UNITED METHODIST REPORTER—P.O. Box 660275, Dallas, TX 75266–0275. Spurgeon M. Dunnam, III, Ed. John Lovelace, Man. Ed. United Methodist. Religious features, to 500 words. Religious verse, 4 to 12 lines. Photos. Pays 4¢ a word, on publication. Send for guidelines. Same address and requirements for *The National Christian Reporter* (interdenominational).

UNITED SYNAGOGUE REVIEW—155 Fifth Ave., New York, NY 10010. Lois Goldrich, Ed. Articles, 1,000 to 1,200 words, on issues of interest to Conservative Jewish community. Query.

UNITY MAGAZINE—Unity School of Christianity, Unity Village, MO 64065. Philip White, Ed. Articles and poems: inspirational, religious, metaphysical, 500 to 1,500 words. Pays 5¢ to 9¢ a word, on acceptance.

VIRTUE—P. O. Box 850, Sisters, OR 97759. Marlee Alex, Ed. Articles and fiction for Christian women. Query only, except for "One Woman's Journal," and "In My Opinion."

VISTA MAGAZINE—P. O. Box 50434, Indianapolis, IN 46250–0434. Articles and adult fiction, on current Christian concerns and issues. First-person pieces, 750 to 1,200 words. Opinion pieces from an evangelical perspective, 500 to 750 words. Pays from 2¢ to 4¢ a word.

WITH—722 Main St., Box 347, Newton, KS 67114. Susan Janzen, Ed. Fiction, 1,000 to 1,250 words; nonfiction, 900 to 1,250 words; and poetry, to 50 lines for Anabaptist-Mennonite teenagers. "We want to help teens understand the issues that affect them directly and indirectly, and help them make choices that reflect an Anabaptist-Mennonite understanding of living by the Spirit of Christ." B&W 8x10 photos accepted. Payment is 4¢ a word, on acceptance (2¢ a word for reprints).

YOUNG SALVATIONIST—The Salvation Army, 799 Bloomfield Ave., Verona, NJ 07044. Robert R. Hostetler, Ed. Articles, 600 to 1,200 words, teach the Christian view to everyday living, for teenagers. Short shorts, first-person testimonies, 600 to 800 words. Pays 4¢ to 6¢ a word, on acceptance. SASE required. Guidelines.

THE YOUNG SOLDIER—The Salvation Army, 799 Bloomfield Ave., Verona, NJ 07044. Robert R. Hostetler, Ed. For children 8 to 12. Must carry a definite Christian message or teach a biblical truth. Fiction, 800 to 1,000 words. Some poetry. Fillers, puzzles, etc. Pays 4¢ a word, $3 to $7 for fillers, puzzles, on acceptance.

HEALTH

ACCENT ON LIVING—P. O. Box 700, Bloomington, IL 61702. Raymond C. Cheever, Pub. Betty Garee, Ed. Articles, 250 to 1,000 words, about physically disabled people, including their careers, recreation, sports, self-help devices, and ideas that can make daily routines easier. Good photos a plus. Pays 10¢ a word, on publication. Query.

ADDICTION & RECOVERY—4959 Commerce Parkway, Cleveland, OH 44128. Brenda L. Lewison, Ed. Articles on all aspects of alcoholism and other drug addiction: treatment, legislation, education, prevention, and recovery. Send SASE for guidelines.

AMERICAN BABY—475 Park Ave. S., New York, NY 10016. Judith Nolte, Ed. Articles, 1,000 to 2,000 words, for new or expectant parents on prenatal or infant care. Pays varying rates, on acceptance.

AMERICAN FITNESS—15250 Ventura Blvd., Suite 310, Sherman Oaks, CA 91403. Peg Jordan, Ed. Rhonda Wilson, Man. Ed. Articles, 500 to 1,500 words, on exercise, health, sports, nutrition, etc. Illustrations, photos, cartoons.

ARTHRITIS TODAY—The Arthritis Foundation, 1314 Spring St. N.W., Atlanta, GA 30309. Cindy McDaniel, Ed. Self-help, how-to, general interest, and inspirational articles (1,000 to 2,500 words) and short fillers (100 to 250 words) to help people with arthritis live more productive, independent, and pain-free lives. Pays from $350, on acceptance.

BETTER HEALTH—1384 Chapel St., New Haven, CT 06511. James F. Malerba, Dir. Wellness and prevention magazine affiliated with The Hospital of Saint Raphael of New Haven. Upbeat articles, 2,000 words, that encourage a healthier lifestyle. Pays $150 to $350, on acceptance. Query with SASE.

EAST WEST: THE JOURNAL OF NATURAL HEALTH & LIVING—17 Station St., Box 1200, Brookline, MA 02147. Features, 1,500 to 2,500 words, on holistic health, natural foods, gardening, etc. Material for "Body," "Healing," "In the Kitchen," and "Beauty and Fitness." Interviews. Photos. Pays 10¢ to 15¢ a word, extra for photos, on publication.

EXPECTING—685 Third Ave., New York, NY 10017. Evelyn A. Podsiadlo, Ed. Articles, 700 to 1,800 words, for expectant mothers. Pays $300 to $500, on acceptance.

HEALTH—3 Park Ave., New York, NY 10016. Articles, 800 to 2,500 words, on medicine, nutrition, fitness, emotional and psychological well-being. Pays up to $2,000, on acceptance. Query.

HEALTH PROGRESS—4455 Woodson Rd., St. Louis, MO 63134. Judy Cassidy, Ed. Journal of the Catholic Health Association. Features, 2,000 to 4,000 words, on hospital management and administration, medical-moral questions, health care, public policy, technological developments in health care and their impacts, nursing, financial and human resource management for healthcare administrators, and innovative programs in hospitals and long-term care facilities. Payment negotiable. Query.

HOSPITALS—211 E. Chicago, IL 60611. Mary Gray, Ed. Articles, 800 to 1,500 words, for hospital administrators, on financing, staffing, coordinating, and providing facilities for health care services. Pays varying rates, on acceptance. Query.

IDEA TODAY—6190 Cornerstone Ct. East, Suite 204, San Diego, CA 92121–3773. Patricia Ryan, Ed. Practical articles, 1,000 to 3,000 words, on new exercise programs, business management, nutrition, sports medicine, and dance-exercise and one-to-one training techniques. Articles must be geared toward the aerobics instructor, exercise studio owner or manager, or personal trainer. No queries on topics for the consumer. No general health ideas wanted. Payment negotiable, on acceptance. Query preferred.

IN HEALTH—475 Gate Five Rd., Suite 225, Sausalito, CA 94965. Leslie Talmadge, Ed. Articles, 850 to 5,000 words, on health and medicine; pieces for "Food," "Fitness," "Vanities," "Drugs," "Mind," "Family," and "Housecalls" departments. Pays 50¢ to 80¢ a word, on acceptance. Query with clips required.

LET'S LIVE—P.O. Box 74908, Los Angeles, CA 90004. Debra Jenkins Robinson, Ed. Articles, 1,000 to 1,500 words, on preventive medicine and nutrition, alternative medicine, diet, exercise, recipes, and natural beauty. Pays $150, on publication. Query.

THE MAIN EVENT—c/o Thomas Boron, Inc., 17–17 Route 208 North, Fair Lawn, NJ 07410. Bob Brody, Contributing Ed. "Sports Journal for Physicians." Articles, 1,000 to 2,000 words, on general sport topics, physician-athletes, fitness, and sports medicine. Pays 30¢ a word, on acceptance. Query required.

MATURE HEALTH—See *Solutions for Better Health*.

MUSCULAR DEVELOPMENT—351 West 54th St., New York, NY 10019. Alan Paul, Ed. Articles, 5 to 10 typed pages, geared to serious weight training athletes, on any aspects of competitive body building, powerlifting, sports and nutrition. Photos. Pays $50 to $300, on publication. Query.

NEW BODY—1700 Broadway, New York, NY 10019. Nayda Rondon, Ed. Well-researched, service-oriented articles, 800 to 1,500 words, on exercise, nutrition, lifestyle, diet, and health for women ages 18 to 35. Writers should have some background in or knowledge of the health field. Pays $100 to $300, on publication. Query.

NEW REALITIES—4000 Albemarle St. N.W., Washington, DC 20016. Joy O'Rourke, Ed. Articles on holistic health, personal growth, humanistic and transpersonal psychology, alternative lifestyles, new spirituality, parapsychology, social and global transformation. Query or send complete manuscript.

NURSING HOMES—4959 Commerce Parkway, Cleveland, OH 44128. Duane Frayer, Ed. Articles, 1,000 to 5,000 words, of interest to administrators, managers, and supervisory personnel in nursing homes; human-interest, academic and clinical pieces; book reviews, 250 to 300 words. Pays $50 for articles, $30 for reviews, on acceptance. Photos, graphics welcome.

NURSING 91—1111 Bethlehem Pike, Springhouse, PA 19477. Maryanne Wagner, Ed. Most articles are clinically oriented, and are written by nurses for nurses. Covers legal, ethical, management, and career aspects of nursing. No poetry. Pays $25 to $250, on publication. Query.

NURSINGWORLD JOURNAL—470 Boston Post Rd., Weston, MA 02193. Eileen Devito, Man. Ed. Articles, 500 to 1,500 words, for and by nurses and nurse-educators, on aspects of current nursing issues. Pays from 25¢ per column inch, on publication.

THE PHYSICIAN AND SPORTSMEDICINE—4530 W. 77th St., Minneapolis, MN 55435. Lauren Pacelli, Acquisitions Mgr. News and feature articles, 500 to 3,000 words, on fitness, sports, and exercise. Medical angle necessary. Pays $150 to $900, on acceptance. Guidelines.

A POSITIVE APPROACH—1600 Malone, Municipal Airport, Millville, NJ 08332. Ann Miller, Ed. Articles, 500 words, on all aspects of the positive-thinking disabled/handicapped person's private and business life. Well-researched articles of interest to the visually and hearing impaired, veterans, the arthritic, and all categories of the disabled and handicapped, on interior design, barrier-free architecture, gardening, wardrobe, computers, and careers. No fiction or poetry. Pays in copies.

SOLUTIONS FOR BETTER HEALTH—(formerly *Mature Health*) 45 W. 34th St., Suite 500, New York, NY 10001. Tim Moriarty, Ed. Articles, 600 to 1,200 words, on exercise, the heart, sex, hypertension, fatigue, diabetes, arthritis, low back pain, nutrition, cholesterol reduction, mental wellness, and health care costs; for people in their forties through their sixties. Query with clips. Pays 40¢ a word, on publication.

TODAY'S OR NURSE—6900 Grove Rd., Thorofare, NJ 08086. John Bond, Ed. Clinical or general articles, from 2,000 words, of direct interest to operating room nurses. Pays $200 honorarium, on acceptance.

VEGETARIAN TIMES—P.O. Box 570, Oak Park, IL 60603. Paul Obis, Pub. Articles, 750 to 2,500 words, on health, nutrition, exercise and fitness, meatless meals, etc. Personal-experience and historical pieces, profiles. Pays $25 to $500, on publication.

VIBRANT LIFE—55 W. Oak Ridge Dr., Hagerstown, MD 21740. Features, 1,000 to 2,000 words, on total health: physical, mental, and spiritual. No disease-related articles or manuscripts geared to people over 50. Seeks upbeat articles on how to live happier and healthier lives; Christian slant. Pays $150 to $300, on acceptance.

VIM & VIGOR—8805 N. 23rd Ave., Suite 11, Phoenix, AZ 85021. Leo Calderella, Ed. Positive articles, with accurate medical facts, on health and fitness, 1,200 to 2,000 words, by assignment only. Pays $350 to $450, on publication. Query.

THE WALKING MAGAZINE—9–11 Harcourt, Boston, MA 02116. Bradford Ketchum, Ed. Articles, 1,500 to 2,500 words, on fitness, health, equipment, nutrition, travel and adventure, famous walkers, and other walking-related topics. Shorter pieces, 150 to 800 words, and essays for "Ramblings" page. Photos welcome. Pays $750 to $1,800 for features, $100 to $500 for department pieces. Guidelines.

YOGA JOURNAL—2054 University Ave., Berkeley, CA 94704. Stephan Bodian, Ed. Articles, 1,200 to 4,000 words, on holistic health, meditation, consciousness, spirituality, and yoga. Pays $50 to $350, on publication.

YOUR HEALTH—1720 Washington Blvd., Box 10010, Ogden, UT 84409. Caroll Shreeve, Pub. Articles, 1,200 words, on individual health care needs: prevention, treatment, low-impact aerobics, fitness, nutrition, etc. Color photos required. Pays 15¢ a word, on acceptance. Guidelines.

EDUCATION

AMERICAN SCHOOL & UNIVERSITY—401 N. Broad St., Philadelphia, PA 19108. Joe Agron, Ed. Articles and case studies, 1,200 to 1,500 words, on design, construction, operation, and management of school and college facilities.

THE BIG APPLE PARENTS' PAPER—928 Broadway, Suite 709, New York, NY 10010. Helen Rosengren Freedman, Ed. Articles (600 to 750 words) for NYC parents. Pays $50 to $75, within 60 days of acceptance (plus $25 cover bonus). Buys first NY-area rights.

CAPSTONE JOURNAL OF EDUCATION—P.O. Box 870231, Tuscaloosa, AL 35487–0231. Alexia M. Kartis, Asst. Ed. Articles, to 5,000 words, on contemporary ideas in educational research. Guidelines.

CAREER WOMAN—See *Minority Engineer.*

CAREERS AND THE HANDICAPPED—See *Minority Engineer.*

CLASSROOM COMPUTER LEARNING—Peter Li, Inc., 2169 E. Francisco Blvd. E., Suite A-4, San Rafael, CA 94901. Holly Brady, Ed. Articles, to 3,000 words, for teachers of grades K through 12, about uses of computers and related technology in the classroom: human-interest and philosophical articles, how-to pieces, software reviews, and hands-on ideas. Pay varies, on acceptance.

EQUAL OPPORTUNITY—See *Minority Engineer.*

FOUNDATION NEWS—1828 L St. N.W., Washington, DC 20036. Arlie W. Schardt, Ed. Articles, to 2,000 words, on national or regional activities supported by, or of interest to, grant makers. Pays to $1,500, on acceptance. Query.

GIFTED EDUCATION PRESS NEWSLETTER—P.O. Box 1586, 10201 Yuma Ct., Manassas, VA 22110. Maurice Fisher, Pub. Articles, to 1,200 words, written by educators, laypersons, and parents of gifted children, on the problems of identifying and teaching gifted children and adolescents. "Interested in incisive analyses of current programs for the gifted, and recommendations for improving the education of gifted students. Particularly interested in the problems of teaching humanities, ethics, literature, and history to the gifted." Pays with subscription.

HOME EDUCATION MAGAZINE—P.O. Box 1083, Tonasket, WA 98855. Helen E. Hagener, Man. Ed. Informative articles, 1,500 to 3,000 words, on all aspects of the growing homeschool movement. Send complete manuscript. Pays about 2¢ word, on publication.

THE HORN BOOK MAGAZINE—14 Beacon St., Boston, MA 02108. Anita Silvey, Ed. Articles, 600 to 2,800 words, on books for young readers, and related subjects, for librarians, teachers, parents, etc. Pays $25 per printed page, on publication. Query.

INDEPENDENT LIVING MAGAZINE—*Minority Engineer.*

INDUSTRIAL EDUCATION—26011 Evergreen Rd., Suite 204, Southfield,

MI 48076. Suzanne Becker, Ed. Educational and instructional articles, 1,000 to 1,500 words, for secondary and post-secondary technical education classes. Photos and drawings. Pays $30, on publication.

INSTRUCTOR MAGAZINE—730 Broadway, New York, NY 10003. Attn: Manuscript Ed. How-to articles on elementary classroom teaching and computers in the classroom, with practical suggestions and project reports. Pays varying rates, on acceptance. SASE required.

ITC COMMUNICATOR—International Training in Communication, P.O. Box 309, West Point, CA 95255. JoAnn Levy, Ed. Educational articles, 200 to 800 words, on leadership, language, speech presentation, meetings procedures, personal and professional development, written and spoken communication techniques. SASE required. Pays in copies.

JOURNAL OF CAREER PLANNING & EMPLOYMENT—62 Highland Ave., Bethlehem, PA 18017. Bill Beebe, Assoc. Ed. Quarterly. Articles, 3,000 to 4,000 words, on topics related to career planning, placement, recruitment, and employment of new college graduates. Pays $200 to $400, on acceptance. Query first with clips. Guidelines available.

KEY TO CHRISTIAN EDUCATION—8121 Hamilton Ave., Cincinnati, OH 45231. Marjorie Miller, Ed. Fillers, articles, to 1,500 words, on Christian education; tips for teachers in the local church. Pays varying rates, on acceptance.

LEARNING 90/91—1111 Bethlehem Pike, Springhouse, PA 19477. Charlene Gaynor, Ed. How-to, why-to, and personal-experience articles, to 3,000 words, for teachers of grades K through 8. Tested classroom ideas for curriculum roundups, to 600 words. Pays to $300 for features, on acceptance.

MEDIA & METHODS—1429 Walnut St., Philadelphia, PA 19102. Michele Sokoloff, Ed. Articles, 800 to 1,500 words, on media, technologies, and methods used to enhance instruction and learning in high school and university classrooms. Pays $50 to $100, on publication. Query.

MINORITY ENGINEER—44 Broadway, Greenlawn, NY 11740. James Schneider, Exec. Ed. Articles, 1,000 to 1,500 words, for college students, on career opportunities in engineering, techniques of job hunting, developments in and applications of new technologies. Interviews. Profiles. Pays 10¢ a word, on publication. Query. Same address and requirements for *Equal Opportunity*, *Career Woman*, *Careers and the Handicapped*, *Independent Living Magazine*; and *Woman Engineer*, a career-guidance quarterly; query Editor Anne Kelly for *Woman Engineer*.

NATIONAL BEAUTY SCHOOL JOURNAL—220 White Plains Rd., Tarrytown, NY 10591. Jacqueline S. Carlsen, Ed. Articles, 1,500 to 2,000 words, on running a cosmetology school; teaching techniques, problems, new procedures, etc. "All articles must be relevant to schools, not to salons." Pays $150, on publication.

PHI DELTA KAPPAN—8th and Union St., Box 789, Bloomington, IN 47402. Pauline Gough, Ed. Articles, 1,000 to 4,000 words, on educational research, service, and leadership; issues, trends, and policy. Pays from $250, on publication.

SCHOOL ARTS MAGAZINE—50 Portland St., Worcester, MA 01608. Kent Anderson, Ed. Articles, 800 to 1,000 words, on art education with special application to the classroom. Photos. Pays varying rates, on publication.

SCHOOL SAFETY—National School Safety Center, 16830 Ventura Blvd., Encino, CA 91436. Ronald D. Stephens, Exec. Ed. Published three times during the school year. Articles, 2,000 to 3,000 words, of use to educators, law enforcers, judges, and legislators on the prevention of drugs, gangs, weapons, bullying, discipline problems, and vandalism; also on-site security and character development as they relate to students and schools. Pays to $500, on publication.

SCHOOL SHOP/TECH DIRECTIONS—Box 8623, Ann Arbor, MI 48107. Susanne Peckham, Man. Ed. Articles, 1 to 10 double-spaced typed pages, for teachers and administrators in industrial, technical, and vocational educational fields, with particular interest in classroom projects and computer uses. Pays $25 to $150, on publication. Guidelines.

TODAY'S CATHOLIC TEACHER—2451 E. River Rd., Dayton, OH 45439. Stephen Brittan, Ed. Articles, 600 to 800 words, 1,000 to 1,200 words, and 1,200 to 1,500 words, on education, parent-teacher relationships, innovative teaching, teaching techniques, etc., of interest to Catholic educators. Pays $15 to $75, on publication. SASE required. Query first. Guidelines.

WILSON LIBRARY BULLETIN—950 University Ave., Bronx, NY 10452. Mary Jo Godwin, Ed. Articles, 2,500 to 3,000 words, on libraries, communications, and information systems. News, reports, features. Pays from $250, extra for photos, on publication.

WOMAN ENGINEER—See *Minority Engineer*.

FARMING AND AGRICULTURE

ACRES USA—10008 E. 60 Terrace, Kansas City, MO 64133. Articles on biological agriculture. Pays 6¢ a word, on acceptance. Query.

AMERICAN BEE JOURNAL—51 N. Second St., Hamilton, IL 62341. Joe M. Graham, Ed. Articles on beekeeping, for professionals. Photos. Pays 75¢ a column inch, extra for photos, on publication.

BEEF—7900 International Dr., Minneapolis, MN 55425. Paul D. Andre, Ed. Articles on beef cattle feeding, cowherds, stocker operations, and related phases of the cattle industry. Pays to $300, on acceptance.

BUCKEYE FARM NEWS—Ohio Farm Bureau Federation, Two Nationwide Plaza, Box 479, Columbus, OH 43216. George D. Robey, Man. Ed. Occasional articles, to 600 words, related to agriculture. Pays on publication. Query.

FARM AND RANCH LIVING—5400 S. 60th St., Greendale, WI 53129. Bob Ottum, Ed. Articles, 2,000 words, on rural people and situations; nostalgia pieces; profiles of interesting farms and farmers, ranches and ranchers. Poetry. Pays $15 to $400, on acceptance and on publication.

FARM INDUSTRY NEWS—7900 International Dr., Minneapolis, MN 55425. Joe Degnan, Ed. Articles for farmers, on new products, machinery, equipment, chemicals, and seeds. Pays $175 to $400, on acceptance. Query required.

FARM JOURNAL—230 W. Washington Sq., Philadelphia, PA 19105. Earl Ainsworth, Ed. Articles, 500 to 1,500 words, with photos, on the business of farming, for farmers. Pays 20¢ to 50¢ a word, on acceptance. Query.

FARM STORE—P.O. Box 2400, 12400 Whitewater Dr., Suite 160, Minnetonka, MN 55343. Jan Johnson, Ed. Articles, 500 to 1,500 words, that offer "business know-how for today's agribusiness professional." Payment varies, on publication. Query.

FLORIDA GROWER & RANCHER—1331 N. Mills Ave., Orlando, FL 32803. Jim Fisher, Ed. Articles and case histories on farmers, growers, and ranchers. Pays on publication. Query; buys little freelance material.

THE FURROW—Deere & Company, John Deere Rd., Moline, IL 61265. George Sollenberger, Exec. Ed. Specialized, illustrated articles on farming. Pays to $1,000, on acceptance.

HARROWSMITH—Telemedia Publishing, Inc., Camden East, Ont., Canada K0K 1J0. Michael Webster, Ed. Articles, 700 to 4,000 words, on country life, homesteading, husbandry, organic gardening, and alternative energy with a Canadian slant. Pays $150 to $1,500, on acceptance. Query with SASE/international reply coupon.

HARROWSMITH COUNTRY LIFE—Ferry Rd., Charlotte, VT 05445. Tom Rawls, Ed. Investigative pieces, 4,000 to 5,000 words, on ecology, energy, health, gardening, do-it-yourself projects, and the food chain. Short pieces for "Screed" (opinions) and "Gazette" (news briefs). Pays $500 to $1,500 for features, $50 to $600 for department pieces, on acceptance. Query required. Send SASE for guidelines.

NORDEN NEWS—See *Topics in Veterinary Medicine*.

THE OHIO FARMER—1350 W. Fifth Ave., Columbus, OH 43212. Andrew L. Stevens, Ed. Articles on farming, rural living, etc., in Ohio. Pays $20 per column, on publication.

PEANUT FARMER—P.O. Box 95075, Raleigh, NC 27625. Dayton Matlick, Ed./Pub. Articles, 500 to 1,500 words, on production and management practices in peanut farming. Pays $50 to $350, on publication.

PENNSYLVANIA FARMER—704 Lisburn Rd., Camp Hill, PA 17011. John R. Vogel, Ed. Articles on farmers in PA, NJ, DE, MD, and WV; timely business-of-farming concepts and successful farm management operations.

RURAL HERITAGE—P.O. Box 516, Albia, IA 52531. D.H. Holle, Pub. How-to and feature articles, 300 to 2,500 words, related to draft horses and rural living. Pays 3¢ to 10¢ a word, $5 to $25 for photos, on publication.

SHEEP! MAGAZINE—W. 2997 Market Rd., Helenville, WI 53137. Dave Thompson, Ed. Articles, to 1,500 words, on successful shepherds, woolcrafts, sheep raising, and sheep dogs. "Especially interested in people who raise sheep successfully as a sideline enterprise." Photos. Pays $80 to $300, extra for photos, on publication. Query first.

SMALL FARMER'S JOURNAL—P.O. Box 2805, Eugene, OR 97402. Address the Editors. How-tos, humor, practical work horse information, livestock and produce marketing, and articles appropriate to the independent family farm. Pays negotiable rates, on publication. Query first.

SUCCESSFUL FARMING—1716 Locust St., Des Moines, IA 50336. Gene Johnston, Man. Ed. Articles on farm production, business, and families; also farm personalities, health, leisure, and outdoor topics. Pays varying rates, on acceptance.

TOPICS IN VETERINARY MEDICINE—(formerly *Norden News*) 812 Springdale Dr., Exton, PA 19341. Kathleen Etchison, Ed. Technical articles, 1,200 to 1,500 words, and clinical features, 500 words, on veterinary medicine. Photos. Pays $200 to $250, $100 for shorter pieces, extra for photos, on publication.

WALLACES FARMER—1501 42nd St., #501, W. Des Moines, IA 50265. Monte Sesker, Ed. Features, 600 to 700 words, on farming in IA, MN, NE, KS, ND, and SD; methods and equipment; interviews with farmers. Query.

THE WESTERN PRODUCER—Box 2500, Saskatoon, Saskatchewan, Canada S7K 2C4. Address Man. Ed. Articles, to 1,000 words, on agricultural and rural subjects, preferably with a Canadian slant. Photos. Pays from 15¢ a word, $15 for B&W photos and cartoons, on acceptance.

ENVIRONMENT, CONSERVATION, WILDLIFE, NATURAL HISTORY

THE AMERICAN FIELD—542 S. Dearborn, Chicago, IL 60605. B.J. Matthys, Man. Ed. Yarns about hunting trips, bird-shooting; articles to 1,500 words, on dogs and field trials, emphasizing conservation of game resources. Pays varying rates, on acceptance.

AMERICAN FORESTS—1516 P St. N.W., Washington, DC 20005. Bill Rooney, Ed. Well-documented articles, to 2,000 words, with photos, on recreational and commercial uses and management of forests. Photos. Pays on acceptance.

THE AMICUS JOURNAL—Natural Resources Defense Council, 40 W. 20th St., New York, NY 10011. Peter Borrelli, Ed. Investigative articles, book reviews, and poetry related to national and international environmental policy. Pays varying rates, on acceptance. Queries required.

ANIMAL KINGDOM—See *Wildlife Conservation*.

ANIMALS—Massachusetts Society for the Prevention of Cruelty to Animals, 350 S. Huntington Ave., Boston, MA 02130. Diana Levey, Ed. Asst. Informative, well-researched articles, to 3,000 words, on animal welfare and pet care, conservation, international wildlife, and environmental issues affecting animals; no personal accounts or favorite pet stories. Pays to $300, on publication. Query.

ATLANTIC SALMON JOURNAL—1435 St. Alexandre, Suite 1030, Montreal, Quebec, Canada H3A 2G4. Terry Davis, Ed. Articles, 1,500 to 3,000 words. Material related to Atlantic salmon: fishing, conservation, ecology, travel, politics, biology, how-tos, anecdotes, cuisine. Pays $100 to $350, on publication.

AUDUBON—950 Third Ave., New York, NY 10022. Les Line, Ed. Bi-monthly. Articles (1,800 to 4,500 words) on conservation and environmental issues, natural history, ecology, and related subjects. Payment varies, on acceptance. Query.

BIRD WATCHER'S DIGEST—P.O. Box 110, Marietta, OH 45750. Mary B. Bowers, Ed. Articles, 600 to 2,500 words, for bird watchers: first-person accounts; how-tos; pieces on endangered species; profiles. Cartoons. Pays from $50, on publication.

BUZZWORM—1818 Sixteenth St., Boulder, CO 80302. Elizabeth Darby Junkin, Man. Ed. Bimonthly consumer magazine covering environmental and natural resources issues worldwide. Topics include endangered species, new ideas in conservation, and personalities. Query with clips and resumé. Pays $200 to $1,500, after publication.

ENVIRONMENTAL ACTION—1525 New Hampshire Ave. N.W., Washington, DC 20036. Barbara Ruben and Hawley Truax, Eds. News and features, varying lengths, on a broad range of political and/or environmental topics: energy, toxics, recycling, solid waste, etc. Book reviews; environmentally-related consumer goods. Pays $250 to $500 for features, $50 for book reviews, $40 to $70 for short news articles, $25 for photos, on publication. Query with clips and resumé required.

EQUINOX—7 Queen Victoria Rd., Camden East, Ont., Canada K0K 1J0. Jody Morgan, Asst. Ed. Articles, 3,000 to 6,000 words, on popular geography, wildlife, astronomy, science, the arts, travel, and adventure. Department pieces, 300 to 800 words, for "Nexus" (science and medicine), and "Habitat" (man-made and natural environment). Pays $1,250 to $2,500, for features, $100 to $500 for short pieces, on acceptance.

FLORIDA WILDLIFE—620 S. Meridian St., Tallahassee, FL 32399–1600. Andrea H. Blount, Ed. Bimonthly of the Florida Game and Fresh Water Fish Commission. Articles, 800 to 1,200 words, that promote native wildlife (flora and fauna), hunting, fishing in Florida's fresh waters, outdoor ethics, and conservation of Florida's natural resources. Pays $50 to $200, on publication.

GARBAGE—435 Ninth St., Brooklyn, NY 11215. Patricia Poore, Ed. Articles, 2,500 to 4,000 words, that tailor scientific and technical information to the environmental interests of a lay audience. Topics include food/health; gardening; how-to (ideas for improving efficiency and cutting down on waste); environmental science and technology; lifestyles. Occasionally publishes short news items. Query with published clips. Payment varies, on acceptance.

HARROWSMITH COUNTRY LIFE—Ferry Rd., Charlotte, VT 05445. Tom Rawls, Ed. Investigative articles, 4,000 to 5,000 words, on ecology, energy, health, gardening, and the food chain. Short pieces for "Screed" (opinions) and "Gazette" (news briefs). Do-it-yourself projects. Pays $500 to $1,500 for features, from $50 to $600 for department pieces, on acceptance. Query with SASE required. Guidelines.

INTERNATIONAL WILDLIFE—8925 Leesburg Pike, Vienna, VA 22184. Jan Boysen, Assoc. Ed. Short features, 700 words, and 1,500- to 2,500-word articles, that make nature (and human use and stewardship of it) understandable and interesting. Pays $500 for one-page features, $1,800 for full-length articles, on acceptance. Query. Guidelines.

THE LOOKOUT—Seamen's Church Institute, 50 Broadway, New York, NY 10004. Carlyle Windley, Ed. Factual articles on the sea and merchant seafarers. Features, 200 to 1,500 words, on the merchant marines, sea oddities, etc. Photos. Pays $25 to $100, on publication.

NATIONAL GEOGRAPHIC—17th and M Sts. N.W., Washington, DC 20036. William P.E. Graves, Ed. First-person, general-interest, heavily-illustrated articles on science, natural history, exploration, and geographical regions. Query required.

NATIONAL PARKS MAGAZINE—1015 31st St. N.W., Washington, DC 20007. Sue Dodge, Ed. Articles, 1,000 to 2,000 words, on natural history, wildlife, outdoors activities, travel, and conservation as they relate to national parks: illustrated features on the natural, historic, and cultural resources of the national park system. Pieces about legislation and other issues and events related to the parks. Pays $100 to $1,000, on acceptance. Query. Send for guidelines.

NATIONAL WILDLIFE & INTERNATIONAL WILDLIFE—8925 Leesburg Pike, Vienna, VA 22184. Mark Wexler, Ed., *National Wildlife*. Jon Fisher, Ed., *International Wildlife*. Articles, 1,000 to 2,500 words, on wildlife, conservation, environment; outdoor how-to pieces. Photos. Pays on acceptance. Query.

NATURAL HISTORY—American Museum of Natural History, Central Park West at 79th St., New York, NY 10024. Alan Ternes, Ed.-in-Chief. Informative articles, to 3,000 words, by experts, on anthropology and natural sciences. Pays $1,000 for features, on acceptance. Query.

OUTDOOR AMERICA—1401 Wilson Blvd., Level B, Arlington, VA 22209. Quarterly publication of the Izaak Walton League of America. Articles, 1,500 to

2,000 words, on natural resource conservation issues and outdoor recreation; especially fishing, hunting, and camping. Pays 20¢ a word for features. Query Articles Ed. with published clippings.

SEA FRONTIERS—4600 Rickenbacker Causeway, Virginia Key, Miami, FL 33149. Bonnie Bilyeu Gordon, Ed. Jean Bradfisch, Exec. Ed. Illustrated articles, 500 to 3,000 words, on scientific advances related to the sea, biological, physical, chemical, or geological phenomena, ecology, conservation, etc., written in a popular style for lay readers. Send SASE for guidelines. Pays 25¢ a word, on acceptance. Query.

SIERRA—730 Polk St., San Francisco, CA 94109. Jonathan F. King, Ed.-in-Chief. Articles, 250 to 2,500 words, on environmental and conservation topics, politics, travel, hiking, backpacking, skiing, rafting, cycling. Book reviews. Photos. Pays from $100 to $1,500, extra for photos, on acceptance. Query with SASE.

SMITHSONIAN MAGAZINE—900 Jefferson Dr., Washington, DC 20560. Marlane A. Liddell, Articles Ed. Articles on history, art, natural history, physical science, profiles, etc. Query.

SPORTS AFIELD—250 W. 55th St., New York, NY 10019. Tom Paugh, Ed. Articles, 2,000 words, with quality photos, on hunting, fishing, natural history, conservation, personal experiences, new hunting/fishing spots. How-to pieces; humor, fiction. Pays top rates, on acceptance.

VIRGINIA WILDLIFE—P.O. Box 11104, Richmond, CA 23230–1104. Monthly of the Commission of Game and Inland Fisheries. Articles, 1,500 to 2,500 words, on conservation and related topics, including fishing, hunting, wildlife management, outdoor safety and ethics, etc. All material must have Virginia tie-in and be accompanied by color photos. Query with SASE. Pays 10¢ a word, extra for photos, on acceptance.

WILDLIFE CONSERVATION —(formerly *Animal Kingdom*) New York Zoological Society, Bronx, NY 10460. Nancy Christie, Sr. Ed. First-person articles, 1,500 to 2,000 words, on "popular" natural history, "based on author's research and experience as opposed to textbook approach." Payment varies, on acceptance. Guidelines.

ZOO LIFE—11661 San Vicente Blvd., Suite 402, Los Angeles, CA 90049. Audrey Tawa, Ed. Quarterly. Articles, 1,500 to 2,000 words, on the work zoos and aquariums are doing in the fields of animal conservation and education. Mention possibility of photos when querying. Pays 20¢ per word, on publication. Payment for photos negotiable. Guidelines.

MEDIA AND THE ARTS

AIRBRUSH ACTION—400 Madison Ave., Lakewood, NJ 08701. Address the editors. Articles, 500 to 3,000 words, on airbrush, graphics, and art-related topics. Pays $75 to $300, on publication. Query.

THE AMERICAN ART JOURNAL—40 W. 57th St., 5th Fl., New York, NY 10019. Jane Van N. Turano, Ed. Quarterly. Scholarly articles, 2,000 to 10,000 words, on American art of the 17th through 20th centuries. Photos. Pays $200 to $400, on acceptance.

AMERICAN INDIAN ART MAGAZINE—7314 E. Osborn Dr., Scottsdale, AZ 85251. Roanne P. Goldfein, Man. Ed. Detailed articles, 10 typed pages, on American Indian arts: painting, carving, beadwork, basketry, textiles, ceramics, jewelry, etc. Pays varying rates for articles, on publication. Query.

AMERICAN THEATRE—355 Lexington Ave., New York, NY 10017. Jim O'Quinn, Ed. Features, 500 to 4,000 words, on the theater and theater-related subjects. Payment negotiable, on publication. Query.

ART & ANTIQUES—89 Fifth Ave., New York, NY 10003. Jeffrey Schaire, Ed. Investigative pieces or personal narratives, 1,500 words, and news items, 300 to 500 words, on art or antiques. Pays 50¢ a word, on publication. Query first.

ART GALLERY INTERNATIONAL: THE CONTEMPORARY COLLECTORS MAGAZINE—P.O. Box 52940, Tulsa, OK 74152. Debra Carter Nelson, Ed. Articles, 1,500 to 2,500 words, on contemporary artists and their recent works; no restrictions on artists' style, medium, or subject matter; a "gallery in print" for readers. Query with clips, visual samples, and SASE. Pays 10¢ a word or $50 per printed page, after publication.

THE ARTIST'S MAGAZINE—1507 Dana Ave., Cincinnati, OH 45207. Michael Ward, Ed. Features, 1,200 to 2,500 words, and department pieces for the working artist. Poems, to 20 lines, on art and the creative process. Single-panel cartoons. Pays $150 to $350 for articles; $50 for cartoons, on acceptance. Guidelines. Query.

ARTS ATLANTIC—P.O. Box 848, Charlottetown, P.E.I., Canada C1A 7L9. Joseph Sherman, Ed. Articles and reviews, 600 to 3,000 words, on visual, performing, and literary arts, crafts in Atlantic Canada. Also, "idea and concept" articles of universal appeal. Pays from 15¢ a word, on publication; flat rates for interviews. Query.

BLUEGRASS UNLIMITED—Box 111, Broad Run, VA 22014. Peter V. Kuykendall, Ed. Articles, to 3,500 words, on bluegrass and traditional country music. Photos. Pays 6¢ to 8¢ a word, extra for photos.

BROADCASTER—7 Labatt Ave., Toronto, Ont., Canada M5A 3P2. Lynda Ashley, Ed. Articles, 500 to 2,000 words, on broadcasting, satellites, and the cable industry. Rates negotiable. Payment on publication.

CLAVIER MAGAZINE—200 Northfield Rd., Northfield, IL 60093. Kingsley Day, Ed. Practical articles, interviews, master classes, and humor pieces, 2,000 words, for keyboard performers and teachers. Pays $35 to $45 per page of magazine text, on publication.

DANCE MAGAZINE—33 W. 60th St., New York, NY 10023. Richard Philp, Ed.-in-Chief. Features on dance, personalities, techniques, health issues, and trends. Photos. Query; limited free-lance market.

DANCE TEACHER NOW—3020 Beacon Blvd., West Sacramento, CA 95691–3436. K.C. Patrick, Ed. Articles, 1,000 to 3,000 words, for professional dance educators, dancers, and other dance professionals on practical information for the teacher and/or business owner, economic and historical issues related to the profession. Profiles of schools, methods, and people who are leaving their mark on dance. Must be thoroughly researched. Pays $200 to $300, on publication. Query preferred.

DARKROOM PHOTOGRAPHY—9171 Wilshire Blvd., Suite 300, Beverly Hills, CA 90210. Thom Harrop, Ed. Articles on photographic techniques and photographic portfolios, 1,000 to 2,500 words, with photos, for all levels of photographers. Pays $100 to $500. Query.

DRAMATICS—Educational Theatre Assoc., 3368 Central Pkwy., Cincinnati, OH 45225–2392. Don Corathers, Ed. Articles, interviews, how-tos, 750 to 4,000 words, for high school students on the performing arts with an emphasis on theater practice: acting, directing, playwriting, technical subjects. Prefer articles that "could

587

be used by a better than average high school teacher to teach students something about the performing arts." Pays $15 to $200 honorariums. Manuscripts preferred; graphics and photos accepted.

THE ENGRAVERS JOURNAL—26 Summit St., Box 318, Brighton, MI 48116. Michael J. Davis, Man. Ed. Articles, varying lengths, on topics related to the engraving industry and small business operations. Pays $60 to $175, on acceptance. Query first.

EXHIBIT—1776 Lake Worth Dr., Lake Worth, FL 33460. Karl H. Meyer, Assoc. Ed. Articles, to 1,000 words, with color transparencies, on fine arts, techniques, new movements, profiles of artists. Query.

FILM QUARTERLY—Univ. of California Press, 2120 Berkeley Way, Berkeley, CA 94720. Ernest Callenbach, Ed. Film reviews, historical and critical articles, book reviews, to 6,000 words. Pays on publication. Query.

FLUTE TALK—Instrumentalist Publishing Co., 200 Northfield Rd., Northfield, IL 60093. Kathleen Goll-Wilson, Ed. Articles, 6 to 12 typed pages, on flute performance and pedagogy; fillers; photos and line drawings. Thorough knowledge of the instrument a must. Pays honorarium, on publication. Queries preferred.

GUITAR PLAYER MAGAZINE—20085 Stevens Creek, Cupertino, CA 95014. Tom Wheeler, Ed. Articles, 1,500 to 5,000 words, on guitarists, guitars, and related subjects. Pays $100 to $400, on acceptance. Buys one-time and reprint rights.

INDUSTRIAL PHOTOGRAPHY—445 Broadhollow Rd., Melville, NY 11747. Steve Shaw, Ed. Articles on techniques and trends in current professional photography; audiovisuals, etc., for industrial photographers and executives. Query.

INTERNATIONAL MUSICIAN—Paramount Bldg., 1501 Broadway, Suite 600, New York, NY 10036. Articles, 1,500 to 2,000 words, for professional musicians. Pays varying rates, on acceptance. Query.

KEYBOARD MAGAZINE—20085 Stevens Creek, Cupertino, CA 95014. Dominic Milano, Ed. Articles, 1,000 to 5,000 words, on keyboard instruments, MIDI and computer technology, and players. Photos. Pays $175 to $500, on acceptance. Query.

MEDIA HISTORY DIGEST—c/o Editor & Publisher, 11 W. 19th St., New York, NY 10011. Hiley H. Ward, Ed. Articles, 1,500 to 2,000 words, on the history of print media, for wide consumer interest. Puzzles and humor related to media history. Pays varying rates, on publication. Query.

MODERN DRUMMER—870 Pompton Ave., Cedar Grove, NJ 07009. Ronald L. Spagnardi, Ed. Articles, 500 to 2,000 words, on drumming: how-tos, interviews. Pays $50 to $500, on publication.

MUSIC MAGAZINE—P. O. Box 96, Station R, Toronto, Ont., Canada M4G 3Z3. Articles, with photos, on musicians, conductors, and composers, for all classical music buffs. Pays $100 to $300, on publication. Query required. Guidelines.

MUSICAL AMERICA—825 Seventh Ave., New York, NY 10019. Shirley Fleming, Ed. Authoritative articles, 1,000 to 1,500 words, on classical music subjects. Pays around 15¢ a word, on acceptance.

NEW ENGLAND ENTERTAINMENT DIGEST—43 Schoosett St., Rt. 139, Pembroke, MA 02359. Michael R. McCaffrey, Pub. Paul J. Reale, Ed. News features and reviews on arts and entertainment in New England. Light verse. Pays $10 to $25, $1 to $2 for verse, on publication.

OPERA NEWS—The Metropolitan Opera Guild, 1865 Broadway, New York, NY 10023. Patrick J. Smith, Ed. Articles, 600 to 2,500 words, on all aspects of opera. Pays 20¢ a word for articles, on publication. Query.

PERFORMANCE—1203 Lake St., Suite 200, Fort Worth, TX 76102–4504. Don Waitt, Pub./Ed.-in-Chief. Reports on the touring industry: concert promoters, booking agents, concert venues and clubs, as well as support services, such as lighting, sound and staging companies. Pays 35¢ per column line, on publication.

PETERSEN'S PHOTOGRAPHIC—8490 Sunset Blvd., Los Angeles, CA 90069. Bill Hurter, Ed. Articles and how-to pieces, with photos, on travel, video, and darkroom photography, for beginners, advanced amateurs, and professionals. Pays $60 per printed page, on publication.

PHOTOMETHODS—CS9043, Hicksville, NY 11802–9043. David Silverman, Ed.-in-Chief. Articles, 1,500 to 3,000 words, on innovative techniques in imaging (still, film, video), working situations, and management. Pays from $75, on publication. Query.

PLAYBILL—71 Vanderbilt Ave., New York, NY 10169. Joan Alleman, Ed.-in-Chief. Sophisticated articles, 700 to 1,800 words, with photos, on theater and subjects of interest to theater-goers. Pays $100 to $500, on acceptance.

PREVUE—P.O. Box 974, Reading, PA 19603. J. Steranko, Ed. Lively articles on films and film-makers; entertainment features and celebrity interviews. Length: 4 to 25 pages. Pays varying rates, on acceptance. Query with clips.

PROFESSIONAL STAINED GLASS—Tonetta Lake Rd., P.O. Box 69, Brewster, NY 10509. Chris Peterson, Man. Ed. Practical articles of interest to stained glass professionals. Abundant opportunity for energetic and enterprising free lancers. Pays $100 to $150, on publication. Query required.

ROLLING STONE—745 Fifth Ave., New York, NY 10151. Articles on American culture, art, and politics. Query required. Rarely accepts free-lance material.

RIGHTING WORDS—Frerdonna Communications, Box 9808, Knoxville, TN 37940. Michael Ward, Pub. Journal of Language and Editing. Articles (3,000 words) on topics of interest to professional editors. Pays from $100, on acceptance.

SHEET MUSIC MAGAZINE—223 Katonah Ave., Katonah, NY 10536. Josephine Sblendorio, Man. Ed. Pieces, 1,000 to 2,000 words, for pianists and organists, on musicians and composers, how-tos, and book reviews (to 500 words); no hard rock or heavy metal subjects. Pays $75 to $200, on publication.

TDR (THE DRAMA REVIEW): A JOURNAL OF PERFORMANCE STUDIES—721 Broadway, 6th Fl., New York, NY 10003. Barbara Harrington, Man. Ed. Eclectic articles on experimental performance and performance theory; cross-cultural, examining the social, political, historical, and theatrical contexts in which performance happens. Submit query or manuscript with SASE. Pays 3¢ a word, on publication.

THEATRE CRAFTS MAGAZINE—135 Fifth Ave., New York, NY 10010. Patricia MacKay, Pub. David Barbour, Ed. Articles, 500 to 2,500 words, for performing arts and entertainment trade magazine covering design, technical, and management aspects of theater, opera, dance, television, and film. Pays on acceptance. Query.

VIDEOMAKER—P.O. Box 4591, Chico, CA 95927. Bradley Kent, Ed. "The Video Camera User's Magazine." Authoritative, how-to articles geared at hobbyist and professional video camera/camcorder users: instructionals, innovative applications, tools and tips, industry developments, new products, etc. Pays varying rates, on publication. Queries preferred.

WASHINGTON JOURNALISM REVIEW—2233 Wisconsin Ave. N.W., Washington, DC 20007. Bill Monroe, Ed. Articles, 500 to 3,000 words, on print or electronic journalism. Pays 20¢ a word, on publication. Query.

HOBBIES, CRAFTS, COLLECTING

ANTIQUE MONTHLY—2100 Powers Ferry Road, Atlanta, GA 30339. Elizabeth McKenzie, Man. Ed. Articles, 750 to 1,200 words, on trends and the exhibition and sales (auctions, antique shops, etc.) of decorative arts and antiques, with B&W photos or color slides. Pays varying rates, on publication.

THE ANTIQUE TRADER WEEKLY—Box 1050, Dubuque, IA 52001. Kyle D. Husfloen, Ed. Articles, 1,000 to 2,000 words, on all types of antiques and collectors' items. Photos. Pays from $5 to $150, extra for photos, on publication. Query preferred. Buys all rights.

ANTIQUES & AUCTION NEWS—P.O. Box 500, Mount Joy, PA 17552. Weekly newspaper. Factual articles, 600 to 1,500 words, on antiques, collectors, and collections. Query required. Photos. Pays $5 to $20, after publication.

ANTIQUEWEEK—P.O. Box 90, Knightstown, IN 46148. Tom Hoepf, Ed. Weekly antique, auction, and collectors newspaper. Articles, 500 to 1,500 words, on antiques, collectibles, restorations, genealogy, auction and antique show reports. Photos. Pays from $1 per inch, $75 to $125 for in-depth articles, on publication. Query. Guidelines.

AOPA PILOT—421 Aviation Way, Frederick, MD 21701. Mark R. Twombly, Ed. Magazine of the Aircraft Owners and Pilots Assn. Articles, to 2,500 words, with photos, on general aviation for beginning and experienced pilots. Pays to $750.

AQUARIUM FISH—P.O. Box 6050, Mission Viejo, CA 92690. Edward Bauman, Ed. Articles, 2,000 words, on freshwater, saltwater, and pond fish, with or without color transparencies. (No "pet fish" stories, please.) Payment varies, on publication.

THE AUTOGRAPH COLLECTOR'S MAGAZINE—P.O. Box 55328, Stockton, CA 95205. Joe Kraus, Ed. Articles, 100 to 1,500 words, on all areas of autograph collecting: preservation, framing, and storage, specialty collections, documents and letters, collectors and dealers. Queries preferred. Pays 5¢ a word, $3 for illustrations, $10 for photos, and $25 for cartoons, on publication.

BIRD TALK—Box 6050, Mission Viejo, CA 92690. Karyn New, Ed. Articles for pet bird owners: care and feeding, training, outstanding personal adventures. Pays 7¢ to 10¢ a word, after publication. Query or send manuscript; good transparencies a plus.

BIRD WATCHER'S DIGEST—P.O. Box 110, Marietta, OH 45740. Mary B. Bowers, Ed. Articles, 600 to 3,000 words, on bird-watching experiences and expeditions: information about rare sightings; updates on endangered species. Pays from $50, on publication. Allow 8 weeks for response.

THE BLADE MAGAZINE—P.O. Box 22007, Chattanooga, TN 37422. J. Bruce Voyles, Ed. Articles, 500 to 3,000 words: historical pieces on knives and old knife factories, etc.; interviews with knifemakers; how-to pieces. Pays from 5¢ a word, on publication. Study magazine first.

BYLINE—Box 130596, Edmond, OK 73013. Marcia Preston, Ed.-in-Chief. Kathryn Fanning, Man. Ed. General fiction, 2,000 to 3,000 words. Nonfiction, 1,200- to 1,600-word features and 300- to 800-word special departments. Poetry, 10 to 30 lines preferred. Nonfiction and poetry must be about writing. Humor, 400 to 800 words, about writing. "We seek practical and motivational material that tells writers how they can succeed, not why they can't. Overdone topics: writers' block, the muse, rejection slips." Queries preferred. Pays $5 to $10 for poetry; $15 to $35 for departments; $50 for features and short fiction, on acceptance.

CARD PLAYER—1455 E. Tropicana Ave., Suite 450, Las Vegas, NV 89119. June Field, Ed./Pub. "The Magazine for Those Who Play to Win." Articles on events, personalities, legal issues, new casinos, tournaments, and prizes. Also articles on strategies, theory and game psychology to improve play. Occasionally use humor, cartoons, puzzles, or anecdotal material. Pays $50, on publication; $25 to $35 for fillers. (For longer stories, features, or special coverage, pays $75 to $100.) Guidelines.

CHESS LIFE—186 Route 9W, New Windsor, NY 12553. Julie Anne Desch, Ed. Articles, 500 to 3,000 words, for members of the U.S. Chess Federation, on news, profiles, technical aspects of chess. Features on all aspects of chess: history, humor, puzzles, etc. Fiction, 500 to 2,000 words, related to chess. Photos. Pays varying rates, on acceptance. Query; limited free-lance market.

CLASSIC TOY TRAINS—21027 Crossroads Cir., Waukesha, WI 53187. Articles, with photos, on toy train layouts and collections. Also train manufacturing history and repair/maintenance. Pays $75 per printed page, on acceptance. Query.

COLLECTOR EDITIONS—170 Fifth Ave., New York, NY 10010. Joan Muyskens Pursley, Ed. Articles, 750 to 1,500 words, on collectibles, mainly glass and porcelain. Pays $150 to $350, within 30 days of acceptance. Query with photos.

COLLECTORS NEWS—P.O. Box 156, Grundy Center, IA 50638. Linda Kruger, Ed. Articles, to 1,500 words, on private collections, antiques, and collectibles, especially 20th century nostalgia, Americana, glass and china, music, furniture, transportation, timepieces, jewelry, and lamps; include B&W photos. Pays 75¢ per column inch; $1 per inch for front page articles, on publication.

COUNTED CROSS-STITCH PLUS—(fomerly *Women's Circle Counted Cross-Stitch*) 306 E. Parr Rd., Berne, IN 46711. Anne Morgan Jefferson, Ed. How-to and instructional counted cross-stitch. Short stories, interviews, and photos of top designers, book reviews, tips. Pays varying rates, on publication.

COUNTRY FOLK ART MAGAZINE—8393 E. Holly Rd., Holly, MI 48442. Julie L. Semrau, Ed. Historical, gardening, collectibles, and how-to pieces, 750 to 2,000 words, with a creative slant on American country folk art. Pays $150 to $300, on acceptance. Query about photos ($25 each). Submit pieces on seasonal topics six months in advance.

COUNTRY HANDCRAFTS—5400 S. 60th St., Greendale, WI 53129. Deborah Hufford, Ed. How-to articles on all types of crafts (needlepoint, quilting, woodworking, etc.) with complete instructions and patterns. Pays from $50 to $300, on acceptance.

CRAFTS 'N THINGS—Dept. W, 701 Lee St., Suite 1000, Des Plaines, IL 60016. Nancy Tosh, Ed. How-to articles on all kinds of crafts projects, with instructions. Pays $35 to $200, on publication. Send manuscript with instructions and photograph of the finished item.

DOG FANCY—P.O. Box 6050, Mission Viejo, CA 92690. Kim Thornton, Ed.

Articles, 1,500 to 3,000 words, on dog care, health, grooming, breeds, activities, events, etc. Photos. Pays 5¢ a word, on publication.

DOLLS, THE COLLECTOR'S MAGAZINE—170 Fifth Ave., New York, NY 10010. Krystyna Poray Goddu, Ed. Articles, 500 to 2,500 words, for knowledgeable doll collectors: sharply focused with a strong collecting angle, and concrete information: value, identification, restoration, etc. Pays $100 to $350, after acceptance. Query.

FIBERARTS—50 College St., Asheville, NC 28801. Ann Batchelder, Ed. Published five times yearly. Articles, 400 to 1,200 words, on contemporary trends in fiber sculpture, weaving, surface design, quilting, stitchery, papermaking, felting, basketry, and wearable art. Query with photos of subject, outline, and synopsis. Pays varying rates, on publication.

FINESCALE MODELER—P.O. Box 1612, Waukesha, WI 53187. Bob Hayden, Ed. How-to articles for people who make nonoperating scale models of aircraft, automobiles, boats, figures. Photos and drawings should accompany articles. One-page model-building hints and tips. Pays from $30 per published page, on acceptance. Query preferred.

GAMBLING TIMES—See *Win Magazine*.

THE HOME SHOP MACHINIST—2779 Aero Park Dr., Box 1810, Traverse City, MI 49685. Joe D. Rice, Ed. How-to articles on precision metalworking and foundry work. Accuracy and attention to detail a must. Pays $40 per published page, extra for photos and illustrations, on publication. Send SASE for writer's guidelines.

INTERNATIONAL DOLL WORLD—306 E. Parr Rd., Berne, IN 46711. Rebekah Montgomery, Ed. Informational articles about doll collecting.

KITPLANES—P.O. Box 6050, Mission Viejo, CA 92690. Dave Martin, Ed. Articles geared to the growing market of aircraft built from kits and plans by home craftsmen, on all aspects of design, construction, and performance, 1,000 to 4,000 words. Pays $150 to $350, on publication.

LOST TREASURE—P.O. Box 1589, Grove, OK 74344. Debi Williams, Man. Ed. Factual articles, 1,000 to 2,500 words, on treasure hunting, metal detecting, prospecting techniques, and legendary lost treasure. Profiles. Photos: $5 each for B&W; $100 for color slides for cover. Pays 4¢ a word; preference given to stories with photos.

MILITARY HISTORY—602 S. King St., Suite 300, Leesburg, VA 22075. C. Brian Kelly, Ed. Bimonthly on the strategy, tactics, and personalities of military history. Department pieces, 2,000 words, on espionage, weaponry, personality, and travel. Features, 4,000 words, with 500-word sidebars. Pays $200 to $400, on publication. Query. Guidelines.

MINIATURE COLLECTOR—P.O. Box 631, Boiling Springs, PA 17007. James Keough, Ed./Pub. Articles, 800 to 1,200 words, with photos, on outstanding 1/12-scale (dollhouse) miniatures and the people who make and collect them. Original, illustrated how-to projects for making miniatures. Pays varying rates, within 30 days of acceptance. Query with photos.

MODEL RAILROADER—21027 Crossroads Cir., Waukesha, WI 53187. Russ Larson, Ed. Articles, with photos of layout and equipment, on model railroads. Pays $75 per printed page, on acceptance. Query.

NEEDLEWORDS—7 Olde Ridge Village, Chadds Ford, PA 19317. Deborah A. Novak, Ed. Nonfiction, 500 to 1,500 words, about counted cross-stitch, drawn thread, or themes revolving around stitching (samplers, needlework tools, etc.). Queries required. Payment varies, on publication.

NEW ENGLAND ANTIQUES JOURNAL—4 Church St., Ware, MA 01082. Jody Young, Gen. Mgr. Well-researched articles, to 2,500 words, on antiques of interest to collectors and/or dealers, auction and antiques show reviews, to 1,000 words, antiques market news, to 500 words; photos desired. Pays to $150, on publication. Query or send manuscript. Reports in 2 to 4 weeks.

THE NEW YORK ANTIQUE ALMANAC—Box 335, Lawrence, NY 11559. Carol Nadel, Ed. Articles on antiques, shows, shops, art, investments, collectibles, collecting suggestions; related humor. Photos. Pays $5 to $75, extra for photos, on publication.

NOSTALGIA WORLD—Box 231, North Haven, CT 06473. Bonnie Roth, Ed. Articles, 500 to 3,000 words, on all kinds of collectibles: records, TV memorabilia (Munsters, Star Trek, Dark Shadows, Elvira, etc.), comics, gum cards, toys, sheet music, monsters, magazines, dolls, movie posters, etc. Pays $10 to $50, on publication.

NUTSHELL NEWS—21027 Crossroads Cir., P.O. Box 1612, Waukesha, WI 53187. Sybil Harp, Ed. Articles, 1,200 to 1,500 words, for architectural scale miniatures enthusiasts, collectors, craftspeople, and hobbyists. Interested in artisan profiles, tours of collections, and how-to projects. Color slides or B&W prints required. Pays 10¢ a word, on publication. Query first.

PETERSEN'S PHOTOGRAPHIC—8490 Sunset Blvd., Los Angeles, CA 90069. Bill Hurter, Ed. How-to articles on all phases of still photography of interest to the amateur and advanced photographer. Pays $60 per printed page for article accompanied by photos, on publication.

PLATE WORLD—9200 N. Maryland Ave., Niles, IL 60648. Alyson Sulaski Wyckoff, Ed. Articles on artists, collectors, manufacturers, retailers of limited-edition (only) collector's plates. No antiques. Internationally oriented. Pays varying rates, on acceptance. Query first with writing samples.

POPULAR MECHANICS—224 W. 57th St., New York, NY 10019. Deborah Frank, Man. Ed. Articles, 300 to 2,000 words, on latest developments in mechanics, industry, science; features on hobbies with a mechanical slant; how-tos on home, shop, and crafts projects. Photos and sketches a plus. Pays to $1,000, $25 to $100 for short pieces, on acceptance. Buys all rights.

THE PROFESSIONAL QUILTER—Oliver Press, Box 75277, St. Paul, MN 55175. Jeannie M. Spears, Ed. Articles, 500 to 1,500 words, for small businesses related to the quilting field: business and marketing skills, personality profiles. Graphics, if applicable; no how-to quilt articles. Pays $25 to $75, on publication. Guidelines.

QUICK & EASY CRAFTS—(formerly *Women's Circle Country Needlecraft*) 306 E. Parr Rd., Berne, IN 46711. Rebekah Montgomery, Ed. How-to and instructional needlecrafts and other arts and crafts, book reviews, and tips. Photos. Pays varying rates, on publication.

RAILROAD MODEL CRAFTSMAN—P.O. Box 700, Newton, NJ 07860. William C. Schaumburg, Ed. How-to articles on scale model railroading; cars, operation, scenery, etc. Pays on publication.

R/C MODELER MAGAZINE—P.O. Box 487, Sierra Madre, CA 91024. Patricia E. Crews, Ed. Technical and semi-technical how-to articles on radio-controlled model aircraft, boats, helicopters, and cars. Query.

RESTORATION—3153 E. Lincoln, Tucson, AZ 85714–2017. W.R. Haessner, Ed. Articles, 1,200 to 1,800 words, on restoring autos, trucks, planes, trains, etc. Photos and art required. Pays $50 per page, on publication. Query.

THE ROBB REPORT—1 Acton Pl., Acton, MA 01720. Attn: Toby Perelmuter. Feature articles on investment opportunities, classic and collectible autos, art and antiques, home interiors, boats, travel, etc. Pays on publication. Query with SASE and published clips.

SCHOOL MATES—U.S. Chess Federation, 186 Route 9W, New Windsor, NY 12550. Jennie L. Simon, Ed. Articles and fiction, to 1,000 words, and short fillers, related to chess for beginning chess players (not necessarily children). "Instructive, but room for fun puzzles, anecdotes, etc. All chess related." Pays about $40 per 1,000 words, on publication.

73 AMATEUR RADIO—WGE Center, Hancock, NH 03449. Bill Brown, Ed. Articles, 1,500 to 3,000 words, for electronics hobbyists and amateur radio operators. Pays $100 per printed page for construction articles, $50 to $75 per printed page for others.

SEW NEWS—P.O. Box 1790, News Plaza, Peoria, IL 61656. Linda Turner Griepentrog, Ed. Articles, to 3,000 words, "that teach a specific technique, inspire a reader to try new sewing projects, or inform a reader about an interesting person, company, or project related to sewing, textiles, or fashion." Emphasis is on fashion (not craft) sewing. Pays $25 to $400, on acceptance. Queries required; no unsolicited manuscripts accepted.

SPORTS CARD TRADER—3 Fairchild Ct., Plainview, NY 11518. Address Editorial Office. Monthly. Fiction and articles, from 1,000 words, related to baseball, football, basketball, and hockey cards; poetry and fillers. Queries preferred. Pays 7¢ per word, on publication.

SPORTS COLLECTORS DIGEST—Krause Publications, 700 E. State St., Iola, WI 54990. Tom Mortenson, Ed. Articles, 750 to 2,000, on old baseball card sets and other collectibles. Pays $50 to $100, on publication.

TEDDY BEAR REVIEW—P.O. Box 1239, Hanover, PA 17331. Chris Revi, Ed. Articles on antique and contemporary teddy bears for makers, collectors, and enthusiasts. Pays $50 to $200, within 30 days of acceptance. Query with photos.

THREADS MAGAZINE—Taunton Press, 63 S. Main St., Box 355, Newtown, CT 06470. Address the Editors. A bimonthly devoted to design, materials, and techniques in sewing and textile arts. Articles and department pieces about materials, tools, techniques, people, and design, especially in garment making, knitting, quilting, and stitchery. Pays $150 per published page, on publication.

TROPICAL FISH HOBBYIST—211 W. Sylvania Ave., Neptune City, NJ 07753. Ray Hunziker, Ed. Articles, 500 to 3,000 words, for beginning and experienced tropical and marine fish enthusiasts. Photos. Pays $35 to $250, on acceptance. Query.

VINTAGE FASHIONS—900 Frederick St., Cumberland, MD 21502. Carolyn Cook, Ed. Articles, to 1,200 words, on vintage clothing (except furs), jewelry, and accessories. Pieces on the care and preservation of vintage items. Photos. Queries preferred. Payment varies, on publication.

WEST ART—Box 6868, Auburn, CA 95604. Martha Garcia, Ed. Features, 350 to 700 words, on fine arts and crafts. No hobbies. Photos. Pays 50¢ per column inch, on publication. SASE required.

WESTERN & EASTERN TREASURES—P.O. Box 1095, Arcata, CA

95521. Rosemary Anderson, Man. Ed. Illustrated articles, to 1,500 words, on metal detecting, treasure hunting, rocks, and gems. Pays 2¢ a word, extra for photos, on publication.

WESTERN FLYER—P.O. Box 98786, Tacoma, WA 98498–0786. Ralph Seeley, Man. Ed. Articles, 500 to 2,500 words, of interest to "general aviation" pilots. "Best shot for non-pilot writers is 'destination' series: attractions and activities near airports not necessarily aviation oriented." Pays $3 per column inch (approximately 40 words); $10 for B&W photos; $50 for color photos; first month following publication.

WIN MAGAZINE—(formerly *Gambling Times*) 16760 Stagg St., #213, Van Nuys, CA 91406. Cecil Suzuki, Ed. Gambling-related articles, 1,000 to 6,000 words. Pays $100 to $150, on publication.

THE WINE SPECTATOR—Opera Plaza, Suite 2014, 601 Van Ness Ave., San Francisco, CA 94102. Jim Gordon, Man. Ed. Features, 600 to 2,000 words, preferably with photos, on news and people in the wine world. Pays from $100, extra for photos, on publication. Query required.

WOMEN'S CIRCLE COUNTED CROSS-STITCH—See *Counted Cross-Stitch Plus*.

WOMEN'S CIRCLE COUNTRY NEEDLECRAFT—See *Quick & Easy Crafts*.

WOODEN BOAT—P.O. Box 78, Brooklin, ME 04616. Jonathan Wilson, Ed. How-to and technical articles, 4,000 words, on construction, repair, and maintenance of wooden boats; design, history, and use of wooden boats; and profiles of outstanding wooden boat builders and designers. Pays $6 per column inch. Query preferred.

THE WORKBASKET—4251 Pennsylvania, Kansas City, MO 64111. Roma Jean Rice, Ed. Instructions and models for original knit, crochet, and tat items. (Designs must fit theme of issue.) How-tos on crafts and gardening, 400 to 1,200 words, with photos. Pays 7¢ a word for articles, extra for photos, on acceptance; negotiable rates for instructional items.

WORKBENCH—4251 Pennsylvania Ave., Kansas City, MO 64111. Robert N. Hoffman, Ed. Articles on do-it-yourself home improvement and maintenance projects and general woodworking articles for beginning and expert craftsmen. Complete working drawings with accurate dimensions, step-by-step instructions, lists of materials, in-progress photos, and photos of the finished product must accompany submission. Queries welcome. Pays from $150 per published page, on acceptance.

YELLOWBACK LIBRARY—P.O. Box 36172, Des Moines, IA 50315. Gil O'Gara, Ed. Articles, 300 to 2,000 words, on boys/girls series literature (Hardy Boys, Nancy Drew, Tom Swift, etc.) for collectors, researchers, and dealers. "Especially welcome are interviews with, or articles by past and present writers of juvenile series fiction." Pays in copies and ads.

YESTERYEAR—P.O. Box 2, Princeton, WI 54968. Michael Jacobi, Ed. Articles on antiques and collectibles, for readers in WI, IL, IA, MN, and surrounding states. Photos. Will consider regular columns on collecting or antiques. Pays from $10, on publication.

ZYMURGY—Box 287, Boulder, CO 80306. Charles N. Papazian, Ed. Articles appealing to beer lovers and homebrewers. Pays $25 to $75, for pieces 750 to 2,000 words, on publication. Query.

AD ASTRA—National Space Society, 922 Pennsylvania Ave. S.E., Washington, DC 20003. Leonard David, Ed.-in-Chief. Lively, non-technical features (to 3,000 words) on all aspects of international space program. Particularly interested in "Living in Space" articles; space settlements; lunar and Mars bases. Pays $150 to $300, on publication. Query; guidelines available.

AIR & SPACE—370 L'Enfant Promenade, 10th Fl., Washington, DC 20024-2518. George Larson, Ed. General-interest articles, 1,000 to 3,500 words, on aerospace experience, past, present, and future; travel, space, history, biographies, essays, commentary. Pays varying rates, on acceptance. Query first.

AMERICAN HERITAGE OF INVENTION & TECHNOLOGY—60 Fifth Ave., New York, NY 10011. Frederick Allen, Ed. Articles, 2,000 to 5,000 words, on history of technology in America, for the sophisticated general reader. Query. Pays on acceptance.

AMIGA WORLD—IDG Communications, 80 Elm St., Peterborough, NH 03458. Linda Barrett, Acquisitions Ed. Articles, 1,500 to 3,000 words, on programming, product tutorials, and product reviews (including games) on the Amiga systems. Pays $450 to $800, on publication. Query first.

ANTIC, THE ATARI RESOURCE—544 Second St., San Francisco, CA 94107. Nat Friedland, Ed. Programs and information for the Atari computer user/owner. Reviews, 500 words, of hardware and software, original programs, etc. Game reviews, 400 words. Pays $50 per review, $60 per published page, on publication. Query.

ARCHAEOLOGY—15 Park Row, New York, NY 10038. Peter A. Young, Ed.-in-Chief. Articles on archaeology by professionals or lay people with a solid knowledge of the field. Pays $500 to $1,000, on acceptance. Query required.

ASTRONOMY—P.O. Box 1612, Waukesha, WI 53187. Richard Berry, Ed.-in-Chief. Articles on astronomy, astrophysics, space programs, research. Hobby pieces on equipment; short news items. Pays varying rates, on acceptance.

BIOSCIENCE—American Institute of Biological Science, 730 11th St. N.W., Washington, DC 20001. Anna Maria Gillis, Features Ed. Articles, 2 to 4 journal pages, on new developments in biology or on science policy, for professional biologists. Pays $200 per journal page, on publication. Query required.

BYTE MAGAZINE—One Phoenix Mill Ln., Peterborough, NH 03458. Frederic Langa, Ed. Features on new technology, how-to articles, and reviews of computers and software, varying lengths, for sophisticated users of personal computers. Payment is competitive. Query. Guidelines.

CBT DIRECTIONS—Weingarten Publications, 38 Chauncy St., Boston, MA 02111. Floyd Kemske, Ed. Articles (2,500 words) and news items (from 500 words) on computer-based training and interactive video for industry and government professionals in program development. Pays $100 to $600, on acceptance. Query.

CLASSROOM COMPUTER LEARNING—Peter Li, Inc., 2169 E. Francisco Blvd., Suite A-4, San Rafael, CA 94901. Holly Brady, Ed. Articles, to 3,000 words, on computer use in the classroom: human-interest, philosophical articles, how-to pieces, software reviews, and hands-on ideas, for teachers of grades K through 12. Pay varies, on acceptance.

COMPUTE!—324 W. Wendover Ave., Suite 200, Greensboro, NC 27408. Peter Scisco, Ed. In-depth feature articles on using the personal computer at home, work, and school. Industry news, interviews with leaders in the pc field, product information, hardware and software reviews. For users of Amiga, Apple, Commodore 64/128, IBM, Tandy, and compatibles.

COMPUTE GAZETTE—324 W. Wendover Ave., Suite 200, Greensboro, NC 27408. David Hensley, Man. Ed. Tom Netsel, Ed. Articles, to 2,000 words, on Commodore 64/128, including home, education, and business applications, games, and programming. Original programs also accepted.

DATA COMMUNICATIONS INTERNATIONAL—1221 Ave. of the Americas, New York, NY 10020. Joseph Braue, Ed.-in-Chief. Technical articles, 2,000 words, on communications networks. Readers are managers of multinational computer networks. Payment varies; made on acceptance and on publication.

DATACENTER MANAGER—International Computer Programs, Inc., 9100 Keystone Crossing, Suite 200, Indianapolis, IN 46240. Mark Taber, Ed. Articles, 2,000 to 3,000 words, on the software and utilities that drive computer systems, communications, and data center operations. Pays $600 to $800, on acceptance.

DESIGN MANAGEMENT—(formerly *Design Graphics World*), Communications Channels, 6255 Barfield Rd., Atlanta, GA 30328. Eric Torrey, Ed. Articles, 1,500 to 2,000 words, on news, trends concerning CAD, engineering and architecture, computer graphics, reprographics, and related design fields. Pays on publication. Query required.

DIGITAL NEWS—33 West St., Boston, MA 02111. Charles Babcock, Ed. Newspaper articles of varying lengths, covering products, applications, and events related to Digital's VAX line of computers. Pay varies, on acceptance. Query required.

ENVIRONMENT—4000 Albemarle St. N.W., Washington, DC 20016. Barbara T. Richman, Man. Ed. Factual articles, 2,500 to 5,000 words, on scientific, technological, and environmental policy and decision-making issues. Pays $100 to $300. Query.

FINAL FRONTIER—P.O. Box 11519, Washington, DC 20008. Tony Reichhardt, Ed. Articles (1,500 to 3,000 words), columns (800 words), and shorts (250 words) about people, events, and "exciting possibilities" of the world's space programs. Pays about 25¢ a word, on acceptance. Query.

THE FUTURIST—World Future Society, 4916 Elmo Ave., Bethesda, MD 20814. Timothy Willard, Man. Ed. Features, 1,000 to 5,000 words, on subjects pertaining to the future: environment, education, science, technology, etc. Pays in copies.

GENETIC ENGINEERING NEWS—1651 Third Ave., New York, NY 10128. John Sterling, Man. Ed. Articles on all aspects of biotechnology; feature articles and news articles. Pays varying rates, on acceptance. Query.

GEOBYTE—American Association of Petroleum Geologists, P.O. Box 979, Tulsa, OK 74101. Ken Milam, Man. Ed. Articles, 20 typed pages, on computer applications in exploration and production of oil, gas, and energy minerals for geophysicists, geologists, and petroleum engineers. Pay varies, on acceptance. Queries preferred.

HOME OFFICE COMPUTING—Scholastic, Inc., 1290 Wall St. W., New York, NY 10005. Bernadette Gray, Exec. Ed. Articles of interest to people operating businesses out of their homes: product reviews, profiles of successful businesses, basic business and technology. Payment varies, on acceptance.

INCIDER—IDG Communications/Peterborough, 80 Elm St., Peterborough, NH 03458. Paul Statt, Sr. Ed. Features, 2,000 to 2,500 words, and product reviews, 1,000 to 1,500 words, of interest to Apple II computer users. Short hints and news, to 100 words. Pays from $25 to $500, on acceptance. Query.

LINK-UP—143 Old Marlton Pike, Medford, NJ 08055. Joseph A. Webb, Ed. Dir. How-to pieces, hardware and software reviews, and current trends, 600 to 2,500 words, for business and education professionals who use computers and modems at work and at home. Pays $90 to $220, on publication. Book reviews, 500 to 800 words, $55. Photos a plus.

LOTUS—P. O. Box 9123, Cambridge, MA 02139. Larry Marion, Ed.-in-Chief. Articles, 1,500 to 2,000 words, on business and professional applications of Lotus software. Query with outline required. Pays to $1 a word, on acceptance.

MICROAGE QUARTERLY—2308 S. 55th St., Tempe, AZ 85282. Jay O'-Callaghan, Ed. Distributed through MicroAge centers. Articles on business uses of microcomputers; prefer writers with experience in microcomputer industry and knowledge of technology and products. Query first. Pays varying rates, on publication.

MODERN ELECTRONICS—76 N. Broadway, Hicksville, NY 10081. Art Salsberg, Ed.-in-Chief. How-to features, technical tutorials, and construction projects related to latest consumer and industrial electronics circuits, products, and personal computer equipment enhancements and modifications. Lengths vary. Query with outline required. Pays $80 to $150 per published page, on acceptance.

NETWORK WORLD—Box 9171, Framingham, MA 01701. John Gallant, Ed. Articles, to 2,500 words, about applications of communications technology for management level users of data, voice, and video communications systems. Pays varying rates, on acceptance.

NIBBLE—52 Domino Dr., Concord, MA 01742. Rich Williams, Man. Ed. Programs and programming methods, as well as short articles, reviews, and general-interest pieces for Apple II Computer users. Include program and article on disk. Send cover letter and sample program runs with manuscript. Pays $200 to $500 for major articles, $50 to $250 for shorter pieces. Send SASE for writers' guidelines.

OMNI—1965 Broadway, New York, NY 10023. Patrice Adcroft, Ed. Articles, 1,000 to 3,500 words, on scientific aspects of the future: space colonies, cloning, machine intelligence, ESP, origin of life, future arts, lifestyles, etc. Pays $800 to $4,000, $150 for short items, on acceptance. Query.

POPULAR ELECTRONICS—500-B Bi County Blvd., Farmingdale, NY 11735. Carl Laron, Ed. Features, 1,500 to 2,500 words, for electronics hobbyists and experimenters. "Our readers are science oriented, understand computer theory and operation, and like to build projects." Fillers and cartoons. Pays $25 to $350, on acceptance.

POPULAR SCIENCE—2 Park Ave., New York, NY 10016. Fred Abatemarco, Ed. Articles, with photos, on developments in applied science and technology. Short illustrated articles on new inventions and products; photo essays, book excerpts. Pays from $150 per printed page, on acceptance.

PUBLISH!—Integrated Media, Inc., 501 Second St., San Francisco, CA 94107. Sandra Rosenzweig, Ed. Features (1,200 to 2,000 words) and reviews (300 to 800 words) on all aspects of computerized publishing. Pays $300 for short articles and reviews, $600 and up for full-length features and reviews, on acceptance. Query Leslie Steere, Man. Ed.

RADIO-ELECTRONICS—500-B Bi-County Blvd., Farmingdale, NY 11735. Brian C. Fenton, Ed. Technical articles, 1,500 to 3,000 words, on all areas related to electronics. Pays $50 to $500, on acceptance.

THE RAINBOW—Falsoft, Inc., 9509 U. S. Highway 42, P. O. Box 385, Prospect, KY 40059. Tony Olive, Submissions Ed. Articles and computer programs for Tandy color computers. Pays varying rates, on publication.

RUN—IDG Communications, 80 Elm St., Peterborough, NH 03458. Dennis Brisson, Ed.-in-Chief. Articles, 6 to 10 typed pages, geared to Commodore home computer users: applications, program listings, hints, and tips to "help readers get the most out of their Commodore." Query first for technical subjects. Pays $100 per printed page.

THE SCIENCES—2 E. 63rd St., New York, NY 10021. Peter G. Brown, Ed. Essays and features, 2,000 to 4,000 words, and book reviews, on all scientific disciplines. Pays honorarium, on publication. Query.

SEA FRONTIERS—4600 Rickenbacker Causeway, Virginia Key, Miami, FL 33149. Bonnie Bilyeu Gordon, Ed. Jean Bradfisch, Exec. Ed. Illustrated articles, 500 to 3,000 words, on scientific advances related to the sea, biological, physical, chemical, or geological phenomena, ecology, conservation, etc., written in a popular style for lay readers. Send SASE for guidelines. Pays 25¢ a word, on acceptance. Query.

SHAREWARE MAGAZINE—1030D E. Duane Ave., Sunnyvale, CA 94086. Tracy Stephenson, Ed. Reviews of shareware programs and articles on related topics, 1,000 to 4,000 words. Payment varies, on publication. Query.

START MAGAZINE—Antic Publishing, 544 Second St., San Francisco, CA 94107. Tom Byron, Ed. Articles, to 4,000 words, and programming features, 1,500 to 2,500 words, for beginning and experienced users of Atari ST computers. Submit hard copy and disk. Pay varies, on publication. Guidelines.

TECHNOLOGY REVIEW—MIT, W59-200, Cambridge, MA 02139. Jonathan Schlefer, Ed. General-interest articles and more technical features, 1,500 to 5,000 words, on technology, the environment, and society. Pay varies, on publication. Query.

VOICE PROCESSING MAGAZINE—P.O. Box 42382, Houston, TX 77242. Tim Cornitius, Ed. Technical articles, 2,000 to 2,400 words, and applications of voice mail and messaging, voice response, call processing, and voice/data networking. Pays flat fee. Query.

ANIMALS

AMERICAN FARRIERS JOURNAL—63 Great Rd., Maynard, MA 01754. Susan Philbrick, Ed. Articles, 800 to 5,000 words, on general farrier issues, hoof care, tool selection, equine lameness, and horse handling. Pays 30¢ per published line, $10 per published illustration or photo, on publication. Query.

ANIMAL KINGDOM—See *Wildlife Conservation*.

AQUARIUM FISH—P.O. Box 6050, Mission Viejo, CA 92690. Edward Bauman, Ed. Articles, 2,000 words, on freshwater, saltwater, and pond fish, with or without color transparencies. (No "pet fish" stories, please.) Payment varies, on publication.

BIRD TALK—Box 6050, Mission Viejo, CA 92690. Karyn New, Ed. Articles for pet bird owners: care and feeding, training, outstanding personal adventures.

Pays 7¢ to 10¢ a word, after publication. Query or send manuscript; good transparencies a plus.

CAT FANCY—P.O. Box 6050, Mission Viejo, CA 92690. Linda Lewis, Ed. Articles, from 1,500 to 3,000 words, on cat care, health, grooming, etc. Pays 5¢ a word, or $150 to $300 for photo story with quality color slides or B&W prints, on publication.

DOG FANCY—P. O. Box 6050, Mission Viejo, CA 92690. Kim Thornton, Ed. Articles, 1,500 to 3,000 words, on dog care, health, grooming, breeds, activities, events, etc. Photos. Pays from 5¢ a word, on publication.

EQUUS—Fleet Street Corp., 656 Quince Orchard Rd., Gaithersburg, MD 20878. Emily Kilby, Ed. 1,000- to 3,000-word articles on all breeds of horses, covering their health, care, the latest advances in equine medicine and research. "Attempt to speak as one horse-person to another." Pays $100 to $400, on acceptance.

FLORIDA WILDLIFE—620 S. Meridian St., Tallahassee, FL 32399–1600. Andrea H. Blount, Ed. Bimonthly of the Florida Game and Fresh Water Fish Commission. Articles, 800 to 1,200 words, that promote native wildlife (flora and fauna), hunting, fishing in Florida's fresh waters, outdoor ethics, and conservation of Florida's natural resources. Pays $50 to $200, on publication.

HORSE & RIDER—P.O. Box 72001, San Clemente, CA 92672. Ray Rich, Ed. Articles, 500 to 3,000 words, with photos, on western riding and general horse care: training, feeding, grooming, etc. Pays varying rates, on publication. Buys all rights. Guidelines.

HORSEMEN'S YANKEE PEDLAR—785 Southbridge St., Auburn, MA 01501. Nancy L. Khoury, Pub. News and feature-length articles, about horses and horsemen in the Northeast. Photos. Pays $2 per published inch, on publication. Query.

HORSEPLAY—P.O. Box 130, Gaithersburg, MD 20884. Cordelia Doucet, Ed. Articles, 1,500 to 3,000 words, on eventing, show jumping, horse shows, dressage, driving, and fox hunting, for horse enthusiasts. Pays 10¢ a word, buys all rights, after publication.

LLAMAS—P.O. Box 1038, Dublin, OH 43017. Susan Ley, Asst. Ed. "The International Camelid Jounal," published 8 times yearly. Articles, 300 to 3,000 words, of interest to llama and alpaca owners. Pays $25 to $300, extra for photos, on acceptance. Query.

MUSHING—P.O. Box 149, Ester, AK 99725. Todd Hoener, Pub. How-tos, profiles, interviews, and features (1,500 to 2,000 words) and department pieces (500 to 1,000 words) for competitive and recreational dog drivers and skijorers. International audience. Photos. Pays $25 to $250, after acceptance. Queries preferred. Guidelines.

PERFORMANCE HORSEMAN—Gum Tree Corner, Unionville, PA 19375. Joanne Tobey, Articles Ed. Factual how-to pieces for the serious western rider, on training improving riding skills, all aspects of care and management, etc. Pays from $300, on acceptance.

PRACTICAL HORSEMAN—Gum Tree Corner, Unionville, PA 19375. Joanne Tobey, Articles Ed. How-to articles on horse care, English riding, and training. Pays on acceptance. Query.

PURE BRED DOGS/AMERICAN KENNEL GAZETTE—51 Madison Ave., New York, NY 10010. Marion Lane, Exec. Ed. Judy Hartop, Sr. Ed. Articles,

1,000 to 2,500 words, relating to pure-bred dogs. Pays from $100 to $300, on acceptance. Query preferred.

SHEEP! MAGAZINE—W. 2997 Market Rd., Helenville, WI 53137. Dave Thompson, Ed. Articles, to 1,500 words, on successful shepherds, woolcrafts, sheep raising, and sheep dogs. "Especially interested in people who raise sheep successfully as a sideline enterprise." Photos. Pays $80 to $300, extra for photos, on publication. Query first.

TROPICAL FISH HOBBYIST—211 W. Sylvania Ave., Neptune City, NJ 07753. Ray Hunziker, Ed. Articles, 500 to 3,000 words, for beginning and experienced tropical and marine fish enthusiasts. Photos. Pays $35 to $250, on acceptance. Query.

VIRGINIA WILDLIFE—P.O. Box 11104, Richmond, VA 23230–1104. Monthly of the Commission of Game and Inland Fisheries. Articles, 1,500 to 2,500 words, with Virginia tie-in, on conservation and related topics, including fishing, hunting, wildlife management, outdoor safety, and ethics, etc. Articles must be accompanied by color photos. Query with SASE. Pays 10¢ a word, extra for photos, on acceptance.

WILDLIFE CONSERVATION—(formerly *Animal Kingdom*) New York Zoological Society, Bronx, NY 10460. Nancy Christie, Sr. Ed. First-person articles, 1,500 to 2,000 words, on "popular" natural history, "based on author's research and experience as opposed to textbook approach." Payment varies, on acceptance. Guidelines.

ZOO LIFE—11661 San Vicente Blvd., Suite 402, Los Angeles, CA 90049. Audrey Tawa, Ed. Quarterly. Articles, 1,500 to 2,000 words, on the work zoos and aquariums are doing in the fields of animal conservation and education. Mention possibility of photos when querying. Pays 20¢ per word, on publication. Payment for photos negotiable. Guidelines.

PARENTING, CHILD CARE, AND DEVELOPMENT

AMERICAN BABY—475 Park Ave. S., New York, NY 10016. Judith Nolte, Ed. Articles, 1,000 to 2,000 words, for new or expectant parents on prenatal and infant care. Pays varying rates, on acceptance.

BABY TALK—636 Ave. of the Americas, New York, NY 10011. Susan Strecker, Ed. Articles, 1,500 to 3,000 words, by parents or professionals, on babies, baby care, etc. Pays varying rates, on acceptance. SASE required.

CHILD—110 Fifth Ave., New York, NY 10011. Freddi Greenberg, Ed. Articles on lifestyles of children and family. Departments: Fashion, Home Environment, Baby Best, and Travel. Pays from $750. Query.

CONCEIVE—P.O. Box 2047, Danville, CA 94526. Catherine C. Knipper, Ed. Articles, 400 to 4,000 words, in lay terms, about current medical technologies and advances for infertile individuals. Pieces addressing the emotional side of infertility and lifestyle alternatives (adoption, child-free living). Pays on publication: $50 to $175; poetry, 4 to 30 lines ($1 a line); fillers ($10 for up to 100 words).

GROWING CHILD/GROWING PARENT—22 N. Second St., Lafayette, IN 47902. Nancy Kleckner, Ed. Articles to 1,500 words on subjects of interest to parents of children under 6, with emphasis on the issues, problems, and choices of being a parent. No personal-experience pieces or poetry. Pays 8¢ to 15¢ a word, on acceptance. Query.

HEALTHY KIDS—Cahners Publishing, 475 Park Ave. S., New York, NY 10016. Phyllis Steinberg, Ed. Published three times yearly, in two editions: Birth-3 and 4–10 Years. Articles, 1,500 to 2,000 words, on the elements of raising a healthy, happy child (basic care, analysis of the growing mind, behavior patterns, nutrition, emergencies, etc.). "All articles should be written by experts or include interviews with appropriate pediatricians and other health-care professionals." Query. Pays $500 to $1,000, on acceptance.

LIVING WITH CHILDREN—127 Ninth Ave. N., Nashville, TN 37234. Articles, 800 to 1,450 words, on parent-child relationships, told from a Christian perspective. Pays 5¢ a word, after acceptance.

LIVING WITH PRESCHOOLERS—127 Ninth Ave. N., Nashville, TN 37234. Articles, 800 to 1,450 words, and anecdotes, for Christian families. Pays 5¢ a word, on acceptance.

LIVING WITH TEENAGERS—127 Ninth Ave. N., Nashville, TN 37234. Articles told from a Christian perspective for parents of teenagers; first-person approach preferred. Poetry, 4 to 16 lines. Pays 5½¢ a word, on acceptance.

MCCALL'S—110 Fifth Ave., New York, NY 10011. Pieces, 800 to 1,000 words, that "describe a problem and solution in a way of interest to parents everywhere," for "The Mothers' Page." Pays $750, on acceptance.

MARRIAGE & FAMILY—Abbey Press Publishing Div., St. Meinrad, IN 47577. Kass Dotterweich, Man. Ed. Expert advice, personal-experience articles with moral, religious, or spiritual slant, to 1,900 words, on marriage and family relationships. Pays 7¢ a word, on acceptance.

NEW YORK FAMILY—420 E. 79th St., New York, NY 10021. Felice Shapiro, Susan Ross, Eds. Articles related to family life in New York City. Pays $50 to $100, on publication. Same requirements for *Westchester Family*, for parents in Westchester County, NY.

PARENTGUIDE NEWS—2 Park Ave., Suite 2012, New York, NY 10016. Leslie Elgort, Ed. Monthly. Articles, 1,000 to 1,500 words, related to New York families and parenting: trends, profiles, special programs and products, etc. Humor, jokes, puzzles, and photos also considered. Payment varies, on publication.

PARENTING—501 Second St., San Francisco, CA 94107. David Markus, Ed. Articles, 500 to 3,500 words, for parents of children up to 10-years-old, especially under 6-years-old. Topics include education, health, fitness, nutrition, child development, psychology, and social issues. Pays to $2,000. Query.

PARENTS—685 Third Ave., New York, NY 10017. Ann Pleshette Murphy, Ed.-in-Chief. Articles, 1,500 to 3,000 words, on growth and development of infants, children, teens; family; women's issues; community; current research. Informal style with quotes from experts. Pays from $1,000, on acceptance. Query.

PARENTS & KIDS—2019A Greenwood Lake Tpke., Hewitt, NJ 07421. John Sailer, Assoc. Pub. Monthly magazine for parents and children in northern New Jersey and southern New York state with articles about parenting techniques, personal experiences, activities for children, reviews of books and videos, etc.

PARENTS AND TEENAGERS—289 N. Monroe Ave., Box 481, Loveland, CO 80539. Joani Schultz, Ed. Dir. Articles, 200 to 1,400 words, with Christian focus on the parenting of teenagers; include quotes of experts, anecdotes, and practical tips. Pays $25 to $100, on acceptance. Query.

SEATTLE'S CHILD—P.O. Box 22578, Seattle, WA 98122. Ann Bergman, Ed. Articles (400 to 2,500 words) of interest to parents, educators, and childcare providers of children under 12, plus investigative reports and consumer tips on issues affecting families in the Puget Sound region. Pays $75 to $400, on publication. Query required.

WESTCHESTER FAMILY—See *New York Family*.

WORKING MOTHER—230 Park Ave., New York, NY 10169. Address Editorial Dept. Articles, to 1,000 words, that help women in their task of juggling job, home, and family. Payment varies, on acceptance.

MILITARY

THE AMERICAN LEGION MAGAZINE—Box 1055, Indianapolis, IN 46206. Michael D. LaBonne, Ed. Articles, 750 to 1,800 words, on current world affairs, public policy, and subjects of contemporary interest. Pays $100 to $1,000, on acceptance. Query.

ARMY MAGAZINE—2425 Wilson Blvd., Arlington, VA 22201–3385. L. James Binder, Ed.-in-Chief. Features, to 5,000 words, on military subjects. Essays, humor, history, news reports, first-person anecdotes. Pays 12¢ to 18¢ a word, $10 to $25 for anecdotes, on publication.

LEATHERNECK—Box 1775, Quantico, VA 22134. William V.H. White, Ed. Articles, to 3,000 words, with photos, on U.S. Marines. Pays $50 per printed page, on acceptance. Query.

LIFE IN THE TIMES—The Times Journal Co., Springfield, VA 22159–0200. Barry Robinson, Ed. Travel articles, 900 words; features on food, 500 to 1,000 words; and short, personal-experience pieces, 750 words, of interest to military people and their families around the world. Pays from $25 to $150 for short pieces, to $350 for general-interest features up to 2,000 words, on acceptance.

MILITARY LIFESTYLE MAGAZINE—1732 Wisconsin Ave. N.W., Washington, DC 20007. Hope Daniels, Ed. Articles, 1,000 to 2,000 words, for military families in the U.S. and overseas, on lifestyles, travel, fashion, nutrition, and health; fiction. Pays $200 to $700, on publication. Query first.

OFF DUTY MAGAZINE—3303 Harbor Blvd., Suite C-2, Costa Mesa, CA 92626. Bruce Thorstad, U.S. Ed. Travel articles, 1,800 to 2,000 words, for active duty military Americans (age 20 to 40) and their families, on U.S. regions or cities. Must have wide scope; no out-of-the-way places. Military angle essential. Photos. Pays from 16¢ a word, extra for photos, on acceptance. Query required. Guidelines. Limited market.

THE RETIRED OFFICER MAGAZINE—201 N. Washington St., Alexandria, VA 22314. Articles, 800 to 2,000 words, of interest to military retirees and their families. Current military/political affairs: recent military history (especially Vietnam and Korea), humor, travel, hobbies, military family lifestyles, wellness, and second-career job opportunities. Photos a plus. Pays to $500, on acceptance. Queries required, no unsolicited manuscripts; address Manuscript Ed. Guidelines.

VFW MAGAZINE—406 West 34th St., Kansas City, MO 64111. Richard K. Kolb, Ed. Magazine for Veterans of Foreign Wars and their families. Articles, 1,000 words, on current issues and history, with veteran angle. Photos. Pays up to $400, extra for photos, on acceptance. Guidelines.

WESTERN

AMERICAN WEST—7000 E. Tanque Verde Rd., Suite 30, Tucson, AZ 85715. Marjory Vals Maud, Exec. Ed. Well-researched, illustrated articles, 1,000 to 2,500 words, linking the contemporary West with its historic past and emphasizing places to see and things to do for the Western traveler. Pays from $200, on acceptance. Query required.

OLD WEST—See *True West.*

PERSIMMON HILL—1700 N.E. 63rd St., Oklahoma City, OK 73111. M.J. Van Deventer, Ed. Published by the National Cowboy Hall of Fame. Articles, 1,500 to 3,000 words, on Western history and art, cowboys, ranching, and nature. Top-quality illustrations a must. Pays from $100 to $250, on acceptance.

TRUE WEST—P.O. Box 2107, Stillwater, OK 74076. John Joerschke, Ed. True stories, 500 to 4,500 words, with photos, about the Old West to 1930. Some contemporary stories with historical slant. Source list required. Pays 3¢ to 6¢ a word, extra for B&W photos, on acceptance. Same address and requirements for *Old West.*

HISTORICAL

AMERICAN HERITAGE—60 Fifth Ave., New York, NY 10011. Byron Dobell, Ed. Articles, 750 to 5,000 words, on U.S. history and background of American life and culture from the beginning to recent times. No fiction. Pays from $300 to $1,500, on acceptance. Query. SASE.

AMERICAN HERITAGE OF INVENTION & TECHNOLOGY—60 Fifth Ave., New York, NY 10011. Frederick Allen, Ed. Articles, 2,000 to 5,000 words, on history of technology in America, for the sophisticated general reader. Query. Pays on acceptance.

AMERICAN HISTORY ILLUSTRATED—2245 Kohn Road, P.O. Box 8200, Harrisburg, PA 17105. Articles, 3,000 to 5,000 words, soundly researched. Style should be popular, not scholarly. No travelogues, fiction, or puzzles. Pays $300 to $650, on acceptance. Query with SASE required.

CHICAGO HISTORY—Clark St. at North Ave., Chicago, IL 60614. Russell Lewis, Ed. Articles, to 4,500 words, on political, social, and cultural history. Pays to $250, on publication. Query.

EARLY AMERICAN LIFE—Box 8200, Harrisburg, PA 17105. Frances Carnahan, Ed. Illustrated articles, 1,000 to 3,000 words, on early American life: arts, crafts, furnishings, architecture; travel features about historic sites and country inns. Pays $50 to $500, on acceptance. Query.

HEARTLAND JOURNAL—Box 55115, Madison, WI 53705. Jeri McCormick and Lenore Coberly, Eds. Articles, 100 to 4,000 words, on "times and places that are gone." Writers must be over 60 years old. Pays in copies.

THE HIGHLANDER—P.O. Box 397, Barrington, IL 60010. Angus Ray, Ed. Bimonthly. Articles, 1,300 to 1,00 words, related to Scottish history. "We are not concerned with modern Scotland or current problems in Scotland." Pays $100 to $150, on acceptance.

HISTORIC PRESERVATION—1785 Massachusetts Ave. N.W., Washington, DC 20036. Anne Elizabeth Powell, Ed. Lively feature articles from published writers, 1,500 to 4,000 words, on residential restoration, preservation issues, and people involved in preserving America's heritage. High-quality photos. Pays $300 to $1,000, extra for photos, on acceptance. Query required.

LABOR'S HERITAGE—10000 New Hampshire Ave., Silver Spring, MD 20903. Stuart Kaufman, Ed. Quarterly journal of The George Meany Memorial Archives. Publishes 15- to 30-page articles to be read by labor scholars, labor union members, and the general public. Pays in copies.

PENNSYLVANIA HERITAGE—P.O. Box 1026, Harrisburg, PA 17108–1026. Michael J. O'Malley III, Ed. Quarterly of the Pennsylvania Historical and Museum Commission. Articles, 3,000 to 4,000 words, that "introduce readers to the state's rich culture and historic legacy...and involve them in such a way as to ensure that Pennsylvania's past has a future." Pays $300 to $500 for articles, and up to $100 for photos or drawings, on acceptance. Guidelines.

COLLEGE, CAREERS

AMPERSAND—2501 W. Burbank Blvd., Suite 302, Burbank, CA 91506. Michael Hogan, Pub. Articles, 1,000 to 2,000 words, of interest to college students. Focus on films and popular entertainment. Query.

THE BLACK COLLEGIAN—1240 S. Broad St., New Orleans, LA 70125. K. Kazi-Ferrouillet, Man. Ed. Articles, to 2,000 words, on experiences of African-American students, careers, and how-to subjects. Pays on publication. Query.

CAMPUS LIFE—465 Gundersen Dr., Carol Stream, IL 60188. Jim Long, Man. Ed. Articles reflecting Christian values and world view, for high school and college students. Humor, general fiction, and true, first-person experiences. "If we have a choice of fiction, how-to, and a strong first-person story, we'll go with the true story every time." Photo essays, cartoons. Pays from $125, on acceptance. Query.

CAMPUS USA—1801 Rockville Pike, Suite 216, Rockville, MD 20852. Gerald S. Snyder, Ed. Articles (500 to 1,500 words) on the tastes, feelings, and moods of today's college students: careers, college financing, travel, movies, fashion, autos, and sports. Pays $150 to $500, on publication. Also publishes *Campus USA Wall-Boards* on computers, business, music, lifestyles, sports, and nightlife. Query required for both publications.

CAREER WOMAN—See *The Minority Engineer*.

CAREERS AND THE HANDICAPPED—See *The Minority Engineer*.

CIRCLE K—3636 Woodview Trace, Indianapolis, IN 46268. Nicholas K. Drake, Exec. Ed. Serious and light articles, 2,000 to 2,500 words, on careers, youth issues, leadership development, self-help, community service and involvement. Pays $200 to $300, on acceptance. Queries preferred.

COLLEGE BROADCASTER—National Assoc. of College Broadcasters, Box 1955, Brown University, Providence, RI 02912. Articles (500 to 2,000 words) on college radio and TV station operations. Published eight times yearly. Query. Pays in copies.

EQUAL OPPORTUNITY—See *The Minority Engineer*.

JOURNAL OF CAREER PLANNING & EMPLOYMENT—62 Highland Ave., Bethlehem, PA 18017. Patricia A. Sinnott, Ed. Quarterly. Articles, 3,000 to 4,000 words, on topics related to career planning, placement, recruitment, and employment of new college graduates. Pays $200 to $400, on acceptance. Query first with clips. Guidelines.

KEY.DC—5323 41st St. N.W., Washington, DC 20015. Soraya Chemaly, Ed. Tabloid. Profiles and informational features, 900 to 2,000 words, of interest to college students in Washington, DC. "Distributed to 22 area colleges and universities. Primarily arts and entertainment with regular profiles and issue/news/information features and supplements." Query for articles and fillers. Pays 5¢ a word for profiles and features; 3¢ word for supplements; on publication.

MINORITY ENGINEER—44 Broadway, Greenlawn, NY 11740. James Schneider, Ed. Articles, 1,000 to 1,500 words, for college students, on career opportunities in engineering, scientific and technological fields; techniques of job hunting; developments in and applications of new technologies. Interviews. Profiles. Pays 10¢ a word, on publication. Query. Same address and requirements for *Woman Engineer*, *Equal Opportunity*, *Career Woman*, and *Careers and the Handicapped*.

STUDENT LEADERSHIP—5206 Maine St., Downers Grove, IL 60515. Robert Kachur, Ed. Articles (to 2,000 words), poetry, for college students. All material should reflect a Christian world view. Queries required.

UCLA MAGAZINE—405 Hilgard Ave., Los Angeles, CA 90024–1391. Mark Wheeler, Ed. Quarterly. Articles (2,000 words) related to UCLA through research, alumni, students, etc. Queries required. Pays to $750, on acceptance.

WHAT'S NEW MAGAZINE—8305 Paces Oaks Blvd., Suite 438, Charlotte, NC 28213. Bob Leja, Ed. General-interest articles, 150 to 300 words, on music, movies, books, cars, travel, sports, food, wine, consumer electronics, computers, arts, and entertainment. Pays varying rates, on publication. Query required.

WOMAN ENGINEER—See *The Minority Engineer*.

ALTERNATIVE MAGAZINES

EAST WEST: THE JOURNAL OF NATURAL HEALTH & LIVING—17 Station St., Box 1200, Brookline, MA 02147. Features, 1,500 to 2,500 words, on holistic health, natural foods, gardening, etc. Material for "Body," "Healing," "In the Kitchen," and "Beauty and Fitness." Interviews. Photos. Pays 10¢ to 15¢ a word, extra for photos, on publication.

FATE—P.O. Box 64383, St. Paul, MN 55164–0383. Donald Michael Kaag, Ed. Factual fillers and true stories, to 300 words, on strange or psychic happenings and mystic personal experiences. Pays $2 to $15.

NEW AGE JOURNAL—342 Western Ave., Brighton, MA 02135. Address Manuscript Ed. Articles for readers who take an active interest in social change, personal growth, health, and contemporary issues. Features, 2,000 to 4,000 words; columns, 750 to 1,500 words; short news items, 50 words; and first-person narratives, 750 to 1,500 words. Pays varying rates. Query.

NEW REALITIES—4000 Albemarle St. N.W., Washington, DC 20016. Joy O'Rouke, Ed. Articles on holistic health, personal growth, humanistic and transpersonal psychology, alternative lifestyles, new spirituality, parapsychology, social and global transformation. Query or send completed manuscript.

WILDFIRE—Bear Tribe Publishing, P.O. Box 9167, Spokane, WA 99209. Matthew Ryan, Ed. Articles (1,000 to 2,500 words) with a strong nature-based focus on spirituality, personal development, alternative lifestyles, natural healings, and ecology. Fiction (900 to 4,500 words) and poetry (20 lines). Pays to $250, on publication.

YOGA JOURNAL—2054 University Ave., Berkeley, CA 94704. Stephan Bodian, Ed. Articles, 1,200 to 4,000 words, on holistic health, spirituality, yoga, and transpersonal psychology; "new age" profiles; interviews. Pays $50 to $350, on publication.

OP-ED MARKETS

Op-ed pages (those that run opposite the editorials in newspapers) offer writers an excellent opportunity to air their opinions, views, ideas, and insights on a wide spectrum of subjects and in various styles, from the highly personal and informal essay to the more serious commentary on politics, foreign affairs, and news events. Humor and nostalgia often find a place here.

THE ARGUS LEADER—P.O. Box 5034, Sioux Falls, SD 57117–5034. Rob Swenson, Editorial Page Ed. Articles, to 850 words, on a wide variety of subjects for Different Voices column. Prefer local writers with an expertise on their subject. No payment made.

THE BALTIMORE SUN—P.O. Box 1377, Baltimore, MD 21278–0001. Hal Piper, Opinion-Commentary Page Ed. Articles, 600 to 1,500 words, for Opinion Commentary page, on a wide range of topics: politics, education, foreign affairs, lifestyles, etc. Humor. Payment varies, on publication. Exclusive rights: MD and DC.

BOSTON HERALD—One Herald Sq., Boston, MA 02106. Editorial Page Ed. Pieces, 600 to 800 words, on economics, foreign affairs, politics, regional interest, and seasonal topics. Payment varies, on publication. Prefer submissions from regional writers. Exclusive rights: MA, RI, and NH.

THE CAPITAL TIMES—P.O. Box 8060, Madison, WI 53708. Phil Haslanger, Ed. Articles, 600 to 700 words, on education, environment, regional interest, and religion. Pays $25, on publication.

THE CHARLOTTE OBSERVER—P.O. Box 32188, Charlotte, NC 28232. Jane McAlister Pope, Ed. Well-written, thought-provoking articles, to 700 words. Prefer local writers. Pays $50, on publication. "No simulataneous submissions in NC or SC."

THE CHICAGO TRIBUNE—435 N. Michigan Ave., Chicago, IL 60611. Richard Liefer, Op-Ed Page Ed. Pieces, to 800 words, on domestic affairs, environment, regional interest, and science. "Writers must be experts in their fields." Pays about $150, on publication. SASE required.

THE CHRISTIAN SCIENCE MONITOR NEWSPAPER—One Norway St., Boston, MA 02115. Scott Baldauf, Ed. Pieces, 700 to 800 words, on domestic affairs, economics, education, environment, foreign affairs, law, and politics. Pays $100 to $150, on acceptance. "We retain all rights for 90 days after publication. Submissions must be exclusive."

THE CHRONICLE—901 Mission St., San Francisco, CA 94103. Stephen Schwartz, Ed. Articles, 800 to 1,000 words, on a wide range of subjects. Pays $50 to $150, on publication. Query with SASE. "No anti-gay or racist pieces." Exclusive rights: Bay area.

THE CLEVELAND PLAIN DEALER—1801 Superior Ave., Cleveland, OH 44114. Jim Strang, Op-Ed Ed. Pieces, 700 to 900 words, on a wide variety of subjects. Pays $50, on publication.

DES MOINES REGISTER—P.O. Box 957, Des Moines, IA 50304. "Opinion" Page Ed. Articles, 500 to 850 words, on all topics. Pays $35 to $75, on publication. Exclusive rights: IA.

THE DETROIT FREE PRESS—321 W. Lafayette St., Detroit, MI 48231. Address Op-Ed Editor. Opinion pieces, to 1,000 words, on domestic and foreign affairs, economics, education, environment, law, politics, and regional interest. Pays $50 to $100, on publication. Query. Exclusive rights: MI and northern OH.

THE DETROIT NEWS—615 Lafayette Blvd., Detroit, MI 48226. Richard Burr, Ed. Pieces, 600 to 900 words, on a wide variety of subjects. Pays $75, on publication.

THE FLINT JOURNAL—200 E. First St., Flint, MI 48502. Articles, 650 words, of regional interest by local writers. No payment. Limited market.

FORT WORTH STAR-TELEGRAM—P.O. Box 1870, Fort Worth, TX 76101. Ann Thompson, Op-Ed Ed. Articles, to 900 words, on a variety of subjects. No human interest, lifestyle, nostalgia, religious, or seasonal material. "Most of our limited space goes to local writers on local topics." Pays $75, on publication. Limited market. Exclusive rights: Dallas area.

THE HOUSTON POST—4747 Southwest Freeway, Houston, TX 77001. Opinions and current affairs pieces, 2½ to 5 pages (double spaced). Pays $40 to $80, on publication. Exclusive rights: Houston area.

INDIANAPOLIS STAR—307 N. Pennsylvania St., Indianapolis, IN 46206–0145. John H. Lyst, Ed. Articles, 650 to 850 words, on economics, education, environment, domestic and foreign affairs, human interest, lifestyles, regional interest, religion, and seasonal material. Pays $40, on publication. Exclusive rights: IN.

LONG BEACH PRESS-TELEGRAM—604 Pine Ave., Long Beach, CA 90844. John J. Fried, Ed. Articles, 750 to 900 words, on lifestyles and regional topics. Writers must be local. "Articles on baby boomer issues are of interest to us." Pays $75, on publication. Exclusive rights: Los Angeles area.

LOS ANGELES TIMES—Times Mirror Sq., Los Angeles, CA 90053. Op-Ed Ed. Commentary pieces, to 800 words, on many subjects. "Not interested in nostalgia or first-person reaction to faraway events." Payment varies, on publication. Limited market. SASE required.

LOUISVILLE COURIER-JOURNAL—525 W. Broadway, Louisville, KY 40202. Op-Ed. Ed. Pieces, 750 words, on regional topics. Author must live in the area. Pays $25 to $50, on publication. Very limited market.

NEWSDAY—235 Pinelawn Rd., Melville, NY 11747. "Viewpoints" Ed. Pieces, 600 to 1,000 words, on a variety of topics. Pays from $150, on publication.

PITTSBURGH POST GAZETTE—50 Blvd. of the Allies, Pittsburgh, PA 15222. Editorial Page Ed. Articles, to 800 words, on a variety of subjects. No humor. Pays $75 to $150, on publication. SASE required.

PORTLAND PRESS HERALD—P.O. Box 1460, Portland, ME 04104. Op-Ed Page Ed. Articles, 750 words, on any topic with regional tie-in. Writers must live in ME or NH. Pays $50, on publication. Query. Exclusive rights: ME and NH.

THE SACRAMENTO BEE—2100 Q St., Sacramento, CA 95852. Rhea Wilson, Opinion Ed. Op-ed pieces, to 1,000 words; topics of state and regional interest only. Pays $150, on publication. Query.

ST. LOUIS POST-DISPATCH—900 N. Tucker Blvd., St. Louis, MO 63101.

Donna Korando, Ed. Articles, 700 words, on economics, education, science, politics, foreign and domestic affairs, and the environment. Pays $70, on publication. "Goal is to have half of the articles by local writers."

ST. PAUL PIONEER PRESS DISPATCH—345 Cedar St., St. Paul, MN 55101. Robert J.R. Johnson, Ed. Uses pieces, to 750 words, on a variety of topics. Prefer authors with a connection to the area. Pays $50, on publication.

SAN FRANCISCO EXAMINER—110 5th St., San Francisco, CA 94103. Op-Ed Ed. Well-written articles, 500 to 650 words, on any subject. "No foreign policy analysis by amateurs." Payment varies, on publication.

SAN JOSE MERCURY NEWS—750 Ridder Park Dr., San Jose, CA 95190. Articles, 750 words, on any subject. Prefer local writers. Pays $75, on publication. Exclusive rights: Bay area.

SEATTLE POST-INTELLIGENCER—P.O. Box 1109, Seattle, WA 98111. Charles J. Dunsire, Editorial Page Ed. Articles, 750 to 800 words, on foreign and domestic affairs, environment, education, politics, regional interest, religion, science, and seasonal material. Prefer writers who live in the area. Pays $75 to $150, on publication. SASE required. Very limited market.

TULSA WORLD—P.O. Box 1770, Tulsa, OK 74102. Articles, about 1,500 words, on subjects of local or regional interest. Payment varies, on publication. Query. Exclusive rights: Tulsa area.

USA TODAY—P.O. Box 500, Washington, DC 20044. Sid Hurlburt, Ed./ Columns. Articles, 380 to 430 words. Very limited market. Query. "Because topics are presented in debate format, most of our guest columns are commissioned to specifically react to the contrary view." Pays $125, on publication.

THE WALL STREET JOURNAL—Editorial Page, 200 Liberty St., New York, NY 10281. Melanie Kirkpatrick, Editorials Ed. Articles, to 1,500 words, on politics, economics, law, education, environment, humor (occasionally), and foreign and domestic affairs. Articles must be of national interest by writers with expertise in the field. Pays $150 to $300, on publication.

WASHINGTON TIMES—3600 New York Ave. N.E., Washington, DC 20002. Charles Wheeler, Ed. Articles, 800 to 1,000 words, on a variety of subjects. No pieces written in the first-person. "Syndicated columnists cover the 'big' issues; find an area that is off the beaten path." Pays $150, on publication. Exclusive rights: DC or Baltimore area.

ADULT MAGAZINES

CAVALIER—2600 Douglas Rd., Suite 602, Coral Gables, FL 33134. Nye Willden, Man. Ed. Articles with photos, and fiction, 1,500 to 3,000 words, for sophisticated young men. Pays to $400 for articles, to $250 for fiction, on publication. Query for articles.

CHIC—9171 Wilshire Blvd., Suite 300, Beverly Hills, CA 90210. Doug Oliver, Exec. Ed. Articles, interviews, erotic fiction, 2,500 to 4,000 words. Query for articles. Pays $750 for articles, $500 for fiction, on acceptance.

FORUM, THE INTERNATIONAL JOURNAL OF HUMAN RELATIONS—1965 Broadway, New York, NY 10023-5965. Don Myrus, Ed. Articles, 2,500 words; interested in well-written, erotic fiction and essays on matters of a sexual nature. Payment varies, on acceptance. Query.

GALLERY—401 Park Ave. S., New York, NY 10016. Marc Lichter, Ed.-in-Chief. Barry Janoff, Man. Ed. Articles, investigative pieces, interviews, profiles, to 3,500 words, for sophisticated men. Short humor, satire, service pieces. Photos. Pays varying rates, half on acceptance, half on publication. Query.

GENESIS—22 West 27th St., 8th Fl., New York, NY 10001. J.J. Kelleher, Ed.-in-Chief. Articles, 2,500 words; celebrity interviews, 2,500 words. Sexually explicit nonfiction features, 3,000 words. Photo essays. Pays 60 days after acceptance. Query.

PENTHOUSE—1965 Broadway, New York, NY 10023. Peter Bloch, Ed. General-interest or investigative articles, to 5,000 words. Interviews, 5,000 words, with introductions. Pays to $1 a word, on acceptance.

PLAYBOY—680 N. Lakeshore Dr., Chicago, IL 60611. John Rezek, Articles Ed. Alice K. Turner, Fiction Ed. Articles, 3,500 to 6,000 words, and sophisticated fiction, 1,000 to 10,000 words (5,000 preferred), for urban men. Humor; satire. Science fiction. Pays to $5,000 for articles, to $5,000 for fiction, $1,000 for short-shorts, on acceptance.

PLAYGIRL—801 Second Ave., New York, NY 10017. Nancie S. Martin, Ed. Articles, 2,000 to 2,500 words, for women 18 to 34. Celebrity interviews, 1,500 to 2,000 words. Humor. Cartoons. Pays varying rates, on acceptance.

FICTION MARKETS

This list gives the fiction requirements of general- and special-interest magazines, including those that publish detective and mystery, science fiction and fantasy, romance and confession stories. Other good markets for short fiction are the *College, Literary and Little Magazines* where, though payment is modest (usually in copies only), publication can help a beginning writer achieve recognition by editors at the larger magazines. Juvenile fiction markets are listed under *Juvenile, Teenage, and Young Adult Magazines*. Publishers of book-length fiction manuscripts are listed under *Book Publishers*.

All manuscripts must be typed double-space and submitted with self-addressed envelopes bearing postage sufficient for the return of the material. Use good white paper; onion skin and erasable bond are not acceptable. *Always* keep a copy of the manuscript, since occasionally a manuscript is lost in the mail. Magazines may take several weeks—often longer—to read and report on submissions. If an editor has not reported on a manuscript after a reasonable amount of time, write a brief, courteous letter of inquiry.

ABORIGINAL SF—P.O. Box 2449, Woburn, MA 01888–0849. Charles C. Ryan, Ed. Stories, 2,500 to 6,000 words, with a unique scientific idea, human or alien character, plot, and theme of lasting value; "must be science fiction, no fantasy, horror, or sword and sorcery." Pays $250. Send SASE for guidelines.

AIM MAGAZINE—P.O. Box 20554, Chicago, IL 60620. Ruth Apilado, Ed. Short stories, 800 to 3,000 words, geared to promoting racial harmony and peace. Pays from $15 to $25, on publication. Annual contest.

ALFRED HITCHCOCK'S MYSTERY MAGAZINE—380 Lexington Ave., New York, NY 10017. Cathleen Jordan, Ed. Well-plotted, plausible mystery, suspense, detection and crime stories, to 14,000 words; "ghost stories, humor, futuristic or atmospheric tales are all possible, as long as they include a crime or the suggestion of one." Pays 5¢ a word, on acceptance. Guidelines with SASE.

ALOHA, THE MAGAZINE OF HAWAII AND THE PACIFIC—49 S. Hotel St., Suite 309, Honolulu, HI 96813. Cheryl Tsutsumi, Ed. Fiction to 4,000 words, with a Hawaii focus. Pays $150 to $300, on publication. Query.

ANALOG: SCIENCE FICTION/SCIENCE FACT—380 Lexington Ave., New York, NY 10017. Stanley Schmidt, Ed. Science fiction with strong characters in believable future or alien setting: short stories, 2,000 to 7,500 words; novelettes, 10,000 to 20,000 words; serials, to 70,000 words. Pays 5¢ to 8¢ a word, on acceptance. Query for novels.

THE ATLANTIC—745 Boylston St., Boston, MA 02116. William Whitworth, Ed. Short stories, 2,000 to 6,000 words, of highest literary quality, with "fully developed narratives, distinctive characterization, freshness in language, and a resolution of some kind." Pays excellent rates, on acceptance.

THE ATLANTIC ADVOCATE—P.O. Box 3370, Fredericton, N.B., Canada E3B 5A2. Marilee Little, Ed. Fiction, 1,000 to 1,500 words, with regional angle. Pays to 10¢ a word, on publication.

ATLANTIC SALMON JOURNAL—1435 St. Alexandre, Suite 1030, Montreal, Quebec, Canada H3A 2G4. Terry Davis, Ed. Fiction, 1,500 to 2,500 words, related to angling or conservation of Atlantic salmon. Pays $100 to $325, on publication.

THE BOSTON GLOBE MAGAZINE—*The Boston Globe*, Boston, MA 02107. Ande Zellman, Ed. Short stories, to 3,000 words. Include SASE. Pays on acceptance.

BOYS' LIFE—1325 Walnut Hill Ln., P.O. Box 152079, Irving, TX 75015–2079. W.E. Butterworth IV, Fiction Ed. Publication of the Boy Scouts of America. Humor, mystery, SF, adventure, 500 to 1,200 words, for 8- to 18-year-old boys; study back issues. Pays from $750, on acceptance. Send SASE for guidelines.

BUFFALO SPREE MAGAZINE—Box 38, Buffalo, NY 14226. Johanna V. Shotell, Ed. Fiction and humor, to 1,800 words, for readers in the western New York region. Pays $75 to $100, on publication.

CAMPUS LIFE—465 Gundersen Dr., Carol Stream, IL 60188. James Long, Man. Ed. Fiction and humor, reflecting Christian values (no overtly religious material), 1,000 to 4,000 words, for high school and college students. Pays from $150 to $400, on acceptance. Limited free-lance market. Queries only; SASE.

CAPPER'S—616 Jefferson Ave., Topeka, KS 66607. Nancy Peavler, Ed. Short novel-length family-oriented or romance stories. Also very limited market for short stories, 5,000 to 7,000 words, that can be divided into two or three installments. Pays $75 to $200. Submit complete manuscript.

CAT FANCY—P.O. Box 6050, Mission Viejo, CA 92690. K.E. Segnar, Ed. Fiction and nonfiction, to 3,000 words, about cats. Pays 5¢ a word, on publication.

CATHOLIC FORESTER—P.O. Box 3012, 425 W. Shuman Blvd., Naperville, IL 60566–7012. Barbara A. Cunningham, Ed. Official publication of the Catholic Order of Foresters. Fiction, to 3,000 words (prefer shorter); "looking for more contemporary, meaningful stories dealing with life today." No sex or violence or "preachy" stories; religious angle not required. Pays from 5¢ a word, on acceptance.

CAVALIER—2600 Douglas Rd., Suite 602, Coral Gables, FL 33134. Maurice DeWalt, Fiction Ed. Sexually oriented fiction, to 3,000 words, for sophisticated young men. Pays to $250, on publication.

CLINTON STREET—P.O. Box 3588, Portland, OR 97208. David Milholland, Ed. Short stories, 2 to 20 pages: "First-person accounts, thought-provoking, non-rhetorical essays, and idea pieces." Pays varying rates, on publication.

COBBLESTONE—30 Grove St., Peterborough, NH 03458. Carolyn P. Yoder, Ed. Fiction must relate to monthly theme, 500 to 1,200 words, for children aged 8 to 14 years. Pays 10¢ to 15¢ a word, on publication. Send SASE for editorial guidelines.

COMMENTARY—165 E. 56th St., New York, NY 10022. Marion Magid, Ed. Fiction, of high literary quality, on contemporary social or Jewish issues. Pays on publication.

COSMOPOLITAN—224 W. 57th St., New York, NY 10019. Betty Kelly, Fiction and Books Ed. Short shorts, 1,500 to 3,000 words, and short stories, 4,000 to 6,000 words, focusing on contemporary man-woman relationships. Solid, upbeat plots, sharp characterization; female protagonists preferred. Pays $800 for short shorts; $1,500 to $2,500 for short stories.

COUNTRY WOMAN—P.O. Box 643, Milwaukee, WI 53201. Kathy Pohl, Man. Ed. Fiction, 750 to 1,000 words, of interest to rural women; protagonist must be a country woman. "Stories should focus on life in the country, its problems and joys, as experienced by country women; must be upbeat and positive." Pays $90 to $125, on acceptance.

CRICKET—Box 300, Peru, IL 61354. Marianne Carus, Pub./Ed.-in-Chief. Fiction, 200 to 1,500 words, for 6- to 14-year-olds. Pays to 25¢ a word, on publication. Return postage required.

DISCOVERIES—6401 The Paseo, Kansas City, MO 64131. Address Middler Ed. Fiction, 600 to 1,000 words, for children grades 3 to 6, defining Christian experiences and values. Pays 3½¢ a word, on acceptance.

DIVER MAGAZINE—295–10991 Shellbridge Way, Richmond, B.C., Canada V6X 3C6. Peter Vassilopoulos, Pub./Ed. Fiction related to diving. Humor. Pays $2.50 per column inch, on publication. Query.

EASYRIDERS MAGAZINE—P. O. Box 3000, Agoura Hills, CA 91301–0800. Keith Ball, Ed. Fiction, 3,000 to 5,000 words. Pays from 10¢ a word, on acceptance.

ELLERY QUEEN'S MYSTERY MAGAZINE—380 Lexington Ave., New York, NY 10017. Eleanor Sullivan, Ed. High-quality detective, crime, and mystery stories, 4,000 to 6,000 words; "we like a mix of classic detection and suspenseful crime." "First Stories" by unpublished writers. Pays 3¢ to 8¢ a word, on acceptance.

ESQUIRE—1790 Broadway, New York, NY 10019. Terry McDonell, Ed.-in-Chief. Send finished manuscript of short story. (Only one at a time.) No full-length novels. No pornography, science fiction, or "true romance" stories.

EVANGEL—Light and Life Press, Box 535002, Indianapolis, IN 46253. Vera

Bethel, Ed. Free Methodist. Fiction, 1,200 words, with personal faith in Christ shown as instrumental in solving problems. Pays $45, on publication.

FAMILY CIRCLE—110 Fifth Ave., New York, NY 10011. Kathy Sagan, Fiction Ed. Very limited market: seeks quality short stories and short shorts that reflect real-life situations and seasonal material. No unsolicited manuscripts.

FAMILY MAGAZINE—P.O. Box 4993, Walnut Creek, CA 94596. Address Editors. Short stories, to 2,000 words, of interest to high school-educated military wives between 20 and 35. Pays from $100 to $300, on publication.

FICTION INTERNATIONAL—English Dept., San Diego State Univ., San Diego, CA 92182. Harold Jaffe and Larry McCaffery, Eds. Post-modernist and politically committed fiction and theory. Submit between Sept. 1st and Jan. 1st.

FIRST FOR WOMEN—P.O. Box 1649, Englewood Cliffs, NJ 07632. Bibi Wein, Fiction Ed. Well-written, mainstream stories, 3,500 to 4,500 words, reflecting the concerns of contemporary women; no formula or experimental fiction. Also: short-shorts, 850 to 1,000 words. A humorous twist is welcome. Pay varies, on acceptance. SASE. Do not query for fiction. Allow 8 to 10 weeks for response.

FLY ROD & REEL—P.O. Box 370, Camden, ME 04843. James E. Butler, Man. Ed. Occasional fiction, 2,000 to 2,500 words, related to fly fishing. Payment varies, on publication.

GALLERY—401 Park Ave. S., New York, NY 10016. Marc Lichter, Ed. Dir. John Bowers, Fiction Ed. Fiction, to 3,000 words, for sophisticated men. Slice-of-life, coming of age, rites of passage, mystery, and adventure genres most preferred. Looking for serious fiction with believable characters and believable actions. Pays varying rates, half on acceptance, half on publication.

GOLF DIGEST—5520 Park Ave., Trumbull, CT 06611. Jerry Tarde, Ed. Unusual or humorous stories, to 2,000 words, about golf; golf "fables," to 1,000 words. Pays 50¢ a word, on acceptance.

GOOD HOUSEKEEPING—959 Eighth Ave., New York, NY 10019. Lee Quarfoot, Fiction Ed. Short stories, 1,000 to 3,000 words, with strong identification figures for women, by published writers and "beginners with demonstrable talent." Novel condensations or excerpts. Pays top rates, on acceptance. Do not send SASE; no manuscripts will be returned.

GUN DOG—1901 Bell Ave., Des Moines, IA 50315. Bob Wilbanks, Man. Ed. Occasional fiction, humor related to gun dogs and bird hunting. Pays $100 to $350, on acceptance.

HICALL—1445 Boonville Ave., Springfield, MO 65802–1894. Deanna Harris, Ed. Fiction, to 1,500 words, for 15- to 19-year-olds. Strong evangelical emphasis a must: believable characters working out their problems according to biblical principles. Pays 3¢ a word for first rights, on acceptance.

HIGHLIGHTS FOR CHILDREN—803 Church St., Honesdale, PA 18431. Kent L. Brown Jr., Ed. Fiction on sports, humor, adventure, mystery, etc., 900 words, for 9- to 12-year-olds. Easy rebus form, 100 to 150 words, and easy-to-read stories, to 600 words, for beginning readers. "We are partial to stories in which the protagonist solves a dilemma through his own resources, rather than through luck or magic." Pays from 14¢ a word, on acceptance. Buys all rights.

HOMETOWN PRESS—2007 Gallatin St., Huntsville, AL 35801. Jeffrey C. Hindman, Ed.-in-Chief. Fiction, 800 to 2,500 words, well-crafted and tightly written, suitable for family reading. New and unpublished writers welcome. SASE for guidelines.

ISAAC ASIMOV'S SCIENCE FICTION MAGAZINE—380 Lexington Ave., New York, NY 10017. Gardner Dozois, Ed. Short science fiction and fantasies, to 15,000 words. Pays 6¢ to 8¢ a word, on acceptance.

LADIES' HOME JOURNAL—100 Park Ave., New York, NY 10017. Fiction with strong identification for women. Short stories and full-length manuscripts accepted through agents only.

LIVE—Gospel Publishing House, 1445 Boonville Ave., Springfield, MO 65802. Christian fiction and true stories, 1,100 to 2,000 words; poems; applying biblical principles to perplexing issues facing adults today. Pays 2¢ to 3¢ a word, on acceptance. Send SASE for guidelines.

LOLLIPOPS—Good Apple, Inc., P. O. Box 299, Carthage, IL 62321–0299. Jerry Aten, Ed. Teaching ideas and activities covering all areas of the curriculum for preschool to second-grade children. Rates vary.

THE LOOKOUT—8121 Hamilton Ave., Cincinnati, OH 45231. Simon J. Dahlman, Ed. Inspirational short-shorts, 1,000 to 1,800 words. Pays to 7¢ a word, on acceptance. No historical fiction, science fiction, or fantasy.

MADEMOISELLE—350 Madison Ave., New York, NY 10017. Eileen Schnurr, Fiction Ed. Short stories, 1,500 to 5,000 words, of interest to young single women. Looking for strong voices, fresh insights, generally classic form; no genre fiction. Male point-of-view about personal relationships welcome. Pays $1,000 for short shorts, to $2,000 for stories, on acceptance.

THE MAGAZINE OF FANTASY AND SCIENCE FICTION—Box 56, Cornwall, CT 06753. Edward Ferman, Ed. Fantasy and science fiction stories, to 10,000 words. Pays 5¢ to 7¢ a word, on acceptance.

MATURE LIVING—127 Ninth Ave. N., Nashville, TN 37234. Judy Pregel, Asst. Ed. Fiction, 900 to 1,200 words, for senior adults. Must be consistent with Christian principles. Pays 5¢ a word, on acceptance.

MIDSTREAM—515 Park Ave., New York, NY 10022. Fiction on Jewish themes, to 3,000 words. Pays 5¢ a word, after publication.

MILITARY LIFESTYLE MAGAZINE—1732 Wisconsin Ave. N.W., Washington, DC 20007. Hope Daniels, Ed. Fiction, to 2,000 words, for military families in the U.S. and overseas. Pays from $300 to $500, on publication.

MODERN SHORT STORIES—4820 Alpine Pl., Bldg. A, Suite 101, Las Vegas, NV 89107. Submit to Glenn Steckler, Submissions Ed., P.O. Box 2513, Telluride, CO 81435. Serious fiction, humor, romance, and science fiction (1,000 to 5,000 words) and shorter stories (1,000 to 2,500 words). "We are interested in publishing the widest variety of material possible and exposing our readership to the newest trends in fiction." Pays $50 to $100 for stories.

MS.—One Times Square, New York, NY 10036. No unsolicited fiction or poetry.

NA'AMAT WOMAN—200 Madison Ave., 21st Fl., New York, NY 10016. Judith A. Sokoloff, Ed. Short stories, approximately 2,500 words, with Jewish theme. Pays 8¢ a word, on publication.

NEVADAN—P.O. Box 70, Las Vegas, NV 89125–0070. K.J. Evans, Ed. Sunday magazine of the *Las Vegas Review-Journal*. Fiction, to 1,000 words, with local or regional angle (Nevada, northern Arizona, southern Utah, and California desert). Query for articles. Send SASE for guidelines and sample issue. Pays $200 to $300 for fiction; to $650 for nonfiction, on publication.

THE NEW YORKER—25 W. 43rd St., New York, NY 10036. Fiction Dept. Short stories, humor, and satire. Pays according to length, on acceptance. Include SASE.

OMNI—1965 Broadway, New York, NY 10023–5965. Ellen Datlow, Fiction Ed. Strong, realistic science fiction, to 12,000 words. Some contemporary hard-edged fantasy. Pays to $2,250, on acceptance.

PENTHOUSE—1965 Broadway, New York, NY 10023. No unsolicited manuscripts.

PLAYBOY—680 N. Lakeshore Dr., Chicago, IL 60611. Alice K. Turner, Fiction Ed. Quality fiction, 1,000 to 8,000 words (average 6,000): suspense, mystery, adventure, and sports short stories; stories about contemporary relationships; science fiction. Active plots, masterful pacing, and strong characterization. Pays from $2,000 to $5,000, on acceptance.

PLOUGHSHARES—Emerson College, 100 Beacon St., Boston, MA 02116. Address Editors. Serious fiction, to 6,000 words. Poetry. Pays $10 to $50, on publication. Reading periods and themes vary; check most recent issue.

PRIME TIMES—2802 International Ln., Suite 210, Madison, WI 53704. Rod Clark, Exec. Ed. Circulates to approximately 300,000 mid-life readers. Excellent fiction, to 2,500 words, shorter lengths preferred; general themes. Pays varying rates, on publication. Query first.

PURPOSE—616 Walnut Ave., Scottdale, PA 15683–1999. James E. Horsch, Ed. Fiction, 1,000 words, on problem solving from a Christian point of view. Poetry, 3 to 12 lines. Pays up to 5¢ a word, to $1 per line for poetry, on acceptance.

RANGER RICK—8925 Leesburg Pike, Vienna, VA 22184–0001. Deborah Churchman, Fiction Ed. Nature- and conservation-related fiction, for 7- to 12-year-olds. Maximum: 900 words. Pays to $550, on acceptance. Buys all rights.

REDBOOK—224 W. 57th St., New York, NY 10019. Dawn Raffel, Fiction Ed. Fresh, distinctive short stories, of interest to women, about love and relationships, friendship, careers, parenting, family dilemmas, confronting basic problems of contemporary life issues. Pays $850 for short-shorts (up to 9 manuscript pages), from $1,000 for short stories (to 20 pages). Allow 12 weeks for reply. Manuscripts without SASE will not be returned. No unsolicited novellas or novels accepted. No guidelines available.

ROAD KING—P.O. Box 250, Park Forest, IL 60466. George Friend, Ed. Short stories, 1,200 to 1,500 words, for and/or about truck drivers. Pays to $400, on acceptance.

ST. ANTHONY MESSENGER—1615 Republic St., Cincinnati, OH 45210. Norman Perry, O.F.M., Ed. Barbara Beckwith, Man. Ed. Fiction that makes readers think about issues, lifestyles, and values. Pays 14¢ a word, on acceptance. Queries or manuscripts accepted.

SASSY—One Times Square, New York, NY 10036. Christina Kelly, Fiction Ed. Short stories written in the magazine's style, 1,000 to 3,000 words, for girls age 14 to 19. Pays $1,500, on acceptance.

SCHOLASTIC SCOPE—Scholastic, Inc., 730 Broadway, New York, NY 10003. Deborah Sussman, Ed. Fiction for 15- to 18-year-olds, with 4th to 6th grade reading ability. Short stories, 400 to 1,200 words, on teenage interests and relationships; family, job, and school situations. Plays to 5,000 words. Pays good rates, on acceptance.

SEA KAYAKER—6327 Seaview Ave. N.W., Seattle, WA 98107. Christopher Cunningham, Ed. Short stories exclusively related to ocean kayaking, 1,000 to 3,000 words. Pays on publication.

SEVENTEEN—850 Third Ave., New York, NY 10022. Adrian LeBlanc, Fiction Ed. High-quality, literary short fiction focusing on the teenage experience. Pays on acceptance.

SPORTS AFIELD—250 W. 55th St., New York, NY 10019. Tom Paugh, Ed. Occasional fiction, on hunting, fishing, and related topics. Outdoor adventure stories. Humor. Pays top rates, on acceptance.

SPORTS CARD TRADER—3 Fairchild Ct., Plainview, NY 11518. Douglas Kale, Ed. Monthly. Fiction, from 1,000 words, related to baseball, football, basketball, and hockey cards. Pays 7¢ per word, on publication.

STRAIGHT—8121 Hamilton Ave., Cincinnati, OH 45231. Carla Crane, Ed. Well-constructed fiction, 1,000 to 1,500 words, showing Christian teens using Bible principles in everyday life. Contemporary, realistic teen characters a must. Most interested in school, church, dating, and family life stories. Pays 3¢ to 7¢ a word, on acceptance. Send SASE for guidelines.

SUNDAY DIGEST—850 N. Grove Ave., Elgin, IL 60120. Ronda Oosterhoff, Ed. Short stories, 1,000 to 1,500 words, with evangelical religious slant. Pays 10¢ a word, on acceptance. Query.

SUNSHINE MAGAZINE—Sunshine Press, Litchfield, IL 62056. Peggy Kuethe, Ed. Wholesome fiction, 900 to 1,200 words; short stories for youths, 400 words. Pays $10 to $100, on acceptance. Guidelines. Include SASE.

SWANK—1700 Broadway, New York, NY 10019. Bob Rosen, Fiction Ed. Graphic erotic short stories, to 2,500 words. Study recent issue before submitting material. Pays on publication. Limited market.

TAMPA BAY LIFE—Bayport Plaza, Suite 990, 6200 Courtney Campbell Causeway, Tampa, FL 33607–1458. David J. Wilson, Ed. Fiction, 1,200 to 2,000 words. Must have a regional base/flavor. Payment varies, on publication.

'TEEN—8490 Sunset Blvd., Los Angeles, CA 90069. Address Fiction Dept. Short stories, 2,500 to 4,000 words: mystery, teen situations, adventure, romance, humor for teens. Pays from $100, on acceptance.

TEENS TODAY—Nazarene Publishing House, 6401 The Paseo, Kansas City, MO 64131. Karen DeSollar, Ed. Short stories, 1,200 to 1,500 words, that deal with teens demonstrating Christian principles in real-life situations. Pays 4¢ a word (3½¢ a word for reprints), on acceptance.

TQ/TEEN QUEST—Box 82808, Lincoln, NE 68501. Karen Christianson, Man. Ed. Fiction, 1,000 to 2,000 words, for Christian teens. Pays 8¢ to 15¢ a word, on acceptance.

UNIQUE—P.O. Box 1224, Bridgeview, IL 60455. Tamara Sellman, Assoc. Ed. Bimonthly. Articles on politics, social issues, and personalities. Stories (mystery, fantasy, horror, science fiction, adventure, and social realism), 1,000 to 6,000 words. Pays 5¢ a word, on acceptance. Guidelines.

VIRTUE—P.O. Box 850, Sisters, OR 97759. Marlee Alex, Ed. Fiction with a Christian slant. Pays 15¢ to 25¢ a word, on acceptance. Query required.

WESTERN PEOPLE—Box 2500, Saskatoon, Sask., Canada S7K 2C4. Short stories, 850 to 1,800 words, on subjects or themes of interest to rural readers in western Canada. Pays $80 to $150, on acceptance. Enclose international reply coupons and SAE.

WIGWAG—14 E. 4th St., New York, NY 10012. Claudia Rowe, Submissions Ed. Fiction of varying lengths. "Readership includes educated people, but more importantly, people who like to read." Payment varies, on publication. Published monthly, except in Jan. and July.

WILDFIRE—Bear Tribe Publishing, P.O. Box 9167, Spokane, WA 99209. Matthew Ryan, Ed. Fiction, 900 to 4,500 words, with a nature-based focus on spirituality, personal development, alternative lifestyles, natural healings, and ecology. Poetry, to 20 lines. Pays $250, on publication.

WILDFOWL—1901 Bell Ave., Suite #4, Des Moines, IA 50315. R. Sparks, Man. Ed. Occasional fiction, humor, related to duck hunters and wildfowl. Pays $200 to $350, on acceptance.

WOMAN'S WORLD—270 Sylvan Ave., Englewood Cliffs, NJ 07632. Jeanne Muchnick, Fiction Ed. Fast-moving short stories, about 3,600 words, with light romantic theme. Mini-mysteries, 1,600 to 1,700 words, with "whodunit" or "howdunit" theme. No science fiction, fantasy, or historical romance. Pays $1,000 for short stories, $500 for mini-mysteries, on acceptance. Submit manuscript with SASE.

WOMEN'S HOUSEHOLD—306 E. Parr Rd., Berne, IN 46711. Allison Ballard, Ed. Romance stories, 1,500 words. Pays $40 to $250, on publication.

WOODMEN OF THE WORLD MAGAZINE—1700 Farnam St., Omaha, NE 68102. George M. Herriott, Ed. Family-oriented fiction. Pays 10¢ a word, on acceptance.

YANKEE—Yankee Publishing Co., Dublin, NH 03444. Judson Hale, Ed. Edie Clark, Fiction Ed. High-quality, literary short fiction, to 3,000 words, with setting in or compatible with New England; no sap buckets or lobster pot stereotypes. Pays $1,000, on acceptance.

DETECTIVE AND MYSTERY

ALFRED HITCHCOCK'S MYSTERY MAGAZINE—380 Lexington Ave., New York, NY 10017. Cathleen Jordan, Ed. Well-plotted mystery, detective, suspense, and crime fiction, up to 14,000 words. Submissions by new writers strongly encouraged. Pays 5¢ a word, on acceptance. Guidelines with SASE.

ARMCHAIR DETECTIVE—129 W. 56th St., New York, NY 10019. Kathy Daniel, Ed. Articles on mystery and detective fiction; short stories; biographical sketches, reviews, etc. Pays $10 a printed page for nonfiction; fiction payment varies; reviews are unpaid.

ELLERY QUEEN'S MYSTERY MAGAZINE—380 Lexington Ave., New York, NY 10017. Eleanor Sullivan, Ed. Detective, crime, and mystery fiction, approximately 4,000 to 6,000 words. No sex, sadism, or sensationalism. Particularly interested in new writers and "first stories." Pays 3¢ to 8¢ a word, on acceptance.

FRONT PAGE DETECTIVE—See *Inside Detective*.

INSIDE DETECTIVE—Reese Communications, Inc., 460 W. 34th St., New York, NY 10001. Rose Mandelsberg, Ed. Timely, true detective stories, 5,000 to

6,000 words, or 10,000 words. No fiction. Pays $250 to $500, extra for photos, on acceptance. Query. Same address and requirements for *Front Page Detective*.

MASTER DETECTIVE—460 W. 34th St., New York, NY 10001. Art Crockett, Ed. Detailed articles, 5,000 to 6,000 words, with photos, on current cases, emphasizing human motivation and detective work. No fiction. Pays to $250, on acceptance. Query.

OFFICIAL DETECTIVE STORIES—460 W. 34th St., New York, NY 10001. Art Crockett, Ed. True detective stories, 5,000 to 6,000 words, on current investigations, strictly from the investigator's point of view. No fiction. Photos. Pays $250, extra for photos, on acceptance. Query.

P.I. MAGAZINE—755 Bronx Ave., Toledo, OH 43609. Bob Mackowiak, Ed. Fiction, 2,500 to 5,000 words, and profiles of professional investigators containing true accounts of their most difficult cases; puzzles. Pays $10 to $25, plus copies, on publication.

TRUE DETECTIVE—460 W. 34th St., New York, NY 10001. Art Crockett, Ed. Articles, from 5,000 words, with photos, on current police cases, emphasizing detective work and human motivation. No fiction. Pays $250, extra for photos, on acceptance. Query.

SCIENCE FICTION AND FANTASY

ABORIGINAL SF—P.O. Box 2449, Woburn, MA 01888–0849. Charles C. Ryan, Ed. Short stories, 2,500 to 5,500 words, and poetry, 1 to 2 typed pages, with strong science content, lively, unique characters, and well-designed plots. No sword and sorcery or fantasy. Pays $250 for fiction, $20 for poetry, $4 for SF jokes, and $20 for cartoons, on publication.

ANALOG: SCIENCE FICTION/SCIENCE FACT—380 Lexington Ave., New York, NY 10017. Stanley Schmidt, Ed. Science fiction, with strong characters in believable future or alien setting: short stories, 2,000 to 7,500 words; novelettes, 10,000 to 20,000 words; serials, to 80,000 words. Also uses future-related articles. Pays to 7¢ a word, on acceptance. Query on serials and articles.

THE ASYMPTOTICAL WORLD—P.O. Box 1372, Williamsport, PA 17703. Michael H. Gerardi, Ed. Psychodramas and fantasy, 1,500 to 2,500 words. Illustrations, photographs. Pays 2¢ a word, on acceptance.

BEYOND: SCIENCE FICTION & FANTASY—P.O. Box 1124, Fair Lawn, NJ 07410. Roberta Rogow, Ed. Science fiction and fantasy: original, exciting, thought-provoking fiction (3,000 to 5,000 words), and poems (10 to 20 lines). Pays ¼¢ a word, on publication.

DARK SIDE—Route 3, Box 272-D, Ripley, MS 38663. Shannon Riley, Ed./Pub. Horror fiction, to 3,000 words; reviews of films and books in the genre and interviews with professional writers and editors/publishers, to 1,200 words; horror and dark poetry, to 40 lines. Digest-size drawings for cover, small inside illustrations. "I seek strong openings, well-developed plots, and endings that are neither predictable nor contrived. Find fresh approaches to known themes!" Pays ½¢ a word for fiction and articles; $5 for poems and small artwork; $10 for cover illustrations, on acceptance. All payments also include 1 free copy. Guidelines.

DRAGON MAGAZINE—P.O. Box 111, Lake Geneva, WI 53147. Roger E. Moore, Ed. Barbara G. Young, Fiction Ed. Articles, 1,500 to 10,000 words, on fantasy and SF role-playing games. Fantasy, 1,500 to 8,000 words. Pays 6¢ to 8¢

a word for fiction, on acceptance. Pays 4¢ a word for articles, on publication. Guidelines (specify article or fiction).

FANTASY MACABRE—P.O. Box 20610, Seattle, WA 98102. Jessica Salmonson, Ed. Fiction, to 3,000 words, including translations. "We look for a tale that is strong in atmosphere, with menace that is suggested and threatening rather than the result of dripping blood and gore." Pays 1¢ a word, to $30 per story, on publication. Also publishes fantasy & terror for poetry-in-prose pieces.

GRUE MAGAZINE—Box 370, Times Square Sta., New York, NY 10108. Peggy Nadramia, Ed. Fiction, 3,500 words, and macabre/surreal poetry of any length. "We seek very visceral, original horror stories with an emphasis on characterization and motivation." Pays ½¢ per word for fiction, $5 per poem, on publication. Allow 3 to 6 months for response.

HAUNTS—Nightshade Publications, Box 3342, Providence, RI 02906. Joseph K. Cherkes, Ed. Horror, science/fantasy, and supernatural short stories with strong characters, 1,500 to 8,000 words. No explicit sexual scenes or gratuitous violence. Pays ¼¢ to ½¢ a word, on publication. Submit June 1 to Dec. 1.

ISAAC ASIMOV'S SCIENCE FICTION MAGAZINE—380 Lexington Ave., New York, NY 10017. Gardner Dozois, Ed. Short, character-oriented science fiction and fantasy, to 15,000 words. Pays 5¢ to 8¢ a word, on acceptance. Send SASE for requirements.

THE LEADING EDGE—3163 JKHB, Provo, UT 84602. Russell W. Asplund, Ed. Tri-annual science fiction and fantasy magazine. Short stories (3,000 to 12,000 words) and some experimental fiction; poems (to 200 lines); and articles (to 8,000 words) on science, scientific speculation, and literary criticism. Fillers and comics. "Do not send originals; manuscripts are marked and critiqued by staff." Pays ½¢ per word with a minimum of $5 for fiction; $4 per published page of poetry; $2 to $4 for fillers; on publication. Guidelines.

THE MAGAZINE OF FANTASY AND SCIENCE FICTION—Box 56, Cornwall, CT 06753. Edward Ferman, Ed. Fantasy and science fiction stories, to 10,000 words. Pays 5¢ to 7¢ a word, on acceptance.

MAGICAL BLEND—Box 11303, San Francisco, CA 94101. Julie Marchasin, Literary Ed. Positive, uplifting articles on spiritual exploration, lifestyles, occult, white magic, new age thought, and fantasy. Fiction and features to 5,000 words. Pays in copies.

NEW BLOOD—540 W. Foothill Blvd., Suite 3730, Glendora, CA 91740. Chris Lacher, Ed. Fiction and poetry considered "too strong" for other periodicals. Interviews and reviews. Pays from 3¢ a word, on acceptance. Eager to work with beginning, less established writers.

NEW DESTINIES—260 Fifth Ave., Suite 3S, New York, NY 10001. Toni Weisskopf, Ed. Magazine published in paperback form. Science fiction, 2,000 words, with companion articles, to 40,000 words. Pays competitive rates, on acceptance. No fantasy. Guidelines.

OMNI—1965 Broadway, New York, NY 10023–1965. Ellen Datlow, Ed. Strong, realistic science fiction, 2,000 to 10,000 words, with good characterizations. Some fantasy. No horror, ghost, or sword and sorcery tales. Pays $1,250 to $2,250, on acceptance.

OWLFLIGHT—1025 55th St., Oakland, CA 94608. Millea Kenin, Ed. Science fiction and fantasy, 3,000 to 8,000 words. Science fiction/fantasy poetry, 8 to

100 lines. Photos, illustrations. Pays 1¢ a word, extra for illustrations, on publication. Send 45¢ SASE for guidelines.

SCIENCE FICTION CHRONICLE—P.O. Box 2730, Brooklyn, NY 11202. Andrew Porter, Ed. News items, 200 to 500 words, for SF and fantasy readers, professionals, and booksellers. Photos and short articles on author signings, events, conventions. Pays 3¢ to 5¢ a word, $5 for photos, on publication.

SPACE AND TIME—138 W. 70th St., #4B, New York, NY 10023. Fantasy fiction, to 12,000 words; science fiction, supernatural, sword and sorcery. Pays ½¢ a word, on acceptance.

THRUST: SCIENCE FICTION & FANTASY REVIEW—8217 Langport Terrace, Gaithersburg, MD 20877. D. Douglas Fratz, Ed. Articles, interviews, 2,000 to 4,000 words, for readers familiar with SF and related literary and scientific topics. Book reviews, 100 to 500 words. Pays 1¢ to 2¢ a word, on publication. Query preferred. SASE for guidelines.

TWISTED—22071 Pinewood Dr., Antioch, IL 60002. Christine Hoard, Ed. Fiction and articles (to 5,000 words); poetry (to 1 page). "No sword and sorcery or hard science fiction. We prefer horror and dark fantasy." Pays in copies.

2 AM—P.O. Box 6754, Rockford, IL 61125–1754. Gretta M. Anderson, Ed. Fiction, of varying lengths. "We prefer dark fantasy/horror; great science fiction and sword and sorcery stories are welcome." Profiles and intelligent commentaries. Poetry, to 50 lines. Pays from ½¢ a word, on acceptance. Guidelines.

WEIRD TALES—P.O. Box 13418, Philadelphia, PA 19101. George H. Scithers, John Betancourt, Darrell Schweitzer, Eds. Fantasy and horror (no SF) up to 20,000 words. Pays 3¢ to 8¢ a word, on acceptance.

CONFESSION AND ROMANCE

INTIMACY—355 Lexington Ave., New York, NY 10017. D. Boyd, Ed. Fiction, 2,000 to 3,000 words, for black women ages 18 to 45; must have contemporary, glamorous plot and contain two romantic and intimate love scenes. Pays $75 to $100, on publication. Same address for *Jive*, geared toward younger women seeking adventure, glamour, and romance. Guidelines.

JIVE—See *Intimacy*.

MODERN ROMANCES—233 Park Ave. S., New York, NY 10003. Cherie Clark King, Ed. Confession stories with reader-identification and strong emotional tone, 2,000 to 10,000 words. Pays 5¢ a word, after publication. Buys all rights.

TRUE EXPERIENCE—233 Park Ave. S., New York, NY 10003. Jean Press Silberg, Ed. Mary Lou Lang, Assoc. Ed. Realistic first-person stories, 4,000 to 8,000 words (short shorts, to 2,000 words), on family life, single life, love, romance, overcoming hardships, psychic/occult occurrences, mysteries. Pays 3¢ a word, after publication.

TRUE LOVE—215 Lexington Ave., New York, NY 10016. Marcia Pomerantz, Ed. Fresh, young, romance stories, on love and topics of current interest. Pays 3¢ a word, a month after publication.

TRUE ROMANCE—233 Park Ave. S., New York, NY 10003. Jean Sharbel, Ed. True, romantic first-person stories, 2,000 to 10,000 words. Love poems. Articles, 300 to 700 words, for young wives and singles. Pays 3¢ a word, a month after publication.

POETRY MARKETS

The following list includes markets for both serious and light verse. Although major magazines pay good rates for poetry, the competition to break into print is very stiff, since editors use only a limited number of poems in each issue. On the other hand, college, little, and literary magazines use a great deal of poetry, and though payment is modest—usually in copies—publication in these journals can establish a beginning poet's reputation, and can lead to publication in the major magazines. Poets will also find a number of competitions offering cash awards for unpublished poems in the *Literary Prize Offers* list.

Poets should also consider local newspapers as possible verse markets. Although they may not specifically seek poetry from free lancers, newspaper editors often print verse submitted to them, especially on holidays and for special occasions.

The market for book-length collections of poetry at commercial publishers is extremely limited. There are a number of university presses that publish poetry collections, however (see *University Presses* and *Poetry Series*), and many of them sponsor annual competitions. Consult the *Literary Prize Offers* list for more information.

ALOHA, THE MAGAZINE OF HAWAII—49 South Hotel St., #309, Honolulu, HI 96813. Cheryl Chee Tsutsumi, Ed. Poetry relating to Hawaii. Pays $25 per poem, on publication.

AMERICA—106 W. 56th St., New York, NY 10019. Patrick Samway, S.J., Literary Ed. Serious poetry, preferably in contemporary prose idiom, 10 to 25 lines. Occasional light verse. Submit 2 or 3 poems at a time. Pays $1.40 per line, on publication. Guidelines.

THE AMERICAN SCHOLAR—1811 Q St. N.W., Washington, DC 20009. Joseph Epstein, Ed. Highly original poetry, 10 to 32 lines, for college-educated, intellectual readers. Pays $50, on acceptance.

THE AMICUS JOURNAL—Natural Resources Defense Council, 40 W. 20th St., New York, NY 10011. Peter Borrelli, Ed. Poetry related to national and international environmental policy. Pays on acceptance.

THE ATLANTIC—745 Boylston St., Boston, MA 02116. Peter Davison, Poetry Ed. Previously unpublished poetry of highest quality. Limited market; only 3 to 4 poems an issue. Interested in new poets. Occasionally uses light verse. Pays excellent rates, on acceptance.

THE ATLANTIC ADVOCATE—P.O. Box 3370, Fredericton, Canada E3B 5A2. Poetry related to Canada's Atlantic provinces. Pays to $5 per column inch, on publication.

CAPPER'S—616 Jefferson St., Topeka, KS 66607. Nancy Peavler, Ed. Traditional poetry and free verse, 4 to 16 lines. Submit up to 6 poems at a time, with SASE. Pays $3 to $6, on acceptance.

CHILDREN'S PLAYMATE—P.O. Box 567, Indianapolis, IN 46206. Elizabeth A. Rinck, Ed. Poetry for children, 6 to 8, on good health, nutrition, exercise, safety, seasonal and humorous subjects. Pays from $10, on publication. Buys all rights.

621

THE CHRISTIAN SCIENCE MONITOR—One Norway St., Boston, MA 02115. April Austin, The Home Forum. Fresh, vigorous nonreligious poems of high quality, on various subjects. Short poems preferred. Pays varying rates, on acceptance. Submit no more than 3 poems at a time.

COBBLESTONE—30 Grove St., Peterborough, NH 03458. Carolyn P. Yoder, Ed. Poetry, to 100 lines, must relate to monthly themes, for 8- to 14-year-olds. Pays varying rates, on publication. Send SASE for guidelines and themes.

COMMONWEAL—15 Dutch St., New York, NY 10038. Rosemary Deen, Poetry Ed. Catholic. Serious, witty poetry. Pays 50¢ a line, on publication. SASE required.

COMPLETE WOMAN—1165 N. Clark St., Chicago, IL 60610. Address Assoc. Ed. Poetry. Pays $10, on publication. SASE necessary for return of material.

COSMOPOLITAN—224 W. 57th St., New York, NY 10019. Teri Karush, Poetry Ed. Poetry about relationships and other topics of interest to young, active women. Pays from $25, on acceptance. SASE required.

COUNTRY WOMAN—P.O. Box 643, Milwaukee, WI 53201. Kathy Pohl, Man. Ed. Traditional rural poetry and light verse, 4 to 30 lines, on rural experiences and country living. Poems must rhyme. Pays $10 to $40, on acceptance.

EVANGEL—Box 535002, Indianapolis, IN 46253. Vera Bethel, Ed. Free Methodist. Devotional or nature poetry, 8 to 16 lines. Pays $5, on publication.

THE EVANGELICAL BEACON—1515 E. 66th St., Minneapolis, MN 55423. George Keck, Ed. Denominational publication of Evangelical Free Church of America. Some poetry related to Christian faith. Pays 4¢ a word, $5 minimum, on publication.

FAMILY CIRCLE—110 Fifth Ave., New York, NY 10011. No unsolicited poetry.

FARM AND RANCH LIVING—5400 S. 60th St., Greendale, WI 53129. Bob Ottum, Ed. Poetry, to 20 lines, on rural people and situations. Photos. Pays $35 to $75, extra for photos, on acceptance and on publication. Query.

GOOD HOUSEKEEPING—959 8th Ave., New York, NY 10019. Rosemary Leonard, Ed. Light, humorous verses, quips, and poems. Pays $25 for four lines, $50 for 6 to 8 lines, on acceptance. Do not send SASE; no manuscripts will be returned.

JOURNEY—Christian Board of Publication, Box 179, St. Louis, MO 63166. Short poems for 12- to 15-year-olds. Pays 30¢ a line, on publication.

LADIES' HOME JOURNAL—100 Park Ave., New York, NY 10017. Short, humorous poetry for "Last Laughs" page only. Must be accessible to women in general. Pays $50 for accepted poetry.

LEATHERNECK—Box 1775, Quantico, VA 22134. W.V. H. White, Ed. Poetry overstocked at present.

MCCALL'S—230 Park Ave., New York, NY 10169. Overstocked.

MARRIAGE & FAMILY —Abbey Press Publishing Div., St. Meinrad, IN 47577. Kass Dotterweich, Man. Ed. Verse on marriage and family. Pays $15, on publication.

MATURE YEARS—201 Eighth Ave. S., P.O. Box 801, Nashville, TN 37202. Donn C. Downall, Ed. United Methodist. Poetry, to 14 lines, on pre-retirement, retirement, seasonal subjects, aging. No saccharine poetry. Pays 50¢ to $1 per line.

MIDSTREAM—515 Park Ave., New York, NY 10022. Murray Zuckoff, Ed. Poetry of Jewish interest. Pays $25, on publication.

THE MIRACULOUS MEDAL—475 E. Chelten Ave., Philadelphia, PA 19144. Robert P. Cawley, C.M., Ed. Catholic. Religious verse, to 20 lines. Pays 50¢ a line, on acceptance.

MODERN BRIDE—475 Park Ave. South, New York, NY 10016. Mary Ann Cavlin, Man. Ed. Short verse of interest to bride and groom. Pays $25 to $35, on acceptance.

THE NATION—72 Fifth Ave., New York, NY 10011. Grace Schulman, Poetry Ed. Poetry of high quality. Pays after publication.

NATIONAL ENQUIRER—Lantana, FL 33464. Michele Cooke, Asst. Ed. Short poems, with traditional rhyming verse, of an amusing, philosophical, or inspirational nature; longer poems of a serious or humorous nature. No experimental poetry. Original epigrams, humorous anecdotes, and "daffynitions." Submit seasonal/holiday material at least 2 months in advance. Pays $25 after publication.

THE NEW YORKER—25 W. 43rd St., New York, NY 10036. First-rate poetry and light verse. Pays top rates, on acceptance. Include SASE.

PENTECOSTAL EVANGEL—1445 Boonville, Springfield, MO 65802. Richard G. Champion, Ed. Journal of Assemblies of God. Religious and inspirational verse, 12 to 30 lines. Pays to 50¢ a line, on acceptance.

PURPOSE—616 Walnut Ave., Scottdale, PA 15683–1999. James E. Horsch, Poetry Ed. Poetry, to 8 lines, with challenging Christian discipleship angle. Pays 50¢ to $1 a line, on acceptance.

ST. JOSEPH'S MESSENGER—P.O. Box 288, Jersey City, NJ 07303. Sister Ursula Maphet, Ed. Light verse and traditional poetry, 4 to 40 lines. Pays $5 to $15, on publication.

THE SATURDAY EVENING POST—1100 Waterway Blvd., Indianapolis, IN 46202. Address Post Scripts Ed. Light verse and humor. Pays $15, on publication.

SEVENTEEN—850 Third Ave., New York, NY 10022. Robert Moritz, Teen Feature Ed. Poetry, to 40 lines, by writers aged 21 and under. Submit up to 5 poems. Pays $15 to $30, after acceptance.

THE UNITED METHODIST REPORTER—P.O. Box 660275, Dallas, TX 75266–0275. Spurgeon M. Dunnam III, Ed. Religious verse, 4 to 16 lines. Pays $2, on acceptance.

WESLEYAN UNIVERSITY PRESS—110 Mt. Vernon St., Middletown, CT 06457–6050. Peter J. Potter, Ed. Books of poetry, 64 to 80 pages. Send complete manuscript. Royalty.

WESTERN PEOPLE—P.O. Box 2500, Saskatoon, Sask., Canada S7K 2C4. Liz Delahey, Man. Ed. Short poetry, with Western Canadian themes. Pays on acceptance. Send International Reply Coupons.

WIGWAG—14 E. 4th St., New York, NY 10012. Elizabeth Macklin, Poetry Ed. Poetry of varying lengths for "people who like to read." Payment varies, on publication. Published monthly, except in Jan. and July.

YANKEE—Yankee Publishing Co., Dublin, NH 03444. Jean Burden, Poetry Ed. Serious poetry of high quality, to 30 lines. Pays $50 per poem for all rights, $35 for first rights, on publication.

POETRY SERIES

The following university presses publish book-length collections of poetry by writers who have never had a book of poems published. Each has specific rules for submission, so before submitting any material, be sure to write well ahead of the deadline dates for further information. Some organizations sponsor competitions for groups of poems; see *Literary Prize Offers*.

CLEVELAND STATE UNIVERSITY POETRY CENTER—Dept. of English, Rhodes Tower, Room 1815, Cleveland, OH 44115. Best volume of poetry submitted between December 15 and March 1 receives publication in the CSU Poetry Series and $1,000. There is a $10 reading fee. Guidelines recommended before submission.

UNIVERSITY OF GEORGIA PRESS—Contemporary Poetry Series, Athens, GA 30602. Poets who have never had a book of poems published may submit book-length poetry manuscripts during the month of September for possible publication. Manuscripts from poets who have published at least one volume of poetry (chapbooks excluded) are considered during the month of January. Send SASE for guidelines before submitting. There is a $10 reading fee.

UNIVERSITY OF PITTSBURGH PRESS—Pitt Poetry Series, Pittsburgh, PA 15260. Poets who have never had a full-length book of poetry published may enter a 48- to 120-page collection of poems to the Agnes Lynch Starrett Poetry Prize between March and April. There is a $10 reading fee. Publication of the winning manuscript and $2,000 are offered. SASE required.

UNIVERSITY OF WISCONSIN PRESS—Poetry Series, 114 N. Murray St., Madison, WI 53715. Ronald Wallace, Administrator. Manuscripts may be submitted during the month of September to the Brittingham Prize in Poetry competition, which offers $500, plus publication in the poetry series, for an unpublished book-length poetry manuscript. Send manuscript-sized SASE with submission and $10 reading fee.

WESLEYAN UNIVERSITY PRESS—110 Mt. Vernon St., Middletown, CT 06457. Considers unpublished book-length poetry manuscripts by poets who have never had a book published, for publication in the Wesleyan New Poets Series. There is no deadline. Submit manuscript, $15 reading fee, and SASE.

YALE UNIVERSITY PRESS—Box 92A, Yale Sta., New Haven, CT 06520. Address Editor, Yale Series of Younger Poets. Conducts Yale Series of Younger Poets Competition, in which the prize is publication of a book-length manuscript of poetry, written by a poet under 40 who has not previously published a volume of poems. Closes in February.

GREETING CARD MARKETS

Greeting card companies often have their own specific requirements for submitting ideas, verse, and artwork. In general, however, each verse or message should be typed, double-space, on a 3x5 or 4x6 card. Use only one side of the card, and be sure to put your name and address in the upper left-hand corner. Keep a copy of every verse or idea you send. (It's also advisable to keep a record of what you've submitted to each publisher.) Always enclose an SASE, and do not send out more than ten verses or ideas in a group to any one publisher. Never send original artwork.

AMBERLEY GREETING CARD COMPANY—11510 Goldcoast Dr., Cincinnati, OH 45249–1695. Ned Stern, Ed. Humorous ideas for birthday, illness, friendship, anniversary, congratulations, "miss you," etc. Send SASE for market letter before submitting ideas. Pays $40. Buys all rights.

BLUE MOUNTAIN ARTS, INC. —P.O. Box 1007, Boulder, CO 80306. Attn: Editorial Staff, Dept. TW. Poetry and prose about love, friendship, family, philosophies, etc. Also material for special occasions and holidays: birthdays, get well, Christmas, Valentine's Day, Easter, etc. No artwork or rhymed verse. Pays $200 per poem published on a notecard.

DAYSPRING GREETING CARDS—Outreach Publications, P.O. Box 1010, Siloam Springs, AR 72761. Joan Aycock, Ed. Relational, inspirational messages that minister love, encouragement, and comfort to the receiver. Holidays, everyday occasions, and special occasion cards. SASE for guidelines. Allow 4 to 6 weeks for response. Pays $30, on acceptance.

FRAVESSI-LAMONT, INC.—11 Edison Pl., Springfield, NJ 07081. Address Editor. Short verse, mostly humorous or sentimental; cards with witty prose. No Christmas material. Pays varying rates, on acceptance.

FREEDOM GREETING CARD COMPANY—P.O. Box 715, Bristol, PA 19007. Submit to Jay Levitt. Traditional and humorous verse and love messages. Inspirational poetry for all occasions. Pays negotiable rates, on acceptance. Query with SASE.

GALLANT GREETINGS CORPORATION—2654 West Medill, Chicago, IL 60647. Ideas for humorous and serious greeting cards.

HALLMARK CARDS, INC.—2501 McGee, Box 419580, Mail Drop 276, Kansas City, MO 64141. Query Carol King for guidelines and release form; include SASE, no samples. Need conversational prose and humor for everyday and seasonal greeting cards. Mostly staff-written; "free lancers must show a high degree of skill and originality."

KALAN—97 S. Union Ave., Lansdowne, PA 19050. Unique and wildly funny messages for birthday and friendship/love studio greeting cards. Humorous ideas for Christmas and Valentine's Day must be sent 9 or 10 months before holiday. One-liners (risqué O.K.) about school, dating, money (or lack thereof), life, sex, etc., for key rings and buttons. Mark submissions "Attn: Editor." Pays $75 per idea purchased. Send SASE for guidelines.

THE MAINE LINE COMPANY—P.O. Box 947, Rockland, ME 04841. Attn: Perri Ardman. Nontraditional humorous cards. Send SASE with two first-class stamps for guidelines. Pays $50 per card.

MERLYN GRAPHICS CORP.—P.O. Box 9087, Canoga Park, CA 91309. B. Galling, Ed. Humorous, risqué, clever greeting card verse. "Funny, not vulgar or x-rated." Pays $50, on publication. Send SASE for guidelines.

NOBLE WORKS—113 Clinton St., Hoboken, NJ 07030. Christopher Noble, Ed. Humorous greeting card ideas and copy. "We like 'Saturday Night Live' style humor." Pays $75 to $150, on publication.

OATMEAL STUDIOS—Box 138 TW, Rochester, VT 05767. Attn: Editor. Humorous, clever, and new ideas needed for all occasions. Query with SASE.

PARAMOUNT CARDS—P.O. Box 6546, Providence, RI 02940–6546. Attn: Editorial Freelance. Everyday material (birthday, illness, sympathy, etc.); prose sentiments (long or short, humorous and conventional); and cute and juvenile sentiments. "We especially need contemporary, alternative market humor." Submit each idea (up to 15) on 3x5 card with name and address on each. Payment varies, on acceptance.

RAINBOW JUNGLE—80 Friend St., Amesbury, MA 01913. Jonathan Peirce, Ed. Greeting card text for holidays, birthdays, anniversaries, personal messages, etc. Poetry, 400 to 600 words long. Pays $25 to $100 for greeting card text, 20¢ a word for poetry, on acceptance.

RECYCLED PAPER PRODUCTS, INC.—3636 N. Broadway, Chicago, IL 60613–4488. Melinda Gordon, Art Mgr. "We're looking for original copy that is hip, flip, and concise." Risqué material considered. Send up to 10 pieces; mock-up ideas (with type and color) preferred. Allow 12 weeks for response. Payment made if design tests well and is picked up for distribution. Guidelines.

RED FARM STUDIO—P.O. Box 347, 334 Pleasant St., Pawtucket, RI 02862. Traditional cards for graduation, wedding, birthday, get-well, anniversary, friendship, new baby, sympathy, Christmas, and Valentine's Day. No studio humor. Pays varying rates. SASE required.

SANGAMON COMPANY—Route 48 West, P.O. Box 410, Taylorville, IL 62568. Address Editorial Dept. Conventional, humorous, inspirational, or conversational prose. Pays competitive rates, on acceptance.

SUNRISE PUBLICATIONS INC.—P.O. Box 2699, Bloomington, IN 47402. Address Editorial Coordinator. Original copy for cards for holidays and everyday. "Submit up to 20 verses, 1 to 4 lines long; simple, to-the-point ideas that could be serious, humorous, or light-hearted, but sincere, without being overly sentimental. Rhymed verse not generally used." SASE required. Allow 2 to 3 months for response. Guidelines. Pays standard rates.

TLC GREETINGS—615 McCall Rd., Manhattan, KS 66502–8512. Michele Johnson, Creative Dir. Humorous and traditional sewing and craft related cards. General humor cards for women for everyday, Christmas, and Valentine's Day. Very few risqué cards purchased. Pays on acceptance. Guidelines.

VAGABOND CREATIONS, INC.—2560 Lance Dr., Dayton, OH 45409. George F. Stanley, Jr., Ed. Greeting cards with graphics only on cover (no copy) and short tie-in copy punch line on inside page: birthday, everyday, Valentine's Day, Christmas, and graduation. Mildly risqué humor with double entendre acceptable. Ideas for illustrated theme stationery. Pays $15, on acceptance.

WARNER PRESS PUBLISHERS—1200 E. Fifth St., Anderson, IN 46012. Cindy Maddox, Product Ed. Sensitive prose and inspirational verse card ideas for boxed assortments; religious themes. Submit everyday ideas Nov. to Jan.; Christmas material June to Aug. Pays $15 to $30, on acceptance. Also accepts poster verses. Send SASE for guidelines before submitting.

WEST GRAPHICS PUBLISHING—238 Capp St., San Francisco, CA 94110. Address Editorial Dept. Outrageous humor concepts, all occasions (especially birthday) and holidays, for photo and illustrated card lines. Submit on 3x5 cards: concept on one side; name, address, and phone number on other. Pays $60 per idea, 30 days after publication.

WILLIAMHOUSE-REGENCY, INC.—28 W. 23rd St., New York, NY 10010. Query Nancy Boecker. Captions for wedding invitations. Payment varies, on acceptance. SASE required.

WILSON FINE ARTS, INC., CAROL—P.O. Box 17394, Portland, OR 97217. Gary Spector, Ed. Carol Wilson, Ed. Humorous copy for greeting cards. Queries preferred. Pays $75 or negotiated royalties, on publication. Guidelines.

COLLEGE, LITERARY AND LITTLE MAGAZINES

FICTION, NONFICTION, POETRY

The thousands of literary journals, little magazines, and college quarterlies published today welcome work from novices and pros alike; editors are always interested in seeing traditional and experimental fiction, poetry, essays, reviews, short articles, criticism, and satire, and as long as the material is well-written, the fact that a writer is a beginner doesn't adversely affect his or her chances for acceptance.

Most of these smaller publications have small budgets and staffs, so they may be slow in their reporting time—several months is not unusual. In addition, they usually pay only in copies of the issue in which published work appears and some—particularly college magazines—do not read manuscripts during the summer.

Publication in the literary journals can, however, lead to recognition by editors of large-circulation magazines, who read the little magazines in their search for new talent. There is also the possibility of having one's work chosen for reprinting in one of the prestigious annual collections of work from the little magazines.

Because the requirements of these journals differ widely, it is always important to study recent issues before submitting work to one of them. Copies of magazines may be in large libraries, or a writer may send a postcard to the editor and ask the price of a sample copy. When submitting a manuscript, always enclose a self-addressed envelope, with sufficient postage for its return.

For a complete list of literary and college publications and little magazines, writers may consult such reference works as *The International Directory of Little Magazines and Small Presses*, published annually by Dustbooks (P.O. Box 100, Paradise, CA 95967).

AEGEAN REVIEW—220 W. 19th St., Suite 2A, New York, NY 10011. Barbara Fields, Ed. Fiction and nonfiction, to 3,000 words, about Greece or by Greeks in translation. Query for drawings. Semiannual. Pays $50 to $100, on publication.

THE AGNI REVIEW—Boston University, Creative Writing Program, 236

Bay State Rd., Boston, MA 02215. Askold Melnyczuk, Ed. Short stories, poetry, essays, and artwork. Pays $8 per page.

ALASKA QUARTERLY REVIEW—Dept. of English, Univ. of Alaska, 3211 Providence Dr., Anchorage, AK 99508. Address Eds. Short stories, novel excerpts, poetry (traditional and unconventional forms). Submit manuscripts between August 15 and May 15. Pays in copies.

ALBATROSS—13498 Darnell Ave., Port Charlotte, FL 33981. Richard Smyth, Richard Brobst, Eds. High-quality poetry: especially interested in ecological and nature poetry; written in narrative form. Interviews with well-known poets. Submit 3 to 5 poems at a time with brief bio. Pays in copies.

ALTERNATIVE FICTION & POETRY—7783 Kensington Ln., Hanover Park, IL 60103. Philip Athans, Ed./Pub. Only very experimental/avant-garde short fiction (less than 8,000 words), poetry, prose, etc. No reviews, nonfiction, SF, horror, or religious. Guidelines. Pays in copies.

THE AMARANTH REVIEW—P.O. Box 56235, Phoenix, AZ 85079. Dana L. Yost, Ed. Semiannual journal of fiction (to 3,500 words) and poetry. Pays in copies and subscription.

AMELIA—329 E St., Bakersfield, CA 93304. Frederick A. Raborg, Jr., Ed. Poetry, to 100 lines; critical essays, to 2,000 words; reviews, to 500 words; belles lettres, to 1,000 words; fiction, to 4,500 words; fine pen and ink sketches; photos. Pays $35 for fiction and criticism, $10 to $25 for other nonfiction and artwork, $2 to $25 for poetry. Annual contest.

THE AMERICAN BOOK REVIEW—Publications Center, Univ. of Colorado, English Dept., Box 494, Boulder, CO 80309. Don Laing, Man. Ed. John Tytell, Rochelle Ratner, Ronald Sukenick, Eds. Book reviews, 700 to 1,200 words. Pays $50 honorarium and copies. Query first.

THE AMERICAN POETRY REVIEW—1704 Walnut St., Philadelphia, PA 19103. Address Eds. Highest quality contemporary poetry. Responds in 10 weeks. SASE a must.

AMERICAN QUARTERLY—National Museum of American History, Smithsonian Institution, Washington, DC 20560. Gary Kulik, Ed. Scholarly essays, 5,000 to 10,000 words, on any aspect of U.S. culture. Pays in copies.

THE AMERICAN SCHOLAR—1811 Q St. N.W., Washington, DC 20009. Joseph Epstein, Ed. Articles, 3,500 to 4,000 words, on science, politics, literature, the arts, etc. Book reviews. Pays $450 for articles, $100 for reviews, on publication.

AMHERST REVIEW—P.O. Box 1811, Amherst College, Amherst, MA 01002. Mark Hayes, Ed. Fiction and other prose, to 6,000 words; poetry to 160 lines. Photos, paintings, drawings, and graphic art. Submit material Sept. through March. SASE required.

ANOTHER CHICAGO MAGAZINE—3709 N. Kenmore, Chicago, IL 60613. Fiction, essays on literature, and poetry. Pays $5 to $25, on acceptance.

ANTAEUS—26 W. 17th St., New York, NY 10011. Daniel Halpern, Ed. Short stories, essays, documents, excerpts, translations, poems. Pays on publication.

ANTIETAM REVIEW—82 W. Washington St., Hagerstown, MD 21740. Ann Knox, Ed.-in-Chief. Fiction, to 5,000 words; poetry and photography. Submissions from regional artists only (MD, PA, WV, VA, DC), from Oct. through Feb. Pays from $25 to $100. Annual Literary Award for fiction.

THE ANTIGONISH REVIEW—St. Francis Xavier Univ., Antigonish, N.S., Canada. George Sanderson, Ed. Poetry; short stories, essays, book reviews, 1,800 to 2,500 words. Pays in copies.

ANTIOCH REVIEW—P.O. Box 148, Yellow Springs, OH 45387. Robert S. Fogarty, Ed. Timely articles, 2,000 to 8,000 words, on social sciences, literature, and humanities. Quality fiction. Poetry. No inspirational poetry. Pays $10 per printed page, on publication.

APALACHEE QUARTERLY—Apalachee Press, P.O. Box 20106, Tallahassee, FL 32316. Barbara Hamby, Pamela Ball, Claudia Johnson, Bruce Boehrer, Paul McCall, Eds. Fiction, to 30 manuscript pages; poems (submit 3 to 5). Pays in copies.

APPALACHIA—299 Gunstock Hill Rd., Gilford, NH 03246. Helen Howe, Poetry Ed. Semiannual publication of the Appalachian Mountain Club. Poems, to 30 lines. Pays in copies.

ARACHNE—162 Sturges St., Jamestown, NY 14701-3233. Susan L. Leach, Ed. Fiction, to 1,500 words. Poetry, submit up to 7. "We are looking for rural material and would like first publication rights." No simultaneous submissions. Quarterly. Pays in copies, on publication.

THE ARCHER—Pro Poets, 2285 Rogers Ln. N.W., Salem, OR 97304. Winifred Layton, Ed. Contemporary poetry, to 30 lines. Pays in copies.

ARIZONA QUARTERLY—Univ. of Arizona, Main Library B-541, Tucson, AZ 85721. Edgar A. Dryden, Ed. Criticism of American literature and culture from a theoretical perspective. No poetry or fiction. Pays in copies.

ARTFUL DODGE—College of Wooster, Wooster, OH 44691. Daniel Bourne and Karen Kovacik, Eds. Fiction, to 20 pages. Literary essays "based on a balance of analysis and insight," to 10 pages. Poetry, including translations of contemporary poets; submit 3 to 6 poems at a time. Long poems encouraged. Annual. Pays $5 plus 2 copies, on publication.

THE ATAVIST—P.O. Box 5643, Berkeley, CA 94705. Robert Dorsett, Loretta Ko, Eds. Poetry and poetry criticism, any length. Translations of original poetry. Pays in copies.

AURA LITERARY/ARTS REVIEW—P.O. Box 76, Univ. Center, UAB, Birmingham, AL 35294. Adam Pierce, Stefanie Truelove, Eds. Fiction and essays on literature, to 7,000 words; book reviews to 4,000 words; poetry; photos. Pays in copies.

BELLES LETTRES—Box 987, Arlington, VA 22216. Janet Mullaney, Ed. Reviews and essays, 250 to 2,000 words, on literature by women. Literary puzzles, interviews, rediscoveries, retrospectives. Query required. Pays in copies.

THE BELLINGHAM REVIEW—The Signpost Press, Inc., 1007 Queen St., Bellingham, WA 98226. Susan Hilton, Ed. Fiction, to 5,000 words, and poetry, any length. Semiannual. Pays in copies and subscription.

BELLOWING ARK—P.O. Box 45637, Seattle, WA 98145. Robert R. Ward, Ed. Short fiction, and poetry and essays of varying lengths, that portray life as a positive, meaningful process. B&W photos; line drawings. Pays in copies.

THE BELOIT FICTION JOURNAL—Box 11, Beloit College, Beloit, WI 53511. Clint McCown, Ed. Short fiction, 1 to 35 pages, on all themes. (No pornography, political propaganda, religious dogma.) Manuscripts read year round. Pays in copies.

BELOIT POETRY JOURNAL—RFD 2, Box 154, Ellsworth, ME 04605. First-rate contemporary poetry, of any length or in any mode. Pays in copies. Send SASE for guidelines.

BITTERROOT—P.O. Box 489, Spring Glen, NY 12483. Menke Katz, Ed.-in-Chief. Poetry, to 50 lines; send poetry books for book reviews; B&W camera-ready drawings. Pays in copies. Annual contests. Send SASE for information.

BLACK BEAR REVIEW—Black Bear Publications, 1916 Lincoln St., Croydon, PA 19020–8026. Ave Jeanne, Ed. Book reviews and contemporary poetry. "We publish poems with social awareness, but any well-written piece is considered." Semiannual. Pays 1 copy.

BLACK RIVER REVIEW—855 Mildred Ave., Lorain, OH 44052. Kaye Coller, Ed. Contemporary poetry, fiction, essays, short book reviews, B&W artwork. No greeting card verse or slick magazine prose. Submit between Jan. 1 and May 1. Pays in copies. Guidelines. SASE required.

THE BLACK WARRIOR REVIEW—P.O. Box 2936, Tuscaloosa, AL 35486–2936. Alicia Griswold, Ed. Fiction; poetry; translations; reviews and essays. Pays varying rates. Annual awards. SASE required.

THE BLOOMSBURY REVIEW—1028 Bannock St., Denver, CO 80204. Tom Auer, Ed. Ray Gonzalez, Poetry Ed. Book reviews, publishing features, interviews, essays, poetry, up to 800 words. Pays $5 to $25, on publication.

BLUE UNICORN—22 Avon Rd., Kensington, CA 94707. Address the Editors. Published in Oct., Feb., and June. "We are looking for originality of image, thought, and music; we rarely use poems over a page long." Submit up to 5 poems. Artwork used occasionally. Pays in one copy.

BLUELINE—English Dept., SUNY, Potsdam, NY 13676. Anthony Tyler, Ed. Reading period Sept. 1 to Dec. 1. Essays, fiction, to 2,500 words, on Adirondack region or similar areas. Poetry, to 44 lines. No more than 5 poems per submission. Pays in copies.

BOSTON REVIEW—33 Harrison Ave., Boston, MA 02111. Margaret Ann Roth, Ed.-in-Chief. Reviews and essays, 800 to 3,000 words, on literature, art, music, film, photography. Original fiction, to 5,000 words. Poetry. Pays $40 to $150.

BOTTOMFISH—21250 Stevens Creek Blvd., Cupertino, CA 95014. Robert Scott, Ed. Stories, vignettes, and experimental fiction, to 5,000 words. Free verse or traditional poetry, any subject, any length. "Our purpose is to give national exposure to new writers and new styles of creative writing." Annual. Pays in copies.

BOULEVARD—2400 Chestnut St., Apt. 3301, Philadelphia, PA 19103. Richard Burgin, Ed. High-quality fiction and articles, to 30 pages; poetry. Published three times a year. Pays to $250, on publication.

BUCKNELL REVIEW—Bucknell Univ., Lewisburg, PA 17837. Interdisciplinary journal in book form. Scholarly articles on arts, science, and letters. Pays in copies.

CAESURA—English Dept., Auburn Univ., Auburn, AL 36849. Lex Williford, Ed. R. T. Smith, Man. Ed. Short stories, to 5,000 words; narrative and lyric poetry, to 150 lines. Pays in copies. Contest for poetry and fiction; prizes depend on funding.

CALLALOO—Dept. of English, University of Virginia, Charlottesville, VA 22903. Charles H. Rowell, Ed. Fiction and poetry by, and critical studies on Afro-

American, Caribbean, and African artists and writers. Payment varies, on publication.

CALLIOPE—Creative Writing Program, Roger Williams College, Bristol, RI 02809. Martha Christina, Ed. Short stories, to 2,500 words; poetry. Pays in copies and subscription. No submissions April through July.

CALYX, A JOURNAL OF ART & LITERATURE BY WOMEN—P.O. Box B, Corvallis, OR 97339. M. Donnelly, Man. Ed. Fiction, 5,000 words, reviews, 1,000 words; poetry, to 6 poems. Pays in copies. Submissions accepted from April through June and Sept. through Nov. Include short bio and SASE. Send for guidelines.

CANADIAN FICTION MAGAZINE—Box 946, Sta. F, Toronto, Ontario, Canada M4Y 2N9. High-quality short stories, novel excerpts, and experimental fiction, to 5,000 words, by Canadians. Interviews with Canadian authors; translations. Pays $10 per page, on publication. Annual prize.

THE CAPE ROCK—Dept. of English, Southeast Missouri State Univ., Cape Girardeau, MO 63701. Harvey E. Hecht, Ed. Poetry, to 70 lines, and B&W photography. (One photographer per issue.) Semiannual. Pays in copies and $200 for best poem in each issue. Pays $100 to photographer.

THE CAPILANO REVIEW—2055 Purcell Way, North Vancouver, B.C., Canada V7J 3H5. Pierre Coupey, Ed. Fiction; poetry; drama; visual arts. Pays $12 to $50.

THE CARIBBEAN WRITER—Univ. of the Virgin Islands, RR 02, Box 10,000, Kingshill, St. Croix, Virgin Islands, U.S. 00850. Erika J. Smilowitz, Ed. Annual. Fiction (to 15 pages, submit up to 2 stories) and poems (no more than five); the Caribbean should be central to the work. Blind submissions policy: place title only on manuscript; name, address, and title of ms. on separate sheet. Reading period is through Oct. for Spring issue of the following year. Pays in copies.

CAROLINA QUARTERLY—Greenlaw Hall CB#3520, Univ. of North Carolina, Chapel Hill, NC 27599–3520. David Kellogg, Ed. Fiction, to 7,000 words, by new or established writers. Poetry (no restrictions on length, though limited space makes inclusion of works of more than 300 lines impractical). Pays $15 for fiction and poetry, on publication.

CATALYST—Atlanta-Fulton Public Library, 1 Margaret Mitchell Sq., Carnegie & Forsyth Sq., Atlanta, GA 30303–1089. Pearl Cleage, Ed. Fiction (to 3,000 words) and poetry by Southern writers, primarily black writers; biannual. Pays to $200, on publication. Send SASE for guidelines and themes.

THE CENTENNIAL REVIEW—110 Morrill Hall, Michigan State Univ., East Lansing, MI 48824–1036. R.K. Meiners, Ed. Articles, 3,000 to 5,000 words, on sciences, humanities, and interdisciplinary topics. Pays in copies.

THE CHARITON REVIEW—Northeast Missouri State Univ., Kirksville, MO 63501. Jim Barnes, Ed. Highest quality poetry and fiction, to 6,000 words. Modern and contemporary translations. Book reviews.

THE CHICAGO REVIEW—Univ. of Chicago, Faculty Exchange Box C, Chicago, IL 60637. Emily McKnight, Anne Myles, David Nicholls, Eds. Essays, interviews, reviews, fiction, translations, poetry. Pays in copies plus one year's subscription.

CHIRON REVIEW—Rt. 2, Box 111, St. John, KS 67576. Michael Hathaway, Ed. Contemporary fiction (to 4,000 words), articles (500 to 1,000 words), and poetry (to 30 lines). Photos. Pays in copies.

CICADA—329 E St., Bakersfield, CA 93304. Frederick A. Raborg, Jr., Ed. Single haiku, sequences or garlands, essays about the forms, haibun and fiction related to haiku or Japan. Pays in copies.

CIMARRON REVIEW—205 Morrill Hall, Oklahoma State Univ., Stillwater, OK 74078–0135. Gordon Weaver, Ed. Poetry, fiction, essays, graphics/artwork. Seeks an individual, innovative style that focuses on contemporary themes. Pays in copies.

CLOCKWATCH REVIEW—Dept. of English, Illinois Wesleyan Univ., Bloomington, IL 61702. James Plath, Ed. Fiction, to 4,000 words, and poetry, to 36 lines. "Our preference is for fresh language, a believable voice, a mature style, and a sense of the unusual with the subject matter." Semiannual. Pays in copies and nominal fee, on publication.

COLLAGES & BRICOLAGES—Office of Int'l Programs, 212 Founders Hall, Clarion Univ. of Pennsylvania, Clarion, PA 16212. Marie-José Fortis, Ed. Fiction, nonfiction, and poetry. Surrealistic and expressionistic drawings in ink. Annual. Pays in copies.

COLORADO REVIEW—English Dept., 359 Eddy, Colorado State Univ., Fort Collins, CO 80523. Poetry, short fiction, translations, interviews, articles on contemporary themes. Submit from September through May 1.

COLUMBIA: A MAGAZINE OF POETRY & PROSE—404 Dodge, Columbia Univ., New York, NY 10027. Address the Editors. Fiction and nonfiction to 5,000 words; poetry; essays; interviews; visual art. Pays in copies. SASE required. Guidelines and annual awards. Reading period: September 1 to April 1.

CONFRONTATION—Dept. of English, C.W. Post of L. I. U., Brookville, NY 11548. Martin Tucker, Ed. Serious fiction, 750 to 6,000 words. Crafted poetry, 10 to 200 lines. Pays $10 to $100, on publication.

THE CONNECTICUT POETRY REVIEW—P.O. Box 3783, New Haven, CT 06525. J. Claire White and James Wm. Chichetto, Eds. Poetry, 5 to 20 lines, and reviews, 700 words. Pays $5 per poem, $10 for a review, on acceptance.

CONNECTICUT RIVER REVIEW—7 Shawnee Ct., Cromwell, CT 06416. Ben Brodinsky, Ed. Poetry journal published twice yearly. Submit 3 to 5 poems, 40 lines or less. Pays in two copies. Guidelines.

COTTON BOLL/ATLANTA REVIEW—Sandy Springs P.O. Box 76757, Atlanta, GA 30358. Mary Hollingsworth, Ed. Short stories to 3,500 words; poetry, to 2 pages. Interviews with known writers. Pays $10 for short stories and $5 for poems, on publication. SASE for guidelines.

CRAB CREEK REVIEW—4462 Whitman N., Seattle, WA 98103. Linda Clifton, Ed. Carol Orlock, Fiction Ed. Clear, dynamic fiction, to 4,000 words, with strong voice and imagery. Nonfiction, to 4,000 words, that "uses image and occasion as a reason to share ideas with an intelligent reader." Poetry, to 80 lines. Published 3 times a year. Pays in copies.

CRAZY QUILT—3341 Adams Ave., San Diego, CA 92116. Address the Editors. Fiction, to 4,000 words, poetry, one-act plays, and literary criticism. Also B&W art, photographs. Pays in copies.

THE CREAM CITY REVIEW—Box 413, Univ. of Wisconsin, Milwaukee, WI 53201. Valerie Ross, Ed. "We serve a national audience interested in a diversity of writing (in terms of style, subject, genre) and writers (gender, race, class, publishing history, etc.). Both well-known and newly published writers of fiction, poetry, and essays are featured, along with B&W artwork and a debate among 3 or more writers on a contemporary literary issue." Payment varies.

THE CRESCENT REVIEW—Box 15065, Winston-Salem, NC 27106. Guy Nancekeville, Ed. Short stories, to 5,000 words. "Especially interested in storytellers who have never been published or who have some connection with the South, but all writers are welcome to submit." Semiannual. Pays in copies.

CUMBERLAND POETRY REVIEW—P.O. Box 120128, Acklen Sta., Nashville, TN 37212. Address Eds. High-quality poetry and criticism; translations. No restrictions on form, style, or subject matter. Pays in copies.

DENVER QUARTERLY—Univ of Denver, Denver, CO 80208. Donald Revell, Ed. Literary, cultural essays and articles; poetry; book reviews; fiction. Pays $5 per printed page, after publication.

DESCANT—Texas Christian Univ., T.C.U. Sta., Fort Worth, TX 76129. Betsy Colquitt, Stanley Trachtenberg, Eds. Fiction, to 6,000 words. Poetry to 40 lines. No restriction on form or subject. Pays in copies. Submit Sept. through May only.

DEVIANCE—P.O. Box 1706, Pawtucket, RI 02862. Lin Collette, Ed. Fiction, to 2,500 words, and nonfiction essays on political and spiritual issues, to 2,500 words. Poetry, any length, and fillers, 25 to 250 words, on "deviant" subjects. No racist, sexist, homophobic work. Query for nonfiction. Published 3 times a year. Pays in copies.

THE DEVIL'S MILLHOPPER—The Devil's Millhopper Press, Coll. of Humanities, Univ. of South Carolina/Aiken,171 University Pkwy., Aiken, SC 29801. Stephen Gardner, Ed. Poetry. Send SASE for guidelines. Pays in copies.

EARTH'S DAUGHTER—Box 41, Central Park St., Buffalo, NY 14215. Fiction (to 1,000 words), poetry (to 40 lines), and B&W photos or drawings. "Finely crafted work with a feminist theme." Published 3 times per year. Pays in copies, on publication.

EMBERS—Box 404, Guilford, CT 06437. Katrina Van Tassel, Mark Johnston, Charlotte Garrett, Eds. A poetry journal published twice yearly. Interested in original new voices as well as published poets.

EOTU, THE MAGAZINE OF EXPERIMENTAL FICTION—#115, 1810 W. State St., Boise, ID 83702. Larry Dennis, Ed. Experimental fiction, to 5,000 words, and experimental poetry, to 2 pages. B&W artwork. "We seek writers working at the edge of their talents and abilities. No taboos—except boring common stuff." Include bio information and SASE. Pays $5 to $25, on acceptance, plus contributor copy.

EVENT—Douglas College, Box 2503, New Westminister, BC, Canada V3L 5B2. Dale Zieroth, Ed. Short fiction, short plays, poetry. Pays modest rates, on publication.

FARMER'S MARKET—P.O. Box 1272, Galesburg, IL 61402. Short stories, essays, and novel excerpts, to 40 pages, and poetry, related to the Midwest. Pays in copies.

FICTION INTERNATIONAL—English Dept., San Diego State Univ., San Diego, CA 92182. Harold Jaffe, Larry McCaffery, Eds. Post-modernist and politically committed fiction and theory. Manuscripts read from September to January 1. Payment varies.

633

THE FIDDLEHEAD—Campus House Univ. of New Brunswick, Fredericton, N.B., Canada E3B 5A3. Serious fiction, 2,500 words, preferably by Canadians. Pays about $10 per printed page, on publication. SAE with international coupons required.

FIELD—Rice Hall, Oberlin College, Oberlin, OH 44074. Stuart Friebert, David Young, Eds. Serious poetry, any length, by established and unknown poets; essays on poetics by poets. Translations by qualified translators. Pays $20 to $30 per page, on publication.

FINE MADNESS—P.O. Box 15176, Seattle, WA 98115–0176. Poetry, any length; short fiction; occasional reviews. Pays varying rates.

FIVE FINGERS REVIEW—553 25th Ave., San Francisco, CA 94121. Socially aware fiction, nonfiction, and poetry that address concerns of the day in surprising ways. Published once or twice a year. Pays in copies.

FOLIO—Dept. of English, American Univ., Washington, DC 20016. James Mitchell and Sara Prigan, Eds. Fiction, reviews, interviews, and essays, to 3,000 words. Photos and drawings. Submissions read Aug. through April. Semiannual. Pays in 1 copy, on publication. Contest.

FOOTWORK, THE PATERSON LITERARY REVIEW—Cultural Affairs Office, Passaic County Comm. College, College Blvd., Paterson, NJ 07509. Maria Gillan, Ed. High quality fiction, to 8 pages, and poetry, to 3 pages, any style. Pays in copies.

FREE INQUIRY—P.O. Box 5, Buffalo, NY 14215–0005. Paul Kurtz, Ed. Tim Madigan, Man. Ed. Articles, 500 to 5,000 words, for "literate and lively readership. Focus is on criticisms of religious belief systems, and how to lead an ethical life without a supernatural basis." Pays in copies.

THE GAMUT—1218 Fenn Tower, Cleveland State Univ., Cleveland, OH 44115. Leonard Trawick, Co-Ed. Lively articles, 2,000 to 6,000 words, on general-interest topics preferably concerned with the region. Quality fiction and poetry. Photos. Pays $25 to $250, on publication. Send SASE for guidelines.

THE GEORGIA REVIEW—Univ. of Georgia, Athens, GA 30602. Stanley W. Lindberg, Ed. Stephen Corey, Assoc. Ed. Short fiction; interdisciplinary essays on arts, sciences, and the humanities; book reviews; poetry. No submissions in June, July, or August.

THE GETTYSBURG REVIEW—Gettysburg College, Gettysburg, PA 17325. Address Dolores Miller. Poetry, fiction, essays, and essay-reviews (on a group of books, films, etc., with an encompassing theme). Pays $2 a line for poetry; $25 per printed page for fiction and nonfiction (1,000 to 20,000 words). Reporting time 3 months.

GRAIN—Box 1154, Regina, Sask., Canada S4P 3B4. Mick Burrs, Ed. Short stories, to 20 typed pages; poems, send up to 6; visual art. Pays $30 to $100 for stories, $100 for cover art, $30 for other art. SAE with international reply coupons required.

GREAT RIVER REVIEW—211 W. 7th St., Winona, MN 55987. Orval Lund, Jr., Ed. Fiction and creative prose, 2,000 to 10,000 words. Quality contemporary poetry; send 4 to 8 poems. Special interest in Midwestern writers and themes.

GREEN'S MAGAZINE—P.O. Box 3236, Regina, Sask., Canada S4P 3H1. David Green, Ed. Fiction for family reading, 1,500 to 4,000 words. Poetry, to 40 lines. Pays in copies.

THE GREENSBORO REVIEW—Univ. of North Carolina, Greensboro, NC 27412. Jim Clark, Ed. Semiannual. Poetry and fiction. Submission deadlines: Sept. 15 and Feb. 15. Pays in copies.

HALF TONES TO JUBILEE—Pensacola Junior College, English Dept., 1000 College Blvd., Pensacola, FL 32504. Walter F. Spara, Ed. Fiction, to 5,000 words, and poetry, to 60 lines. Pays in copies.

HAUNTS —Nightshade Publications, Box 3342, Providence, RI 02906. Joseph K. Cherkes, Ed. Short stories, 1,500 to 8,000 words: horror, science-fantasy, and supernatural tales with strong characters. Pays ¼¢ to ½¢ a word, on publication.

HAWAII REVIEW—Dept. of English, Univ. of Hawaii, 1733 Donagho Rd., Honolulu, HI 96882. Elizabeth Lovell, Ed.-in-Chief. Quality fiction, poetry, interviews, nonfiction essays, and literary criticism reflecting both regional and universal concerns.

HAYDEN'S FERRY REVIEW—Matthew's Center, Arizona State Univ., Tempe, AZ 85287–1502. Selima Keegan, Ed. Fiction, essays, and poetry (submit up to 6 poems). Photos and drawings (clearly marked slides). Include brief bio and SASE. Semiannual. Pays in copies.

HEARTLAND JOURNAL—Box 55115, Madison, WI 53705. Jeri McCormick, Ed. Lenore Coberly, Sr. Ed. Fiction, poetry, children's page, articles, essays, B&W drawings, color slides of artwork. Open-minded about subject matter and length. Writers must be over 60 years old. Pays in copies. Contest.

HERESIES: A FEMINIST PUBLICATION ON ART AND POLITICS— Box 1306, Canal Street Sta., New York, NY 10013. Thematic issues. Fiction, to 20 double-spaced typed pages; nonfiction; poetry; art; photography.

HIGH PLAINS LITERARY REVIEW—180 Adams St., Suite 250, Denver, CO 80206. Robert O. Greer, Ed.-in-Chief. Essays, 3,000 to 6,000 words. Pays $5 a page for prose. Overstocked. Not currently accepting submissions.

THE HIGHLANDER—P.O. Box 397, Barrington, IL 60010. Angus Ray, Ed. Bimonthly. Articles, 1,300 to 1,900 words, related to Scottish history. "We are not concerned with modern Scotland or current problems in Scotland." Pays $100 to $150, on acceptance.

THE HOLLINS CRITIC—P.O. Box 9538, Hollins College, VA 24020. John Rees Moore, Ed. Poetry, to 2 pages. Published 5 times a year. Pays $25, on publication.

HOME LIFE—127 Ninth Ave. N., Nashville, TN 37234. Charlie Warren, Ed. Southern Baptist. Short lyrical verse: humorous, marriage and family, seasonal, and inspirational. Pays to $24 for poetry, 5¢ a word for articles, on acceptance.

HOME PLANET NEWS—P.O. Box 415, Stuyvesant Sta., New York, NY 10009. Enid Dame and Donald Lev, Eds. Quarterly art tabloid. Fiction, to 8 typed pages; reviews, 3 to 5 pages; and poetry, any length. "We are looking for quality poetry, fiction and discerning literary and art reviews." Query for nonfiction. Pays in copies and gift subscription.

HOWLING DOG—10917 W. Outer Dr., Detroit, MI 48223. Mark Donovan, Ed. "Strange" fiction, to 1,500 words. Free verse, avant-garde, wild poetry to 5 pages. "We are looking for pieces with a humorous perspective toward society's problems." Semiannual. Pays in copies, on publication.

HURRICANE ALICE: A FEMINIST QUARTERLY—207 Lind Hall, 207

Church St. S.E., Minneapolis, MN 55455. Articles, fiction, essays, interviews, and reviews, 500 to 3,000 words, with feminist perspective. Pays in copies.

ILLINOIS WRITERS REVIEW—P.O. Box 1087, Champaign, IL 61820. Kevin Stein and Jim Elledge, Eds. Critical reviews, essays, and commentary on contemporary writing, 750 to 2,500 words. B&W cover art and photos. Semiannual. Pays $25, on publication.

INDIANA REVIEW—316 N. Jordan Ave., Bloomington, IN 47405. Renée Manfredi, Fiction Ed. Jon Tribble, Poetry Ed. Fiction with an emphasis on an honest voice as well as style. Poems that are well executed and ambitious. Pays $5 a page.

INLET—Dept. of English, Virginia Wesleyan College,, Norfolk, VA 23502. Joseph Harkey, Ed. Short fiction, 1,000 to 3,000 words (short lengths preferred). Poems of 4 to 40 lines; all forms and themes. Submit between September and March 1st, each year. Pays in copies.

INTERIM—Dept. of English, Univ. of Nevada, Las Vegas, NV 89154. A. Wilber Stevens, Ed. Fiction, to 7,500 words, and poetry. Semiannual. Pays in copies and 2-year subscription.

INVISIBLE CITY—P.O. Box 2853, San Francisco, CA 94126. John McBride, Paul Vangelisti, Eds. Reviews, translations; especially interested in contemporary European literature. Pays in copies.

THE IOWA REVIEW—EPB 308, Univ. of Iowa, Iowa City, IA 52242. David Hamilton, Ed. Essays, poems, stories, reviews. Pays $10 a page for fiction and nonfiction, $1 a line for poetry, on publication.

JACARANDA REVIEW—Dept. of English, Univ. of California, Los Angeles, CA 90024. Bruce Kijewski, Fiction Ed. Carolie Parker and David Case, Poetry Eds. Fiction, to 50 pages, and poetry (submit up to 3 poems). Semiannual. No payment.

KALEIDOSCOPE—United Cerebral Palsy & Services for the Handicapped, 326 Locust St., Akron, OH 44302. Darshan Perusek, Ph.D., Ed. Fiction, essays, interviews, articles, and biographies relating to the arts, to 5,000 words. Poetry and fillers, any length. Photos a plus. Submissions by disabled writers encouraged. Semiannual. Pays $50 for fiction, to $50 for poetry, to $25 for book reviews, to $25 for photos. Guidelines recommended.

KANSAS QUARTERLY—Dept. of English, Denison Hall 122, Kansas State Univ., Manhattan, KS 66506. Literary criticism, art, and history. Fiction and poetry. Pays in copies. Two series of annual awards. Query for articles and special topics.

KARAMU—Dept. of English, Eastern Illinois Univ., Charleston, IL 61920. Peggy Brayfield, Ed. Contemporary or experimental fiction. Poetry. Pays in copies.

THE KENYON REVIEW—Kenyon College, Gambier, OH 43022. Fiction, nonfiction, and humor. Quarterly. Pays $10 a printed page for prose and $15 a printed page for poetry and reviews, on publication.

KIOSK—302 Clemens Hall, SUNY Buffalo, Buffalo, NY 14201. Stephanie Foote and Marten Clibbens, Eds. "Quirky experimental fiction and poetry," as well as interviews and essays. Pays in copies.

LAKE EFFECT—P.O. Box 315, Oswego, NY 13126. Jean O'Connor Fuller, Man. Ed. Short stories, essays, poetry, and humor for a general audience. Pays $25 for fiction and nonfiction, $5 for poems, on publication. Query for nonfiction only.

THE LAKE STREET REVIEW—Box 7188, Powderhorn Sta., Minneapolis, MN 55407. Kevin Fitzpatrick, Ed. Fiction, essays, and creative nonfiction, 500 to 4,500 words. Poems (submit 3 to 5 at a time), any length, and B&W drawings. Annual. Pays in copies, on publication.

THE LEADING EDGE—3163 JKHB, Provo, UT 84602. Russell W. Asplund, Ed. Tri-annual science fiction and fantasy magazine. Short stories (3,000 to 12,000 words); poetry (to 200 lines); and articles (to 8,000 words) on science, scientific speculation, and literary criticism. Fillers and comics. "Do not send originals; manuscripts are marked and critiqued by staff." Pays ½¢ per word with $5 minimum for fiction; $4 per published page of poetry; $2 to $4 for fillers; on publication. SASE for guidelines.

LILITH, THE JEWISH WOMEN'S MAGAZINE—250 W. 57th St., New York, NY 10107. Susan Weidman Schneider, Ed. Fiction, 1,500 to 2,000 words, on issues of interest to Jewish women.

THE LION AND THE UNICORN—English Dept., Brooklyn College, Brooklyn, NY 11210. Geraldine DeLuca, Roni Natov, Eds. Articles, from 2,000 words, offering criticism of children's and young adult books, for teachers, scholars, artists, and parents. Query preferred. Pays in copies.

LITERARY MAGAZINE REVIEW—English Dept., Kansas State Univ., Manhattan, KS 66506. Reviews and articles concerning literary magazines, 1,000 to 1,500 words, for writers and readers of contemporary literature. Pays modest fees and in copies. Query.

THE LITERARY REVIEW—Fairleigh Dickinson Univ., 285 Madison Ave., Madison, NJ 07940. Walter Cummins, Martin Green, Harry Keyishian, William Zander, Eds. Serious fiction; poetry; translations; reviews; essays and reviews on contemporary literature. Pays in copies.

LONG SHOT—P.O. Box 6231, Hoboken, NJ 07030. Danny Shot, Caren Lee Michaelson, Jack Wiler, Eds. Fiction, poetry and nonfiction, to 10 pages. B&W drawings. "No taboos." Pays in copies.

THE LONG STORY—11 Kingston St., N. Andover, MA 01845. Stories, 8,000 to 20,000 words; prefer committed fiction. Pays in copies, on publication.

LYRA—P.O. Box 3188, Guttenberg, NJ 07093. Lourdes Gil and Iraida Iturralde, Eds. Fiction, to 12 double-spaced pages. Essays, translations, interviews, and reviews, 3 to 15 pages. Poetry, any length. Quarterly. Pays in copies and $25 to $30 per book review, on acceptance.

THE MALAHAT REVIEW—Univ. of Victoria, P.O. Box 3045, Victoria, BC, Canada V8W 3P4. Constance Rooke, Ed. Fiction and poetry, including translations. Pays from $20 per page, on acceptance.

THE MANHATTAN REVIEW—440 Riverside Dr., #45, New York, NY 10027. Highest quality poetry. Pays in copies.

MASSACHUSETTS REVIEW—Memorial Hall, Univ. of Massachusetts, Amherst, MA 01003. Literary criticism; articles on public affairs, scholarly disciplines. Short fiction. Poetry. No submissions between June and October. Pays modest rates, on publication. SASE required.

MICHIGAN HISTORICAL REVIEW—Clark Historical Library, Central Michigan Univ., Mt. Pleasant, MI 48859. Address Ed. Scholarly articles related to Michigan's political, social, economic, and cultural history; articles on American,

Canadian, and Midwestern history that directly or indirectly explore themes related to Michigan's past. SASE required.

THE MICKLE STREET REVIEW—326 Mickle St., Camden, NJ 08102. Articles, poems, and artwork related to Walt Whitman. Pays in copies.

MID-AMERICAN REVIEW—Dept. of English, Bowling Green State Univ., Bowling Green, OH 43403. Ken Letko, Ed. High-quality fiction, poetry, articles, translations, and reviews of contemporary writing. Fiction to 20,000 words. Reviews, articles, 500 to 2,500 words. Pays to $50, on publication. Doesn't read manuscripts June through Aug.

MIDWEST QUARTERLY—Pittsburg State Univ., Pittsburg, KS 66762. James B. M. Schick, Ed. Scholarly articles, 2,500 to 5,000 words, on contemporary issues. Pays in copies.

THE MINNESOTA REVIEW—English Dept., SUNY-Stony Brook, Stony Brook, NY 11794. Address the Editors. "Politically committed fiction (3,000 to 6,000 words), nonfiction (5,000 to 7,500 words), and poetry (3 pages maximum), for socialist, marxist, or feminist audience." Pays in copies.

MISSISSIPPI REVIEW—Center for Writers, Univ. of Southern Mississippi, Southern Sta., Box 5144, Hattiesburg, MS 39406–5144. Frederick Barthelme, Ed. Serious fiction, poetry, criticism, interviews. Pays in copies.

THE MISSISSIPPI VALLEY REVIEW—Dept. of English, Western Illinois Univ., Macomb, IL 61455. Forrest Robinson, Ed. Short fiction, to 20 typed pages. Poetry; send 3 to 5 poems. Pays in copies. No guidelines.

THE MISSOURI REVIEW—Dept. of English, 107 Tate Hall, Univ. of Missouri-Columbia, Columbia, MO 65211. Greg Michalson, Man. Ed. Poems, of any length. Fiction and essays. Pays $20 per printed page, on publication.

MODERN HAIKU—P.O. Box 1752, Madison, WI 53701. Robert Spiess, Ed. Haiku and articles about haiku. Pays $1 per haiku, $5 a page for articles.

MONTHLY REVIEW—122 W. 27th St., New York, NY 10001. Paul M. Sweezy, Harry Magdoff, Eds. Analytical articles, 5,000 words, on politics and economics, from independent socialist viewpoint. Pays $50, on publication.

THE MOUNTAIN—P.O. Box 1010, Galax, VA 24333. Address the Editors. Fiction (3,000 to 8,000 words) and general-interest nonfiction (500 to 6,000 words) reflecting mountain region life and on topics of a national political interest. Humor, 10 to 150 words. Pay varies, on publication.

MUSE—P.O. Box 45, Burlington, NC 27216–0045. J. William Griffin, Ed. Poems (up to 36 lines preferred) on any subject, in any form or style. Send up to five poems, typed single spaced. Also articles (to 1,500 words) about writing poetry. Pays $5 per poem; 3¢ word for articles, on publication.

THE NATIONAL STORYTELLING JOURNAL—See *Storytelling Magazine*.

NEBO: A LITERARY JOURNAL—Dept. of English and Foreign Languages, Arkansas Tech. Univ., Russellville, AR 72801–2222. Poetry (submit up to 10); mainstream fiction to 3,000 words; critical essays to 10 pages. Pays 1 copy. Offices closed May through Aug. SASE for guidelines.

NEGATIVE CAPABILITY—62 Ridgelawn Dr. E., Mobile, AL 36608. Sue Walker, Ed. Poetry, any length; fiction, essays, art. Pays $20 per story. Contests.

NER/BLQ—*New England Review and Bread Loaf Quarterly*, Middlebury

College, Middlebury, VT 05753. T.R. Hummer and Maura High, Eds. Fiction, nonfiction, and poetry of varying lengths. "No formula writing; other than that, we're very eclectic." Pays $5 per page, on acceptance, and in copies and subscription.

NEW DELTA REVIEW—c/o Dept. of English, Louisiana State Univ., Baton Rouge, LA 70803–5001. Kathleen Fitzpatrick, Ed. Fiction and nonfiction, 500 to 3,500 words. Poetry, any length. B&W photos or drawings. "We want pieces with raw power behind them." Semiannual. Pays in copies.

NEW LAUREL REVIEW—828 Lesseps St., New Orleans, LA 70117. Lee Meitzen Grue, Ed. Fiction, 10 to 20 pages; nonfiction, to 10 pages; poetry, any length. Library market. No inspirational verse. International readership. Annual. Pays 1 copy.

NEW LETTERS—5100 Rockhill Rd., Kansas City, MO 64110. James McKinley, Ed. Fiction, 10 to 25 pages. Poetry, submit 3 to 6 at a time.

NEW MEXICO HUMANITIES REVIEW—Box A, New Mexico Tech, Socorro, NM 87801. Poetry and fiction, any length, any theme; personal and scholarly essays; articles dealing with southwestern and Native American themes; book reviews. Pays in subscriptions.

NEW ORLEANS REVIEW—Loyola Univ., New Orleans, LA 70118. John Mosier, Ed. Literary or film criticism, to 6,000 words. Serious fiction and poetry.

THE NEW PRESS—75–28 66th Dr., Middle Village, NY 11379. Bob Abramson, Ed. Fiction and nonfiction, to 2,500 words. Poetry to 40 lines. Quarterly. Pays in copies and occasional honorarium.

THE NEW RENAISSANCE—9 Heath Rd., Arlington, MA 02174. Louise T. Reynolds, Ed. An international magazine of ideas and opinions, emphasizing literature and the arts. Query for articles; send complete manuscript for essays. Payment varies, after publication.

NEXUS—Wright State Univ., 006 Univ. Center, Dayton, OH 45435. Chris Rue, Ed. Poetry, hard-hitting fiction, surrealism. Essays on obscure poets, artists, and musicians. Pays in copies.

NIMROD—2210 S. Main St., Tulsa, OK 74114. Quality poetry and fiction, experimental and traditional. Publishes two issues annually, one awards and one thematic. Pays in copies. Annual awards for poetry and fiction. Send #10 SASE for guidelines.

THE NORTH AMERICAN REVIEW—Univ. of Northern Iowa, Cedar Falls, IA 50614. Peter Cooley, Poetry Ed. Poetry of high quality. Pays 50¢ a line, on acceptance.

NORTH ATLANTIC REVIEW—15 Arbutus Lane, Stony Brook, NY 11790–1408. John Gill, Ed. Semiannual. Fiction and nonfiction, to 5,000 words; poetry, any length; fillers, humor, photographs and illustrations. Pays in copies.

THE NORTH DAKOTA QUARTERLY—Univ. of North Dakota, Box 8237, Grand Forks, ND 58202. Nonfiction essays in the humanities; fiction, reviews, graphics, and poetry. Limited market. Pays in copies.

THE NORTHERN REVIEW—Dept. of English, Univ. of Wisconsin/Stevens Point, Stevens Point, WI 54481. Address Man. Ed. Essays, articles (1,200 to 4,000 words), interviews, reviews, fiction, and poetry on or exploring northern themes. Pays in copies.

THE NORTHLAND QUARTERLY—51 E. Fourth St., Suite 412, Winona, MN 55987. Jody Namio Wallace, Ed. Articles and fiction (1,500 to 3,500 words) on progressive issues, contemporary relationships, experimental fiction. Also includes reviews, art, essays. Poetry, any length. Query for articles. Pays in copies.

NORTHWEST REVIEW—369 PLC, Univ. of Oregon, Eugene, OR 97403. Cecelia Hagen, Fiction Ed. Fiction, commentary, essays, and poetry. Reviews. Pays in copies. Send SASE for guidelines.

THE OHIO REVIEW—Ellis Hall, Ohio Univ., Athens, OH 45701–2979. Wayne Dodd, Ed. Short stories, poetry, essays, reviews. Pays $5 per page for prose, $1 a line for poetry, plus copies, on publication. SASE required. Submissions not read in June, July, or August.

ONIONHEAD—Arts on the Park, Inc., 115 N. Kentucky Ave., Lakeland, FL 33801. Address Editorial Council. Short stories (to 4,000 words), essays (to 2,500 words), and poetry (to 60 lines), on provocative social, political, and cultural observations and hypotheses. Pays in copies.

OREGON EAST—Hoke College Center, EOSC, La Grande, OR 97850. Short fiction, nonfiction (to 3,000 words), poetry (to 60 lines), and high-contrast graphics. Pays in copies. Submissions by March 1, notification by June.

ORPHIC LUTE—526 Paul Pl., Los Alamos, NM 87544. Patricia Doherty Hinnebusch, Ed. Well-crafted lyric poetry, traditional and contemporary, third-person perspective. Submit 4 to 5 poems at a time. Pays in copies.

OTHER VOICES—820 Ridge Rd., Highland Park, IL 60035. Dolores Weinberg, Lois Hauselman, Sharon Fiffer, Eds. Semiannual. Fresh, accessible short stories and novel excerpts, to 5,000 words. Pays in copies and modest honorarium.

OUROBOROS—3912 24th St., Rock Island, IL 61201. Erskine Carter, Ed. Short stories (to 3,500 words) and poetry (submit 7 to 10 poems at a time). Guidelines. Pays in copies.

PAINTBRUSH—Language & Literature, Northeast Missouri State Univ., Kirksville, MO 63501. Ben Bennani, Ed. Book reviews, to 1,500 words, and serious, sophisticated poetry (submit 3 to 5). Query preferred for book reviews. Semiannual. Pays in copies.

PAINTED BRIDE QUARTERLY—230 Vine St., Philadelphia, PA 19106. Louis Camp, and Joanne DiPaolo, Eds. Fiction, nonfiction, and poetry of varying lengths. Pays in copies and subscription.

PANDORA—2844 Grayson, Ferndale, MI 48220. Meg Mac Donald, Ed. Ruth Berman, Poetry Ed. Polly Vedder, Art Ed. Science fiction and speculative fantasy, to 4,000 words; poetry. "Looking for work that is role-expanding, with characters readers care about. No futile endings, 'It was a dream/joke, etc.'" Pays to 2¢ a word for fiction, on publication. Payment varies for poetry and artwork.

PANHANDLER—English Dept., Univ. of West Florida, Pensacola, FL 32514. Michael Yots and Stanton Millet, Eds. Fiction, 1,500 to 4,000 words, "that tells a story"; poetry, any length, with a strong sense of colloquial language. Semiannual. Pays in copies.

THE PARIS REVIEW—541 E. 72nd St., New York, NY 10021. Address Fiction and Poetry Eds. Fiction and poetry of high literary quality. Pays on publication.

PARNASSUS—41 Union Sq. W., Rm. 804, New York, NY 10003. Herbert Leibowitz, Ed. Critical essays and reviews on contemporary poetry. International in scope. Pays in cash and copies.

PARTISAN REVIEW—236 Bay State Rd., Boston, MA 02215. William Phillips, Ed. Serious fiction, poetry, and essays. Payment varies. No simultaneous submissions.

PASSAGES NORTH—Kalamazoo College, 1200 Academy, Kalamazoo, MI 49007. Ben Mitchell, Ed. Quality short fiction and contemporary poetry. Pays in copies, frequent prizes, and honoraria.

THE PENNSYLVANIA REVIEW—Univ. of Pittsburgh, Dept. of English, 526 Cathedral of Learning, Pittsburgh, PA 15260. Fiction, to 5,000 words, book reviews, interviews with authors, and poetry (send up to six at once). Pays $5 a page for prose, $5 for poetry. Submissions not accepted April 1 to Sept. 1.

PEQUOD—New York Univ. English Dept., 19 University Pl., 2nd Fl., New York, NY 10003. Mark Rudman, Ed. Semiannual. Short stories, essays, and literary criticism to 10 pages; poetry and translations to 3 pages. Pays $10 to $25, on publication.

PERMAFROST—English Dept., Univ. of Alaska, Fairbanks, AK 99775. Poetry, short fiction to 7,500 words, essays, and B&W photos and graphics. Reading periods: Sept. 1 to Dec. 1 and Jan. 15 to April 1. Pays in copies.

PIEDMONT LITERARY REVIEW—Bluebird Lane, Rt. #1, Box 512, Forest, VA 24551. Evelyn Miles, Man. Ed. Quarterly. Prose, to 2,500 words. Submit prose to Dr. Olga Kronmeyer, 25 West Dale Dr., Lynchburg, VA 24501. Poems, any length and style. Submit up to 5 poems to Gail White, 1017 Spanish Moss Ln., Breaux Bridge, LA 70517. Submit Asian verse to Dorothy McLaughlin, 10 Atlantic Rd., Somerset, NJ 08873. Pays one copy.

PIG IRON—P.O. Box 237, Youngstown, OH 44501. Nate Leslie, Jim Villani, Eds. Fiction and nonfiction, to 8,000 words. Poetry, to 100 lines. Pays $5 per published page, on publication. Query for themes.

PIVOT—250 Riverside Dr., #23, New York, NY 10025. Martin Mitchell, Ed. Poetry, to 75 lines. Annual. Pays 2 copies, on publication.

PLAINS POETRY JOURNAL—Box 2337, Bismarck, ND 58502. Jane Greer, Ed. Poetry using traditional conventions in vigorous, compelling ways; no "greeting card"-type verse. No subject is taboo. Pays in copies.

PLOUGHSHARES—Emerson College, 100 Beacon St., Boston, MA 02116. Pays $10 to $50, on publication. Reading periods vary, check recent issue; guidelines.

POEM—c/o English Dept., U.A.H., Huntsville, AL 35899. Nancy Frey Dillard, Ed. Serious lyric poetry. Pays in copies.

POET AND CRITIC—203 Ross Hall, Iowa State Univ., Ames, IA 50011. Neal Bowers, Ed. Poetry, reviews, essays on contemporary poetry. Pays in copies.

POET LORE—7815 Old Georgetown Rd., Bethesda, MD 20814. Sunil Freeman, Man. Ed. Original poetry, all kinds. Translations, reviews. Pays in copies. Annual narrative contest.

POETRY—60 West Walton St., Chicago, IL 60610. Joseph Parisi, Ed. Poetry of highest quality. Pays $2 a line, on publication.

POETRY EAST—DePaul University, 802 W. Belden Ave., Chicago, IL 60614–3214. Marilyn Woitel, Man. Ed. Published in spring and fall. Poetry, essays, and translations. "Please send a sampling of your best work. Do not send book-length manuscripts without querying first." Pays in copies.

POETRY/LA—P.O. Box 84271, Los Angeles, CA 90073. Helen Friedland,

Ed. Semiannual. Quality poems by poets living, working, or attending school within a 100-mile radius of Los Angeles. Pays in copies.

PORTLAND REVIEW—c/o Portland State Univ., P.O. Box 751, Portland, OR 97207. Nancy Row, Ed. Short fiction, essays, and poetry (1 poem per page). B&W photos and drawings. Published 3 times a year. Payment is 1 copy.

PRAIRIE SCHOONER—201 Andrews Hall, Univ. of Nebraska, Lincoln, NE 68588–0334. Hilda Raz, Ed. Short stories, poetry, essays, book reviews, and translations. Pays in copies. Annual contests. SASE required.

PRISM INTERNATIONAL—E459–1866 Main Mall, Dept. of Creative Writing, Univ. of British Columbia, Vancouver, B.C., Canada V6T 1W5. Debbie Howlett, Ed. High-quality fiction, poetry, drama, creative nonfiction, and literature in translation, varying lengths. Include international reply coupons. Pays $30 per published page. Annual short fiction contest.

PROOF ROCK—P.O. Box 607, Halifax, VA 24558. Don Conner, Fiction Ed. Serena Fusek, Poetry Ed. Fiction, to 2,500 words. Poetry, to 32 lines. Reviews. Pays in copies.

PUDDING—60 N. Main St., Johnstown, OH 43031. Jennifer Welch Bosveld, Ed. Poems on popular culture and social concerns, especially free verse and experimental, with fresh language, concrete images, and specific detail. Short articles about poetry in human services.

PUERTO DEL SOL—New Mexico State Univ., Box 3E, Las Cruces, NM 88003. Kevin McIlvoy, Ed. Short stories, to 30 pages; novel excerpts, to 65 pages; articles, to 45 pages, and reviews, to 15 pages. Poetry, photos. Pays in copies.

THE QUARTERLY—201 East 50th, New York, NY 10022. Gordon Lish, Ed. "The Magazine of New American Writing." Fiction, nonfiction, and poetry, no limits on length. Payment varies, on publication.

QUARTERLY WEST—317 Olpin Union, Univ. of Utah, Salt Lake City, UT 84112. C.F. Pinketon and Tom Schmid, Eds. Short shorts and novellas; critical nonfiction and essays. Poetry (submit up to 3 poems at a time). Query for novellas. Pays $15 to $300 for fiction and nonfiction, $1 a line for poetry, on publication.

QUEEN'S QUARTERLY—Queens Univ., Kingston, Ont., Canada K7L 3N6. Articles, to 8,000 words, on a wide range of topics, and fiction, to 5,000 words. Poetry: send no more than 6 poems. B&W art. Pays to $300, on publication.

RACCOON—Ion Books, Inc., Box 111327, Memphis, TN 38111–1327. David Spicer, Ed. Poetry and poetic criticism, varying lengths. Pays in subscription for poetry, $50 for criticism, fiction.

RAG MAN—P.O. Box 12, Goodhue, MN 55027. Beverly Voldseth, Ed. Fiction and nonfiction, to 1,000 words. Poetry any length. No religious writing. Semiannual. Pays in copies.

RAMBUNCTIOUS REVIEW—1221 W. Pratt Blvd., Chicago, IL 60626. Mary Dellutri, Richard Goldman, Nancy Lennon, Beth Hausler, Eds. Fiction to 15 pages, poetry (submit up to 5 at a time). Pays in copies. Submit material September through May. Contests.

RED CEDAR REVIEW—Dept. of English, Morrill Hall, Michigan State Univ., East Lansing, MI 48825. Fiction, 10 to 15 pages; poetry; interviews; book reviews; graphics. Pays in copies.

THE REDNECK REVIEW OF LITERATURE—P.O. Box 730, Twin Falls,

642

ID 83301. Penelope Reedy, Ed. Fiction, to 2,500 words, of the contemporary American West; essays and book reviews, 300 to 1,500 words; poetry. Semiannual. Pays in copies, on publication.

RELIGION AND PUBLIC EDUCATION—E262 Lagomarcino Hall, Iowa State Univ., Ames, IA 50011. Charles R. Kniker, Ed.-in-Chief. Paul Blakeley, Poetry Ed. Poems with mythological or religious values or themes. Pays in copies.

RESONANCE—P.O. Box 215, Beacon, NY 12508. Evan Pritchard, Ed. Fiction, to 1,200 words; thematic nonfiction, to 1,200 words; poetry, to 46 lines. Quarterly. Pays 1 copy.

REVIEW: LATIN AMERICAN LITERATURE AND ARTS—Americas Society, 680 Park Ave., New York, NY 10021. Alfred J. MacAdam, Ed. Published twice yearly. Work in English translation by and about young and established Latin American writers; essays and book reviews considered. Send queries for 1,000- to 1,500-word manuscripts, and short poem translations. Payment varies, on acceptance.

RHINO—8403 W. Normal Ave., Niles, IL 60648. Kay Meier and Martha Vertreace, Eds. "Authentic emotion in well-crafted poetry." January to June reading period. Pays in copies.

RIVER CITY—Dept. of English, Memphis State Univ., Memphis, TN 38152. Poems, short stories, essays. Awards. Pays in copies.

RIVERSIDE QUARTERLY—P.O. Box 464, Waco, TX 76703. Leland Sapiro, Ed. Science fiction and fantasy, to 3,500 words; criticism; poetry; reviews. Send fiction to Redd Boggs, Box 1111, Berkeley, CA 94701; poetry to Sheryl Smith, 515 Saratoga, Santa Clara, CA 95050. Pays in copies.

ROANOKE REVIEW—Roanoke College, Salem, VA 24153. Robert R. Walter, Ed. Quality short fiction, to 10,000 words, and poetry, to 100 lines. Pays in copies.

ROMANCING THE PAST—17239 S. Oak Park Ave. #207, Tinley Park, IL 60477. Michelle Regan, Ed. Nostalgia and historic material: fiction and nonfiction, to 10 pages, and poetry. Quarterly. Pays in copies.

SAN FERNANDO POETRY JOURNAL—18301 Halstead St., Northridge, CA 91325. Richard Cloke, Ed. Quality poetry, 20 to 100 lines, with social content; scientific, philosophic, and historical themes. Pays in copies.

SAN JOSE STUDIES—San Jose State Univ., San Jose, CA 95192. Fauneil J. Rinn, Ed. Poetry, fiction, and essays on interdisciplinary topics. Pays in copies. Annual awards.

SANSKRIT LITERARY/ART PUBLICATION—Univ. of North Carolina/Charlotte, Charlotte, NC 28223. Tina McEntire, Ed.-in-Chief. Poetry, short fiction, photos, and fine art. Published annually.

SATORI—P.O. Box 318, Tivoli, NY 12583. Pat Sims and Gary Green, Eds. Traditional and experimental fiction, 250 to 2,000 words. Experimental and visual poetry, to 3 pages. Query for essays, 1,000 to 2,000 words. Quarterly. Pays in copies.

SCANDINAVIAN REVIEW—725 Park Ave., New York, NY 10021. Essays on contemporary Scandinavia. Fiction and poetry, translated from Nordic languages. Pays from $100, on publication.

SCRIVENER—McGill Univ., 853 Sherbrooke St. W., Montreal, Quebec, Canada H3A 2T6. Ernest Alston, Julie Crawford, Eds. Poetry, 5 to 15 lines; prose, to 20 pages; reviews, to 5 pages; essays, to 10 pages. Photography and graphics. Pays in copies.

THE SEATTLE REVIEW—Padelford Hall, GN-30, Univ. of Washington, Seattle, WA 98195. Donna Gerstenberger, Ed. Short stories (to 20 pages), poetry, essays on the craft of writing, and interviews with northwest writers. Payment varies.

SENECA REVIEW—Hobart & William Smith Colleges, Geneva, NY 14456. Deborah Tall, Ed. Poetry, translations, and essays on contemporary poetry. Pays in copies.

SHOOTING STAR REVIEW—7123 Race St., Pittsburgh, PA 15208. Sandra Gould Ford, Pub. Fiction and folktales, to 3,500 words, essays, to 2,500 words, and poetry, to 50 lines, on the African-American experience. Query for book reviews only. Pays $8 to $30, and in copies. Send SASE for topic deadlines.

SING HEAVENLY MUSE! WOMEN'S POETRY & PROSE—P.O. Box 13299, Minneapolis, MN 55414. Short stories and essays, to 5,000 words. Poetry. Query for themes and reading periods. Pays in copies.

SLIPSTREAM—Box 2071, New Market Sta., Niagara Falls, NY 14301. Fiction, 2 to 18 pages, and contemporary poetry, any length. Pays in copies. Query for themes. (Also accepting cassette tape submissions for audio poetics tape series: spoken word, collaborations, songs, audio experimentation.)

THE SMALL POND MAGAZINE—P.O. Box 664, Stratford, CT 06497. Napoleon St. Cyr, Ed. Fiction, to 2,500 words; poetry, to 100 lines. Query for nonfiction. Published 3 times a year. Pays in copies.

SMALL PRESS REVIEW—Box 100, Paradise, CA 95967. Len Fulton, Ed. News pieces and reviews, to 200 words, about small presses and little magazines. Pays in copies.

SNOWY EGRET—R.R. #1, Box 354, Poland, IN 47868. Karl Barnebey, Ed. Poetry, fiction, and nonfiction to 10,000 words. Natural history from artistic, literary, philosophical, and historical perspectives. Pays $2 per page for prose; $2 to $4 for poetry, on publication. Send poetry to Alan Seaburg, Poetry Ed., 67 Century St., West Medford, MA 02155.

SONORA REVIEW—Dept. of English, Univ. of Arizona, Tucson, AZ 85721. Jean Marcus, Ed.-in-Chief. Fiction, poetry, translations, interviews, literary nonfiction. Pays in copies. Annual prizes for fiction and poetry.

SOUTH COAST POETRY JOURNAL—English Dept., CSUF, Fullerton, CA 92634. John J. Brugaletta, Ed. Poetry, to 40 lines, and B&W line drawings. "We look for excellent poetry, without regard for any other consideration." Semiannual. Pays in 1 copy, on publication.

SOUTH DAKOTA REVIEW—Box 111, Univ. Exchange, Vermillion, SD 57069. John R. Milton, Ed. Exceptional fiction, 3,000 to 5,000 words, and poetry, 10 to 25 lines. Critical articles, especially on American literature, Western American literature, theory and esthetics, 3,000 to 5,000 words. Pays in copies.

THE SOUTHERN CALIFORNIA ANTHOLOGY—c/o Master of Professional Writing Program, WPH 404, University of Southern California, Los Angeles, CA 90089–4034. Stacie Strong, Ed.-in-Chief. Fiction, to 20 pages, and poetry, to 5 pages. Pays in copies.

SOUTHERN EXPOSURE—P.O. Box 531, Durham, NC 27702. Eric Bates, Ed. Quarterly forum on "Southern movements for social change." Short stories, to

4,500 words, essays, investigative journalism, and oral histories, 500 to 4,500 words. Pays $25 to $200, on publication. Query.

SOUTHERN HUMANITIES REVIEW—9088 Haley Center, Auburn Univ., AL 36849. Thomas L. Wright, Dan R. Latimer, Eds. Short stories, essays, and criticism, 3,500 to 5,000 words; poetry, to 2 pages.

SOUTHERN POETRY REVIEW—Dept. of English, Univ. of North Carolina, Charlotte, NC 28223. Robert W. Grey, Ed. Poems. No restrictions on style, length, or content.

SOUTHERN REVIEW—43 Allen Hall, Louisiana State Univ., Baton Rouge, LA 70803. James Olney, Ed. Emphasis on contemporary literature in United States and abroad with special interest in southern culture and history. Fiction and essays, 4,000 to 8,000 words. Serious poetry of highest quality. Pays $12 a page for prose, $20 a page for poetry, on publication.

SOUTHWEST REVIEW—6410 Airline Rd., Southern Methodist Univ., Dallas, TX 75275. Willard Spiegelman, Ed. Fiction, essays, and interviews with well-known writers, 3,000 to 7,500 words. Poetry. Pays varying rates.

SOU'WESTER—Dept. of English, Southern Illinois Univ. at Edwardsville, Edwardsville, IL 62026–1438. Dickie Spurgeon, Ed. Fiction, to 10,000 words. Poetry, especially poems over 100 lines. Pays in copies.

SPECTRUM—Univ. of California/ Santa Barbara, Box 14800, Santa Barbara, CA 93106. Short stories, essays on literature, memoirs, poetry. Pays in copies. Annual contest.

SPECTRUM—Anna Maria College, Box 72-A, Paxton, MA 01612. Robert H. Goepfert, Ed. Scholarly articles (3,000 to 15,000 words); short stories (to 10 pages) and poetry (to 2 pages); book reviews, photos and artwork. Pays $20 plus 2 copies. SASE required.

THE SPOON RIVER QUARTERLY—Dept. of English, Stevenson Hall, Illinois State Univ., Normal, IL 61761. Lucia Cordell Getsi, Ed. Poetry, any length. Pays in copies.

SPSM&H—329 E St., Bakersfield, CA 93304. Frederick A. Raborg, Jr., Ed. Single sonnets, sequences, essays about the form, short fiction in which the sonnet plays a part, books, and anthologies. Pays in copies.

STAND MAGAZINE—P.O. Box 5923, Huntsville, AL 35814. Jessie Emerson, Ed. Fiction, 3,500 to 4,000 words, and poetry to 100 lines. No formulaic verse. Pays varying rates, on publication.

STORY QUARTERLY—P.O. Box 1416, Northbrook, IL 60065. Anne Brashler, Diane Williams, Eds. Short stories and interviews. Pays in copies.

STORYTELLING MAGAZINE—(formerly *The National Storytelling Journal*) P.O. Box 309, Jonesborough, TN 37659. Articles, 500 to 2,500 words, related to storytelling: "Articles can have folkloric, historical, personal, educational, or travel bias, as long as they're related to storytelling." Pays 5¢ a word.

STUDIES IN AMERICAN FICTION—English Dept., Northeastern Univ., Boston, MA 02115. James Nagel, Ed. Reviews, 750 words; scholarly essays, 2,500 to 6,500 words, on American fiction. Pays in copies.

THE SUN—The Sun Publishing Co., 107 N. Roberson St., Chapel Hill, NC 27516. Sy Safransky, Ed. Articles, essays, interviews, and fiction to 10,000 words; poetry; photos, illustrations, and cartoons. "We're interested in all writing that makes sense and enriches our common space." Pays $100 for fiction and essays, $25 for poetry, on publication.

SUNRUST—P.O. Box 58, New Wilmington, PA 16142. James Ashbrook Perkins, Nancy Esther James, Eds. Nonfiction, to 2,000 words, and poetry, to 75 lines, about rural life, nature, memories of the past, and small communities. Submissions accepted December 1 to January 31 and June 1 to July 31. Guidelines. Pays in copies.

SWAMP ROOT—Route 2, Box 1098, Hiwassee One, Jacksboro, TN 37757. Al Masarik, Ed. Poetry, any length, any style. Essays, reviews, letters, and interviews related to poetry. Query for artwork. SASE required. Published 3 times a year. Pays in copies and subscription.

SYCAMORE REVIEW—Purdue Univ., Dept. of English, West Lafayette, IN 47907. Henry Hughes, Ed.-in-Chief. Poetry, short fiction (no genre fiction), personal essays, and translations for semiannual publication; manuscripts to 10,000 words. Pays in copies. Reading period: September to April.

TAR RIVER POETRY—Dept. of English, East Carolina Univ., Greenville, NC 27834. Peter Makuck, Ed. Poems, all styles. Interested in skillful use of figurative language. No flat statement poetry. Submit between September and May. Pays in copies.

THE TEXAS REVIEW—English Dept., Sam Houston State Univ., Huntsville, TX 77341. Paul Ruffin, Ed. Fiction, poetry, articles, to 20 typed pages. Reviews. Pays in copies and subscription.

THIRTEEN—Box 392, Portlandville, NY 13834–0392. Ken Stone, Ed. Thirteen-line poetry. Quarterly. Pays 1 copy.

THE THREEPENNY REVIEW—P.O. Box 9131, Berkeley, CA 94709. Wendy Lesser, Ed. Fiction, to 5,000 words. Poetry, to 100 lines. Essays, on books, theater, film, dance, music, art, television, and politics, 1,500 to 3,000 words. Pays to $100, on acceptance. Limited market. Query first with SASE for guidelines.

TIGHTROPE—323 Pelham Rd., Amherst, MA 01002. Ed Rayher, Ed. Fiction and nonfiction, to 10 pages; poetry, any length. Limited-edition, letterpress publication. Semiannual. Pays in copies.

TOUCHSTONE—P.O. Box 8308, Spring, TX 77387. Bill Laufer, Pub. Quarterly. Fiction, 750 to 2,000 words: mainstream, experimental. Interviews, essays, reviews. Poetry, to 40 lines. Pays $2 to $5 for poems; $5 reviews; to $5 per page for prose.

TRANSLATION—The Translation Center, 412 Dodge Hall, Columbia Univ., New York, NY 10027. Frank MacShane, Dir. Semiannual. New translations of contemporary foreign fiction and poetry.

TRIQUARTERLY—Northwestern Univ., 2020 Ridge Ave., Evanston, IL 60208. Serious, aesthetically informed and inventive poetry and prose, for an international and literate audience. Pays $40 per page for prose, $3 per line for poetry. Reading period Oct. 1 to April 30.

TRIVIA—P.O. Box 606, N. Amherst, NY 01059. Lise Weil, Ed. Semiannual journal of feminist writing. Literary essays, experimental prose, translations, and reviews. "After readings": essay reviews on books written by women. Submit up to 20 pages. Pays in copies. Guidelines.

2 AM—P.O. Box 6754, Rockford, IL 61125–1754. Gretta Anderson, Ed. Poetry, articles, reviews, and personality profiles (500 to 2,000 words), as well as fantasy, horror, and some science fiction/sword-and-sorcery short stories (500 to 5,000 words). Pays ½¢ a word, on acceptance.

THE UNIVERSITY OF PORTLAND REVIEW—Univ. of Portland, Portland, OR 97203. Thompson H. Faller, Ed. Scholarly articles and contemporary fiction, 500 to 2,500 words. Poetry. Book reviews. Pays in copies.

UNIVERSITY OF WINDSOR REVIEW—Dept. of English, Univ. of Windsor, Windsor, Ont., Canada N9B 3P4. Joseph A. Quinn, Ed. Short stories, poetry. Pays $10 to $25, on publication.

THE VILLAGER—135 Midland Ave., Bronxville, NY 10708. Amy Murphy, Ed. Fiction, 900 to 1,500 words: mystery, adventure, humor, romance. Short, preferably seasonal poetry. Pays in copies.

VIRGINIA QUARTERLY REVIEW—One W. Range, Charlottesville, VA 22903. Quality fiction and poetry. Serious essays and articles, 3,000 to 6,000 words, on literature, science, politics, economics, etc. Pays $10 per page for prose, $1 per line for poetry, on publication.

VISIONS—4705 South 8th Rd., Arlington, VA 22204. Bradley R. Strahan, Ed. Poetry, to 40 lines, and B&W drawings. (Query first for artwork.) "Nothing amateurish or previously published." Published 3 times a year. Pays in copies.

WASCANA REVIEW—c/o Dept. of English, Univ. of Regina, Regina, Sask., Canada S4S 0A2. Joan Givner, Ed. Short stories, 2,000 to 6,000 words; critical articles; poetry. Pays $3 per page for prose, $10 for poetry, after publication.

WASHINGTON REVIEW—P.O. Box 50132, Washington, DC 20004. Clarissa Wittenberg, Ed. Poetry; articles on literary, performing and fine arts in the Washington, D.C., area. Fiction, 1,000 to 2,500 words. Area writers preferred. Pays in copies.

WEBSTER REVIEW—Webster Univ., 470 E. Lockwood, Webster Groves, MO 63119. Nancy Schapiro, Ed. Fiction; poetry; interviews; essays; translations. Pays in copies.

WEST BRANCH—Bucknell Hall, Bucknell Univ., Lewisburg, PA 17837. Karl Patten, Robert Taylor, Eds. Poetry and fiction. Pays in copies and subscriptions.

WESTERN HUMANITIES REVIEW—Univ. of Utah, Salt Lake City, UT 84112. Pamela Houston, Man. Ed. Quarterly. Fiction and essays, to 30 pages, and poetry. Pays $50 for poetry, $150 for short stories and essays, on acceptance.

WIND—R1-Box 809K, Pikesville, KY 41501. Quentin Howard, Ed. Short stories and poems. Book reviews from small presses, to 250 words. Semiannual. Pays in copies.

WINDFALL—Dept. of English, UW-Whitewater, Whitewater, WI 53190. Ron Ellis, Ed. Intense, highly crafted, lyric poetry. (Occasionally consider poems longer than 1 page.) No dot matrix or poor copies will be considered. Semiannual. Pays 1 copy.

THE WINDLESS ORCHARD—Dept. of English, Indiana-Purdue Univ., Ft. Wayne, IN 46805. Robert Novak, Ed. Contemporary poetry. Pays in copies. SASE required.

WITHOUT HALOS—Ocean County Poets Collective, P.O. Box 1342, Point Pleasant Beach, NJ 08742. Frank Finale, Ed. Submit 3 to 5 poems (to 2 pages) between Jan. 1 and June 30. Pays in copies.

WITNESS—31000 Northwestern Hwy., Suite 200, Farmington Hills, MI 48018. Peter Stine, Ed. Quarterly, thematic journal. Fiction and essays, 5 to 20 pages, and poems (submit up to 3). Pays $6 per page for prose, $10 per page for poetry, on publication.

WOMAN OF POWER—Box 827, Cambridge, MA 02238–0827. Char McKee, Ed. A magazine of feminism, spirituality, and politics. Fiction and nonfiction, to 3,500 words. Poetry; submit up to 5 poems at a time. Send SASE for issue themes and guidelines. Pays in copies and subscription.

THE WORCESTER REVIEW—6 Chatham St., Worcester, MA 01609. Rodger Martin, Ed. Poetry (submit up to 5 poems at a time), fiction, critical articles about poetry, and articles and reviews with a New England connection. Semiannual. Pays in copies.

THE WORMWOOD REVIEW—P.O. Box 8840, Stockton, CA 95208–0840. Marvin Malone, Ed. Poetry and prose-poetry, 4 to 400 lines. "We encourage wit and conciseness." Quarterly. Pays 3 to 20 copies or cash equivalent.

WRITERS FORUM—Univ. of Colorado, Colorado Springs, CO 80933–7150. Alex Blackburn, Ed. Annual. Mainstream and experimental fiction, 1,000 to 10,000 words. Poetry (1 to 5 poems per submission). Emphasis on western themes and writers. Send material October through May. Pays in copies.

WYOMING, THE HUB OF THE WHEEL—The Willow Bee Publishing House, Box 9, Saratoga, WY 82331. Lenore A. Senior, Man. Ed. Fiction and nonfiction, to 2,500 words; poetry, to 80 lines. "An international literary/art magazine devoted to peace, the human race, positive relationships, and the human spirit and possibilities." Pays in copies.

XANADU—Box 773, Huntington, NY 11743. Pat Nesbitt, Mildred Jeffrey, Barbara Lucas, Eds. Poetry on a variety of topics; no length restrictions. Pays in copies.

YALE REVIEW—1902A Yale Sta., New Haven, CT 06520. Penelope Laurans, Ed. Serious poetry, to 200 lines, and fiction, 3,000 to 5,000 words. Pays nominal sum.

ZYZZYVA—41 Sutter, Suite 1400, San Francisco, CA 94104. Howard Junker, Ed. Publishes work of west coast writers only: fiction, essays, and poetry. Pays $25 to $100, on acceptance.

HUMOR, FILLERS, SHORT ITEMS

Magazines noted for their excellent filler departments, plus a cross-section of publications using humor, short items, jokes, quizzes, and cartoons, follow. However, almost all magazines use some type of filler material, and writers can find dozens of markets by studying copies of magazines at a library or newsstand.

THE AMERICAN FIELD—542 S. Dearborn, Chicago, IL 60605. W.F.

Brown, Ed. Short fact items and anecdotes on hunting dogs and field trials for bird dogs. Pays varying rates, on acceptance.

THE AMERICAN NEWSPAPER CARRIER—P.O. Box 2225, Kernersville, NC 27285. W.H. Lowry, Ed. Short, humorous pieces, to 1,200 words, for preteen and teenage newspaper carriers. Pays $25, on publication.

ARMY MAGAZINE—2425 Wilson Blvd., Arlington, VA 22201–3385. L. James Binder, Ed.-in-Chief. True anecdotes on military subjects. Pays $10 to $35, on publication.

THE ATLANTIC—745 Boylston St., Boston, MA 02116. Sophisticated humorous or satirical pieces, 1,000 to 3,000 words. Some light poetry. Pays from $750 for prose, on acceptance.

ATLANTIC SALMON JOURNAL—1435 St. Alexandre, Suite 1030, Montreal, Quebec, Canada H3A 2G4. Terry Davis, Ed. Fillers, 50 to 100 words, on salmon politics, conservation, and nature. Cartoons. Pays $25 for fillers, $50 for cartoons, on publication.

BICYCLING—33 E. Minor St., Emmaus, PA 18098. Anecdotes, helpful cycling tips, and other items for "Paceline" section, 150 to 250 words. Pays $50, on publication.

BIKEREPORT—Bikecentennial, P.O. Box 8308, Missoula, MT 59807. Daniel D'Ambrosio, Ed. News shorts from the bicycling world for "In Bicycle Circles." Pays $5 to $10, on publication.

CAPPER'S—616 Jefferson St., Topeka, KS 66607. Nancy Peavler, Ed. Household hints, recipes, jokes. Pays varying rates, on publication.

CASCADES EAST—716 N. E. 4th St., P. O. Box 5784, Bend, OR 97708. Geoff Hill, Ed. Fillers, related to travel, history, and recreation in central Oregon. Pays 3¢ to 10¢ a word, extra for photos, on publication.

CATHOLIC DIGEST—P.O. Box 64090, St. Paul, MN 55164. No fiction. Articles, 200 to 500 words, on instances of kindness rewarded, for "Hearts Are Trumps." Stories about conversions, for "Open Door." Reports of tactful remarks or actions, for "The Perfect Assist." Accounts of good deeds, for "People Are Like That." Humorous pieces, 50 to 300 words, on parish life, for "In Our Parish." Amusing signs, for "Signs of the Times." Jokes; fillers. Pays $4 to $50, on publication. Manuscripts cannot be acknowledged or returned.

CHICKADEE—56 The Esplanade, Suite 306, Toronto, Ont., Canada M5E 1A7. Humorous poetry, 10 to 15 lines, about animals and nature, for children. Pays on publication. Enclose international reply coupons.

CHILDREN'S PLAYMATE—1100 Waterway Blvd., P. O. Box 567, Indianapolis, IN 46206. Elizabeth Rinck, Ed. Puzzles, games, mazes for 6- to 8-year-olds, emphasizing health, safety, and nutrition. Pays about 8¢ a word (varies on puzzles), on acceptance.

CHRISTIAN HERALD—40 Overlook Dr., Chappaqua, NY 10514. Bob Chuvala, Ed. For "The Two of Us": memorable, humorous, or touching moments in the life of a Christian marriage. For "Kids of the Kingdom": funny or revealing things that happened to you in the process of raising, teaching, or working with Christian kids. Both columns, 75 to 200 words. Pay $25, on acceptance.

THE CHURCH MUSICIAN—127 Ninth Ave. N., Nashville, TN 37234. W. M. Anderson, Ed. For Southern Baptist music leaders. Humorous fillers with a music slant. No clippings. Pays around 5¢ a word, on acceptance. Same address and requirements for *Glory Songs* and *The Senior Musician*.

COLUMBIA JOURNALISM REVIEW—Columbia University, 700 Journalism Bldg., New York, NY 10027. Gloria Cooper, Man. Ed. Amusing mistakes in news stories, headlines, photos, etc. (original clippings required), for "Lower Case." Pays $25, on publication.

CORPORATE CASHFLOW—(formerly *Cashflow*) 6255 Barfield Rd., Atlanta, GA 30328. Dick Gamble, Ed. Fillers, to 1,000 words, on varied aspects of treasury management and corporate finance, for treasury managers in public and private companies. Pays on publication. Query.

COUNTRY—5400 S. 60th St, Greendale, WI 53129. Fillers, 50 to 200 words, for rural audience. Pays on acceptance. Address Deb Mulvey.

COUNTRY WOMAN—P. O. Box 643, Milwaukee, WI 53201. Kathy Pohl, Man. Ed. Short rhymed verse, 4 to 20 lines, and fillers, to 250 words, on the rural experience. All material must be positive and upbeat. Pays $10 to $50, on acceptance.

CURRENT COMEDY—165 W. 47th St., New York, NY 10036. Gary Apple, Ed. Original, funny, performable one-liners and brief jokes on news, fads, topical subjects, etc. Jokes for roasts, retirement dinners, and for speaking engagements. Humorous material specifically geared for public speaking situations such as microphone feedback, hecklers, etc. Pays $12, after publication. SASE for guidelines.

THE ELKS MAGAZINE—425 W. Diversey Pkwy., Chicago, IL 60614. Fred D. Oakes, Ed. Informative or humorous pieces, to 2,500 words. Pays from $150, on acceptance. Query.

ENTERTAINER MAGAZINE—803 Scott St., Covington, KY 41011. Dennis O'Connor, Pub. Pop music reviews, 600 words. Pays $25 and copies, on publication.

FACES—30 Grove St., Peterborough, NH 03458. Carolyn Yoder, Ed. Puzzles, mazes, crosswords, and picture puzzles, related to monthly themes, for children. Send SASE for list of themes before submitting.

FAMILY CIRCLE—Box 2822, Grand Central Sta., New York, NY 10017. "Between Friends," a column of innovative reader tips on a wide range of topics, including diet, fitness, health, child care, travel, finances, etc. Pays $100. Submit postcards only; unpublished entries cannot be acknowledged or returned.

FARM AND RANCH LIVING—5400 S. 60th St., Greendale, WI 53129. Bob Ottum, Ed. Fillers on rural people and living, 200 words. Pays from $15, on acceptance and publication.

FATE—P.O. Box 64383, St. Paul, MN 55164–0383. Donald Michael Kraig, Ed. Factual fillers, to 300 words, on strange or psychic happenings. True stories, to 300 words, on psychic or mystic personal experiences. Pays $2 to $15.

FIELD & STREAM—2 Park Ave., New York, NY 10016. Duncan Barnes, Ed. Fillers on hunting, fishing, camping, etc., to 1,000 words. Cartoons. Pays $250 to $750 for fillers, $100 for cartoons, on acceptance.

FLY FISHERMAN—2245 Kohn Rd., Box 8200, Harrisburg, PA 17105. Philip Hanyok, Assoc. Ed. Fillers, 100 words, on equipment tackle tips, knots, and fly-tying tips. Pays from $35, on acceptance.

GALLERY—401 Park Ave. S., New York, NY 10016–8802. Marc Lichter,

Ed. Dir. Barry Janoff, Man. Ed. Short humor, satire, and short service features for men. Pays varying rates, half on acceptance and half on publication. Query.

GAMES—810 Seventh Ave., New York, NY 10019. Will Shortz, Ed. Pencil puzzles, visual brainteasers, and pop culture tests. Humor and playfulness a plus. Pays varying rates, on publication. Query.

GLAMOUR—350 Madison Ave., New York, NY 10017. Articles, 1,000 words, for "Viewpoint" section: opinion pieces for women. Pays $500, on acceptance. Send SASE.

GLORY SONGS—See *The Church Musician*.

GOLF DIGEST—5520 Park Ave., Trumbull, CT 06611. Lisa Sweet, Ed. Asst. Short fact items, anecdotes, quips, jokes, light verse related to golf. True humorous or odd incidents, to 200 words. Pays from $25, on acceptance.

GOLF ILLUSTRATED—3 Park Ave., New York, NY 10016. Golf-related fillers; one- to two-paragraph news or personal-experience snippets, preferably of humorous or offbeat nature. Pays $25 to $100, on acceptance.

GOOD HOUSEKEEPING—959 Eighth Ave., New York, NY 10019. Rosemary Leonard, Ed. Two to eight lines of witty poetry, light verse, and quips with broad appeal, easy to illustrate for "Light Housekeeping" page. Seasonal material welcome. Pays $25 to $50, on acceptance.

GUIDEPOSTS—747 Third Ave., New York, NY 10017. Rick Hamlin, Features Ed. Inspirational anecdotes, to 250 words. Pays $10 to $50, on acceptance.

HEARTH & HOME—P. O. Box 2008, Laconia, NH 03247. Ken Daggett, Ed. Profiles and interviews, 1,000 to 1,800 words, with specialty retailers selling both casual furniture and hearth products (fireplaces, woodstoves, accessories, etc.). Pays $150 to $250, on acceptance.

HOME LIFE—127 Ninth Ave. N., Nashville, TN 37234. Charlie Warren, Ed. Southern Baptist. Personal-experience pieces, 100 to 500 words, on Christian marriage and family relationships. Pays to 5¢ a word, on acceptance.

HOME MECHANIX—2 Park Ave., New York, NY 10016. Michael Morris, Ed. Time- or money-saving tips for the home, garage, or yard; seasonal reminders for homeowners. Pays $50, on acceptance.

HUMOR MAGAZINE—Box 41070, Philadelphia, PA 19127. Edward Savaria, Jr., Ed. Quarterly. Fiction, interviews, and profiles, up to 1,000 words; short poetry, jokes, and fillers. "We would edit out all truly gross humor and anything that elicits loud groans. Please, no X-rated jokes or stories." Pays on acceptance: $50 to $300 for stories and articles; $5 to $25 for jokes and fillers.

INDEPENDENT LIVING—44 Broadway, New York, NY 11740. Anne Kelly, Ed. Short humor, to 500 words, and cartoons for magazine addressing lifestyles and home health care of persons who have disabilities. Pays 10¢ a word, on publication. Query.

LADIES' HOME JOURNAL—"Last Laughs," 100 Park Ave., New York, NY 10017. Brief, true anecdotes about the amusing things children say for "Out of the Mouths of Babes" column and short poetry about the funny business of being a woman today. All material must be original. Pays $50 for children's anecdotes; $100 for poems and other humor. Due to the volume of mail received, submissions cannot be acknowledged or returned.

MCCALL'S—Child Care Dept., 230 Park Ave., New York, NY 10169. Parenting tips and ideas, or words of wisdom on raising children. Pays $10. Include home phone and Social Security number with submission.

MAD MAGAZINE—485 Madison Ave., New York , NY 10022. Humorous pieces on a wide variety of topics. Two- to eight-panel cartoons; sketches not necessary. SASE for guidelines. Pays top rates, on acceptance.

MATURE LIVING—127 Ninth Ave. N., MSN 140, Nashville, TN 37234. Brief, humorous, original items; 25 line profiles with action photos; "Grandparents Brag Board" items; Christian inspirational pieces for senior adults, 125 words. Pays $5 to $15.

MATURE YEARS—201 Eighth Ave. S., P.O. Box 801, Nashville, TN 37202. Donn C. Downall, Ed. Poems, cartoons, puzzles, jokes, anecdotes, to 300 words, for older adults. Allow two months for manuscript evaluation. Include name, address, Social Security number with all submissions.

MID-WEST OUTDOORS—111 Shore Dr., Hinsdale, IL 60521. Gene Laulunen, Man. Ed. Where to and how to fish in the Midwest, 400 to 1,500 words, with two photos. Pays $15 to $35, on publication.

MODERN BRIDE—475 Park Ave. S., New York, NY 10016. Mary Ann Cavlin, Man. Ed. Humorous pieces, 500 to 1,500 words, for brides. Pays on acceptance.

MODERN MATURITY—3200 E. Carson St., Lakewood, CA 90712. Ian Ledgerwood, Ed. Money-saving tips; jokes, cartoons; etc. Submit seasonal material six months in advance. Pays from $50, on acceptance. Query.

NATIONAL ENQUIRER—Lantana, FL 33464. Michele Cooke, Asst. Ed. Short, humorous or philosophical fillers, witticisms, anecdotes, jokes, tart comments. Original items only. Short poetry with traditional rhyming verse, of amusing, philosophical, or inspirational nature. No obscure or artsy poetry. Occasionally uses longer poems of a serious or humorous nature. Submit seasonal/holiday material at least three months in advance. SASE required with all submissions. Pays $25, after publication.

NATIONAL REVIEW—150 E. 35th St., New York, NY 10016. William F. Buckley, Ed. Satire, to 900 words. Short, satirical poems. Pays $35 to $200, on publication.

NEW CHOICES FOR THE BEST YEARS—28 W. 23rd St., New York, NY 10010. Carol Mauro, Exec. Ed. Short humor pieces for lifestyle/service magazine for people ages 45 to 60. Payment varies, on acceptance.

NEW JERSEY MONTHLY—P.O. Box 920, Morristown, NJ 07963–0920. Sarah Fryberger, Assoc. Ed. Short pieces related to life in New Jersey. Pays 30¢ a word, on acceptance.

NEW YORK—755 Second Ave., New York, NY 10017. Chris Smith, Assoc. Ed. Short, lively pieces, to 400 words, highlighting events and trends in New York City for "Fast Track." Profiles to 300 words for "Brief Lives." Pays $25 to $300, on publication. Include SASE.

NORTHWEST LIVING!—130 Second Ave. S., Edmonds, WA 98020–3512. Terry W. Sheely, Ed. Shorts, 100 to 400 words, related to the natural resources of the Northwest. Query first with SASE. Pays on publication.

OUTDOOR LIFE—2 Park Ave., New York, NY 10016. Clare Conley, Ed.-in-Chief. Short instructive items and one-pagers on hunting, fishing, boating, and outdoor equipment. Photos. Pays on acceptance.

PARENTS—685 Third Ave., New York, NY 10017. Ann Pleshette Murphy, Ed. Short items on solutions of child care-related problems for "Parents Exchange." Pays $50, on publication.

PARISH FAMILY DIGEST—200 Noll Plaza, Huntington, IN 46750. Corine B. Erlandson, Ed. Family- or Catholic parish-oriented humor. Anecdotes, to 250 words, of unusual parish experiences. Pays $5, on acceptance.

PENNYWHISTLE PRESS—Box 500-P, Washington, DC 20044. Anita Sama, Ed. Puzzlers, word games, stories, for 7- to 14-year-olds. Pays varying rates, on acceptance.

PLAYBOY—680 N. Lakeshore Dr., Chicago, IL 60611. Address Party Jokes Ed. or After Hours Ed. Jokes; short original material on new trends, lifestyles, personalities; humorous news items. Pays $100 for jokes, on publication; $50 to $350 for "After Hours" items, on publication.

POPULAR MECHANICS—224 W. 57th St., New York, NY 10019. Deborah Frank, Man. Ed. How-to pieces, from 300 words, with photos and sketches, on home improvement and shop and craft projects. Pays $25 to $300, on acceptance. Buys all rights.

READER'S DIGEST—Pleasantville, NY 10570. Anecdotes for "Life in These United States," "Humor in Uniform," "Campus Comedy," and "All in a Day's Work." Pays $400, on publication. Short items for "Toward More Picturesque Speech." Pays $50. Anecdotes, fillers, for "Laughter, the Best Medicine," "Personal Glimpses," "Points to Ponder," "Quotable Quotes," etc. Pays $30 per two-column line. No submissions acknowledged or returned. Consult "Contributor's Corner" page for guidelines.

RHODE ISLAND MONTHLY—60 Branch Ave., Providence, RI 02904. Vicki Sanders, Man. Ed. Shorts pieces (to 250 words) on Rhode Island and southeastern Massachusetts: places, customs, people and events; pieces to 150 words on products and services; to 200 words on food, chefs, and restaurants. Pays $25 to $50, on publication.

RIVER RUNNER—P.O. Box 697, Fallbrook, CA 92028. Rand Green, Ed. Dir. Ken Hulick, Ed. Tips for whitewater boaters of all levels. Pays from 10¢ a word, on publication.

ROAD KING—P. O. Box 250, Park Forest, IL 60466. Address Features Ed. Trucking-related cartoons and anecdotes to 200 words, for "Trucker's Life." Pays $25 for cartoons, $25 for anecdotes, on publication. SASE required.

THE ROTARIAN—1560 Sherman Ave., Evanston, IL 60201. Willmon L. White, Ed. Occasional humor articles. Payment varies, on acceptance.

RURAL HERITAGE—P. O. Box 516, Albia, IA 52531. Current articles, 100 to 750 words, related to draft horses, rural events, or crafts. Pays 3¢ to 10¢ a word, on publication.

SACRAMENTO—1021 Second St., Sacramento, CA 95814. "City Lights," interesting and unusual people, places, and behind-the-scenes news items, 75 to 250 words. All material must have Sacramento tie-in. Pays $40 to $100 on publication.

THE SATURDAY EVENING POST—1100 Waterway Blvd., Indianapolis, IN 46202. Chuck Willig, Post Scripts Ed. Humor and satire, to 300 words; light verse, cartoons, jokes, for "Post Scripts." Pays $15, on publication.

SCHOOL SHOP/TECH DIRECTIONS—Prakken Publishing, Box 8623, 416 Longshore Dr., Ann Arbor, MI 48107. Susanne Peckham, Man. Ed. Puzzles and cartoons of interest to technology and industrial education teachers and administrators. Pay varies, on publication.

SCORE, CANADA'S GOLF MAGAZINE—287 MacPherson Ave., Toronto, Ont., Canada M4V 1A4. John Gordon, Man. Ed. Fillers, 50 to 100 words, related to Canadian golf scene. Rarely uses humor or poems. Pays $10 to $25, on publication. Include international reply coupons.

THE SENIOR MUSICIAN—See *The Church Musician*.

SKI MAGAZINE—2 Park Ave., New York, NY 10016. Dick Needham, Ed. Short, 100- to 300-word items on events and people in skiing for "Ski Life" department. Humor, 300 to 2,000 words, related to skiing. Pays on acceptance.

SNOWMOBILE—319 Barry Ave. S. Suite 101, Wayzata, MN 55391. Dick Hendricks, Ed. Short humor and cartoons on snowmobiling and winter "Personality Plates" sighted. Pays varying rates, on publication.

SPORTS AFIELD—250 W. 55th St., New York, NY 10019. Unusual, useful tips, anecdotes, 100 to 300 words, for "Almanac" section: hunting, fishing, camping, boating, etc. Photos. Pays 10¢ per column inch, on publication.

SPORTS CARD TRADER—3 Fairchild Ct., Plainview, NY 11518. Douglas Kale, Ed. Monthly. Fillers and poetry related to baseball, football, basketball, and hockey cards. Pays 7¢ per word, on publication.

STAR—660 White Plains Rd., Tarrytown, NY 10591. Topical articles, 50 to 800 words, on human-interest subjects, show business, lifestyles, the sciences, etc., for family audience. Pays varying rates.

TOUCH—Box 7259, Grand Rapids, MI 49510. Carol Smith, Man. Ed. Bible puzzles on themes from NIV version, for Christian girls aged 8 to 14. Pays $5 to $10 per puzzle, on acceptance. Send SASE for theme update.

TRAILER BOATS MAGAZINE—20700 Belshaw Ave., Carson, CA 90746. Chuck Coyne, Ed. Fillers and humor, preferably with illustrations, on boating and related activities. Pays $5 per column inch, extra for photos, on publication.

TRAVEL SMART—Dobbs Ferry, NY 10522. Interesting, unusual travel-related tips. Practical information for vacation or business travel. Query for over 250 words. Pays $5 to $100.

UNIQUE—P.O. Box 1224, Bridgeview, IL 60455. Hugh M. Cook, Ed. Bi-monthly. Articles on politics, social issues, and personalities. Humorous essays, 1,000 to 2,500 words. Pays 5¢ a word, on acceptance.

VOLKSWAGEN WORLD—P. O. Box 3951, 888 W. Big Beaver, Troy, MI 48007–3951. Marlene Goldsmith, Ed. Anecdotes, to 100 words, about Volkswagen owners' experiences; humorous photos of current model Volkswagens. Pays $40, on acceptance.

WASHINGTON'S ALMANAC—200 W. Thomas, Seattle, WA 98119. Gail E. Hudson, Man. Ed. Fillers and short humor pieces related to Washington state. Pays varying rates, on publication.

WISCONSIN TRAILS—P.O. Box 5650, Madison, WI 53705. Short fillers about Wisconsin: places to go, things to see, etc., 500 words. Pays $100, on publication.

WOMAN'S DAY—1633 Broadway, New York, NY 10019. Address "Neighbors" editor. Heart-warming anecdotes about a "good neighbor"; creative solutions to community or family problems. For "Tips to Share": short pieces of personal, instructive or family experiences, practical suggestions for homemakers. Pays $75, on publication.

WOODENBOAT MAGAZINE—Box 78, Brooklin, ME 04616. Jon Wilson, Ed. News of wooden boat-related activities and projects. Pays $5 to $50, on publication.

JUVENILE, TEENAGE, AND YOUNG ADULT MAGAZINES

JUVENILE MAGAZINES

BEAR ESSENTIALS NEWS FOR KIDS—P.O. Box 26908, Tempe, AZ 85285. Educational and entertaining articles, 300 to 600 words, for children in grades K through 3 and 4 through 8, including: world news in kids' terms; unique school projects; profiles of interesting achievers; family entertainment; science; youth sports and health; bilingual and multicultural topics; hobbies/young careers; pets and pet care; cartoon humor; educational activities, trivia, or puzzles. Also uses 50- to 150-word pieces for a companion Teachers Guide, providing classroom-use ideas related to articles. Payment is 10¢ a word, on publication; $10 to $35 for photos. Buys all rights. SASE required.

CHICKADEE—The Young Naturalist Foundation, 56 The Esplanade, Suite 306, Toronto, Ont., Canada M5E 1A7. Catherine Ripley, Ed. Animal and adventure stories, 200 to 800 words, for children ages 3 to 8. Also, puzzles, activities, and observation games, 50 to 100 words. Pays varying rates, on publication. Send complete manuscript and $1 check or money order for return postage.

CHILD LIFE—1100 Waterway Blvd., P.O. Box 567, Indianapolis, IN 46206. Steve Charles, Ed. Articles, 500 to 1,200 words, for 7- to 9-year-olds. Fiction and humor stories, to 1,200 words. Puzzles. Photos. Pays about 8¢ a word, extra for photos, on publication. Buys all rights.

CHILDREN'S ALBUM—P.O. Box 6086, Concord, CA 94524. Kathy Madsen, Ed. Fiction and poetry by children 8 to 14. Science and crafts projects, with step-by-step instructions. Pays $50 per page. Guidelines.

CHILDREN'S DIGEST—1100 Waterway Blvd., P.O. Box 567, Indianapolis, IN 46202. Elizabeth Rinck, Ed. Health publication for preteens. Informative articles, 500 to 1,200 words, and fiction (especially realistic, adventure, mystery, and humorous), 500 to 1,500 words, with health, safety, exercise, nutrition, or hygiene as theme. Historical and biographical articles. Poetry. Pays 8¢ a word, from $10 for poems, on publication.

CHILDREN'S PLAYMATE—Editorial Office, 1100 Waterway Blvd., P.O. Box 567, Indianapolis, IN 46206. Elizabeth Rinck, Ed. Humorous and health-related short stories, 500 to 700 words, for 6- to 8-year-olds. Simple science articles and how-to crafts pieces with brief instructions. "All About" features, about 500 words, on health, nutrition, safety, and exercise. Poems. Pays about 8¢ a word, $10 minimum for poetry, on publication.

CHILDREN'S SURPRISES—P.O. Box 236, Chanhassen, MN 55317. Peggy Simenson, Jeanne Palmer, Eds. "Activities for today's kids and parents." Educational activities, puzzles, games in reading, language, math, science, cooking, music, and art. Articles about history, animals, and geography. Pays $15 to $35, on publication.

CLUBHOUSE—Box 15, Berrien Springs, MI 49103. Elaine Trumbo, Ed. Action-oriented Christian stories: features, 800 to 1,200 words. Children in stories should be wise, brave, funny, kind, etc. Pays to $30 to $35 for stories.

COBBLESTONE—30 Grove St., Peterborough, NH 03458. Carolyn Yoder, Ed. Theme-related biographies, fiction, poetry, and short accounts of historical events, to 1,200 words, for children aged 8 to 14 years. Pays 10¢ to 15¢ a word for prose, varying rates for poetry, on publication. Send SASE for editorial guidelines with monthly themes.

CRICKET—Box 300, Peru, IL 61354. Marianne Carus, Ed.-in-Chief. Articles and fiction, 200 to 1,500 words, for 6- to 12-year-olds. Poetry, to 30 lines. Pays to 25¢ a word, to $3 a line for poetry, on publication. SASE required. Guidelines.

DISCOVERIES—6401 The Paseo, Kansas City, MO 64131. Stories, 500 to 1,000 words, for 3rd to 6th graders, with Christian emphasis. Poetry, 4 to 20 lines. Cartoons. Pays 3½¢ a word (2¢ a word for reprints), 25¢ a line for poetry (minimum of $2), on acceptance. Send SASE with manuscript.

THE DOLPHIN LOG—The Cousteau Society, 8440 Santa Monica Blvd., Los Angeles, CA 90069. Pam Stacey, Ed. Articles, 500 to 1,200 words, on a variety of topics related to our global water system: marine biology, ecology, natural history, and water-related stories, for children aged 7 to 15. Pays $25 to $150, on publication. Query.

FREE SPIRIT: NEWS & VIEWS ON GROWING UP—Free Spirit Publishing, Inc., 400 First Ave. N., Suite 616, Minneapolis, MN 55401. Judy Galbraith, Ed. Published 5 times a year. Nonfiction, 800 to 1,200 words, related to the lives of teens and preteens (school, peer relationships, family, health, etc.). Readers are 10- to 14-years-old. No fiction. Queries preferred. Pays to $100, on publication.

THE FRIEND—50 E. North Temple, 23rd Floor, Salt Lake City, UT 84150. Vivian Paulsen, Man. Ed. Stories and articles, 1,000 to 1,200 words. (Prefers completed manuscripts.) "Tiny tot" stories, to 250 words. Pays from 8¢ a word, from $15 per poem, on acceptance.

HIGHLIGHTS FOR CHILDREN—803 Church St., Honesdale, PA 18431. Kent L. Brown, Ed. Fiction and articles, to 900 words, for 2- to 12-year-olds. Fiction should have strong plot, believable characters, story that holds reader's interest from beginning to end. No crime or violence. For articles, cite references used and qualifications. Easy rebus-form stories. Easy-to-read stories, 400 to 600 words, with strong plots. Pays from 14¢ a word, on acceptance.

HOPSCOTCH—P.O. Box 1292, Saratoga Springs, NY 12866. Donald P. Evans, Ed. Bimonthly. Articles and fiction (600 to 1,200 words) and short poetry for girls ages 6 to 12. "We believe young girls deserve the right to enjoy a season of childhood before they become young adults; we are not interested in such topics as sex, romance, cosmetics, hairstyles, etc." Pays 5¢ per word; $150 for cover photos, made on publication.

HUMPTY DUMPTY'S MAGAZINE—1100 Waterway Blvd., P.O. Box 567, Indianapolis, IN 46206. Christine French Clark, Ed. General-interest publication with an emphasis on health for children ages 4 to 6. Easy-to-read fiction, to 600 words, some with health and nutrition, safety, exercise, or hygiene as theme; humor and light approach preferred. Creative nonfiction, including photo stories. Crafts with clear, brief instructions. No-cook recipes using healthful ingredients. Short verse, narrative poems. Pays about 8¢ a word, from $10 for poems, on publication. Buys all rights.

JACK AND JILL—Box 567, Indianapolis, IN 46206. Steve Charles, Ed. Articles, 500 to 1,000 words, for 6- to 8-year-olds, on sports, nature, science, health, safety, exercise. Features, 1,000 to 1,200 words, on history, biography, life in other countries, etc. Fiction, to 1,200 words. Short poems, games, puzzles, projects. Photos. Pays about 8¢ a word, extra for photos, varying rates for fillers, on publication.

JUNIOR TRAILS—1445 Boonville Ave., Springfield, MO 65802. Sinda Zinn, Ed. Fiction (1,000 to 1,500 words) with a Christian focus, believable characters, and moral emphasis. Articles (500 to 1,000 words) on science, nature, biography. Pays 2¢ or 3¢ a word, on acceptance.

KID CITY—See *3-2-1 Contact*.

LADYBUG—P.O. Box 300, Peru, IL 61354. Theresa Gaffey, Man. Ed. Picture stories, read-aloud stories, fantasy, folk and fairy tales, 300 to 750 words; poetry, to 20 lines; songs and rhymes; crafts, activities, and games, to 4 pages. Pays on publication: 25¢ a word for stories and articles; up to $3 a line for poetry.

LOLLIPOPS—Good Apple, Inc., P.O. Box 299, Carthage, IL 62321–0299. Learning games and activities covering all areas of the curriculum; arts and crafts ideas; stories, for ages 4 to 7. Pays varying rates, on publication. Query first.

MY FRIEND—Daughters of St. Paul, 50 St. Paul's Ave., Boston, MA 02130. Sister Anne Joan, Ed. "The Catholic Magazine for Kids." Readers are 6- to 12-years-old. Fiction, to 400 words, for primary readers; 400 to 600 words for intermediate readers. Nonfiction: general-information articles, lives of saints, etc., 150 to 600 words. Some humorous poetry, 6 to 8 lines. Buys first rights. Pays 3¢ to 7¢ a word (to $45). Query for artwork. Guidelines available.

NATIONAL GEOGRAPHIC WORLD—1145 17th St. N.W., Washington, DC 20036. Pat Robbins, Ed. Picture magazine for young readers, ages 8 and older. Games and puzzles; proposals for picture stories. Queries required for stories.

ODYSSEY—21027 Crossroads Circle, P.O. Box 1612, Waukesha, WI 53187. Nancy Mack, Ed. Features, 600 to 1,500 words, on astronomy and space science for 8- to 14-year-olds. Short experiments, projects, and games. Pays $100 to $350, on publication.

ON THE LINE—616 Walnut, Scottdale, PA 15683–1999. Mary Clemens Meyer, Ed. Weekly paper for 10- to 14- year olds. Uses nature and how-to articles, 500 to 650 words; fiction, 900 to 1,200 words; poetry, puzzles, cartoons. Pays to 4¢ a word, on acceptance.

OWL—The Young Naturalist Foundation, 56 The Esplanade, Suite 306, Toronto, Ont., Canada M5E 1A7. Sylvia Funston, Ed.-in-Chief. Articles, 500 to 1,000 words, for children ages 8 to 12 about animals, science, people, technology, new discoveries, activities. Pays varying rates, on publication. Send for guidelines.

PENNYWHISTLE PRESS—Box 500-P, Washington, DC 20044. Anita

Sama, Ed. Fiction for 7- to 12-year-olds, 450 to 500 words. Long poems, 15 to 25 lines. Puzzles and word games. Payment varies, on publication.

PLAYS, THE DRAMA MAGAZINE FOR YOUNG PEOPLE—120 Boylston St., Boston, MA 02116. Elizabeth Preston, Man. Ed. Needs one-act plays, programs, skits, creative dramatic material, suitable for school productions at junior high, middle, and lower grade levels. Plays with one set preferred. Uses comedies, dramas, satires, farces, melodramas, dramatized classics, folktales and fairy tales, puppet plays. Pays good rates, on acceptance. Buys all rights. Guidelines. SASE.

POCKETS—1908 Grand Ave., Box 189, Nashville, TN 37202. Janet Bugg, Ed. Ecumenical magazine for children ages 6 to 12. Fiction and scripture stories, 600 to 1,500 words; short poems; and articles about the Bible, 400 to 600 words. Pays from 10¢ a word, $25 to $50 for poetry, on acceptance. Guidelines and themes.

RADAR—8121 Hamilton Ave., Cincinnati, OH 45231. Margaret Williams, Ed. Articles, 400 to 650 words, on nature, hobbies, crafts. Short stories, 900 to 1,000 words: mystery, sports, school, family, with 12-year-old as main character; serials of 2,000 words. Christian emphasis. Poems to 12 lines. Pays to 3¢ a word, to 40¢ a line for poetry, on acceptance.

RANGER RICK—1400 16th St. N.W., Washington, DC 20036. Gerald Bishop, Ed. Articles, to 900 words, on wildlife, conservation, natural sciences, and kids in the outdoors, for 6- to 12-year-olds. Nature-related fiction and science fiction welcome. Games, crafts, poems, and puzzles. Pays to $550, on acceptance.

REFLECTIONS—P.O. Box 368, Duncan Falls, OH 43734. Dean Harper, Ed. "A National Magazine Publishing Student Writing." Published twice a year. Fiction and nonfiction, 300 to 2,000 words; poetry, any length. "Our magazine goes into K through 12th grades of schools and general offices. The purpose is to encourage writing." Queries not necessary. Pays in copies.

SESAME STREET MAGAZINE—See *3–2–1 Contact*.

SHOE TREE—National Assoc. for Young Writers, 215 Valle del Sol Dr., Santa Fe, NM 87501. Sheila Cowing, Ed.-in-Chief. Fiction, fantasy, science fiction, nonfiction, and poetry by writers ages 6 to 14. "We judge on quality of writing." Pays in copies.

SHOFAR—43 Northcote Dr., Melville, NY 11747. Gerald H. Grayson, Ed. Short stories, 500 to 750 words; articles, 250 to 750 words; poetry, to 50 lines; short fillers, games, puzzles, and cartoons, for Jewish children, 8 to 13. All material must have a Jewish theme. Pays 10¢ a word, on publication. Submit holiday pieces at least three months in advance.

SKIPPING STONES—80574 Hazelton Rd., Cottage Grove, OK 97424. Arun N. Toké, Man. Ed. "A Multi-Cultural Children's Quarterly." Nonfiction, of approximately 500 words, relating to cultural celebrations, life in other countries, and traditions for children ages 7 to 13. "Especially invited to submit are children, youth, and adults from other cultural backgrounds, minorities, blacks, and underpriviledged people. We print articles, writings, poetry, art, photographs, and stories from all parts of the world and in many different languages." Payment is one copy, on publication. Guidelines.

STONE SOUP, THE MAGAZINE BY CHILDREN—Box 83, Santa Cruz, CA 95063. Gerry Mandel, Ed. Stories, poems, plays, book reviews by children under 14. Pays in copies.

STORY FRIENDS—Mennonite Publishing House, Scottdale, PA 15683. Marjorie Waybill, Ed. Stories, 350 to 800 words, for 4- to 9-year-olds, on Christian faith and values in everyday experiences. Quizzes, riddles. Poetry. Pays to 5¢ a word, to $5 per poem, on acceptance.

3–2–1 CONTACT—Children's Television Workshop, 1 Lincoln Plaza, New York, NY 10023. Jonathan Rosenbloom, Ed. Entertaining and informative articles, 600 to 1,000 words, for 8- to 14-year-olds, on all aspects of science, computers, scientists, and children who are learning about or practicing science. Pays $75 to $400, on acceptance. No fiction. Also publishes *Kid City* and *Sesame Street Magazine*. Query.

TOUCH—Box 7259, Grand Rapids, MI 49510. Carol Smith, Man. Ed. Upbeat fiction and features, 1,000 to 1,500 words, for Christian girls ages 8 to 14; personal life, nature, crafts. Poetry, fillers, puzzles. Pays 2½¢ a word, extra for photos, on acceptance. Query with SASE for theme update.

TURTLE MAGAZINE FOR PRESCHOOL KIDS—1100 Waterway Blvd., Box 567, Indianapolis, IN 46206. Beth Wood Thomas, Ed. Stories about safety, exercise, health, and nutrition, for preschoolers. Humorous, entertaining fiction, 600 words. Simple poems. Stories-in-rhyme; easy-to-read stories, to 500 words, for beginning readers. Pays about 8¢ a word, on publication. Buys all rights. Send SASE for guidelines.

U.S. KIDS—245 Long Hill Rd., Middletown, CT 06457. Nancy Webb, Ed. Articles and fiction, 250 to 400 words, on issues related to kids age 5 to 10, fiction, true life adventures, science and nature topics. Pays $150 to $300, on acceptance. Query. Guidelines.

VENTURE—Christian Service Brigade, P.O. Box 150, Wheaton, IL 60189. Deborah Christensen, Man. Ed. Fiction and nonfiction, 1,000 to 1,500 words, for 10- to 15-year old boys involved in Stockade and Battalion. "Articles and stories should reflect the simple truths of the Gospel and its life-changing power." Humor and fillers and B&W 8x10 photos also accepted. Pays 5¢ to 10¢ a word, on publication.

WEE WISDOM—Unity Village, MO 64065. Judy Gehrlein, Ed. Character-building stories, to 800 words, for children through age 12. Pays varying rates, on acceptance.

WONDER TIME—6401 The Paseo, Kansas City, MO 64131. Evelyn J. Beals, Ed. Stories, 200 to 550 words, for 6- to 8-year-olds, with Christian emphasis to correlate with Sunday school curriculum. Poetry, 4 to 12 lines. Pays 3½¢ a word, from 25¢ a line for verse, $3 minimum, on acceptance.

YOUNG AMERICAN, AMERICA'S NEWSPAPER FOR KIDS—P.O. Box 12409, Portland, OR 97212. Kristina T. Linden, Ed. Upbeat, positive, sophisticated material for children ages 6 to 15. Fiction, to 1,000 words; articles, to 350 words, on science, humor, history, and newsworthy young people; poetry. Pays from 7¢ a word, from $10 for photos, on publication.

YOUNG JUDEAN—50 W. 58th St., New York, NY 10019. Mordecai Newman, Ed. Articles, 500 to 1,000 words, with photos, for 9- to 12-year-olds, on Israel, Jewish holidays, Jewish-American life, Jewish history. Fiction, 800 to 1,500 words, on Jewish themes. Poetry, from 8 lines. Fillers, humor, reviews. Pays 5¢ a word.

ZILLIONS—Consumers Union of the United States, 256 Washington St., Mt. Vernon, NY 10553. Jeanne Kiefer, Man. Ed. Bimonthly. Articles, 1,000 to 1,500 words, on consumer education (money, product testing, etc.), for children, preteens, and young teens. "We are the *Consumer Reports* for kids." Pays $500 to $1,000, on publication. Guidelines.

TEENAGE AND YOUNG ADULT

ALIVE NOW!—P.O. Box 189, Nashville, TN 37202. Mary Ruth Coffman, Ed. Short essays, 250 to 400 words, with Christian emphasis for adults and young adults. Poetry, one page. Photos. Pays $15 to $20, on publication.

BOP—3500 W. Olive Ave., Suite 850, Burbank, CA 91505. Julie Laufer, Ed. Interviews and features, 500 to 1,000 words, for teenage girls, on stars popular with teenagers. Photos. Pays varying rates, on acceptance. Query preferred. Same requirements for *The Big Bopper*.

BOYS' LIFE—1325 Walnut Hill Ln., Irving, TX 75038–3096. William B. McMorris, Ed. Publication of Boy Scouts of America. Articles and fiction, 1,000 to 1,200 words, for 8- to 18-year-old boys. Photos. Pays from $500 for major articles and $750 fiction, on acceptance. Query first.

CHALLENGE—See *Pioneer*.

EXPLORING—1325 Walnut Hill Ln., Box 152079, Irving, TX 75015–2079. Scott Daniels, Exec. Ed. Publication of Boy Scouts of America. Articles, 500 to 1,800 words, for 14- to 21-year-old boys and girls, on education, careers, Explorer activities (hiking, canoeing, camping) and program ideas for meetings. No controversial subjects. Pays $150 to $500, on acceptance. Query. Send SASE for guidelines.

FREEWAY—Box 632, Glen Ellyn, IL 60138. Billie Sue Thompson, Ed. First-person true stories, personal experience, how-tos, fillers, and humor, to 1,000 words, with photos, for 13- to 22-year-olds. Must have Christian emphasis. Pays to 8¢ a word.

GRIT—208 W. Third St., Williamsport, PA 17701. Joanne Decker, Assignment Ed. Articles, 400 to 800 words, with photos, on young people involved in unusual hobbies, occupations, athletic pursuits, and personal adventures. Pays 15¢ a word, extra for photos, on acceptance.

HICALL—1445 Boonville Ave., Springfield, MO 65802–1894. Deanna Harris, Ed. Articles, 500 to 1,000 words, and fiction, to 1,500 words, for 12- to 19-year-olds; strong evangelical emphasis. Pays on acceptance.

IN TOUCH—Box 50434, Indianapolis, IN 46250–0434. Rebecca Higgins, Ed. Articles, 500 to 1,000 words, on contemporary issues, athletes, and singers from conservative Christian perspective, for 13- to 19-year-olds. Pays 2¢ to 4¢ a word. Send SASE for guidelines.

KEYNOTER—3636 Woodview Trace, Indianapolis, IN 46268. Tamara P. Burley, Exec. Ed. Articles, 1,500 to 2,500 words, for high school leaders: general-interest features; self-help; pieces on contemporary teenage problems. No fillers or poetry. Photos. Pays $75 to $250, extra for photos, on acceptance. Query preferred.

LISTEN MAGAZINE—12501 Old Columbia Pike, Silver Spring, MD 20904. Gary B. Swanson, Ed. Articles (1,200 to 1,500 words) providing teens with "a vigorous, positive, educational approach to the problems arising out of the use of tobacco, alcohol, and other drugs." Pays 5¢ to 7¢ a word, on acceptance.

MERLYN'S PEN, THE NATIONAL MAGAZINE OF STUDENT WRITING—P.O. Box 1058, East Greenwich, RI 02818. R. James Stahl, Ed. Writing by students in grades 7 through 10 only. Short stories, to 3,500 words; reviews; travel pieces and poetry, to 100 lines. Pays in copies. Guidelines available.

NEW ERA—50 E. North Temple, Salt Lake City, UT 84150. Richard M. Romney, Ed. Articles, 150 to 3,000 words, and fiction, to 3,000 words, for young Mormons. Poetry. Photos. Pays 5¢ to 20¢ a word, 25¢ a line for poetry, on acceptance. Query.

PIONEER—1548 Poplar Ave., Memphis, TN 38104. Tim Bearden, Ed. Southern Baptist. Articles, to 1,500 words, for 12- and 14-year-old boys, on teen problems, current events. Photo essays on Christian sports personalities. Pays 4½¢ a word, extra for photos, on acceptance. Same address and requirements for *Challenge*.

SCHOLASTIC SCOPE—730 Broadway, New York, NY 10003. Deborah Sussman, Sr. Ed. For 15- to 18-year-olds with 4th to 6th grade reading ability. Fiction, 400 to 1,500 words, and plays, to 5,000 words, on subjects relevant to contemporary teens. Humor O.K. Also adaptations of classics. Profiles, 400 to 800 words, of interesting teenagers, with photos. Pays $125 for 500- to 600-word articles, from $200 for plays and short stories, from $150 for longer pieces, on acceptance.

SEVENTEEN—850 Third Ave., New York, NY 10022. Roberta Myers, Articles Ed. Articles, to 2,500 words, on subjects of interest to teenagers. Sophisticated, well-written fiction, 1,500 to 3,500 words, for young adults. Poetry, to 40 lines, by teens. Short news and features, to 750 words, for "Talk." Articles, 1,000 words, by teenagers, for "View." Pays varying rates, on acceptance.

STRAIGHT—8121 Hamilton Ave., Cincinnati, OH 45231. Carla J. Crane, Ed. Articles on current situations and issues, humor, for Christian teens. Well-constructed fiction, 1,000 to 1,200 words, showing teens using Christian principles. Poetry by teenagers. Photos. Pays about 3¢ a word, on acceptance. Guidelines.

TEEN POWER—Box 632, Glen Ellyn, IL 60138. Amy Swanson, Ed. True-to-life fiction or first person (as told to), true teen experience stories with Christian insights and conclusion, 700 to 1,000 words. Include photos. Pays 7¢ to 10¢ a word, extra for photos, on acceptance.

TQ/TEEN QUEST—Box 82808, Lincoln, NE 68501. Karen Christianson, Ed. Articles, to 1,800 words, and well-crafted fiction, to 2,500 words, for conservative Christian teens. B&W photos and color slides. Pays 5¢ to 10¢ a word, extra for photos, on publication.

WRITING!—60 Revere Dr., Northbrook, IL 60062–1563. Alan Lenhoff, Ed. Interviews, 1,200 words, for "Writers at Work" department, for high school students. Pays $200, on publication. Query.

YM—685 Third Ave., New York, NY 10017. David Keeps, Sr. Articles Ed., Entertainment. Mary Garner, Man. Ed., Articles. Articles, to 1,500 words, on entertainment, lifestyle, fashion, beauty, relationships, health, for women from 12 to 22. Query with clips. SASE. Payment varies, on acceptance.

YOUNG AND ALIVE—4444 S. 52nd St., Lincoln, NE 68506. Richard Kaiser, Ed. Feature articles, 800 to 1,400 words, for blind and visually impaired young adults, on adventure, biography, camping, health, hobbies, and travel. Photos. Pays 3¢ to 5¢ a word, extra for photos, on acceptance. Write for guidelines.

YOUNG SALVATIONIST—The Salvation Army, 799 Bloomfield Ave., Verona, NJ 07044. Capt. Robert R. Hostetler, Ed. Articles for teens, 800 to 1,200 words, with Christian perspective; fiction, 800 to 1,200 words; short fillers. "Young Soldier" section: fiction, 600 to 800 words; games and puzzles for children. Pays 3¢ to 5¢ a word, on acceptance.

THE DRAMA MARKET

Community, regional, and civic theaters and college dramatic groups offer the best opportunities today for playwrights to see their plays produced, whether for staged production or for dramatic readings. Indeed, aspiring playwrights who can get their work produced by any of these have taken an important step toward breaking into the competitive dramatic field —many well-known playwrights received their first recognition in the regional theaters. Payment is generally nominal, but regional and university theaters usually buy only the right to produce a play, and all further rights revert to the author. Since most directors like to work closely with the authors on any revisions necessary, theaters will often pay the playwright's expenses while in residence during rehearsals. The thrill of seeing your play come to life on the stage is one of the pleasures of being on hand for rehearsals and performances.

Aspiring playwrights should query college and community theaters in their region to find out which ones are interested in seeing original scripts. Dramatic associations of interest to playwrights include the Dramatists Guild (234 W. 44th St., New York, NY 10036) and Theatre Communications Group, Inc. (355 Lexington Ave., New York, NY 10017), which publishes the annual *Dramatists Sourcebook*. *The Playwright's Companion*, published by Feedback Theatrebooks, P.O. Box 5187, Bloomington, IN 47402–5187, is an annual directory of theatres and prize contests seeking scripts.

Some of the theaters on the following list require that playwrights submit all or some of the following with scripts—cast list, synopsis, resumé, recommendations, return postcard—and with scripts and queries, SASEs must always be enclosed. Playwrights may also wish to register their material with the U.S. Copyright Office. For additional information about this, write Register of Copyrights, Library of Congress, Washington, DC 20559.

REGIONAL AND UNIVERSITY THEATERS

ACADEMY THEATRE—P.O. Box 77070, Atlanta, GA 30357. Linda C. Anderson, Lit. Mgr. Plays "stretching the boundaries of imagination, with elements of surrealism, poetic language, and imagery in comedy and drama format." Prefers local playwrights for Genesis Series Productions. Considers regional and national playwrights for new play premieres in subscription series productions. Royalty is negotiable.

ACTORS THEATRE OF LOUISVILLE—316 W. Main St., Louisville, KY 40202. Michael Bigelow Dixon, Lit. Mgr. Ten-minute comedies and dramas (to 10 pages); include SASE. Annual contest. Guidelines.

A. D. PLAYERS—2710 W. Alabama, Houston, TX 77098. Jeannette Clift George, Artistic Dir. Carol E. Anderson, Lit. Mgr. Full-length or one-act comedies, dramas, musicals, children's plays, and adaptations with Christian world view. Submit script with SAS postcard, resumé, cast list, and synopsis. (Christmas plays should be submitted before Oct.) Reports in 2 months. Readings. Pays negotiable rates.

ALABAMA SHAKESPEARE FESTIVAL—The State Theatre, #1 Festival

Drive, Montgomery, AL 36117. Kent Thompson, Art. Dir. Full-length adaptations and plays dealing with southern or black issues. Send resumé and synopsis in June.

ALLEY THEATRE—615 Texas Ave., Houston, TX 77002. Christopher Baker, Lit. Mgr. Full-length plays and musicals, including translations and adaptations, plays for young audiences. Query with synopsis, 10 sample pages, and resumé.

ALLIANCE THEATRE COMPANY—1280 Peachtree St. N.E., Atlanta, GA 30309. Sandra Deer, Lit. Mgr. Full-length comedies and dramas. Query with synopsis and cast list. Pay varies.

AMERICAN LINE—810 W. 183rd St., #5C, New York, NY 10033. Robert Hoehler, Art. Dir. Produces one-act and full-length plays for two- to four-week runs in midtown Manhattan. Contemporary situations, tightly written plays "with a message" reflecting a multi-cultural mix. Query with synopsis and SASE in September and May. Royalties negotiable.

AMERICAN LIVING HISTORY THEATER—P.O. Box 2677, Hollywood, CA 90078. Dorene Ludwig, Artistic Dir. One-act, historically accurate (primary source materials only) dramas. Submit script with SASE. Reports in 1 to 6 months. Pays varying rates.

AMERICAN PLACE THEATRE—111 W. 46th St., New York, NY 10036. Cynthia Jenner, Dramaturg. "No unsolicited manuscripts accepted. We welcome scripts from writers who have had full or workshop productions of their plays and professional theaters. Writers may send a synopsis and the first 20 pages with SASE. We seek challenging, innovative works and do not favor obviously commercial material."

AMERICAN REPERTORY THEATRE—64 Brattle St., Cambridge, MA 02138. Robert Scanlan, Lit. Dir. No unsolicited manuscripts. Submit one-page description of play, 10 page sample; nothing returned without SASE; 3 to 4 months for response.

AMERICAN STAGE—P.O. Box 1560, St. Petersburg, FL 33731. Victoria Holloway, Artistic Dir. Full-length comedies and dramas. Send synopsis with short description of cast and production requirements with SAS postcard. Pays negotiable rates. Submit Sept. to Jan.

AMERICAN STAGE COMPANY—FDU, Box 336, Teaneck, NJ 07666. Ted Rawlins, Prod. Dir. Full-length comedies, dramas, and musicals for cast of 5 or 6 and single set. Submit synopsis with resumé, cast list, and return postcard to Sheldon Epps, Art. Assoc. Read in spring, reports in 2 to 3 months. No unsolicited scripts.

AMERICAN STANISLAVSKI THEATRE—485 Park Ave., #6A, New York, NY 10022. Sonia Moore, Artistic Dir. Full-length or one-act drama with important message. No offensive language. For cast aged 16 to 45. Submit script with SAS postcard in April and May; reports in Sept. No payment.

AMERICAN THEATRE OF ACTORS—314 W. 54th St., New York, NY 10019. James Jennings, Art. Dir. Full-length dramas for a cast of 2 to 6. Submit complete play and SASE. Reports in 1 to 2 months.

ARENA STAGE—Sixth and Maine Ave. S.W., Washington, DC 20024. Laurence Maslon, Lit. Mgr./Dramaturg. Submit one-page synopsis, first 10 pages of dialogue, and resumé. No unsolicited manuscripts. Allow 1 month reply for queries, 3 months for manuscripts.

ARKANSAS ARTS CENTER CHILDREN'S THEATRE—Box 2137, Little

Rock, AR 72203. Bradley Anderson, Artistic Dir. Seeks solid, professional (full-length or one-act) scripts, especially work adapted from contemporary and classic literature. Some original work. Pays flat rate.

ARKANSAS REPERTORY THEATRE COMPANY—601 S. Main, P.O. Box 110, Little Rock, AR 72203–0110. Brad Mooy, Lit. Mgr. Full-length comedies, dramas, and musicals; prefer up to 8 characters. Send synopsis, cast list, resumé, and return postage. Reports in 5 to 6 months.

ARTREACH TOURING THEATRE—3074 Madison Rd., Cincinnati, OH 45209. Kathryn Schultz Miller, Artistic Dir. One-act dramas and adaptations for touring children's theater; cast to 3, simple sets. Submit script with synopsis, cast list, resumé, recommendations, and SASE. Payment varies.

ASOLO STATE THEATRE—P.O. Drawer E, Sarasota, FL 34230. John Ulmer, Artistic Dir. Full-length dramas, comedies, musicals, and children's plays. Small stage. Pays royalty or varying rates. Readings and workshops offered. No unsolicited manuscripts. Query with synopsis.

BAILIWICK REPERTORY—3212 N. Broadway, Chicago, IL 60657–3515. David Zak, Art. Dir. Produces 5 full-length, 5 late-night, and 45 one-act festival plays per year. Large casts or musicals are O.K. Plays are highly theatrical and politically aware. "Know the rules, then break them creatively and boldly. Creative staging is a must." Submit complete manuscript. Submit one-act plays before Dec. 1. (One-act-play festival runs March through April.) Reports in 3 months. Pays 4% to 8% royalty.

BARTER THEATER—P.O. Box 867, Abingdon, VA 24210. Rex Partington, Producing Dir. Full-length dramas, comedies, adaptations, musicals, and children's plays. Full workshop and reading productions. Allow 6 to 8 months for report. Payment rates negotiable.

BERKSHIRE THEATRE FESTIVAL—Box 797, Stockbridge, MA 01262. Richard Dunlap, Artistic Dir. Full-length comedies, musicals, and dramas; cast to 8. Submit through agent only.

BOARSHEAD THEATER—425 S. Grand Ave., Lansing, MI 48933. John Peakes, Artistic Dir. Full-length comedies and dramas with simple sets and cast to 10. Send precis, 5 to 10 pages of dialogue, cast list with descriptions, and resumé. SAS postcard for reply.

BRISTOL RIVERSIDE THEATRE—Box 1250, Bristol, PA 19007. Susan D. Atkinson, Art. Dir. Full-length and one-act plays with up to 10 actors on simple set. Submit synopsis with return postcard in summer. Pays a percentage of box office proceeds. Offers workshops and readings.

CALIFORNIA UNIVERSITY THEATRE—California, PA 15419. Dr. Roger C. Emelson, Chairman. Unusual, avant-garde, and experimental one-act and full-length plays (comedy and drama), children's plays, and adaptations. Cast size varies. Submit synopsis in Jan. with short, sample scene(s). Payment available.

CHELSEA STAGE, INC.—(formerly Hudson Guild Theater) 441 W. 26th St., New York, NY 10001. Geoffrey Sherman, Art. Dir. Full-length comedies, dramas, and musicals for 8-person cast. (No fly or wing space in theater.) Submit synopsis, letter of inquiry, and SASE to Rebecca Kreinen, Lit. Mgr. All musicals must be accompanied by tape of music. Response time varies from 3 to 6 months. Pays $1,000.

CHILDSPLAY, INC.—Box 517, Tempe, AZ 85280. David Saar, Art. Dir. Plays running 45 to 90 minutes: dramas, musicals, children's plays, and adaptations.

Sets must travel. Cast size, 4 to 8. Submissions accepted July through November. Reports in 2 to 6 months. Payment varies.

CIRCLE IN THE SQUARE/UPTOWN—1633 Broadway, New York, NY 10019. Theodore Mann, Artistic Dir. Full-length comedies, dramas, and adaptations. Send synopsis with resumé, cast list, and 10-page dialogue sample to Seth Goldman, Lit. Advisor. No unsolicited scripts. SASE required.

CIRCLE REPERTORY COMPANY—161 Ave. of the Americas, New York, NY 10013. Adrienne Hiegel, Lit. Mgr. Send full-length dramas with cast list. Offers criticism "as often as possible." Pays $2,500. Reports in 5 months. Readings.

CITY THEATRE COMPANY—Bellefield Annex, 315 S. Bellefield Ave., Pittsburgh, PA 15260. Scott Cummings, Lit. Dir. Full-length comedies and dramas; query Sept. to May. Cast to 12; simple sets. Readings. Royalty.

CLASSIC STAGE COMPANY—136 E. 13th St., New York, NY 10003. Patty Taylor, Managing Dir. Carey Perloff, Artistic Dir. Full-length adaptations and translations of existing classic literature. Submit synopsis with cast list and SASE, Sept. to May. Offers readings. Pays on royalty basis.

COLUMBIA COLLEGE—Theatre-Music Center, 72 E. 11th St., Chicago, IL 60605. Sheldon Patinkin, Art. Dir. The New Musicals Project is designed to support playwrights, lyricists, and composers during writing process. Submit original bound script, treatment of idea, or outline of idea with narrative synopsis and history of project. Include biographical information and tape of music. Workshop participation is from May through September. Allow 3 months for response. Offers weekly salary, directorial and dramaturg assistance, staged readings or workshops with cast, and studio recording of score.

CREATIVE THEATRE—102 Witherspoon St., Princeton, NJ 08540. Eloise Bruce, Art. Dir. Participatory plays for children, grades K through 6; cast of 4 to 6; arena or thrust stage. Submit manuscript with synopsis and cast list. Pay varies.

THE CRICKET THEATRE—1407 Nicollet Ave., Minneapolis, MN 55403. William Partlan, Art. Dir. Send synopsis, resumé, and 10 page sample of work; "prefer contemporary plays." Cast to 11. Reports in 6 months.

DELAWARE THEATRE COMPANY—P.O. Box 516, Wilmington, DE 19899. Cleveland Morris, Artistic Dir. Full-length comedies, dramas, musicals, and adaptations, with cast to 10; prefer single set. Send cast list, synopsis, and SASE. Reports in 6 months. Pays royalty.

DENVER CENTER THEATRE COMPANY—1050 13th St., Denver, CO 80204. Send full-length, previously unproduced scripts with cast to 12, June through December. Stipend and housing. Annual New Play Festival, "U.S. West Fest."

DETROIT REPERTORY THEATRE—13103 Woodrow Wilson Ave., Detroit, MI 48238. Barbara Busby, Lit. Mgr. Full-length comedies and dramas. Enclose SASE. Pays royalty.

STEVE DOBBINS PRODUCTIONS—25 Van Ness Ave., Lower Level, San Francisco, CA 94102. Michael Lojkovic, Lit. Dir. Full-length comedies, dramas, and musicals. Cast to 12. Query with synopsis and resumé. No unsolicited manuscripts. Reports in 6 months. Offers workshops and readings. Pays 6% of gross.

DORSET THEATRE FESTIVAL—Box 519, Dorset, VT 05251. Jill Charles, Art. Dir. Full-length comedies, musicals, dramas, and adaptations; cast to 8; simple set preferred. Agent submissions and professional recomendations only. Pays varying rates. Residencies at Dorset Colony House for Writers available Sept. to May. (See "Writers Colonies" list.)

DRIFTWOOD SHOWBOAT—Box 1032, Kingston, NY 12401. Fred Hall, Resident Company Art. Dir. Full-length family comedies for 2- to 6-person cast, single setting. No profanity. Submit cast list, synopsis, and return postcard Sept. to June.

ECCENTRIC CIRCLES THEATRE—400 W. 43rd St., #4N, New York, NY 10036. Rosemary Hopkins, Art. Dir. Full-length comedies, dramas, and musicals with simple sets and a cast size to 10. Submit manuscript with resumé and SASE. Reports in 6 weeks.

EMPIRE STATE INSTITUTE FOR THE PERFORMING ARTS—Empire State Plaza, Albany, NY 12223. Patricia B. Snyder, Prod. Dir. Query for new musicals and plays for family audiences, with synopsis, cast list. Submit between June and August. Payment varies.

THE EMPTY SPACE THEATRE—P.O. Box 1748, Seattle , WA 98111–1748. Kurt Beattie, Lit. Mgr. Unsolicited scripts accepted only from WA, OR, WY, MT, and ID. Outside five-state N.W. region: scripts accepted through agents or established theater groups only.

ENSEMBLE STUDIO THEATRE—549 W. 52nd St., New York, NY 10019. Address Literary Mgr. Send full-length or one-act comedies and dramas, with resumé and SASE, Sept. to April. Pay varies. Readings.

FLORIDA STUDIO THEATRE—1241 N. Palm Ave., Sarasota, FL 33577. Jack Fournier, New Play Development. Innovative smaller cast plays that are pertinent and contemporary. Query first with synopsis and SASE. Also accepting musicals.

GE VA THEATRE—75 Woodbury Blvd., Rochester, NY 14607. Ann Patrice Carrigan, Lit. Dir. Query for comedies and dramas with synopsis and cast list. Readings.

GEER THEATRICUM BOTANICUM, WILL—Box 1222, Topanga, CA 90290. All types of scripts for outdoor theater, with large playing area. Submit synopsis with SASE. Pays varing rates.

EMMY GIFFORD CHILDREN'S THEATER—3504 Center St., Omaha, NE 68105. James Larson, Artistic Dir. Unsolicited scripts accepted with SASE.

THE GOODMAN THEATRE—200 S. Columbus Dr., Chicago, IL 60603. Tom Creamer, Dramaturg. Queries required for full-length comedies or dramas and must come through recognized literary agents or producing organizations. No unsolicited scripts or synopses accepted.

THE GUTHRIE THEATER—725 Vineland Pl., Minneapolis, MN 55403. Full-length comedies, dramas, and adaptations. Manuscripts accepted only from recognized theatrical agents. Query with detailed synopsis and cast size. Reports in 1 to 2 months.

HARRISBURG COMMUNITY THEATRE—513 Hurlock St., Harrisburg, PA 17110. Thomas G. Hostetter, Artistic Dir. Full-length comedies, dramas, musicals, and adaptations; cast to 20; prefers simple set. Submit script with cast list, resumé, synopsis, and SAS postcard. Best time to submit: June to August. Reporting time: 6 months. Pays negotiable rates.

HEDGEROW THEATRE—146 Rose Valley Rd., Moylan, PA 19086. David Zum Brunnen, Art. Dir. Mark Lofta, Lit. Assoc. Full-length comedies, dramas, musicals, children's plays, and adaptation for 15-person cast. Small theater seats 150. Send script in the spring or summer with resumé, return postcard, cast list, and SASE. Reports in 2 months.

HIPPODROME STATE THEATRE—25 S.E. Second Pl., Gainesville, FL 32601. Mary Hausch, Producing Art. Dir. Full-length plays with unit sets and casts up to 15. Submit in summer and fall. Enclose return postcard and synopsis.

HOLLYWOOD THEATER COMPANY—12838 Kling St., Studio City, CA 91604. Rai Tasco, Art. Dir. Full-length comedies and dramas for integrated cast. Include cast list and stamped return postcard with submission.

HONOLULU THEATRE FOR YOUTH—2846 Ualena St., Honolulu, HI 96819. Pam Sterling, Resident Dir. Plays, 60 to 90 minutes playing time, for young people/family audiences. Adult casts. Contemporary issues, Pacific themes, etc. Unit sets, small cast. Query or send manuscript with synopsis, cast list, and SASE. Royalties negotiable.

HORIZON THEATRE COMPANY—P. O. Box 5376, Station E, Atlanta, GA 30307. Jeffrey and Lisa Adler, Co-Artistic Directors. Full-length comedies, dramas, and satires that use "heightened" realism and other highly theatrical forms. Cast to 10. Submit synopsis with cast list, resumé, and recommendations. Pays percentage. Readings. Reports in 3 months.

HUDSON GUILD THEATRE—See Chelsea Stage, Inc.

ILLINOIS THEATRE CENTER—400 Lakewood Blvd., Park Forest, IL 60466. Steve S. Billig, Artistic Dir. Full-length comedies, dramas, musicals, and adaptations, for unit/fragmentary sets, and cast to 8. Send summary and return postcard. No unsolicited manuscripts. Pays negotiable rates. Workshops and readings offered.

ILLUSTRATED STAGE COMPANY—Box 640063, San Francisco, CA 94164–0063. Steve Dobbins, Art. Dir. Full-length comedies, dramas, and musicals for a cast to 18. Query with synopsis and SASE. No unsolicited manuscripts. Offers workshops and readings.

INVISIBLE THEATRE—1400 N. First Ave, Tucson, AZ 85719. Deborah Dickey, Literary Mgr. Reads queries for full-length comedies, dramas, musicals, adaptations, Jan. to May. Cast to 10; simple set. Pays royalty.

JEWISH REPERTORY THEATRE—344 E. 14th St., New York, NY 10003. Ran Avni, Artistic Dir. Full-length comedies, dramas, musicals, and adaptations, with cast to 10, relating to the Jewish experience. Pays varying rates. Enclose return postcard.

KUMU KAHUA—Kennedy Theatre, Univ. of Hawaii at Manoa, 1770 East-West Rd., Honolulu 96822. Dennis Carroll, Man. Dir. Full-length plays specially relevant to life in Hawaii. Prefer simple sets for arena and in-the-round productions. Submit resumé and synopsis January through April. Pays $25 per performance. Readings. Contests.

LAMB'S PLAYERS THEATRE—500 Plaza Blvd., P. O. Box 26, National City, CA 92050. Kerry Cederberg, Lit. Mgr. Full-length dramas, translations, adaptations, musicals. Special interest in works with Christian world view. Query with synopsis required.

LONG ISLAND STAGE—P. O. Box 9001, Rockville Centre, New York 11571–9001. Clinton J. Atkinson, Art. Dir. Full-length dramas and adaptations. Query with SASE in late spring/early summer. Pays varying rates.

LOS ANGELES DESIGNERS' THEATRE—P. O. Box 1883, Studio City, CA 91614–0883. Richard Niederberg, Artistic Dir. Full-length comedies, dramas, muscials, fantasies, or adaptations. Religious, political, social, and controversial themes encouraged. Nudity, "adult" language, etc., O.K. Payment varies.

THE MAGIC THEATRE—Bldg. D, Fort Mason, San Francisco, CA 94123. Eugenie Chan, Lit. Mgr. Comedies and dramas, ethnic-American, workshop productions. Query with synopsis, resumé, and 3 to 5 pages of sample dialogue. Pays varying rates.

MANHATTAN THEATRE CLUB—453 W. 16th, New York, NY 10011. Address Kate Loewald. Full-length and one-act comedies, dramas, and musicals. No unsolicited manuscripts. Send synopsis with 10 to 15 pages of dialogue, cast list, resumé, recommendations, and SASE. Pays negotiable rates. Allow 6 months for reply.

MAXWELL ANDERSON PLAYWRIGHTS SERIES, INC.—6 Sagmore Rd., Stamford, CT 06902. Dr. Philip Devine, Exec. Prod. Send script with SASE. Reports in 2 months. Pays travel expenses, to $100, for playwright to attend rehearsals.

MILL MOUNTAIN THEATRE—Center in the Square, One Market Square, Roanoke, VA 24011. Jo Weinstein, Lit. Mgr. Full-length or one-act comedies, dramas, musicals; include publicity, resumé. One-act plays limited to 25 to 40 minutes. Payment varies.

MISSOURI REPERTORY THEATRE—4949 Cherry St., Kansas City, MO 64110. Felicia Londré, Dramaturg. Full-length comedies and dramas. Query with synopsis, cast list, resumé, and return postcard. Pays standard royalty.

MUSIC-THEATRE GROUP—735 Washington St., New York, NY 10014. Innovative musicals, to 1 ½ hours. Query only, with synopsis and return postcard. Best submission time: Sept. to Dec.

MUSICAL THEATRE WORKS—440 Lafayette St., New York, NY 10003. Brook R. Garrett, Lit. Mgr. Full-length musicals, cast to 10; simple sets. Submit manuscript with SASE and cassette score. No payment.

NATIONAL BLACK THEATRE—2033 Fifth Ave., Harlem, NY 10035. Submit to Tundi Samuel. Drama, musicals, and children's plays. "Scripts should reflect African and African-American lifestyle. Historical, inspirational, and ritualistic forms appreciated." Workshops and readings.

NATIONAL PLAYWRIGHTS CONFERENCE, EUGENE O'NEILL THEATRE CENTER—234 W. 44th St., Suite 901, New York, NY 10036. Annual competition to select new stage and television plays for development during the summer at organization's Waterford, CT, location. Submission deadline: Dec. 1. Send #10-size SASE in the fall for guidelines to National Playwright's Conference, c/o above address. Pays stipend, plus travel/living expenses during conference.

NEW TUNERS/PERFORMANCE COMMUNITY—1225 W. Belmont Ave., Chicago, IL 60657. Allan Chambers, Dramaturg. Full-length musicals only, for cast to 15; no wing/fly space. Send manuscript with cassette tape of score, cast list, resumé, and return postcard. Pays on royalty basis.

NEW YORK SHAKESPEARE FESTIVAL/PUBLIC THEATER—425 Lafayette St., New York, NY 10003. Gail Merrifield, Dir. of Plays and Musicals. Plays and musical works for the theater, translations, and adaptations. Submit manuscript, cassette (with musicals) and SASE.

ODYSSEY THEATRE ENSEMBLE—12111 Ohio Ave., Los Angeles, CA 90025. Ron Sossi, Artistic Dir. Full-length comedies, dramas, musicals, and adaptations: provocative subject matter, or plays that stretch and explore the possibilities of theater. Query Jan Lewis, Lit. Mgr. with synopsis and return postcard. Pays variable rates. Allow 2 to 6 months for reply. Workshops and readings.

OLD GLOBE THEATRE—Simon Edison Center for the Performing Arts, Box 2171, San Diego, CA 92112. Address Mark Hofflund. Full-length comedies, dramas, and musicals. No unsolicited manuscripts. Submit through agent, or query with synopsis.

OLDCASTLE THEATRE COMPANY—Southern Vermont College, Box 1555, Bennington, VT 05201. Eric Peterson, Dir. Full-length comedies, dramas, and musicals for a small cast (up to 10) and a single stage set. Submit synopsis and cast list in the winter. Reports in 2 months. Offers workshops and readings. Pays expenses for playwright to attend rehearsals. Royalty.

PAPER MILL PLAYHOUSE—Brookside Dr., Millburn, NJ 07041. Maryan F. Stephens, Lit. Advisor. Full-length plays and musicals. Submit synopsis, resumé, and tape for musicals; reporting time, 4 to 6 months.

PENGUIN REPERTORY COMPANY—Box 91, Stony Point, NY 10980. Joe Brancato, Artistic Dir. Full-length comedies and dramas with cast size to 5. Submit script, resumé, and SASE. Payment varies.

PENNSYLVANIA STAGE COMPANY—837 Linden St., Allentown, PA 18101. Full-length plays with cast to 8; one set. Send synopsis, cast list, and SASE to Literary Dept. Pays negotiable rates. Allow 6 months for reply. Readings.

PEOPLE'S LIGHT AND THEATRE COMPANY—39 Conestoga Rd., Malvern, PA 19355. Alda Cortese, Lit. Mgr. One-act or full-length comedies, dramas, adaptations. Query with synopsis, resumé, ten pages of script required. Reports in 6 months. Payment negotiable.

PIER ONE THEATRE—Box 894, Homer, AK 94603. Lance Petersen, Lit. Dir. Full-length and one-act comedies, dramas, musicals, children's plays, and adaptations. Submit complete script; include piano score with musicals. New works given staged readings. "We think new works in the theater are extremely important!" Pays 8% of ticket sales for mainstage musicals; other payment varies.

PLAYHOUSE ON THE SQUARE—51 S. Cooper in Overton Sq., Memphis, TN 38104. Jackie Nichols, Artistic Dir. Full-length comedies, dramas; cast to 15. Query. Pays $500.

PLAYWRIGHTS HORIZONS—416 W. 42nd St., New York, NY 10036. Address Literary Dept. Full-length, original comedies, dramas, and musicals by American authors. Send resumé and SASE. Pays varying rates.

PLAYWRIGHTS' PLATFORM—164 Brayton Rd., Boston, MA 02135. B. A. Creasey, Pres. Script development workshops and public readings for New England playwrights only. Full-length and one-act plays of all kinds. No sexist or racial material accepted. Residents of New England send scripts with short synopsis, resumé, return postcard, and SASE.

POPLAR PIKE PLAYHOUSE—7653 Old Poplar Pike, Germantown, TN 38138. Frank Bluestein, Art. Dir. Full-length and one-act comedies, dramas, musicals, and children's plays. Submit synopsis with return postcard and resumé. Pays $300.

PRINCETON REPERTORY COMPANY—13 Witherspoon St., Princeton,

NJ 08542. Victoria Liberatori, Art. Dir. Full-length comedies and dramas for a cast to 8. One set. Submit synopsis with resumé and cast list, or complete manuscript. "Scripts with socially relevant themes that move beyond domestic drama preferred. The treatment of these themes might be lyrical, surreal, realistic, or high concept." Workshops and readings offered. Response within 1 year.

THE PUERTO RICAN TRAVELING THEATRE—141 W. 94th St., New York, NY 10025. Miriam Colon Valle, Artistic Dir. Full-length and one-act comedies, dramas, and musicals; cast to 8; simple sets. Payment negotiable.

THE REPERTORY THEATRE OF ST. LOUIS—Box 28030, St. Louis, MO 63119. Agent submissions only.

THE ROAD COMPANY—Box 5278 EKS, John City, TN 37603. Robert H. Leonard, Artistic Dir. Christine Murdock, Lit. Mgr. Full-length and one-act comedies, dramas with social/political relevance to small-town audiences. Send synopsis, cast list, and production history, if any. Pays negotiable rates. Reports in 6 to 12 months.

ROUND HOUSE THEATRE—12210 Bushey Dr., Silver Spring, MD 20902. Address Production Office Mgr. Full-length comedies, dramas, adaptations, and musicals; cast to 10; prefer simple set. Send 1 page synopsis. No unsolicited manuscripts.

SALT AND PEPPER MIME COMPANY/NEW ENSEMBLE ACTORS THEATRE—320 E. 90th St., New York, NY 10128. Ms. Scottie Davis, Art. Dir. One acts, all types, childrens plays, mini musicals, especially dealing with African-American, Hispanic, and Native American cultures. Cast size to 4. Send resumé, return postcard, cast list, and synopsis. "Very interested in pieces adaptable to the surrealistic concept." Scripts reviewed from July to Oct. Payment of royalties based on rates established at beginning of run. Works also considered for readings, story-players, and experimental development.

SEATTLE GROUP THEATRE—3940 Brooklyn Ave. N.E., Seattle, WA 98105. William S. Yellow Robe, Jr., Lit. Mgr. Full-length satires, dramas, musicals, and translations, cast to 10; simple set. Special interest in plays suitable for multi-ethnic cast; serious plays on social/cultural issues; satires. Query with synopsis, self-addressed postcard, sample dialogue, and resumé required. Reporting time: 6 weeks.

SEATTLE REPERTORY THEATRE—155 Mercer St., Seattle, WA 98109. Daniel Sullivan, Art. Dir. Full-length comedies, dramas, and adaptations. Submit synopsis, 10-page sample, return postcard, and resumé to Mark Bly, Art. Assoc. New plays series with workshops each spring.

SOCIETY HILL PLAYHOUSE—507 S. 8th St., Philadelphia, PA 19147. Walter Vail, Dramaturg. Full-length dramas and comedies; cast to 6; simple set. Submit synopsis and SASE. Reports in 6 months. Nominal payment.

SOUTH COAST REPERTORY—P. O. Box 2197, Costa Mesa, CA 92628. John Glore, Lit. Mgr. Full-length comedies, dramas, musicals, juveniles. Query first with synopsis and resumé. Payment varies.

SOUTHERN APPALACHIAN REPERTORY THEATRE—P.O. Box 620, Mars Hills, NC 28754. James W. Thomas, Art. Dir. Full-length comedies, dramas, musicals, and plays with Appalachian theme for a small stage. Submit resumé, recommendations, full script, and SASE to Jan W. Blalock, Asst. Man. Dir. Send SASE for information on Southern Appalachian Playwright's Conference. Pays

$500 royalty if play is selected for production during the summer season. Deadline for submissions is Dec. 15 each year.

THE SPUYTEN DUYVIL THEATRE CO.—c/o Isabel Glasser, 22 W. 15th St. #18D, New York, NY 10011. Full-length comedies and dramas with single set and cast size to 5. SASE required.

STAGE LEFT THEATRE—3244 N. Clark, Chicago, IL 60657. Dennis McCullough, Art. Dir. Full-length comedies, dramas, and adaptations for cast of 3 to 12. "We are committed to producing material that is politically and socially conscious." Submit in the spring/summer. Reports in 4 to 6 weeks. Offers workshops and readings. Payment varies.

STAGE ONE: THE LOUISVILLE CHILDREN'S THEATRE—425 W. Market St., Louisville, KY 40202. Adaptations of classics and original plays for children ages 4 to 18. Submit script with resumé and SASE. Reports in 4 months.

STAGES THEATRE—3201 Allen Parkway, Suite 101, Houston, TX 77019. Joe Turner Cantu, Interim Art. Dir. Full-length and one-act comedies, dramas, and children's scripts. Cast to 12; simple set. For season submission: submit script, synopsis, resumé. and SASE. Texas Playwrights Festival submissions (from Texas natives or residents) accepted Fall through early Spring. Texas Playwrights Festival submissions cannot be returned.

STREET PLAYERS THEATRE—P.O. Box 2687, Norman, OK 73070. Robert Woods, Art. Dir. Full-length comedies, dramas, and children's plays for 4 to 7 actors, with single sets or open staging. Queries preferred. Reporting time 6 months. Pays $250, after production.

TAPER FORUM, MARK—135 N. Grand Ave., Los Angeles, CA 90012. Oliver Mayer, Lit. Assoc. Full-length comedies, dramas, musicals, juvenile, adaptations. Query first.

TEN MINUTE MUSICALS PROJECT—Box 461194, West Hollywood, CA 90046. Michael Koppy, Prod. One-act musicals. Include audio cassette, libretto, and lead sheets with submission. "We are looking for complete short musicals." Pays $250. Also offers workshops.

THEATER ARTISTS OF MARIN—Box 473, San Rafael, CA 94915. Charles Brousse, Art. Dir. Full-length comedies, dramas, and musicals for a cast of 2 to 8. Submit synopsis with cast list and return postcard. Reports in 4 to 6 months. Pays $400 before opening. Three showcase productions each year.

THEATRE AMERICANA—Box 245, Altadena, CA 91001. Full-length comedies and dramas, preferably with American theme. No musicals or children's plays. Send bound manuscript with cast list, resumé, and SASE, by April 1. No payment. Allow 3 to 6 months for reply. Submit no more than two entries per season.

THEATRE ON THE SQUARE—450 Post St., San Francisco, CA 94102. Jonathan Reinis, Art. Dir. Full-length comedies, dramas, and musicals for 15-person cast. Submit cast list and script with SASE. Reports in 30 days.

THEATREWORKS/USA—890 Broadway, 7th Fl., New York, NY 10003. Barbara Pasternack, Lit. Man. Small-cast children's musicals only. Playwrights must be within commutable distance to New York City. Submit in spring, summer. Pays royalty.

WALNUT STREET THEATRE COMPANY—9th and Walnut Sts., Philadelphia, PA 19107. Ernest Tremblay, Lit. Mgr. Full-length comedies, dramas, muscials, and adaptations; also, 1- to 5-character plays for second stage. Submit 10 pages sample with return postcard, cast list, and synopsis. Reports in 5 months. Payment varies.

THE WESTERN STAGE—156 Homestead Ave., Salinas, CA 93901. Tom Humphrey, Art. Dir. The Steinbeck Playwriting Prize. Submissions Oct. 1 to Dec. 31 to Joyce Lower, Dramaturg. Full-length plays in the spirit of John Steinbeck. No one-act plays or adaptations. Prize includes readings, workshops, residency, a full-scale production, royalties, and support during reworking (up to $4,000).

WISDOM BRIDGE THEATRE—1559 W. Howard St., Chicago, IL 60626. Jeff Ortmann, Producing Dir. Plays dealing with contemporary social/political issues; small scale musicals, literary adaptations; cast to 12.

YOUNG MIME THEATRE, GARY—23724 Park Madrid, Calabasas, CA 91302. Gary Young, Art. Dir. Comedy monologues and two-person vignettes, for children and adults, 1 minute to 90 minutes in length; casts of 1 or 2, and portable set. Pays varying rates. Enclose return postcard, resumé, recommendations, cast list, and synopsis.

PLAY PUBLISHERS

ART CRAFT PLAY COMPANY—Box 1058, Cedar Rapids, IA 52406. Three-act comedies, mysteries, musicals, and farces, and one-act comedies or dramas, with one set, for production by junior or senior high schools. Pays on royalty basis or by outright purchase.

BAKER'S PLAYS—100 Chauncy St., Boston, MA 02111. Scripts for amateur production: one-act plays for competition, children's plays, musicals, religious drama, full-length plays for high school production. Three- to four-month reading period. Include SASE.

CHILDREN'S PLAYMATE—1100 Waterway Blvd., P. O. Box 567, Indianapolis, IN 46206. Elizabeth A. Rinck, Ed. Plays, 200 to 600 words, for children ages 6 to 8: special emphasis on health, nutrition, exercise, and safety. Pays about 8¢ a word, on publication.

CONTEMPORARY DRAMA SERVICE—Meriwether Publishing Co., Box 7710, 885 Elkton Dr., Colorado Springs, CO 80903. Arthur Zapel, Ed. Books on theater arts subjects and anthologies. Textbooks for speech and drama. Easy-to-stage comedies, skits, one-acts, musicals, puppet scripts, full-length plays for schools and churches. (Jr. high through college level; no elementary level material.) Adaptations of classics and improvised material for classroom use. Comedy monologues and duets. Chancel drama for Christmas and Easter church use. Enclose synopsis. Pays by fee arrangement or on royalty basis.

THE DRAMATIC PUBLISHING CO.—311 Washington St., P. O. Box 109, Woodstock, IL 60098. Full-length and one-act plays, musical comedies for amateur, children's, and stock groups. Must run at least thirty minutes. Pays on royalty basis. Address Sarah Clark. Reports within 10 to 14 weeks.

DRAMATICS—Educational Theatre Assoc., 3368 Central Pkwy., Cincinnati, OH 45225–2392. Don Corathers, Ed. One-act and full-length plays for high school production. Pays $100 to $200, on acceptance.

ELDRIDGE PUBLISHING COMPANY—P. O. Drawer 216, Franklin, OH 45005. Nancy Vorhis, Ed. Dept. One-, two-, and three-act plays and operettas for school, churches, community groups, etc. Special interest in comedies and Christmas plays. Include cassette for operettas. Pays varying rates. Responds in 2 to 3 months.

FRENCH,INC., SAMUEL—45 W. 25th St., New York, NY 10010. Lawrence R. Harbison, Ed. Full-length plays for dinner, community, stock, college, and high school theaters. One-act plays (30 to 45 minutes). Children's plays, 45 to 60 minutes. Pays on royalty basis.

HEUER PUBLISHING COMPANY—Drawer 248, Cedar Rapids, IA 52406. C. Emmett McMullen, Ed. One-act comedies and dramas for contest work; three-act comedies, mysteries, or farces, and musicals, with one interior setting, for high school production. Pays royalty or flat fee.

PIONEER DRAMA SERVICE—P. O. Box 22555, Denver, CO 80222. Full-length and one-act plays; plays for young audiences; musicals, melodramas, and Christmas plays. No unproduced plays, plays with largely male casts or multiple sets. Query. Outright purchase or royalty.

PLAYS, THE DRAMA MAGAZINE FOR YOUNG PEOPLE—120 Boylston St., Boston, MA 02116. Elizabeth Preston, Man. Ed. One-act plays, with simple settings, for production by young people, 7 to 17: holiday plays, comedies, dramas, farces, skits, dramatized classics, puppet plays, melodramas, dramatized folktales, and creative dramatics. Maximum lengths: lower grades, 10 double-spaced pages; middle grades, 15 pages; junior and senior high, 20 pages. Casts may be mixed, all-male or all-female. Send SASE for manuscript specification sheet. Queries suggested for adaptations. Pays good rates, on acceptance. Buys all rights.

SCHOLASTIC SCOPE—730 Broadway, New York, NY 10003. Deborah Sussman, Ed. For ages 15 to 18 with 4th- to 5th-grade reading ability. Plays, 1,000 to 6,000 words, on problems of contemporary teenagers, relationships between people in family, job, and school situations. Some mysteries, comedies, and science fiction; plays about minorities. Also plays adapted from the classics. Pays good rates, on acceptance.

SCHOLASTIC VOICE—730 Broadway, New York, NY 10003. Forrest Stone, Ed. For ages 14 to 18 with at least an 8th-grade reading level. Plays, 1,000 to 3,000 words, on any subject. Magazine is distributed though schools. Pays good rates, on acceptance.

THE TELEVISION MARKET

The almost round-the-clock television offerings on commercial, educational, and cable TV stations may lead free-lance writers to believe that opportunities to sell scripts or program ideas are infinite. Unfortunately, this is not true. With few exceptions, producers and programmers do not consider scripts submitted directly to them, no matter how good they are. In general, free lancers can achieve success in this nearly closed field by concentrating on getting their fiction (short and in novel form) and nonfiction published in magazines or books, combed diligently by television producers for possible adaptations. A large percentage of the material offered over all types of networks (in addition to the motion pictures made in Hollywood or especially for TV) is in the form of adaptations of published material.

Writers who want to try their hand at writing directly for this very limited market should be prepared to learn the special techniques and acceptable format of script writing. Also, experience in playwriting and a knowledge of dramatic structure gained through working in amateur, community, or professional theaters can be helpful.

Since virtually all TV producers will read scripts and queries submitted only through recognized agents, we've included a list of agents who have indicated to us that they are willing to read queries for TV scripts. Society of Authors' Representatives (10 Astor Pl., 3rd Floor, New York, NY 10003) will send out a listing of agents upon receipt of an SASE, and *Literary Market Place* (Bowker), available in most libraries, also has list of agents. Before submitting scripts to producers or to agents, authors should query to learn whether they prefer to see the material in script form, or as an outline or summary. A list of network (ABC, NBC, CBS, FOX) shows and production companies may be found in *Ross Reports Television*, published monthly by Television Index, Inc., (40–29 27th St., Long Island City, NY 11101).

Writers may wish to register their story, treatment, series format, or script with the Writers Guild of America. This registration does not confer statutory rights, but it does supply evidence of authorship and date of authorship. Registration is effective for five years (and is renewable after that). The WGA's registration service is available to guild members and non-members for a reasonable fee. For more information, write the Writers Guild of America Registration Service East, Inc., 555 W. 57th St., New York, NY 10019. Dramatic material can also be registered with the U.S. Copyright Office (Register of Copyrights, Library of Congress, Washington, DC 20559). Finally, those interested in writing for television may want to read such daily trade newspapers as *Daily Variety* (5700 Wilshire Blvd., Suite 120, Los Angeles, CA 90036) and *Hollywood Reporter* (6715 Sunset Blvd., Hollywood, CA 90028).

TELEVISION SCRIPT AGENTS

MARCIA AMSTERDAM AGENCY—41 W. 82nd St., #9A, New York, NY 10024. Query with SASE.

PEMA BROWNE LTD—Pine Rd., HCR Box 104B, Neversink, NY 12765. No scripts for ongoing shows. Reads queries. Prefers writers with credits.

THE CALDER AGENCY—17420 Ventura Blvd., Suite 4, Encino, CA 91316. Reads queries and synopses for features only; no episode TV material. Movies for TV and long form O.K.

BILL COOPER ASSOCIATES—224 W. 49th St., New York, NY 10019. Will look at developed ideas for comedies, dramas, and motion pictures.

ANN ELMO AGENCY, INC.—60 E. 42nd St., New York, NY 10165. Prefer queries on TV or screen feature material. Writers with screen credits only.

ROBERT A. FREEDMAN—Dramatic Agency, Inc., 1501 Broadway, #2310, New York, NY 10036. Query with SASE.

OTTO R. KOZAK LITERARY AGENCY—P.O. Box 152, Long Beach, NY 11561. Query with SASE.

THE LANTZ OFFICE—888 Seventh Ave., New York, NY 10106. Limited market. Query.

HAROLD OBER ASSOCIATES, INC.—425 Madison Ave., New York, NY 10017. Query with SASE.

THE SHUKAT COMPANY, LTD.—340 W. 55th St., #1A, New York, NY 10036. Query.

WRITERS AND ARTISTS AGENCY—19 West 44th St., Suite 1000, New York, NY 10036. Reads queries with SASEs. Considers screenplays, teleplays, and plays. Send bio and resumé.

BOOK PUBLISHERS

The following list includes the major publishers of trade books (adult and juvenile fiction and nonfiction) and a representative number of small publishers from across the country. All companies in the list publish both hardcover and paperback books, unless otherwise indicated.

Before sending a complete manuscript to an editor, it is advisable to send a brief query letter describing the proposed book. The letter should also include information about the author's special qualifications for dealing with a particular topic and any previous publication credits. An outline of the book (or a synopsis for fiction) and a sample chapter may also be included.

It is common practice to submit a book manuscript to only one publisher at a time, although it is becoming more and more acceptable for writers, even those without agents, to submit the same query or proposal to more than one editor at the same time.

Book manuscripts may be sent in typing paper boxes (available from a stationer) and sent by first-class mail, or, more common and less expensive, by "Special Fourth Class Rate—Manuscript." For rates, details of insurance, and so forth, inquire at your local post office. With any submission to a publisher, be sure to enclose sufficient postage for the manuscript's return.

Royalty rates for hardcover books usually start at 10% of the retail price of the book and increase after a certain number of copies have been sold. Paperbacks generally have a somewhat lower rate, about 5% to 8%. It is customary for the publishing company to pay the author a cash advance against royalties when the book contract is signed or when the finished manuscript is received. Some publishers pay on a flat fee basis.

ABBEY PRESS—St. Meinrad, IN 47577. Keith McClellan, O.S.B., Pub. Nonfiction books on marriage, parenting, family, pastoral care, and spiritual growth with a mainline Judeo-Christian religious slant. Query with table of contents, writing sample, and SASE.

ABINGDON PRESS—201 Eighth Ave. S., Nashville, TN 37202. Mary Catherine Dean, Ed. Religious books: mainline, social issues. Query with outline and one or two sample chapters. Guidelines.

ACADEMY CHICAGO, PUBLISHERS—213 West Institute Pl., Chicago, IL 60610. Anita Miller, Ed. General quality adult fiction; classic mysteries with emphasis on character and/or puzzle. History; biographies; travel; books by and about women. Royalty. Also interested in reprinting books dropped by other houses, including academic titles and anthologies. Query with four sample chapters. SASE required.

ACCENT BOOKS—Box 15337, 12100 W. 6th Ave., Denver, CO 80215. Mary Nelson, Exec. Ed. Fiction and nonfiction from evangelical Christian perspective. "Request guidelines before querying." Query with sample chapters and SASE. Royalty. Paperback only.

ACE BOOKS —Imprint of Berkley Publishing Group, 200 Madison Ave., New York, NY 10016. Susan Allison, V.P., Ed.-in-Chief. Science fiction and fantasy. Royalty. Query with first three chapters and outline.

ACROPOLIS BOOKS—11250 Roger Bacon Dr.,#22 Acropolis Bldg., Reston, VA 22090. Kathleen Hughes, Pub. Nonfiction titles. Query with outline and sample chapters. Length varies. Royalty.

ADAMA BOOKS—306 W. 38th St., New York, NY 10018. Bennett Shelkowitz, Man. Dir. Adult nonfiction. Young-adult fiction and nonfiction. Children's picture books. Books with international focus or related to political or social issues.

ADDISON-WESLEY PUBLISHING CO.—Rt. 128, Reading, MA 01867. General Publishing Group: Adult nonfiction on current topics: education, health, psychology, computers, software, business, biography, child care, etc. Royalty.

ALASKA NORTHWEST BOOKS—A Div. of GT/E Discovery Publications, 22026 20th Ave. S.E., Bothell, WA 98021. Maureen Zimmerman, Mgr. Nonfiction, 50,000 to 100,000 words, with an emphasis on natural world and history of Alaska, Western Canada, and Pacific Northwest: travel books; biographies; cookbooks; field guides; guidebooks. Send query or sample chapters with outline. New imprint will include Pacific Rim material.

THE AMERICAN PSYCHIATRIC PRESS—1400 K St. N.W., Washington, DC 20005. Carol C. Nadelson, M.D., Ed.-in-Chief. Books that interpret scientific and medical aspects of psychiatry for a lay audience and that address specific psychiatric problems. Authors must have appropriate credentials to write on medical topics. Query required. Royalty.

AND BOOKS—702 S. Michigan, South Bend, IN 46618. Janos Szebedinsky, Ed. Adult nonfiction. Topics include computers, fine arts, health, philosophy, sports and recreation, regional subjects, biographies, and religion.

APPALACHIAN MOUNTAIN CLUB BOOKS—5 Joy St., Boston, MA 02108. Regional (New England) nonfiction titles (250 to 400 pages) for adult audience; juvenile and young adult nonfiction. Topics include guidebooks on backcountry (non-motorized) recreation, nature, mountain history/biography, search and rescue, and environmental management. Send queries with outline and sample chapters to the editor. Multiple queries considered. Royalty.

APPLE BOOKS—See Scholastic, Inc.

ARCADE PUBLISHING —Subsidiary of Little, Brown, and Co., 141 Fifth Ave., New York, NY 10010. Richard Seaver, Pub./Ed. Fiction, nonfiction, and children's books. Query first.

ARCHWAY PAPERBACKS—Pocket Books, 1230 Ave. of the Americas, New York, NY 10020. Patricia MacDonald, Exec. Ed. Young-adult contemporary fiction (suspense thrillers, survival adventure, strong boy/girl stories) and nonfiction (popular current topics), for ages 11 and up. Query and SASE required; include outline and sample chapter.

ARCO PUBLISHING—Div. of Simon & Schuster, Gulf & Western Bldg., One Gulf & Western Plaza, 16th Fl., New York, NY 10023. Charles Wall, Exec. Ed. Nonfiction, originals and reprints, from 50,000 words. Career guides, test preparation. Royalty. Unsolicited manuscripts not accepted.

ARCSOFT PUBLISHERS—P.O. Box 132, Woodsboro, MD 21798. Anthony Curtis, Pres. Nonfiction hobby books for beginners: personal computing, space science, desktop publishing, journalism. Hobby electronics for laymen and consumers, beginners and novices. Outright purchase and royalty basis. Query. Paper only.

THE ATLANTIC MONTHLY PRESS—19 Union Square West, New York, NY 10003. Ann Godoff, Ed.-in-Chief. Fiction, general nonfiction. Hardcover and trade paperback. Royalty. SASE required.

AVERY PUBLISHING GROUP—120 Old Broadway, Garden City Park, NY 11040. Nonfiction, from 40,000 words, on health, childbirth, child care, health, cooking. Query first. Royalty.

AVIATION PUBLISHERS—Ultralight Publications, Inc., One Aviation Way, Lock Box 234, Hummelstown, PA 17036. Michael A. Markowski, Ed. Nonfiction, from 30,000 words, on aviation, cars, model cars and planes, boats, trains, health, self-help, and inspiration. Query with outline and sample chapters. Royalty.

AVON BOOKS—105 Madison Ave., New York, NY 10016. Carolyn Reidy, Pres./Pub. Robert McCoy, Exec. Ed. Genre fiction, general nonfiction, historical romance, 60,000 to 200,000 words. Science fiction, 75,000 to 100,000 words. Query with synopsis and sample chapters. Ellen Edwards, Historical Romance; John Douglas, Science Fiction. Camelot Books: Ellen Krieger, Ed. Fiction and nonfiction for 7- to 10-year-olds. Query. Flare Books: Ellen Krieger, Ed. Fiction and nonfiction for 12-year-olds and up. Query. Royalty. Paperback only.

BACKCOUNTRY PUBLICATIONS—Div. of The Countryman Press, Inc., P. O. Box 175, Woodstock, VT 05091. Carl Taylor, Ed. Regional guidebooks, 150 to 300 pages, on hiking, walking, canoeing, bicycling, mountain biking, cross-country skiing, and fishing. Send outline and sample chapter. Royalty.

BAEN BOOKS—Baen Enterprises, P.O. Books 1403, Riverdale, NY 10471–1403. Jim Baen, Pres. and Ed.-in-Chief. Strongly plotted science fiction; innovative fantasy. Query with synopsis and manuscript. Advance and royalty. Guidelines available for letter-sized SASE.

BAKER BOOK HOUSE—P. O. Box 6287, Grand Rapids, MI 49516–6287. Religious nonfiction. Dan Van't Kerkhoff, Ed., general trade and professional books. Allan Fisher, Ed., academic and reference books. Royalty.

BALLANTINE BOOKS—201 E. 50th St., New York, NY 10022. Robert Wyatt, Ed.-in-Chief. General fiction and nonfiction. Query.

BALSAM PRESS—122 E. 25th St., New York, NY 10010. Barbara Krohn, Exec. Ed. General and illustrated adult nonfiction. Query. Royalty.

BANTAM BOOKS—Div. of Bantam, Doubleday, Dell, 666 Fifth Ave., New York, NY 10103. Linda Grey, Pres. Jeff Stone, Pub. Adult Fiction and Nonfiction. General and educational fiction and nonfiction, 75,000 to 100,000 words. Judy Gitenstein, Ed. Dir., Books for Young Readers: fiction and science fiction, ages 6 to 12. Beverly Horowitz, Ed. Dir., Books for Young Adults: fiction and non-formula romance for teens. Bantam Travel Guides, Dick Scott, Pub. Only agented queries and manuscripts.

BARRON'S—250 Wireless Blvd., Hauppauge, NY 11788. Grace Freedson, Acquisitions Ed. Nonfiction for juveniles (science, nature, history, hobbies, and how-to) and picture books for ages 3 to 6. Nonfiction for adults (business, childcare, sports). Queries required. Guidelines.

BAUHAN, PUBLISHER, WILLIAM L.—Dublin, NH 03444. William L. Bauhan, Ed. Biographies, fine arts, gardening, and history books with an emphasis on New England. Submit query with outline and sample chapter.

BEACON PRESS—25 Beacon St., Boston, MA 02108. Wendy Strothman, Dir. Lauren Bryant, Sr. Ed. General nonfiction: world affairs, sociology, psychology, women's studies, political science, art, anthropology, literature, history, philosophy, religion. Series: Asian Voices (fiction and nonfiction); Barnard New Women Poets; Black Women Writers (fiction); Men and Masculinity (nonfiction); Night Lights (juveniles). Query first. SASE required.

BEAR & COMPANY, INC.—P.O. Drawer 2860, Santa Fe, NM 87504. Barbara Clow, Ed. Nonfiction "that will help transform our culture philosophically, environmentally, and spiritually." Query with outline and sample chapters. SASE required. Royalty.

BERKLEY PUBLISHING GROUP—200 Madison Ave., New York, NY 10016. Roger Cooper, Pub. Leslie Gelbman, Ed.-in-Chief. General-interest fiction and nonfiction: science fiction, suspense and espionage novels; romance. Submit through agent only. Publishes both reprints and originals. Paper only.

BETHANY HOUSE PUBLISHERS—6820 Auto Club Rd., Minneapolis, MN 55438. Address Editorial Dept. Fiction, nonfiction. Religious. Query required. Royalty.

BETTER HOMES AND GARDENS BOOKS—See Meredith Corporation.

BINFORD & MORT PUBLISHING—1202 N.W. 17th Ave., Portland, OR 97209. J. F. Roberts, Ed. Books on subjects related to the Pacific Coast and the Northwest. Lengths vary. Query first. Royalty.

BLAIR, PUBLISHER, JOHN F.—1406 Plaza Dr., Winston-Salem, NC 27103. Stephen D. Kirk, Ed. Dept. Biography, history, fiction, folklore, and guidebooks, with southeastern tie-in. Length: at least 75,000 words. Royalty. Query.

BONUS BOOKS—160 E. Illinois St., Chicago, IL 60611. Sharon Turner Mulvihill, Asst. Ed. Nonfiction; topics vary widely. Query with sample chapters and SASE. Royalty.

BOOKMAKERS GUILD—9655 W. Colfax Ave., Lakewood, CO 80215. Jill A. Nieman, Man. Ed. Adult books of fiction (150 to 350 pages) and nonfiction (250 to 500 pages) focusing on the growth and development of families and children. Picture books and juvenile fiction, 24 to 48 pages, juvenile nonfiction, 100 to 250 pages, and young adult books, 96 to 300 pages. Query with outline and sample chapters. Royalty.

BOOKS FOR PROFESSIONALS—See Harcourt, Brace, Jovanovich.

BOUREGY & CO., INC., THOMAS—Avalon Books, 401 Lafayette St., New York, NY 10003. Barbara J. Brett, Ed. Hardcover library books. Wholesome contemporary romances, and mystery romances about young single (never married) women. Wholesome westerns and contemporary adventure novels. Length: 35,000 to 50,000 words. Query with first chapter and outline. SASE required. Guidelines for SASE.

BRADBURY PRESS—866 Third Ave., New York, NY 10022. Barbara Lalicki, Ed. Hardcover: fiction (general, humor, science fiction), grades 4 to 12; nonfiction (science, sports, history) up to grade 6; picture books, to age 8. Submit complete manuscript. Royalty.

BRANDEN PUBLISHING COMPANY—17 Station St., Box 843, Brookline Village, MA 02147. Adolph Caso, Ed. Novels, biographies, and autobiographies. Especially books by or on women, 250 to 350 pages. Also considers queries on history, computers, business, performance arts, and translations. Query only with SASE. Royalty.

BRICK HOUSE PUBLISHING—Box 134, 11 Thoreau Rd., Acton, MA 01720. Robert Runck, Ed. Books on business, personal finance, careers, travel, and home design and maintenance. Query with outline and sample chapters. Royalty.

BRIDGE PUBLISHING—2500 Hamilton Blvd., South Plainfield, NJ 07080. Nonfiction books: biography, autobiography, self-help, psychology, and religion. "Books must be written from an evangelical Christian perspective, but need not be explicitly religious in nature."

BRISTOL PUBLISHING ENTERPRISES—P.O. Box 1737, San Leandro, CA 94577. Patricia J. Hall, Ed. Mature reader series: nonfiction for 50 + population, approximately 40,000 words. Nitty Gritty Cookbooks: 120-recipe manuscripts. Query with outline, sample chapters, SASE. Royalty.

BROADMAN PRESS—127 Ninth Ave. N., Nashville, TN 37234. Harold. S. Smith, Mgr. Religious and inspirational fiction and nonfiction. Query. Royalty.

BUCKNELL UNIVERSITY PRESS—Bucknell Univ., Lewisburg, PA 17837. Mills Edgerton, Ed. Scholarly nonfiction. Query. Royalty.

BULFINCH PRESS—(formerly New York Graphic Society Books) Div. of Little, Brown and Co., 34 Beacon St., Boston, MA 02108. Books on fine arts and photography. Query with outline or proposal and vita.

BYRON PREISS VISUAL PUBLICATIONS—24 W. 25th St., New York, NY 10010. David M. Harris, Ed. Book packager; creates series to sell to publishers. Interested in adult books (60,000 words) of science fiction, fantasy, mystery. Produces juvenile fiction and nonfiction (science and wildlife) and young adult fiction and nonfiction. "We need people who can write well and are willing to write to our specifications." Submit writing samples rather than specific manuscripts. Royalty.

CAMELOT BOOKS—See Avon Books.

CAROLRHODA BOOKS—241 First Ave. N., Minneapolis, MN 55401. Rebecca Poole, Ed. Complete manuscripts for ages 7 to 12: biography, science, nature, history, photo essays; historical fiction, 10 to 15 pages, for ages 6 to 10. Guidelines. Hardcover.

CARROLL AND GRAF PUBLISHERS, INC.—260 Fifth Ave., New York, NY 10001. Kent E. Carroll, Exec. Ed. General fiction and nonfiction. Query with SASE. Royalty.

CASSANDRA PRESS—P.O. Box 868, San Rafael, CA 94915. New Age, holistic health, metaphysical, and psychological books. Query with outline and sample chapters, or complete manuscript. Royalty.

THE CATHOLIC UNIVERSITY OF AMERICA PRESS—620 Michigan

Ave. N.E., Washington, DC 20064. David J. McGonagle, Dir. Scholarly nonfiction. Query with prospectus, annotated table of contents, or introduction and author's resumé. Royalty.

CBI PUBLISHING—See Van Nostrand Reinhold.

CHARTER/DIAMOND BOOKS—Imprint of Berkley Publishing Co., 200 Madison Ave., New York, NY 10012. Leslie Gelbman, Ed.-in-Chief. Adventure, suspense fiction, horror, erotica, historical romances, regencies, women's contemporary fiction, family sagas, and historical novels. Westerns, male action/adventure. Will consider unsolicited manuscripts. Royalty or outright purchase. Paperback.

CHATHAM PRESS—P. O. Box A, Old Greenwich, CT 06807. Roger H. Lourie, Man. Dir. Books on the Northeast coast, New England maritime subjects, and the ocean. Query with outline, sample chapters, illustrations, and SASE large enough for the return of material. Royalty.

CHELSEA GREEN PUBLISHING CO.—Route 113, P.O. Box 130, Post Mills, VT 05058–0130. Ian Baldwin, Jr., Ed. Fiction and nonfiction on natural history, biography, history, politics, and travel. Query with outline. Royalty.

CHICAGO REVIEW PRESS—814 N. Franklin St., Chicago, IL 60610. Linda Matthews, Ed. Nonfiction: project books for young people ages 10 to 18, anthropology, travel, nature, and regional topics. Query with outline and sample chapters.

CHILTON BOOK CO.—One Chilton Way, Radnor, PA 19089. Alan F. Turner, Ed. Dir. Antiques and collectibles, sewing and crafts, business, computers, and automotive topics. Query with outline, sample chapter, and return postage. Royalty. Wallace-Homestead Books.

CHINA BOOKS—2929 24th St., San Francisco, CA 94110. Robert Schildgen, Ed. Fiction and nonfiction, 200 to 500 pages, and poetry, 100 to 200 pages, related to China, China's autonomous regions, or Chinese Americans. Translations welcome. Send query with outline and sample chapters. (Multiple queries considered.) Royalty.

THE CHRISTOPHER PUBLISHING HOUSE—24 Rockland St., Hanover, MA 02339–2221. Susan E. Lukas, Ed. Religious nonfiction, how-tos, textbooks, and poetry, 64 pages and up. Royalty.

CHRONICLE BOOKS—275 Fifth St., San Francisco, CA 94103. Topical nonfiction, history, biography, fiction, art, photography, architecture, nature, food, regional, and children's books. Send proposal with SASE.

CITADEL PRESS—See Lyle Stuart, Inc.

CLARION BOOKS—215 Park Ave. S., New York, NY 10003. Dorothy Briley, Ed.-in-Chief/Pub. Fiction, nonfiction, and picture books: short novels and lively stories for ages 8 to 12, historical fiction, humor; picture books for infants to age 7; biography, natural history, social studies, American and world history for readers 5 to 8 and 9 and up. Royalty. Hardcover.

CLIFFHANGER PRESS—P.O. Box 29527, Oakland, CA 94604–9527. Nancy Chirich, Ed. Mystery and suspense. Unagented manuscripts only. Query with first three chapters, outline, and SASE. Royalty. Guidelines.

CLOVERDALE PRESS—96 Morton St., New York, NY 10014. Book packager. Adult nonfiction; YA, middle- and lower-grade fiction and nonfiction. "Since our requirements vary considerably and frequently according to our publishers' needs, please send query letter before submitting material." Address YA and juvenile to Marion Vaarn; adult to Lisa Howell.

COFFEE HOUSE PRESS—27 N. 4th St., Suite 400, Minneapolis, MN 55401. Address E. Dietz. Essays, fiction (no genres), and poetry (over 48 pages). Query or send complete manuscript. Royalty.

COLLIER BOOKS—See Macmillan Publishing Co.

COMPCARE PUBLISHERS—2415 Annapolis Ln., Minneapolis, MN 55441. Margaret Marsh, Man. Ed. Adult nonfiction; young-adult nonfiction: books on recovery from addictive/compulsive behavior; emotional health; growth in personal, couple, and family relationships. Submit complete manuscript. Royalty.

CONCORDIA PUBLISHING HOUSE—3558 S. Jefferson Ave., St. Louis, MO 63118. Practical nonfiction with explicit religious content, conservative Lutheran doctrine. Children's fiction with explicit Christian content. No poetry. Query. Royalty.

CONSUMER REPORTS BOOKS—51 E. 42nd St., Suite 800, New York, NY 10017. Address Exec. Ed. Medicine/health, finances, automotive, homeowners, food and cooking topics. Submit complete manuscript, or send contents, outline, and three chapters, with resumé.

CONTEMPORARY BOOKS, INC.—180 N. Michigan Ave., Chicago, IL 60601. Nancy Crossman, Ed. Dir. Trade nonfiction, 100 to 400 pages, on health, fitness, sports, cooking, humor, business, popular culture, biography, real estate, finance, women's issues. Query with outline and sample chapters. Royalty.

COOK PUBLISHING CO., DAVID C.—850 N. Grove Ave., Elgin, IL 60120. Paul Mouw, Man. Ed., Life Journey, General Titles. Catherine Davis, Man. Ed., Chariot, Children's Books. Fiction that "helps children better understand themselves and their relationship with God"; nonfiction that illuminates the Bible; picture books, ages 1 to 7; fiction for ages 8 to 10, 10 to 12, and 12 to 14. Lengths and payment vary. Query required. Guidelines.

CRAFTSMAN BOOK COMPANY—6058 Corte del Cedro, P.O. Box 6500, Carlsbad, CA 92008. Laurence D. Jacobs, Ed. How-to construction and estimating manuals for builders, 450 pages. Query. Softcover. Royalty.

CREATIVE ARTS BOOK CO.—833 Bancroft Way, Berkeley, CA 94710. D.S. Ellis, Pub. Adult nonfiction, including photography, technical books, art, and music. Query with outline and sample chapters. Royalty.

THE CROSSING PRESS—97 Hangar Way, Watsonville, CA 95076. Elaine Goldman Gill, John Gill, Pubs. Fiction, health, men's studies, feminist studies, science fiction, mysteries, gay topics, cookbooks. Royalty.

CROWELL, THOMAS Y.—See Harper Junior Books Group.

CROWN PUBLISHERS—225 Park Ave. S., New York, NY 10003. Andrea E. Cascardi, Ed.-in-Chief. Children's fiction (including humor and mystery), nonfiction (biography, science, sports, nature, music, and history), and picture books for ages 3 and up. Query with outline and sample chapter; send manuscript for picture books. Guidelines.

DANIEL AND COMPANY, JOHN—P.O. Box 21922, Santa Barbara, CA 93121. John Daniel, Pub. Books (under 200 pages) in the field of belles lettres and literary memoirs; stylish and elegant writing; essays and short fiction dealing with social issues; one poetry title per year. Send synopsis or outline with no more that 50 sample pages and SASE. Allow 6 to 8 weeks for response. Royalty.

DAW BOOKS, INC.—375 Hudson St., New York, NY 10014. Elizabeth R. Wollheim, Ed.-in-Chief. Science fiction and fantasy, 60,000 to 120,000 words. Royalty.

DEL REY BOOKS—201 E. 50th St., New York, NY 10022. Shelly Shapiro, SF Ed. Lester del Rey, V.P. and Fantasy Ed. Science fiction and fantasy; first novelists welcome. Material must be well-paced with logical resolutions. Fantasy with magic basic to plotline. Length, 70,000 to 120,000 words. Complete manuscripts preferred, or send outline with 3 sample chapters. Royalty.

DELACORTE PRESS—666 Fifth Ave., New York, NY 10103. Jackie Farber, Robert Miller, Eds. Adult fiction and nonfiction. Juvenile and YA fiction (George Nicholson, Ed.). Accepts fiction (mystery, YA, romance, fantasy, etc.) from agents only.

DELL PUBLISHING—666 Fifth Ave., New York, NY 10103. Dell Books: family sagas, historical romances, war action, general fiction, occult/horror/psychological suspense, true crime, men's adventure. Delta: General-interest nonfiction, psychology, feminism, health, nutrition, child care, science. Delta Trade Paperbacks: nonfiction, self-help, how-to. Laurel: Nonfiction. History, politics, language, reference. Juvenile Books: Yearling (kindergarten through 6th grade; no unsolicited manuscripts); and Laurel-Leaf (grades 7 through 12; no unsolicited manuscripts). Submissions policy for Dell Books: Send four-page narrative synopsis for fiction, or an outline for nonfiction. Enclose SASE. Address submissions to the appropriate Dell division, Editorial Dept., Book Proposal.

DELTA BOOKS AND DELTA TRADE PAPERBACKS—See Dell Publishing Co.

DEMBNER BOOKS—80 Eighth Ave., New York, NY 10011. S. Arthur Dembner, Ed. Popular reference books, popular medicine, mystery fiction. No first-person tragedy, no romance or pornography, no fads. Send synopsis and two sample chapters with SASE. Modest advances against royalties.

DEVIN-ADAIR PUBLISHERS, INC.—6 N. Water St., Greenwich, CT 06830. C. de la Belle Issue, Pub. J. Andrassi, Ed. Books on conservative affairs, Irish topics, Americana, self-help, health, gardening, cooking, and ecology. Send outline, sample chapters, and SASE. Royalty.

DIAL BOOKS FOR YOUNG READERS—375 Hudson St., New York, NY 10014. Phyllis Fogelman, Pub./Ed.in-Chief. Picture books; Easy-to-Read Books; middle-grade readers; young-adult fiction and some nonfiction. Submit complete manuscript for picture books and Easy-to-Reads; outline and sample chapters for nonfiction and novels. Enclose SASE. Royalty. Hardcover only.

DILLON PRESS—242 Portland Ave. S., Minneapolis, MN 55415. Tom Schneider, Sr. Ed. Lisa Erskine, Nonfiction Ed. Juvenile nonfiction: international festivals and foods, Third World countries and U.S. states, major world cities, world geography/places of interest, environmental topics, contemporary and historical biographies for elementary and middle-grade levels, unusual or remarkable animals. Length, 10 to 90 pages. Royalty and outright purchase. Guidelines.

DOUBLEDAY AND CO.—666 Fifth Ave., New York, NY 10103. Hardcover: mystery/suspense fiction, science fiction, 70,000 to 80,000 words. Send query and outline to appropriate editor: Crime Club or Science Fiction. Wendy Barish, Pub., Books for Young Readers: "Only special books, appropriate for gifts in the bookstore market." Paperback: Martha Levin, Pub., Anchor Press. Adult trade books: general fiction and nonfiction, sociology, psychology, philosophy, women's, etc. Susan Moldow, Ed.-in-Chief. "Currency" line: business books for a general audience on "the art of getting things done"; address Harriet Rubin, Editorial Director. Query. SASE required.

DUNNE BOOKS, THOMAS—Imprint of St. Martin's Press, 175 Fifth Ave., New York, NY 10010. Thomas L. Dunne, Ed. Adult fiction (mysteries, trade, SF, etc.) and nonfiction (history, biographies, science, politics, etc.). Query with outline and sample chapters and SASE. Royalty.

DUTTON CHILDREN'S BOOKS—Div. of Penguin USA, 375 Hudson St., New York, NY 10014. Lucia Monfried, Ed.-in-Chief. Picture books, easy-to-read books; fiction and nonfiction for preschoolers to young adults. Submit outline and sample chapters with query for fiction and nonfiction, complete manuscripts for picture books and easy-to-read books. Manuscripts should be well-written with fresh ideas and child appeal.

DUTTON, E.P.—Div. of Penguin USA, 375 Hudson St., New York, NY 10014. Michaela Hamilton, Exec. Ed. Fiction and nonfiction books. Manuscripts accepted only from agents and/or personal recommendation.

EERDMANS PUBLISHING COMPANY, INC., WM. B—255 Jefferson Ave. S.E., Grand Rapids, MI 49503. Jon Pott, Ed.-in-Chief. Protestant, Roman Catholic, and Orthodox theological nonfiction; American religious history; some fiction. Royalty.

EMC CORP.—300 York Ave., St. Paul, MN 55101. Eileen Slater, Ed. Vocational, career, and consumer education textbooks. Royalty. No unsolicited manuscripts.

ENSLOW PUBLISHERS—Bloy St. & Ramsey Ave., Box 777, Hillside, NJ 07205. R. M. Enslow, Jr., Ed/Pub. Nonfiction books for young people. Areas of emphasis are children's and young adult books for ages 10 to 16 in the fields of science, social studies, and biography. Other specialties for young people are reference books for all ages and easy reading books for teenagers.

ERIKSSON, PUBLISHER, PAUL S.—208 Battell Bldg., Middlebury, VT 05753. General nonfiction; some fiction. Query first. Royalty.

EVANS & CO., INC., M.—216 E. 49th St., New York, NY 10017. Books on humor, health, self-help, popular psychology, and cookbooks. Western and romance fiction for adults; fiction and nonfiction for young adults. Query with outline, sample chapter, and SASE. Royalty.

FABER AND FABER—50 Cross St., Winchester, MA 01890. Novels, story collections, and nonfiction books on topics of popular culture; novels for juveniles and young adults. Query with SASE. Royalty.

FACTS ON FILE PUBLICATIONS—460 Park Ave. S., New York, NY 10016. Gerard Helferich, Assoc. Pub. Reference and trade books on nature, business, science, health, language, history, the performing arts, etc. Query with outline and sample chapter. Royalty. Hardcover.

FARRAR, STRAUS & GIROUX—19 Union Sq. West, New York, NY 10003. Adult and juvenile fiction and nonfiction.

FELL PUBLISHERS, INC.—2131 Hollywood Blvd., Hollywood, FL 33020. Allan Taber, Ed. Nonfiction (100 to 300 pages): general interest, how-tos, business, and health. Query with letter or outline and sample chapter, include SASE. Royalty.

THE FEMINIST PRESS AT THE CITY UNIVERSITY OF NEW YORK —311 E. 94th St., New York, NY 10128. Florence Howe, Pub. Reprints of significant "lost" fiction, memoirs, autobiographies, or other feminist work from the past; biography; original anthologies for classroom adoption; handbooks; bibliographies. "We are especially interested in international literature and the theme, women and peace." Royalty.

FINE, INC., DONALD I.—19 West 21st St., New York, NY 10010. Literary and commercial fiction. General nonfiction. No queries or unsolicited manuscripts. Submit through agent only.

FIREBRAND BOOKS—141 The Commons, Ithaca, NY 14850. Nancy K. Bereano, Ed. Feminist and lesbian fiction and nonfiction. Royalty. Paperback.

FIRESIDE BOOKS—Imprint of Simon & Schuster, 1230 Ave. of the Americas, New York, NY 10020. General nonfiction; cultural and issue-oriented fiction. Royalty basis or outright purchase. Submit outline and one chapter. Trade paperback reprints and originals.

FLARE BOOKS—See Avon Books.

FODOR'S TRAVEL GUIDES—201 E. 50th St., New York, NY 10022. Michael Spring, Ed. Travel guides for both foreign and US destinations. "We hire writers who live in the area they will write about." Books follow established format; send writing sample.

FORTRESS PRESS—426 S. Fifth St., Box 1209, Minneapolis, MN 55440. Dr. Marshall D. Johnson, Dir. Books in the areas of biblical studies, theology, ethics, and church history for academic and professional markets, including libraries. Query first.

FOUR WINDS PRESS—Imprint of Macmillan Publishing Co., 866 Third Ave., New York, NY 10022. Neal Porter, Pub. Cindy Kane, Ed.-in-Chief. Juveniles: picture books, fiction for all ages. Nonfiction for young children. Query with SASE required for nonfiction. No simultaneous submissions. Hardcover only. Presently overstocked.

THE FREE PRESS—See Macmillan Publishing Co.

FRIENDS UNITED PRESS—101 Quaker Hill Dr., Richmond, IN 47374. Ardith Talbot, Ed. Nonfiction and fiction, 200 pages, on Quaker history, biography, and Quaker faith experience. Query with outline and sample chapters. Royalty.

GARDEN WAY PUBLISHING COMPANY—Storey Communications, Schoolhouse Rd., Pownal, VT 05261. Kim Foster, Assoc. Ed. How-to books on gardening, cooking, building, animals, country living. Royalty or outright purchase. Query with outline and sample chapter.

GARRETT PARK PRESS—P.O. Box 190, Garrett Park, MD 20896. Robert Calvert, Jr., Pub. Reference books on career education, international affairs, occupational guidance, social studies, and financial aid. Query required. Multiple queries considered but not encouraged. Royalty.

GINIGER CO. INC., THE K.S.—250 W. 57th St., Suite 519, New York, NY 10107. General nonfiction; reference and religious.Query with SASE; no unsolicited manuscripts. Royalty.

THE GLOBE PEQUOT PRESS—138 W. Main St., Chester, CT 06412. Laura Strom, Assoc. Ed. Nonfiction with national and regional focus; nature and outdoor guides; environment and natural sciences; how-tos; gardening; journalism and media; biographies. Query with sample chapter, contents, and one-page synopsis. SASE required. Royalty.

GOLD EAGLE BOOKS—See Worldwide Library.

GOLDEN PRESS—See Western Publishing Co., Inc.

GRAYWOLF PRESS—2402 University Ave., Suite 203, St. Paul, MN 55114. Scott M. Walker, Ed. Literary fiction (short story collections and novels), poetry, and essays. Query with sample chapters.

GREENE PRESS, INC., STEPHEN—Div. of Penguin USA, 15 Muzzey St., Lexington, MA 02173. Tom Begner, Pres. General nonfiction; fitness, sports, and nature. Royalty.

GREENWILLOW BOOKS—Imprint of William Morrow and Co., Inc., 105 Madison Ave., New York, NY 10016. Susan Hirschman, Ed.-in-Chief. Children's books for all ages. Picture books.

GROSSET AND DUNLAP, INC.—Div. of Putnam & Grosset Books, 200 Madison Ave., New York, NY 10016. Material accepted through agents only.

GROVE WEIDENFELD—841 Broadway, New York, NY 10003–4793. Alan D. Williams, Pub. "Looking to publish distinguished fiction and nonfiction." Queries required.

GULLIVER BOOKS—See Harcourt Brace Jovanovich.

HAMMOND INC.—Maplewood, NJ 07040. Charles Lees, Ed. Nonfiction: cartographic reference, travel. Payment varies. Query with outline and sample chapters. SASE required.

HANCOCK HOUSE PUBLISHERS—1431 Harrison Ave., Blaine, WA 98230. David Hancock, Ed. Nonfiction: gardening, outdoor guides, Western history, Native American, real estate, and investing. Royalty.

HARBINGER HOUSE—2802 N. Alvernon Way, Tucson, AZ 85712. Zdenek Gerych, Ed.-in-Chief. Jeffrey H. Lockridge, Children's Books Ed. Adult nonfiction focusing on social issues and personal growth; very little adult fiction. Children's picture books; stories for middle readers; nonfiction (Natural History Series). Submit resumé, outline/synopsis, 2 sample chapters, and SASE. For short children's book, submit entire manuscript with SASE. Royalty.

HARCOURT BRACE JOVANOVICH—1250 Sixth Ave., San Diego, CA 92101. Adult trade nonfiction and fiction. Books for Professionals: test preparation guides and other student self-help materials. Miller Accounting Publications, Inc.: professional books for practitioners in accounting and finance; college accounting texts. Juvenile fiction and nonfiction for beginning readers through young adults under imprints: HBJ Children's Books, Gulliver Books, and Voyager Paperbacks. Adult books: no unsolicited manuscripts or queries. Children's books: unsolicited manuscripts accepted by HBJ Children's Books only. No simultaneous submissions. Send query or manuscript to Manuscript Submissions, Children's Book Division.

HARLEQUIN BOOKS/CANADA—225 Duncan Mill Rd., Don Mills, Ont., Canada M3B 3K9. Harlequin Romance: Paula Eykelhof, Ed. Contemporary romance novels, 50,000 to 55,000 words, any setting, ranging in plot from the traditional and gentle to the more sophisticated. Query first. Harlequin Regency: Marmie Charndoff, Ed. Short traditional novels set in 19th century Europe, 50,000 to 60,000 words. Query first. Harlequin Superromance: Marsha Zinberg, Sr. Ed. Contemporary romance, 85,000 words, with North American or foreign setting. Query first.

Harlequin Temptation: Birgit Davis-Todd, Sr. Ed. Sensually charged contemporary romantic fantasies, 60,000 to 65,000 words. Query first.

HARLEQUIN BOOKS/U.S.—300 E. 42nd St., 6th Fl., New York, NY 10017. Debra Matteucci, Sr. Ed. Contemporary romances, 70,000 to 75,000 words. Send for tip sheets. Paperback. Harlequin American Romance: Believable contemporary situations, set in the U.S. Harlequin Intrigue: Set against backdrop of suspense and adventure. Worldwide locales. Query.

HARPER JUNIOR BOOKS GROUP—10 E. 53rd St., New York, NY 10022. Katherine Magnusson, Admin. Coord. West Coast: P. O. Box 6549, San Pedro, CA 90732. Linda Zuckerman, Exec. Ed. (Query one address only.) Juvenile fiction, nonfiction, and picture books imprints include: Thomas Y. Crowell Co., Publishers: juveniles, etc.; J. B. Lippincott Co. and Harper & Row: juveniles, picture books, etc.; Trophy Books: paperback juveniles. All publish from preschool to young adult titles. Query, send sample chapters or complete manuscript. Royalty.

HARPER PAPERBACKS—Harper & Row, 10 E. 53rd St., New York, NY 10022. Eddie Bell, Pub. Agent submissions only.

HARPERCOLLINS PUBLISHERS—(formerly Harper & Row) 10 E. 53rd St., New York, NY 10022. Fiction and nonfiction (biography, economics, history, etc.). Adult Trade Dept.: Agents only, Helen Moore, Man. Ed. College texts: address College Dept. Children's books: address Junior Books Dept., Attn. Sedora Belin, 9th Floor. Unsolicited material accepted. Religion, theology, etc.: address Harper San Francisco, Ice House One-401, 151 Union St., San Francisco, CA 94111-1299. No unsolicited manuscripts; query only.

HARVEST HOUSE PUBLISHERS—1075 Arrowsmith, Eugene, OR 97402. Eileen L. Mason, Ed. Nonfiction with evangelical theme: how-tos, educational, counseling, marriage, women, contemporary issues. No biographies, history, fiction, children's books, or poetry. Query first. SASE required.

HEALTH COMMUNICATIONS, INC.—3201 S.W. 15th St., Deerfield Beach, FL 33442. Marie Stilkind, Ed. Books on self-help recovery for adults (250 pages) and juveniles (100 pages). Query with outline and sample chapter, or send manuscript. Royalty.

HEALTH PLUS PUBLISHERS—Box 22001, Phoenix, AZ 85028. Paula E. Clure, Ed. Books on health and fitness. Query with outline and sample chapters.

HEALTH PRESS—P.O. Box 367, Santa Fe, NM 87501. Kathleen Schwartz, Ed. Health-related adult books, 100 to 300 published pages. "We're seeking cutting-edge, original manuscripts that will excite and help reader. Author must have credentials, or preface/intro must be written by MD, Ph.D., etc. Controversial topics are desired; must be well researched and documented." Prefers completed manuscript, but will consider queries with outline and sample chapters. Multiple queries considered. Royalty.

HEARST BOOKS AND HEARST MARINE BOOKS—See William Morrow and Co.

HEARTFIRE ROMANCES—See Zebra Books.

HEATH & COMPANY, D. C.—125 Spring St., Lexington, MA 02173. Textbooks for schools and colleges. Professional books (Lexington Books Div.). Software and related educational material. Query Vince Duggan.

HELDMAN BOOKS, IRMA—275 Central Park W., New York, NY 10024.

Irma Heldman, Ed. Mystery and suspense, mainstream fiction, from 65,000 words; query for nonfiction. SASE required. Advance and royalty.

HEMINGWAY WESTERN STUDIES SERIES—Boise State Univ., 1910 University Dr., Boise, ID 83725. Tom Trusky, Ed. Nonfiction relating to the Inter-Mountain West (Rockies) in areas of history, political science, anthropology, natural sciences, film, fine arts, literary history or criticism. Publishes up to two books annually.

HERALD PRESS—616 Walnut Ave., Scottdale, PA 15683. Christian books for adults and children (age 9 and up): inspiration, Bible study, self-help, devotionals, current issues, peace studies, church history, missions, evangelism, family life. Send one-page summary and two sample chapters. Royalty.

HIPPOCRENE BOOKS—171 Madison Ave., New York, NY 10016. George Blagowidow, Ed. Military history and travel books. Send outline and sample chapters. Multiple queries considered. Royalty.

HOLIDAY HOUSE, INC.—425 Madison Ave., New York, NY 10014. Margery S. Cuyler, Vice Pres. General juvenile and young adult fiction and nonfiction. Query with outline and sample chapter. Hardcover only. Royalty.

HOLT AND CO., HENRY—115 W. 18th St., New York, NY 10011. William Strachan, Ed.-in-Chief. Fiction and nonfiction (mysteries, history, autobiographies, natural history, travel, art, and how-to) of highest literary quality. Query with SASE required. Royalty.

HOUGHTON MIFFLIN COMPANY—2 Park St., Boston, MA 02108. Fiction: literary, historical, suspense. Nonfiction: history, biography, psychology. No unsolicited manuscripts. Query Submissions Dept. with SASE. Children's Book Division, address Mary Lee Donovan: picture books, fiction, and nonfiction for all ages. Query. Royalty.

H. P. BOOKS—Div. of Price Stern Sloan, 360 N. La Cienga Blvd., Los Angeles, CA 90048. Illustrated how-tos on cooking, gardening, photography, health and fitness, automotive, etc. Query with SASE. Royalty.

HUNTER PUBLISHING, INC.—300 Raritan Center Pkwy., Edison, NJ 08818. Michael Hunter, Ed. Travel guides. Query with outline.

INDIANA UNIVERSITY PRESS—10th and Morton Sts., Bloomington, IN 47405. Scholarly nonfiction, especially cultural studies, literary criticism, music, history, women's studies, archaeology, anthropology, etc. Query with outline and sample chapters. Royalty.

INTIMATE MOMENTS—See Silhouette Books.

JAMESON BOOKS—722 Columbus St., Ottawa, IL 61350. J. G. Campaigne, Ed. American historical fiction for "Frontier Library" series. Some nonfiction. Query with outline and sample chapters. Royalty.

JOHNSON BOOKS, INC.—1880 S. 57th Court, Boulder, CO 80301. Rebecca Herr, Ed. Dir. Nonfiction: environmental subjects, archaeology, geology, natural history, astronomy, travel guides, outdoor guidebooks, fly fishing, regional. Query. Royalty.

JONATHAN DAVID PUBLISHERS, INC.—68-22 Eliot Ave., Middle Village, NY 11379. Alfred J. Kolatch, Ed.-in-Chief. General nonfiction (how-to, sports, cooking and food, self-help, etc.) and specializing in Judaica. Query with outline, sample chapter, and resumé required. SASE. Royalty or outright purchase.

JOVE BOOKS—200 Madison Ave., New York, NY 10016. Fiction and nonfiction. No unsolicited manuscripts.

JOY STREET BOOKS —Imprint of Little, Brown & Co., 34 Beacon St., Boston, MA 02108. Melanie Kroupa, Ed.-in-Chief. Juvenile picture books; fiction and nonfiction for middle readers and young adults. Especially interested in fiction for 8- to 12-year-olds and innovative nonfiction. Query with outline and sample chapters for nonfiction; send complete manuscript for fiction. Royalty.

KAR-BEN COPIES—6800 Tildenwood Lane, Rockville, MD 20852. Judye Groner, Ed. Books on Jewish themes for pre-school and elementary-age children (to age 6): picture books, fiction, and nonfiction. Complete manuscript preferred. Flat fee and royalty.

KEATS PUBLISHING, INC.—27 Pine St., Box 876, New Canaan, CT 06840. D.R. Bensen, Ed. Nonfiction: health, inspiration, how-to. Query. Royalty.

KESTRAL BOOKS—See Penguin USA.

KNOPF, INC., ALFRED A.—201 E. 50th St., New York, NY 10022. Stephanie Spinner, Assoc. Pub. Frances Foster and Anne Schwartz, Sr. Eds. Reg Kahney, Sr. Ed. Nonfiction. Sherry Gerstein, Paperback Ed. Distinguished picture books, fiction and nonfiction for middle grades and YAs. (Address Alfred A. Knopf Books for Young Readers, 225 Park Ave. S., New York, NY 10003.) Query for nonfiction; send manuscript for fiction. Ashbel Green, V.P. and Sr. Ed.; distinguished fiction and general nonfiction; query. Royalty. Guidelines.

KODANSHA INTERNATIONAL—114 Fifth Ave., New York, NY 10011. Attn: Editorial Dept. Books, 50,000 to 200,000 words, on popular science, sports, business management, travel, biography, gardening, health, history, and cooking, for an international adult audience. Query with outline and sample chapters. Royalty.

LARK BOOKS—50 College St., Asheville, NC 28801. Rob Pulleyn, Pub. Publishes "distinctive books for creative people" in crafts, how-to, and "coffee table" categories. Query with outline. Royalty.

LAUREL BOOKS AND LAUREL-LEAF BOOKS—See Dell Publishing Co.

LEISURE BOOKS—Div. of Dorchester Publishing Co., 276 Fifth Ave., New York, NY 10001. Frank Walgren, Sub. Ed. Historical romance novels, from 90,000 words; men's adventure series, Western series from 50,000 words. Query with synopsis, sample chapters, and SASE. Royalty.

LEXINGTON BOOKS—See D.C. Heath & Co.

LIBERTY HOUSE—Imprint of Tab Books, Div. of McGraw-Hill, Inc., 10 E. 21st St., Suite 1101, New York, NY 10010. David J. Conti, Ed. Dir. Personal finance, investing, legal self-help, real estate, small business books; approach should be practical, realistic, results-oriented. Query with outline, sample chapters if available. Royalty.

LION PUBLISHING—1705 Hubbard Ave., Batavia, IL 60510. Robert Bittner, Ed. Fiction and nonfiction written from a Christian viewpoint for a general audience. Guidelines. Royalty.

LIPPINCOTT COMPANY, J.B.—See Harper Junior Books Group.

LITTLE, BROWN & CO.—34 Beacon St., Boston, MA 02106. Maria Modugno, Ed.-in-Chief. Fiction, general nonfiction, sports books; divisions for law and medical texts. Royalty. Query Children's Book Dept. for juvenile fiction and nonfiction (science, history, and nature) and picture books (ages 3 to 8). Guidelines.

LODESTAR—Div. of Penguin Books USA, Inc., 2 Park Ave., New York, NY 10016. Virginia Buckley, Ed. Dir. Fiction (YA, mystery, fantasy, science fiction, western) and nonfiction (science, sports, nature, history) considered for ages 9 to 11, 10 to 14, and 12 and up. Also fiction and nonfiction picture books for ages 4 to 8. Send manuscript for fiction; query for nonfiction.

LONGMAN FINANCIAL SERVICES PUBLISHING—Div. of Longman Group USA, 520 N. Dearborn, Chicago, IL 60610. Anita A. Constant, V.P./Pub. Books on financial services, real estate, banking, etc. Query with outline and sample chapters. Royalty and flat fee.

LOTHROP, LEE & SHEPARD BOOKS—Imprint of William Morrow & Co., Inc., 105 Madison Ave., New York, NY 10016. Susan Pearson, Ed.-in-Chief. Juvenile, picture books, fiction, and nonfiction. Query. Royalty.

LOVEGRAM ROMANCES—See Zebra Books.

LOVESWEPT—Imprint of Bantam Books, 666 Fifth Ave., New York, NY 10103. Carolyn Nichols, Assoc. Pub. Highly sensual, adult contemporary romances, approx. 55,000 words. Study field before submitting. Query required. Paperback only.

LOYOLA UNIVERSITY PRESS—3441 N. Ashland Ave., Chicago, IL 60657. Joseph Downey, S. J., Ed. Religious material for college-educated Catholic readers. Nonfiction, 200 to 400 pages. Query with outline. Royalty.

LYONS & BURFORD, PUBLISHERS—31 W. 21st St., New York, NY 10010. Peter Burford, Ed. Books, 100 to 300 pages, related to the outdoors (camping, natural history, etc.). Query with outline. Royalty.

MCELDERRY BOOKS, MARGARET K.—Macmillan Publishers, 866 Third Ave., New York, NY 10022. Margaret K. McElderry, Ed. Picture books; quality fiction, including fantasy, science fiction, beginning chapter books, humor, and realism; nonfiction. For ages 3 to 5, 6 to 9, 8 to 12, 10 to 14, and 12 and up.

MCKAY COMPANY, DAVID—201 E. 50th St., New York, NY 10022. Nonfiction. Unsolicited manuscripts neither acknowledged nor returned.

MACMILLAN PUBLISHING CO., INC.—866 Third Ave., New York, NY 10022. General Books Division: Religious, sports, science, and reference books. No fiction. Paperbacks, Collier Books. College texts and professional books in social sciences, humanities, address The Free Press. Royalty.

MADISON BOOKS—4720 Boston Way, Lanham, MD 20706. Full-length, nonfiction manuscripts on history, biography, popular culture, contemporary affairs, trade reference. Query required. Royalty.

MEADOWBROOK PRESS—18318 Minnetonka Blvd., Deephaven, MN 55391. Upbeat, useful books on pregnancy, childbirth and parenting, travel, humor, children's activities, 60,000 words. Query with outline, sample chapters, and qualifications. Royalty or flat fee.

MENTOR BOOKS—See Penguin USA.

MERCURY HOUSE—201 Filbert St., Suite 400, San Francisco, CA 94133. Ms. Alev Lytle Croutier, Exec. Ed. Quality fiction and nonfiction. Query with outline and sample chapters.

MEREDITH CORP. BOOK GROUP—Better Homes and Gardens Books,

1716 Locust St., Des Moines, IA 50336. David A. Kirchner, Man. Ed. Books on gardening, crafts, health, decorating, etc., mostly staff written. "Interested in freelance writers with expertise in these areas more than in queries for book manuscripts." Limited market. Query.

MESSNER, JULIAN—Div. of Simon & Schuster, Prentice Hall Bldg., Rt. 9W, Englewood Cliffs, NJ 07632. Bonnie Brook, Ed.-in-Chief. Curriculum-oriented nonfiction. General nonfiction, ages 8 to 14, includes science, nature, biography, history, and hobbies. Lengths vary. Royalty.

METAMORPHOUS PRESS—P.O. Box 10616, 3249 N.W. 29th Ave., Portland, OR 97210. Gene Radeka, Acquisitions Ed. Business, education, health, how-to, humor, performance arts, psychology, sports and recreation, and women's topics. Also children's books that promote self-esteem and self-reliance. "We select books that provide the tools to help people improve their lives and the lives of those around them." Query with sample chapter and outline.

METEOR PUBLISHING—3369 Progress Dr., Bensalem, PA 19020. Kate Duffy, Ed.-in-Chief. Contemporary romance novels, 65,000 words, sold through direct mail only. Royalty.

MILKWEED EDITIONS—528 Hennepin Ave., Suite 505, Minneapolis, MN 55403. Emilie Buchwald, Ed. "We publish excellent fiction, poetry, essays, and collaborative books—the kind of writing that makes for good reading." This small press publishes about 10 books a year. Writers are encouraged to query first with sample chapters. Royalty.

MILLER ACCOUNTING PUBLICATIONS, INC.—See Harcourt, Brace, Jovanovich.

MILLS & SANDERSON, PUBLISHERS—412 Marrett Rd., Suite 6, Lexington, MA 02173. Georgia Mills, Ed. Books, 250 pages, on travel, fitness, and lifestyle enhancement. Query. Royalty.

MINSTREL BOOKS—Imprint of Pocket Books, 1230 Ave. of the Americas, New York, NY 10020. Patricia MacDonald, Exec. Ed. Fiction for girls and boys ages 6 to 11: scary stories, fantasies, funny stories, school stories, adventures, animal stories. Query first with detailed plot outline, sample chapter, and SASE. Royalty.

MOON HANDBOOKS—Moon Publications, Inc., 722 Wall St., Chico, CA 95928. Mark Morris, Ed. Travel guides of varying lengths. Will consider multiple submissions. Query. Royalty.

MOREHOUSE PUBLISHING—78 Danbury Rd., Wilton, CT 06897. E. Allen Kelley, Pub. Theology, pastoral care, church administration, spirituality, Anglican studies, history of religion, books for children, youth, elders, etc. Query with outline, contents, and sample chapter. Royalty.

MORROW AND CO., INC., WILLIAM—105 Madison Ave., New York, NY 10016. James Landis, Pub./Ed.-in-Chief. Adult fiction and nonfiction: no unsolicited manuscripts. Morrow Junior Books: David Reuther, Ed.-in-Chief. Children's books for all ages. Hearst Marine Books: Connie Roosevelt, Ed. Hearst Books: Ann Bramson, Ed. General nonfiction. Submit through agent only.

MORROW QUILL PAPERBACKS—Div. of William Morrow, 105 Madison Ave., New York, NY 10016. Andrew Dutter, Ed. Trade paperbacks. Adult nonfiction. No unsolicited manuscripts.

THE MOUNTAINEERS BOOKS—306 Second Ave. W., Seattle, WA 98119. Margaret Foster-Finan, Ed. Mgr. Nonfiction books on noncompetitive aspects of outdoor sports such as mountaineering, backpacking, canoeing, kayaking, bicycling, skiing. Field guides, regional histories, biographies of outdoor people; accounts of expeditions. Guidebooks should be nonproduct or service oriented. Nature books. Submit sample chapters and outline. Royalty.

MUIR PUBLICATIONS, JOHN—P.O. Box 613, Santa Fe, NM 87504–0613. Ken Luroff, Ed. Books for children and adults on travel and other cultural and environmental topics; easy-to-use car repair manuals. Send manuscript or query with sample chapters. Royalty.

MULTNOMAH PRESS—10209 S.E. Division St., Portland, OR 97266. Conservative, evangelical nonfiction. Some juvenile fiction with Christian world view. Request guidelines and manuscript questionnaire. Royalty.

MUSTANG PUBLISHING CO., INC.—Box 3004, Memphis, TN 38173. Rollin A. Riggs, Pres. Nonfiction paperbacks for 18- to 40-year-olds. Send queries for 100- to 300-page books, with outlines and sample chapters. Royalty. SASE required.

THE MYSTERIOUS PRESS—129 W. 56th St., New York, NY 10019. William Malloy, Ed.-in-Chief. Mystery/suspense novels. Agented manuscripts only.

NAIAD PRESS, INC.—Box 10543, Tallahassee, FL 32302. Barbara Grier, Ed. Adult fiction, 60,000 to 65,000 words, with lesbian themes and characters: mysteries, romances, gothics, ghost stories, westerns, regencies, spy novels, etc. Query with letter and one page précis only. Royalty.

NATUREGRAPH PUBLISHERS—P. O. Box 1075, Happy Camp, CA 96039. Barbara Brown, Ed. Nonfiction: Native American culture, natural history, outdoor living, land and gardening, holistic learning and health, Indian lore, crafts, and how-to. Query. Royalty.

THE NAVAL INSTITUTE PRESS—Annapolis, MD 21402. Nonfiction (60,000 to 100,000 words): How-tos on boating and navigation; battle histories; biography; ship guides. Occasional fiction (75,000 to 110,000 words). Query with outline and sample chapters. Royalty.

NELSON, INC., THOMAS—Nelson Place at Elm Hill Pike, P. O. Box 141000, Nashville, TN 37214–1000. William D. Watkins, Man. Ed. Religious adult nonfiction. Teen and adult nonfiction. Query with outline and sample chapter.

NEW SOCIETY PUBLISHERS—4527 Springfield Ave., Philadelphia, PA 19143. Books on fundamental social change through nonviolent social action. Request guidelines before submitting proposal. SASE required.

NEW WORLD LIBRARY—P.O. Box 13257, Northgate Sta., San Rafael, CA 94913. Submissions Ed. Nonfiction, to 300 pages, especially high quality, inspirational/self-help books, that encourage environmental awareness. "Aim for intelligent, aware audience, interested in personal and planetary transformation." Query with outline. Multiple queries accepted. Royalty.

NEW YORK GRAPHIC SOCIETY BOOKS—See Bulfinch Press.

NEWCASTLE PUBLISHING—13419 Saticoy St., N. Hollywood, CA 91605. Al Saunders, Pub. Nonfiction manuscripts (200 to 250 pages) for older adults dealing with personal health, health care issues, and relationships. "We are not looking for fads or trends. We want books with a long shelf life." Multiple queries considered. Royalty.

NEWMARKET PRESS—18 E. 48th St., New York, NY 10017. Keith Hollaman, Man. Ed. Nonfiction on health, self-help, child care, parenting, biography, and history. Some fiction. Query first. Royalty.

NORTH COUNTRY PRESS—P.O. Box 440, Belfast, ME 04915. William M. Johnson, Pub. Fiction and nonfiction with a Maine and/or New England tie-in. "Our goal is to publish high-quality books for people who love New England." Query with SASE, outline, and sample chapters. Royalty.

NORTHWORD PRESS, INC.—Box 1360, 7520 Highway 51, Minocqua, WI 54548. Tom Klein, Ed. Natural history and natural heritage books, from 25,000 words. Send outline with sample chapters, or complete manuscript. Royalty or flat fee.

NORTON AND CO., INC., W.W.—500 Fifth Ave., New York, NY 10110. Liz Malcolm, Ed. High-quality fiction and nonfiction. No occult, paranormal, religious, genre fiction (formula romance, SF, westerns), cookbooks, arts and crafts, YA, or children's books. Query with synopsis, 2 to 3 chapters, and resumé. Return postage and packaging required. Royalty.

ONEWORLD PUBLICATIONS, INC.—Country Route 9, P.O. Box 357, Chatham, NY 12037. Leo Hallen, Sales and Marketing Dir., Books for Thoughtful People. "We deal with issues bearing on the collective life of humanity and its changing needs as we approach the 21st century. As a broad guide, all works should be in tune with Baha'i ideals." Queries preferred.

OPEN COURT PUBLISHING COMPANY—Box 599, Peru, IL 61354. Scholarly books on philosophy, psychology, religion, oriental thought, history, public policy, and related topics. Send sample chapters with outline and resumé. Royalty.

ORCHARD BOOKS—Div. of Franklin Watts, 387 Park Ave., New York, NY 10016. Norma Jean Sawicki, Pub. Hardcover picture books and fiction for juveniles; fiction for young adults. Nonfiction and photo essays for young children. Submit complete manuscript. Royalty.

OSBORNE/MCGRAW HILL—2600 Tenth St., Berkeley, CA 94710. Cynthia Hudson, Ed.-in-Chief. Microcomputer books for general audience. Query. Royalty.

OXFORD UNIVERSITY PRESS—200 Madison Ave., New York, NY 10016. Authoritative books on literature, history, philosophy, etc.; college textbooks, medical, and reference books. Query. Royalty.

OXMOOR HOUSE, INC.—Box 2262, Birmingham, AL 35201. John Logue, Ed. Nonfiction: art, photography, gardening, decorating, cooking, sports, and crafts. Royalty.

PACER BOOKS FOR YOUNG ADULTS—Imprint of Berkley Publishing Group, 200 Madison Ave., New York, NY 10016. Fiction: adventure, fantasy, and role-playing fantasy gamebooks. No unsolicited manuscripts; queries only. Address Melinda Metz. Paperback only.

PANTHEON BOOKS—Div. of Random House, 201 E. 50th St., New York, NY 10022. Nonfiction: academic level for general reader on history, political science, sociology, etc.; picture books; folklore. Some fiction. Query required. Royalty.

PARA PUBLISHING—P.O. Box 4232, Santa Barbara, CA 93140–4232. Dan Poynter, Ed. Adult nonfiction books on parachutes and skydiving only. Author must present evidence of having made at least 1,000 jumps. Company publishes an average of 5 new books each year. Query. Royalty.

PARAGON HOUSE—90 Fifth Ave., New York, NY 10011. Ken Stuart, Ed.-in-Chief. Serious nonfiction, including biography, history, reference, and how-to. Query or send manuscript. Royalty.

PARKER PUBLISHING COMPANY, INC.—West Nyack, NY 10994. James Bradler, Pres. Self-help how-to books, 65,000 words: health, money opportunities, business, and books on sports and coaching. Royalty.

PASSPORT BOOKS—4255 W. Touhy Ave., Lincolnwood, IL 60646–1975. Michael Ross, Ed. Dir. Adult nonfiction, 200 to 400 words, picture books up to 120 words, and juvenile nonfiction. Send outline and sample chapters for books on foreign language, travel, and culture. Multiple queries considered. Royalty and flat fee.

PATH PRESS—53 W. Jackson Blvd., Chicago, IL 60604. Herman C. Gilbert, Ed. Quality books by and about African-Americans and Third-World peoples. Submit outline and sample chapters. Royalty.

PEACHTREE PUBLISHERS, LTD.—494 Armour Circle N.E., Atlanta, GA 30324. Wide variety of fiction and nonfiction. No religious material, SF/fantasy, romance, mystery/detective, historical fiction; no business, scientific, or technical books. Send outline and sample chapters for fiction and nonfiction. SASE required. Royalty.

PELICAN PUBLISHING CO., INC.—1101 Monroe St., Gretna, LA 70053. Nina Kooj, Ed. General nonfiction: Americana, regional, architecture, how-to, travel, cookbooks, inspirational, motivational, music, parenting, etc. Juvenile fiction. Royalty.

PELION PRESS—See The Rosen Publishing Group.

PENGUIN USA—375 Hudson St., New York, NY 10014. Signet Books and Signet Classics: Commercial fiction (historicals, sagas, thrillers, action/adventure novels, westerns, horror, science fiction and fantasy) and nonfiction (self-help, how-to, etc.). Plume Books: hobbies, business, health, cooking, child care, psychology, etc. Mentor Books: Nonfiction originals for the college and high school market. No unsolicited manuscripts. Kestral Books: Fiction and nonfiction, including biography, history, and sports, for ages 7 to 14; humor and picture books for ages 2 to 6. Query Children's Books Dept. with outline and sample chapter. SASE required. Adult fiction and nonfiction. Adult hardcovers. Frederick Warne: Children's hardcovers and paperbacks. Penguin Books: Adult fiction and nonfiction paperbacks. Puffin Books: Children's fiction and nonfiction paperbacks. No unsolicited material. Royalty.

THE PERMANENT PRESS—R.D. 2, Noyac Rd., Sag Harbor, NY 11963. Judith Shepard, Ed. Seeks original and arresting novels, trade books, biographies. Query. Royalty.

PHAROS BOOKS—200 Park Ave., New York, NY 10166. Hana Umlauf Lane, Ed. Current issues, personal finance, food, health, history, true crime, how-to, humor, politics, reference, and sports. Nonfiction reference books for children, ages 6 and up. Query with sample chapter and outline. Royalty.

PHILOMEL BOOKS—Div. of The Putnam & Grosset Group, 200 Madison Ave., New York, NY 10016. Patricia Lee Gauch, Ed.-in-Chief. Pamela Wiseman, Sr. Ed. Fiction, picture books, and some biographies. Fresh, original work with compelling characters and "a truly childlike spirit." Query required.

THE PILGRIM PRESS/UNITED CHURCH PRESS—475 Riverside Dr.,

10th Fl., New York, NY 10015. Larry E. Kalp, Pub. Religious and general-interest nonfiction. Query with outline and sample chapters. Royalty.

PINEAPPLE PRESS—P.O. Drawer 16008, Southside Sta., Sarasota, FL 34239. June Cussen, Ed. Serious fiction and nonfiction, 60,000 to 125,000 words. Query with outline, sample chapters, and SASE. Royalty.

PIPPIN PRESS—229 E. 85th St., Gracie Sta., Box 92, New York, NY 10028. Barbara Francis, Pub. High-quality picture books for pre-schoolers; middle-group fiction, humor and mysteries; imaginative nonfiction for children of all ages. Query with outline. Royalty.

PLENUM PUBLISHING CORP.—233 Spring St., New York, NY 10013. Linda Greenspan Regan, Sr. Ed. Trade nonfiction, approximately 300 pages, on science, social science, and humanities. Query required. Hardcover. Royalty.

PLUME BOOKS—See Penguin USA.

POCKET BOOKS—Div. of Simon and Schuster, 1230 Ave. of the Americas, New York, NY 10020. William R. Grose, Ed. Dir. Original fiction and nonfiction. Mystery line: police procedurals, private eye, and amateur sleuth novels; query with outline and sample chapters to Jane Chelius, Sr. Ed. Royalty.

POINT—See Scholastic, Inc.

POPULAR PRESS—Bowling Green State Univ., Bowling Green, OH 43403. Ms. Pat Browne, Ed. Nonfiction, 250 to 400 pages, examining some aspect of popular culture. Query with outline. Flat fee or royalty.

POSEIDON PRESS—Imprint of Simon & Schuster, 1230 Ave. of the Americas, New York, NY 10020. Ann Patty, V.P./Pub. General fiction and nonfiction. No unsolicted material. Royalty.

POTTER, CLARKSON —201 E. 50th St., New York, NY 10022. Carol Southern, Assoc. Pub./Ed.-in-Chief. General trade books. Submissions accepted through agents only.

PRAEGER PUBLISHERS—Imprint of Greenwood Publishing Group, 1 Madison Ave., New York, NY 10010. Ron Chambers, Pub. General nonfiction; scholarly and reference books. Query with outline. Royalty.

PRENTICE HALL, BUSINESS & PROFESSIONAL PUBLISHING DIV. —Div. of Simon & Schuster, Englewood Cliffs, NJ 07632. Ted Nardin, V.P. and Ed.-in-Chief. Nonfiction, how-to, and reference books on business, self-improvement, education, and technical subjects. Hardcover and paperback. Royalty.

PRENTICE HALL PRESS—Div. of Simon & Schuster, 15 Columbus Cir., 15th Fl., New York, NY 10023. Literary nonfiction, history, self-help, New Age, health, travel, sports, equestrian, military, and illustrated gift books. No unsolicited manuscripts.

PRESIDIO PRESS—31 Pamaron Way, Novato, CA 94949. Nonfiction: contemporary military history from 50,000 words. Selected military fiction. Query. Royalty.

PRICE STERN SLOAN PUBLISHERS, INC.—360 N. La Cienega Blvd., Los Angeles, CA 90048. Children's books; adult trade nonfiction, including humor. Query with SASE required. Royalty.

PRIMA PUBLISHING AND COMMUNICATIONS—P.O. Box 1260, Rocklin, CA 95677. Ben Dominitz, Pub. Nonfiction on variety of subjects, including business, health, and cookbooks. "We want books with originality, written by highly qualified individuals." Royalty.

PRUETT PUBLISHING COMPANY—2928 Pearl, Boulder, CO 80301. Jim Pruett, Pres. Gerald Keenan, Sr. Ed. Nonfiction: outdoors and recreation, western U.S. history and travel, adventure travel and railroadiana. Query. Royalty.

PUFFIN BOOKS—See Penguin USA.

PUTNAM'S SONS, G.P.—Div. of Putnam Publishing Co., 200 Madison Ave., New York, NY 10016. General fiction and nonfiction. No unsolicited manuscripts or queries.

QUEST BOOKS—Imprint of The Theosophical Publishing House, 306 W. Geneva Rd., P. O. Box 270, Wheaton, IL 60189–0270. Shirley Nicholson, Sr. Ed. Nonfiction books on Eastern and Western religion and philosophy, holism, healing, meditation, yoga, astrology. Query. Royalty.

QUILL—Imprint of William Morrow and Co., Inc., 105 Madison Ave., New York, NY 10016. Andy Dutter, Ed. Trade paperback nonfiction. Submit through agent only.

RANDOM HOUSE, INC.—201 E. 50th St., New York, NY 10022. J. Shulman, Ed.-in-Chief, Juvenile Books. Stuart Flexner, Ed.-in-Chief, Reference Books. General fiction and nonfiction; reference and college textbooks. Fiction and nonfiction for beginning readers; paperback fiction line for 7- to 9-year-olds; 35 pages max. (Address Random House Juvenile Div., 225 Park Ave. S., New York, NY 10003.) Query with three chapters and outline for nonfiction; complete manuscript for fiction and SASE. Royalty.

REGNERY GATEWAY—1130 17th St. N.W., Suite 600, Washington, DC 20036. Nonfiction books on public policy. Query. Royalty.

RODALE PRESS—33 E. Minor St., Emmaus, PA 18098. Pat Corpora, Pub. Books on health, gardening, homeowner projects, cookbooks, inspirational topics, pop psychology, woodworking, natural history. Query with outline and sample chapter. Royalty and outright purchase. In addition: "We're always looking for truly competent free lancers to write chapters for books conceived and developed in-house"; payment on a "writer-for-hire" basis; address Bill Gottlieb, V.P.

RONIN PUBLISHING—P.O. Box 1035, Berkeley, CA 94701. Address Editors. Books on career issues and on psychoactive drugs. Query required. Royalty.

ROSEN PUBLISHING GROUP—29 E. 21st St., New York, NY 10010. Roger Rosen, Pres. Ruth C. Rosen, Ed. Young adult books, to 40,000 words, on career and personal guidance, journalism, self-help, etc. Pelion Press: music, art, history. Pays varying rates.

ROSSET & CO.—61 Fourth Ave., New York, NY 10003. Barney Rosset, Pub. Fiction and nonfiction on a variety of topics. Send complete manuscript or sample chapters and SASE.

RUTLEDGE HILL PRESS—513 Third Ave. S., Nashville, TN 37210. Ronald E. Pitkin, V.P. Southern-interest fiction and market-specific nonfiction. Query with outline and sample chapters. Royalty.

ST. ANTHONY MESSENGER PRESS—1615 Republic St., Cincinnati, OH 45210. Lisa Biedenbach, Man. Ed. Inspirational nonfiction for Catholics, supporting a Christian lifestyle in our culture; prayer aids, education, practical spirituality, parish ministry, liturgy resources. Query with 500-word summary. Royalty.

ST. MARTIN'S PRESS—175 Fifth Ave., New York, NY 10010. General adult fiction and nonfiction. Query first. Royalty.

SANDLAPPER PUBLISHING, INC.—P.O. Box 1932, Orangeburg, SC

29116–1932. Frank N. Handal, Book Ed. Books on South Carolina history, culture, cuisine. Nonfiction about South Carolina or fiction set in South Carolina. Submit query with outline and sample chapters.

SASQUATCH BOOKS—1931 Second Ave., Seattle, WA 98101. Books by local authors on a wide range of topics related to the Pacific Northwest: travel, natural history, gardening, cooking, history, and public affairs. Books must have a Pacific Northwest angle; length is 60,000 to 80,000 words. Query with SASE. Royalty.

SCARECROW PRESS—P.O. Box 4167, Metuchen, NJ 08840. Norman Horrocks, V.P./Editorial. Reference works and bibliographies (150 words and up) in the areas of cinema, TV, radio, and theatre, mainly for use by libraries. Query or send complete manuscript; multiple queries considered. Royalty.

SCHOCKEN BOOKS—Div. of Pantheon Books, 201 E. 50th St., New York, NY 10022. General nonfiction: Judaica, women's studies, education, art history. Query with outline and sample chapter. Royalty.

SCHOLASTIC, INC.—730 Broadway, New York, NY 10003. Point: Regina Griffin, Sr. Ed. Young adult fiction for readers 12 and up. Apple Books: Regina Griffin, Sr. Ed. Fiction for readers ages 8 to 12. Submit complete manuscript with cover letter and SASE. Royalty. Sunfire: Ann Reit, Ed. American historical romances, for girls 12 and up, 55,000 words. Query with outline and three sample chapters. Write for tip sheets.

SCOTT, FORESMAN AND CO.—1900 E. Lake Ave., Glenview, IL 60025. Richard E. Peterson, Pres. Elementary and secondary textbooks and supplemental material. Royalty.

SCRIBNER'S SONS, CHARLES—866 Third Ave., New York, NY 10022. Barbara Grossman, Pub. Fiction, general nonfiction, science, history, and biography; query first. Clare Costello, Ed., Books for Young Readers: fantasy, mystery, YA, SF, and problem novels; picture books, ages 5 and up; and nonfiction (science and how-tos). Query with outline and sample chapter.

SEVEN SEAS PRESS—International Marine, Box 220, Camden, ME 04843. Jonathan Eaton, VP/Ed. James Babb, Acquisitions Ed. Books on boating (sailing and power), other marine topics.

SHAW PUBLISHERS, HAROLD—388 Gunderson Dr., Box 567, Wheaton, IL 60189. Ramona Cramer Tucker, Dir. of Ed. Services. Nonfiction, 120 to 220 pages, with an evangelical Christian perspective. Teen and adult fiction and literary books. Query. Flat fee.

SIERRA CLUB BOOKS—100 Bush St., San Francisco, CA 94104. Nonfiction: environment, natural history, the sciences, outdoors and regional guidebooks, nature photography; juvenile fiction and nonfiction. Query with SASE. Royalty.

SIGNET BOOKS AND SIGNET CLASSIC—See Penguin USA.

SILHOUETTE BOOKS—300 E. 42nd St., New York, NY 10017. Isabel Swift, Ed. Mgr. Silhouette Romances: Tara Gavin, Sr. Ed. Contemporary romances, 53,000 to 58,000 words. Special Edition: Leslie Kazanjian, Sr. Ed. Sophisticated contemporary romances, 75,000 to 80,000 words. Silhouette Desire: Lucia Macro,

Sr. Ed. Sensuous contemporary romances, 53,000 to 60,000 words. Intimate Moments: Leslie Wainger, Sr. Ed./Ed. Coord. Sensuous, exciting contemporary romances, 80,000 to 85,000 words. Historical romance: 95,000 to 105,000 words, set in England, France, and North America between 1700 and 1900; query with synopsis and three sample chapters to Eliza Shallcross/Tracy Farrell, Eds. Query with synopsis and SASE to appropriate editor. Tipsheets available.

SIMON & SCHUSTER—1230 Ave. of the Americas, New York, NY 10020. Adult books: No unsolicited material. Children's Book Division: Olga Litowinsky, Ed. Material for middle-grade readers. "Everything from storybooks for 7-year-olds up to novels for 10- to 14-year-olds."

SMITH PUBLISHER, GIBBS/PEREGRINE SMITH BOOKS—P. O. Box 667, Layton, UT 84401. Steve Chapman, Fiction Ed. John Well, Nonfiction Ed. Adult fiction and nonfiction. Query. Royalty.

SOHO PRESS—One Union Sq., New York, NY 10003. Juris Jurjevics, Ed. Adult fiction (mysteries, thrillers) and nonfiction, from 75,000 words. Send SASE and complete manuscript. Royalty.

SOUTHERN ILLINOIS UNIVERSITY PRESS—Box 3697, Carbondale, IL 62901. Curtis L. Clark, Ed. Nonfiction in the humanities, 200 to 400 pages. Query with outline and sample chapters. Royalty.

SOUTHERN METHODIST UNIVERSITY PRESS—Box 415, Dallas, TX 75275. Suzanne Comer, Sr. Ed. Fiction: serious literary fiction, short story collections, set in Texas or the Southwest, 150 to 400 pages. Nonfiction: scholarly studies in ethics, composition/rhetoric, theater, film, North African archaeology, belles lettres, scholarly writing about Texas or Southwest, 150 to 400 pages. No juvenile material or poetry. Query. Royalty or flat fee.

SPECTRA BOOKS—Imprint of Bantam Books, 666 Fifth Ave., New York, NY 10103. Lou Aronica, Pub. Science fiction and fantasy, with emphasis on storytelling and characterization. Query with SASE; no unsolicited manuscripts. Royalty.

STANDARD PUBLISHING—8121 Hamilton Ave., Cincinnati, OH 45231. Address Mark Plunkett. Fiction: juveniles, based on Bible or with moral tone. Nonfiction: biblical, Christian education. Conservative evangelical. Query preferred.

STANFORD UNIVERSITY PRESS—Stanford Univ., Stanford, CA 94305–2235. Norris Pope, Ed. Adult nonfiction. Query with outline and sample chapters. Royalty.

STECK-VAUGHN COMPANY—National Education Corp., 11 Prospect St., Madison, NJ 07940. Walter Kossmann, Ed. Nonfiction books, 5,000 to 30, 000 words, for school and library market: biographies for grades 6 and up; and science, social studies, and history books for primary grades through high school. Query with outline and sample chapters; SASE required. Flat fee and royalty.

STEMMER HOUSE PUBLISHERS, INC.—2627 Caves Rd., Owings Mills, MD 21117. Barbara Holdridge, Ed. Juvenile fiction and adult fiction and nonfiction. Specialize in art, design, and horticultural titles. Query with SASE. Royalty.

STERLING PUBLISHING CO., INC.—387 Park Ave. S., New York, NY 10016. Sheila Anne Barry, Acquisitions Mgr. How-to, hobby, woodworking, health, craft, wine, New Age, puzzles, juvenile humor and activities, juvenile science, and sports and games books. Query with outline, sample chapter, and sample illustrations. Royalty.

STONE WALL PRESS, INC.—1241 30th St. N.W., Washington, D.C. 20007. Nonfiction on natural history, outdoors, conservation, 200 to 300 manuscript pages. Query first. Royalty.

STONEYDALE PRESS—205 Main St., Drawer B, Stevensville, MT 59870. Dale A. Burk, Ed. Adult nonfiction, primarily how-to on outdoor recreation with emphasis on big game hunting. "We're a very specialized market." Query with outline and sample chapters. Royalty.

STORY LINE PRESS—Three Oaks Farm, Brownsville, OR 97327–9718. Robert McDowell, Ed. Fiction, nonfiction, and poetry of varying lengths. Query. Royalty.

STRAWBERRY HILL PRESS—2594 15th Ave., San Francisco, CA 94127. Carolyn Soto, Ed. Nonfiction: biography, autobiography, history, cooking, health, how-to, philosophy, performance arts, and Third World. Query first with sample chapters, outline, and SASE. Royalty.

STUART, INC., LYLE—120 Enterprise Ave., Secaucus, NJ 07094. Allan J. Wilson, Ed. General nonfiction. Citadel Press: biography, film, history, limited fiction. Query required. Royalty.

SUMMIT BOOKS—1230 Ave. of the Americas, New York, NY 10020. General-interest fiction and nonfiction of high literary quality. No category books. Query through agents only. Royalty.

SUNFIRE—See Scholastic, Inc.

TAB BOOKS, INC.—Blue Ridge Summit, PA 17294. Ron Powers, Dir. of Acquisitions, Ed. Dept. Nonfiction: electronics, computers, how-to, aviation, science fair projects, self-help, business, solar and energy, science and technology, back to basics, automotive, marine and outdoor life, hobby and craft, military history, graphic design, and engineering. Fiction: military. Royalty or flat fee.

TAMBOURINE BOOKS—Imprint of William Morrow & Co., Inc., 105 Madison Ave., New York, NY 10016. Paulette C. Kaufmann, V.P./Ed.-in-Chief. Picture books and nonfiction for ages 7 to 10 for general trade market. "We hope to find new talented writers and illustrators who are working outside the New York area."

TARCHER, INC., JEREMY P.—5858 Wilshire Blvd., Suite 200, Los Angeles, CA 90036. Jeremy P. Tarcher, Ed.-in-Chief. General nonfiction: psychology, spirituality, creativity, personal development, health and fitness, women's concerns, science for the layperson, etc. Query with outline, sample chapter, credentials, and SASE. Royalty.

TAYLOR PUBLISHING CO.—1550 W. Mockingbird Ln., Dallas, TX 75235. Nonfiction: cooking, gardening, sports and recreation, true crime, health, self-help, humor/trivia, lifestyles. Query with outline and sample chapters. Royalty.

TEMPLE UNIVERSITY PRESS—Broad and Oxford Sts., Philadelphia, PA 19122. Michael Ames, Ed. Adult nonfiction. Query with outline and sample chapters. Royalty.

TEN SPEED PRESS—P.O. Box 7123, Berkeley, CA 94707. Mariah Bear, Ed. Self-help and how-to on careers, recreation, etc.; natural science, history, cookbooks. Query with outline and sample chapters. Royalty. Paperback.

THUNDER'S MOUTH PRESS—54 Greene St., Suite 4S, New York, NY 10013. Neil Ortenberg, Ed. Literary fiction and poetry collections; books on historical and political topics. Query first. Length requirement: poetry, 96 pages; fiction, to 200 pages. Royalty.

TICKNOR & FIELDS—Subsidiary of Houghton Mifflin Company, 215 Park Ave. S., New York, NY 10003. John Herman, Ed. Dir. General nonfiction and fiction. Royalty.

TIMES BOOKS—Div. of Random House, Inc., 201 E. 50th St., New York, NY 10022. Steve Wasserman, Ed. Dir. General nonfiction specializing in business, science, and current affairs. No unsolicited manuscripts or queries accepted.

TOR BOOKS—49 W. 24th St., New York, NY 10010. Beth Meacham, Ed.-in-Chief: Science fiction and fantasy. Exec. Ed.: Thrillers, espionage, and mysteries. Melissa Ann Singer, Ed.: Horror and dark fantasy. Wanda June Alexander, Assoc. Ed.: Historicals. Length: from 60,000 words. Query with outline and sample chapters. Royalty.

TROLL ASSOCIATES—100 Corporate Dr., Mahwah, NJ 07430. M. Francis, Ed. Juvenile fiction and nonfiction. Query preferred. Royalty or flat fee.

TROPHY BOOKS—See Harper Junior Books Group.

TROUBADOR PRESS—Imprint of Price Stern Sloan, 360 N. Cienega Blvd., Los Angeles, CA 90048. Juvenile illustrated games, activity, paper doll, coloring, and cut-out books. Query with outline and SASE. Royalty or flat fee.

TSR BOOKS, INC.—P.O. Box 756, Lake Geneva, WI 53147. Address Manuscript Ed. "Seeking highly original works of science fiction, horror, mystery, and fantasy," 100,000 words, for Dragonlance, Forgotten Realms, and Buck Rogers book lines. Query required.

UAHC PRESS—838 Fifth Ave., New York, NY 10021. Sharyn Ruff, Marketing Mgr. Fiction and nonfiction from pre-school to adult. No poetry. Material that deals with traditional and controversial themes in Judaism for Jewish and non-Jewish readers. Query with detailed table of contents, outline, and sample chapter or complete manuscript.

UNIVERSE BOOKS—381 Park Ave. S., New York, NY 10016. Adele J. Ursone, Sr. Ed. Fine arts and art history, photography, design, art calendars. Query with SASE. Royalty.

UNIVERSITY OF ALABAMA PRESS—P.O. Box 870380, Tuscaloosa, AL 35487. Scholarly and general regional nonfiction. Submit to appropriate editor: Malcolm MacDonald, Ed. (history, public administration, political science); Nicole Mitchell, Ed. (English, rhetoric and communication, Judaic studies, women's studies); Judith Knight, Ed. (archaeology, anthropology). Send complete manuscript. Royalty.

UNIVERSITY OF ARIZONA PRESS—1230 N. Park Ave., Suite 102, Tucson, AZ 85719. Gregory McNamee, Sr. Ed. Barbara Beatty, Acquiring Ed., Sciences. Joanne O'Hare, Acquiring Ed., Humanities. Scholarly nonfiction, to 100,000 words: anthropology, history, the sciences, natural history, Native American and Latin American studies, regional or national topics, books of personal essays. Query with outline and sample chapters or send complete manuscript. Royalty.

UNIVERSITY OF CALIFORNIA PRESS—2120 Berkeley Way, Berkeley, CA 94720. Address Acquisitions Department. Scholarly nonfiction. Query with outline and sample chapters.

UNIVERSITY OF GEORGIA PRESS—Univ. of Georgia, Athens, GA 30602. Karen Orchard, Ed. Short story collections and poetry, scholarly nonfiction and literary criticism, Southern and American history, regional studies, biography and autobiography. For nonfiction, query with outline and sample chapters. Poetry collections considered in Sept. and Jan. only; short fiction in June and July only.

A $10 fee is required for all poetry and fiction submissions. Royalty. SASE for competition guidelines.

UNIVERSITY OF ILLINOIS PRESS—54 E. Gregory Dr., Champaign, IL 61820. Richard L. Wentworth, Ed.-in-Chief. Short story collections, 140 to 180 pages; nonfiction; and poetry, 70 to 100 pages. Rarely considers multiple submissions. Query. Royalty.

UNIVERSITY OF MINNESOTA PRESS—2037 University Ave. S.E., Minneapolis, MN 55414. Terry Cochran, Ed.-in-Chief. Fiction: minority and Third World, 40,000 to 100,000 words. Nonfiction: media studies, literary theory, philosophy, cultural criticism, regional titles, 50,000 to 225,000 words. Query with detailed prospectus or introduction, table of contents, a sample chapter, and a recent resumé. Royalty.

UNIVERSITY OF NEW MEXICO PRESS—Univ. of New Mexico Press, Albuquerque, NM 87131. Elizabeth C. Hadas, Ed. Dir. David V. Holtby, Jeffrey Grathwohl, Dana Asbury, and Barbara Guth, Eds. Scholarly nonfiction on social and cultural anthropology, archaeology, Western history, art, and photography. Query. Royalty.

UNIVERSITY OF NORTH CAROLINA PRESS—P.O. Box 2288, Chapel Hill, NC 27515–2288. David Perry, Ed. General-interest books (75,000 to 125,000 words) on the lore, crafts, cooking, gardening, travel, and natural history of the southeast. Query preferred. Royalty.

UNIVERSITY OF TENNESSEE PRESS—293 Communications Bldg., Knoxville, TN 37996–0325. Nonfiction, 200 to 300 pages. Query with outline and sample chapters. Royalty.

UNIVERSITY OF UTAH PRESS—101 U.S.B., Salt Lake City, UT 84112. David Catron, Ed. Nonfiction and fiction from 200 pages, and poetry from 60 pages. (Submit poetry during March only.) Query. Royalty.

UNIVERSITY PRESSES OF FLORIDA—15 N.W. 15th St., Gainesville, FL 32603. Walda Metcalf, Sr. Ed. and Asst. Dir. Nonfiction, 150 to 450 manuscript pages, on regional studies, women's studies, Latin American studies, contemporary literary criticism, sociology, anthropology, archaeology, international affairs, labor studies, and history. Royalty.

VAN NOSTRAND REINHOLD—115 Fifth Ave., New York, NY 10003. Chester C. Lucido, Jr., Pres./C.E.O. Business, professional, scientific, and technical publishers of applied reference works: Hospitality; Architecture; Graphic and Interior Design; Gemology; Chemistry; Industrial and Environmental Health and Safety; Food Science and Technology; Computer Science and Engineering. Royalty.

VANDAMERE PRESS—P.O. Box 5243, Arlington, VA 22205. Arthur F. Brown, Ed. Adult nonfiction and juvenile fiction and nonfiction, any length. Areas of special interest: history; Washington, DC area; career guides; parenting; mid-Atlantic area; children's books; and travel. Prefer outline with sample chapter for first submission. Multiple queries considered. Royalty.

VIKING—Imprint of Penguin USA, 375 Hudson St., New York, NY 10014. No unagented manuscripts.

VOYAGER PAPERBACKS—See Harcourt Brace Jovanovich.

WALKER AND COMPANY—720 Fifth Ave., New York, NY 10019. Fiction: mysteries, suspense, westerns, regency romance, espionage, and horror. Nonfiction: Americana, biography, history, science, natural history, medicine, psychology, parenting, sports, outdoors, reference, popular science, self-help, business, and music. Juvenile nonfiction, including biography, science, history, music, and nature. Fiction and problem novels for YA. Query with synopsis. Royalty.

WALLACE-HOMESTEAD—See Chilton Book Co.

WARNE, FREDERICK—See Penguin USA.

WARNER BOOKS—666 Fifth Ave., New York, NY 10103. Mel Parker, Ed.-in-Chief. Fiction: historical romance, contemporary women's fiction, unusual big-scale horror and suspense. Nonfiction: business books, health and nutrition, self-help. Query with sample chapters.

WATTS, INC., FRANKLIN—387 Park Ave. S., New York, NY 10016. Philippe Gray, Asst. to Ed. Dir. Nonfiction for grades K to 12, including science, history, and biography. Adult nonfiction dealing with family life, submit to Judith Rothman, Pub. Query with SASE required.

WESLEYAN UNIVERSITY PRESS—110 Mt. Vernon St., Middletown, CT 06457–6050. Wesleyan Poetry: new poets, 64 pages; published poets, 64 to 80 pages. Send complete manuscript. Royalty.

WESTERN PUBLISHING CO., INC.—850 Third Ave., New York, NY 10022. Robin Warner, Pub., Children's Books; Thea Feldman, Ed. Dir., Children's Books. Adult nonfiction: field guides, cookbooks, etc. Children's books, fiction and nonfiction: picture books, storybooks, concept books, novelty books. Royalty and flat fee. No unsolicited manuscripts. Same address and requirements for Golden Press.

WESTMINSTER/JOHN KNOX PRESS—100 Witherspoon St., Louisville, KY 40202. Davis Perkins, Ed. Dir. Books that inform, interpret, challenge, and encourage Christian faith and living. Royalty. Send SASE for "Guidelines for a Book Proposal."

WHITMAN, ALBERT—5747 W. Howard St., Niles, IL 60648. Kathleen Tucker, Ed. Picture books; novels, biographies, mysteries, and general nonfiction for middle-grade readers. Submit complete manuscript for picture books, three chapters and outline for longer fiction; query for nonfiction. Royalty.

WILDERNESS PRESS—2440 Bancroft Way, Berkeley, CA 94704. Thomas Winnett, Ed. Nonfiction: sports, recreation, and travel in the western U.S. Royalty.

WILEY & SONS, JOHN—605 Third Ave., New York, NY 10158–0012. Gwenyth Jones, Pub. Nonfiction manuscripts, 250 to 350 pages: science/nature; business/management; real estate; travel; cooking; biography; psychology; microcomputers; language; history; current affairs; health; finance. Send proposals, with outline, author vita, market information, and sample chapter. Royalty.

WILSHIRE BOOK COMPANY—12015 Sherman Rd., N. Hollywood, CA 91605. Melvin Powers, Ed. Dir. Psychological self-help with strong motivational messages. Adult fables. Query or send synopsis. Royalty.

WINDSWEPT HOUSE PUBLISHERS—Mt. Desert, ME 04660. Jane Weinberger, Ed. Children's picture books, 150 words, with illustrations. Query first for how-to and teenage novels. Currently overstocked.

WINGBOW PRESS—2929 Fifth St., Berkeley, CA 94710. Randy Fingland, Ed. Nonfiction: women's interests, health, psychology. Query preferred. Royalty.

WOODBINE HOUSE—5615 Fishers Lane, Rockville, MD 20852. Susan Stokes, Ed. Nonfiction of all types; especially interested in science, history, special education, travel, military, natural history, and general reference. No personal accounts. Query or submit complete manuscript with SASE. Guidelines for SASE. Royalty or flat fee.

WORD PUBLISHING—5221 O'Connor Blvd., Irving, TX 75039. Joey Paul, Acquiring Ed. Nonfiction, 65,000 to 85,000 words, dealing with the relationship and/or applications of biblical principles to everyday life. Query with outline and sample chapters. Royalty.

WORDWARE PUBLISHING—1506 Capital Ave., Plano, TX 75074. Russell A. Stultz, Ed. Computer reference books and business/professional books. Query with outline and sample chapters. Flat fee.

WORKMAN PUBLISHING CO., INC.—708 Broadway, New York, NY 10003. Address Editors. General nonfiction. Normal contractual terms based on agreement.

WORLDWIDE LIBRARY—Div. of Harlequin Books, 225 Duncan Mill Rd., Don Mills, Ont., Canada M3B 3K9. Randall Toye, Ed. Dir. Action adventure series and futuristic fiction for Gold Eagle imprint; mystery fiction. Query. Paperback only.

YANKEE BOOKS—P.O. Box 1248, 62 Bay View St., Camden, ME 04843. Linda Spencer, Sr. Ed. Books relating specifically to New England: cooking, crafts, environmental issues, gardening, nature, humor, popular history. No fiction.Query or send proposal. Royalty.

YEARLING BOOKS—See Dell Publishing Co., Inc.

ZEBRA BOOKS—475 Park Ave. S., New York, NY 10016. Ann La Farge, Sr. Ed. Carin Cohen Ritter, Sr. Ed. Popular fiction: horror; historical romance (Heartfire Romances, 107,000 words, and Lovegram Romances, 130,000 words); traditional Gothics (first person, 100,000 words); regencies (80,000 to 120,000 words); sagas (150,000 words); glitz (100,000 words); men's adventure; westerns; thrillers, etc. Query with synopsis and sample chapters preferred.

ZOLOTOW BOOKS, CHARLOTTE—Imprint of Harper & Row, 10 E. 53rd St., New York, NY 10022. Address Editors. Juvenile fiction and nonfiction "with integrity of purpose, beauty of language, and an out-of-ordinary look at ordinary things." Royalty.

ZONDERVAN PUBLISHING HOUSE—1415 Lake Dr. S.E., Grand Rapids, MI 49506. Christian titles. General fiction and nonfiction; academic and professional books. Address Manuscript Review Ed. Query with outline, sample chapter, and SASE. Royalty. Guidelines.

UNIVERSITY PRESSES

University presses generally publish books of a scholarly nature or of specialized interest by authorities in a given field. A few publish fiction and poetry. Many publish only a handful of titles a year. Always query first. Do not send a manuscript until you have been invited to do so by the editor.

Several of the following presses and their detailed editorial submission requirements are included in the *Book Publishers* list.

BUCKNELL UNIVERSITY PRESS—Bucknell University, Lewisburg, PA 17837.

CAMBRIDGE UNIVERSITY PRESS—40 W. 20th St., New York, NY 10011–4211.

THE CATHOLIC UNIVERSITY OF AMERICA PRESS—620 Michigan Ave. N.E., Washington, DC 20064.

COLUMBIA UNIVERSITY PRESS—562 West 113th St., New York, NY 10025.

FORDHAM UNIVERSITY PRESS—University Box L, Bronx, NY 10458–5172.

GEORGIA STATE UNIVERSITY BUSINESS PRESS—University Plaza, Atlanta, GA 30303–3093.

HARVARD UNIVERSITY PRESS—79 Garden St., Cambridge, MA 02138.

INDIANA UNIVERSITY PRESS—10th and Morton Sts., Bloomington, IN 47405.

KENT STATE UNIVERSITY PRESS—Kent State Univ., Kent, OH 44242.

LOUISIANA STATE UNIVERSITY PRESS—LSU, Baton Rouge, LA 70893.

LOYOLA UNIVERSITY PRESS—3441 N. Ashland Ave., Chicago, IL 60657.

MEMPHIS STATE UNIVERSITY PRESS—Memphis State Univ., Memphis, TN 38152.

MICHIGAN STATE UNIVERSITY PRESS—1405 S. Harrison Rd., East Lansing, MI 48823–5202.

THE MIT PRESS—Acquisitions Dept., 55 Hayward St., Cambridge, MA 02142.

OHIO STATE UNIVERSITY PRESS—180 Pressey Hall, 1070 Carmark Rd., Columbus, OH 43210.

OHIO UNIVERSITY PRESS/SWALLOW PRESS—Scott Quadrangle, Athens, OH 45701.

OREGON STATE UNIVERSITY PRESS—101 Waldo Hall, Corvallis, OR 97331.

THE PENNSYLVANIA STATE UNIVERSITY PRESS—Barbara Bldg., Suite C, 820 N. University Dr., University Park, PA 16802.

PRINCETON UNIVERSITY PRESS—41 William St., Princeton, NJ 08540.

SOUTHERN ILLINOIS UNIVERSITY PRESS—Box 3697, Carbondale, IL 62901.

SOUTHERN METHODIST UNIVERSITY PRESS—Box 415, Dallas, TX 75275.

STANFORD UNIVERSITY PRESS—Stanford University, Stanford, CA 94305–2235.

STATE UNIVERSITY OF NEW YORK PRESS—State University Plaza, Albany, NY 12246.

SYRACUSE UNIVERSITY PRESS—1600 Jamesville Ave., Syracuse, NY 13244–5160.

TEMPLE UNIVERSITY PRESS—Broad and Oxford Sts., Philadelphia, PA 19122.

UNIVERSITY OF ALABAMA PRESS—P.O. Box 870380, Tuscaloosa, AL 35487.

UNIVERSITY OF ARIZONA PRESS—1230 N. Park Ave., Suite 102, Tucson, AZ 85719.

UNIVERSITY OF CALIFORNIA PRESS—2120 Berkeley Way, Berkeley, CA 94720.

UNIVERSITY OF CHICAGO PRESS—5801 Ellis Ave., Chicago, IL 60637.

UNIVERSITY OF GEORGIA PRESS—University of Georgia, Athens, GA 30602.

UNIVERSITY OF ILLINOIS PRESS—54 E. Gregory Dr., Champaign, IL 61820.

UNIVERSITY OF MASSACHUSETTS PRESS—Box 429, Amherst, MA 01004.

UNIVERSITY OF MICHIGAN PRESS—839 Greene St., P.O. Box 1104, Ann Arbor, MI 48106.

UNIVERSITY OF MINNESOTA PRESS—2037 University Ave. S.E., Minneapolis, MN 55414.

UNIVERSITY OF MISSOURI PRESS—2910 LeMone Blvd., Columbia, MO 65201.

UNIVERSITY OF NEBRASKA PRESS—901 North 17th St., Lincoln, NE 68588–0520.

UNIVERSITY OF NEW MEXICO PRESS—UNM, Albuquerque, NM 87131.

UNIVERSITY OF NORTH CAROLINA PRESS—P.O. Box 2288, Chapel Hill, NC 27515–2288.

UNIVERSITY OF OKLAHOMA PRESS—1005 Asp Ave., Norman, OK 73019–0445.

UNIVERSITY OF PITTSBURGH PRESS—127 North Bellefield Ave., Pittsburgh, PA 15260.

UNIVERSITY OF SOUTH CAROLINA PRESS—1716 College St., Columbia, SC 29208.

UNIVERSITY OF TENNESSEE PRESS—293 Communications Bldg., Knoxville, TN 37996–0325.

UNIVERSITY OF UTAH PRESS—101 U.S.B., Salt Lake City, UT 84112.

UNIVERSITY OF WISCONSIN PRESS—114 N. Murray St., Madison, WI 53715–1199.

UNIVERSITY PRESS OF COLORADO—P.O. Box 849, Niwot, CO 80544.

THE UNIVERSITY PRESS OF KENTUCKY—663 S. Limestone St., Lexington, KY 40506–0336.

UNIVERSITY PRESS OF MISSISSIPPI—3825 Ridgewood Rd., Jackson, MS 39211.

UNIVERSITY PRESS OF NEW ENGLAND—17½ Lebanon St., Hanover, NH 03755.

THE UNIVERSITY PRESS OF VIRGINIA—Box 3608, University Sta., Charlottesville, VA 22903.

UNIVERSITY PRESSES OF FLORIDA—15 N.W. 15th St., Gainesville, FL 32603.

WAYNE STATE UNIVERSITY PRESS—5959 Woodward Ave., Detroit, MI 48202.

WESLEYAN UNIVERSITY PRESS—110 Mt.Vernon St., Middletown, CT 06457–6050.

YALE UNIVERSITY PRESS—92A Yale Sta., New Haven, CT 06520.

SYNDICATES

Syndicates are business organizations that buy material from writers and artists to sell to newspapers all over the country and the world. Authors are paid either a percentage of the gross proceeds or an outright fee.

Of course, features by people well known in their fields have the best chance of being syndicated. In general, syndicates want columns that have been popular in a local newspaper, perhaps, or magazine. Since most syndicated fiction has been published previously in magazines or books, beginning fiction writers should try to sell their stories to magazines before submitting them to syndicates.

Always query syndicates before sending manuscripts, since their needs change frequently, and be sure to enclose SASEs with queries and manuscripts.

ARKIN MAGAZINE SYNDICATE—1817 N.E. 164th St., N. Miami Beach, FL 33162. Joseph Arkin, Ed. Dir. Articles, 750 to 2,200 words, for trade and professional magazines. Must have small-business slant, written in layman's language, and offer solutions to business problems. Articles should apply to many businesses, not just a specific industry. No columns. Pays 3¢ to 10¢ a word, on acceptance. Query preferred.

BUSINESS FEATURES SYNDICATE—P. O. Box 9844, Ft. Lauderdale, FL 33310. Dana K. Cassell, Ed. Articles, 1,500 to 2,000 words, for the independent retailer or small service business owner, on marketing, security, personnel, merchandising, general management. Pays 50% of sales.

CONTEMPORARY FEATURES SYNDICATE—P. O. Box 1258, Jackson,

TN 38302. Lloyd Russell, Ed. Articles, 1,000 to 10,000 words: how-to, money savers, business, etc. Self-help pieces for small business. Pays from $25, on acceptance.

HARRIS & ASSOCIATES FEATURES—12084 Caminito Campana, San Diego, CA 92128. Dick Harris, Ed. Sports and family-oriented features, to 1,200 words; fillers and short humor, 500 to 800 words. Queries preferred. Pays varying rates.

HERITAGE FEATURES SYNDICATE—214 Massachusetts Ave. N.E., Washington, DC 20002. Andy Seamans, Man. Ed. Public policy news features; syndicates weekly columns and editorial cartoons. Query with SASE a must.

HISPANIC LINK NEWS SERVICE—1420 N St. N.W., Washington, DC 20005. Charles A. Ericksen, Ed. Trend articles, opinion and personal experience pieces, and general features with Hispanic focus, 650 to 700 words; editorial cartoons. Pays $25 for op-ed columns and cartoons, on acceptance. Send SASE for guidelines.

THE HOLLYWOOD INSIDE SYNDICATE—Box 49957, Los Angeles, CA 90049. John Austin, Dir. Feature material, 750 to 2,500 words, on TV and film personalities. Story suggestions for 3-part series. Pieces on unusual medical and scientific breakthroughs. Pays on percentage basis for features, negotiated rates for ideas, on acceptance.

KING FEATURES SYNDICATE—235 E. 45th St., New York, NY 10017. Merry Clark, Dir. of Ed. Projects. Columns, comics; all contributions on contract for regular columns. "We do not consider nor buy individual articles. We are interested in ideas for nationally syndicated columns." Submit cover letter, 6 sample columns of 650 words each, bio sheet and any additional clips, and SASE. No simultaneous submissions. Query with SASE for guidelines.

LOS ANGELES TIMES SYNDICATE—Times Mirror Sq., Los Angeles, CA 90053. Commentary, features, columns, editorial cartoons, comics, puzzles and games; news services. Query for articles.

NATIONAL NEWS BUREAU—1318 Chancellor St., Philadelphia, PA 19107. Articles, 500 to 800 words, interviews, consumer news, how-tos, travel pieces, reviews, entertainment pieces, features, etc. Pays on publication.

NEW YORK TIMES SYNDICATION SALES—130 Fifth Ave., New York, NY 10011. Barbara Gaynes, Man. Ed. Previously published health, lifestyle, and entertainment articles only, to 2,000 words. Query with published article or tear sheet and SASE. Pays varying rates, on publication.

NEWSPAPER ENTERPRISE ASSOCIATION, INC.—200 Park Ave., New York, NY 10166. Gail Robinson, Man. Ed. Ideas for new concepts in syndicated columns. No single stories or stringers. Payment by contractual arrangement.

OCEANIC PRESS SERVICE—P. O. Box 6538, Buena Park, CA 90622–6538. Peter Carbone, General Mgr. Buys reprint rights for foreign markets, on previously published novels, self-help, and how-to books; interviews with celebrities; illustrated features on celebrities, family, health, beauty, personal relations, etc.; cartoons, comic strips. Pays on acceptance or 50:50 syndication. Query.

SINGER MEDIA CORP.—3164 W. Tyler Ave., Anaheim, CA 92801. Kurt D. Singer, Ed. U.S. and/or foreign reprint rights to romantic short stories, historical and romantic novels, gothics, westerns, and mysteries published during last 25 years; business management titles. Biography, women's-interest material, all

706

lengths. Home repair, real estate, crosswords, psychological quizzes. Interviews with celebrities. Illustrated columns, humor, cartoons, comic strips. Pays on percentage basis or by outright purchase.

TRIBUNE MEDIA SERVICES—64 E. Concord St., Orlando, FL 32801. Michael Argirion, Ed. Continuing columns, comic strips, features, electronic data bases.

UNITED FEATURE SYNDICATE—200 Park Ave., New York, NY 10166. James Robison, Exec. Ed. Syndicated columns; no one-shots or series. Payment by contractual arrangement. Send samples with SASE.

UNITED PRESS INTERNATIONAL—1400 Eye St. N.W., Washington, DC 20005. Bill G. Ferguson, Man. Ed. Seldom accepts free-lance material.

LITERARY PRIZE OFFERS

Each year many important literary contests are open to free-lance writers. The short summaries given below are intended merely as guides. Closing dates, requirements, and rules are tentative. Modest entry fees are often required. Every effort has been made to ensure the accuracy of information provided here. However, due to the ever-changing nature of literary competitions, writers are advised to check the monthly "Prize Offers" column of *The Writer* Magazine (120 Boylston St., Boston, MA 02116) for the most up-to-date contest requirements. Writers should send for guidelines before submitting to any contest.

ACADEMY OF AMERICAN POETS—177 E. 87th St., New York, NY 10128. Offers Walt Whitman Award: publication and $1,000 cash prize for a book-length poetry manuscript by a poet who has not yet published a volume of poetry. Closes in November.

ACTORS THEATRE OF LOUISVILLE—316 W. Main St., Louisville, KY 40202. Conducts Ten-Minute Play Contest. Offers $1,000 for previously unproduced ten-page script. Closes in December.

AMERICAN ACADEMY OF ARTS AND LETTERS—633 W. 155th St., New York, NY 10032. Offers Richard Rodgers Production Award, which consists of subsidized production in New York City by a non-profit theater for a musical, play with music, thematic review, or any comparable work other than opera. Closes in November.

THE ASSOCIATED WRITING PROGRAMS ANNUAL AWARDS SERIES—Old Dominion University, Norfolk, VA 23529–0079. Conducts Annual Awards Series in Poetry, Short Fiction, the Novel, and Nonfiction. In each category the prize is book publication and a $1,000 honorarium. Closes in February.

ASSOCIATION OF JEWISH LIBRARIES—15 Goldsmith St., Providence, RI 02906. Address Lillian Schwartz, Secretary. Conducts Sydney Taylor Manuscript Competition for best fiction manuscript for readers 8 to 12. Prize is $1,000. Closes in January.

BARNARD COLLEGE—Women Poets at Barnard, Columbia University, 3009 Broadway, New York, NY 10027–6598. The Barnard New Women Poets Prize offers $1,500 and publication by Beacon Press for an unpublished poetry manuscript, 50 to 100 pages, by a female poet who has never published a book of poetry. Closes in September.

BEVERLY HILLS THEATRE GUILD/JULIE HARRIS PLAYWRIGHT AWARD—2815 N. Beachwood Dr., Los Angeles, CA 90068. Address Marcella Meharg. Offers prize of $5,000, plus possible $2,000 for productions in Los Angeles area, for previously unproduced and unpublished full-length play. A $1,000 second prize and $500 third prize are also offered. Closes in November.

THE CHICAGO TRIBUNE/NELSON ALGREN AWARDS FOR SHORT FICTION—435 N. Michigan Ave., Chicago, IL 60611. Sponsors Nelson Algren Awards for Short Fiction, with a first prize of $5,000 and three runners-up prizes of $1,000 for outstanding unpublished short stories of 10,000 words or less, by American writers. Closes in January.

EUGENE V. DEBS FOUNDATION—Dept. Of History, Indiana State Univ., Terre Haute, IN 47809. Offers Bryant Spann Memorial Prize of $1,000 for published or unpublished article or essay on themes relating to social protest or human equality. Closes in April.

DELACORTE PRESS—Dept. BFYR, 666 Fifth Ave., New York, NY 10103. Sponsors Delacorte Press Prize for outstanding first young adult novel. The prize consists of one Delacorte hardcover and one Dell paperback contract, an advance of $6,000 on royalties, and a $1,500 cash prize. Closes in December.

HIGHLIGHTS FOR CHILDREN—803 Church St., Honesdale, PA 18431. Conducts children's short fiction contest, with three $1,000 prizes and publication offered for stories up to 900 words. Closes in February.

HONOLULU MAGAZINE/PARKER PEN—36 Merchant St., Honolulu, HI 96813. Sponsors annual fiction contest, with cash prize of $1,000, plus publication in *Honolulu*, for unpublished short story with Hawaiian theme, setting, and/or characters. Closes in November.

HOUGHTON MIFFLIN COMPANY—2 Park St., Boston, MA 02108. Offers Literary Fellowship for fiction or nonfiction project of exceptional literary merit written by an American author whose work has already been accepted for publication by Houghton Mifflin. Work under consideration must be unpublished and in English. Fellowship consists of $10,000, of which $2,500 is an outright grant and $7,500 is an advance against royalties. There is no deadline. Send SASE for guidelines; unsolicited material will not be read.

HUMBOLDT STATE UNIVERSITY—English Dept., Arcata, CA 95521–4957. Attn. Patricia Roller. Sponsors Raymond Carver Short Story Contest, with a prize of $500, plus publication in the literary journal *Toyon*, and a $250 second prize for an unpublished short story by a writer living in the U.S. Closes in November.

INTERNATIONAL SOCIETY OF DRAMATISTS—ISD Fulfillment Center, P. O. Box 1310, Miami, FL 33153. Sponsors Adriatic Award: a prize of $250 for a full-length play. Closes in November.

IUPUI CHILDREN'S THEATRE PLAYWRITING COMPETITION—Indiana University-Purdue University at Indianapolis, 525 N. Blackford St., Indianapolis, IN 46202–3120. Offers four $1,000 prizes plus staged readings for plays for young people. Closes in October of even-numbered years.

JEROME PLAYWRIGHT-IN-RESIDENCE FELLOWSHIPS—The Playwrights' Center, 2301 Franklin Ave. East, Minneapolis, MN 55406. Annually awards six emerging playwrights a $5,000 stipend and 12-month residency; housing and travel are not provided. Closes in March.

JEWISH COMMUNITY CENTER THEATRE IN CLEVELAND—3505 Mayfield Rd., Cleveland Heights, OH 44118. Elaine Rembrandt, Dir. of Cultural Arts. Offers cash award of $1,000 and a staged reading in the Dorothy Silver Playwriting Competition for an original, previously unproduced full-length play, on some aspect of the Jewish experience. Closes in December.

CHESTER H. JONES FOUNDATION—P. O. Box 498, Chardon, OH 44024. Conducts the National Poetry Competition, with more than $1,900 in cash prizes (including a $1,000 first prize) for original, unpublished first poems. Closes in March.

THE JOURNAL: THE LITERARY MAGAZINE OF THE OHIO STATE—The Ohio State University Press, 180 Pressey Hall, 1070 Carmack Rd. Attn: David Citino, Poetry Editor. Awards $1,000 plus publication for at least 48 pages of original, unpublished poetry. Closes in September.

LINCOLN COLLEGE—Lincoln, IL 62656. Address Janet Overton. Offers the Billie Murray Denny Poetry Award for original poem by poet who has not previously published a volume of poetry. First prize of $1,000, 2nd prize of $500, and 3rd prize of $250 are offered. Closes in May.

LIVE OAK THEATRE NEW PLAY AWARDS—311 Nueces St., Austin, TX 78701. Offers $1,000 each plus possible production for Best New American Play and Best New Play by a Texas Playwright for unproduced, unpublished, full-length scripts. Closes in November.

MADEMOISELLE MAGAZINE—350 Madison Ave., New York, NY 10017. Sponsors Fiction Writers Contest, with first prize of $2,500, plus publication, and second prize of $500, for short fiction by a writer aged 18 to 30. Closes in March.

MILKWEED NATIONAL FICTION PRIZE—P.O. Box 3226, Minneapolis, MN 55403. Annual contest for a novel, novella, or collection of short fiction, for which the winner receives $3,000 advance plus publication. Open to writers who have previously published a book-length collection of fiction or at least three short stories or a novella in commercial or literary journals with national distribution. Closes in September.

MILL MOUNTAIN THEATRE NEW PLAY COMPETITION—Center in the Square, One Market Square, Roanoke, VA 24011. Jo Weinstein, Lit. Mgr. Sponsors New Play Competition with a $1,000 prize and staged reading, with possible full production, for unpublished, unproduced, full-length or one-act play. Cast size to ten. Closes in January.

THE MOUNTAINEERS BOOKS—306 Second Ave. W., Seattle, WA 98119. Address Donna DeShazo, Dir. Offers The Barbara Savage/"Miles From Nowhere" Memorial Award for a book-length, nonfiction personal-adventure narrative. The prize consists of a $3,000 cash award, plus publication and a $12,000 guaranteed advance against royalties. Closes in March of even-numbered years.

MULTICULTURAL PLAYWRIGHTS' FESTIVAL—The Group Theatre, 3940 Brooklyn Ave. N.E., Seattle, WA 98105. Awards two American citizens of

Asian, Black, Chicano/Hispanic, or Native American ethnicity $1,000 plus production for previously unproduced one-act or full-length play. Closes in November.

NATIONAL ENDOWMENT FOR THE ARTS—Nancy Hanks Center, 1100 Pennsylvania Ave. N.W., Washington, DC 20506. Address Director, Literature Program. Offers fellowships to writers of poetry, fiction, and creative nonfiction. Deadlines vary; write for guidelines.

NATIONAL PLAY AWARD—630 N. Grand Ave., Suite 405, Los Angeles, CA 90012. National Play Award consists of $7,500 cash prize, plus $5,000 for production, for an original, previously unproduced play. Sponsored by National Repertory Theatre Foundation. Closes in July of even-numbered years.

THE NATIONAL POETRY SERIES—26 W. 17th St., New York, NY 10001. Sponsors Annual Open Competition for unpublished book-length poetry manuscript. The prize is publication. Closes in February.

NEGATIVE CAPABILITY SHORT FICTION CONTEST—62 Ridgelawn Dr. East, Mobile, AL 36608. Attn: Sue Walker. Sponsors the $1,000 Short Fiction Award for previously unpublished stories. Closes in December.

NEW DRAMATISTS—Arnold Weissburger Playwriting Competition, 424 W. 44th St., New York, NY 10036. Sponsors competition for full-length, unpublished, unproduced scripts; $5,000 is awarded the winning playwright. Closes in December.

THE NEW ENGLAND THEATRE CONFERENCE—50 Exchange St., Waltham, MA 02154. First prize of $500 and second prize of $250 are offered for unpublished and unproduced one-act plays in the John Gassner Memorial Playwriting Award Competition. Closes in April.

NEW VOICES—551 Tremont St., Boston, MA 02116. Conducts Clauder Competition for a full-length play by a New England writer. The prize is $3,000 and workshop production. Closes in June of odd-numbered years.

NILON AWARD FOR MINORITY FICTION—English Dept. Publications Ctr., University of Colorado, Campus Box 494, Boulder, CO 80309–0494. Awards $1,000 plus joint publication by Fiction Collective Two and CU-Boulder for original, unpublished, English Language, book-length fiction (novels, novellas, short story collections) by U.S. citizens of the following ethnic minorities: African-American, Hispanic, Asian, Native American or Alaskan Native, and Pacific Islander. Closes in November.

NORTHEASTERN UNIVERSITY PRESS—English Dept., 406 Holmes, Northeastern Univ., Boston, MA 02115. Guy Rotella, Chairman. Offers Samuel French Morse Poetry Prize—$500 plus publication of full-length poetry manuscript —by U.S. poet who has published no more than one book of poems. August is deadline for inquiries; contest closes in September.

O'NEILL THEATER CENTER—234 W. 44th St., Suite 901, New York, NY 10036. Offers stipend, staged readings, and room and board at the National Playwrights Conference, for new stage and television plays. Send SASE for guidelines. Closes in December.

THE PARIS REVIEW—541 E. 72nd St., New York, NY 10021. Sponsors the Aga Khan Prize for Fiction: $1,000, plus publication, for previously unpublished short story. Closes in June. Offers Bernard F. Connors Prize: $1,000, plus publication, for previously unpublished poem. Closes in May. Offers John Train Humor

710

Prize: $1,500, plus publication, for unpublished work of humorous fiction, nonfiction, or poetry. Closes in March.

PEN/JERARD FUND AWARD—568 Broadway, New York, NY 10012. Address John Morrone, Programs & Publications. Offers $3,000 to beginning female writers for a work-in-progress of general nonfiction. Applicants must have published at least one article in a national magazine or major literary magazine, but not more than one book of any kind. Closes in January.

PEN SYNDICATED FICTION PROJECT—P.O. Box 15650, Washington, DC 20003. For short fiction, unpublished or published in literary magazines. Offers $500 for rights to each story selected and $100 each time it is published by a newspaper. All selected stories are used on the Project's radio show, "The Sound of Writing." Closes in January.

PLAYBOY MAGAZINE COLLEGE FICTION CONTEST—680 N. Lakeshore Dr., Chicago, IL 60611. Sponsors college fiction contest, with first prize of $3,000 and publication in *Playboy*, for a short story by a college student; second prize is $500. Closes in January.

POETRY SOCIETY OF AMERICA—15 Gramercy Park, New York, NY 10003. Conducts annual contests (The Celia B. Wagner Memorial Award, the John Masefield Memorial Award, the Elias Lieberman Student Poetry Award, and the Ruth Lake Memorial Award) in which cash prizes are offered for unpublished poems. Closes in December.

PRIVATE EYE WRITERS OF AMERICA—PWA/St. Martin's Press, 175 Fifth Ave., New York, NY 10010. Winner of The Best First Private Eye Novel Contest receives publication with St. Martin's Press plus $10,000 against royalties; open to previously unpublished writers of private eye novels. Closes in August.

PURDUE UNIVERSITY PRESS—South Campus Courts—B, W. Lafayette, IN 47907. Attn: Margaret Hunt, Man. Ed. The Verna Emery Poetry Competition for an unpublished collection of poetry (65 pages) awards $500 plus publication for original poems. Closes in February.

REGARDIE'S MAGAZINE—1010 Wisconsin Ave., Suite 600, Washington, DC 20007. Sponsors the annual Money, Power, Greed Fiction Contest for short stories, 2,000 to 10,000 words, about the world of movers and shakers in and around Washington. Publication and a $5,000 first prize, $3,000 second prize, and $2,000 third prize are offered. Closes in April.

RIVER CITY WRITING AWARDS—River City, Dept. of English, Memphis State University, Memphis, TN 38152. Sharon Bryan, Ed. Awards $2,000 first prize, plus publication, $500 second prize, and $300 third prize, for previously unpublished short stories, to 7,500 words. Closes in December.

ST. MARTIN'S PRESS/MALICE DOMESTIC CONTEST—Thomas Dunne Books, 175 Fifth Ave., New York, NY 10010. Co-sponsored by Macmillan London, offers publication plus a $10,000 advance against royalties, for Best First Traditional Mystery Novel. Closes in November.

SAN DIEGO POETS PRESS—P.O. Box 8638, La Jolla, CA 92038. Sponsors the American Book Series contest for a poet's first book of poetry. Winner receives $500 plus publication. Closes in September.

SHIRAS/PANOWSKI PLAYWRITING COMPETITION—Playwriting Award Information, Forest Roberts Theatre, Northern Michigan Univ., Marquette, MI 49855. Conducts annual Shiras Institute/Albert & Mildred Panowski Playwriting Competition, with prize of $2,000, plus production, for original, full-length, previously unproduced and unpublished play. Closes in November.

SIENA COLLEGE PLAYWRIGHTS COMPETITION—Playwriting Competition, Dept. of Fine Arts, Theatre Program, Siena College, Loudonville, NY 12211. Offers $2,000 plus expenses for a campus residency for the winning full-length script; contemporary settings preferred; no musicals. Closes in June of even-numbered years.

SIERRA REPERTORY THEATRE—P. O. Box 3030, Sonora, CA 95370. Attn: Dennis Jones, Producing Dir. Offers annual playwriting award of $500, plus production, for original, previously unpublished, unproduced full-length play or musical. Closes in May.

SOCIETY OF AMERICAN TRAVEL WRITERS—1155 Connecticut Ave. N.W., Suite 500, Washington, DC 20036. Sponsors Lowell Thomas Travel Journalism Award for published and broadcast work by U.S. and Canadian travel journalists. Prizes total $8,500. Closes in February.

STANLEY DRAMA AWARD—Wagner College, Dept. of Humanities, 631 Howard Ave., Staten Island, NY 10301. Awards $2,000 for an original, previously unpublished and unproduced full-length play. Closes in September.

STORY LINE PRESS—Three Oaks Farm, Brownsville, OR 97327–9718. Sponsors the Nicholas Roerich Prize of $1,000 plus publication for an original, unpublished book of poetry by a poet who has never been published in book form. Closes in October.

SUNSET CENTER—P. O. Box 5066, Carmel, CA 93921. Attn: Director. Offers prize of up to $1,000 for an original, unproduced full-length play in its annual Festival of Firsts Playwriting Competition. Closes in August.

SUNTORY AWARDS FOR MYSTERY FICTION—c/o Dentsu Inc., 1–11 Tsukiji, Chuo-ku, Tokyo 104, Japan. Co-sponsored by Bungei Shunju publishers and Asahi Broadcasting. Offers 5 million yen first prize and 1 million yen Readers Choice award, plus possible publication and television production for 40,000- to 80,000-word English or Japanese language mystery, suspense, detective, or espionage novel. Closes in January.

SYRACUSE UNIVERSITY PRESS—1600 Jamesville Ave., Syracuse, NY 13244–5160. Address Director. Sponsors John Ben Snow Prize: $1,500, plus publication, for an unpublished book-length nonfiction manuscript about New York State, especially upstate or central New York. Closes in December.

THEATRE AMERICANA—P.O. Box 245, Altadena, CA 91001. Sponsors the $500 David James Ellis Memorial Award for an original, unproduced full-length play in two or three acts (no musicals or children's plays). Preference is given to American authors and to plays of the American scene. Closes in April.

THEATRE MEMPHIS—630 Perkins Extended, Memphis, TN 38117–4799. Conducts New Play Competition for a full-length play or related one-acts. The prize is $2,500 and production. Closes in October of even-numbered years.

UNITED FOUNDATIONS—Trust for Creators, P.O. Box 4162, Laguna Beach, CA 92652–4162. Awards the Robert Anson Heinlein Memorial Prize of $1,000 plus one- to three-month residency in the United Foundations' Creators Community for unpublished speculative fiction or science fiction in English or French, by writers ages 7 to 35: Closes in December and September. Also, the Karoline Von Dworschak Memorial Prize for English, German, or French language

712

fiction and nonfiction to female authors under 30 years of age; one- to three-month residencies are awarded; closes in March.

U.S. NAVAL INSTITUTE—Membership Dept., A.B.E.C., Annapolis, MD 21402. Conducts the Arleigh Burke Essay Contest, with prizes of $2,000, $1,000, and $750, plus publication, for essays on the advancement of professional, literary or scientific knowledge in the naval or maritime services, and the advancement of the knowledge of sea power. Closes in December.

UNIVERSITY OF ARKANSAS PRESS—Arkansas Poetry Award, Fayetteville, AR 72701. Awards publication of a 50- to 80-page poetry manuscript to a writer has never had a book published. Closes in May.

UNIVERSITY OF GEORGIA PRESS—Athens, GA 30602. Offers Flannery O'Connor Award for Short Fiction: a prize of $1,000, plus publication, for a book-length collection of short fiction. Closes in July.

UNIVERSITY OF HAWAII AT MANOA—Dept. of Drama and Theatre, 1770 East-West Rd., Honolulu, HI 96822. Conducts annual Kumu Kahua Playwriting Contest with $500 prize for a full-length play, and $200 for a one-act, set in Hawaii and dealing with some aspect of the Hawaiian experience. Also conducts contest for plays written by Hawaiian residents. Write for conditions-of-entry brochure. Closes in January.

UNIVERSITY OF IOWA—Dept. of English, English-Philosophy Bldg., University of Iowa, Iowa City, IA 52242. Offers The John Simmons Short Fiction Award and the Iowa Short Fiction Award, each offering $1,000, plus publication, for an unpublished full-length collection of short stories (150 pages or more). Closes in September.

UNIVERSITY OF MASSACHUSETTS PRESS—Juniper Prize, Univ. of Massachusetts Press, c/o Mail Office, Amherst, MA 01003. Offers the annual Juniper Prize of $1,000, plus publication, for a book-length manuscript of poetry; awarded in odd-numbered years to writers who have never published a book of poetry (even-numbered years to writers who have published a book of poetry) Closes in September.

UNIVERSITY OF PITTSBURGH PRESS—127 N. Bellefield Ave., Pittsburgh, PA 15260. Sponsors Drue Heinz Literature Prize of $7,500, plus publication and royalty contract, for unpublished collection of short stories. Closes in August. Also sponsors the Agnes Lynch Starrett Poetry Prize of $2,000, plus publication in the Pitt Poetry Series, for book-length collection of poems by poet who has not yet published a volume of poetry. Closes in April.

UNIVERSITY OF WISCONSIN PRESS—Poetry Series, 114 N. Murray St., Madison, WI 53715. Ronald Wallace, Administrator. Offers Brittingham Prize in Poetry: $500, plus publication, for an unpublished book-length poetry manuscript. Closes in September.

WORD WORKS—P. O. Box 42164, Washington, DC 20015. Offers the Washington Prize of $1,000 plus publication for an unpublished volume of poetry by a living American poet. Closes in March.

YALE UNIVERSITY PRESS—Box 92A, Yale Sta., New Haven, CT 06520. Address Editor, Yale Series of Younger Poets. Conducts Yale Series of Younger Poets Competition, in which the prize is publication of a book-length manuscript of poetry, written by a poet under 40 who has not previously published a volume of poems. Closes in February.

WRITERS COLONIES

Writers colonies offer isolation and freedom from everyday distractions and a quiet place for writers to concentrate on their work. Though some colonies are quite small, with space for just three or four writers at a time, others can provide accommodations for as many as thirty or forty. The length of a residency may vary, too, from a couple of weeks to five or six months. These programs have strict admissions policies, and writers must submit a formal application or letter of intent, a resumé, writing samples, and letters of recommendation. Write for application information first, enclosing a stamped, self-addressed envelope.

BLUE MOUNTAIN CENTER—Hosts month-long residencies for artists and writers. Apply by sending a brief biographical sketch, a statement of your plan for work at Blue Mountain, names and phone numbers of three references, five slides or approximately 10 pages of work, an indication of your preference for an early, late summer, or fall residence, and a $20 application fee (due no later than February 1), to Harriet Barlow, Director, Blue Mountain Center, Blue Mountain Lake, NY 12812. There is no charge to residents for their time at Blue Mountain, although all visitors are invited to contribute to the studio construction fund. Brochure available upon request.

CENTRUM—Centrum sponsors month-long residencies at Fort Worden State Park, a Victorian fort on the Strait of Juan De Fuca in Washington. Nonfiction, fiction, and poetry writers may apply for residency awards, which include housing and a $75 a week stipend. Families are welcome, but no separate working space is provided. Application deadlines: October 1 and April 1. For details, send SASE to Centrum, P.O. Box 1158, Port Townsend, WA 98368; or call (206) 385-3102.

CUMMINGTON COMMUNITY OF THE ARTS—Residencies for artists of all disciplines. Living/studio space in individual cottages or in two main houses on 100 acres in the Berkshires. Work exchange available. During July and August, artists with children are encouraged to apply; there is a children's program with supervised activities. Application deadlines: January 1st for May, June; March 1st for July, August; June 1st for September, October, November. Contact Executive Director, Cummington Community of the Arts, RR#1, Box 145, Cummington, MA 01026.

DORLAND MOUNTAIN ARTS COLONY—Novelists, playwrights, poets, nonfiction writers, composers, and visual artists are encouraged to apply for residencies of one to three months. Dorland is a nature preserve located in the Palomar Mountains of Southern California. Fee of $150 a month includes cottage, fuel, and firewood. Application deadlines are March 1 and September 1. Send SASE to Admissions Committee, Dorland Mt. Arts Colony, Box 6, Temecula, CA 92390.

DORSET COLONY HOUSE—Writers and playwrights are offered low-cost room with kitchen facilities at the historic Colony House in Dorset, Vermont. Periods of residency are one to three weeks, and are available between September 15 and May 15. Application deadlines are open. For more information, send SASE to John Nassivera, Director, Dorset Colony House, Dorset, VT 05251.

FINE ARTS WORK CENTER IN PROVINCETOWN—Fellowships, including living and studio space and monthly stipends, are available at the Fine Arts Work Center on Cape Cod, for writers to work independently. Residencies are for seven months only; apply before February 1 deadline. For details, send SASE to

714

Director, Fine Arts Work Center, P.O. Box 565, 24 Pearl St., Provincetown, MA 02657.

THE HAMBIDGE CENTER—Two-week to two-month residencies are offered to writers, artists, composers, historians, humanists, and scientists at the Hambidge Center for Creative Arts and Sciences located on 600 acres of quiet woods in the north Georgia mountains. Send SASE for application form to Executive Director, The Hambidge Center, P.O. Box 339, Rabun Gap, GA 30568.

THE MACDOWELL COLONY—Studios, room and board at the MacDowell Colony of Peterborough, New Hampshire, for writers to work without interruption in semi-rural woodland setting. Selection is competitive. Apply at least six months in advance of season desired; residencies up to eight weeks. For details and application forms, send SASE to Admissions Coordinator, The MacDowell Colony, 100 High St., Peterborough, NH 03458.

THE MILLAY COLONY FOR THE ARTS—At Steepletop in Austerlitz, New York (former home of Edna St. Vincent Millay), studios, living quarters, and meals are provided to writers at no cost. Residencies are for one month. Application deadlines are February 1, May 1, and September 1. For information and an application form, write to the Millay Colony for the Arts, Inc., Steepletop, Austerlitz, NY 12017.

MONTALVO CENTER FOR THE ARTS—One- to three-month, low-cost residencies at the Villa Montalvo in the foothills of the Santa Cruz Mountains south of San Francisco, for writers working on specific projects. There are a few small fellowships available to writers with demonstrable financial need. Send self-addressed envelope and 85¢ stamp for application forms to Montalvo Residency Program, P.O. Box 158, Saratoga, CA 95071.

RAGDALE FOUNDATION—Residencies from two weeks to two months are available for writers, artists, and composers. Located in Lake Forest, Illinois, 30 miles north of Chicago, on 40 acres of prairie. Low fees; some full and partial fee waivers available. Deadlines are January 15 for May-August; May 15 for September-December; and September 15 for January-April. Late applications considered when space is available. For application, send SASE to Ragdale Foundation, 1260 N. Green Bay Rd., Lake Forest, IL 60045.

UCROSS FOUNDATION—Residencies, two weeks to four months, at the Ucross Foundation in the foothills of the Big Horn Mountains in Wyoming, for writers, artists, and scholars to concentrate on their work without interruptions. Two residency sessions are scheduled annually: January-May and August-November. There is no charge for room, board, or studio space. Application deadlines are March 1 for fall session and October 1 for spring session. For more information, send SASE to Director, Residency Program, Ucross Foundation, 2836 US Hwy 14–16 East, Clearmont, WY 82835.

VIRGINIA CENTER FOR THE CREATIVE ARTS—Residencies of one to three months at the Mt. San Angelo Estate in Sweet Briar, Virginia, for writers to work without distraction. Apply at least three months in advance. A limited amount of financial assistance is available. For more information, send SASE to William Smart, Director, Virginia Center for the Creative Arts, Sweet Briar, VA 24595.

HELENE WURLITZER FOUNDATION OF NEW MEXICO—Rent-free and utility-free studios at the Helene Wurlitzer Foundation in Taos, New Mexico, are offered to creative writers and artists in all media. Length of residency varies from three to six months. The Foundation is closed from October 1 through March

31 annually. For details, write to Henry A. Sauerwein, Jr., Exec. Dir., The Helene Wurlitzer Foundation of New Mexico, Box 545, Taos, NM 87571.

YADDO—Artists, writers, and composers are invited for stays from two weeks to two months at Yaddo in Saratoga Springs, New York. Voluntary payment of $20 a day is requested. No artist deemed worthy of admission by the judging panels will be denied admission on the basis of an inability to contribute. Requests for applications should be sent with SASE before January 15 or August 1 to Myra Sklarew, President, Yaddo, Box 395, Saratoga Springs, NY 12866. An application fee of $20 is required.

WRITERS CONFERENCES

Each year, hundreds of writers conferences are held across the country. The following list, arranged geographically, represents a sampling of conferences; each listing includes the location of the conference, the month during which it is usually held, and the name of the person from whom specific information may be received. Additional conferences are listed annually in the May issue of *The Writer* Magazine (120 Boylston St., Boston, MA 02116).

ALASKA

SITKA SUMMER WRITERS SYMPOSIUM—Sitka, AK. June. Write Box 2420, Sitka, AK 99835.

ANNUAL TRAVEL WRITING CONFERENCE—Juneau, AK. June. Write UAS Cont. Ed., 11120-W Glacier Hwy., Juneau, AK 99801–8682.

ARIZONA

PIMA WRITERS' WORKSHOP—Tucson, AZ. May. Write Peg Files, Dir., Pima College, 2202 W. Anklam Rd., Tucson, AZ 85775–0901.

ARKANSAS

ARKANSAS WRITER'S CONFERENCE—Little Rock, AR. June. Write Clovita Rice, Dir., 1115 Gillette Dr., Little Rock, AR 72207.

CALIFORNIA

SAN DIEGO STATE UNIVERSITY WRITERS CONFERENCE—San Diego, CA. January. Write SDSU Extended Studies, San Diego, CA 92182.

ANNUAL WRITERS CONFERENCE IN CHILDREN'S LITERATURE —Universal City, CA. August. Write Lin Oliver, Dir., SCBW, P.O. Box 296, Mar Vista Station, Los Angeles, CA 90066.

ANNUAL WOMEN'S NATIONAL BOOK ASSOCIATION CONFERENCE—Culver City, CA. October. Send SASE to Sue Mac Laurin, Los Angeles Chapter, WNBA, P.O. Box 807, Burbank, CA 91503–0807.

COLORADO

ANNUAL SOCIETY OF CHILDREN'S BOOK WRITERS ROCKY MOUNTAIN RETREAT—Estes Park, CO. June. Write Mary Bahr Fritts, Dir., 807 Hercules Pl., Colorado Springs, CO 80906.

ASPEN WRITERS CONFERENCE—Aspen, CO. July. Write Karen Chamberlain, Dir., P.O. Drawer 7726, Aspen, CO 81612.

ANNUAL STEAMBOAT SPRINGS WRITERS CONFERENCE—Steamboat Springs, CO. August. Write Harriet Freiberger, Dir., P.O. Box 771913, Steamboat Springs CO 80477.

CONNECTICUT

WESLEYAN WRITERS CONFERENCE—Middletown, CT. June. Write Anne Greene, Dir., Wesleyan Writers Conf., Wesleyan Univ., Middletown, CT 06457.

WASHINGTON, DC

ANNUAL WASHINGTON INDEPENDENT WRITERS SPRING CONFERENCE—Washington, DC. May. Write WIW Conference, 733 Fifteenth St. N.W., Suite 220, Washington, D.C. 20005.

FLORIDA

KEY WEST LITERARY SEMINAR—Key West, FL. January. Write Key West Literary Seminars, P.O. Box 391, Sugarloaf Shores, FL 33044.

FLORIDA SPACE COAST WRITERS CONFERENCE—Melbourne, FL. March. Write Dr. Edwin J. Kirschner, F.S.C.W.C., Box 804, Melbourne, FL 32902.

ANNUAL FLORIDA STATE WRITERS CONFERENCE—Tampa, FL. May. Write Florida Freelance Writers Assn., Box 9844-REV, Fort Lauderdale, FL 33310.

GEORGIA

ANNUAL COUNCIL OF AUTHORS AND JOURNALISTS CONFERENCE—St. Simmons Island, GA. June. Write Ann Ritter, Dir., 1214 Laurel Hill Dr., Decatur, GA 30033.

ILLINOIS

ANNUAL CHRISTIAN WRITERS INSTITUTE CONFERENCE—Wheaton, IL. May. Write June Eaton, Dir., Christian Writers Inst., 388 E. Gundersen Dr., Wheaton, IL 60188.

OF DARK AND STORMY NIGHTS ANNUAL CONFERENCE—Evanston, IL. June. Write Mystery Writers of America, Midwest Chapter, Box 8, Techny, IL 60082.

ILLINOIS WESLEYAN UNIVERSITY WRITERS' CONFERENCE—
Bloomington, IL. August. Write Bettie Wilson Story, Dir., IWUWC, Illinois Wesleyan Univ., Bloomington, IL 61702.

INDIANA

INDIANA UNIVERSITY WRITERS' CONFERENCE—Bloomington, IN. June. Write Maura Stanton, Dir., IUWC, Ballantine 464, Bloomington, IN 47405.

MIDWEST WRITERS CONFERENCE—Muncie, IN. August. Write Earl L. Conn, Dept. of Journalism, Ball State Univ., Muncie, IN 47306.

IOWA

IOWA SUMMER WRITING FESTIVAL—Iowa City, IA. June and July. Write Peggy Houston, Dir., Iowa Summer Writing Festival,116 International Center, Univ. of Iowa, Iowa City, IA 52242.

KENTUCKY

CARTER CAVES WRITER'S WORKSHOP—Olive Hill, KY. June. Write Lee Pennington, 11905 Lilac Way, Middletown, KY 40243.

ANNUAL WRITING WORKSHOP FOR PEOPLE OVER 57—Lexington, KY. July. Write Roberta James, Donovan Scholars Program, Ligon House, 658 S. Limestone St., Univ. of Kentucky, Lexington, KY 40506–0442.

ANNUAL GREEN RIVER WRITERS' RETREAT—Louisville, KY. July. Write Deborah Spears, Dir., 403 S. Sixth, Ironton, OH 45638.

LOUISIANA

DEEP SOUTH WRITERS CONFERENCE—Lafayette, LA. September. Send SASE to Box 44691, Univ. of Southwestern Louisiana, Lafayette, LA 70504–4691.

MAINE

ANNUAL MAINE WRITERS WORKSHOP—Oceanville, ME. July and August. Write George F. Bush, Dir., P.O. Box 905, RD 1, Stonington, ME 04681.

STONECOAST WRITERS' CONFERENCE—Gorham, ME. July and August. Write Kenneth Rosen, English Dept., Univ. of Southern Maine, 96 Falmouth St., Portland, ME 04103.

STATE OF MAINE WRITERS CONFERENCE—Ocean Park (Old Orchard Beach), ME. August. Write Richard F. Burns, Box 296, Ocean Park, ME 04063.

MARYLAND

WESTERN MARYLAND WRITERS' WORKSHOP IN POETRY—Frostburg, MD. July. Write Barbara Wilson, Dir., WMWW, Frostburg State Univ., Frostburg, MD 21532.

MASSACHUSETTS

EASTERN WRITERS CONFERENCE—Salem, MA. June. Write Rod Kessler, English Dept., Salem State College, Salem, MA 01970.

NEW ENGLAND WRITERS' CONFERENCE AT SIMMONS COLLEGE—Boston, MA. June. Write Theodore Vrettos, Simmons College, 300 The Fenway, Boston, MA 02115.

HARVARD SUMMER WRITING PROGRAM—Cambridge, MA. June through August. Write Harvard Summer School, Dept. 457, 20 Garden St., Cambridge, MA 02138.

CAPE COD WRITERS' CONFERENCE—Craigville, MA. August. Write Marion Vuilleumier, Dir., CCWC c/o Cape Cod Conservatory of Music & Arts, Route 132, West Barnstable MA 02668.

MICHIGAN

CLARION WORKSHOP OF SCIENCE FICTION AND FANTASY WRITING—E. Lansing, MI. June through August. Write Mary Sheridan, E-28 Holmes Hall, Lyman Briggs School, Michigan State Univ., East Lansing, MI 48825-1107.

MINNESOTA

YOUNG PLAYWRIGHTS' SUMMER CONFERENCE—St. Paul, MN. June. Write Sally MacDonald, Outreach Dir., The Playwrights' Center, 2310 Franklin Ave. E., Minneapolis, MN 55406.

MINNEAPOLIS WRITERS WORKSHOP FICTION CONFERENCE—Minneapolis, MN. August. Send SASE to Colleen Campbell, Dir., P.O. Box 24356, Minneapolis, MN 55436.

MISSOURI

ANNUAL MARK TWAIN WRITERS CONFERENCE—Hannibal, MO. June. Write Dr. James C. Hefley, Hannibal-LaGrange College, Hannibal, MO 63401.

MONTANA

WESTERN MONTANA WRITERS CONFERENCE—Dillon, MT. July. Write Sally Garrett-Dingley, Dir., Summer School Office, Western Montana College, Dillon, MT 59725.

YELLOW BAY WRITERS' WORKSHOP—Flathead Lake, MT. August. Write Center for Cont. Ed., Univ. of Montana, Missoula, MT 59812.

NEW HAMPSHIRE

MILDRED I. REID WRITERS CONFERENCE—Contoocook, NH. July and August. Write Mildred I. Reid, Writers Colony, Penacook Rd., Contoocook, NH 03229.

ANNUAL FESTIVAL OF POETRY—Franconia, NH. July and August. Write Donald Sheehan, Dir., The Frost Place, Franconia, NH 03580.

ANNUAL SEACOAST WRITERS CONFERENCE—Portsmouth, NH. September. Write Urban Forestry Center, P.O. Box 6553, Portsmouth, NH 03802–6553.

NEW JERSEY

METROPOLITAN WRITERS CONFERENCE—South Orange, NJ. July. Write Jane Degnan, Bayley Hall, Seton Hall Univ., South Orange, NJ 07079.

NEW MEXICO

TAOS INSTITUTE OF ARTS—Taos, NM. June and July. Write Lawrence Houghteling, Dir., P.O. Box 1389, Taos, NM 87571.

SANTA FE WRITERS' CONFERENCE—Santa Fe, NM. August. Write Recursos De Santa Fe, 826 Camino De Monte Rey, Santa Fe, NM 87501.

NEW YORK

VASSAR INSTITUTE OF PUBLISHING AND WRITING—Poughkeepsie, NY. June. Write Vassar Institute of Publishing and Writing, Vassar College, Box 300, Poughkeepsie, NY 12601.

SOUTHAMPTON WRITERS' CONFERENCE—Southampton, NY. June. Write William Roberson, Dir., Library, LIU-Southampton Campus, Southampton, NY 11968.

ANNUAL SUMMER WRITERS' CONFERENCE—Hempstead, NY. July. Write Lewis Sheena, Hofstra Univ., Memorial Hall, U.C.C.E., Rm. 232, Hempstead, NY 11550.

CHAUTAUQUA INSTITUTION ANNUAL WRITER'S WORKSHOP—Chautauqua, New York. July. Write Christopher McMillan, Dir., Schools Office, Box 1098, Chautauqua Institution, Chautauqua, NY 14722.

ANNUAL BROCKPORT WRITERS FORUM SUMMER WORKSHOP—Brockport, NY. July. Write Dr. Stan Rubin, Dir., Summer Workshops, Hartwell Hall, SUNY College, Brockport, NY 14420–2211.

FEMINIST WOMEN'S WRITING WORKSHOPS, INC.—Aurora, NY. July. Send SASE to Mary Gilliland, Dir., FWWW, P.O. Box 6583, Ithaca, NY 14851.

ANNUAL IWWG SUMMER WRITERS CONFERENCE—Saratoga Springs, NY. July and August. Write Hannelore Hahn, Exec. Dir., International Women's Writing Guild, P.O. Box 810, Gracie Station, NY 10028.

NORTH CAROLINA

BLUE RIDGE CHRISTIAN WRITERS CONFERENCE—Asheville, NC. July. Write Yvonne Lehman, P.O. Box 188, Black Mountain, NC 28711.

OHIO

ANNUAL CUYAHOGA WRITERS' CONFERENCE—Cleveland, OH. May. Write Margaret Taylor, Dir., CWC, 4250 Richmond, RD., Cleveland, OH 44122.

ANTIOCH WRITERS' WORKSHOP—Yellow Springs, OH. July. Write Sandra Love, Dir., 133 N. Walnut St., Yellow Springs, OH 45387.

ANNUAL SKYLINE WRITERS' CONFERENCE AND WORKSHOP— N. Royalton, OH. August. Write Linda Buchsbaum, 737 Bridle Ln., Berea, OH 44017.

OKLAHOMA

OKLAHOMA WRITER'S FEDERATION—Oklahoma City, OK. May. Write Gordon Greene, Dir., 109 W. Kerr, Oklahoma City, OK 73110.

ANNUAL WRITERS OF CHILDREN'S LITERATURE CONFERENCE —Lawton, OK. June. Write Dr. George E. Stanley, P.O. Box 16355, Cameron Univ. Station, Lawton, OK 73505.

OREGON

HAYSTACK PROGRAM IN THE ARTS AND SCIENCES—Cannon Beach, OR. July and August. Write Steve Harmon, Dir., Portland State Univ., Summer Session, P.O. Box 751, Portland, OR 97207.

ANNUAL WILLAMETTE WRITERS CONFERENCE—Portland, OR. August. Write Jeanne Owen, Dir., 9045 S.W. Barbur Blvd., Portland, OR 97219.

PENNSYLVANIA

PHILADELPHIA WRITERS' CONFERENCE—Philadelphia, PA. June. Send SASE to Anthony T. Bruno, 253 Harrison Ave., Glenside, PA 19038.

ST. DAVIDS CHRISTIAN WRITERS' CONFERENCE—St. Davids, PA. June. Write S. Eaby, Registrar, 1775 Eden Rd., Lancaster, PA 17601–3523.

SOUTH CAROLINA

FRANCIS MARION WRITERS' RETREAT—Florence, SC. May. Write Robert Parham, Dir., Francis Marion College, Florence, SC 29501.

SOUTH DAKOTA

BLACK HILLS WRITERS CONFERENCE—Hill City, SD. July. Write Paul Lippman, Dir., Authors and Artists Agency, 4444 Lakeside Dr., Burbank, CA 91505.

WESTERN WOMEN IN THE ARTS WRITERS AND ARTISTS RE- TREAT—Rapid City, SD. September. Write Barbara VanNorman, Rt. 8, Box 3020, Rapid City, SD 57702.

TENNESSEE

ANNUAL RANDALL HOUSE PUBLICATIONS WRITERS' CONFERENCE—Nashville, TN. May. Write Dr. Malcolm C. Fry, 114 Bush Rd., P.O. Box 17306, Nashville, TN 37217.

TEXAS

ANNUAL "CRAFT OF WRITING" CONFERENCE—Richardson, TX. September. Write Janet Harris, Dir., P.O. Box 830688, M/S, CN,1.1, Richardson, TX 75083–0688

UTAH

WRITERS AT WORK—Park City, UT. June. Write Jennifer Kohler, Dir., Writers at Work, P.O. Box 58857, Salt Lake City, UT 84158.

VERMONT

BENNINGTON WRITING WORKSHOPS—Bennington, VT. July. Write Brian Swann, Bennington Writing Workshops, Bennington College, Box C, Bennington, VT 05201.

ANNUAL BREAD LOAF WRITERS' CONFERENCE—Ripton, VT. August. Write Bread Loaf Writers' Conference, Middlebury College, W. Middlebury, VT 05753.

VIRGINIA

ANNUAL HIGHLAND SUMMER CONFERENCE—Radford, VA. June. Write Dr. Grace Toney Edwards, Dir., Box 5917, Radford Univ., Radford, VA 24142.

BLUE RIDGE WRITERS CONFERENCE—Roanoke, VA. October. Write Rodney A. Franklin, Coord., Blue Ridge Writers Conference, 1917 Warrington Rd., S.W., Roanoke, VA 24015.

WASHINGTON

SEATTLE PACIFIC CHRISTIAN WRITERS' CONFERENCE—Seattle, WA. June. Write Linda Wagner, Dir., Humanities Dept., Seattle Pacific Univ., Seattle, WA 98119.

PORT TOWNSEND WRITERS' CONFERENCE—Port Townsend, WA. July. Write Carol Jane Bangs, Dir., CENTRUM, Box 1158, Port Townsend, WA 98368.

PACIFIC NORTHWEST WRITERS CONFERENCE—Tacoma, WA. July. Write Executive Secretary, PNWC, 17345 Sylvester Rd. S.W., Seattle, WA 98166.

WEST VIRGINIA

ANNUAL GOLDEN ROD WRITERS CONFERENCE—Morgantown, WV. October. Write George M. Lies, P.O. Box 239, Morgantown, WV 26505.

WISCONSIN

UW-MADISON SCHOOL OF THE ARTS AT RHINELANDER—Rhinelander, WI. July. Write Kathy G. Berigan, Admin. Coord., Box 727, Lowell Hall, 610 Langdon St., Madison, WI 53703.

CANADA

SASKATCHEWAN WRITERS' GUILD CONFERENCE—Regina, Sask. June. Write Paul Wilson, Dir., Saskatchewan Writers' Guild, Box 3986, Regina, SK, Canada S4P 3R9.

MARITIME WRITERS' WORKSHOP—Fredericton, New Brunswick. July. Write Heather Browne Prince, Dir., Dept. of Extension, Univ. of New Brunswick, P.O. Box 4400, Fredericton, NB, Canada E3B 5A3.

INTERNATIONAL

CREATIVE WRITING IN THE COUNTRYSIDE—Somerset, England. July and August. Write Beatrice Levin, Dir., Leonard Wills Field Centre, Nettlecomb Court, Somerset, England TA 4HT.

WRITERS TOUR OF GREECE—Athens, Greece. August and September. Write Richard L. Purthill, Dept. of Philosophy, Western Washington Univ., Bellingham, WA 98225.

STATE ARTS COUNCILS

State arts councils sponsor grants, fellowships, and other programs for writers. To be eligible for funding, a writer *must* be a resident of the state in which he is applying. For more information, write to the addresses below.

ALABAMA STATE COUNCIL ON THE ARTS
Albert B. Head, Executive Director
One Dexter Ave.
Montgomery, AL 36130

ALASKA STATE COUNCIL ON THE ARTS
Christine D'Arcy, Director
619 Warehouse Ave., Suite 220
Anchorage, AK 99501–1682

ARIZONA COMMISSION ON THE ARTS
Shelley Cohn, Executive Director
417 W. Roosevelt
Phoenix, AZ 85003

ARKANSAS ARTS COUNCIL
The Heritage Center, Suite 200
225 E. Markham
Little Rock, AR 72201

CALIFORNIA ARTS COUNCIL
JoAnn Anglin, Public Information Officer
1901 Broadway, Suite A
Sacramento, CA 95818

COLORADO COUNCIL ON THE ARTS AND HUMANITIES
Barbara Neal, Executive Director
750 Pennsylvania St.
Denver, CO 80203–3699

CONNECTICUT COMMISSION ON THE ARTS
John Ostrout, Acting Executive Director
227 Lawrence St.
Hartford, CT 06106

DELAWARE DIVISION OF THE ARTS
Cecelia Fitzgibbon, Director
Carvel State Building
820 N. French St.
Wilmington, DE 19801

FLORIDA ARTS COUNCIL
Ms. Peyton Fearington
Dept. of State
Div. of Cultural Affairs
The Capitol
Tallahassee, FL 32399–0250

GEORGIA COUNCIL FOR THE ARTS
Literary Coordinator
2082 E. Exchange Pl., Suite 100
Tucker, GA 30084

HAWAII STATE FOUNDATION ON CULTURE AND THE ARTS
Wendell P.K. Silva, Executive Director
335 Merchant St., Room 202
Honolulu, HI 96813

IDAHO COMMISSION ON THE ARTS
304 W. State St.
Boise, ID 83720

ILLINOIS ARTS COUNCIL
Richard Gage, Communication Arts Program Director
State of Illinois Center
100 W. Randolph, Suite 10–500
Chicago, IL 60601

INDIANA ARTS COMMISSION
47 South Pennsylvania St.
Indianapolis, IN 46204

IOWA STATE ARTS COUNCIL
Julie Baily, Director of Partnership Programs
State Capitol Complex
Des Moines, IA 50319

KANSAS ARTS COMMISSION
Robert T. Burtch, Information Coordinator
700 Jackson, Suite 1004
Topeka, KS 66603–3731

KENTUCKY ARTS COUNCIL
Berry Hill, Louisville Rd.
Frankfort, KY 40601

LOUISIANA COUNCIL FOR MUSIC AND PERFORMING ARTS
Literature Program Associate
7524 St. Charles Ave.
New Orleans, LA 70118

MAINE ARTS COMMISSION
David Cadigan
State House, Station 25
Augusta, ME 04333

MARYLAND STATE ARTS COUNCIL
Linda Vlasak, Program Director
Artists-in-Education
15 W. Mulberry St.
Baltimore, MD 21201

MASSACHUSETTS CULTURAL COUNCIL
Tesair Lauve, Literature Coordinator
80 Boylston St., 10th Fl.
Boston, MA 02116

MICHIGAN COUNCIL FOR THE ARTS
Barbara K. Goldman, Executive Director
1200 Sixth Ave., Suite 1180
Detroit, MI 48226–2461

MINNESOTA STATE ARTS BOARD
Karen Mueller
Artist Assistance Program Associate
432 Summit Ave.
St. Paul, MN 55102

COMPAS: WRITERS AND ARTISTS IN THE SCHOOLS
Molly LaBerge, Executive Director
Daniel Gabriel, Director
305 Landmark Center
75 W. 5th St.
St. Paul, MN 55102

MISSISSIPPI ARTS COMMISSION
Jane Crater Hiatt, Executive Director
239 N. Lamar St., Suite 207
Jackson, MS 39201

MISSOURI ARTS COUNCIL
Robin VerHage, Program Administrator for Literature
Wainwright Office Complex
111 N. 7th St., Suite 105
St. Louis, MO 63101–2188

MONTANA ARTS COUNCIL
Julia A. Smith, Director, Artist Services
New York Block
48 North Last Chance Gulch
Helena, MT 59620

725

NEBRASKA ARTS COUNCIL
Jennifer S. Clark, Executive Director
1313 Farnam On-the-Mall
Omaha, NE 68102–1873

NEVADA STATE COUNCIL ON THE ARTS
William L. Fox, Executive Director
329 Flint St.
Reno, NV 89501

NEW HAMPSHIRE STATE COUNCIL ON THE ARTS
Phenix Hall, 40 N. Main St.
Concord, NH 03301–4974

NEW JERSEY STATE COUNCIL ON THE ARTS
Grants Office
4 N. Broad St. CN-306
Trenton, NJ 08625

NEW MEXICO ARTS DIVISION
Artists Residency Program
224 E. Palace Ave.
Santa Fe, NM 87501

NEW YORK STATE COUNCIL ON THE ARTS
Jewelle L. Gomez, Acting Director, Literature Program
915 Broadway
New York, NY 10010

NORTH CAROLINA ARTS COUNCIL
Deborah McGill, Literature Director
Dept. of Cultural Resources
Raleigh, NC 27601–2807

NORTH DAKOTA COUNCIL ON THE ARTS
Donna Evenson, Executive Director
Black Building, Suite 606
Fargo, ND 58102

OHIO ARTS COUNCIL
727 E. Main St.
Columbus, OH 43205–1796

STATE ARTS COUNCIL OF OKLAHOMA
Ellen Jonsson, Deputy Director
Jim Thorpe Bldg., Room 640
Oklahoma City, OK 73105

OREGON ARTS COMMISSION
835 Summer St., N.E.
Salem, OR 97301

PENNSYLVANIA COUNCIL ON THE ARTS
Peter Carnahan, Literature and Theatre Programs
Diane Young, Artists-in-Education Program
Room 216, Finance Bldg.
Harrisburg, PA 17120

RHODE ISLAND STATE COUNCIL ON THE ARTS
Iona B. Dobbins, Executive Director
95 Cedar St., Suite 103
Providence, RI 02903

SOUTH CAROLINA ARTS COMMISSION
Steve Lewis, Director, Literary Arts Program
1800 Gervais St.
Columbia, SC 29201

SOUTH DAKOTA ARTS COUNCIL
108 W. 11th St.
Sioux Falls, SD 57102

TENNESSEE ARTS COMMISSION
320 Sixth Ave., N., Suite 100
Nashville, TN 37243–0780

TEXAS COMMISSION ON THE ARTS
P.O. Box 13406, Capitol Station
Austin, TX 78711

UTAH ARTS COUNCIL
G. Barnes, Literary Arts Coordinator
617 East South Temple
Salt Lake City, UT 84102

VERMONT COUNCIL ON THE ARTS
Grants Officer
136 State St.
Montpelier, VT 05602

VIRGINIA COMMISSION FOR THE ARTS
Peggy J. Baggett, Executive Director
James Monroe Bldg., 17th Fl.
101 N. 14th St.
Richmond, VA 23219

WASHINGTON STATE ARTS COMMISSION
110 9th and Columbia Bldg., MS GH-11
Olympia, WA 98504–4111

WEST VIRGINIA DEPT. OF EDUCATION AND THE ARTS
Culture and History Division
Arts and Humanities Section
The Cultural Center, Capitol Complex
Charleston, WV 25305

WISCONSIN ARTS BOARD
Mr. Arley Curtz, Executive Director
131 W. Wilson St., Suite 301
Madison, WI 53703

WYOMING ARTS COUNCIL
Joy Thompson, Director
2320 Capitol Ave.
Cheyenne, WY 82002

ORGANIZATIONS FOR WRITERS

THE ACADEMY OF AMERICAN POETS
177 E. 87th St.
New York, NY 10128
Mrs. Edward T. Chase, *President*
Founded in 1934 to "encourage, stimulate, and foster the art of poetry," the AAP sponsors a series of poetry readings in New York and other locations in the United States, and awards many prizes, including an annual fellowship of $20,000 for "distinguished poetic achievement." Membership is open to all: $45 annual fee includes subscription to the monthly newsletter and free copies of prize book selections.

AMERICAN MEDICAL WRITERS ASSOCIATION
9650 Rockville Pike
Bethesda, MD 20814
Lillian Sablack, *Executive Director*
Members of this association are engaged in communication about medicine and its allied professions. Any person actively interested in or professionally associated with any medium of medical communication is eligible for membership. The annual dues are $65.

AMERICAN SOCIETY OF JOURNALISTS AND AUTHORS, INC.
1501 Broadway, Suite 1907
New York, NY 10036
Alexandra Cantor, *Executive Director*
This nationwide organization of independent writers of nonfiction is dedicated to promoting high standards of nonfiction writing through monthly meetings, annual writers' conferences, etc. ASJA offers extensive benefits and services including referral service, numerous discount services, and the opportunity to explore professional issues and concerns with other writers. Members also receive a monthly newsletter. Membership is open to professional freelance writers of nonfiction; qualifications are judged by Membership Committee. Call or write for application details. Annual dues, $120. Phone number: (212)997-0947; fax number (212) 768-7414.

THE AUTHORS LEAGUE OF AMERICA, INC.
(The Authors Guild and The Dramatists Guild)
234 W. 44th St.
New York, NY 10036
The Authors League of America is a national organization of over 14,000 authors and dramatists, representing them on matters of joint concern, such as copyright, taxes, and freedom of expression. Membership in the league is restricted to authors and dramatists who are members of The Authors Guild and The Dramatists Guild. Matters such as contract terms and subsidiary rights are in the province of the two guilds.
A writer who has published a book in the last seven years with an established publisher, or one who has published several magazine pieces with periodicals of general circulation within the last eighteen months, may be eligible for active voting membership in The Authors Guild. A new writer may be eligible for associate membership on application to the Membership Committee. Dues: $90 a year.
The Dramatists Guild is a professional association of playwrights, composers, and lyricists, established to protect dramatists' rights and to improve

728

working conditions. Services include use of the Guild's contracts, business counseling, publications, and symposia in major cities. All playwrights (produced or not) are eligible for membership.

THE INTERNATIONAL SOCIETY OF DRAMATISTS
Box 1310
Miami, FL 33153

Open to playwrights, agents, producers, screenwriters, and others involved in the theater. Publishes *Dramatist's Bible*, a directory of script opportunities, and *The Globe*, a newsletter with information and news of theaters across the country. Also provides free referral service for playwrights.

MYSTERY WRITERS OF AMERICA, INC.
236 W. 27th St., Rm. 600
New York, NY 10001
Priscilla Ridgway, *Executive Secretary*

The MWA exists for the purpose of raising the prestige of mystery and detective writing, and of defending the rights and increasing the income of all writers in the field of mystery, detection, and fact crime writing. Each year, the MWA presents the Edgar Allan Poe Awards for the best mystery writing in a variety of fields. The four classifications of membership are: *active* (open to any writer who has made a sale in the field of mystery, suspense, or crime writing); *associate* (for professionals in allied fields/writers in other fields); *corresponding* (writers living outside the U.S.); *affiliate* (for unpublished writers and mystery enthusiasts). Annual dues: $65; $25 for corresponding members.

NATIONAL ASSOCIATION OF SCIENCE WRITERS, INC.
P.O. Box 294
Greenlawn, NY 11740

The NASW promotes the dissemination of accurate information regarding science through all media, and conducts a varied program to increase the flow of news from scientists, to improve the quality of its presentation, and to communicate its meaning to the reading public.

Anyone who has been actively engaged in the dissemination of science information is eligible to apply for membership. Active members must be principally involved in reporting on science through newspapers, magazines, TV, or other media that reach the public directly. Associate members report on science through limited-circulation publications and other media. Annual dues: $45.

THE NATIONAL WRITERS CLUB
1450 S. Havana, Suite 620
Aurora, CO 80012
James Lee Young, *Executive Director*

New and established writers, poets, and playwrights throughout the U.S. and Canada may become members of The National Writers Club, a full-time, customer service-oriented association founded in 1937. Membership includes bimonthly newsletter, *Authorship*. Dues: $60 annually, ($50 Associates), plus a $15 one-time initiation fee. Add $20 outside the USA, Canada, and Mexico for annual membership fee. Phone: (303) 751–7844.

NATIONAL WRITERS UNION
13 Astor Pl., 7th Fl.
New York, NY 10003

The National Writers Union, a new labor organization dedicated to bringing about equitable payment and fair treatment of free-lance writers through collective action, has over 3,000 members, including book authors, poets, free-lance journalists, and technical writers in eleven locals nationwide. The NWU offers its members contract and agent information, health insurance plans, press credentials, grievance handling, a union newspaper, and sponsors events across the country. Membership is open to writers who have published a book, play, three articles, five poems, one short story or an equivalent amount of newsletter, publicity, technical, commercial, government or institutional copy, or have written an equivalent amount of unpublished material and are actively seeking publication. Dues range from $55 to $135.

OUTDOOR WRITERS ASSOCIATION OF AMERICA, INC.
2017 Cato Ave., Suite 101
State College, PA 16801
Sylvia G. Bashline, *Executive Director*

The OWAA is a non-profit, international organization representing pro-fessional communicators who report and reflect upon America's diverse inter-ests in the outdoors. Membership (by nomination only) includes a monthly publication, *Outdoors Unlimited*; annual conference; annual membership direc-tory; contests. OWAA also provides scholarships to qualified students.

PEN AMERICAN CENTER
568 Broadway
New York, NY 10012

PEN American Center is one of more than 90 centers that make up International PEN, a worldwide association of literary writers, offering confer-ences, writing programs, and financial and educational assistance. Membership is open to writers who have published two books of literary merit, as well as editors, agents, playwrights, and translators who meet specific standards. (Apply to nomination committee.) PEN sponsors annual awards and grants and publishes the quarterly *PEN Newsletter* and the biennial directory, *Grants and Awards Available to American Writers*.

THE POETRY SOCIETY OF AMERICA
15 Gramercy Park
New York, NY 10003
Elise Paschen, *Executive Director*

Founded in 1910, The Poetry Society of America seeks through a variety of programs to gain a wider audience for American poetry. The Society offers 19 annual prizes for poetry (with many contests open to non-members as well as members), and sponsors workshops, poetry readings, and publications. Maintains the Van Vooris Library of American Poetry. Dues: $35 annually.

POETS AND WRITERS, INC.
72 Spring St.
New York, NY 10012
Elliot Figman, *Executive Director*

Poets & Writers, Inc. was founded in 1970 to foster the development of poets and fiction writers and to promote communication throughout the liter-ary community. A non-membership organization, it offers a nationwide infor-mation center for writers; *Poets & Writers Magazine* and other publications; as well as sponsored readings and workshops.

PRIVATE EYE WRITERS OF AMERICA
1952 Hendrick St.
Brooklyn, NY 11234
Robert J. Randisi, *Executive Director*

Private Eye Writers of America is a national organization that seeks to promote a wider recognition and appreciation of private eye literature. Writers who have published a work of fiction—short story, novel, TV script, or movie screen play—with a private eye as the central character are eligible to join as active members. Serious devotees of the P.I. story may become associate members. Dues: $24 (active), $18 (associate). Annual Shamus Award for the best in P.I. fiction.

ROMANCE WRITERS OF AMERICA
13700 Veterans Memorial Dr., Suite 315
Houston, TX 77014
Bobbi Stinson, *Office Supervisor*
   The RWA is an international organization with over 80 local chapters across the U.S. and Canada, open to any writer, published or unpublished, interested in the field of romantic fiction. Annual dues of $45, plus $10 application fee for new members; benefits include annual conference, contest, market information, and bimonthly newsmagazine, *Romance Writers' Report*.

SCIENCE FICTION WRITERS OF AMERICA, INC.
P.O. Box 4335
Spartanburg, SC 29305
Peter Dennis Pautz, *Executive Secretary*
   The purpose of the SFWA, a professional organization of science fiction and fantasy writers, is to foster and further the interests of writers of fantasy and science fiction. SFWA presents the Nebula Award annually for excellence in the field and publishes the *Bulletin* for its members.
   Any writer who has sold a work of science fiction or fantasy is eligible for membership. Dues: $65 per year for active members, $46 for affiliates, plus $10 installation fee; send for application and information. The *Bulletin* is available to nonmembers for $12.50 (four issues) within the U.S.; $16 overseas.

SMALL PRESS WRITERS AND ARTISTS ORGANIZATION
5116 S.143rd St.
Omaha, NE 68137
Marthayn Pelegrimas, *Secretary*
   Founded in 1977, the SPWAO is an international service organization of 400 writers, artists, poets, and publishers dedicated to the promotion of excellence in the small press fields of science fiction, fantasy, and horror. Members receive the bimonthly *SPWAO Newsletter*, critiques by fellow members, grievance arbitration, and research assistance. Initial dues: $17.50; annual renewal is $15.

SOCIETY FOR TECHNICAL COMMUNICATION
901 N. Stuart St., #304
Arlington, VA 22203
William C. Stolgitis, *Executive Director*
   The Society for Technical Communication is a professional organization dedicated to the advancement of the theory and practice of technical communication in all media. The 15,000 members in the U.S. and other countries include technical writers and editors, publishers, artists and draftsmen, researchers, educators, and audiovisual specialists.

SOCIETY OF AMERICAN TRAVEL WRITERS
1155 Connecticut Ave., Suite 500
Washington, D.C. 20036
Ken Fischer, *Administrative Coordinator*

The Society of American Travel Writers represents writers and other professionals who strive to provide travelers with accurate reports on destinations, facilities, and services.

Membership is by invitation. Active membership is limited to salaried travel writers and others employed as freelancers, who have a steady volume of published or distributed work about travel. Initiation fee for active members is $200, for associate members $400. Annual dues: $100 (active); $200 (associate).

SOCIETY OF CHILDREN'S BOOK WRITERS
P.O. Box 66296
Mar Vista Station
Los Angeles, CA 90066
Lin Oliver, *Executive Director*

This national organization of authors, editors, publishers, illustrators, filmmakers, librarians, and educators offers a variety of services to people who write, illustrate for or share an interest in children's literature. Full memberships are open to those who have had at least one children's book or story published. Associate memberships are open to all those with an interest in children's literature. Yearly dues are $35.

SOCIETY OF PROFESSIONAL JOURNALISTS
16 S. Jackson St.
Greencastle, IN 46135
Ira D. Perry, *Executive Director*

With over 16,000 members and 300 chapters, the SPJ serves the interests of print, broadcast, and wire journalists. Services include legal counsel on journalism issues, jobs-for-journalists career search program, professional development seminars, and awards that encourage journalism. Members receive *The Quill*, a monthly magazine that explores current issues in the field. SPJ promotes ethics and freedom of information programs.

Members must spend at least 50 percent of their working hours in journalism. National dues: $55 for professionals; $27.50 for students.

WESTERN WRITERS OF AMERICA
P.O. Box 823
Sheridan, WY 82801
Barbara Ketcham, *Secretary/Treasurer*

Published writers of fiction, nonfiction, and poetry pertaining to the traditions, legends, development, and history of the American West may join the nonprofit Western Writers of America. Its chief purpose is to promote a more widespread distribution, readership, and appreciation of the West and its literature. Dues are $60 a year. Sponsors annual Spur Awards, Saddleman Award, and Medicine Pipe Bearer's Award for Published Work.

WRITERS GUILD OF AMERICA, EAST, INC.
555 W. 57th St.
New York, NY 10019
Mona Mangan, *Executive Director*

WRITERS GUILD OF AMERICA, WEST, INC.
8955 Beverly Blvd.
West Hollywood, CA 90048
Brian Walton, *Executive Director*

The Writers Guild of America (East and West) represents writers in the fields of radio, television, and motion pictures in both news and entertainment.

In order to qualify for membership, a writer must fulfill current requirements for employment or sale of material in one of these three fields.

The basic dues are $25 per quarter for the Writers Guild West and $12.50 per quarter for Writers Guild East. In addition, there are quarterly dues based on percentage of the member's earnings in any one of the fields over which the Guild has jurisdiction. The initiation fee is $1,000 for Writers Guild East and $1,500 for Writers Guild West. (Writers living east of the Mississippi join Writers Guild East, and those living west of the Mississippi, Writers Guild West.)

AMERICAN LITERARY AGENTS

Most literary agents do not accept new writers as clients. Since the agent's income is a percentage (10% to 20%) of the amount he receives from the sales he makes for his clients, he must have as clients writers who are selling fairly regularly to good markets. Always query an agent first. Do not send any manuscripts until the agent has asked you to do so. The following is a list of members of the Society of Authors' Representatives (10 Astor Pl., 3rd Floor, New York, NY 10003). Addresses that include zip codes in parentheses are located in New York City (the majority of agents in this list are in New York). An extensive list of agents can be found in *Literary Market Place*, a directory found in most libraries, and in *Literary Agents of North America* (Research Associates International, Box 6503-B, GCPO, New York, NY 10163–6022). Other lists of agents and information on the author/agent relationship can be obtained by sending a self-addressed, stamped envelope to the Society of Authors' Representatives (address above) or to the Independent Literary Agents Assn., Inc., c/o Ellen Levine Literary Agency, 15 E. 26th St., Suite 1801, New York, NY 10010.

BRET ADAMS, LTD. 448 W. 44th St. (10036)

JULIAN BACH LITERARY AGENCY, INC. 747 Third Ave. (10017)

LOIS BERMAN The Little Theatre Bldg., 240 W. 44th St. (10036)

GEORGES BORCHARDT, INC. 136 E. 57th St. (10022)

BRANDT & BRANDT LITERARY AGENTS, INC. 1501 Broadway (10036)

THE HELEN BRANN AGENCY, INC. 94 Curtis Rd., Bridgewater, CT 06752

BROADWAY PLAY PUBLISHING 357 W. 20th St. (10011)

CURTIS BROWN, LTD. 10 Astor Pl. (10003)

KNOX BURGER ASSOCIATES, LTD. 39½ Washington Square S. (10012)

COLLIER ASSOCIATES 2000 Flat Run Rd., Seaman, OH 45679

FRANCES COLLIN LITERARY AGENCY 110 W. 40th St., Suite 1403 (10018)

DON CONGDON ASSOCIATES, INC. 156 Fifth Ave., Suite 625 (10010)

WILLIAM CRAVER WRITERS AND ARTISTS AGENCY 70 W. 36th St., Suite 501 (10018)

JOAN DAVES 21 W. 26th St. (10010–1003)

ANITA DIAMANT 310 Madison Ave., #1508 (10017)

CANDIDA DONADIO & ASSOCIATES, INC. 231 W. 22nd St. (10011)

ANN ELMO AGENCY, INC. 60 E. 42nd St. (10165)

JOHN FARQUHARSON, LTD. 250 W. 57th St., Suite 1007 (10107)

THE FOX CHASE AGENCY, INC. Public Ledger Bldg. #930, Independence Square, Philadelphia, PA 19106

ROBERT A. FREEDMAN DRAMATIC AGENCY, INC. 1501 Broadway, #2310 (10036)

SAMUEL FRENCH, INC. 45 W. 25th St. (10010)

GRAHAM AGENCY 311 W. 43rd St. (10036)

BLANCHE C. GREGORY, INC. Two Tudor City Place (10017)

HELEN HARVEY 410 W. 24th St., (10011)

JOHN W. HAWKINS & ASSOCIATES, INC. 71 W. 23rd St., Suite 1600 (10010)

INTERNATIONAL CREATIVE MANAGEMENT, INC. 40 W. 57th St. (10019)

JCA LITERARY AGENCY, INC. 27 W. 20th St., Suite 1103 (10011)

KIDDE, HOYT & PICARD 335 E. 51st St. (10022)

LUCY KROLL AGENCY 390 West End Ave. (10024)

THE LANTZ OFFICE 888 Seventh Ave. (10106)

LESCHER & LESCHER, LTD. 67 Irving Pl. (10003)

ELLEN LEVINE LITERARY AGENCY 15 E. 26th St., Suite 1801 (10010)

STERLING LORD LITERISTIC, INC. 1 Madison Ave. (10010)

GERARD MCCAULEY AGENCY, INC. P.O. Box AE, Katonah, NY 10536

MCINTOSH & OTIS, INC. 310 Madison Ave. (10017)

ELISABETH MARTON 96 Fifth Ave. (10011)

HAROLD MATSON COMPANY, INC. 276 Fifth Ave. (10001)

MARY MEAGHER The Gersh Agency N.Y., 130 W. 42nd St., 24th Floor (10036)

HELEN MERRILL, LTD. 435 W. 23rd St., #1A (10011)

WILLIAM MORRIS AGENCY, INC. 1350 Ave. of the Americas (10019)

JEAN V. NAGGAR LITERARY AGENCY 336 E. 73rd St. (10021)

HAROLD OBER ASSOCIATES, INC. 40 E. 49th St. (10017)

FIFI OSCARD ASSOCIATES, INC. 19 W. 44th St. (10036)

PINDER LANE PRODUCTIONS, LTD. 159 W. 53rd St. (10019)

RAINES & RAINES 71 Park Ave. (10016)

FLORA ROBERTS, INC. Penthouse A, 157 W. 57th St. (10019)

ROSENSTONE/WENDER 3 E. 48th St. (10017)

RUSSELL & VOLKENING, INC. 50 W. 29th St. (10001)

SUSAN SCHULMAN AGENCY 454 W. 44th St. (10036)

THE SHUKAT COMPANY, LTD. 340 W. 55th St., #1A (10019)

PHILIP G. SPITZER LITERARY AGENCY 788 Ninth Ave. (10019)

ROSLYN TARG LITERARY AGENCY, INC. 105 W. 13th St., #15E
(10011)

THE WALLACE AGENCY 177 E. 70th St. (10021)

THE WENDY WEIL AGENCY, INC. 747 Third Ave. (10017)

MARY YOST ASSOCIATES, INC. 59 E. 54th St., #72 (10022)

INDEX TO MARKETS